The Complete
Lincoln-Douglas Debates
of 1858

The Lincoln–Douglas Campaign
in Illinois, 1858

I leave you, hoping that the lamp of liberty will burn in your bosoms until there shall no longer be a doubt that all men are created free and equal.

LINCOLN AT CHICAGO
July 10, 1858

I say that this government was established on the white basis. It was made by white men, for the benefit of white men and their posterity forever, and never should be administered by any except white men.

DOUGLAS AT CHARLESTON
September 18, 1858

The Complete
Lincoln-Douglas Debates
of 1858

Edited and with an Introduction by

PAUL M. ANGLE

With a new Foreword by

DAVID ZAREFSKY

THE UNIVERSITY OF CHICAGO PRESS

CHICAGO & LONDON

This book was compiled

and edited under the auspices of

THE CHICAGO HISTORICAL SOCIETY

Philip K. Wrigley Fund

The University of Chicago Press, Chicago 60637
The University of Chicago Press, Ltd., London
© 1958, 1991 by The University of Chicago
All rights reserved. Published 1958
Midway reprint edition 1985
Paperback edition 1991
Printed in the United States of America
00 99 98 97 96 95 94 93 92 91 5 4 3 2 1

Library of Congress Cataloging-in-Publication Data

Lincoln, Abraham, 1809–1865.
   [Created equal?]
   The complete Lincoln-Douglas debates of 1858 / edited and with an introduction by Paul M. Angle; with a
new foreword by David Zarefsky.
     p.   cm.
   Reprint. Originally published. Created equal? Chicago : University of Chicago Press, 1958.
   Includes index.
   ISBN 0-226-02084-3 (pbk.)
   1. Lincoln-Douglas debates, 1858. 2. Lincoln,
Abraham, 1809–1865. 3. Douglas, Stephen Arnold,
1813–1861. 4. United States—Politics and government—1857–1861. I. Douglas, Stephen Arnold,
1813–1861. II. Angle, Paul M. (Paul McClelland),
1900–1975. III. Title.
[E457.4.L775   1991]
973.6′8′0922—dc20   90-19583
                                              CIP

TABLE OF CONTENTS

FOREWORD, 1991

When this volume was first published in 1958, on the centennial of the Lincoln-Douglas debates, political debate had fallen out of fashion. Improvements in transportation and communication after the Civil War removed the logistical advantage to scheduling joint appearances between candidates, and the political calculus in most elections made it in at least one contender's interest not to debate. Not even the technology of radio served as the impetus to more widespread national debate.

Only two years later, though, the first-ever presidential debates of 1960 renewed interest in this special form of campaign persuasion. The four exchanges between John F. Kennedy and Richard Nixon are widely believed to have affected the outcome of that extremely close election. They were closely studied, not only by academics but also by politicians searching for maneuvers to emulate or mistakes to avoid. The debates did not herald a renaissance of political debate, however—at any rate not immediately. For each of the next three presidential contests, at least one of the major-party candidates had an interest in avoiding debate. In 1976, though, both candidates had reason to debate, the League of Women Voters was a willing sponsor, and the law permitted television coverage of debates as news events without the requirement that equal time be offered to all minor-party candidates. Again the debates may have made a crucial difference, and debates have been held in each election since, under the sponsorship of either the League or a bipartisan Commission on Presidential Debates which was established in 1988. And there has been a trickle-down effect of the new interest in political debate, so that these exchanges have become common on the state and local as well as the national level, during the primary season as well as that of the general election, and in multiple-candidate races as well as in one-on-one situations.

In some respects, the debates of the late twentieth century are quite unlike those between Lincoln and Douglas. None are three hours long. Rarely are there as many as seven debates in the same race. And, following the precedent of the Kennedy-Nixon debates, most contemporary political debates employ a panel of questioners, usually journalists, rather than relying exclusively on the candidates themselves for sustained development of arguments. The result is to chop up the debate time so that each candidate must speak very briefly to a wide range of issues, whereas in the Lincoln-Douglas debates the shortest speaking opportunity was 30 minutes in length and the candidates were free to determine the issues and to discuss them in depth.

Despite these differences, however, the Lincoln-Douglas debates remain our culture's model of what public political debate ought to be. Scarcely a campaign goes by without a challenge by one candidate to replace advertising-dominated campaigns with a return to the tradition of Lincoln and Douglas. The debates of 1858 have receded into folk-lore and the image which Americans hold of those encounters is far more compelling than the text of what actually was said. Consequently, in Reinhard Luthin's aphoristic phrase, the debates have been "vastly more admired than read."[1]

The central issue in the 1858 campaign, slavery in the territories, is ably explicated by Paul M. Angle in the introduction to the original edition of this book. It loomed large in the campaign not because it directly affected the people of Illinois but because of the political position of Senator Douglas. He was the most prominent Democrat in the country, with the possible exception only of President James Buchanan, and he was conspicuously identified with issues regarding territories. He chaired the Senate Committee on Territories. He was the author of the Kansas-Nebraska Act, which provided that "popular sovereignty" rather than the Missouri Compromise would determine the status of slavery in those new regions. He was scrambling to reconcile his cherished principle of popular sovereignty with the Supreme Court's 1857 Dred Scott decision. And he had broken with Buchanan over the Lecompton constitution, under which Kansas sought admission as a slave state. This constitution was perfectly legal, having been drafted by a duly constituted convention and ratified by Kansas voters in a properly scheduled election. For this reason Buchanan maintained that it represented the will of the people. But the convention was unrepresentative and free-state forces had boycotted the ratification vote because the ballot offered no option by which slavery could be excluded altogether. A clear majority of Kansans opposed the document. Douglas therefore concluded that it did *not* represent the will of the people but instead made popular sovereignty a sham. On that basis he withdrew his support of the President.

Besides these specific considerations, the territories became the fo-

1. Reinhard Luthin, *The Real Abraham Lincoln* (Englewood Cliffs, N.J.: Prentice-Hall, 1960), 197.

cal point of the slavery controversy in part because they were the only places where the status of the "peculiar institution" was unsettled and in part because, while the immediate stakes were modest, the symbolic significance of the conflict was not. The struggle for the territories was a struggle for the future, for the definition of America's national destiny.

From this background information, the first-time reader of the debates might expect to find lengthy discussions of the wisdom or morality of slavery in the territories. The transcripts will show this expectation to be unfounded. Although there are brief discussions of the morality of slavery and its extension, for the most part the debates are dominated by conspiracy charges, legal disputes, and historical arguments.

Douglas opened the first debate by accusing Lincoln of plotting secretly to convert both the Whig and Democratic parties to abolitionism, as part of a larger plot not only to contain slavery but to abolish it altogether—a goal espoused by virtually no political leader in 1858. The "House Divided" speech was cited by Douglas as proof of Lincoln's intentions. Lincoln, in the same debate, alleged that Douglas was conspiring, along with Chief Justice Roger B. Taney and Presidents Franklin Pierce and James Buchanan, to spread slavery across the nation—to the states as well as the territories, the north as well as the south. The means for doing so would be a second Dred Scott decision which would prevent *states* from outlawing slavery. Despite the paucity of evidence to support either of these charges, both echoed throughout the debates.

And there were other conspiracy allegations as well. Lincoln accused Douglas of plotting with other Illinois Democrats to forge or misrepresent the 1854 platform of the state Republican party. There was no single statewide organization in 1854, but Douglas had cited various local documents in an attempt to show that the new party favored abolition. Douglas alleged that Lincoln and Buchanan were working together to use federal patronage as a way to withdraw public subsidies for Douglas newspapers and to remove Douglas supporters from public office, all for the purpose of intimidating the voters of Illinois. Virtually the entire fourth debate is devoted to a complex charge made by Lincoln, that Douglas had been secretly plotting to prevent Kansans from having a chance to vote on whether or not to adopt the Lecompton constitution, even while publicly proclaiming that his position was the opposite. This argument had been made by Illinois senator Lyman Trumbull and other Senate Republicans; Lincoln brought it to the campaign trail.

In addition to the conspiracy charges, the debates also were marked

by arcane legal disputes. These began with the interpretation of the
Dred Scott decision and led into larger questions about the nature and
ownership of the territories and the reach of the national government
within a federal system. With respect to Dred Scott, the first issue is
whether the decision was final. That will seem a strange question to
late-twentieth-century Americans, who generally have accepted that
the Supreme Court has the last word in interpreting the Constitution,
except for the possibility of constitutional amendment. But it was an
unsettled question in antebellum America; after all, Dred Scott was
only the second decision overturning an act of Congress, the first decision to limit the powers of another branch of government, and the
first with significant policy implications.[2] Douglas defended the finality
of the decision, partly for political reasons and partly to defend the
integrity of the Court. To do otherwise, he suggested in the fifth and
sixth debates, would be to replace the rule of law with rule of a mob—
an outcome with which he tried to stigmatize Lincoln. For his part,
the Republican accepted the finality of the decision only with respect
to the case of Dred Scott himself, not as a binding political rule. He
noted that it was not uncommon for courts to reverse themselves and
suggested that the remedy for Dred Scott was to elect a Republican
president who would appoint Republican justices.

Beyond the issue of finality was the question of what the Dred Scott
decision actually meant. Lincoln was sure that it undercut the basis of
Douglas's popular sovereignty position. The Little Giant, however, insisted that the two could be reconciled because the right established
by Dred Scott was barren and worthless without the positive protection of local legislation, which a community could choose to provide or
to withhold. Lincoln found this reasoning to be specious, but insisted
that if it were valid it would also justify northern states in nullifying
the federal fugitive-slave law. The validity of Douglas's belief, however, turned on a more fundamental question: Who owned the territories? Lincoln argued that they were held in trust by the federal government as the common property of all the people. Consequently,
whatever power was denied to the Congress by the Dred Scott decision was also denied to the territorial legislatures, who were agents of
Congress. Douglas saw the matter differently. He viewed the territories as incipient states, and therefore entitled to the same degree of
self-determination as states might enjoy over their own affairs.

This dispute, in turn, hinged on the meaning of the terms "states"
and "territories" in the Constitution. Lincoln argued straightforwardly

2. Harry V. Jaffa, *Crisis of the House Divided: An Interpretation of the Issues
in the Lincoln-Douglas Debates* (1959. Reprint, Chicago: University of Chicago Press, 1982), 285.

that Article IV, Section 3, gave Congress authority to make all regulations affecting the territories. For Douglas, however, the reference to "territories" designated geographic, not political, units. The authority of Congress over the territories stemmed rather from the congressional power to admit new states. In his usage the term "states" embraced both the current and the future states. Although Douglas's usage instinctively seems tortured, it did have some historical basis. And it enabled him to stigmatize Lincoln's policy as colonialism and thereby to appeal to the widespread anti-British prejudice of the time.

The third major argument pattern, in addition to conspiracy and legal claims, was historical dispute. Each candidate sought to identify his own policy with the founding fathers' and to characterize his opponent as a deviant from their wisdom. Douglas wasted no time in introducing this argument. Taking note of Lincoln's prediction in the "House Divided" speech that the nation could not remain half-slave and half-free, the Little Giant asserted that this prediction was at odds with the wisdom of "Washington, Jefferson, Franklin, Madison, Hamilton, Jay, and the great men of that day,"[3] who deliberately made the government divided into free and slave states and left each state free to regulate its own affairs as it saw fit. This same charge, with only slight variation, was made in every debate except one. Douglas was sure that he interpreted the founders correctly, and he appealed to historical evidence. At the time of the drafting of the Constitution, twelve of the thirteen states permitted slavery. If the founders had subscribed to Lincoln's doctrine, the twelve slaveholding states would have outvoted the one free state and fastened slavery on the entire nation. That they did not do so proved that Douglas's view was more in keeping with their own, and enabled the Little Giant to chide Lincoln for setting himself up as wiser than the revered founders of the government.

For his part, Lincoln claimed that *he* was the true heir of the founding fathers. As evidence he cited the "created equal" phrase in the Declaration of Independence; Jefferson's role in drafting the Northwest Ordinance, which outlawed slavery in the territory north and west of the Ohio River; and the abolition of the foreign slave trade. Lincoln denied Douglas's assertion that the founders made the country half-slave and half-free. Rather, he argued, they *found* it that way, and, not knowing what else to do, left the situation alone until the institution disappeared naturally in the fullness of time. But that they intended it to disappear was obvious, both from their specific actions and from the care they took to see that the Constitution never con-

3. This volume, 109–10, 113.

tained the word "slavery" so that the document could survive unblemished in a future age.

The fact that the statements of the founding fathers were equivocal meant that neither candidate would score a decisive victory on this argument. There was a second historical argument, however, which involved appealing to the memory of Henry Clay, widely regarded as the symbolic descendant of the founding fathers as well as the patron saint of the old-line Whigs of central Illinois, whose votes ultimately would decide the senatorial election. Lincoln had been a Clay Whig for much of his life, and claimed with justification that he stood exactly where Clay would have stood on the slavery issue, accepting the presence of the peculiar institution but desiring not to extend it to new territories. Douglas, however, appealed to Clay's role as a compromiser and tried to portray popular sovereignty as the type of compromise Clay would have endorsed, a middle ground between the fire-eating southerners and the radical abolitionism which he attributed to Lincoln. Although Lincoln was rightly upset by Douglas's pretensions to Clay's mantle, the Little Giant's position seemed to gain credibility when he received the endorsement of Kentucky senator John J. Crittenden, Clay's successor in the Senate.

If so much of the Lincoln-Douglas debates consisted of conspiracy, legal, and historical arguments which were tangential to the main issue, two questions naturally suggest themselves. Why did two such able advocates seemingly skirt the central issue of their time? And, if they did, why do we continue nevertheless to regard the encounters between Lincoln and Douglas as the paradigm case of American political debate? The answers to both questions are complex.

The political realities of Illinois in the late 1850s provide part of the answer to the first question. The southern one-third of the state was solidly Democratic, even in places tending toward proslavery. The only question for these voters was whether Douglas or Buchanan would command their allegiance, and as the campaign proceeded it became clearer that this question would be answered in favor of Douglas. The northern one-third of the state was solidly Republican, even in some places tending toward abolitionism—a view well beyond the mainstream of the Republican party. The swing voters were those in the central one-third of the state, roughly between Ottawa and Springfield. Many of these voters were former Whigs who were unsure of their political allegiance after their own party's demise. They were mildly antislavery, regarding the institution as an evil that would disappear in God's good time. But they were strongly anti-abolition, believing the imminent demise of slavery to be far too radical a measure for the political system to absorb. Above all, they were political moderates who believed that any change should be slow and gradual.

To appeal to these voters, it was obviously desirable that each candidate position himself in the middle of the political spectrum and locate his opponent at the extremes. Thus Lincoln maintained that only those who saw no end, ever, to slavery should support Douglas, whereas anyone who thought the institution was bad and should be terminated at any time in the future should support him. Conversely, Douglas insisted that he should receive the support of former Whigs unless they favored not only immediate emancipation but the social and political equality of the races—a view taken by no respectable mainstream politician but one which Douglas attributed to Lincoln. The conspiracy argument is a staple of American politics, going back at least to the colonial allegations that the British government was plotting to deny American colonists the rights of Englishmen.[4] Its primary function in 1858 was to facilitate the positioning of candidates as moderate or radical, thereby making them more or less palatable to the swing voters of central Illinois.

But there is a deeper reason for the argument choices of the Lincoln-Douglas debates. The discussion which *did* take place about the basic moral issues revealed that the candidates' positions were not just different but incommensurable. Lincoln's was a morality of natural rights which began with the premise that slavery was wrong. He was willing to recognize its actual existence in the southern states as protected by the Constitution, but he was not willing to extend it into new territory, and he was not willing to contest what he took to be the prevailing sentiment before 1854, that slavery was on the course of ultimate extinction. The heart of the issue, as he saw it, was that he and the Republicans believed slavery to be wrong whereas Douglas and the Democrats did not. He could ridicule Douglas for regarding slavery as a trifling matter and castigate him for his moral indifference.

Douglas, though, was not an amoral man. Rather, his highest moral value was procedural: the principle of local self-government, the right of each community to make its own decisions about its domestic affairs. Douglas was not an apologist for slavery; he sought to remove the issue from the national agenda. Decisions about slavery should not be made on the basis of whether it was right or wrong. That was a question for the inhabitants of each community to determine. For Douglas the principle of local self-government was the prerequisite for preserving

4. This early use of conspiracy argument is examined in Bernard Bailyn, *The Ideological Origins of the American Revolution* (Cambridge, Mass.: Belknap Press, Harvard University Press, 1967).

and expanding the Union, a goal which the Little Giant regarded as more important than slavery or any other moral issue. If local self-government meant anything, it meant that those not affected by a decision had no business trying to influence that decision. If Lincoln could accuse him of moral indifference, he could respond that the Republican was presumptuous in the extreme when he tried to make moral decisions for others. Moral judgment of the slaveholders was not a subject for political debate but a matter for their consciences and their God.[5]

In short, one candidate relied on a substantive view of morality; the other on a procedural view. These positions did not directly engage each other, and each candidate could dismiss the other's challenges as beside the point. The issue of slavery occupied a position not unlike that of the abortion controversy in the late twentieth century. There too, a substantive view about the morality of abortion is met by a procedural view of who should have the right to decide such a complex moral issue. Since the positions were not comparable, discussion stalemated quickly. Extended development of the competing views would have served no purpose other than to restate assertions. It is perhaps fitting that the moral argument received the fullest examination in the final debate. Had these statements been made in the first encounter, it is hard to imagine where the debates could have gone from there.

In the face of the stalemated moral argument, Lincoln and Douglas talked instead about matters legal and historical. But these were not just filler. Rather, they functioned as surrogates for the moral issue, enabling the discussion to proceed. What made the moral arguments incommensurable was the absence of common ground. Instead of withdrawing from the contest, the debaters sought out other argument patterns on which common ground was available. They reached for the appeals that united rather than divided their listeners. Reverence for the Constitution was such an appeal. Conceived in controversy and only narrowly obtaining ratification, the document quickly became glorified as something that was fought for, not fought over. As a consequence, there was great advantage for anyone who could identify his or her own position with that of the Constitution and who could denigrate opponents as traducers of it. Prevailing in such a situation, where the values were shared, became a surrogate for winning the moral issue, where values were deeply divided.

Much the same thinking applies to the historical argument. The 1850s were characterized by sentimental worship of the founding fa-

5. This volume, 351.

thers which was so intense that one writer has called it "filiopiety."[6] Since the authority of the founders was a shared warrant for arguments, the candidate who could establish that his position was more in keeping with that of the founding fathers would achieve the same result as if he had prevailed on the moral issue itself. In short, the predominance of the legal and historical arguments reflects the advocates' attempt to carry the dispute forward by making an argument for one claim in terms of something else.

The fact that the Lincoln-Douglas debates were able to proceed in the face of incommensurable moral positions is also one reason why the texts merit close scrutiny. Certainly in contemporary discourse it is far more common for opposing advocates to proclaim their rival moral positions, repeating the same key phrases and symbols without extending the argument. In a sense, neither really can understand the other's whole framework of assumptions and belief. Rather, each side places the other's arguments into its own worldview and concludes that the opponents are inept. What results is public discourse marked by judgmental statements and personal attacks, which in each case are "taken by the other side as evidence that its own statements are valid."[7] Each side is reduced to self-persuasion.

The Lincoln-Douglas debates dealt with this problem by invoking common constitutional and historical values to serve as the premises for surrogate arguments. They were not slogans, symbols, or "sound bites," but fully developed substantial arguments. These debates, then, offer a powerful example of how a discussion can proceed in the face of noncomparable moral positions. They stand in contrast to a pattern of reciprocated diatribe which only intensifies the opposing positions and polarizes the conflict. In an age in which many moral disputes, such as abortion, medical ethics, creation science, gay rights, or capital punishment, seem to reflect incommensurable premises, the Lincoln-Douglas debates are worthy of study and modeling.

Moreover, if they are not eloquent, statesmanlike discussions of the morality of slavery—the stereotype with which people often approach them—the Lincoln-Douglas debates do illustrate the masterful use of argument strategies and tactics in the public forum. Both candidates were masters at selecting effective arguments from the arsenal of possibilities, making the most of the arguments they picked, minimizing

6. See George B. Forgie, *Patricide in the House Divided: A Psychological Interpretation of Lincoln and His Age* (New York: Norton, 1979).
7. W. Barnett Pearce, Stephen W. Littlejohn, and Alison Alexander, "The New Christian Right and the Humanist Response: Reciprocated Diatribe," *Communication Quarterly* 35 (Spring 1987): 177, 187.

their own burdens of proof while adding to those of the opponent, employing humor and ridicule gracefully, asking questions that got to the heart of the matter and put the opponent on the spot, drawing on available sources of evidence and using the opponent's own words and actions as evidence, adapting the arguments to the audience's level of understanding, and involving the audience in the evolution of the argument. Often discussed as only matters of technique, these skills are vital to the art of argumentation. Without them, no debate could proceed beyond the statement of opposing positions. There would be no way to analyze or test these positions, no way to resolve the conflict. These skills are not always present in contemporary public debate, but they are skills for which the Lincoln-Douglas debates can serve as an outstanding model.

Appreciating either the significance of these skills or the use of surrogate arguments to avoid deadlock, however, requires close attention to the actual texts of the debates. Often they are not studied that way. They are regarded as important historical events rather than as significant texts. Their effects, not their content, have been the focus of attention. The romantic and picturesque aspects of the seven encounters may receive more emphasis than the substance of the debates or the relation between the argument and the culture of the time.[8] But what is particularly important about the debates is that they were a sustained public discussion of the issue most troubling the nation. They were attempts to reach and persuade audiences who brought to the discussion their own predispositions and concerns. To see the debates from such a rhetorical perspective, one must focus closely on the dynamics within the actual text. This reissue of the transcripts edited by Paul Angle makes the text easily accessible.

David Zarefsky

---

8. On this point, see J. G. Randall, *Lincoln the President: Springfield to Gettysburg* (New York: Dodd, Mead, 1945), 1: 121.

INTRODUCTION

One hundred years ago, in 1858, Abraham Lincoln, with the back-ing of the young and vigorous Republican party, undertook to con-test the re-election of Stephen A. Douglas, Democrat, to the United States Senate. For three months Lincoln and Douglas stumped the state of Illinois, engaging in seven formal debates and speaking more than a hundred times at their own party rallies.

In their political effect, the debates were of far-reaching impor-tance. Through them, Douglas won another term in the Senate, but to achieve that immediate victory he was forced to take positions that made him unacceptable to the southern wing of his party and cost him the chance—and very good it was—of being elected Presi-dent in 1860. Lincoln, on the other hand, acquired the nation-wide reputation without which he could not have been nominated for the presidency two years later. But for the debates, it is conceivable that in the next two or three years American history might have run a far different course.

As important as their effect on the fortunes of the contestants was the part played by the debates in crystallizing public opinion. The issues the two candidates discussed were national, not local: the extension of slavery to the national territories, the status of the Negro, and the power of the states and territories to regulate their "domestic institutions"—meaning slavery and the Negro—as they saw fit.

Within seven years the Civil War, and the Thirteenth Amend-ment to the Constitution, settled the first of these issues for all time by abolishing slavery. For nearly a century thereafter it appeared that the other two, if not definitely settled, had at least lost their power to divide the nation. Events since May, 1954, when the Su-preme Court of the United States handed down its decision deseg-regating the public schools, have shown that the status of the Negro, and the right of the states to regulate that status, are questions as live today and as dangerously charged with emotion as they were when Lincoln and Douglas discussed them a hundred years ago.

To place the Lincoln-Douglas campaign in its proper setting one must go back at least to 1850. In that year the nation came close to dissolution. Vast new territory had been acquired through the Mexican War, only recently ended. Would these lands be opened to slavery? Over this issue sections clashed, tempers flared. Henry Clay and Daniel Webster, the country's most revered elder statesmen, supported a compromise. The spirit of accommodation grew stronger, and disunion was averted. Gradually all factions except militant abolitionists and southern fire-eaters acquiesced in the compromise measures. Slavery, most people believed, would not be a source of discord for many years to come.

By the Mexican War the United States had extended its boundaries to the Pacific on the west and the Rio Grande on the south. The population of the whole country was growing rapidly: from 17,000,000 in 1840 to 23,000,000 in 1850, and the rate of increase would continue. The East had had a network of railroads for twenty years; now, in 1854, the iron rails were crisscrossing Lincoln's own state. Telegraph lines, accompanying the expanding railroads, had already released millions from isolation. Farmers, given cheap transportation to markets, were prospering as they had never prospered before. New towns were springing up wherever the railroads reached; older communities pulsed with new life.

Early in 1848 gold had been discovered in California. A few months later fortune hunters rushed for the west coast. Thousands made their way across the plains, other thousands fought for passage across the Isthmus of Panama or even around the Horn. California, a sleepy pastoral paradise, suddenly churned with restless, reckless men, intent on wresting fortunes overnight from gold-laden hills and streams. In 1850 the state was admitted to the Union. The federal census takers put its population at 92,600; by 1854 that number had doubled.

The presence of this large, fast-growing settlement on the far Pacific pointed up the necessity of moving forward with a project which had gripped the American imagination for years: the construction of a transcontinental railroad. A route far to the south had its proponents, chief among them Jefferson Davis, senator from Mississippi, but the North was determined that a central route should be selected. To this conviction no one held more strongly than Stephen A. Douglas, senator from Illinois and rival of Abraham Lincoln in the rough-and-tumble political battles of that state.

One step was essential to the location of a transcontinental railroad along the central route. The vast territory of Nebraska, stretching westward from Missouri and Iowa, must be organized and a government established. Settlers, already clamoring for admission to the region, would protect the railroad while it was under construction and at the same time provide the freight and passengers without which it could not function.

Douglas, as chairman of the Senate Committee on Territories, had the responsibility of sponsoring the necessary legislation. A personal passion for developing the West gave urgency to his official sense of responsibility. He had written the laws that had brought five states into the Union and had created five territories, and he had attempted time after time to crown his work with the organization of Nebraska, only to be balked by conflicting sectional interests. Those interests persisted in 1854, and could be counted on to cause trouble; yet the times seemed to be more propitious than they had ever been before. In the first place, Indian titles had been extinguished in 1853, thus paving the way for white settlement. In the second place, Senator Augustus Caesar Dodge of Iowa had introduced a bill for the organization of Nebraska in mid-December, 1853; it had been referred to Douglas' Committee, and the Illinois senator could not have avoided taking some action even had he been disposed to do nothing.

Instead of taking up Dodge's bill, Douglas, on January 4, 1854, introduced his own measure. In its original form, the bill simply organized a territorial government for Nebraska, and disposed of the problem of slavery—the rock on which all previous measures had foundered—with a clause reading: "And when admitted as a State or States, the said Territory, or any portion of the same, shall be received into the Union, with or without slavery, as their constitution may prescribe at the time of their admission." This was the identical language of the Utah and New Mexico acts, passed in 1850 as parts of the compromise measures of that year. Yet the meaning of the clause was far from clear. Under it, could slaves be held in Nebraska during the territorial period? The Missouri Compromise, adopted in 1820, prohibited slavery north of the line of 36° 30′, and all Nebraska lay above that line. In a report filed with the bill the Committee on Territories stated that "eminent statesmen" believed the Missouri Compromise to be unconstitutional, but the committee members were not prepared to recommend either an explicit affirmation or a repeal of the slavery-restriction clause.

Obviously, they were trying to dodge an issue. They failed. David R. Atchison of Missouri, president pro tempore of the Senate and belligerent advocate of slavery, took a hand immediately. What pressures he exerted are not clear, but there is no doubt of their effectiveness. On January 10 Douglas explained that when his bill was first printed one section had been omitted by a clerical error.

That section was now added. It read: "In order to avoid all mis-construction, it is hereby declared to be the true intent and meaning of this act, so far as the question of slavery is concerned, to carry into practical operation the following propositions and principles, established by the Compromise measures of 1850," namely, that fugitive slaves were recoverable in territories as well as states; that all cases involving title to slaves could be appealed to the Supreme Court of the United States; and most important, "that all questions pertaining to slavery in the Territories and in the new States to be formed therefrom, are to be left to the decision of the people re-siding therein, through their appropriate representatives." In short, this section would enact the principle of popular sovereignty and kill the slavery restriction provision of the Missouri Compromise.

Senator Atchison was content with the bill as it now stood, but several of his southern colleagues were not. Chief among them was Senator Archibald Dixon of Kentucky. Dixon saw that the Missouri Compromise restriction would remain in force until the people of the newly organized territory could act on the slavery question through their representatives. By that time the proponents of slavery might well be outnumbered by its opponents. Only by explicitly repealing the Missouri Compromise would the South have an equal chance to plant slavery in Nebraska. On January 16 Dixon offered an amendment, in the form of a new section, which stated that the Missouri Compromise restriction did not apply to the proposed Nebraska Territory or to any other territory of the United States.

Douglas was alarmed. He had hoped to avoid a bitter fight over the slavery question in Nebraska. Dixon's amendment, it was clear, would precipitate a battle. Douglas begged the Kentuckian to with-draw his amendment; he refused.

The chairman of the Committee on Territories now faced a hard necessity. If his bill were to pass, he would need the support of southern senators and representatives. The price of that support was acceptance of Dixon's amendment. Douglas would also need the full backing of the administration. In the next few days he obtained both. After discussing repeal of the Missouri Compromise with Dixon, Douglas gave his promise: "By God, sir, you are right, and I will incorporate it in my bill, though I know it will raise a hell of a storm." A long conference with President Pierce brought a statement to the effect that support of the Nebraska Bill would be considered a test of Democratic orthodoxy.

On January 23 Douglas reported the bill in perfected form. It now provided for the organization of two territories—Kansas and Ne-braska—instead of one. It also met the demands of Dixon and the proslavery senators in this fashion: "The Constitution, and all laws of the United States which are not locally inapplicable, shall have the same force and effect within the said Territories as elsewhere in the United States, except the eighth section of the act preparatory to the admission of Missouri to the Union, approved March 6, 1820, which was superseded by the principles of the legislation of 1850, commonly called the compromise measures, and is declared inoperative." Later, Douglas would change "superseded" to "inconsistent with," and "inoperative" to "null and void." With those substitutions, the Kansas-Nebraska Act took final form.

Before this stage had been reached, the bill had aroused violent protest. The opposition, organized and stimulated by Chase of Ohio, Seward of New York, and Sumner of Massachusetts, mounted as time passed. Yet the outcome, in the Senate at least, was never in doubt. Southern senators stood solid behind the bill, though several doubted its wisdom, and the administration held most northern Democrats in line. On the final vote, taken at 5:00 A.M. on March 4 after a continuous session of seventeen hours, thirty-seven members voted aye, fourteen nay. Many senators had left the chamber in exhaustion, but their absence made no difference. Had all been present, the opposition could have mustered no more than twenty votes.

In the House, with many northern Democrats more responsive to the sentiment of their constituents than their colleagues in the Senate, the division was much closer. For weeks the administration forces held the bill in committee, but by the middle of May they were sure that they had enough votes for passage. On the twenty-second, after a debate that several times threatened to lead to violence, the vote stood 113 to 100. Eight days later Franklin Pierce affixed his signature. The Kansas-Nebraska Act was now the law of the land.

The opposition refused to accept the accomplished fact. Denunciation of the new policy continued, not only from free-soilers and abolitionists, but also from the far larger number of moderates who thought that the slavery question had been settled in 1850 and were shocked to find it suddenly and recklessly reopened. Editorials condemned Douglas and the administration and demanded the repeal of the law. Mass meetings in cities large and small heard angry speakers attack the new policy and its makers. The opposition cut across old party lines, with many northern Democrats joining free-soilers and Whigs.

In Springfield, Illinois, Lincoln saw that the future had suddenly turned dark and ominous. In the third-person autobiography he wrote in 1860, he recorded the change: "His profession had almost superseded the thought of politics in his mind, when the repeal of the Missouri Compromise aroused him as he had never been before." No man concerned for his country, he believed, could remain silent. Richard Yates, the Whig who represented the Springfield district, had fought the Nebraska Bill in the House. The Nebraska forces would make every effort to prevent his re-election; the opponents of the measure must come to his support. Lincoln edged back into politics. In late August he made the first of several speeches urging that Yates be re-elected. Experienced at gauging the reaction of audiences, Lincoln was surprised at the reception accorded him. "His speeches at once attracted a more marked attention than they had ever before done," he wrote of himself. "As the canvass proceeded, he was drawn to different parts of the state, outside of Mr. Yates' district"—specifically, to Bloomington, Peoria, Urbana, Chicago, and Quincy.

The crowds who attended these meetings heard a new Lincoln. In earlier years he had brought roars of laughter with raillery and personal jibes and had grappled for any small argumentative advantage. Now he spoke from deep conviction that the nation was in danger—spoke without humor but with an eloquence that he had never before achieved. By fall he had matured his argument. When he spoke on October 4 at Springfield, where Douglas had presented the case for the Nebraska Bill on the preceding day, the hundreds who jammed the hall of the House of Representatives knew that they were listening to a great speech. On the evening of the sixteenth Lincoln repeated it at Peoria,[1] where Douglas had spoken in the afternoon.

In opening, Lincoln reviewed national policy with reference to slavery in the territories. Then he attacked the repeal of the Missouri Compromise. Contrary to Douglas' assertion, the public had never demanded that the Compromise be repealed. Douglas' measure was intrinsically wrong: by the Compromise of 1850 both North and South had divided the "bone of contention"; now one party to that division, the South, had seized the share of the other party. "It is as if two starving men had divided their only loaf; the one had hastily swallowed his half, and then grabbed the other half just as he was putting it to his mouth!" Popular sovereignty, the right of the people of a territory to decide for themselves whether

---

[1] The text of the speech to be found in *The Collected Works of Abraham Lincoln*, ed. Roy P. Basler *et al.*, II, 247–83, is the one which Lincoln delivered at Peoria. It was printed originally in the Springfield *Illinois Journal* in instalments beginning with the issue of October 21 and concluding with October 28, 1854.

or not to have slavery, Lincoln countered with another principle: "I insist, that if there is ANY THING which it is the duty of the WHOLE PEOPLE to never entrust to any hands but their own, that thing is the preservation and perpetuity, of their own liberties, and institutions."

But the Kansas-Nebraska Act was now law. What could be done about it? Repeal it, Lincoln urged, and restore the Missouri Compromise by sending Anti-Nebraskans to Congress. "Some men, mostly, whigs," he admitted, "who condemn the repeal of the Missouri Compromise, nevertheless hesitate to go for its restoration, lest they be thrown in company with the abolitionist. Will they allow me as an old whig to tell them good humoredly, that I think this is very silly? Stand with anybody that stands RIGHT. Stand with him while he is right, and PART with him when he goes wrong. Stand WITH the abolitionist in restoring the Missouri Compromise; and stand AGAINST him when he attempts to repeal the fugitive slave law. In the latter case you stand with the southern disunionist. What of that? you are still right. In both cases you are right. In both cases you oppose the dangerous extremes. In both you stand on middle ground and hold the ship level and steady. In both you are national and nothing less than national. This is the good old whig ground. To desert such ground, because of any company, is to be less than a whig—less than a man—less than an American."

Lincoln closed on a note of high eloquence. "Our republican robe is soiled, and trailed in the dust. Let us repurify it. Let us turn and wash it white, in the spirit, if not the blood, of the Revolution. Let us turn slavery from its claims of 'moral right,' back upon its existing legal rights, and its arguments of 'necessity.' Let us return it to the position our fathers gave it; and there let it rest in peace. Let us re-adopt the Declaration of Independence, and with it, the practices, and policy, which harmonize with it. Let north and south—let all Americans—let all lovers of liberty everywhere—join in the great and good work. If we do this, we shall not only have saved the Union; but we shall have so saved it, as to make, and keep it, forever worthy of the saving. We shall have so saved it, that the succeeding millions of free happy people, the world over, shall rise up, and call us blessed, to the latest generations."

Lincoln was willing enough to make alliances, but he was far from ready to leave his old party. On October 4, 1854, a group of abolitionists from northern Illinois calling themselves Republicans held a convention in Springfield. Immediately after making his speech Lincoln slipped out of town to avoid being compromised by them. When they made him a member of their state central committee, he protested that the action had been taken without his consent and, in effect, refused to serve.

Although his refusal sprang from conviction, Lincoln was now—in late November, 1854—in a position where he could not afford to be labeled an extremist. In an effort to further the Anti-Nebraska cause he had allowed himself to be named as a candidate for the Illinois House of Representatives. On November 7, without effort on his part, he had been elected. As soon as the statewide returns were in, it was apparent that the Anti-Nebraskans had been successful beyond their expectations: they had elected a majority of members of the legislature. The senatorial term of James Shields, staunch supporter of Douglas, was expiring, and the Anti-Nebraskans could elect one of their own number if they would unite. Lincoln, by his efforts in the campaign, had earned the place of honor. To strengthen his position, he declined to accept his seat in the House and undertook by every means at his command to obtain pledges of support.

The legislature did not meet in joint session until February 8, 1855. On the first ballot Lincoln received forty-four votes, Shields forty-one, and Lyman Trumbull, an Anti-Nebraska Democrat, five. It was soon apparent that Joel Matteson, Democratic governor of Illinois, rather than Shields was the real candidate of the Douglas forces. With Trumbull's five supporters, Lincoln would win; but if they held back, Matteson would eventually attract a few wavering Anti-Nebraskans and be elected. For ballot after ballot Trumbull's men refused to yield: they could not, they said, bring themselves to vote for a Whig. After the ninth ballot Lincoln saw that only by throwing his own votes to Trumbull could Matteson be defeated. The Whig leader released his supporters, and on the next ballot Trumbull was elected.

Thus Lincoln failed to obtain the one office which he wanted above all others. But the fact that he was the indubitable choice of the great majority of Anti-Nebraskans, and his magnanimity and devotion to principle in bringing about Trumbull's election, made him the undisputed leader of the Anti-Nebraska movement in Illinois. Barring some unexpected development, he would oppose Douglas when the Senator's term expired in 1858.

Meanwhile, an ominous state of affairs had arisen in Kansas. The residents of western Missouri, touching the eastern border of the new territory, were proslavery in sentiment and expected Kansas to enter the Union as a slave state. Even before the territory was organized, many Missourians crossed the border and took up land. At the same time settlers from states of the Old Northwest, not much concerned about the slavery question one way or the other, began to acquire farms. In New England, abolitionists sensed danger and organized the New England Emigrant Aid Company for the purpose of sending a sufficient number of militantly antislavery settlers to Kansas to make it a free state.

The Missourians resented interference and resolved to beat the Emigrant Aid Company at its own game. In late November, 1854, when an election was held to choose a territorial delegate, nearly two thousand Missourians crossed the border to vote. The free-state forces, small and as yet unorganized, made no protest but resolved to recruit their strength for the election at which a territorial legislature would be chosen. On March 30, 1855, when the election took place, the Missourians again swarmed over the border. Of the 6,307 votes counted, it was said that the invaders cast more than three-fourths. The free-state forces protested strenuously, but certificates were issued to most of the winning candidates, and the proslavery party emerged with a heavy legislative majority.

In Springfield, Lincoln watched the practical workings of popular sovereignty and came to certain conclusions which he expressed in a letter to his old friend Joshua Speed, a fair-minded Kentuckian. "You say if you were President," Lincoln wrote, "you would send an army and hang the leaders of the Missouri outrages upon the Kansas elections; still, if Kansas fairly votes herself a slave state, she must be admitted, or the Union must be dissolved. But how if she votes herself a slave state *unfairly*—that is, by the very means for which you say you would hang men? Must she still be admitted, or the Union be dissolved?"

That, Lincoln predicted, would be the question with which the country would be faced. "In your assumption that there may be a *fair* decision of the slavery question in Kansas," he continued, "I plainly see you and I would differ about the Nebraska law. I look upon that enactment not as a *law*, but as violence from the beginning. It was conceived in violence, passed in violence, is maintained in violence, and is being executed in violence. I say it was *conceived* in violence, because the destruction of the Missouri Compromise, under the circumstances, was nothing less than violence. It was *passed* in violence, because it could not have been passed at all but for the votes of many members, in violent disregard of the known will of their constituents. It is *maintained* in violence because the elections since, clearly demand its repeal, and this demand is openly disregarded. *You* say men ought to be hung for the way they are executing that law; and *I* say the way it is being executed is quite as good as any of its antecedents. It is being executed in the precise way which was intended from the first; else why does no Nebraska man express astonishment or condemnation?"

What was to be done? Lincoln could answer for himself. "In my humble sphere, I shall advocate the restoration of the Missouri Compromise, so long as Kansas remains a territory; and when, by all these foul means, it seeks to come into the Union as a slave state, I shall oppose it. . . . In my opposition to the admission of Kansas I shall have some company; but we may be beaten. If we are, I shall not, on that account, attempt to dissolve the Union. On the contrary, if we succeed, there will be enough of us to take care of the Union."

With the old political parties disintegrating as their members took sides on the slavery question, where did Lincoln stand? "That is a disputed point," he admitted. "I think I am a whig; but others say there are no whigs, and that I am an abolitionist. When I was at Washington I voted for the Wilmot Proviso[2] as good as forty times, and I never heard of any one attempting to unwhig me for that. I now do no more than oppose the extension of slavery."

On one point Lincoln was certain. He would have nothing to do with the nativistic American, or Know-Nothing, party, to which many former Whigs were turning. "I am not a Know-Nothing," he concluded. ". . . How could I be? How can any one who abhors the oppression of Negroes, be in favor of degrading classes of white people? Our progress in degeneracy appears to me to be pretty rapid. As a nation, we began by declaring that 'all men are created equal.' We now practically read it 'all men are created equal, except negroes.' When the Know Nothings get control, it will read 'all men are created equal, except negroes, and foreigners, and catholics.' When it comes to this I should prefer emigrating to some country where they make no pretence of loving liberty—to Russia, for instance, where despotism can be taken pure, without the base alloy of hypocrisy."[3]

In Kansas the situation became progressively worse. A census taken in 1855 revealed that there were only 192 slaves in the territory, and sensible men everywhere knew that slavery could never thrive there. But Kansas had become a symbol. The South had decided that the prospective state must come into the Union with slavery; the North was equally determined that Kansas must be free.

The territorial legislature met at Lecompton in July, 1855, unseated the few free-state members who had been elected, legalized

[2] A measure providing that slavery should never exist in any territory to be acquired from Mexico.

[3] To Joshua Fry Speed, Springfield, August 24, 1855, *Collected Works of Abraham Lincoln*, II, 320–23.

slavery, and passed a stringent slave code. The free-state settlers, despairing of accomplishing anything within the existing framework of government, decided to organize a state government of their own and apply for admission to the Union. On October 23 they held a convention at Topeka and framed a constitution which prohibited slavery.

Kansas now had two rival governments and two bitterly hostile factions of settlers. Civil war seemed imminent. Bloodshed was narrowly averted in early December, when more than a thousand armed men, mostly proslavery Missourians, gathered in camps along the Wakarusa River in the vicinity of Lawrence, the antislavery center, and threatened to destroy the town. The defenders were badly outnumbered, but so many of them were armed with Sharps rifles—a superior, breech-loading weapon—that the invaders lost heart and dispersed.

The free-state men moved to organize the government which they had initiated at Topeka. On December 15 they ratified the constitution framed by their representatives and elected a governor. The proslavery settlers took the position that the election was extralegal and stayed away from the polls. Before the end of January, 1856, President Pierce upheld them by declaring the Topeka constitution and the election held under it to be revolutionary.

By 1856 the slavery question, kept constantly in the foreground by the troubles in Kansas, had brought a new party into existence. In the beginning, most of the Whigs and Democrats who could not stomach the Nebraska Bill called themselves "Anti-Nebraskans" or "fusionists," but a few groups adopted the name "Republican," hallowed by association with Thomas Jefferson. Some such groups, as in Illinois, were too radical to win the immediate adherence of moderate antislavery men. But as time went on, increasing numbers of Anti-Nebraskans saw the necessity of building a party organization if the policy they represented were to be made effective. Unless they were willing to accept the Know-Nothing creed—and some were—they joined the Republicans. The new party lost its radical cast as it grew, and became acceptable to ever growing numbers who had shunned it in its early days.

By 1856, the Republicans were strong enough to elect Nathaniel P. Banks of Massachusetts Speaker of the House of Representatives, although 133 ballots were necessary to do the trick. The victory convinced the leaders of the new party that it could elect a President in the forthcoming campaign. Before the national convention the Republicans were the beneficiaries of a dramatic and disgraceful incident in the United States Senate. There, on the nineteenth of May,

Charles Sumner, the able, pompous, humorless senator from Massachusetts, delivered a carefully prepared speech on the troubles in Kansas. Sumner often exceeded reasonable bounds of restraint, but this time he outdid himself in offensive allusions to the state of South Carolina and to her elderly senator, Andrew P. Butler. Two days later Preston Brooks, a member of the House and Butler's nephew, caned Sumner into unconsciousness as he sat pinned at his desk in the Senate chamber. Indignation meetings were held in dozens of northern cities and editors fumed while the South showered testimonial canes on Brooks and hailed him as a hero. The episode intensified sectional animosities, and brought new thousands into the Republican ranks.

By this time Abraham Lincoln had ended his Hamlet-like soliloquy and joined the Republican party. On Washington's Birthday, 1856, he met with a group of Anti-Nebraska editors and helped to build the framework of a state organization. The meeting adopted resolutions protesting the further extension of slavery, appointed a state central committee, and issued a call for a state convention to meet at Bloomington on May 29. At that gathering, attended by delegates from seventy of the one hundred Illinois counties, Lincoln made a closing address of such fervor that even the reporters lost themselves in his impassioned oratory and forgot to take notes.

The Republican National Convention met at Philadelphia on June 17, chose John C. Frémont, colorful but politically inexperienced explorer, as the presidential nominee, and selected William L. Dayton, former senator from New Jersey, as Frémont's running mate. Early in the month the Democrats had nominated James Buchanan of Pennsylvania and John C. Breckinridge of Kentucky to run on a platform which indorsed popular sovereignty. The Illinois delegation had pressed hard for Douglas but had had to yield to the general feeling that the senator, then only forty-three years old, could afford to wait for the honor. The situation was complicated by the presence in the field of a third ticket, that of the Know-Nothings, consisting of former President Millard Fillmore and Andrew J. Donelson, who had served as Andrew Jackson's presidential secretary. Though waning in strength, the Know-Nothings might draw enough votes from Frémont to give the election to Buchanan.

In many northern states the Republicans campaigned as if they were crusaders. Nothing like their zeal had been seen since the "Tippecanoe and Tyler Too" hysteria of 1840. "The drive and energy of the republicans astounded their opponents," Arthur Charles Cole writes of Illinois. "Huge parades and processions with gay banners and gorgeous floats preceded the meetings. At Peoria thirty-one young women dressed in white with wreaths of flowers about their brows, with one in mourning garb to represent Kansas, were embarked on a boat, drawn by eight splendid white horses; it was the 'Constitution,' 'bound for the White House.' This device was adopted all over the state; often the young women were led by one more beautiful and splendidly attired than the rest to represent 'the queen of hearts,' the 'adored Jessie,' dashing wife of Colonel Frémont. Free dinners and barbecues, widely advertised in staring posters, drew together crowds of thousands; the roar of artillery, the fluttering of banners, and the melody of bands of wind and string instruments, aided in attaching the sturdy yeomanry of the Illinois prairies to the republican cause."[4]

No Republican worked harder for the party than Abraham Lincoln. Writing four years later, he said that he had made more than fifty speeches during the campaign. Yet the divisive effect of the Know-Nothings could not be overcome. In Illinois, Buchanan polled 105,348 votes, Frémont 96,189, and Fillmore 37,444; in the nation the totals were Buchanan, 1,838,169; Frémont, 1,341,364; and Fillmore, 874,534. But the Republicans, while failing to win the presidency, made substantial gains in the House, Senate, and state offices. In Illinois they won all the state offices and elected four of nine congressmen. Lincoln emerged as the acknowledged leader of the party in the state, as two years earlier he had stood at the head of the Anti-Nebraska forces.

Throughout the year 1856 the situation in Kansas had worsened steadily. As spring advanced, violence increased to such an extent that newspapers headed their dispatches, "The War in Kansas." On May 11, the United States marshal summoned a posse to aid him in executing certain writs in Lawrence. While the posse was assembling, one free-state man was shot. Three of his comrades attempted to avenge his death. One was killed. Ten days later the posse entered Lawrence. The marshal served his writs without trouble. But the members of the posse, described by one historian as "a swearing, whiskey-drinking, ruffianly horde, seven hundred and fifty in number,"[5] had plans of their own. They destroyed the offices of the town's two newspapers, smashed the presses, and threw the type into the streets. With their four cannon they opened fire on the Free State Hotel. The balls bounced off the stout stone building but started fires in the inflammable interior that brought about its destruction. The posse proceeded to sack the town.

[4] *The Era of the Civil War, 1848–1870* (Springfield, Ill., 1919), p. 148.

[5] James Ford Rhodes, *History of the United States from the Compromise of 1850* (New York, 1892), II, 158.

At Osawatomie, fifty miles away, John Brown, antislavery fanatic, brooded over the destruction of Lawrence and counted up the number of free-state men who had been killed since the "war" began. Five. Their deaths must be expiated by an equal number of deaths in the proslavery ranks. Brown called for volunteers, without, however, disclosing his intentions. Four sons, a son-in-law, and two other men responded. On the night of May 24 the party visited three homesteads. At the first they murdered the father and two sons; at each of the other houses they found one victim. The murdered men, though all proslavery in sentiment, had not been notorious wrongdoers. For their deaths there was no justification except in the tortured mind of a man who had come to identify himself with an avenging God.

Turmoil in the territory continued until John W. Geary was appointed governor in mid-September. By pursuing a strictly impartial course, Geary soon won the respect of the responsible men in both factions. The disorders became less frequent until the new governor could report, on November 7, that "the general peace of the territory remains unimpaired, confidence is being gradually restored, business is resuming its ordinary channels, citizens are preparing for winter, and there is readiness among the good people of all parties to sustain my administration."

With Kansas quiet, the slavery question might have died down. But the United States Supreme Court was now to blow it into flame. For some time the court had had before it the case of Dred Scott. Dred, a Negro, had been the slave and personal servant of an army surgeon, Dr. John Emerson. Emerson, a Missourian, had taken Dred with him on tours of duty at Rock Island, Illinois, and later at Fort Snelling, Minnesota, and had then carried the slave back to his home state. In 1846, after Emerson's death, Dred sued for his liberty on the ground that residence on free soil—Rock Island and Fort Snelling were both north of the 36° 30′ line of the Missouri Compromise—had made him a free man. He obtained a verdict in his favor, but on appeal the Supreme Court of Missouri held that by voluntarily returning from free territory he had resumed the status of slave.

By various means the case was brought into the courts of the United States and eventually reached the Supreme Court. In 1856 distinguished counsel argued it twice. By this time the case had attracted national attention, for the decision could hardly fail to have great political significance. Buchanan, in his inaugural address of March 4, 1857, went so far as to predict that it would settle the question of slavery in the territories.

The decision came two days after the President spoke. It took the form of nine separate opinions, six of which coincided in general with that of the Chief Justice, Roger B. Taney, while two, by Justices Curtis and McLean, were dissents. One need not attempt to follow all the legal tortuosities of the various opinions. Taney came to the nub of the case in two conclusions: (1) that "Dred Scott was not a citizen of Missouri within the meaning of the Constitution of the United States, and not entitled as such to sue in its courts"; (2) "that the Act of Congress which prohibited a citizen from holding and owning" slave property north of the line of 36° 30' "is not warranted by the Constitution, and is therefore void." In plain words, a Negro could not be a citizen of the United States, the Missouri Compromise was unconstitutional, and Congress had no power to exclude slavery from the national territories.

The Republican press and Republican orators denounced the decision without restraint. It was a "deliberate iniquity," a "wilful perversion," "the greatest crime in the judicial annals of the Republic," and "entitled to just so much moral weight as would be the judgment of a majority of those congregated in any Washington barroom."[6] Such a reaction was to be expected, for the decision left the Republicans without a solution for the slavery problem. They had been working for the repeal of the Nebraska Bill and the restoration of the Missouri Compromise. Now they were told, by the court of last resort, that Congress had had no power to enact the Compromise. Obviously, the court would hold any attempt at restoration unconstitutional.

If the Dred Scott decision played hob with the Republican program, it also demolished Douglas' popular sovereignty—or appeared to. If Congress had no power to exclude slavery from a territory, how could the people residing there exercise a choice? Douglas made no public comment on the decision until June 12, 1857, when he spoke at Springfield on the invitation of the federal grand jury. The slavery issue, he asserted, had been reduced to the limits of the decision in the Dred Scott case. That decision must be respected; to resist it would be to strike "a deadly blow" at the "whole republican system of government." If resistance should be aroused for partisan purposes, there would be raised "a distinct and naked issue between the friends and the enemies of the constitution—the friends and the enemies of the supremacy of the laws."

The decision itself, Douglas continued, would have no effect upon the practical operation of popular sovereignty. To be sure, the court had decided that the right to hold slaves in national territories could not be extinguished. But that was "a barren and a worthless right,

___

[6] James G. Randall, *The Civil War and Reconstruction* (Boston, 1937), p. 155.

unless sustained, protected and enforced, by appropriate police regulations and local legislation, prescribing adequate remedies for its
violation. These regulations and remedies must necessarily depend
entirely upon the will and wishes of the people of the territory, as
they can only be prescribed by the local legislatures." Hence, Douglas concluded with curious logic, "the great principle of popular
sovereignty and self-government is sustained and firmly established
by the authority of this decision."

Having solved his dilemma, Douglas took the offensive. Republicans and abolitionists had characterized Taney's opinion that a
Negro could not be a citizen of the United States as "cruel, inhuman,
and infamous." Wherein is the cruelty, the inhumanity, the infamy?
Douglas asked. He then launched into an argument to show that the
Founding Fathers had not intended to include Negroes in their
declaration that all men were created equal. "The history of the
times clearly show that our fathers did not regard the negro race as
any kin to them, and determined so to lay the foundations of society
and government that they should never be of any kin to their posterity. But," Douglas concluded, "when you confer upon the African
race the privileges of citizenship, and put them upon an equality
with white men at the polls, in the jury box, on the bench, in the
executive chair, and in the councils of the nation, upon what principle will you deny their equality at the festive board and in the
domestic circle?"[7]

Douglas here propounded the two issues upon which he would
campaign for re-election in the coming year: a reconciliation of the
Dred Scott decision and popular sovereignty, and an appeal to the
anti-Negro sentiments of his constituents, many of whom were of
southern origin.

Lincoln sat in Douglas' audience on June 12. Two weeks later the
Republican leader made his reply. Douglas had denounced opposition to the Dred Scott decision. "But who resists it?" Lincoln asked.
"Who has, in spite of the decision, declared Dred Scott free, and resisted the authority of his master over him?" Republicans, Lincoln
continued, went no further than to refuse to accept the decision "as
not having yet quite established a settled doctrine for the country."

Lincoln had no aversion to meeting Douglas' contention that the
founders of the Republic had looked on the Negro as an inferior
person. "There is a natural disgust in the minds of nearly all white
people," Lincoln admitted, "to the idea of an indiscriminate amalgamation of the white and black races; and Judge Douglas evidently is

[7] *Remarks of the Hon. Stephen A. Douglas on Kansas, Utah, and the Dred
Scott Decision* (Chicago *Daily Times*, 1857).

basing his chief hope, upon the chances of being able to appropriate the benefit of this disgust to himself. If he can, by much drumming and repeating, fasten the odium of that idea upon his adversaries, he thinks he can struggle through the storm. He therefore clings to this hope, as a drowning man to the last plank. He makes an occasion for lugging it in from the opposition to the Dred Scott decision. He finds the Republicans insisting that the Declaration of Independence includes ALL men, black as well as white; and forthwith he boldly denies that it includes negroes at all, and proceeds to argue gravely that all who contend it does, do so only because they want to vote, and eat, and sleep, and marry with negroes! He will have it that they cannot be consistent else. Now I protest against that counterfeit logic which concludes that, because I do not want a black woman for a *slave* I must necessarily want her for a *wife*. I need not have her for either, I can just leave her alone. In some respects she certainly is not my equal; but in her natural right to eat the bread she earns with her own hands without asking leave of any one else, she is my equal, and the equal of all others."

"I had thought the Declaration contemplated the progressive improvement in the condition of all men everywhere," Lincoln continued; "but no, it merely 'was adopted for the purpose of justifying the colonists in the eyes of the civilized world in withdrawing their allegiance from the British crown, and dissolving their connection with the mother country.' Why, that object having been effected some eighty years ago, the Declaration is of no practical use now—mere rubbish—old wadding left to rot on the battlefield after the victory is won."

But when it came to a positive solution of the slavery question, Lincoln could offer nothing better than colonization.[8] Even here he had to admit that the Republican party had not gone on record officially in favor of this expedient. Yet Republican support could be inferred, since true Republicans held that "the negro is a man; that his bondage is cruelly wrong, and that the field of his oppression ought not to be enlarged."

By contrast, "the Democrats deny his [the Negro's] manhood; deny, or dwarf to insignificance, the wrong of his bondage; so far as possible, crush all sympathy for him, and cultivate and excite hatred and disgust against him; compliment themselves as Union-savers for doing so; and call the indefinite outspreading of his bondage 'a sacred right of self-government.'"

"The plainest print," Lincoln concluded, "cannot be read through a gold eagle; and it will be ever hard to find many men who will

[8] The establishing of Negro "colonies" outside of the United States.

send a slave to Liberia, and pay his passage while they can send him to a new country, Kansas for instance, and sell him for fifteen hundred dollars, and the rise."[9]

Lincoln too had found one of the issues—the moral iniquity of slavery—on which he would make his campaign in 1858.

When Douglas spoke on June 12 he had touched briefly on Kansas. The territory, he said, was "about to speak for herself, through her delegates assembled in convention to form a constitution, preparatory to her admission into the Union on an equal footing with the original States. Peace and prosperity now prevail within her borders. The law under which her delegates are about to be elected is believed to be just and fair in all its objects and provisions. There is every reason to hope and believe that the law will be fairly interpreted and impartially executed, so as to insure to every *bona fide* inhabitant the free and quiet exercise of the elective franchise."

As a reporter Douglas was correct, for the quiet which Governor Geary had noted six months earlier had been disturbed by no serious incidents. As prophet, Douglas could hardly have been wider of the mark.

The election to which he referred, held for the purpose of electing delegates to a constitutional convention, took place on June 15, 1857. Free-state settlers, convinced that they would be counted out at the polls, abstained from voting, with the result that only pro-slavery delegates were chosen. Meeting at Lecompton in the fall of the year, they framed a constitution which provided for the usual forms of state government. An article on slavery, however, declared that the "right of property . . . is higher than any constitutional sanction, and the right of the owner of a slave . . . is . . . as inviolable as the right of the owner of any property whatever." Instead of providing for the submission of the entire constitution to the voters, the delegates decided that the people should be permitted to vote only for the constitution "with slavery" or for the constitution "with no slavery." If the vote favored the constitution "with no slavery," the institution was to exist "no longer," except that "the right of property in slaves now in this Territory shall in no measure be interfered with." Moreover, amendment was prohibited before the year 1865.

The vote on ratification took place on December 21, 1857. Again the free-state men stayed away from the polls, with the result that the returns showed more than six thousand votes for the constitution with slavery and fewer than six hundred for the constitution without slavery.

Robert J. Walker, now territorial governor, had become convinced

[9] *Collected Works of Abraham Lincoln*, II, 398–410.

that the proslavery element was maintaining its ascendancy only by fraud and intimidation. Buchanan refused to heed Walker's reports and, heartily sick of the whole mess, resolved to ram the acceptance of the Lecompton constitution through Congress as an administration measure. Douglas, aware that the limited submission to the people was a travesty on popular sovereignty, broke with the President. A heated interview ended with a threat from Buchanan: "Mr. Douglas, I desire you to remember that no Democrat ever yet differed with an administration of his own choosing without being crushed. Beware of the fate of Talmadge and Rives."[10]

"Mr. President," Douglas shot back, "I wish you to remember that General Jackson is dead."

In the Senate, the administration had the votes, and the bill to admit Kansas under the Lecompton constitution passed, 33 to 25. But in the House it soon became evident that a compromise of some sort would have to be devised. A formula was found in a measure known as the English Bill, which called for the submission of the Lecompton constitution in its entirety to the people of Kansas and offered a federal land grant if it should be accepted. After some hesitation Douglas denounced the compromise as a bribe, but the English Bill passed both houses and became law on May 4, 1858. Two months later, Kansans, voting in a fair election, buried the Lecompton constitution by a vote of 11,300 to 1,788.

By his courageous course Douglas had won the respect of many Republicans, particularly in the East. More than one leader of the party in that section suggested that Illinois Republicans might well drop any notion of opposing him in 1858. Lincoln was deeply disturbed, not only for the effect such a course would have on his own fortunes, but also because he believed that Douglas would never recede from a political philosophy which the Republican party could not accept. In letters written in the winter of 1857–58 and the following spring, Lincoln expressed his concern. He need not, however, have worried, for the party in Illinois resented outside interference and went ahead with its plans to throw its strongest candidate against the Little Giant.

To superficial observers, in the spring of 1858, Lincoln's chances of success seemed to be excellent. In 1856 the Republicans had trailed the Democrats by less than 10,000 votes, and they were stronger now than then. The Know-Nothing party had disappeared. Two years earlier the Republicans had faced a united, aggressive Democracy; now the opposition would be divided. But practical politicians knew that more would be required than a majority of the

10 Two Democrats whom Jackson had broken for insurgency.

votes cast. United States senators were elected by the legislature in joint session. The state had not been reapportioned since 1852, and the fast-growing northern section, heavily Republican, was under-represented in comparison with the central and southern parts. Besides, only half of the Senate seats were to be filled. (Senators served four-year terms, with half of their number chosen every two years.) Senators who had been elected in 1856 might or might not represent political opinion in 1858.

The key to the election lay in the central third of the state. The northern third would go Republican, the southern third Democratic. The central counties made up the old Whig stronghold. The Whig party was dead. In the new alignment—Republicans vs. Democrats—which side would a majority of old Whigs choose?

The question determined the strategy of the campaign. Aside from the debates, Lincoln spoke at only four places north of Galesburg and at only three south of Alton. Douglas, as an official representative of the entire state, could not appear to slight any section, but even he made two-thirds of his speeches in the critical center.

The rallies between the debates had an importance that is not generally recognized. The formal meetings, with the candidates face to face, offered drama which the press exploited fully, and, with the exception of the one held at Jonesboro, drew large crowds. But they reached only a fraction of the voters, and only a fraction of the voters saw the newspapers which reported the speeches. To the others, the campaign had to be brought home. This both candidates succeeded in doing between early August and election day. Never before had aspirants for political office undertaken such a grind. Each man traveled thousands of miles on the primitive railroads of the day; each had to put up with the scanty comforts and poor food of small-town hotels; each had to speak almost every day in the open air, taxing his voice to the limit; each had to say the right word to thousands of ardent yet touchy partisans. It would not have been surprising had both men broken under the strain, but there is no record that either missed a single scheduled meeting. Toward the end, Douglas' voice showed signs of failure, but Lincoln appeared to be as fresh as he was at the beginning of the ordeal.

The campaign had no precedent in other respects. No previous local election had aroused such a degree of national interest. This was partly because the questions involved were national questions, partly because not only the political future of Stephen A. Douglas but also that of James Buchanan was at stake, and partly because the campaign was the first to be reported in modern fashion. In two ways, it made journalistic history. For the first time correspondents traveled with candidates, and for the first time a series of political speeches was reported stenographically.[11]

The two leading party organs of the state—the Chicago *Press and Tribune*, Republican, and the Chicago *Times*, Democratic—were responsible for these innovations. The *Press and Tribune*[12] assigned Horace White, a twenty-four-year-old editorial writer, to travel with Lincoln and report the progress of his campaign and hired Robert R. Hitt, also twenty-four, to take down the debates in shorthand. Two years earlier Hitt had opened an office in Chicago to become the city's first expert stenographer. The *Times* imported its men, hiring Henry Binmore from the St. Louis *Republican* and James B. Sheridan from the Philadelphia *Press*. Both men could write shorthand, and, unlike the *Press and Tribune* team, both filed "color" stories.

Throughout the campaign, each party charged the opposing party paper with printing garbled reports of speeches. There seems to be no real basis for the accusation. Edwin Earle Sparks, after comparing the *Press and Tribune* and *Times* versions of the same speech, could find no discrepancies which could not be accounted for by the difficulties which the reporters faced—"the open air, the rude platforms, the lack of accommodations for writing, the jostling of the crowds of people, and the occasional puffs of wind which played havoc with sheets of paper"—and by the natural tendency of the reporters for each paper to take more care with the speeches of the party candidate than with those of his opponent.[13]

This judgment applies only to verbatim reporting. In other stories, fairness was not to be expected. According to Binmore and Sheridan, Douglas' meetings were invariably triumphs, and Lincoln's—when they had an opportunity to describe them—pitiable failures. Exactly the opposite impression would be given by Horace White in the *Press and Tribune*. Misrepresentation extended even to such tangibles as attendance, with Democratic reporters ever ready to claim an audience for a Douglas meeting four times as large as White would concede and the Republicans no less willing to make similarly exaggerated claims in Lincoln's behalf. That readers could have accepted such accounts at their face value seems incredible.

Although there were only seven formal debates, five earlier

[11] To assign "firsts" is always dangerous, but these assertions seem to be warranted by all the evidence with which I am familiar.

[12] The word "Press" was not dropped until 1861. The *Times* had no relationship to the present Chicago *Sun-Times*.

[13] *The Lincoln-Douglas Debates of 1858*, ed. Edwin Earle Sparks (Springfield, Ill., 1908), pp. 81–82.

speeches must be considered integral parts of the campaign and have therefore been included in this book. They are: Lincoln's "House Divided" speech of June 16, 1858, with which he opened his campaign; Douglas' initial speech at Chicago on July 9 and Lincoln's reply the following evening; and the speeches of both men at Springfield on July 17. That both Lincoln and Douglas recognized these addresses as parts of the pattern is indicated by the fact that, when they made arrangements for the debates, they limited their joint meetings to the seven congressional districts in which neither had spoken. Chicago and Springfield represented the other two districts.

In the debates there was, of course, much repetition, and there must have been even more in the unrecorded speeches. Each audience was new, and not until the campaign had been in progress for several weeks could either speaker be sure that the principal issues were generally understood. In the "House Divided" speech Lincoln charged that the advocates of slavery had embarked on a policy which would fasten the institution on all the states of the Union and that one Senator (Douglas), two Presidents (Pierce and Buchanan), and a Chief Justice of the United States (Taney) had entered into a conspiracy to bring about that result. At Chicago, on July 9, Douglas picked up Lincoln's declaration that a house divided could not stand, twisted it into an assertion "that there must be uniformity in the local laws and domestic institutions of each and all the States of the Union," and countered with popular sovereignty—the right of the people in each state and territory to choose their own domestic institutions. He cited his attitude on the Lecompton constitution as proof of his fidelity to this principle and took credit for the refusal of Congress to admit Kansas under this document. He ignored Lincoln's conspiracy charge but scored those who were attacking the Supreme Court for its decision in the Dred Scott case. In conclusion, Douglas stated candidly and at some length his conviction that the Negro was not the equal of the white man and that the government of the United States "was made by the white man, for the benefit of the white man, to be administered by white men, in such manner as they should determine."

On the following day, at Chicago, Lincoln found himself on the defensive. He had to deny that his "House Divided" assertion meant what Douglas said it meant. He had to clear his party of the charge that its members were "resisting" the Dred Scott decision. They were not resisting, but they would do what they could to force the Court to reverse itself. As far as the defeat of the Lecompton constitution was concerned, that was accomplished mainly by Republican votes. On the status of the Negro, Lincoln made a distinction. He admitted that the black man was not the equal of the white in all respects, but, he insisted, "in relation to the principle that all men are created equal, let it be as nearly reached as we can. If we cannot give freedom to every creature, let us do nothing that will impose slavery upon any other creature."

On the whole, Lincoln was pleased with his effort in this first encounter. Five days later, from Springfield, he wrote to Gustave Koerner: "I have just returned from Chicago. Douglas took nothing by his motion there. In fact, by his rampant indorsement of the Dred Scott decision he drove back a few republicans who were favorably inclined towards him. . . . I was present at his reception in Chicago, and it certainly was very large and imposing; but judging from the opinions of others better acquainted with faces there, and by the strong call for me to speak when he closed, I really believe we could have voted him down in that very crowd. Our meeting, twenty-four hours after, called only twelve hours before it came together and got up without trumpery, was nearly as large, and five times as enthusiastic."

When Douglas spoke at Springfield on July 17 he covered much the same ground as he had covered at Chicago, but in more detail. Again he took credit for defeating the Lecompton constitution. Again he hit at Lincoln's "House Divided" doctrine, but here he gave the argument a new twist. The Republicans, he charged, intended to achieve uniformity in the country by abolishing slavery in the states where it existed. As to the Dred Scott decision, how would Lincoln reverse it? To what tribunal could he take an appeal? Lincoln's argument that the decision had destroyed popular sovereignty was nonsense. Slavery could not exist unless it was sustained by friendly local legislation—the same doctrine that the speaker had advanced in his Dred Scott speech of June 12, 1857. In conclusion, Douglas charged again that Lincoln aimed at Negro equality, while he, Douglas, intended to maintain both government and society on the basis of white superiority.

When Lincoln spoke on the evening of the same day he called attention, first, to the disadvantages under which the Republicans labored: the inequitable apportionment of legislative seats, the holdover senators who no longer represented the political complexion of their districts. He then restated, in essence, the points he had made at Chicago, adding little to the development of the general argument. He concluded with a reiteration of his belief, elaborately developed in the "House Divided" speech, that a conspiracy existed which aimed at perpetuating and nationalizing slavery. "Judge

Douglas," Lincoln stated, "has carefully read and re-read that speech. He has not, so far as I know, contradicted those charges. . . . I charge him with having been a party to that conspiracy and to that deception for the sole purpose of nationalizing slavery."

When the two candidates met at Ottawa for the first of the formal debates, each had already laid down the platform on which he would campaign. Douglas would stand on popular sovereignty as a basic American principle, harmonize it with the Dred Scott decision through his doctrine of unfriendly local legislation, charge Lincoln with advocating sectional conflict, and press the contention that the Negro was an inferior being who was not entitled to the social and political equality which, he alleged, Lincoln sought to bring about. To Lincoln's conspiracy charge Douglas opposed a categorical denial: "All I have to say is, that I am not green enough to let him make a charge which he acknowledges he does not know to be true, and then take up my time in answering it, when I know it to be false and nobody else knows it to be true." Although Lincoln would repeat the allegation, he failed to support it with evidence, and gave it diminishing emphasis in his later speeches.

At Ottawa, and in the succeeding debates, Lincoln took the position that the repeal of the Missouri Compromise was the breaking of a contract and that the Dred Scott decision had nullified popular sovereignty. To a degree, he would be on the defensive. He would be compelled to explain and qualify his "'House Divided" declaration, and he must deny that he was promoting Negro equality. This necessity, however, gave him an opportunity to take a high moral position on slavery and the Negro in contrast to Douglas' candid indifference.

These issues furnished the subject matter of all the debates except the fourth, at Charleston, where a bitter squabble between Douglas and Lyman Trumbull became the principal topic. There were, however, developments within the general framework. At Ottawa Douglas propounded a series of questions designed to pin Lincoln down to specific avowals with which his opponent could grapple. Lincoln, with characteristic caution, did not reply until the next debate at Freeport, and then he accompanied his answers with interrogatories of his own. The second of these would have a major place in succeeding encounters. It reads: "Can the people of a United States territory, in any lawful way, against the wish of any citizen of the United States, exclude slavery from its limits prior to the formulation of a state constitution?"

Before asking the question, Lincoln had sought the advice of a number of leading Republicans. Several advised against it. All knew what the answer would be, for ever since the summer of 1857 Douglas had been contending that in spite of Supreme Court decisions slavery could not exist unless it was sustained by local laws and ordinances. Should he be given the opportunity to elaborate this answer before many thousands? His Illinois constituents would probably find it convincing. It would hurt him in the South, where a nullification of what had been gained by the Dred Scott decision would not be popular, and it might well cost Douglas the presidential nomination in 1860. But this was 1858, with an Illinois seat in the Senate, and not the presidency, at stake. Lincoln pondered the problem, then asked the question.

Who "won" the debates? From the standpoint of forensics, the answer to that question must always be a matter of opinion. Certain comments, however, are relevant. Some historians have argued that the speakers were concerned only with slavery in the territories and that the chance of slavery's being established there was so small that the issue was a false one. It has been contended, moreover, that experience with the Prohibition amendment in the 1920's proves that Douglas' solution was an eminently practical one: that Prohibition became a nullity wherever local opinion was opposed to it.

Such positions ignore a basic reality, namely, that any issue, no matter how hollow, which stirs large numbers of people is a historical fact of first importance. Concede that the American people should not have become aroused over the presence of a couple of hundred slaves in Kansas, and concede that even that small number could have been forced out had Douglas' doctrine of local legislation been adopted; the fact is that the people did become aroused and by taking sides accentuated a cleavage that soon led to civil war.

Moreover, the assertion that the debates dealt only with slavery in the territories is simply not true. Lincoln lifted the discussion far above that narrow issue when he attacked the morality of the slave system. To be sure, his attitude toward the Negro, whether slave or free, was essentially the same as that of Douglas. Neither would place the Negro on an equality with the white man, either politically or socially. But Douglas made it quite clear that he would be satisfied, permanently, with the Negro's inferior status, while that status tortured Lincoln's conscience. Unlike Douglas, Lincoln looked forward to a time when slavery would no longer stain American democracy and when the Negro would at least have an equal chance to advance to the limit of his capabilities.

Considered in relation to their effect on votes, the debates gave neither contestant a claim to a clear victory. The Republicans could boast that more Illinois voters stood with Lincoln than with Douglas —125,430 as against 121,609—but even in the popular vote they had to be content with a plurality, for the Buchanan Democrats polled 5,071. On the other hand, Douglas won re-election by a safe margin. When the Illinois legislature met in joint session on January 5, 1859, he received fifty-four votes to Lincoln's forty-six. Informed of the result by telegraph, Douglas wired back from Washington: "Let the voice of the people rule"—a singularly inept comment in view of the popular vote.

But Douglas' victory was a costly one. His answer to Lincoln's second Freeport question—that the territories need not have slavery in spite of the Dred Scott decision—seemed to southern extremists to be a prodigal discarding of a hard-won right. Douglas' position was not new, as we have seen, but never before had he been compelled to expound, reiterate, and elaborate it before a national audience. Since it labeled him as indifferent to the spread of slavery, rather than as an advocate of the institution, the extreme proslavery leaders of the Democratic party counted him out. In 1860 they would split the party and insure Lincoln's election rather than accept Douglas as the nominee.

On the other hand, Lincoln's defeat turned out to be, in his own words, "a slip and not a fall." Before the campaign of 1858 he was hardly known outside of Illinois. But in the following year he accepted speaking engagements in Iowa, Ohio, Indiana, Wisconsin, and Kansas. In 1860 he spoke at Cooper Union in New York City and at many cities in New England. When the Republican National Convention met in May, Lincoln was not a leading candidate. But when considerations of availability killed off Seward and Chase, the leading contenders, Lincoln was well enough known so that he could be chosen. Without the reputation he had made in the debates, no amount of political wirepulling could have brought about his selection.

In one other respect, the debates contributed to Lincoln's success in 1860. Published in the spring of that year by Follett, Foster and Company of Columbus, Ohio, they became an important campaign document. Some thirty thousand copies were sold, and read by several times that number.

Toward the end of the Alton debate Lincoln had referred to the "eternal struggle" between right and wrong. "That is the real issue," he had said. "That is the issue that will continue in this country when these poor tongues of Judge Douglas and myself shall be silent." His prophecy was sound, yet the "poor tongues" still speak.

A NOTE ABOUT THE TEXTS

Three weeks after the election in 1858 Lincoln set out to make a scrapbook of the newspaper reports of the speeches, Douglas' as well as his own, made in the course of the debates. He had difficulty procuring back issues, but by the end of the year he had obtained all needed copies. A Springfield printer considered bringing out the speeches in book form but gave up the idea. Some time in 1859 a group of Ohio Republicans, seeing in Lincoln a presidential possibility, took it up and arranged for publication by the firm of Follett, Foster and Company at Columbus. Manufacture of the book was under way by January, 1860; the first copies were offered for sale in the latter part of March, almost two months before Lincoln received the presidential nomination at the hands of the Republican National Convention.

For copy, the publisher used Lincoln's scrapbook. There, in addition to the seven formal debates, Lincoln had included his "House Divided" speech and his speeches at Chicago on July 10 and at Springfield on July 17, as well as Douglas' speeches at Chicago on July 9 and at Springfield on July 17. For the text of the debates Lincoln had taken the Chicago *Times* reports of Douglas' speeches, the *Press and Tribune* reports of his own. For the earlier speeches he had had to rely on various sources: the Chicago *Times* and the *Illinois State Register* for those of Douglas; the Chicago *Daily Democrat* and the *Illinois State Journal* for his own.[1]

"The copies I send you," he wrote in forwarding the scrapbook to Columbus, "are reported and printed, by the respective friends of Senator Douglas and myself, at the time—that is, his by his friends, and mine by mine. It would be an unwarrantable liberty for us to change a word or a letter in his, and the changes I have made in mine, you perceive, are verbal only, and very few in number."

In the speeches as printed here, Lincoln's changes have been incorporated without identification. Thus the basic text is that of the scrapbook as revised by Lincoln. But there have been three departures. (1) In the scrapbook Lincoln deleted all cheering and

[1] Exact references are given for all speeches as they appear in this compilation.

[xlv]

other interruptions from the audience. These have been restored. (2) The original newspaper accounts contained many typographical errors. These have been corrected. (3) In the sources, capitalization is wildly erratic. Here it has been made reasonably uniform.

For a text of the debates showing all Lincoln's changes and all variations between different reports of the same speech, the reader is referred to Roy P. Basler, Marion Dolores Pratt, and Lloyd A. Dunlap (eds.), *The Collected Works of Abraham Lincoln* (9 vols.; New Brunswick, N.J.: Rutgers University Press, 1953–55). The original Lincoln-Douglas Debate scrapbook is now in the Library of Congress.

CHAPTER ONE

THE CAMPAIGN OPENS

Just before the Illinois State Republican Convention recessed on the afternoon of June 16, 1858, Charles L. Wilson, editor of the Chicago Journal and a delegate from Cook County, submitted a resolution:

"Resolved, That Abraham Lincoln is the first and only choice of the Republicans of Illinois for the United States Senate, as the successor of Stephen A. Douglas."

Shouts of applause signified unanimous approval.

That evening the Hall of the House of Representatives in the Illinois State House was packed to the limit of its capacity. The day had been hot; the chamber was stifling. But Lincoln had spoken no more than a few sentences before the audience forgot its discomfort. Deliberately, and with frequent emphasis, he outlined the issues he would press in the ensuing campaign.

Lincoln at Springfield, June 16, 1858[1]

Mr. President and Gentlemen of the Convention:

If we could first know *where* we are, and *whither* we are tending, we could then better judge *what* to do, and *how* to do it.

We are now far into the *fifth* year, since a policy was initiated,

---

[1] From the *Illinois State Journal*, June 18, 1858, with obvious typographical errors corrected.

The short paragraphs of this speech are a result of the way it was written: on stray slips of paper and old envelopes over a period of weeks. Before delivering it Lincoln made a fair copy, underlining many words and phrases for emphasis. Horace White, present as a reporter for the Chicago *Press and Tribune,* stated that Lincoln asked him to take the speech to the *Illinois State Journal* immediately after its delivery. Later in the evening Lincoln visited the composing room and read the proofs. "He said to me," White wrote, "that he had taken a great deal of pains with this speech, and that he wanted it to go before the people just as he had prepared it." William H. Herndon and Jesse W. Weik, *Abraham Lincoln, The True Story of a Great Life* (New York, 1892), II, 66, 92.

with the *avowed* object, and *confident* promise, of putting an end to slavery agitation.

Under the operation of that policy, that agitation has not only, *not ceased,* but has *constantly augmented.*

In *my* opinion, it *will* not cease, until a *crisis* shall have been reached, and passed.

"A house divided against itself cannot stand."

I believe this government cannot endure, permanently half *slave* and half *free.*

I do not expect the Union to be *dissolved—*I do not expect the house to *fall—*but I *do* expect it will cease to be divided.

It will become *all* one thing, or *all* the other.

Either the *opponents* of slavery, will arrest the further spread of it, and place it where the public mind shall rest in the belief that it is in course of ultimate extinction; or its *advocates* will push it forward, till it shall become alike lawful in *all* the states, *old* as well as *new—North* as well as *South.*

Have we no *tendency* to the latter condition?

Let any one who doubts, carefully contemplate that now almost complete legal combination—piece of *machinery* so to speak—compounded of the Nebraska doctrine, and the Dred Scott decision. Let him consider not only *what work* the machinery is adapted to do, and *how well* adapted; but also, let him study the *history* of its construction, and trace, if he can, or rather *fail,* if he can, to trace the evidences of design, and concert of action, among its chief bosses, from the beginning.

But, so far, *Congress* only, had acted; and an *indorsement* by the people, *real* or apparent, was indispensable, to *save* the point already gained, and give chance for more.

The new year of 1854 found slavery excluded from more than half the states by state constitutions, and from most of the national territory by congressional prohibition.

Four days later, commenced the struggle, which ended in repealing that congressional prohibition.

This opened all the national territory to slavery; and was the first point gained.

This necessity had not been overlooked; but had been provided for, as well as might be, in the notable argument of *"squatter sovereignty,"* otherwise called *"sacred right of self government,"* which latter phrase, though expressive of the only rightful basis of any government, was so perverted in this attempted use of it as to amount to just this: That if any *one* man, choose to enslave *another,* no *third* man shall be allowed to object.

[2]

That argument was incorporated into the Nebraska Bill itself, in the language which follows: *"It being the true intent and meaning of this act not to legislate slavery into any territory or state, nor exclude it therefrom; but to leave the people thereof perfectly free to form and regulate their domestic institutions in their own way, subject only to the Constitution of the United States."*

Then opened the roar of loose declamation in favor of "Squatter Sovereignty," and "Sacred right of self government."

"But," said opposition members, "let us be more *specific*—let us *amend* the bill so as to expressly declare that the people of the territory *may* exclude slavery." "Not we," said the friends of the measure; and down they voted the amendment.

While the Nebraska Bill was passing through Congress, a *law* case, involving the question of a negro's freedom, by reason of his owner having voluntarily taken him first into a free state and then a territory covered by the congressional prohibition, and held him as a slave, for a long time in each, was passing through the U.S. Circuit Court for the District of Missouri; and both Nebraska Bill and law suit were brought to a decision in the same month of May, 1854. The negro's name was "Dred Scott," which name now designates the decision finally made in the case.

Before the *then* next presidential election, the law case came *to*, and was argued *in* the Supreme Court of the United States; but the *decision* of it was deferred until *after* the election. Still, *before* the election, Senator Trumbull, on the floor of the Senate, requests the leading advocate of the Nebraska Bill to state *his opinion* whether the people of a territory can constitutionally exclude slavery from their limits; and the latter answers, "That is a question for the Supreme Court."

The election came. Mr. Buchanan was elected, and the *indorsement*, such as it was, secured. That was the *second* point gained. The indorsement, however, fell short of a clear popular majority by nearly four hundred thousand votes, and so, perhaps, was not overwhelmingly reliable and satisfactory.

The *outgoing* President, in his last annual message, as impressively as possible *echoed back* upon the people the *weight* and *authority* of the indorsement.

The Supreme Court met again; *did not* announce their decision, but ordered a re-argument.

The presidential inauguration came, and still no decision of the court; but the *incoming* President, in his inaugural address, fervently exhorted the people to abide by the forthcoming decision, *whatever it might be.*

[3]

Then, in a few days, came the decision.

The reputed author of the Nebraska Bill finds an early occasion to make a speech at this capitol indorsing the Dred Scott decision, and vehemently denouncing all opposition to it.

The new President, too, seizes the early occasion of the Silliman letter to *indorse* and strongly *construe* that decision, and to express his *astonishment* that any different view had ever been entertained.

At length a squabble springs up between the President and the author of the Nebraska Bill, on the *mere* question of *fact*, whether the Lecompton constitution was or was not, in any just sense, made by the people of Kansas; and in that squabble the latter declares that all he wants is a fair vote for the people, and that he *cares* not whether slavery be voted *down* or voted *up*. I do not understand his declaration that he cares not whether slavery be voted down or voted up, to be intended by him other than as an *apt definition* of the *policy* he would impress upon the public mind—the *principle* for which he declares he has suffered much, and is ready to suffer to the end.

And well may he cling to that principle. If he has any parental feeling, well may he cling to it. That principle, is the only *shred* left of his original Nebraska doctrine. Under the Dred Scott decision, "squatter sovereignty" squatted out of existence, tumbled down like temporary scaffolding—like the mould at the foundry served through one blast and fell back into loose sand—helped to carry an election, and then was kicked to the winds. His late *joint* struggle with the Republicans, against the Lecompton constitution, involves nothing of the original Nebsaska doctrine. That struggle was made on a point, the right of a people to make their own constitution, upon which he and the Republicans have never differed.

The several points of the Dred Scott decision, in connection with Senator Douglas' "care not" policy, constitute the piece of machinery, in its *present* state of advancement. This was the third point gained.

The *working* points of that machinery are:

First, that no negro slave, imported as such from Africa, and no descendant of such slave can ever be a *citizen* of any state, in the sense of that term as used in the Constitution of the United States.

This point is made in order to deprive the negro, in every possible event, of the benefit of this provision of the United States Constitution, which declares that—

"The citizens of each state shall be entitled to all privileges and immunities of citizens in the several states."

Secondly, that "subject to the Constitution of the United States," neither *Congress* nor a *territorial legislature* can exclude slavery from any United States territory.

This point is made in order that individual men may *fill up* the territories with slaves, without danger of losing them as property, and thus to enhance the chances of *permanency* to the institution through all the future.

Thirdly, that whether the holding a negro in actual slavery in a free state, makes him free, as against the holder, the United States courts will not decide, but will leave to be decided by the courts of any slave state the negro may be forced into by the master.

This point is made, not to be pressed *immediately;* but, if acquiesced in for a while, and apparently *indorsed* by the people at an election, *then* to sustain the logical conclusion that what Dred Scott's master might lawfully do with Dred Scott, in the free state of Illinois, every other master may lawfully do with any other *one,* or one *thousand* slaves, in Illinois, or in any other free state.

Auxiliary to all this, and working hand in hand with it, the Nebraska doctrine, or what is left of it, is to *educate* and *mould* public opinion, at least *Northern* public opinion, to not *care* whether slavery is voted *down* or voted *up.*

This shows exactly where we now *are;* and *partially* also, whither we are tending.

It will throw additional light on the latter, to go back, and run the mind over the string of historical facts already stated. Several things will *now* appear less *dark* and *mysterious* than they did *when* they were transpiring. The people were to be left "perfectly free" "subject only to the Constitution." What the *Constitution* had to do with it, outsiders could not *then* see. Plainly enough *now,* it was an exactly fitted *niche,* for the Dred Scott decision to afterwards come in, and declare the *perfect freedom* of the people, to be just no freedom at all.

Why was the amendment, expressly declaring the right of the people to exclude slavery, voted down? Plainly enough *now,* the adoption of it, would have spoiled the niche for the Dred Scott decision.

Why was the court decision held up? Why, even a Senator's individual opinion withheld, till *after* the presidential election? Plainly enough *now,* the speaking out *then* would have damaged the *"perfectly free"* argument upon which the election was to be carried.

Why the *outgoing* President's felicitation on the indorsement? Why the delay of a reargument? Why the incoming President's *advance* exhortation in favor of the decision?

These things *look* like the cautious *patting* and *petting* a spirited horse, preparatory to mounting him, when it is dreaded that he may give the rider a fall.

And why the hasty after-indorsements of the decision by the President and others?

We can not absolutely *know* that all these exact adaptations are the result of preconcert. But when we see a lot of framed timbers, different portions of which we know have been gotten out at different times and places and by different workmen—Stephen, Franklin, Roger and James,[2] for instance—and when we see these timbers joined together, and see they exactly make the frame of a house or a mill, all the tenons and mortices exactly fitting, and all the lengths and proportions of the different pieces exactly adapted to their respective places, and not a piece too many or too few—not omitting even scaffolding—or, if a single piece be lacking, we can see the place in the frame exactly fitted and prepared to yet bring such piece in—in *such* a case, we find it impossible to not *believe* that Stephen and Franklin and Roger and James all understood one another from the beginning, and all worked upon a common *plan* or *draft* drawn up before the first lick was struck.

It should not be overlooked that, by the Nebraska Bill, the people of a *state* as well as *territory*, were to be left *"perfectly free"* *"subject only to the Constitution."*

Why mention a *state?* They were legislating for *territories,* and not *for* or *about* states. Certainly the people of a state *are* and *ought to be* subject to the Constitution of the United States; but why is mention of this *lugged* into this merely *territorial* law? Why are the people of a *territory* and the people of a *state* therein *lumped* together, and their relation to the Constitution therein treated as being *precisely* the same?

While the opinion of the *Court,* by Chief Justice Taney, in the Dred Scott case, and the separate opinions of all the concurring judges, expressly declare that the Constitution of the United States neither permits Congress nor a territorial legislature to exclude slavery from any United States territory, they all *omit* to declare whether or not the same constitution permits a *state,* or the people of a state, to exclude it.

Possibly, this was a mere *omission;* but who can be *quite* sure, if McLean or Curtis[3] had sought to get into the opinion a declaration of unlimited power in the people of a *state* to exclude slavery from their limits, just as Chase and Macy[4] sought to get such declaration,

---

[2] Stephen A. Douglas, Franklin Pierce, Roger B. Taney, James Buchanan.

[3] Justices John McLean and Benjamin R. Curtis, who filed dissenting opinions.

[4] Senator Salmon P. Chase of Ohio and Representative Daniel Macy of Indiana.

in behalf of the people of a territory, into the Nebraska Bill—I ask, who can be quite *sure* that it would not have been voted down, in the one case, as it had been in the other.

The nearest approach to the point of declaring the power of a state over slavery, is made by Judge Nelson.[5] He approaches it more than once, using the precise idea, and *almost* the language too, of the Nebraska Act. On one occasion his exact language is, "except in cases where the power is restrained by the Constitution of the United States, the law of the state is supreme over the subject of slavery within its jurisdiction."

In what *cases* the power of the *states is* so restrained by the U.S. Constitution, is left an *open* question, precisely as the same question, as to the restraint on the power of the *territories* was left open in the Nebraska Act. Put *that* and *that* together, and we have another nice little niche, which we may, ere long, see filled with another Supreme Court decision, declaring that the Constitution of the United States does not permit a *state* to exclude slavery from its limits.

And this may especially be expected if the doctrine of "care not whether slavery be voted *down* or voted *up*," shall gain upon the public mind sufficiently to give promise that such a decision can be maintained when made.

Such a decision is all that slavery now lacks of being alike lawful in all the states.

Welcome or unwelcome, such decision *is* probably coming, and will soon be upon us, unless the power of the present political dynasty shall be met and overthrown.

We shall *lie down* pleasantly dreaming that the people of *Missouri* are on the verge of making their state *free;* and we shall *awake* to the *reality*, instead, that the *Supreme* Court has made *Illinois* a *slave* state.

To meet and overthrow the power of that dynasty, is the work now before all those who would prevent that consummation.

That is *what* we have to do.

But *how* can we best do it?

There are those who denounce us *openly* to their *own* friends, and yet whisper *us softly*, that *Senator Douglas* is the *aptest* instrument there is, with which to effect that object. *They* do *not* tell us, nor has *he* told us, that he *wishes* any such object to be effected. They wish us to *infer* all, from the facts, that he now has a little quarrel with the present head of the dynasty; and that he has

[5] Justice Samuel Nelson.

[7]

regularly voted with us, on a single point, upon which, he and we, have never differed.

They remind us that *he* is a very *great man*, and that the largest of *us* are very small ones. Let this be granted. But "a *living dog* is better than a *dead lion*." Judge Douglas, if not a *dead* lion *for this work*, is at least a *caged* and *toothless* one. How can he oppose the advances of slavery? He don't *care* anything about it. His avowed *mission is impressing* the "public heart" to *care* nothing about it.

A leading Douglas Democratic newspaper thinks Douglas' superior talent will be needed to resist the revival of the African slave trade.

Does Douglas believe an effort to revive that trade is approaching? He has not said so. Does he *really* think so? But if it is, how can he resist it? For years he has labored to prove it a *sacred right* of white men to take negro slaves into the new territories. Can he possibly show that it is *less* a sacred right to *buy* them where they can be bought cheapest? And, unquestionably they can be bought *cheaper in Africa* than in *Virginia*.

He has done all in his power to reduce the whole question of slavery to one of a mere *right of property;* and as such, how can *he* oppose the foreign slave trade—how can he refuse that trade in that "property" shall be "perfectly free"—unless he does it as a *protection* to the home production? And as the home *producers* will probably not *ask* the protection, he will be wholly without a ground of opposition.

Senator Douglas holds, we know, that a man may rightfully be *wiser to-day* than he was *yesterday*—that he may rightfully *change* when he finds himself wrong.

But, can we for that reason, run ahead, and *infer* that he *will* make any particular change, of which he, himself, has given no intimation? Can we *safely* base *our* action upon any such *vague* inference?

Now, as ever, I wish to not *misrepresent* Judge Douglas' *position*, question his *motives*, or do ought that can be personally offensive to him.

Whenever, *if ever*, he and we can come together on *principle* so that *our great cause* may have assistance from *his great ability*, I hope to have interposed no adventitious obstacle.

But clearly, he is not *now* with us—he does not *pretend* to be— he does not *promise* to *ever* be.

Our cause, then, must be intrusted to, and conducted by its own undoubted friends—those whose hands are free, whose hearts are in the work—who *do care* for the result.

[8]

Two years ago the Republicans of the nation mustered over thirteen hundred thousand strong.

We did this under the single impulse of resistance to a common danger, with every external circumstance against us.

Of *strange, discordant,* and even, *hostile* elements, we gathered from the four winds, and *formed* and fought the battle through, under the constant hot fire of a disciplined, proud, and pampered enemy.

Did we brave all *then,* to *falter* now?—*now*—when that same enemy is *wavering,* dissevered and belligerent?

The result is not doubtful. We shall not fail—if we stand firm, we shall not fail.

Wise councils may *accelerate* or *mistakes delay* it, but, sooner or later the victory is *sure* to come.

After the adjournment of Congress, Douglas remained in the East for several weeks. When he returned to Chicago on July 9 the Democracy gave him a hero's welcome. The Chicago Times[6] *reported what it headlined as the "grand ovation."*

Yesterday Senator Douglas was received in Chicago, and the occasion, as well as the manner of that reception, was of the most magnificent character. Some few days ago it was heard that he was at Cleveland, and forthwith arrangements were hastily made to give him a reception worthy of his great services. With that view it was determined to appoint a committee to meet him at Michigan City, and escort him to the city. . . .

An extra train of cars was ready at 1 o'clock yesterday. . . . It was not contemplated, either by the committee or anyone else, that many persons, besides such as were on the committee, would desire to go that distance in the middle of an intensely hot day, over a sandy and exposed road, and accordingly no effort was made to make up a long train. But full an half-hour before the time for starting, hundreds of citizens, many of whom came from remote parts of the state, had collected at the depot. . . .

While the crowd was gathering, fine bands of music were employed, which, by their inspiriting strains, helped to awaken the most general and intense enthusiasm. In the meantime, also, a great number of large national flags were being elevated at conspicuous points near the depot and elsewhere, and banners of different shapes and colors, besides streamers, pendants, etc., were disposed in all directions. A grand sight it was!

[6] July 10, 1858.

. . . All things being ready, the cars moved off amid shouts from the outside, and answering shouts and music from within. In all, the company numbered Four Hundred. A splendid banner, that of the Young Men's Democratic Club, was carried upon the locomotive. . . .

The train proceeded to Michigan City, where it was met by a host of gallant Indianians, who accompanied the Judge from Laporte to Michigan City. Some malicious person having secretly spiked the only gun of the town, the Democracy obtained a large anvil, and placing it in the middle of the principal street, made the welkin echo with its repeated discharges.

The delegation from Chicago—including Democrats from Logan, Peoria, Tazewell, La Salle, Marshall, McHenry, Knox, Will, Boone, Kankakee, Champaign, Stephenson, Kane, De Kalb, Du Page, and other counties of the state, formed into line, and preceded by a band of music, marched to the Tremont House, where they met Senator Douglas. After exchanging personal salutations with his friends, Judge Douglas returned, in a few happy remarks, his thanks for this marked expression of their continued friendship.

THE RETURN TO THE CITY

At a few minutes after five o'clock the procession was formed and proceeded to the depot, Judge Douglas being now the guest of the committee. The train soon started, and all along the road—at every station, at almost every farmhouse and laborer's cabin—in every cornfield, and at every point where laborers were engaged—there was exhibited by cheers, by waving of handkerchiefs and other demonstrations, that cordial "welcome home" to the great representative of popular rights.

At the outer depot of the Illinois Central Railroad the national flag had been raised by the operatives, and a swivel belched forth its roaring notes of welcome. The hardy hands of the mechanics resounded with applause, and cheers and huzzas continued until the train had passed on to the city.

As the train passed along from Twelfth Street to the depot, crowds of ladies were assembled on the doorsteps of the residences on Michigan Avenue, waving banners and handkerchiefs; the lake park was crowded by persons hastily proceeding to the depot. Long before the train could enter the station house, thousands had crossed over the breakwater, got upon the track, and climbed into the cars, and when the latter reached the depot they were literally crammed inside and covered on top by ardent and enthusiastic friends and supporters of the illustrious Illinoisan.

[10]

Capt. Smith's artillery were, in the meantime, firing from Dearborn Park a salute of 150 guns (guns were also firing in the West and North Divisions) the booming of the cannon alone rising above the cheering plaudits of the assembled multitude.

The hotels and principal buildings of the city were adorned with flags. The Adams House, near the Central depot, was most handsomely decorated. The national flag, a banner bearing the motto, "Douglas, the Champion of Popular Sovereignty," as well as numerous flags belonging to vessels in the harbor were suspended across the street, presenting a grand display. The doors, windows, balconies, and roofs of the Adams House, as well as the private residences in the neighborhood, and the large stores and warehouses along Lake Street were crowded with ladies and other persons—all cheering and welcoming the Senator. At the depot, a procession consisting of the "Montgomery Guards," Capt. Gleson, and the "Emmet Guards," Lieut. Stuart commanding, acting as a military escort, was then formed. Judge Douglas was in an open barouche drawn by six horses, and was followed by the Committee of Arrangements in other carriages. The procession proceeded up Lake to Wabash Avenue, down Wabash Avenue to Dearborn Street, and thence by Dearborn Street to the Tremont House.

Throughout the whole route of the procession, the Senator was greeted from house top and window, from street, from awning post and balcony by every demonstration of grateful welcome.

THE SCENE AT THE TREMONT

As early as half-past six o'clock people began to collect around the Tremont House. The omnibuses from Union Park, and from the southern and northern limits of the city, were crowded with suburban residents, and people came on foot from the remotest parts of the city, taking up eligible standing places around the hotel. At about half-past seven, the booming of cannon on the lake shore having announced the arrival of the train, it was the signal for the assembling of thousands of others who rapidly filled up every vacant spot in Lake Street, from State, for the distance of a block and a half. Dearborn Street was also thronged from Lake to Randolph. . . . In addition to this, every roof and window within hearing distance was occupied, a large portion of the occupants being ladies. The assemblage of people who welcomed in vociferous and prolonged shouts of joy the return of Senator Douglas numbered at the least calculation *thirty thousand.*

Chicago has never before witnessed such a sight. A field of human forms parted with difficulty as the procession passed through, and closed instantly behind it, with the surge and roar of the waters of a sea; an ocean of upturned faces, extending beyond the furthest limits to which the Senator's powerful voice could reach, and from which broke one spontaneous burst of applause as he appeared upon the balcony before them! Over all, the light of the illumination, and the glare and glitter of fireworks, spread an appearance which is indescribable!

Learning that Lincoln was present, Douglas offered his rival a chair on the Tremont House balcony. The Senator then made the opening speech of his campaign.

Douglas at Chicago, July 9, 1858[7]

Mr. Chairman and fellow-citizens:

I can find no language which can adequately express my profound gratitude for the magnificent welcome which you have extended to me on this occasion. This vast sea of human faces indicates how deep an interest is felt by our people in the great questions which agitate the public mind, and which underlie the foundations of our free institutions. A reception like this, so great in numbers that no human voice can be heard to its countless thousands—so enthusiastic that no one individual can be the object of such enthusiasm—clearly shows that there is some great principle which sinks deep in the heart of the masses, and involves the rights and the liberties of a whole people, that has brought you together with a unanimity and a cordiality never before excelled, if, indeed, equalled on any occasion. I have not the vanity to believe that it is any personal compliment to me.

It is an expression of your devotion to that great principle of self-government, to which my life for many years past has been, and in the future will be devoted. If there is any one principle dearer and more sacred than all others in free governments, it is that which asserts the exclusive right of a free people to form and adopt their own fundamental law, and to manage and regulate their own internal affairs and domestic institutions.

When I found an effort being made during the recent session of Congress to force a constitution upon the people of Kansas against their will, and to force that state into the Union with a constitution which her people had rejected by more than 10,000, I felt bound as a man of honor and a representative of Illinois, bound by every

[7] Chicago *Times*, July 11, 1858.

consideration of duty, of fidelity, and of patriotism, to resist to the utmost of my power the consummation of that fraud. With others I did resist it, and resisted it successfully until the attempt was abandoned. We forced them to refer that constitution back to the people of Kansas, to be accepted or rejected as they shall decide at an election, which is fixed for the first Monday of August next. It is true that the mode of reference, and the form of the submission was not such as I could sanction with my vote, for the reason that it discriminated between free states and slave states; providing that if Kansas consented to come in under the Lecompton constitution it should be received with a population of 35,000; but that if she demanded another constitution, more consistent with the sentiments of her people and their feelings, that it should not be received into the Union until she has 93,420 inhabitants. I did not consider that mode of submission fair, for the reason that any election is a mockery which is not free—that any election is a fraud upon the right of the people which holds out inducements for affirmative votes, and threatens penalties for negative votes. But whilst I was not satisfied with the mode of submission, whilst I resisted it to the last, demanding a fair, a just, a free mode of submission, still, when the law passed placing it within the power of the people of Kansas at that election to reject the Lecompton constitution, and then make another in harmony with their principles and their opinions, I did not believe that either the penalties on the one hand, or the inducements on the other, would force that people to accept a constitution to which they are irreconcilably opposed. All I can say is, that if their votes can be controlled by such considerations, all the sympathy which has been expended upon them has been misplaced, and all the efforts that have been made in defence of their right to self-government have been made in an unworthy cause.

Hence, my friends, I regard the Lecompton battle as having been fought and the victory won, because the arrogant demand for the admission of Kansas under the Lecompton constitution unconditionally, whether her people wanted it or not, has been abandoned, and the principle which recognizes the right of the people to decide for themselves has been submitted to its place.

Fellow-citizens: While I devoted my best energies—all my energies, mental and physical—to the vindication of the great principle, and whilst the result has been such as will enable the people of Kansas to come into the Union, with such a constitution as they desire, yet the credit of this great moral victory is to be divided among a large number of men of various and different political creeds. I was rejoiced when I found in this great contest the Republican party coming up manfully and sustaining the principle that the people of each territory, when coming into the Union, have the right to decide for themselves whether slavery shall or shall not exist within their limits. I have seen the time when that principle was controverted. I have seen the time when all parties did not recognize the right of a people to have slavery or freedom, to tolerate or prohibit slavery, as they deemed best; but claimed that power for Congress of the United States, regardless of the wishes of the people to be affected by it, and when I found upon the Crittenden-Montgomery Bill the Republicans and Americans of the North, and I may say, too, some glorious Americans and Old Line Whigs from the South, like Crittenden and his patriotic associates, joined with a portion of the Democracy to carry out and vindicate the right of the people to decide whether slavery should or should not exist within the limits of Kansas, I was rejoiced within my secret soul, for I saw an indication that the American people, when they come to understand the principle, would give it their cordial support.

The Crittenden-Montgomery Bill was as fair and as perfect an exposition of the doctrine of popular sovereignty as could be carried out by any bill that man ever devised. It proposed to refer the Lecompton constitution back to the people of Kansas, and give them the right to accept or reject it as they pleased at a fair election, held in pursuance of law, and in the event of their rejecting it and forming another in its stead, to permit them to come into the Union on an equal footing with the original states. It was fair and just in all of its provisions! I gave it my cordial support, and was rejoiced when I found that it passed the House of Representatives, and at one time I entertained high hope that it would pass the Senate.

I regard the great principle of popular sovereignty as having been vindicated and made triumphant in this land as a permanent rule of public policy in the organization of territories and the admission of new states. Illinois took her position upon this principle many years ago. You all recollect that in 1850, after the passage of the compromise measures of that year, when I returned to my home there was great dissatisfaction expressed at my course in supporting those measures. I appeared before the people of Chicago at a mass meeting, and vindicated each and every one of those measures; and by reference to my speech on that occasion, which was printed and circulated broad-cast throughout the state at the time, you will find that I then and there said that those measures were all founded upon the great principle that every people ought to possess the right to form and regulate their own domestic institutions in their own way, and that that right being possessed by the people of the states, I saw no reason why the same principle should not be extended to all of the territories of the United States. A general election was held in this state a few months afterwards, for members of the legislature, pending which, all these question were thoroughly canvassed and discussed, and the nominees of the different parties instructed in regard to the wishes of their constituents upon them. When that election was over, and the legislature assembled, they proceeded to consider the merits of those compromise measures and the principles upon which they were predicated. And what was the result of their action? They passed resolutions, first repealing the Wilmot proviso instructions, and in lieu thereof adopted another resolution, in which they declared the great principle which asserts the right of the people to make their own form of government and establish their own institutions. That resolution is as follows:

Resolved, That our liberty and independence are based upon the right of the people to form for themselves such a government as they may choose; that this great principle, the birthright of freemen, the gift of Heaven, secured to us by the blood of our ancestors, ought to be extended to future generations, and no limitation ought to be applied to this power in the organization of any territory of the U.S. of either territorial government or state constitution, provided the government so established shall be Republican, and in conformity with the Constitution of the United States.

That resolution, declaring the great principle of self-government as applicable to the territories and new states, passed the House of Representatives of this state by a vote of sixty-one in the affirmative, to only four in the negative. Thus you find that an expression of public opinion, enlightened, educated, intelligent public opinion on this question by the Representatives of Illinois, in 1851, approaches nearer to unanimity than has ever been obtained on any controverted question. That resolution was entered on the journal of the legislature of the state of Illinois, and it has remained there from that day to this, a standing instruction to her Senators and a request to her Representatives in Congress, to carry out that principle in all future cases.—Illinois therefore stands pre-eminent as the state which stepped forward early and established a platform applicable to this slavery question, concurred in alike by Whigs and Democrats, in which it was declared to be the wish of our people that thereafter the people of the territories should be left perfectly free to form and regulate their domestic institutions in their own way, and that no limitation should be placed upon that right in any form.

[15]

Hence what was my duty, in 1854, when it became necessary to bring forward a bill for the organization of the territories of Kansas and Nebraska? Was it not my duty, in obedience to the Illinois platform, to your standing instructions to your Senators, adopted with almost entire unanimity, to incorporate in that bill the great principle of self-government, declaring that it was "the true intent and meaning of the act not to legislate slavery into any state or territory, or to exclude it therefrom, but to leave the people thereof perfectly free to form and regulate their domestic institutions in their own way, subject only to the Constitution of the United States?" I did incorporate that principle in the Kansas-Nebraska Bill, and perhaps I did as much as any living man in the enactment of that bill, thus establishing the doctrine in the public policy of the country. I then defended that principle against assaults from one section of the Union. During this last winter it became my duty to vindicate it against assaults from the other section of the Union. I vindicated it boldly and fearlessly, as the people of Chicago can bear witness, when it was assailed by Freesoilers; and during this winter I vindicated and defended it as boldly and as fearlessly when it was attempted to be violated by the almost united South. I pledged myself to you on every stump in Illinois in 1854, I pledged myself to the people of other states, North and South—whenever I spoke—and in the United States Senate and elsewhere, in every forum in which I could reach the public mind or the public ear, I gave the pledge that I, so far as the power should be in my hands, would vindicate the principle of the right of the people to form their own institutions, to establish free states or slave states as they chose, and that that principle should never be violated either by fraud, by violence, by circumvention, or by any other means, if it was in my power to prevent it. I now submit to you my fellow-citizens, whether I have not redeemed that pledge in good faith! Yes, my friends, I have redeemed it in good faith, and it is a matter of heartfelt gratification to me to see these assembled thousands here to-night bearing their testimony to the fidelity with which I have advocated that principle and redeemed my pledges in connection with it.

I will be entirely frank with you. My object was to secure the right of the people of each state and of each territory, North or South, to decide the question for themselves, to have slavery or not, just as they chose; and my opposition to the Lecompton constitution was not predicated upon the ground that it was a pro-slavery constitution, nor would my action have been different had it been a free-soil constitution. My speech against the Lecompton fraud was made on the 9th of December, while the vote on the slavery clause in that constitution was not taken until the 21st of the same month, nearly two weeks after. I made my speech against the Lecompton monstrosity solely on the ground that it was a violation of the fundamental principles of free government; on the ground that it was not the act and deed of the people of Kansas; that it did not embody their will; that they were averse to it; and hence I denied the right of Congress to force it upon them, either as a free state or a slave state. I deny the right of Congress to force a slave-holding state upon an unwilling people. I deny their right to force a free state upon an unwilling people. I deny their right to force a good thing upon a people who are unwilling to receive it. The great principle is the right of every community to judge and decide for itself, whether a thing is right or wrong, whether it would be good or evil for them to adopt it; and the right of free action, the right of free thought, the right of free judgment upon the question is dearer to every true American than any other under a free government. My objection to the Lecompton contrivance was that it undertook to put a constitution on the people of Kansas against their will, in opposition to their wishes, and thus violated the great principle upon which all our institutions rest. It is no answer to this argument to say that slavery is an evil and hence should not be tolerated. You must allow the people to decide for themselves whether it is a good or an evil. You allow them to decide for themselves whether they desire a Maine liquor law or not; you allow them to decide for themselves what kind of common schools they will have; what system of banking they will adopt, or whether they will adopt any at all; you allow them to decide for themselves the relations between husband and wife, parent and child, the guardian and ward; in fact, you allow them to decide for themselves all other questions, and why not upon this question? Whenever you put a limitation upon the right of any people to decide what laws they want, you have destroyed the fundamental principle of self-government.

In connection with this subject, perhaps, it will not be improper for me on this occasion to allude to the position of those who have chosen to arraign my conduct on this same subject. I have observed from the public prints that but a few days ago the Republican party of the state of Illinois assembled in convention at Springfield, and not only laid down their platform, but nominated a candidate for the United State Senate as my successor. I take great pleasure in saying that I have known, personally and intimately, for about a quarter of a century, the worthy gentleman who has been nominated for my place, and I will say that I regard him as a kind, amiable, and intelligent gentleman, a good citizen and an honorable

[17]

opponent; and whatever issue I may have with him will be of principle, and not involving personalities.— Mr. Lincoln made a speech before that Republican Convention which unanimously nominated him for the Senate—a speech evidently well prepared and carefully written—in which he states the basis upon which he proposes to carry on the campaign during this summer. In it he lays down two distinct propositions which I shall notice, and upon which I shall take a direct and bold issue with him.

His first and main proposition I will give in his own language, scripture quotations and all, (laughter) I give his exact language—" 'A house divided against itself cannot stand.' I believe this government cannot endure, permanently, half *slave* and half *free*. I do not expect the Union to be *dissolved*. I do not expect the house to *fall*; but I do expect it to cease to be divided. It will become *all* one thing or *all* the other."

In other words, Mr. Lincoln asserts as a fundamental principle of this government, that there must be uniformity in the local laws and domestic institutions of each and all the states of the Union; and he therefore invites all the non-slaveholding states to band together, organize as one body, and make war upon slavery in Kentucky, upon slavery in Virginia, upon the Carolinas, upon slavery in all of the slave-holding states in this Union, and to persevere in that war until it shall be exterminated. He then notifies the slaveholding states to stand together as a unit and make an aggressive war upon the free states of this Union with a view of establishing slavery in them all; of forcing it upon Illinois, of forcing it upon New York, upon New England, and upon every other free state, and that they shall keep up the warfare until it has been formally established in them all. In other words, Mr. Lincoln advocates boldly and clearly a war of sections, a war of the North against the South, of the free states against the slave states—a war of extermination—to be continued relentlessly until the one or the other shall be subdued and all the states shall either become free or become slave.

Now, my friends, I must say to you frankly, that I take bold, unqualified issue with him upon that principle. I assert that it is neither desirable nor possible that there should be uniformity in the local institutions and domestic regulations of the different states of this Union. The framers of our government never contemplated uniformity in its internal concerns. The fathers of the Revolution, and the sages who made the Constitution well understood that the laws and domestic institutions which would suit the granite hills of New Hampshire would be totally unfit for the rice plantations of South Carolina; they well understood that the laws which would suit the agricultural districts of Pennsylvania and New York would be totally unfit for the large mining regions of the Pacific, or the lumber regions of Maine. They well understood that the great varieties of soil, of production and of interests, in a republic as large as this, required different local and domestic regulations in each locality, adapted to the wants and interests of each separate state, and for that reason it was provided in the federal Constitution that the thirteen original states should remain sovereign and supreme within their own limits in regard to all that was local, and internal, and domestic, while the federal government should have certain specified powers which were general and national, and could be exercised only by the federal authority.

The framers of the Constitution well understood that each locality, having separate and distinct interests, required separate and distinct laws, domestic institutions, and police regulations adapted to its own wants and its own condition; and they acted on the presumption, also, that these laws and institutions would be as diversified and as dissimilar as the states would be numerous, and that no two would be precisely alike, because the interests of the two would [not] be precisely the same. Hence, I assert, that the great fundamental principle which underlies our complex system of state and federal governments, contemplated diversity and dissimilarity in the local institutions and domestic affairs of each and every state then in the Union, or thereafter to be admitted into the confederacy. I therefore conceive that my friend, Mr. Lincoln, has totally misapprehended the great principles upon which our government rests. Uniformity in local and domestic affairs would be destructive of state rights, of state sovereignty, of personal liberty and personal freedom. Uniformity is the parent of despotism the world over, not only in politics, but in religion. Wherever the doctrine of uniformity is proclaimed, that all the states must be free or all slave, that all labor must be white or all black, that all the citizens of the different states must have the same privileges or be governed by the same regulations, you have destroyed the greatest safeguard which our institutions have thrown around the rights of the citizen.

How could this uniformity be accomplished, if it was desirable and possible? There is but one mode in which it could be obtained, and that must be by abolishing the state legislatures, blotting out state sovereignty, merging the rights and sovereignty of the states in one consolidated empire, and vesting Congress with the plenary power to make all the police regulations, domestic and local laws, uniform throughout the limits of the Republic. When you shall have done this you will have uniformity. Then the states will all be slave or all be free; then negroes will vote everywhere or nowhere; then you will have a Maine liquor law in every state or none; then you will have uniformity in all things local and domestic by the authority of the federal government. But when you attain that uniformity, you will have converted these thirty-two sovereign, independent states, into one consolidated empire, with the uniformity of despotism reigning triumphant throughout the length and breadth of the land.

From this view of the case, my friends, I am driven irresistibly to the conclusion that diversity, dissimilarity, variety in all our local and domestic institutions, is the great safeguard of our liberties; and that the framers of our institutions were wise, sagacious, and patriotic when they made this government a confederation of sovereign states with a legislature for each, and conferred upon each legislature the power to make all local and domestic institutions to suit the people it represented, without interference from any other state or from the general Congress of the Union. If we expect to maintain our liberties we must preserve the rights and sovereignty of the states, we must maintain and carry out that great principle of self-government incorporated in the compromise measures of 1850: endorsed by the Illinois legislature in 1851; emphatically embodied and carried out in the Kansas-Nebraska Bill, and vindicated this year by the refusal to bring Kansas into the Union with a constitution distasteful to her people.

The other proposition discussed by Mr. Lincoln in his speech consists in a crusade against the Supreme Court of the United States on account of the Dred Scott decision. On this question, also, I desire to say to you unequivocally, that I take direct and distinct issue with him. I have no warfare to make on the Supreme Court of the United States, either on account of that or any other decision which they have pronounced from that bench. The Constitution of the United States has provided that the powers of government (and the constitution of each state has the same provision) shall be divided into three departments, executive, legislative, and judicial. The right and the province of expounding the Constitution, and construing the law, is vested in the judiciary established by the Constitution.—As a lawyer, I feel at liberty to appear before the Court and controvert any principle of law while the question is pending before the tribunal; but when the decision is made, my private opinion, your opinion, all other opinions must yield to the majesty of that authoritative adjudication. I wish you to bear in mind that this involves a great principle, upon which our rights, our liberty and our property all depend. What security have you for your property, for your reputation, and for your personal rights, if the courts are not upheld, and their decisions respected when once firmly rendered by the highest tribunal known to the Constitution? I do not choose, therefore, to go into any argument with Mr. Lincoln in reviewing the various decisions which the Supreme Court has made, either upon the Dred Scott case, or any other. I have no idea of appealing from the decision of the Supreme Court upon a constitutional question to the decisions of a tumultuous town meeting. I am aware that once an eminent lawyer of this city, now no more, said that the state of Illinois had the most perfect judicial system in the world, subject to but one exception, which could be cured by a slight amendment, and that amendment was to so change the law as to allow an appeal from the decisions of the Supreme Court of Illinois, on all constitutional questions, to Justice of the Peace.

My friend, Mr. Lincoln, who sits behind me, reminds me that that proposition was made when I was Judge of the Supreme Court. Be that as it may, I do not think that fact adds any greater weight or authority to the suggestion. It matters not with me who was on the bench, whether Mr. Lincoln or myself, whether a Lockwood or a Smith, a Taney or a Marshall; the decision of the highest tribunal known to the Constitution of the country must be final till it has been reversed by an equally high authority. Hence, I am opposed to this doctrine of Mr. Lincoln, by which he proposes to take an appeal from the decision of the Supreme Court of the United States, upon this high constitutional question to a Republican caucus sitting in the country. Yes, or any other caucus or town meeting, whether it be Republican, American, or Democratic. I respect the decisions of that august tribunal; I shall always bow in deference to them. I am a law-abiding man. I will sustain the Constitution of my country as our fathers have made it. I will yield obedience to to the laws, whether I like them or not, as I find them on the statute book. I will sustain the judicial tribunals and constituted authorities in all matters within the pale of their jurisdiction as defined by the Constitution.

But I am equally free to say that the reason assigned by Mr. Lincoln for resisting the decision of the Supreme Court in the Dred Scott case does not in itself meet my approbation. He objects to it because that decision declared that a negro descended from African parents who were brought here and sold as slaves is not, and cannot be a citizen of the United States. He says it is wrong, because it deprives the negro of the benefits of that clause of the Constitution which says that citizens of one state shall enjoy all the privi-

leges and immunities of citizens of the several states; in other
words, he thinks it wrong because it deprives the negro of the
privileges, immunities, and rights of citizenship, which pertain, according to that decision, only to the white man. I am free to say to
you that in my opinion this government of ours is founded on the
white basis. It was made by the white man, for the benefit of the
white man, to be administered by white men, in such manner as
they should determine. It is also true that a negro, an Indian, or any
other man of an inferior race to a white man, should be permitted
to enjoy, and humanity requires that he should have all the rights,
privileges and immunities which he is capable of exercising consistent with the safety of society. I would give him every right and
every privilege which his capacity would enable him to enjoy, consistent with the good of the society in which he lived. But you may
ask me what are these rights and these privileges. My answer is that
each state must decide for itself the nature and extent of these
rights. Illinois has decided for herself. We have decided that the
negro shall not be a slave, and we have at the same time decided
that he shall not vote, or serve on juries, or enjoy political privileges.
I am content with that system of policy which we have adopted for
ourselves. I deny the right of any other State to complain of our
policy in that respect, or to interfere with it, or to attempt to change
it. On the other hand, the state of Maine has decided that in that
state a negro man may vote on an equality with the white man. The
sovereign power of Maine had the right to prescribe that rule for
herself. Illinois has no right to complain of Maine for conferring the
right of negro suffrage, nor has Maine any right to interfere with,
or complain of Illinois because she has denied negro suffrage.

The state of New York has decided by her constitution that a
negro may vote, provided that he own $250 worth of property, but
not otherwise. The rich negro can vote, but the poor one cannot.
Although that distinction does not commend itself to my judgment,
yet I assert that the sovereign power of New York had a right to
prescribe that form of the elective franchise. Kentucky, Virginia,
and other states have provided that negroes, or a certain class of
them in those states, shall be slaves, having neither civil or political
rights. Without endorsing the wisdom of that decision, I assert that
Virginia has the same power by virtue of her sovereignty to protect
slavery within her limits, as Illinois has to banish it forever from our
own borders. I assert the right of each state to decide for itself on
all these questions and I do not subscribe to the doctrine of my
friend, Mr. Lincoln, that uniformity is either desirable or possible.

I do not acknowledge that the states must all be free or must all be slave.

I do not acknowledge that the negro must have civil and political rights everywhere or nowhere. I do not acknowledge that the Chinese must have the same rights in California that we would confer upon him here. I do not acknowledge that the cooley imported into this country must necessarily be put upon an equality with the white race. I do not acknowledge any of these doctrines of uniformity in the local and domestic regulations in the different states.

Thus you see, my fellow-citizens, that the issues between Mr. Lincoln and myself, as respective candidates for the U.S. Senate, as made up, are direct, unequivocal, and irreconcilable. He goes for uniformity in our domestic institutions, for a war of sections, until one or the other shall be subdued. I go for the great principle of the Kansas-Nebraska Bill, the right of the people to decide for themselves.

On the other point, Mr. Lincoln goes for a warfare upon the Supreme Court of the United States, because of their judicial decision in the Dred Scott case. I yield obedience to the decisions of that Court—to the final determination of the highest judicial tribunal known to our Constitution. He objects to the Dred Scott decision because it does not put the negro in the possession of the rights of citizenship on an equality with the white man. I am opposed to negro equality. I repeat that this nation is a white people—a people composed of European descendants—a people that have established this government for themselves and their posterity, and I am in favor of preserving not only the purity of the blood, but the purity of the government from any mixture or amalgamation with inferior races. I have seen the effects of this mixture of superior and inferior races—this amalgamation of white men and Indians and negroes; we have seen it in Mexico, in Central America, in South America, and in all the Spanish-American states, and its result has been degeneration, demoralization, and degradation below the capacity for self-government.

I am opposed to taking any step that recognizes the negro man or the Indian as the equal of the white man. I am opposed to giving him a voice in the administration of the government. I would extend to the negro, and the Indian, and to all dependent races every right, every privilege, and every immunity consistent with the safety and welfare of the white races; but equality they never should have, either political or social, or in any other respect whatever.

My friends, you see that the issues are distinctly drawn. I stand by the same platform that I have so often proclaimed to you and to the people of Illinois heretofore. I stand by the Democratic organization, yield obedience to its usages, and support its regular nominations. I endorse and approve the Cincinnati platform, and I adhere to and intend to carry out as part of that platform, the great principle of self-government, which recognizes the right of the people in each state and territory to decide for themselves their domestic institutions. In other words, if the Lecompton issue shall arise again, you have only to turn back and see where you have found me during the last six months, and then rest assured that you will find me in the same position, battling for the same principle, and vindicating it from assault from whatever quarter it may come, so long as I have the power to do it.

Fellow-citizens, you now have before you the outlines of the propositions which I intend to discuss before the people of Illinois during the pending campaign. I have spoken without preparation and in a very desultory manner, and may have omitted some points which I desired to discuss, and may have been less explicit on others than I could have wished. I have made up my mind to appeal to the people against the combination which has been made against me. The Republican leaders have formed an alliance, an unholy, unnatural alliance with a portion of the unscrupulous federal office-holders. I intend to fight that allied army wherever I meet them. I know they deny the alliance while avowing the common purpose, but yet these men who are trying to divide the Democratic party for the purpose of electing a Republican Senator in my place, are just as much the agents, the tools, the supporters of Mr. Lincoln as if they were avowed Republicans, and expect their reward for their services when the Republicans come into power. I shall deal with these allied forces just as the Russians dealt with the allies at Sebastopol. The Russians when they fired a broadside at the common enemy did not stop to inquire whether it hit a Frenchman, an Englishman or a Turk, nor will I stop to inquire, nor shall I hesitate, whether my blows hit the Republican leaders or their allies, who are holding the federal offices and yet acting in concert with the Republicans to defeat the Democratic party and its nominees. I do not include all of the federal office holders in this remark. Such of them as are Democrats and show their Democracy by remaining inside of the Democratic organization and supporting its nominees, I recognize as Democrats, but those who, having been defeated inside of the organization, go outside and attempt to divide and destroy the party in concert with the Republican leaders, have ceased to be Democrats, and belong to the allied army whose avowed object is to elect the Republican ticket by dividing and destroying the Democratic party.

My friends, I have exhausted myself, and I certainly have fatigued you, in the long and desultory remarks which I have made. It is now two nights since I have been in bed, and I think I have a right to a little sleep. I will, however, have an opportunity of meeting you face to face, and addressing you on more than one occasion before the November election. In conclusion, I must again say to you, justice to my own feelings demands it, that my gratitude for the welcome you have extended to me on this occasion knows no bounds, and can be described by no language which I can command. I see that I am literally at home when among my constituents. This welcome has amply repaid me for every effort that I have made in the public service during nearly twenty-five years that I have held office at your hands. It not only compensates me for the past, but it furnishes an inducement and incentive for future effort which no man, no matter how patriotic, can feel who has not witnessed the magnificent reception you have extended to me to-night on my return.

Twenty-four hours after Douglas spoke, Lincoln replied. The Chicago *Press and Tribune* reported the meeting.[8]

The audience assembled to hear Hon. Abraham Lincoln on Saturday evening was, in point of numbers, about three-fourths as large as that of the previous evening, when Douglas held forth; and in point of enthusiasm, about four times as great. The crowd extended from the corner of Lake and Dearborn Streets the whole length of the Tremont House, and, as on the evening previous, the balconies, windows and roofs of the adjoining buildings were filled with attentive spectators—ladies and gentlemen. The only advertisement of the meeting consisted of a notice in the Saturday morning papers, and a few handbills distributed during the day. The essential difference in the two demonstrations was simply that the Lincoln audience was enthusiastically for Lincoln, and the Douglas audience was but qualifiedly in favor of anybody. This will be admitted by any fair-minded man who witnessed both demonstrations. The Douglas authorities estimate the crowd of Friday evening at 30,000—or something more than the whole male adult population of the city. We presume that 12,000 is a liberal reckoning for that evening, and that 9,000 would about cover the gathering of Saturday night. . . .

Mr. Lincoln was introduced by C. L. Wilson, Esq., and as he made his appearance he was greeted with a perfect storm of applause.

[8] July 11, 1858.

Lincoln at Chicago, July 10, 1858[9]

My Fellow Citizens:

On yesterday evening, upon the occasion of the reception given to Senator Douglas, I was furnished with a seat very convenient for hearing him, and was otherwise very courteously treated by him and his friends, and for which I thank him and them. During the course of his remarks my name was mentioned in such a way, as I suppose renders it at least not improper that I should make some sort of reply to him. I shall not attempt to follow him in the precise order in which he addressed the assembled multitude upon that occasion, though I shall perhaps do so in the main.

A QUESTION OF VERACITY—THE ALLIANCE

There was one question to which he asked the attention of the crowd, which I deem of somewhat less importance—at least of propriety for me to dwell upon—than the others, which he brought in near the close of his speech, and which I think would not be entirely proper for me to omit attending to, and yet if I were not to give some attention to it now, I should probably forget it altogether. [Applause]. While I am upon this subject, allow me to say that I do not intend to indulge in that inconvenient mode sometimes adopted in public speaking, of reading from documents; but I shall depart from that rule so far as to read a little scrap from his speech, which notices this first topic of which I shall speak—that is, provided I can find it in the paper. (Examines the *Press and Tribune* of this morning). A voice—"Get out your specs."

I have made up my mind to appeal to the people against the combination that has been made against me!—the Republican leaders have formed an alliance, an unholy and unnatural alliance, with a portion of unscrupulous federal office-holders. I intend to fight that allied army wherever I meet them. I know they deny the alliance, but yet these men who are trying to divide the Democratic party for the purpose of electing a Republican Senator in my place, are just as much the agents and tools of the supporters of Mr. Lincoln. Hence I shall deal with this allied army just as the Russians dealt with the allies at Sebastopol—that is, the Russians did not stop to inquire, when they fired a broadside, whether it hit an Englishman, a Frenchman, or a Turk. Nor will I stop to inquire, nor shall I hesitate, whether my blows shall hit these Republican leaders or their allies who are holding the federal offices and yet acting in concert with them.

[9] Speech as reported in the Chicago *Daily Democrat*, July 13, 1858, with Lincoln's additions and corrections.

Well now, gentlemen, is not that very alarming? [Laughter.] Just to think of it! right at the outset of this canvass, I, a poor, kind, amiable, intelligent, [laughter] gentleman, [laughter and renewed cheers] I am to be slain in this way. Why,, my friend, the Judge, is not only, as it turns out, not a dead lion, nor even a living one—he is the rugged Russian Bear! [Roars of laughter and loud applause.]

But if they will have it—for he says that we deny it—that there is any such alliance, as he says there is—and I don't propose hanging very much upon this question of veracity—but if he will have it that there is such an alliance—that the administration men and we are allied, and we stand in the attitude of English, French and Turk, he occupying the position of the Russian, in that case, I beg that he will indulge us while we barely suggest to him, that these allies took Sebastopol. [Long and tremendous applause.]

Gentlemen, only a few more words as to this alliance. For my part, I have to say, that whether there be such an alliance, depends, so far as I know, upon what may be a right definition of the term *alliance*. If for the Republican party to see the other great party to which they are opposed divided among themselves, and not try to stop the division and rather be glad of it—if that is an alliance I confess I am in; but if it is meant to be said that the Republicans had formed an alliance going beyond that, by which there is contribution of money or sacrifice of principle on the one side or the other, so far as the Republican party is concerned, if there be any such thing, I protest that I neither know anything of it, nor do I believe it. I will however say—as I think this branch of the argument is lugged in—I would before I leave it, state, for the benefit of those concerned, that one of those same Buchanan men did once tell me of an argument that he made for his opposition to Judge Douglas. He said that a friend of our Senator Douglas had been talking to him, and had among other things said to him: "Why, you don't want to beat Douglas?" "Yes," said he "I do want to beat him, and I will tell you why. I believe his original Nebraska Bill was right in the abstract, but it was wrong in the time that it was brought forward. It was wrong in the application to a territory in regard to which the question had been settled; it was brought forward at a time when nobody asked him; it was tendered to the South when the South had not asked for it, but when they could not well refuse it; and for this same reason he forced that question upon our party: it has sunk the best men all over the nation, everywhere; and now when our President, struggling with the difficulties of this man's getting up, has reached the very hardest point to turn

[27]

in the case, he deserts him, and I am for putting him where he will trouble us no more." [Applause.]

Now, gentlemen, that is not my argument—that is not my argument at all. I have only been stating to you the argument of a Buchanan man. You will judge if there is any force in it. [Applause.]

WHAT IS POPULAR SOVEREIGNTY?

Popular sovereignty! everlasting popular sovereignty! [Laughter and continued cheers.] Let us for a moment inquire into this vast matter of popular sovereignty. What is popular sovereignty? We recollect that at an early period in the history of this struggle, there was another name for this same thing—*Squatter Sovereignty*. It was not exactly popular sovereignty but squatter sovereignty. What do those terms mean? What do those terms mean when used now? And vast credit is taken by our friend, the Judge, in regard to his support of it, when he declares the last years of his life have been, and all the future years of his life shall be, devoted to this matter of popular sovereignty. What is it? Why, it is the sovereignty of the people! What was squatter sovereignty? I suppose if it had any significance at all it was the right of the people to govern themselves, to be sovereign of their own affairs while they were squatted down in a country not their own, while they had squatted on a territory that did not belong to them, in the sense that a state belongs to the people who inhabit it—when it belonged to the nation—such right to govern themselves was called "Squatter Sovereignty."

Now I wish you to mark. What has become of that squatter sovereignty? What has become of it? Can you get anybody to tell you now that the people of a territory have any authority to govern themselves, in regard to this mooted question of slavery, before they form a state constitution? No such thing at all, although there is a general running fire, and although there has been a hurrah made in every speech on that side, assuming that policy had given the people of a territory the right to govern themselves upon this question; yet the point is dodged. To-day it has been decided—no more than a year ago it was decided by the Supreme Court of the United States, and is insisted upon to-day, that the people of a territory have no right to exclude slavery from a territory, that if any one man chooses to take slaves into a territory, all the rest of the people have no right to keep them out. This being so, and this decision being made one of the points that the Judge approved, and one in the approval of which he says he means to keep me down—put me down I should not say, for I have never been up. He says he is in favor of it, and sticks to it, and expects to win his battle on that decision, which says that there is no such thing as squatter sovereignty; but that any one man may take slaves into a territory, and all the other men in the territory may be opposed to it, and yet by reason of the Constitution they cannot prohibit it. When that is so, how much is left of this vast matter of squatter sovereignty I should like to know?—(a voice)—"it has all gone."

When we get back, we get to the point of the right of the people to make a constitution. Kansas was settled, for example, in 1854. It was a territory yet, without having formed a constitution, in a very regular way, for three years. All this time negro slavery could be taken in by any few individuals, and by that decision of the Supreme Court, which the Judge approves, all the rest of the people cannot keep it out; but when they come to make a constitution they may say they will not have slavery. But it is there; they are obliged to tolerate it in some way, and all experience shows that it will be so —for they will not take the negro slaves and absolutely deprive the owners of them. All experience shows this to be so. All that space of time that runs from the beginning of the settlement of the territory until there is sufficiency of people to make a state constitution —all that portion of time popular sovereignty is given up. The seal is absolutely put down upon it by the court decision, and Judge Douglas puts his own upon the top of that, yet he is appealing to the people to give him vast credit for his devotion to popular sovereignty. (Applause.)

Again, when we get to the question of the right of the people to form a state constitution as they please, to form it with slavery or without slavery—if that is anything new, I confess I don't know it. Has there ever been a time when anybody said that any other than the people of a territory itself should form a constitution? What is now in it, that Judge Douglas should have fought several years of his life, and pledged himself to fight all the remaining years of his life for? Can Judge Douglas find anybody on earth that said that anybody else should form a constitution for a people?

(A VOICE, "Yes.") Well, I should like you to name him; I should like to know who he was. (SAME VOICE—"John Calhoun.")

MR. LINCOLN—No, sir, I never heard of even John Calhoun[10] saying such a thing. He insisted on the same principle as Judge Douglas; but his mode of applying it in fact, was wrong. It is enough for my purpose to ask this crowd, when ever a Republican said anything

[10] John Calhoun was a Democratic politician from Springfield, Illinois, whom President Pierce had appointed Surveyor-General of Kansas. In the territory he lined up with the pro-slavery forces, and was elected President of the Lecompton Convention. Nevertheless, he was strongly in favor of submitting the Lecompton Constitution to the people for ratification or rejection.

against it? They never said anything against it, but they have constantly spoken for it; and whosoever will undertake to examine the platform, and the speeches of responsible men of the party, and of irresponsible men, too, if you please, will be unable to find one word from anybody in the Republican ranks, opposed to that popular sovereignty which Judge Douglas thinks that he has invented. [Applause.] I suppose that Judge Douglas will claim in a little while, that he is the inventor of the idea that the people should govern themselves: [cheers and laughter]; that nobody ever thought of such a thing until he brought it forward. We do remember, that in that old Declaration of Independence, it is said that "We hold these truths to be self-evident that all men are created equal; that they are endowed by their Creator with certain inalienable rights; that among these are life, liberty, and the pursuit of happiness; that to secure these rights, governments are instituted among men, deriving their just powers from the consent of the governed." There is the origin of popular sovereignty. [Loud applause.] Who, then, shall come in at this day and claim that he invented it? [Laughter and applause.]

LECOMPTON CONSTITUTION

The Lecompton constitution connects itself with this question, for it is in this matter of the Lecompton constitution that our friend Judge Douglas claims such vast credit. I agree that in opposing the Lecompton constitution so far as I can perceive, he was right. ["Good," "good."] I do not deny that at all; and gentlemen, you will readily see why I could not deny it, even if I wanted to. But I do not wish to; for all the Republicans in the nation opposed it, and they would have opposed it just as much without Judge Douglas' aid, as with it. They had all taken ground against it long before he did. Why, the reason that he urges against that constitution, I urged against him a year before. I have the printed speech in my hand. The argument that he makes, why that constitution should not be adopted, that the people were not fairly represented nor allowed to vote, I pointed out in a speech a year ago, which I hold in my hand now, that no fair chance was to be given to the people. ["Read it," "read it."] I shall not waste your time by trying to read it. ["Read it," "read it."] Gentlemen, reading from speeches is a very tedious business, particularly for an old man that has to put on spectacles, and the more so if the man be so tall that he has to bend over to the light. [Laughter.]

A little more, now, as to this matter of popular sovereignty and the Lecompton constitution. The Lecompton constitution, as the

Judge tells us, was defeated. The defeat of it was a good thing or it was not. He thinks the defeat of it was a good thing, and so do I, and we agree in that. Who defeated it?

A VOICE—Judge Douglas.

MR. LINCOLN—Yes, he furnished himself, and if you suppose he controlled the other Democrats that went with him, he furnished *three* votes, while the Republicans furnished *twenty*. [Applause.]

That is what he did to defeat it. In the House of Representatives he and his friends furnished some twenty votes, and the Republicans furnished *ninety odd*. [Loud applause.] Now who was it that that did the work?

A VOICE—Douglas.

MR. LINCOLN—Why, yes, Douglas did it! To be sure he did.

Let us, however, put that proposition another way. The Republicans could not have done it without Judge Douglas. Could he have done it without them? [Applause.] Which could have come the nearest to doing it without the other? [Renewed applause. "That's it," "that's it"; "good," "good."]

A VOICE—Who killed the bill?

ANOTHER VOICE—Douglas.

MR. LINCOLN—Ground was taken against it by the Republicans long before Douglas did it. The proportion of opposition to that measure is about five to one.

A VOICE—Why don't they come out on it?

MR. LINCOLN—You don't know what you are talking about, my friend. I am quite willing to answer any gentleman in the crowd who asks an *intelligent* question. [Great applause.]

Now, who in all this country has ever found any of our friends of Judge Douglas' way of thinking, and who have acted upon this main question, that has ever thought of uttering a word in behalf of Judge Trumbull? [A voice—"we have."] I defy you to show a printed resolution passed in a Democratic meeting—I take it upon myself to defy any man to show a printed resolution of a Democratic meeting, large or small, in favor of Judge Trumbull, or any of the five to one Republicans who beat that bill. Every thing must be for the Democrats! They did every thing, and the five to one that really did the thing, they snub over, and they do not seem to remember that they have an existence upon the face of the earth. [Applause.]

LINCOLN AND DOUGLAS

Gentlemen: I fear that I shall become tedious, ("Go on, go on.") I leave this branch of the subject to take hold of another. I take up that part of Judge Douglas' speech in which he respectfully attended to me. [Laughter.]

Judge Douglas made two points upon my recent speech at Springfield. He says they are to be the issues of this campaign. The first one of these points he bases upon the language in a speech which I delivered at Springfield, which I believe I can quote correctly from memory. I said there that "we are now far into the fifth year since a policy was instituted for the avowed object and with the confident promise of putting an end to slavery agitation; under the operation of that policy, that agitation had not only not ceased, but has constantly augmented."—(A voice—"That's the very language.") "I believe it will not cease until a crisis shall have been reached and passed. A house divided against itself cannot stand. I believe this government cannot endure permanently half slave and half free." [Applause.] "I do not expect the Union to be dissolved,"—I am quoting from my speech—"I do not expect the house to fall, but I do expect it will cease to be divided. It will become all one thing or the other. Either the opponents of slavery will arrest the spread of it, and place it where the public mind shall rest in the belief that it is in the course of ultimate extinction, or its advocates will push it forward until it shall become alike lawful in all the states, North as well as South." ["Good, good."]

That is the paragraph. In this paragraph which I have quoted in your hearing, and to which I ask the attention of all, Judge Douglas thinks he discovers great political heresy. I want your attention particularly to what he has inferred from it. He says I am in favor of making all the states of this Union uniform in all their internal regulations; that in all their domestic concerns I am in favor of making them entirely uniform. He draws this inference from the language I have quoted to you. He says that I am in favor of making war by the North upon the South for the extinction of slavery; that I am also in favor of inviting (as he expresses it) the South to a war upon the North, for the purpose of nationalizing slavery. Now, it is singular enough, if you will carefully read that passage over, that I did not say that I was in favor of anything in it. I only said what I expected would take place. I made a prediction only—it may have been a foolish one perhaps. I did not even say that I desired that slavery should be put in course of ultimate extinction. I do say so now, however, [great applause] so there need be no longer any difficulty about that. It may be written down in the great speech. [Applause and laughter.]

Gentlemen, Judge Douglas informed you that this speech of mine was probably carefully prepared. I admit that it was. I am not master of language; I have not a fine education; I am not capable of entering into a disquisition upon dialectics, as I believe you call it; but I do not believe the language I employed bears any such construction as Judge Douglas put upon it. But I don't care about a quibble in regard to words. I know what I meant, and I will not leave this crowd in doubt, if I can explain it to them, what I really meant in the use of that paragraph.

I am not, in the first place, unaware that this government has endured eighty-two years, half slave and half free. I know that. I am tolerably well acquainted with the history of the country, and I know that it has endured eighty-two years, half slave and half free. I *believe*—and that is what I meant to allude to there—I *believe* it has endured because, during all that time, until the introduction of the Nebraska Bill, the public mind did rest, all the time, in the belief that slavery was in course of ultimate extinction. ["Good!" "Good!" and applause.] That was what gave us the rest that we had through that period of eighty-two years; at least, so I believe. I have always hated slavery, I think as much as any Abolitionist. [Applause.] I have been an Old Line Whig. I have always hated it, but I have always been quiet about it until this new era of the introduction of the Nebraska Bill began. I always believed that everybody was against it, and that it was in course of ultimate extinction. (Pointing to Mr. Browning,[11] who stood nearby.) Browning thought so; the great mass of the nation have rested in the belief that slavery was in course of ultimate extinction. They had reason so to believe.

The adoption of the Constitution and its attendant history led the people to believe so; and that such was the belief of the framers of the Constitution itself. Why did those old men, about the time of the adoption of the Constitution, decree that slavery should not go into the new territory, where it had not already gone? Why declare that within twenty years the African slave trade, by which slaves are supplied, might be cut off by Congress? Why were all these acts? I might enumerate more of these acts—but enough. What were they but a clear indication that the framers of the Constitution intended and expected the ultimate extinction of that institution? [Cheers.] And now, when I say, as I said in my speech that Judge Douglas has quoted from, when I say that I think the opponents of slavery will resist the farther spread of it, and place it where the public

[11] Orville H. Browning, a lawyer of Quincy, Illinois, and a former Whig who was now a prominent Republican.

mind shall rest with the belief that it is in course of ultimate extinction, I only mean to say, that they will place it where the founders of this government originally placed it.

I have said a hundred times, and I have now no inclination to take it back, that I believe there is no right, and ought to be no inclination in the people of the free states to enter into the slave states, and interfere with the question of slavery at all. I have said that always. Judge Douglas has heard me say it—if not quite a hundred times, at least as good as a hundred times; and when it is said that I am in favor of interfering with slavery where it exists, I know it is unwarranted by anything I have ever *intended*, and, as I believe, by anything I have ever *said*. If, by any means, I have ever used language which could fairly be construed, (as, however, I believe I never have,) I now correct it.

[Here the shouts of the Seventh Ward delegation announced that they were coming in procession. They were received with enthusiastic cheers.]

So much, then, for the inference that Judge Douglas draws, that I am in favor of setting the sections at war with one another. I know that I never meant any such thing, and I believe that no fair mind can infer any such thing from anything I have ever said. ["Good," "good."]

Now in relation to his inference that I am in favor of a general consolidation of all the local institutions of the various states. I will attend to that for a little while, and try to inquire, if I can, how on earth it could be that any man could draw such an inference from anything I said. I have said, very many times, in Judge Douglas' hearing, that no man believed more than I in the principle of self-government; that it lies at the bottom of all my ideas of just government, from beginning to end. I have denied that his use of that term applies properly. But for the thing itself, I deny that any man has ever gone ahead of me in his devotion to the principle, whatever he may have done in efficiency in advocating it. I think that I have said it in your hearing—that I believe each individual is naturally entitled to do as he pleases with himself and the fruit of his labor, so far as it in no wise interferes with any other man's rights—[applause]—that each community, as a state, has a right to do exactly as it pleases with all the concerns within that state that interfere with the rights of no other state, and that the general government, upon principle, has no right to interfere with anything other than that general class of things that does concern the whole. I have said that at all times. I have said, as illustrations, that I do not believe in the right of Illinois to interfere with the cranberry laws of Indiana, the oyster laws of Virginia, or the liquor laws of Maine. I have said these things over and over again, and I repeat them here as my sentiments.

How is it, then, that Judge Douglas infers, because I hope to see slavery put where the public mind shall rest in the belief that it is in the course of ultimate extinction, that I am in favor of Illinois going over and interfering with the cranberry laws of Indiana? What can authorize him to draw any such inference? I suppose there might be one thing that at least enabled *him* to draw such an inference that would not be true with me or with many others, that is, because he looks upon all this matter of slavery as an exceedingly little thing—this matter of keeping one-sixth of the population of the whole nation in a state of oppression and tyranny unequalled in the world. He looks upon it as being an exceedingly little thing—only equal to the question of the cranberry laws of Indiana—as something having no moral question in it—as something on a par with the question of whether a man shall pasture his land with cattle, or plant it with tobacco—so little and so small a thing, that he concludes, if I could desire that anything should be done to bring about the ultimate extinction of that little thing, I must be in favor of bringing about an amalgamation of all the other little things in the Union. Now, it so happens—and there, I presume, is the foundation of this mistake—that the Judge thinks thus; and it so happens that there is a vast portion of the American people that do *not* look upon that matter as being this very little thing. They look upon it as a vast moral evil; they can prove it is such by the writings of those who gave us the blessings of liberty which we enjoy, and that they so looked upon it, and not as an evil merely confining itself to the states where it is situated; and while we agree that, by the Constitution we assented to, in the states where it exists we have no right to interfere with it because it is in the Constitution and we are by both duty and inclination to stick by that Constitution in all its letter and spirit from beginning to end. [Great applause.]

So much then as to my disposition—my wish—to have all the state legislatures blotted out, and to have one general consolidated government, and a uniformity of domestic regulations in all the states, by which I suppose it is meant if we raise corn here, we must make sugar cane grow here too, and we must make those which grow North, grow in the South. All this I suppose he understands I am in favor of doing. Now, so much for all this nonsense—for I must call it so. The Judge can have no issue with me on a question of establishing uniformity in the domestic regulations of the states.

DRED SCOTT DECISION

A little now on the other point—the Dred Scott decision. Another one of the issues he says that is to be made with me, is upon his devotion to the Dred Scott decision, and my opposition to it.

I have expressed heretofore, and I now repeat, my opposition to the Dred Scott decision, but I should be allowed to state the nature of that opposition, and I ask your indulgence while I do so. What is fairly implied by the term Judge Douglas has used "resistance to the decision?" I do not resist it. If I wanted to take Dred Scott from his master, I would be interfering with property, and that terrible difficulty that Judge Douglas speaks of, of interfering with property, would arise. But I am doing no such thing as that, but all that I am doing is refusing to obey it as a political rule. If I were in Congress, and a vote should come up on a question whether slavery should be prohibited in a new territory, in spite of that Dred Scott decision, I would vote that it should. [Applause; "good for you;" "we hope to see it;" "that's right."]

MR. LINCOLN—That is what I would do. ["You will have a chance soon."] Judge Douglas said last night, that before the decision he might advance his opinion, and it might be contrary to the decision when it was made; but after it was made he would abide by it until it was reversed. Just so! We let this property abide by the decision, but we will try to reverse that decision. [Loud applause—cries of "good."] We will try to put it where Judge Douglas would not object, for he says he will obey it until it is reversed. Somebody has to reverse that decision, since it is made, and we mean to reverse it, and we mean to do it peaceably.

What are the uses of decisions of courts? They have two uses. As rules of property they have two uses. First—they decide upon the question before the court. They decide in this case that Dred Scott is a slave. Nobody resists that. Not only that, but they say to everybody else, that persons standing just as Dred Scott stands is as he is. That is, they say that when a question comes up upon another person it will be so decided again, unless the court decides in another way, [cheers—cries of "good,"] unless the court overrules its decision. [Renewed applause.] Well, we mean to do what we can to have the court decide the other way. That is one thing we mean to try to do.

The sacredness that Judge Douglas throws around this decision, is a degree of sacredness that has never been before thrown around any other decision. I have never heard of such a thing. Why, decisions apparently contrary to that decision, or that good lawyers thought were contrary to that decision, have been made by that very court before. It is the first of its kind; it is an astonisher in legal history. [Laughter.] It is a new wonder of the world. [Laughter and applause.] It is based upon falsehood in the main as to the facts—allegations of facts upon which it stands are not facts at all in many instances, and no decision made on any question—the first instance of a decision made under so many unfavorable circumstances—thus placed has ever been held by the profession as law, and it has always needed confirmation before the lawyers regarded it as settled law. But Judge Douglas will have it that all hands must take this extraordinary decision, made under these extraordinary circumstances, and give their vote in Congress in accordance with it, yield to it and obey it in every possible sense. Circumstances alter cases. Do not gentlemen here remember the case of that same Supreme Court, some twenty-five or thirty years ago, deciding that a national bank was constitutional? I ask, if somebody does not remember that a national bank was declared to be constitutional? ["Yes," "yes."] Such is the truth, whether it be remembered or not. The bank charter ran out, and a re-charter was granted by Congress. That re-charter was laid before General Jackson. It was urged upon him, when he denied the constitutionality of the bank, that the Supreme Court had decided that it was constitutional; and that General Jackson then said that the Supreme Court had no right to lay down a rule to govern a co-ordinate branch of the government, the members of which had sworn to support the Constitution—that each member had sworn to support that Constitution as he understood it. I will venture here to say, that I have heard Judge Douglas say that he approved of General Jackson for that act. What has now become of all his tirade about "resistance to the Supreme Court?" ["Gone up," "Gone to the Theatre."]

My fellow citizens, getting back a little, for I pass from these points, when Judge Douglas makes his threat of annihilation upon the "alliance." He is cautious to say that that warfare of his is to fall upon the leaders of the Republican party. Almost every word he utters and every distinction he makes, has its significance. He means for the Republicans that do not count themselves as leaders, to be his friends; he makes no fuss over them; it is the leaders that he is making war upon. He wants it understood that the mass of the Republican party are really his friends. It is only the leaders that are doing something, that are intolerant, and that require extermination at his hands. As this is clearly and unquestionably the light in which he presents that matter, I want to ask your attention, addressing myself to the Republicans here, that I may ask you some questions, as to where you, as the Republican party, would be placed if you sustained Judge Douglas in his present position by a re-election? I do not claim, gentlemen, to be unselfish, I do not pretend that I would not like to go to the United States Senate, (laughter), I make no such hypocritical pretense, but I do say to you that in this mighty issue, it is nothing to you—nothing to the mass of the people of the nation, whether or not Judge Douglas or myself shall ever be heard of after this night, it may be a trifle to either of us, but in connection with this mighty question, upon which hang the destinies of the nation, perhaps, it is absolutely nothing; but where will you be placed if you re-endorse Judge Douglas? Don't you know how apt he is—how exceedingly anxious he is at all times to seize upon anything and everything to persuade you that something *he* has done *you* did yourselves? Why, he tried to persuade you last night that our Illinois legislature instructed him to introduce the Nebraska Bill. There was nobody in that legislature ever thought of such a thing; and when he first introduced the bill, he never thought of it; but still he fights furiously for the proposition, and that he did it because there was a standing instruction to our Senators to be always introducing Nebraska bills. [Laughter and applause.] He tells you he is for the Cincinnati platform, he tells you he is for the Dred Scott decision. He tells you, not in his speech last night, but substantially in a former speech, that he cares not if slavery is voted up or down—he tells you the struggle on Lecompton is past—it may come up again or not, and if it does he stands where he stood when in spite of him and his opposition you built up the Republican party. If you endorse him you tell him you do not care whether slavery be voted up or down, and he will close, or try to close your mouths with his declaration repeated by the day, the week, the month and the year. Is that what you mean? (Cries of "no," one voice "yes.") Yes, I have no doubt you who have always been for him if you mean that. No doubt of that (a voice "hit him again") soberly I have said, and I repeat it I think in the position in which Judge Douglas stood in opposing the Lecompton constitution he was right, he does not know that it will return, but if it does we may know where to find him, and if it does not we may know where to look for him and that is on the Cincinnati platform. Now I could ask the Republican party after all the hard names that Judge Douglas has called them by—all his repeated charges of their inclination to marry with and hug negroes—all his declarations of Black Republicanism—by the way we are improving, the black has got rubbed off—but with all that, if he be endorsed by Republican votes where do you stand? Plainly you stand ready saddled, bridled and harnessed and waiting to be driven over to the slavery extension camp of the nation [a voice "we will hang ourselves first"]—just ready to be driven over tied together in a lot—to be driven over, every man with a rope around his neck, that halter being held by Judge Douglas. That is the question. If Republican men have been in earnest in what they have done, I think they had better not do it, but I think that the Republican party is made up of those who, as far as they can peaceably, will oppose the extension of slavery, and who will hope for its ultimate extinction. If they believe it is wrong in grasping up the new lands of the continent, and keeping them from the settlement of free white laborers, who want the land to bring up their families upon; if they are in earnest, although they may make a mistake, they will grow restless, and the time will come when they will come back again and re-organize, if not by the same name, at least upon the same principles as their party now has. It is better, then, to save the work while it is begun. You have done the labor; maintain it—keep it. If men choose to serve you, go with them; but as you have made up your organization upon principle, stand by it; for, as surely as God reigns over you, and has inspired your mind, and given you a sense of propriety, and continues to give you hope, so surely you will still cling to these ideas, and you will at last come back again after your wanderings, merely to do your work over again. [Loud applause.]

We were often—more than once at least—in the course of Judge Douglas' speech last night, reminded that this government was made for white men—that he believed it was made for white men. Well, that is putting it into a shape in which no one wants to deny it, but the Judge then goes into his passion for drawing inferences that are not warranted. I protest, now and forever, against that counterfeit logic which presumes that because I do not want a negro woman for a slave, I do necessarily want her for a wife. [Laughter and cheers.] My understanding is that I need not have her for either, but as God made us separate, we can leave one another alone and do one another much good thereby. There are white men enough to marry all the white women, and enough black men to marry all the black women, and in God's name let them be so married. The Judge regales us with the terrible enormities that take place by the mixture of the races; that the inferior race bears the superior down. Why, Judge, if we do not let them get together in the territories they won't mix there. [Immense applause.]

A Voice—"Three cheers for Lincoln." [The cheers were given with a hearty good will.]

Mr. Lincoln—I should say at least that that is a self-evident truth. Now, it happens that we meet together once every year, sometime about the 4th of July, for some reason or other. These 4th of July gatherings I suppose have their uses. If you will indulge me, I will state what I suppose to be some of them.

We are now a mighty nation, we are thirty—or about thirty millions of people, and we own and inhabit about one-fifteenth part of the dry land of the whole earth. We run our memory back over the pages of history for about eighty-two years and we discover that we were then a very small people in point of numbers, vastly inferior to what we are now, with a vastly less extent of country,— with vastly less of everything we deem desirable among men,—we look upon the change as exceedingly advantageous to us and to our posterity, and we fix upon something that happened away back, as in some way or other being connected with this rise of prosperity. We find a race of men living in that day whom we claim as our fathers and grandfathers; they were iron men, they fought for the principle that they were contending for; and we understood that by what they then did it has followed that the degree of prosperity that we now enjoy has come to us. We hold this annual celebration to remind ourselves of all the good done in this process of time, of how it was done and who did it, and how we are historically connected with it; and we go from these meetings in better humor with ourselves—we feel more attached the one to the other, and more firmly bound to the country we inhabit. In every way we are better men in the age, and race, and country in which we live for these celebrations. But after we have done all this we have not yet reached the whole. There is something else connected with it. We have besides these men—descended by blood from our ancestors— among us perhaps half our people who are not descendants at all of these men, they are men who have come from Europe—German, Irish, French and Scandinavian—men that have come from Europe themselves, or whose ancestors have come hither and settled here, finding themselves our equals in all things. If they look back through this history to trace their connection with those days by blood, they find they have none, they cannot carry themselves back into that glorious epoch and make themselves feel that they are part of us, but when they look through that old Declaration of Independence they find that those old men say that "We hold these truths to be self-evident, that all men are created equal," and then they feel that that moral sentiment taught in that day evidences their relation to those men, that it is the father of all moral principle in them, and that they have a right to claim it as though they were blood of the blood, and flesh of the flesh of the men who wrote that Declaration, (loud and long continued applause) and so they are. This is the electric cord in that Declaration that links the hearts of patriotic and liberty-loving men together, that will link those patriotic hearts as long as the love of freedom exists in the minds of men throughout the world. [Applause.]

Now, sirs, for the purpose of squaring things with this idea of "don't care if slavery is voted up or voted down," for sustaining the Dred Scott decision [A voice—"Hit him again"], for holding that the Declaration of Independence did not mean anything at all, we have Judge Douglas giving his exposition of what the Declaration of Independence means, and we have him saying that the people of America are equal to the people of England. According to his construction, you Germans are not connected with it. Now I ask you in all soberness, if all these things, if indulged in, if ratified, if confirmed and endorsed, if taught to our children, and repeated to them, do not tend to rub out the sentiment of liberty in the country, and to transform this government into a government of some other form. Those arguments that are made, that the inferior race are to be treated with as much allowance as they are capable of enjoying; that as much is to be done for them as their condition will allow. What are these arguments? They are the arguments that kings have made for enslaving the people in all ages of the world. You will find that all the arguments in favor of king-craft were of this class; they always bestrode the necks of the people, not that they wanted to do it, but because the people were better off for being ridden. That is their argument, and this argument of the Judge is the same old serpent that says you work and I eat, you toil and I will enjoy the fruits of it. Turn it whatever way you will—whether it come from the mouth of a king, an excuse for enslaving the people of his country, or from the mouth of men of one race as a reason for enslaving the men of another race, it is all the same old serpent, and I hold if that course of argumentation that is made for the purpose of convincing the public mind that we should not care about this, should be granted, it does not stop with the negro. I should like to know if taking this old Declaration of Independence, which declares that all men are equal upon principle and making exceptions to it where will it stop. If one man says it does not mean a negro, why not another say it does not mean some other man? If that Declaration is not the truth, let us get the statute book, in which we find it and tear it out! Who is so bold as to do it! [Voices—"me" "no one," &c.] If it is not true let us tear it out! [cries of "no, no,"] let us stick to it then, [cheers] let us stand firmly by it then. [Applause.]

It may be argued that there are certain conditions that make necessities and impose them upon us, and to the extent that a necessity is imposed upon a man he must submit to it. I think that was the condition in which we found ourselves when we established this government. We had slavery among us, we could not get our constitution unless we permitted them to remain in slavery, we could not secure the good we did secure if we grasped for more, and having by necessity submitted to that much, it does not destroy the principle that is the charter of our liberties. Let that charter stand as our standard.

My friend has said to me that I am a poor hand to quote Scripture. I will try it again, however. It is said in one of the admonitions of the Lord, "As your Father in Heaven is perfect, be ye also perfect." The Savior, I suppose, did not expect that any human creature could be perfect as the Father in Heaven; but He said, "As your Father in Heaven is perfect, be ye also perfect." He set that up as a standard, and he who did most towards reaching that standard, attained the highest degree of moral perfection. So I say in relation to the principle that all men are created equal, let it be as nearly reached as we can. If we cannot give freedom to every creature, let us do nothing that will impose slavery upon any other creature. [Applause.] Let us then turn this government back into the channel in which the framers of the Constitution originally placed it. Let us stand firmly by each other. If we do not do so we are turning in the contrary direction, that our friend Judge Douglas proposes—not intentionally—as working in the traces tend to make this one universal slave nation. [A voice—"that is so."] He is one that runs in that direction, and as such I resist him.

My friends, I have detained you about as long as I desired to do, and I have only to say, let us discard all this quibbling about this man and the other man—this race and that race and the other race being inferior, and therefore they must be placed in an inferior position—discarding our standard that we have left us. Let us discard all these things, and unite as one people throughout this land, until we shall once more stand up declaring that all men are created equal.

My friends, I could not, without launching off upon some new topic, which would detain you too long, continue to-night. [Cries of "go on."] I thank you for this most extensive audience that you have furnished me to-night. I leave you, hoping that the lamp of liberty will burn in your bosoms until there shall no longer be a doubt that all men are created free and equal.

CHAPTER TWO

THE SPRINGFIELD SPEECHES

Douglas at Springfield, July 17, 1858[1]

One week after Douglas returned to Chicago he set out for Bloomington and Springfield, where he was scheduled to speak on the 16th and 17th. Flags and banners decked his train, and crowds cheered him at every station. At Joliet the Senator spent twenty minutes shaking hands with faithful supporters, drawing from one sunburned farmer the comment, "By God, that did me good!" At Joliet, too, the train added a flatcar on which a small cannon had been mounted. For the remainder of the trip "Popular Sovereignty," as the gun was called, gave notice to each town that the "Little Giant" was approaching.

Bloomington extended a boisterous welcome. After an enthusiastic greeting at the station, Douglas was seated in an open carriage and escorted by the Bloomington Rifles and a band to the London House. That evening he spoke for two hours from a platform in the court house square. The following morning he proceeded by special train to Springfield, arriving there at 3:00 p.m. The train stopped at a grove near the edge of town where a stand had been erected. A heavy rain earlier in the afternoon had made the grounds muddy and uncomfortable but did not interfere with the program. After an introduction by Benjamin S. Edwards, a former Republican who had recently announced his conversion, Douglas made the second major speech of his campaign.[2]

Mr. Chairman and Fellow-citizens of Springfield and old Sangamon:

My heart is filled with emotions at the allusions which have been so happily and so kindly made in the welcome just extended to me —a welcome so numerous and so enthusiastic, bringing me to my

---

[1] *Illinois State Register*, July 19, 1858.

[2] In strict accuracy, the third speech, since he spoke at Bloomington on the 16th. The Springfield speech, covering the same ground as that at Bloomington, was more polished, and definitely superior.

home among my old friends, that language cannot express my gratitude. I do feel at home whenever I return to old Sangamon and receive those kind and friendly greetings which have never failed to meet me when I have come among you; but never before have I had such occasion to be grateful and to be proud of the manner of the reception as on the present. While I am willing, sir, to attribute a part of this demonstration to those kind and friendly personal relations to which you have referred, I cannot conceal from myself that the controlling and pervading element in this great mass of human beings is devotion to that principle of self-government to which so many years of my life have been devoted; and rejoice more in considering it an approval of my support of a cardinal principle than I would if I could appropriate it to myself as a personal compliment.

You but speak rightly when you assert that during the last session of Congress there was an attempt to violate one of the fundamental principles upon which our free institutions rest. The attempt to force the Lecompton constitution upon the people of Kansas against their will, would have been, if successful, subversive of the great fundamental principles upon which all our institutions rest. If there is any one principle more sacred and more vital to the existence of a free government than all others, it is the right of the people to form and ratify the constitution under which they are to live. It is the corner stone of the temple of liberty, it is the foundation upon which the whole structure rests, and whenever it can be successfully evaded self-government has received a vital stab. I deemed it my duty, as a citizen and as a representative of the state of Illinois, to resist, with all my energies and with whatever of ability I could command, the consummation of that effort to force a constitution upon an unwilling people. [Applause.]

I am aware that other questions have been connected, or attempted to be connected, with that great struggle, but they were mere collateral questions, not affecting the main point. My opposition to the Lecompton constitution rested solely upon the fact that it was not the act and deed of that people, and that it did not embody their will. I did not object to it upon the ground of the slavery clause contained in it. I should have resisted it with the same energy and determination even if it had been a free state instead of a slaveholding state; and as an evidence of this fact I wish you to bear in mind that my speech against that Lecompton act was made on the 9th day of December, nearly two weeks before the vote was taken on the acceptance or rejection of the slavery clause. I did not then know, I could not have known, whether the slavery clause would be accepted or rejected, the general impression was that it would be rejected, and in my speech I assumed that impression to be true; that probably it would be voted down; and then I said to the U.S. Senate, as I now proclaim to you, my constituents, that you have no more right to force a free state upon an unwilling people than you have to force a slave state upon them against their will. ["That's so," and cheers.] You have no right to force either a good or a bad thing upon a people who do not choose to receive it. And then, again, the highest privilege of our people is to determine for themselves what kind of institutions are good and what kind of institutions are bad, and it may be true that the same people, situated in a different latitude and different climate, and with different productions and different interests, might decide the same question one way in the North and another way in the South, in order to adapt their institutions to the wants and wishes of the people to be affected by them.

You are all familiar with the Lecompton struggle, and I will occupy no more time upon the subject, except to remark that when we drove the enemies of the principle of popular sovereignty from the effort to force the Lecompton constitution upon the people of Kansas, and when we compelled them to abandon the attempt and to refer that constitution to that people for acceptance or rejection, we obtained a concession of the principle for which I had contended throughout the struggle. When I saw that the principle was conceded, and that the constitution was not to be forced on Kansas against the wishes of the people, I felt anxious to give the proposition my support; but, when I examined it, I found that the mode of reference to the people and the form of submission, upon which the vote was taken, was so objectionable as to make it unfair and unjust.

Sir, it is an axiom with me that in every free government an unfair election is no election at all. Every election should be free, should be fair, with the same privileges and the same inducements for a negative as for an affirmative vote. The objection to what is called the "English" proposition, by which the Lecompton constitution was referred back to the people of Kansas was this, that if the people chose to accept the Lecompton constitution they could come in with only 35,000 inhabitants, while if they determined to reject it in order to form another more in accordance with their wishes and sentiments, they were compelled to stay out until they should have 93,420 inhabitants. In other words, it was making a distinction and discrimination between free states and slave states under the federal constitution. I deny the justice, I deny the right, of any distinction or discrimination between the states North or South, free or slave. Equality among the states is a fundamental principle of this government. ("Stand up to that," and cheers.) Hence while I will never consent to the passage of a law that a slave state may come in with 35,000 while a free state shall not come in unless it have 93,000, on the other hand I shall not consent to admit a free state with a population of 35,000, and require 93,000 in a slaveholding state. ("Good," and cheers.)

My principle is to recognize each state of the Union as independent, sovereign and equal in its sovereignty. I will apply that principle not only to the original thirteen states, but to the states which have since been brought into the Union, and also to every state that shall hereafter be received, "as long as water shall run and grass grow." (Cheers.) For these reasons I felt compelled by a sense of duty, by a conviction of principle, to record my vote against what is called the English Bill; but yet the bill became a law, and under that law an election has been ordered to be held on the first Monday in August for the purpose of determining the question of the acceptance or rejection of the proposition submitted by Congress. I have no hesitation in saying to you, as the chairman of your committee has justly said in his address, that whatever the decision of the people of Kansas may be at that election, it must be final and conclusive of the whole subject; ("that's it") for if at that election a majority of the people of Kansas shall vote for the acceptance of the congressional proposition, Kansas at that moment becomes a state of the Union, the law admitting her becomes irrepealable, and thus the controversy terminates forever; if, on the other hand, the people of Kansas shall vote down that proposition, as it is now generally admitted they will, by a large majority, then from that instant the Lecompton constitution is *dead*, dead beyond the power of resurrection, and thus the controversy terminates. (Cheers.) And when the monster shall die I shall be willing, and trust that all of you will be willing, to acquisce in the death of the Lecompton constitution. (Cheers.) The controversy may now be considered as terminated, for in three weeks from now it will be finally settled, and all the ill feeling, all the embittered feeling which grew out of it shall cease, unless an attempt should be made in the future to repeat the same outrage upon popular rights. I need not tell you that my past course is a sufficient guarantee that if the occasion shall ever arise again whilst I occupy a seat in the United States Senate, you will find me carrying out the same principle, ("good") that I have this winter, with all the energy and all the power I may be able to command. ("We will stand by you," "That's it," "Good," &c.) I have the gratification of saying to you that I do not believe that that controversy will ever arise again; first, because the fate of Lecompton is a *warning* to the people of every territory and of every state to be cautious how the example is repeated, ("that's so," and laughter;) and secondly, because the President of the United States, in his annual message has said that he trusts the example in the Minnesota case, wherein Congress passed a law, called an enabling act, requiring the constitution to be submitted to the people for acceptance or rejection, will be followed in all future cases. ("That was right.") I agree with you that it was right. I said so on the day after the message was delivered, in my speech in the Senate on the Lecompton constitution, and I have frequently in the debate tendered to the President and his friends, tendered to the Lecomptonites, my voluntary pledge that if he will stand by that recommendation, and they will stand by it, that they will find me working hand in hand with them in the effort to carry it out. (Cheers.) All we have to do, therefore, is to adhere firmly in the future, as we have done in the past, to the principle contained in the recommendation of the President in his annual message, that the example in the Minnesota case shall be carried out in all future cases of the admission of territories into the Union as states. ("That's the doctrine.") Let that be done and the principle of popular sovereignty will be maintained in all of its vigor and all of its integrity. I rejoice to know that Illinois stands prominently and proudly forward among the states which first took their position firmly and immovably upon this principle of popular sovereignty, applied to the territories as well as to the states. You all recollect when in 1850 the peace of the country was disturbed in consequence of the agitation of the slavery question, and the effort to force the Wilmot proviso upon all the territories, that it required all the talent and all the energy, all the wisdom, all the patriotism, of a Clay and a Webster, united with other great party leaders, to devise a system of measures by which peace and harmony could be restored to our distracted country. Those compromise measures eventually passed and were recorded on the statute book, not only as the settlement of the then existing difficulties but as furnishing a rule of action which should prevent in all future time the recurrence of like evils, if they were firmly and fairly carried out. Those compromise measures rested, as I said in my speech at Chicago, on my return home that year, upon the principle that every people ought to have the right to form and regulate their own domestic institutions in their own way, subject only to the Constitution. They were founded upon the principle that, while every state possessed that right under the

Constitution, that the same right ought to be extended to and exercised by the people of the territories. ("Good.") When the Illinois legislature assembled, a few months after the adoption of these measures, the first thing the members did was to review their action upon this slavery agitation, and to correct the errors into which their predecessors had fallen. You remember that their first act was to repeal the Wilmot proviso instructions to our U.S. Senators, which had been previously passed, and in lieu of them to record another resolution upon the journal, with which you must all be familiar—a resolution brought forward by Mr. Ninian Edwards, and adopted by the House of Representatives by a vote of 61 in the affirmative and 4 in the negative. That resolution I can quote to you in almost its precise language. It declared that the great principle of self-government was the birth right of freemen; was the gift of heaven; was achieved by the blood of our Revolutionary fathers and must be continued and carried out in the organization of all the territories and the admission of all new states. That became the Illinois platform by the united voices of the Democratic party and of the Whig party in 1851; all the Whigs and all the Democrats in the legislature uniting in an affirmative vote upon it and there being only 4 votes in the negative, of Abolitionists, of course, ("of course." "They could not be anything else," and laughter). That resolution stands upon the journal of your legislature to this day and hour unrepealed, and a standing, living, perpetual instruction to the Senators from Illinois in all time to come to carry out that principle of self-government and allow no limitation upon it in the organization of any territories or the admission of any new states. In 1854 when it became my duty as the chairman of the Committee on Territories to bring forward a bill for the organization of Kansas and Nebraska, I incorporated that principle in it and Congress passed it, thus carrying the principle into practical effect. I will not recur to the scenes which took place all over this country in 1854 when that Nebraska Bill passed. I could then travel from Boston to Chicago by the light of my own effigies, in consequence of having stood up for it. ("It did not hurt you," "Hurra for Douglas," &c.) I leave it to you to say how I met that storm, and whether I quailed under it; ("never," "no") whether I did not "face the music," justify the principle and pledge my life to carry it out. ("You did," and three cheers.)

A friend here reminds me, too, that when making speeches then, justifying the Nebraska Bill and the great principle of self-government, that I predicted that in less than five years you would have to get out a search warrant to find an anti-Nebraska man. ["That's so," "good," &c.] Well, I believe I did make that prediction. I did not claim the power of a prophet, but it occurred to me that among a free people, and an honest people and an intelligent people, that five years was long enough for them to come to an understanding that the great principle of self-government was right, not only in the states, but in the territories. I rejoiced this year to see my prediction, in that respect, carried out and fulfilled by the unanimous vote, in one form or another, of both Houses of Congress. If you will remember that pending this Lecompton controversy that gallant old Roman, Kentucky's favorite son, the worthy successor of the immortal Clay—I allude, as you know, to the gallant John J. Crittenden—[cheers] brought forward a bill, now known as the Crittenden-Montgomery Bill, in which it was proposed that the Lecompton constitution should be referred back to the people of Kansas, to be decided for or against it, at a fair election, and if a majority of the people were in favor of it, that Kansas should come into the Union as a slaveholding state, but that if a majority were against it that they should make a new constitution and come in with slavery or without it, as they thought proper. ["That was right."] Yes, my dear sir, it was not only right, but it was carrying out the principle of the Nebraska Bill in its letter and in its spirit. Of course I voted for it, [cheers,] and so did every Republican Senator and Representative in Congress. [Laughter.] I have found some Democrats so perfectly straight that they blame me for voting for the principle of the Nebraska Bill because the Republicans voted the same way. [Great laughter. "What did they say?"]

What did they say? Why, many of them said that Douglas voted with the Republicans. Yes! not only that, but with the *Black* Republicans. [Renewed laughter.] Well, there are different modes of stating that proposition. The New York *Tribune* says that Douglas did not vote with the Republicans, but that on that question the Republicans went over to Douglas and voted with him. ["Good," and cheers.]

My friends, I have never yet abandoned a principle because of the support I found men yielding to it, and I shall never abandon my Democratic principles, merely because Republicans come to them. [Great applause.] For what do we travel over the country and make speeches in every political canvass, if it is not to enlighten the minds of these Republicans; ["Good," great laughter and cheers,] to remove the scales from their eyes, and to impart to them the light of Democratic vision, so that they may be able to carry out the constitution of our country as our fathers made it. ["Good, good."] And if by preaching our principles to the people we succeed in convincing the Republicans of the errors of their ways, and bring them over to us, are we bound to turn traitors to our principles, merely because they give them their support? ["Never," and cheers.] All I have to say is that I hope the Republican party will stand firm, in the future, by the vote they gave on the Crittenden-Montgomery Bill. [Cheers.] I hope we will find, in the resolutions of their county and congressional conventions, no declarations of "no more slave states to be admitted into this Union," but in lieu of that declaration that we will find the principle that the people of every state and every territory shall come into the Union with slavery or without it, just as they please, without any interference on the part of Congress. ["That's the doctrine."]

My friends, whilst I was at Washington, engaged in this great battle for sound constitutional principles, I find from the newspapers that the Republican party of this state assembled in this capital, in state convention, and not only nominated, as it was wise and proper for them to do, a man for my successor in the Senate, but laid down a platform, and their nominee made a speech, carefully written and prepared, and well delivered, which that convention accepted as containing the Republican creed. I have no comment to make on that part of Mr. Lincoln's speech, in which he represents me as forming a conspiracy with the Supreme Court and with the late President of the United States and the present chief magistrate, having for my object the passage of the Nebraska Bill, the Dred Scott decision and the extension of slavery—a scheme of political tricksters, composed of Chief Justice Taney and his eight associates, two Presidents of the United States, and one Senator of Illinois. ["Hit him again," cheers and great laughter.] If Mr. Lincoln deems me a conspirator of that kind, all I have to say is that I do not think so badly of the President of the United States and the Supreme Court of the United States, the highest judicial tribunal on earth, as to believe that they were capable in their action and decision of entering into political intrigues for partisan purposes. [Three cheers were here given for the Supreme Court of the United States.] I therefore shall only notice those parts of Mr. Lincoln's speech, in which he lays down his platform of principles and tells you what he intends to do if he is elected to the Senate of the United States.

[An old gentleman here rose on the platform and said: "Be particular now Judge, be particular."]

MR. DOUGLAS—My venerable friend here says that he will be gratified if I will be particular, and in order that I may be so I will read the language of Mr. Lincoln as reported by himself and published to the country. ("Good, good.") Mr. Lincoln lays down his main proposition in these words:

"A house divided against itself cannot stand." I believe this Union cannot endure permanently half free and half slave. I do not expect the Union will be dissolved, I do not expect the house to fall, but I do expect it will cease to be divided. It will become all one thing or all the other. [Laughter.]

Mr. Lincoln does not think this Union can continue to exist composed of half slave and half free states; they must all be free or all slave. ("That's Abolition doctrine.") I do not doubt that this is Mr. Lincoln's conscientious conviction. ("Nor I.") I do not doubt that he thinks it is the highest duty of every patriotic citizen to preserve this glorious Union, and to adopt these measures as necessary to its preservation. He tells you that the only mode to preserve the Union is to make all the states free or all slave. ("God forbid.") It must be the one or it must be the other. Now that being essential, in his estimation, to the preservation of this glorious union, how is he going to accomplish it? He says that he wants to go to the Senate in order to carry out this favorite patriotic policy of his, of making all the states free, so that the house shall no longer be divided against itself. (Great laughter.) When he gets to the Senate by what means is he going to accomplish it? By an act of Congress. Will he contend that Congress has any power under the Constitution to abolish slavery in any state of this Union, or to interfere with it directly or indirectly? Of course he will not contend that. ("Hurra for Douglas.") Then what is to be his mode of carrying out his principle, by which slavery shall be abolished in all the states? Mr. Lincoln certainly does not speak at random. He is a lawyer, an eminent lawyer, and his profession is to know the remedy for every wrong. What is his remedy for this imaginary wrong which he supposes to exist? The Constitution of the United States provides that it may be amended by Congress passing an amendment by a two-thirds majority of each House, which shall be ratified by three-fourths of the states, and the inference is that Mr. Lincoln intends to carry this slavery agitation into Congress with the view of amending the Constitution so that slavery can be abolished in all the states of the Union. In other words he is not going to allow one portion of the Union to be slave and another portion to be free; he is not going to permit the house to be divided against itself. ("He can't help it.") He is going to remedy it by lawful and constitutional means. What are to be these means? How can he abolish slavery in those states where it exists? There is but one mode by which a political organ-

[51]

ization, composed of men in the free states, can abolish slavery in the slaveholding states, and that would be to abolish the state legislatures, blot out of existence the state sovereignties, invest Congress with full and plenary power over all the local and domestic police regulations of the different states of this Union. Then there would be uniformity in the local concerns and domestic institutions of the different states; then the house would no longer be divided against itself; then the states would all be free, or they would all be slave, then you would have uniformity prevailing throughout this whole land in the local and domestic institutions, but it would be a uniformity not of liberty but a uniformity of despotism that would triumph. (Three cheers.) I submit to you, my fellow citizens, whether this is not the logical consequence of Mr. Lincoln's proposition. ("Right.") I have called on Mr. Lincoln to explain what he did mean, if he did not mean this, and he has made a speech at Chicago, in which he attempts to explain. And how does he explain? I will give him the benefit of his own language, precisely as it was reported in the Republican papers of that city, after undergoing his revision. [Laughter.]

I have said a hundred times, and have now no inclination to take it back, that I believe there is no right and ought to be no inclination in the people of the free states to enter into the slave sates and interfere with the question of slavery at all.

He believes there is no right on the part of the free people of the free states to enter the slave states and interfere with the question of slavery, hence he does not propose to go into Kentucky and stir up a civil war and a servile war between the blacks and the whites. All he proposes is to invite the people of Illinois and every other free state to band together as one sectional party, governed and divided by a geographical line, to make war upon the institution of slavery in the slaveholding states. He is going to carry it out by means of a political party, that has its adherents only in the free states; a political party, that does not pretend that it can give [get?] a solitary vote in the slave states of the Union, and by this sectional vote he is going to elect a President of the United States, form a cabinet and administer the government on sectional grounds, being the power of the North over that of the South. In other words, he invites a war of the North against the South, a warfare of the free states against the slaveholding states. He asks all men in the free states to conspire to exterminate slavery in the Southern states so as to make them all free, and then he notifies the South that unless they are going to submit to our efforts to exterminate their institutions, they must band together and plant slavery in Illinois and every Northern state. He says that the states must all be free or must all be slave. On this point I take issue with him directly. I assert that Illinois has a right to decide the slavery question for herself. We have decided it, and I think we have done it wisely, but whether wisely or unwisely it is our business, and the people of no other state have any right to interfere with us directly or indirectly. Claiming as we do this right for ourselves we must concede it to every other state to be exercised by them respectively. ["That's the doctrine."]

Now, Mr. Lincoln says, that he will not enter into Kentucky to abolish slavery there, but that all he will do is to fight slavery in Kentucky from Illinois. [Laughter.] He will not go over there to set fire to the match. I do not think he would. Mr. Lincoln is a very prudent man. [Laughter.] He would not deem it wise to go over into Kentucky to stir up this strife but he would do it from this side of the river. [Great laughter and cheers.] Permit me to inquire whether the wrong, the outrage of interference by one state with the local concerns of another is worse when you actually invade them than it would be if you carried on the warfare from another state. For the purpose of illustration, suppose the British government should plant a battery on the Niagara River opposite Buffalo and throw their shells over into Buffalo, where they should explode and blow up the houses and destroy the town. We call the British government to an account and they say, in the language of Mr. Lincoln, we did not enter into the limits of the United States to interfere with you, [great laughter] we planted the battery on our own soil and had a right to shoot from our own soil, and if our shells and balls fell in Buffalo and killed your inhabitants, why, it is your lookout, not ours. Thus, Mr. Lincoln is going to plant his Abolition batteries all along the banks of the Ohio River and throw his shells into Virginia and Kentucky and into Missouri, and blow up the institution of slavery, and when we arraign him for his unjust interference with the institutions of the other states, he says, "Why, I never did enter into Kentucky to interfere with her; I do not propose to do it, I only propose to take care of my own head by keeping on this side of the river, out of harm's way." (Shouts of laughter and cheers.) But yet, he says he is going to persevere in this system of sectional warfare, and I have no doubt he is sincere in what he says. (Laughter.) He says that the existence of the Union depends upon his success in firing into these slave states until he exterminates them. [Renewed laughter.] He says that unless he shall play his batteries successfully, so as to abolish slavery in every one of the states, that the Union shall be dissolved; [Laughter] and he

[53]

says that a dissolution of the Union would be a terrible calamity. Of course it would. We are all friends of the Union. We all believe —I do—that our lives, our liberties, our hopes in the future depend upon the preservation and perpetuity of this glorious Union. I believe that the hopes of the friends of liberty throughout the world depend upon the perpetuity of the American Union. ("Hear him," and intense enthusiasm.) But while I believe that my mode of preserving the Union is a very different one from that of Mr. Lincoln, I believe that the Union can only be preserved by maintaining inviolate the Constitution of the U.S. as our fathers have made it. ("That's it," and cheers.) That Constitution guarantees to the people of every state the right to have slavery or not have it; to have negroes or not have them; to have Maine liquor laws or not have them; to have just such institutions as they choose, each state being left free to decide for itself. ("That's right," and cheers.) The framers of that Constitution never conceived the idea that uniformity in the domestic institutions of the different states was either desirable or possible. They well understood that the laws and institutions which would be well adapted to the granite hills of New Hampshire would be unfit for the rice plantations of South Carolina; they well understood that each one of the thirteen states had distinct and separate interests, and required distinct and separate local laws and local institutions. ("That's sound doctrine; hurrah for Douglas.") And in view of that fact they provided that each state should retain its sovereign power within its own limits, with the right to make just such laws and just such institutions as it saw proper, under the belief that no two of them would be alike. If they had supposed that uniformity was desirable and possible, why did they provide for a separate legislature for each state? Why did they not blot out state sovereignty and state legislatures, and give all the power to Congress, in order that the laws might be uniform? For the very reason that uniformity, in their opinion, was neither desirable or possible. We have increased from thirteen states to thirty-two states, and just in proportion as the number of states increases and our territory expands, there will be a still greater variety and dissimilarity of climate, of production, and of interest, requiring a corresponding dissimilarity and variety in the local laws and institutions adapted thereto. The laws that are necessary in the mining regions of California, would be totally useless and vicious on the prairies of Illinois; the laws that would suit the lumber regions of Maine or of Minnesota, would be totally useless and valueless in the tobacco regions of Virginia and Kentucky; the laws which would suit the manufacturing districts of New England, would be totally unsuited to the planting regions of the Carolinas, of Georgia and of Louisiana. Each state is supposed to have interests separate and distinct from each and every other, and hence must have laws different from each and every other state, in order that its laws shall be adapted to the condition and necessities of the people. ["Hurrah for Douglas."] Hence I insist that our institutions rest on the theory that there shall be dissimilarity and variety in the local laws and institutions of the different states instead of all being uniform; and you find, my friends, that Mr. Lincoln and myself differ radically and totally on the fundamental principles of this government. He goes for consolidation, for uniformity in our local institutions, for blotting out state rights and state sovereignty, and consolidating all the power in the federal government, for converting these thirty-two sovereign states into one empire, and making uniformity throughout the length and breadth of the land. On the other hand, I go for maintaining the authority of the federal government within the limits marked out by the Constitution, and then for maintaining and preserving the sovereignty of each and all of the states of the Union, in order that each state may regulate and adopt its own local institutions in its own way, without interference from any power whatsoever. [Cheers.] Thus you find there is a distinct issue of principles—principles irreconcilable—between Mr. Lincoln and myself. He goes for consolidation and uniformity in our government. I go for maintaining the confederation of the sovereign states under the Constitution, as our fathers made it, leaving each state at liberty to manage its own affairs and own internal institutions.

Mr. Lincoln makes another point upon me, and rests his whole case upon these two points. His last point is, that he will wage a warfare upon the Supreme Court of the United States because of the Dred Scott decision. He takes occasion, in his speech made before the Republican convention, in my absence, to arraign me, not only for having expressed my acquiescence in that decision, but to charge me with being a conspirator with that court in devising that decision three years before Dred Scott ever thought of commencing a suit for his freedom. [Laughter.] The object of his speech was to convey the idea to the people that the court could not be trusted, that the late President could not be trusted, that the present one could not be trusted, and that Mr. Douglas could not be trusted; that they were all conspirators in bringing about that corrupt decision, to which Mr. Lincoln is determined he will never yield a willing obedience.

He makes two points upon the Dred Scott decision. The first is that he objects to it because the court decided that negroes descended of slave parents are not citizens of the United States; and secondly, because they have decided that the act of Congress, passed 8th of March, 1820, prohibiting slavery in all of the territories north of 36°30′, was unconstitutional and void, and hence did not have effect in emancipating a slave brought into that territory. And he will not submit to that decision. He says that he will not fight the judges or the United States marshals in order to liberate Dred Scott, but that he will not respect that decision, as a rule of law binding on this country, in the future. Why not? Because, he says, it is unjust. How is he going to remedy it? Why, he says he is going to reverse it. How? He is going to take an appeal. To whom is he going to appeal? [Laughter.] The Constitution of the United States provides that the Supreme Court is the ultimate tribunal, the highest judicial tribunal on earth, and Mr. Lincoln is going to appeal from that. To whom? I know he appealed to the Republican State Convention of Illinois, [laughter,] and I believe that convention reversed the decision, but I am not aware that they have yet carried it into effect. [Renewed laughter.] How are they going to make that reversal effectual? Why, Mr. Lincoln tells us in his late Chicago speech. He explains it as clear as light. He says to the people of Illinois that if you elect him to the Senate he will introduce a bill to re-enact the law which the court pronounced unconstitutional. [Shouts of laughter, and voices, "*spot* the law."] Yes, he is going to spot the law. The court pronounces that law, prohibiting slavery, unconstitutional and void, and Mr. Lincoln is going to pass an act reversing that decision and making it valid. I never heard before of an appeal being taken from the Supreme Court to the Congress of the United States to reverse its decision. I have heard of appeals being taken from Congress to the Supreme Court to declare a statute void. That has been done from the earliest days of Chief Justice Marshall, down to the present time.

The supreme court of Illinois do not hesitate to pronounce an act of the legislature void, as being repugnant to the constitution, and the Supreme Court of the United States is vested by the Constitution with that very power. The Constitution says that the judicial power of the United States shall be vested in the Supreme Court, and such inferior courts as Congress shall, from time to time, ordain and establish. Hence it is the province and duty of the Supreme Court to pronounce judgment on the validity and constitutionality of an act of Congress. In this case they have done so, and Mr. Lincoln will not submit to it, and he is going to reverse it by another act of Congress of the same tenor. [Laughter.] My opinion is that Mr. Lincoln ought to be on the supreme bench himself, when the Republicans get into power, if that kind of law knowledge qualifies a man for the bench. But Mr. Lincoln intimates that there is another mode by which he can reverse the Dred Scott decision. How is that? Why, he is going to appeal to the people to elect a President who will appoint judges who will reverse the Dred Scott decision. Well, let us see how that is going to be done. First, he has to carry on his sectional organization, a party confined to the free states, making war upon the slaveholding states until he gets a Republican President elected. ["He never will, sir," and great cheering.] I do not believe he ever will. ["Bravo," and applause.] But suppose he should; when that Republican President shall have taken his seat—Mr. Seward, for instance—will he then proceed to appoint judges? No! he will have to wait until the present judges die before he can do that, and perhaps his four years would be out before a majority of these judges found it agreeable to die; [laughter and cheers,] and it very possible, too, that Mr. Lincoln's senatorial term would expire before these judges would be accommodating enough to die. ["That's right."] If it should so happen I do not see a very great prospect for Mr. Lincoln to reverse the Dred Scott decision. But suppose they should die, then how are the new judges to be appointed? Why, the Republican President is to call up the candidates and catechise them, and ask them, "How will you decide this case if I appoint you judge?" [Shouts of laughter.] Suppose, for instance, Mr. Lincoln to be a candidate for a vacancy on the supreme bench to fill Chief Justice Taney's place, [renewed laughter] and when he applied to Seward, the latter would say, "Mr. Lincoln, I cannot appoint you until I know how you will decide the Dred Scott case." Mr. Lincoln tells him, and then [Seward] asks him how he will decide Tom Jones' case, and Bill Wilson's case, and thus catechises the judge as to how he will decide any case which may arise before him. Suppose you get a Supreme Court composed of such judges, who have been appointed by a partisan President upon their giving pledges how they would decide a case before it arise, what confidence would you have in such a court? ["None, none."]

Would not your court be prostituted beneath the contempt of all mankind! What man would feel that his liberties were safe; his right of person or property was secure if the supreme bench, that august tribunal, the highest on earth, was brought down to that low, dirty pool wherein the judges are to give pledges in advance how they will decide all the questions which may be brought before them. ("Hurra for Douglas.") It is a proposition to make that court the corrupt, unscrupulous tool of a political party. But Mr. Lincoln cannot conscientiously submit, he thinks, to the decision of a court composed of a majority of Democrats. If he cannot, how can he expect us to have confidence in a court composed of a majority of Republicans, selected for the purpose of deciding against the Democracy, and in favor of the Republicans? (Cheers.) The very proposition carries with it the demoralization and degradation destructive of the judicial department of the federal government.

I say to you, fellow citizens, that I have no warfare to make upon the Supreme Court because of the Dred Scott decision. I have no complaints to make against that court, because of that decision. My private opinions on some points of the case may have been one way and on other points of the case another; in some things concurring with the court and in others dissenting, but what have my private opinions in a question of law to do with the decision after it has been pronounced by the highest judicial tribunal known to the Constitution? (Cheers.) You, sir, [addressing the chairman], as an eminent lawyer, have a right to entertain your opinions on any question that comes before the court and to appear before the tribunal and maintain them boldly and with tenacity until the final decision shall have been pronounced, and then, sir, whether you are sustained or overruled your duty as a lawyer and a citizen is to bow in deference to that decision. I intend to yield obedience to the highest tribunals in the land in all cases whether their opinions are in conformity with my views as a lawyer or not. When we refuse to abide by judicial decisions what protection is there left for life and property? To whom shall you appeal? To mob law, to partisan caucuses, to town meetings, to revolution? Where is the remedy when you refuse obedience to the constituted authorities? I will not stop to inquire whether I agree or disagree with all the opinions expressed by Judge Taney or any other judge. It is enough for me to know that the decision has been made. It has been made by a tribunal appointed by the Constitution to make it; it was a point within their jurisdiction, and I am bound by it. [Cheers.]

But, my friends, Mr. Lincoln says that this Dred Scott decision destroys the doctrine of popular sovereignty, for the reason that the court has decided that Congress had no power to prohibit slavery in the territories, and hence he infers that it would decide that the territorial legislatures could not prohibit slavery there. I will not stop to inquire whether the court will carry the decision that far or not. It would be interesting as a matter of theory, but of no importance in practice; for this reason, that if the people of a territory want slavery they will have it, ["that's so,"] and if they do not want it they will drive it out, and you cannot force it on them.

["That's good," "That's the doctrine," and cheers.] Slavery cannot exist a day in the midst of an unfriendly people with unfriendly laws. There is truth and wisdom in a remark made to me by an eminent Southern Senator, when speaking of this technical right to take slaves into the territories. Said he:

I do not care a fig which way the decision shall be, for it is of no particular consequence; slavery cannot exist a day or an hour in any territory or state unless it has affirmative laws sustaining and supporting it, furnishing police regulations and remedies, and an omission to furnish them would be as fatal as a constitutional prohibition. Without affirmative legislation in its favor slavery could not exist any longer than a new born infant could survive under the heat of the sun on a barren rock without protection. It would wilt and die for the want of support.

So it would be in the territories. See the illustration in Kansas. The Republicans have told you, during the whole history of that territory, down to last winter, that the pro-slavery party in the legislature had passed a pro-slavery code, establishing and sustaining slavery in Kansas, but that this pro-slavery legislature did not truly represent the people, but was imposed upon them by an invasion from Missouri, and hence the legislature were one way and the people another. Granting all this, and what has been the result? With laws supporting slavery, but the people against, there are not as many slaves in Kansas today as there were on the day the Nebraska Bill passed and the Missouri Compromise was repealed. [Cheers.] Why? Simply because slave owners knew that if they took their slaves into Kansas, where a majority of the people were opposed to slavery, that it would soon be abolished, and that they would lose their right of property in consequence of taking them there. For that reason they would not take or keep them there. If there had been a majority of the people in favor of slavery and the climate had been favorable, they would have taken them there, but the climate not being suitable, the interest of the people being opposed to it, and a majority of them against it, the slave owner did not find it profitable to take his slaves there, and consequently there are not as many slaves there today as on the day the Missouri Compromise was repealed. This shows clearly that if the people do not want slavery they will keep it out and that if they do want it they will protect it.

You have a good illustration of this in the territorial history of this state. You all remember that by the Ordinance of 1787 slavery was prohibited in Illinois, yet you all know, particularly you old settlers, who were here in territorial times, that the territorial legislature, in defiance of that ordinance, passed a law allowing you to go into Kentucky, buy slaves and bring them into the territory, having them sign indentures to serve you and your posterity 99 years, and their posterity thereafter to do the same. This hereditary slavery was introduced in defiance of the act of Congress. That was the exercise of popular sovereignty, the right of a territory to decide the question for itself in defiance of the act of Congress. On the other hand, if the people of a territory are hostile to slavery they will drive it out. Consequently this theoretical question raised upon the Dred Scott decision, is worthy of no consideration whatsoever, for it is only brought into these political discussions and used as a hobby upon which to ride into office, or out of which to manufacture political capital.

But Mr. Lincoln's main objection to the Dred Scott decision I have reserved for my conclusion. His principal objection to that decision is that it was intended to deprive the negro of the rights of citizenship in the different states of the Union. Well, suppose it was, and there is no doubt that that was its legal effect, what is his objection to it? Why, he thinks that a negro ought to be permitted to have the rights of citizenship. He is in favor of negro citizenship, and opposed to the Dred Scott decision, because it declares that a negro is not a citizen, and hence is not entitled to vote. Here I have a direct issue with Mr. Lincoln. I am not in favor of negro citizenship. ("Nor I," responded the crowd, "Hurrah for Douglas," "good, good," &c.) I do not believe that a negro is a citizen or ought to be a citizen. ("Hurrah for Douglas.") I believe that this government of ours was founded, and wisely founded, upon the white basis. ("That's right," "Hurrah," and "Bravo," &c.) It was made by white men for the benefit of white men and their posterity, to be executed and managed by white men, ("Glory to you," "Hurrah for Douglas," and great applause). I freely concede that humanity requires us to extend all the protection, all the privileges, all the immunities, to the Indian and the negro which they are capable of enjoying consistent with the safety of society. ("That's right.") You may then ask me what are those rights, what is the nature and extent of the rights which a negro ought to have. My answer is that this is a question for each state and each territory to decide for itself. ("Good.") In Illinois we have decided that a negro is not a slave, but we have at the same time determined that he is not a citizen and shall not enjoy any political rights. ("That's right.") I concur in the wisdom of that policy and am content with it. ("Hurrah for Douglas.") I assert that the sovereignty of Illinois had a right to determine that question as we have decided it, and I deny that any other state has a right to interfere with us or call us to account for that decision. In the state of Maine they have decided by their constitution that the negro shall exercise the elective franchise and hold office on an equality with the white man. Whilst I do not concur in the good sense or correct taste of that decision on the part of Maine, I have no disposition to quarrel with her. It is her business and not ours. If the people of Maine desire to be put on an equality with the negro (laughter), I do not know that anybody in this state will attempt to prevent it. ("Not at all.") If the white people of Maine think a negro their equal, and that he has a right to come and kill their vote by a negro vote, they have a right to think so, I suppose, and I have no disposition to interfere with them. Then again, passing over to New York, we find in that state they have provided that a negro may vote provided he holds $250 worth of property, but that he shall not unless he does; that is to say, they will allow a negro to vote if he is rich, but a poor fellow they will not allow to vote. In New York they think a rich negro is equal to a white man. Well, that is a matter of taste with them. (Laughter.) If they think so in that state and do not carry the doctrine outside of it and propose to interfere with us, I have no quarrel to make with them. It is their business. There is a great deal of philosophy and good sense in a saying of Fridley of Kane. Fridley had a law suit before a justice of the peace, and the justice decided it against him. This he did not like, and standing up and looking at the justice for a moment, "Well, Square," said he, "if a man chooses to make darnation fool of himself I suppose there is no law against it." (Laughter.) That is all I have to say about these negro regulations and this negro voting in other states where they have systems different from ours. If it is their wish to have it so, be it so. There is no cause to complain. Kentucky has decided that it is not consistent with her safety and her prosperity to allow a negro to have either political rights or his freedom, and hence she makes him a slave. That is her business, not mine. It is her right under the constitution of the country. The sovereignty of Kentucky, and that alone, can decide that question, and when she decides it there is no power on earth to which you can appeal to reverse it. ("Hurrah for old Kaintuck.") Therefore, leave Kentucky as the Constitution has left her, a sovereign, independent state, with the exclusive right to have slavery or not, as she chooses, and so long as I hold power I will maintain and defend her right against any assaults from whatever quarter they may come. (Cheers.)

I will never stop to inquire whether I approve or disapprove of the domestic institutions of a state. I maintain her sovereign rights. I defend her sovereignty from all assault, in the hope that she will join in defending us when we are assailed by any outside power. ["Good, good," and cheers.] How are we to protect our sovereign rights, to keep slavery out, unless we protect the sovereign rights of every other state to decide the question for itself. Let Kentucky, or South Carolina, or any other state, attempt to interfere in Illinois and tell us that we shall establish slavery, in order to make it uniform, according to Mr. Lincoln's proposition, throughout the Union. [Laughter.] Let them come here and tell us that we must and shall have slavery, and I will call on you to follow me and shed the last drop of our heart's blood in repelling the invasion and chastizing their insolence. [Cheers.] And if we would fight for our reserved rights and sovereign power in our own limits, we must respect the sovereignty of each other state. ["That's the doctrine."]

Hence, you find that Mr. Lincoln and myself come to a direct issue on this whole doctrine of slavery. He is going to wage a war against it everywhere, not only in Illinois but in his native state of Kentucky. And why? Because he says that the Declaration of Independence contains this language: "We hold these truths to be self-evident, that all men are created equal; that they are endowed by their Creator with certain inalienable rights; that among these are life, liberty and the pursuit of happiness," and he asks whether that instrument does not declare that all men are created equal. ["Not niggers."] Mr. Lincoln then goes on to say that that clause of the Declaration of Independence includes negroes. ["I say not."] Well, if you say not I do not think you will vote for Mr. Lincoln. [Laughter, and the same voice, "I'll be d——d if I do."] Mr. Lincoln goes on to argue that the language "all men" included the negroes, Indians, and all inferior races.

In his Chicago speech he says in so many words that it includes the negroes, that they were endowed by the Almighty with the right of equality with the white man, and therefore that that right is divine—a right under the higher law; that the law of God makes them equal to the white man, and therefore that the law of the white man cannot deprive them of that right. This is Mr. Lincoln's argument. He is conscientious in his belief. I do not question his sincerity, I do not doubt that he, in his conscience, believes that the Almighty made the negro equal to the white man. He thinks that the negro is his brother. [Laughter.] I do not think that the negro is any kin of mine at all. [Laughter and cheers.] And here is the difference between us. I believe that the Declaration of Independence, in the words "all men are created equal," was intended to allude only to the people of the United States, to men of European birth or descent, being white men, that they were created equal, and hence that Great Britain had no right to deprive them of their political and religious priviliges; but the signers of that paper did not intend to include the Indian or the negro in that declaration, ["never," &c.] for if they had would they not have been bound to abolish slavery in every state and colony from that day? ["Certainly," and cheers.] Remember, too, that at the time the Declaration was put forth every one of the thirteen colonies were slave-holding colonies; every man who signed the Declaration represented slaveholding constituents. ["Hurrah for Douglas."] Did those signers mean by that act to charge themselves and all their constituents with having violated the law of God, in holding the negro in an inferior condition to the white man? ["No, certainly not."] And yet, if they included negroes in that term they were bound, as conscientious men, that day and that hour, not only to have abolished slavery throughout the land, but to have conferred political rights and privileges on the negro, and elevated him to an equality with the white man. ["They did not do it."] I know they did not do it, and the very fact that they did not shows that they did not understand the language they used to include any but the white race. Did they mean to say that the Indian, on this continent, was created equal to the white man, and that he was endowed by the Almighty with inalienable rights—rights so sacred that they could not be taken away by any constitution or law that man could pass? Why, their whole action towards the Indian showed that they never dreamed that they were bound to put him on an equality. I am not only opposed to negro equality, but I am opposed to Indian equality. I am opposed to putting the coolies, now importing into this country, on an equality with us, or putting the Chinese or any other inferior race on an equality with us. I hold that the white race, the European race, I care not whether Irish, German, French, Scotch, English, or to what nation they belong, so they are the white race to be our equals, ["Good, that's the doctrine," and cheers,] and I am for placing them, as our fathers did, on an equality with us. [Cheers.] Emigrants from Europe and their descendants constitute the people of the U.S. [Renewed applause.] The Declaration of Independence only included the white people of the U.S. ["Not the negro."] The Constitution of the U.S. was framed by the white people, it ought to be administered by them, leaving each state to make such regulations concerning the negro as it chooses, allowing him political rights or not as it chooses, and allowing him civil rights or not as it may determine for itself.

Let us only carry out those principles, and we will have peace and harmony in the different states. But Mr. Lincoln's conscientious

scruples on this point govern his action and I honor him for following them, although I abhor the doctrine which he preaches. [Laugh-
ter.] His conscientious scruples lead him to believe that the negro
is entitled by divine right to the civil and political privileges of
citizenship on an equality with the white man. ["Hurra for
Douglas."]

For that reason he says he wishes the Dred Scott decision reversed. He wishes to confer those priviliges of citizenship on the
negro. Let us see how he will do it. He will first be called upon to
strike out of the constitution of Illinois that clause which prohibits
free negroes and slaves from Kentucky or any other state coming
into Illinois. When he blots out that clause, when he lets down the
door or opens the gate for all the negro population to flow in and
cover our prairies in mid-day they will look dark and black as night
(laughter), when we shall have done this, his mission will yet be
unfulfilled. Then it will be that he will apply his principles of negro
equality, that is if he can get the Dred Scott decision reversed in
the meantime. He will then change the constitution again, and
allow negroes to vote and hold office, and will make them eligible
to the legislature so that thereafter they can have the right men for
U.S. Senators. [Laughter.] He will allow them to vote to elect the
legislature, the judges and the governor, and will make them eligible
to the office of judge or governor, or to the legislature. He will put
them on an equality with the white man. What then? Of course,
after making them eligible to the judiciary, when he gets Cuffee
elevated to the bench, he certainly will not refuse his judge the
privilege of marrying any woman he may select! I submit to you
whether these are not the legitimate consequences of his doctrine.
["Certainly."] If it be true, as he says, that by the Declaration of
Independence and by divine law, the negro is created the equal of
the white man; if it be true that the Dred Scott decision is unjust
and wrong, because it deprives the negro of citizenship and equality
with the white man, then does it not follow that if he had the power
he would make negroes citizens, and give them all the rights and
privileges of citizenship on an equality with white men? I think that
is the inevitable conclusion. I do not doubt Mr. Lincoln's conscientious conviction on the subject, and I do not doubt that he will
carry out that doctrine if he ever has the power; but I resist it
because I am utterly opposed to any political amalgamation or any
other amalgamation on this continent. We are witnessing the result
of giving civil and political rights to inferior races in Mexico, in
Central America, in South America, and in the West India Islands.
Those young men who went from here to Mexico to fight the battles

of their country in the Mexican war, can tell you the fruits of negro equality with the white man. They will tell you that the result of that equality is social amalgamation, demoralization and degradation, below the capacity for self-government.

My friends, if we wish to preserve this government we must maintain it on the basis on which it was established, to wit: the white basis. We must preserve the purity of the race not only in our politics but in our domestic relations. We must then preserve the sovereignty of the states, and we must maintain the federal Union by preserving the federal constitution inviolate. Let us do that and our Union will not only be perpetual but may extend until it shall spread over the entire continent.

Fellow-citizens—I have already detained you too long. ["Go on, go on, do not stop yet."] I have exhausted myself and wearied you, and owe you an apology for the desultory manner in which I have discussed these topics. I will have an opportunity of addressing you again before the November election comes off. ["You will be welcome," &c.] I come to you to appeal to your judgment as American citizens, to take your verdict of approval or disapproval upon the discharge of my public duty and my principles as compared with those of Mr. Lincoln. ["We'll return you," and cheers.] If you conscientiously believe that his principles are more in harmony ["we do not"] with the feelings of the American people and the interests and honor of the Republic, elect him. ["We'll not do it, never, never."] If, on the contrary, you believe that my principles are more consistent with those great principles upon which our fathers framed this government, then I shall ask you to so express your opinion at the polls. ["Hurrah for Douglas, we will do it," &c.] I am aware that it is a bitter and severe contest, but I do not doubt what the decision of the people of Illinois will be. ["We do not doubt it. It will be for you."] I do not anticipate any personal collision between Mr. Lincoln and myself. You all know that I am an amiable, good-natured man, ["Hurrah for Douglas"] and I take great pleasure in bearing testimony to the fact that Mr. Lincoln is a kind-hearted, amiable, good-natured gentleman, with whom no man has a right to pick a quarrel, even if he wanted one. He is a worthy gentleman. I have known him for twenty-five years, and there is no better citizen, no kinder hearted man. He is a fine lawyer, possesses high ability, and there is no objection to him, except the monstrous revolutionary doctrines with which he is identified and which he conscientiously entertains, and is determined to carry out if he gets the power. ["He never shall, &c.]

He has one element of strength upon which he relies to accomplish his object, and that is his alliance with certain men in this state claiming to be Democrats, whose avowed object is to use their power to prostrate the Democratic nominees. ["Hurrah for Douglas; they can't do it," &c.] He hopes he can secure the few men claiming to be friends of the Lecompton constitution, and for that reason you will find he does not say a word against the Lecompton constitution or its supporters. He is as silent as the grave upon that subject. Behold Mr. Lincoln courting Lecompton votes, in order that he may go to the Senate as the representative of Republican principles! [Laughter.] You know that that alliance exists. I think you will find that it will ooze out before the contest is over. ["That's my opinion," and cheers.] It must be a contest of principle.—Either the radical Abolition principles of Mr. Lincoln must be maintained, or the strong, constitutional, national Democratic principles with which I am identified must be carried out. I shall be satisfied whatever way you decide. I have been sustained by the people of Illinois with a steadiness, a firmness and an enthusiasm which makes my heart overflow with gratitude. If I was now to be consigned to private life, I would have nothing to complain of. I would even then owe you a debt of gratitude which the balance of my life could not repay. But, my friends, you have discharged every obligation you owe to me. I have been a thousand times paid by the welcome you have extended to me since I have entered the state on my return home this time. Your reception not only discharges all obligations, but it furnishes inducement to renewed efforts to serve you in the future. If you think Mr. Lincoln will do more to advance the interests and elevate the character of Illinois than myself, it is your duty to elect him; if you think he would do more to preserve the peace of the country and perpetuate the Union than myself, then elect him. ["No," "no," "never."] I leave the question in your hands and again tender you my profound thanks for the cordial and heartfelt welcome tendered to me this evening.

Lincoln at Springfield, July 17, 1858[3]

On the evening of the 17th Lincoln spoke at the State House. "Although there was no regular announcement of the speech," the Illinois State Journal *remarked, "only a few handbills having been distributed during the afternoon, the State House was crowded by*

[3] *Illinois State Journal,* July 20, 21, 1858, as revised by Lincoln for publication in a separate pamphlet.

an immense audience. Mr. Lincoln made a most able effort which was received with tremendous cheering."

Fellow Citizens:

Another election, which is deemed an important one, is approaching, and, as I suppose, the Republican party will, without much difficulty elect their state ticket. But in regard to the legislature, we, the Republicans, labor under some disadvantages. In the first place, we have a legislature to elect upon an apportionment of the representation made several years ago, when the proportion of the population was far greater in the south (as compared with the north) than it now is; and inasmuch as our opponents hold almost entire sway in the south, and we a correspondingly large majority in the north, the fact that we are now to be represented as we were years ago, when the population was different, is to us a very great disadvantage. We had, in the year 1855, according to law, a census or enumeration of the inhabitants, taken for the purpose of a new apportionment of representation. We know what a fair apportionment of representation upon that census would give us. We know that it could not if fairly made, fail to give the Republican party from six to ten more members of the legislature than they can probably get as the law now stands. It so happened at the last session of the legislature, that our opponents, holding the control of both branches of the legislature, steadily refused to give us such an apportionment as we were rightfully entitled to have upon the census already taken. [A rocket goes up near the window.] I expect that we shall have as much of that as we can conveniently get along with. I was saying that the legislature steadily refused to give us such an apportionment as we were rightfully entitled to have upon the census taken of the population of the state. The legislature would pass no bill upon that subject, except such as was at least as unfair to us as the old one, and in which in some instances, two men in the Democratic regions were allowed to go as far towards sending a member of the legislature as three were in the Republican regions. Comparison was made at the time as to representative and senatorial districts, which completely demonstrated that such was the fact. Such a bill was passed, and tendered to the Republican Governor for his signature; but principally for the reasons I have stated, he withheld his approval, and the bill fell without becoming a law.

Another disadvantage under which we labor is, that there are one or two Democratic Senators who will be members of the next legislature, and will vote for the election of Senator, who are holding over in districts in which we could, on all reasonable calculation, elect men of our own, if we only had the chance of an election. When we consider that there are but twenty-five Senators in the Senate, taking two from the side where they rightfully belong and adding them to the other, is to us a disadvantage not to be lightly regarded. Still, so it is; we have this to contend with. Perhaps there is no ground of complaint on our part. In attending to the many things involved in the last general election for President, Governor, Auditor, Treasurer, Superintendent of Public Instruction, Members of Congress, of the legislature, county officers, and so on, we allowed these things to happen by want of sufficient attention, and we have no cause to complain of our adversaries, so far as this matter is concerned. But we have some cause to complain of the refusal to give us a fair apportionment.

There is still another disadvantage under which we labor, and to which I will ask your attention. It arises out of the relative positions of the two persons who stand before the state as candidates for the Senate. Senator Douglas is of world wide renown. All the anxious politicians of his party, or who have been of his party for years past, have been looking upon him as certainly, at no distant day, to be be the President of the United States. They have seen in his round, jolly, fruitful face, postoffices, landoffices, marshalships, and cabinet appointments, chargeships and foreign missions, bursting and sprouting out in wonderful exuberance ready to be laid hold of by their greedy hands. [Great laughter.] And as they have been gazing upon this attractive picture so long, they cannot, in the little distraction that has taken place in the party, bring themselves to give up the charming hope; but with greedier anxiety they rush about him, sustain him, and give him marches, triumphal entries, and receptions beyond what even in the days of his highest prosperity they could have brought about in his favor. On the contrary nobody has ever expected me to be President. In my poor, lean, lank, face, nobody has ever seen that any cabbages were sprouting out. [Tremendous cheering and laughter.] These are disadvantages all, taken together, that the Republicans labor under. We have to fight this battle upon principle, and upon principle alone. I am, in a certain sense, made the standard-bearer in behalf of the Republicans. I was made so merely because there had to be some one so placed—I being in no wise, preferable to any other one of the twenty-five—perhaps a hundred we have in the Republican ranks. Then I say I wish it to be distinctly understood and borne in mind, that we have to fight this battle without many—perhaps without any—of the external aids which are brought to bear against us. So I hope those with whom

I am surrounded have principle enough to nerve themselves for the task and leave nothing undone, that can be fairly done, to bring about the right result.

After Senator Douglas left Washington, as his movements were made known by the public prints, he tarried a considerable time in the city of New York; and it was heralded that, like another Napoleon, he was lying by, and framing the plan of his campaign. It was telegraphed to Washington City, and published in the *Union,* that he was framing his plan for the purpose of going to Illinois to pounce upon and annihilate the treasonable and disunion speech which Lincoln had made here on the 16th of June. Now, I do suppose that the Judge really spent some time in New York maturing the plan of the campaign, as his friends heralded for him. I have been able, by noting his movements since his arrival in Illinois, to discover evidences confirmatory of that allegation. I think I have been able to see what are the material points of that plan. I will, for a little while, ask your attention to some of them. What I shall point out, though not showing the whole plan, are, nevertheless, the main points, as I suppose.

They are not very numerous. The first is popular sovereignty. The second and third are attacks upon my speech made on the 16th of June. Out of these three points—drawing within the range of popular sovereignty the question of the Lecompton constitution—he makes his principal assault. Upon these his successive speeches are substantially one and the same. On this matter of popular sovereignty I wish to be a little careful. Auxiliary to these main points, to be sure, are their thunderings of cannon, their marching and music, their fizzlegigs and fireworks; but I will not waste time with them. They are but the little trappings of the campaign.

Coming to the substance—the first point—"Popular Sovereignty." It is to be labelled upon the cars in which he travels; put upon the hacks he rides in; to be flaunted upon the arches he passes under, and the banners which wave over him. It is to be dished up in as many varieties as a French cook can produce soups from potatoes. Now, as this is so great a staple of the plan of the campaign, it is worth while to examine it carefully; and if we examine only a very little, and do not allow ourselves to be misled, we shall be able to see that the whole thing is the most arrant quixotism that was ever enacted before a community. What is the matter of popular sovereignty? The first thing, in order to understand it, is to get a good definition of what it is, and after that to see how it is applied.

I suppose almost every one knows, that in this controversy, whatever has been said, has had reference to the question of negro slavery. We have not been in a controversy about the right of the people to govern themselves in the *ordinary* matters of domestic concern in the states and territories. Mr. Buchanan in one of his late messages, (I think when he sent up the Lecompton constitution,) urged that the main points to which the public attention had been directed, was not in regard to the great variety of small domestic matters, but was directed to the question of negro slavery; and he asserts, that if the people had had a fair chance to vote on that question, there was no reasonable ground of objection in regard to minor questions. Now, while I think that the people had *not* had given, or offered them, a fair chance upon that slavery question; still, if there had been a fair submission to a vote upon that main question, the President's proposition would have been true to the uttermost. Hence, when hereafter, I speak of popular sovereignty, I wish to be understood as applying what I say to the question of slavery only, not to other minor domestic matters of a territory or a state.

Does Judge Douglas, when he says that several of the past years of his life have been devoted to the question of "popular sovereignty," and that all the remainder of his life shall be devoted to it, does he mean to say that he has been devoting his life to securing to the people of the territories the right to exclude slavery from the territories? If he means so to say, he means to deceive; because he and every one knows that the decision of the Supreme Court, which he approves and makes especial ground of attack upon me for disapproving, forbids the people of a territory to exclude slavery. This covers the whole ground, from the settlement of a territory till it reaches the degree of maturity entitling it to form a state constitution. So far as all that ground is concerned, the Judge is not sustaining popular sovereignty, but absolutely opposing it. He sustains the decision which declares that the popular will of the territories has no constitutional power to exclude slavery during their territorial existence. [Cheers.] This being so, the period of time from the first settlement of a territory till it reaches the point of forming a state constitution, is not the thing that the Judge has fought for or is fighting for, but on the contrary, he has fought for, and is fighting for, the thing that annihilates and crushes out that same popular sovereignty.

Well, so much being disposed of, what is left? Why, he is contending for the right of the people, when they come to make a state constitution, to make it for themselves, and precisely as best suits themselves. I say again, that is quixotic. I defy contradiction when I declare that the Judge can find no one to oppose him on that proposition. I repeat, there is nobody opposing that proposition on *principle*. Let me not be misunderstood. I know that, with reference to the Lecompton constitution, I may be misunderstood; but when you understand me correctly, my proposition will be true and accurate. Nobody is opposing, or has opposed, the right of the people, when they form a constitution, to form it for themselves. Mr. Buchanan and his friends have not done it; they, too, as well as the Republicans and the anti-Lecompton Democrats, have not done it; but, on the contrary, they together have insisted on the right of the people to form a constitution for themselves. The difference between the Buchanan men on the one hand, and the Douglas men and the Republicans on the other, has not been on a question of principle, but on a question of *fact*.

The dispute was upon the question of fact, whether the Lecompton constitution had been fairly formed by the people or not. Mr. Buchanan and his friends have not contended for the contrary principle any more than the Douglas men or the Republicans. They have insisted that whatever of small irregularities existed in getting up the Lecompton constitution, were such as happen in the settlement of all new territories. The question was, was it a fair emanation of the people? It was a question of fact, and not of principle. As to the principle, all were agreed. Judge Douglas voted with the Republicans upon that matter of fact.

He and they, by their voices and votes, denied that it was a fair emanation of the people. The administration affirmed that it was. With respect to the evidence bearing upon that question of fact, I readily agree that Judge Douglas and the Republicans had the right on their side, and that the administration was wrong. But I state again that as a matter of principle there is no dispute upon the right of a people in a territory, merging into a state to form a constitution for themselves without outside interference from any quarter. This being so, what is Judge Douglas going to spend his life for? Is he going to spend his life in maintaining a principle that nobody on earth opposes? [Cheers.] Does he expect to stand up in majestic dignity, and go through his *apotheosis* and become a god, in the maintaining of a principle which neither a man nor a mouse in all God's creation is opposing? [Tremendous cheering.] Now something in regard to the Lecompton constitution more specially; for I pass from this other question of popular sovereignty as the most errant humbug that has ever been attempted on an intelligent community.

As to the Lecompton constitution, I have already said that on the question of fact as to whether it was a fair emanation of the people or not, Judge Douglas with the Republicans and some Americans had greatly the argument against the administration; and while I repeat this, I wish to know what there is in the opposition of Judge Douglas to the Lecompton constitution that entitles him to be considered the only opponent to it—as being *par excellence* the very *quintessence* of that opposition. I agree to the rightfulness of his opposition. He in the Senate and his class of men there formed the number *three* and no more. In the House of Representatives his class of men—the anti-Lecompton Democrats—formed a number of about twenty. It took one hundred and twenty to defeat the measure against one hundred and twelve. Of the votes of that one hundred and twenty, Judge Douglas' friends furnished twenty, to add to which, there were six Americans and ninety-four Republicans. I do not say that I am precisely accurate in their numbers, but I am sufficiently so for any use I am making of it.

Why is it that twenty shall be entitled to all the credit of doing that work, and the hundred none of it? Why, if, as Judge Douglas says, the honor is to be divided and due credit is to be given to other parties, why is just so much given as is consonant with the wishes, the interests and advancement of the twenty? My understanding is, when a common job is done, or a common enterprise prosecuted, if I put in five dollars to your one, I have a right to take out five dollars to your one. But he does not so understand it. He declares the dividend of credit for defeating Lecompton upon a basis which seems unprecedented and incomprehensible.

Let us see. Lecompton in the raw was defeated. It afterwards took a sort of cooked up shape, and was passed in the English Bill. It is said by the Judge that the defeat was a good and proper thing. If it was a good thing, why is he entitled to more credit than others, for the performance of that good act, unless there was something in the antecedents of the Republicans that might induce every one to expect them to join in that good work, and at the same time, something leading them to doubt that he would? Does he place his superior claim to credit, on the ground that he performed a good act which was never expected of him? He says I have a proneness for quoting scripture. If I should do so now, it occurs that perhaps he places himself somewhat upon the ground of the parable of the lost sheep which went astray upon the mountains, and when the owner of the hundred sheep found the one that was lost, and threw it upon his shoulders, and came home rejoicing, it was said that there was more rejoicing over the one sheep that was lost and had been found, than over the ninety and nine in the fold. [Great cheering, renewed cheering.] The application is made by the Saviour in this parable, thus, "Verily, I say unto you, there is more rejoicing in heaven over one sinner that repenteth, than over ninety and nine just persons that need no repentance." [Cheering.]

And now, if the Judge claims the benefit of this parable, *let him repent.* [Vociferous applause.] Let him not come up here and say: I am the only just person; and you are the ninety-nine sinners! *Repentance,* before *forgiveness* is a provision of the Christian system, and on that condition alone will the Republicans grant his forgiveness. [Laughter and cheers.]

How will he prove that we have ever occupied a different position in regard to the Lecompton constitution or any principle in it? He says he did not make his opposition on the ground as to whether it was a free or slave constitution, and he would have you understand that the Republicans made the opposition because it ultimately became a slave constitution. To make proof in favor of himself on this point, he reminds us that he opposed Lecompton before the vote was taken declaring whether the state was to be free or slave. But he forgets to say that our Republican Senator Trumbull, made a speech against Lecompton, even before he did.

Why did he oppose it? Partly, as he declares, because the members of the convention who framed it were not fairly elected by the people; that the people were not allowed to vote unless they had been registered; and that the people of whole counties, in some instances, were not registered. For these reasons he declares the constitution was not an emanation, in any true sense, from the people. He also has an additional objection as to the mode of submitting the constitution back to the people. But bearing on the question of whether the delegates were fairly elected, a speech of his, made something more than twelve months ago, from this stand, becomes important. It was made a little while before the election of the delegates who made Lecompton. In that speech he declared there was every reason to hope and believe the election would be fair; and if any one failed to vote, it would be his own culpable fault.

I, a few days after, made a sort of answer to that speech. In that answer, I made, substantially, the very argument with which he combatted his Lecompton adversaries in the Senate last winter. I pointed to the facts that the people could not vote without being registered, and that the time for registering had gone by. I commented on it as wonderful that Judge Douglas could be ignorant of these facts, which every one else in the nation so well knew.

I now pass from popular sovereignty and Lecompton. I may have occasion to refer to one or both.

When he was preparing his plan of campaign, Napoleon like, in

New York, as appears by two speeches I have heard him deliver since his arrival in Illinois, he gave special attention to a speech of mine, delivered here on the 16th of June last. He says that he carefully read that speech. He told us that at Chicago a week ago last night, and he repeated it at Bloomington last night. Doubtless, he repeated it again to-day, though I did not hear him. In the two first places—Chicago and Bloomington—I heard him; to-day I did not. [A voice—"Yes; he said the same thing."] He said he had carefully examined that speech; *when*, he did not say; but there is no reasonable doubt it was when he was in New York preparing his plan of campaign. I am glad he did read it carefully. He says it was evidently prepared with great care. I freely admit it was prepared with care. I claim not to be more free from errors than others—perhaps scarcely so much; but I was very careful not to put anything in that speech as a matter of fact, or make any inferences which did not appear to me to be true, and fully warrantable. If I had made any mistake I was willing to be corrected; if I had drawn any inference in regard to Judge Douglas, or any one else, which was not warranted, I was fully prepared to modify it as soon as discovered. I planted myself upon the truth, and the truth only, so far as I knew it, or could be brought to know it.

Having made that speech with the most kindly feeling towards Judge Douglas, as manifested therein, I was gratified when I found that he had carefully examined it, and had detected no error of fact, nor any inference against him, nor any misrepresentations, of which he thought fit to complain. In neither of the two speeches I have mentioned, did he make any such complaint. I will thank any one who will inform me that he, in his speech to day, pointed out anything I had stated, respecting him, as being erroneous. I presume there is no such thing. I have reason to be gratified that the care and caution used in that speech, left it so that he, most of all others interested in discovering error, has not been able to point out one thing against him which he could say was wrong. He seizes upon the doctrines he supposes to be included in that speech, and declares that upon them will turn the issues of this campaign. He then quotes, or attempts to quote, from my speech. I will not say that he willfully misquotes, but he does fail to quote accurately. His attempt at quoting is from a passage which I believe I can quote accurately from memory. I shall make the quotation now, with some comments upon it, as I have already said, in order that the Judge shall be left entirely without excuse for misrepresenting me. I do so now, as I hope, for the last time. I do this in great caution, in order that if he repeats his misrepresentation, it shall be plain to all that he does

so willfully. If, after all, he still persists, I shall be compelled to re-
construct the course I have marked out for myself, and draw upon
such humble resources as I have, for a new course, better suited to
the real exigencies of the case. I set out in this campaign, with the
intention of conducting it strictly as a gentleman, in substance at
least, if not in the outside polish. The latter I shall never be, but
that which constitutes the inside of a gentleman I hope I understand, and am not less inclined to practice than others. [Cheers.] It
was my purpose and expectation that this canvass would be conducted upon principle, and with fairness on both sides; and it shall
not be my fault, if this purpose and expectation shall be given up.

He charges, in substance, that I invite a war of sections; that I
propose all the local institutions of the different states shall become
consolidated and uniform. What is there in the language of that
speech which expresses such purpose, or bears such construction? I
have again and again said that I would not enter into any of the
states to disturb the institution of slavery. Judge Douglas said, at
Bloomington, that I used language most able and ingenious for concealing what I really meant; and that while I had protested against
entering into the slave states, I nevertheless did mean to go on the
banks of [the] Ohio and throw missiles into Kentucky to disturb
them in their domestic institutions.

I said, in that speech, and I meant no more, that the institution of
slavery ought to be placed in the very attitude where the framers of
this government placed it, and left it. I do not understand that the
framers of our Constitution left the people of the free states in the
attitude of firing bombs or shells into the slave states. I was not
using that passage for the purpose for which he infers I did use it. I
said: "We are now far advanced into the fifth year since a policy
was created for the avowed object and with the confident promise
of putting an end to slavery agitation. Under the operation of that
policy that agitation has not only not ceased, but has constantly
augmented. In my opinion it will not cease till a crisis shall have
been reached and passed. 'A house divided against itself can not
stand.' I believe that this government cannot endure permanently
half slave and half free. It will become all one thing or all the
other. Either the opponents of slavery will arrest the further spread
of it, and place it where the public mind shall rest in the belief that
it is in the course of ultimate extinction, or its advocates will push
it forward till it shall become alike lawful in all the states, old as
well as new, North as well as South."

Now you all see, from that quotation, I did not express my *wish*
on anything. In that passage I indicated no wish or purpose of my

own; I simply expressed my *expectation*. Cannot the Judge perceive the distinction between a *purpose* and an *expectation?* I have often expressed an expectation to die, but I have never expressed a *wish* to die. I said at Chicago, and now repeat, that I am quite aware this government has endured, half slave and half free, for eighty-two years. I understand that little bit of history. I expressed the opinion I did, because I perceived—or thought I perceived—a new set of causes introduced. I did say, at Chicago, in my speech there, that I do wish to see the spread of slavery arrested and to see it placed where the public mind shall rest in the belief that it is in course of ultimate extinction. I said that because I supposed, when the public mind shall rest in that belief, we shall have peace on the slavery question. I have believed—and now believe—the public mind did rest in that belief up to the introduction of the Nebraska Bill.

Although I have ever been opposed to slavery, so far I rested in the hope and belief that it was in course of ultimate extinction. For that reason, it had been a minor question with me. I might have been mistaken; but I had believed, and now believe, that the whole public mind, that is the mind of the great majority, had rested in that belief up to the repeal of the Missouri Compromise. But upon that event, I became convinced that either I had been resting in a delusion, or the institution was being placed on a new basis—a basis for making it perpetual, national and universal. Subsequent events have greatly confirmed me in that belief. I believe that bill to be the beginning of a conspiracy for that purpose. So believing, I have since then considered that question a paramount one. So believing, I have thought the public mind will never rest till the power of Congress to restrict the spread of it, shall again be acknowledged and exercised on the one hand, or on the other, all resistance be entirely crushed out. I have expressed that opinion, and I entertain it to-night. It is denied that there is any tendency to the nationalization of slavery in these states.

Mr. Brooks, of South Carolina, in one of his speeches, when they were presenting him with canes, silver plate, gold pitchers and the like, for assaulting Senator Sumner, distinctly affirmed his opinion that when this Constitution was formed, it was the belief of no man that slavery would last to the present day.

He said, what I think, that the framers of our Constitution placed the institution of slavery where the public mind rested in the hope that it was in course of ultimate extinction. But he went on to say that the men of the present age, by their experience, have become wiser than the framers of the Constitution; and the invention of the cotton gin has made the perpetuity of slavery a necessity in this country.

As another piece of evidence tending to the same point:—Quite recently in Virginia, a man—the owner of slaves—made a will providing that after his death certain of his slaves should have their freedom if they should so choose, and go to Liberia, rather than remain in slavery. They chose to be liberated. But the persons to whom they would descend as property, claimed them as slaves. A suit was instituted, which finally came to the Supreme Court of Virginia, and was therein decided against the slaves, upon the ground that a negro cannot make a choice—that they had no legal power to choose—could not perform the condition upon which their freedom depended.

I do not mention this with any purpose of criticizing, but to connect it with the arguments as affording additional evidence of the change of sentiment upon this question of slavery in the direction of making it perpetual and national. I argue now as I did before, that there is such a tendency, and I am backed not merely by the facts, but by the open confession in the slave states.

And now as to the Judge's inference, that because I wish to see slavery placed in the course of ultimate extinction—placed where our fathers originally placed it—I wish to annihilate the state legislatures—to force cotton to grow upon the tops of the Green Mountains—to freeze ice in Florida—to cut lumber on the broad Illinois prairies—that I am in favor of all these ridiculous and impossible things.

It seems to me it is a complete answer to all this, to ask, if, when Congress did have the fashion of restricting slavery from free territory; when courts did have the fashion of deciding that taking a slave into a free country made him free—I say it is a sufficient answer, to ask, if any of this ridiculous nonsense about consolidation, and uniformity, did actually follow. Who heard of any such thing, because of the Ordinance of '87? because of the Missouri Restriction? because of the numerous court decisions of that character?

Now, as to the Dred Scott decision; for upon that he makes his last point at me. He boldly takes ground in favor of that decision.

This is one-half the onslaught, and one-third of the entire plan of the campaign. I am opposed to that decision in a certain sense, but not in the sense which he puts on it. I say that in so far as it decided in favor of Dred Scott's master and against Dred Scott and his family, I do not propose to disturb or resist the decision.

I never have proposed to do any such thing. I think, that in respect for judicial authority, my humble history would not suffer in a comparison with that of Judge Douglas. He would have the citizen conform his vote to that decision; the member of Congress, his; the President, his use of the veto power. He would make it a rule of political action for the people and all the departments of the government. I would not. By resisting it as a political rule, I disturb no right of property, create no disorder, excite no mobs.

When he spoke at Chicago, on Friday evening of last week, he made this same point upon me. On Saturday evening I replied and reminded him of a Supreme Court decision which he opposed for at least several years. Last night, at Bloomington, he took some notice of that reply; but entirely forgot to remember that part of it.

He renews his onslaught upon me, forgetting to remember that I have turned the tables against himself on that very point. I renew the effort to draw his attention to it. I wish to stand erect before the country as well as Judge Douglas, on this question of judicial authority; and therefore I add something to the authority in favor of my own position. I wish to show that I am sustained by authority, in addition to that heretofore presented. I do not expect to convince the Judge. It is part of the plan of his campaign, and he will cling to it with a desperate gripe. Even, turn it upon him—turn the sharp point against him, and gaff him through—he will still cling to it till he can invent some new dodge to take the place of it.

In public speaking it is tedious reading from documents; but I must beg to indulge the practice to a limited extent. I shall read from a letter written by Mr. Jefferson in 1820, and now to be found in the seventh volume of his correspondence, at page 177. It seems he had been presented by a gentleman by the name of Jarvis with a book, or essay, or periodical, called the "Republican," and he was writing in acknowledgement of the present, and noting some of its contents. After expressing the hope that the work will produce a favorable effect upon the minds of the young, he proceeds to say:

> That it will have this tendency may be expected, and for that reason I feel an urgency to note what I deem an error in it, the more requiring notice as your opinion is strengthened by that of many others. You seem in pages 84 and 148, to consider the judges as the ultimate arbiters of all constitutional questions—a very dangerous doctrine indeed and one which would place us under the despotism of an oligarchy. Our judges are as honest as other men, and not more so. They have, with others, the same passions for party, for power, and the privilege of their corps. Their maxim is, "boni judicis est ampliare jurisdictionem"; and their power is the more dangerous as they are in office for life, and not responsible, as the other functionaries are, to the elective control. The constitution has erected no such single tribunal, knowing that to whatever hands confided, with the corruptions of time and party, its members would become despots. It has more wisely made all the departments co-equal and co-sovereign within themselves.

Thus we see the power claimed for the Supreme Court by Judge Douglas, Mr. Jefferson holds, would reduce us to the despotism of an oligarchy.

Now, I have said no more than this—in fact, never quite so much as this—at least I am sustained by Mr. Jefferson.

Let us go a little further. You remember we once had a national bank. Some one owed the bank a debt; he was sued and sought to avoid payment, on the ground that the bank was unconstitutional. The case went to the Supreme Court, and therein it was decided that the bank was constitutional. The whole Democratic party revolted against that decision. General Jackson himself asserted that he, as President, would not be bound to hold a national bank to be constitutional, even though the Court had decided it to be so. He fell in precisely with the view of Mr. Jefferson, and acted upon it under his official oath, in vetoing a charter for a national bank. The declaration that Congress does not possess this constitutional power to charter a bank, has gone into the Democratic platform, at their national conventions, and was brought forward and reaffirmed in their last convention at Cincinnati. They have contended for that declaration, in the very teeth of the Supreme Court, for more than a quarter of a century. In fact, they have reduced the decision to an absolute nullity. That decision, I repeat, is repudiated in the Cincinnati platform; and still, as if to show that effrontery can go no farther, Judge Douglas vaunts in the very speeches in which he denounces me for opposing the Dred Scott decision, that he stands on the Cincinnati platform.

Now, I wish to know what the Judge can charge upon me, with respect to decisions of the Supreme Court which does not lie in all its length, breadth, and proportions at his own door. The plain truth is simply this: Judge Douglas is *for* Supreme Court decisions when he likes and against them when he does not like them. He is for the Dred Scott decision because it tends to nationalize slavery —because it is part of the original combination for that object. It so happens, singularly enough, that I never stood opposed to a decision of the Supreme Court till this. On the contrary, I have no recollection that he was ever particularly in favor of one till this. He never was in favor of any, nor opposed to any, till the present one, which helps to nationalize slavery.

Free men of Sangamon—free men of Illinois—free men everywhere—judge ye between him and me, upon this issue.

He says this Dred Scott case is a very small matter at most—that it has no practical effect; that at best, or rather, I suppose, at worst, it is but an abstraction. I submit that the proposition that the thing which determines whether a man is free or a slave, is rather *con-*

crete than *abstract*. I think you would conclude that it was, if your liberty depended upon it, and so would Judge Douglas if his liberty depended upon it. But suppose it was on the question of spreading slavery over the new territories that he considers it as being merely an abstract matter, and one of no practical importance. How has the planting of slavery in new countries always been effected? It has now been decided that slavery cannot be kept out of our new territories by any legal means. In what does our new territories now differ in this respect, from the old colonies when slavery was first planted within them? It was planted as Mr. Clay once declared, and as history proves true, by individual men in spite of the wishes of the people; the mother government refusing to prohibit it, and withholding from the people of the colonies the authority to prohibit it for themselves. Mr. Clay says this was one of the great and just causes of complaint against Great Britain by the colonies, and the best apology we can now make for having the institution amongst us. In that precise condition our Nebraska politicians have at last succeeded in placing our own new territories; the government will not prohibit slavery within them, nor allow the people to prohibit it.

I defy any man to find any difference between the policy which originally planted slavery in these colonies and that policy which now prevails in our own new territories. If it does not go into them, it is only because no individual wishes it to go. The Judge indulged himself, doubtless, to-day, with the question as to what I am going to do with or about the Dred Scott decision. Well, Judge, will you please tell me what you did about the bank decision? Will you not graciously allow us to do with the Dred Scott decision precisely as you did with the bank decision? You succeeded in breaking down down the moral effect of that decision; did you find it necessary to amend the Constitution? or to set up a court of negroes in order to do it?

There is one other point. Judge Douglas has a very affectionate leaning towards the Americans and Old Whigs. Last evening, in a sort of weeping tone, he described to us a death bed scene. He had been called to the side of Mr. Clay, in his last moments, in order that the genius of "popular sovereignty" might duly descend from the dying man and settle upon him, the living and most worthy successor. He could do no less than promise that he would devote the remainder of his life to "popular sovereignty"; and then the great statesman departs in peace. By this part of the "plan of the campaign," the Judge has evidently promised himself that tears shall be drawn down the cheeks of all Old Whigs, as large as half grown apples.

Mr. Webster, too, was mentioned; but it did not quite come to a death-bed scene, as to him. It would be amusing, if it were not disgusting, to see how quick these compromise-breakers administer on the political effects of their dead adversaries, trumping up claims never before heard of, and dividing the assets among themselves. If I should be found dead tomorrow morning, nothing but my insignificance could prevent a speech being made on my authority, before the end of next week. It so happens that in that "popular sovereignty" with which Mr. Clay was identified, the Missouri Compromise was expressly reserved; and it was a little singular if Mr. Clay cast his mantle upon Judge Douglas on purpose to have that compromise repealed.

Again, the Judge did not keep faith with Mr. Clay when he first brought in his Nebraska bill. He left the Missouri Compromise unrepealed, and in his report accompanying the bill, he told the world he did it on purpose. The manes of Mr. Clay must have been in great agony, till thirty days later, when "popular sovereignty" stood forth in all its glory.

One more thing. Last night Judge Douglas tormented himself with horrors about my disposition to make negroes perfectly equal with white men in social and political relations. He did not stop to show that I have said any such thing, or that it legitimately follows from any thing I have said, but he rushes on with his assertions. I adhere to the Declaration of Independence. If Judge Douglas and his friends are not willing to stand by it, let them come up and amend it. Let them make it read that all men are created equal except negroes. Let us have it decided, whether the Declaration of Independence, in this blessed year of 1858, shall be thus amended. In his construction of the Declaration last year he said it only meant that Americans in America were equal to Englishmen in England. Then, when I pointed out to him that by that rule he excludes the Germans, the Irish, the Portuguese, and all the other people who have come amongst us since the Revolution, he reconstructs his construction. In his last speech he tells us it meant Europeans.

I press him a little further, and ask if it meant to include the Russians in Asia? or does he mean to exclude that vast population from the principles of our Declaration of Independence? I expect ere long he will introduce another amendment to his definition. He is not at all particular. He is satisfied with any thing which does not endanger the nationalizing of negro slavery. It may draw white men down, but it must not lift negroes up. Who shall say, "I am the superior, and you are the inferior?"

My declarations upon this subject of negro slavery may be misrepresented, but can not be misunderstood. I have said that I do not understand the Declaration to mean that all men were created equal in all respects. They are not our equal in color; but I suppose that it does mean to declare that all men are equal in some respects; they are equal in their right to "life, liberty, and the pursuit of happiness." Certainly the negro is not our equal in color—perhaps not in many other respects; still, in the right to put into his mouth the bread that his own hands have earned, he is the equal of every other man, white or black. In pointing out that more has been given you, you can not be justified in taking away the little which has been given him. All I ask for the negro is that if you do not like him, let him alone. If God gave him but little, that little let him enjoy.

When our government was established, we had the institution of slavery among us. We were in a certain sense compelled to tolerate its existence. It was a sort of necessity. We had gone through our struggle and secured our own independence. The framers of the Constitution found the institution of slavery amongst their other institutions at the time. They found that by an effort to eradicate it, they might lose much of what they had already gained. They were obliged to bow to the necessity. They gave power to Congress to abolish the slave trade at the end of twenty years. They also prohibited it in the territories where it did not exist. They did what they could and yielded to the necessity for the rest. I also yield to all which follows from that necessity. What I would most desire would be the separation of the white and black races.

One more point on this Springfield speech which Judge Douglas says he has read so carefully. I expressed my belief in the existence of a conspiracy to perpetuate and nationalize slavery. I did not profess to know it, nor do I now. I showed the part Judge Douglas had played in the string of facts, constituting to my mind, the proof of that conspiracy. I showed the parts played by others.

I charged that the people had been deceived into carrying the last presidential election, by the impression that the people of the territories might exclude slavery if they chose, when it was known in advance by the conspirators, that the Court was to decide that neither Congress nor the people could so exclude slavery. These charges are more distinctly made than any thing else in the speech.

Judge Douglas has carefully read and re-read that speech. He has not, so far as I know, contradicted those charges. In the two speeches which I heard he certainly did not. On his own tacit admission I renew that charge. I charge him with having been a party to that conspiracy and to that deception for the sole purpose of nationalizing slavery.

CHAPTER THREE

TAKING THE STUMP

A few days after his speech of the 17th Lincoln went to Chicago, undoubtedly to consult with Norman B. Judd, chairman of the Republican State Central Committee, and other party associates. A short letter resulted.

Hon. S. A. Douglas   Chicago, Ills.

My Dear Sir   July 24, 1858.

Will it be agreeable to you to make an arrangement for you and myself to divide time, and address the same audiences during the present canvass? Mr. Judd, who will hand you this, is authorized to receive your answer; and, if agreeable to you, to enter into the terms of such arrangement. Your Obt. Servt

             A. Lincoln

Douglas replied on the same day. Before his letter could be delivered, Lincoln had returned to Springfield.

           Chicago, July 24, 1858

Hon. A. Lincoln:—Dear Sir:

Your note of this date, in which you inquire if it would be agreeable to me to make an arrangement to divide the time and address the same audiences during the present canvass, was handed me by Mr. Judd. Recent events have interposed difficulties in the way of such an arrangement.

I went to Springfield last week for the purpose of conferring with the Democratic State Central Committee upon the mode of conducting the canvass, and with them, and under their advice, made a list of appointments covering the entire period until late in October. The people of the several localities have been notified of the times and places of the meetings. Those appointments have all been made for Democratic meetings, and arrangements have been made by which the Democratic candidates for Congress, for the legislature, and other offices will be present and address the people. It is evident therefore, that these various candidates, in connection with myself, will occupy the whole time of the day and evening, and leave no opportunity for other speeches.

Besides, there is another consideration which should be kept in mind. It has been suggested recently that an arrangement had been made to bring out a third candidate for the United States Senate, who, with yourself, should canvass the state in opposition to me, with no other purpose than to insure my defeat, by dividing the Democratic party for your benefit. If I should make this arrangement with you, it is more than probable that this other candidate, who has a common object with you, would desire to become a party to it, and claim the right to speak from the same stand; so that he and you in concert might be able to take the opening and closing speech in every case.

I cannot refrain from expressing my surprise, if it was your original intention to invite such an arrangement, that you should have waited until after I had made my appointments, inasmuch as we were both here in Chicago together for several days after my arrival, and again at Bloomington, Atlanta, Lincoln and Springfield, where it was well known I went for the purpose of consulting with the State Central Committee, and agreeing upon the plan of the campaign.

While, under these circumstances, I do not feel at liberty to make any arrangements which would deprive the Democratic candidates for Congress, state offices, and the legislature from participating in the discussion at the various meetings designated by the Democratic State Central Committee, I will, in order to accommodate you as far as it is in my power to do so, take the responsibility of making an arrangement with you for a discussion between us at one prominent point in each congressional district in the state, except the second and sixth districts, where we have both spoken, and in each of which cases you had the concluding speech. If agreeable to you I will indicate the following places as those most suitable in the several congressional districts at which we should speak to wit: Freeport, Ottawa, Galesburg, Quincy, Alton, Jonesboro and Charleston. I will confer with you at the earliest convenient opportunity in regard to the mode of conducting the debate, the times of meeting at the several places, subject to the condition, that where appointments have already been made by the Democratic State Central Committee at any of those places, I must insist upon you meeting me at the times specified.

Very respectfully,

Your most obd't servant,

S. A. DOUGLAS

*Meanwhile, Douglas had started on the round of appointments
that would occupy him almost daily until the end of October. July
27 found him at Clinton, where he spoke for three hours in the late
afternoon. The reporter for the Chicago Times, who devoted almost
two columns to the meeting,[1] incorporated a reference to Lincoln
that was typical of the partisan journalism of the day.*

Lincoln was present during the delivery of the speech, sitting immediately in front of Senator Douglas, but rendered invisible from
the stand by a gentleman in green goggles, whom he used as a
shield and cover. After Senator Douglas had concluded, and the
cheers which greeted him ceased, green goggles rose and proposed three cheers for Lincoln, which were given by about ten men
who stood immediately around him. Mr. Lincoln then gradually
lengthened out his long, lank proportions until he stood upon his
feet, and with a desperate attempt at looking pleasant, said that he
would not take advantage of Judge Douglas' crowd, but would address "sich" as would like to hear him in the evening at the court
house. Having made this announcement in a tone and with the air
of a perfect "Uriah Heep," pleading his humility, and asking the forgiveness of Heaven for enemies, he stood "washing his hands with
invisible soap in imperceptible water," until his friends, seeing that
his mind was wandering, took him in charge and bundled him off
the ground. . . .

According to appointment Lincoln's meeting came off in the evening. Most of the people who were present at Senator Douglas'
meeting returned home immediately afterwards, and the contrast
between the two was most striking. Not more than 250 people were
present at Lincoln's meeting. His speech, like the man, was dis-
jointed, labored, and inelegant. . . .

Mr. Lincoln's course in following Senator Douglas is condemned
even by his friends. He explains it by saying that he challenged
Judge Douglas to meet the people and address them together, which
challenge had not been accepted.

*Two days later, in the early afternoon, Douglas spoke at Monti-
cello, and then started by carriage for Bement, where he was to take
a train for Paris. The Chicago Times reporter described an encounter on the road.[2]*

About two miles out of the town the procession met Mr. Lincoln,
who was on his way to Monticello. As he passed, Senator Douglas
called to him to stop, that he wanted to see him. Lincoln jumped
out of his carriage and shook hands with the Senator, who said to
him, "Come, Lincoln, return to Bement. You see we have only a

[1] Issue of July 30, 1858.   [2] Issue of August 1, 1858.

mile or two of people here. I will promise you a much larger meeting there than you will have at Monticello." "No, Judge," replied
Lincoln, "I can't. The fact is I did not come over here to make a
speech. I don't intend to follow you any more; I don't call this following you. I have come down here from Springfield to see you and
give you my reply to your letter. I have it in my pocket, but have
not compared it with the copy yet. We can compare the two now,
can't we?" Senator Douglas told him that he had better compare
the two at Monticello, and, when he had his answer ready, send it
to him at Bement, where he intended to remain until the one o'clock
P.M.[3] train for the East. This Lincoln promised to do, and, after
again assuring the Senator that he must not consider his visit to
Monticello "following" him—that such a "conclusion" would be erroneous—the two separated, after shaking hands.

*Lincoln delivered the letter as he had promised; Douglas replied
the following day.*

HON. S. A. DOUGLAS   SPRINGFIELD,
DEAR SIR   July 29. 1858

Yours of the 24th. in relation to an arrangement to divide time
and address the same audiences, is received; and, in apology for
not sooner replying, allow me to say that when I sat by you at dinner yesterday I was not aware that you had answered my note, nor
certainly, that my own note had been presented to you. An hour
after I saw a copy of your answer in the Chicago *Times;* and,
reaching home, I found the original awaiting me. Protesting that
your insinuations of attempted unfairness on my part are unjust;
and with the hope that you did not very considerately make them,
I proceed to reply. To your statement that "It has been suggested
recently that an arrangement had been made to bring out a third
candidate for the U.S. Senate who, with yourself, should canvass
the state in opposition to me &c." I can only say that such suggestion must have been made by yourself; for certainly none such has
been made by, or to me; or otherwise, to my knowledge. Surely you
did not *deliberately* conclude, as you insinuate, that I was expecting
to draw you into an arrangement, of terms to be agreed on by yourself, by which a third candidate, and myself, "in concert, might be
able to take the opening and closing speech in every case."

As to your surprise that I did not sooner make the proposal to
divide time with you, I can only say I made it as soon as I resolved
to make it. I did not know but that such proposal would come from
you; I waited respectfully to see. It may have been well known to

[3] Obviously, the 1:00 A.M. train the following morning, July 30.

you that you went to Springfield for the purpose of agreeing on the plan of campaign; but it was not so known to me. When your appointments were announced in the papers, extending only to the 21st. of August, I, for the first time, considered it certain that you would make no proposal to me; and then resolved, that if my friends concurred, I would make one to you. As soon thereafter as I could see and consult with friends satisfactorily, I did make the proposal. It did not occur to me that the proposed arrangement could derange your plan, after the latest of your appointments already made. After that, there was, before the election, largely over two months of clear time.

For you to say that we have already spoken at Chicago and Springfield, and that on both occasions I had the concluding speech, is hardly a fair statement. The truth rather is this. At Chicago, July 9th, you made a carefully prepared conclusion on my speech of June 16th.; twentyfour hours after I made a hasty conclusion on yours of the 9th.; you had six days to prepare, and concluded on me again at Bloomington on the 16th.; twentyfour hours after I concluded on you again at Springfield. In the mean time you had made another conclusion on me at Springfield, which I did not hear, and of the contents of which I knew nothing when I spoke; so that your speech made in day-light, and mine at night of the 17th. at Springfield were both made in perfect independence of each other. The dates of making all these speeches, will show, I think, that in the matter of time for preparation, the advantage has all been on your side; and that none of the external circumstances have stood to my advantage.

I agree to an arrangement for us to speak at the seven places you have named, and at your own times, provided you name the times at once, so that I, as well as you, can have to myself the time not covered by the arrangement. As to other details, I wish perfect reciprocity, and no more. I wish as much time as you, and that conclusions shall alternate. That is all. Your obedient Servant

A. LINCOLN

P.S. As matters now stand, I shall be at no more of your exclusive meetings; and for about a week from to-day a letter from you will reach me at Springfield. A. L.

BEMENT, PIATT Co., ILL., July 30, 1858

HON. A. LINCOLN, Springfield, Ill.

DEAR SIR:

Your letter, dated yesterday, accepting my proposition for a joint discussion at one prominent point in each Congressional District, as stated in my previous letter, was received this morning.

The times and places designated, are as follows:

Ottawa, La Salle County	August	21st, 1858
Freeport, Stephenson County	do	27th, do
Jonesboro, Union County	September 15th, do
Charleston, Coles County	do	18th, do
Galesburg, Knox County	October	7th, do
Quincy, Adams County	do	13th, do
Alton, Madison County	do	15th, do

I agree to your suggestion that we shall alternately open and close the discussion. I will speak at Ottawa one hour, you can reply, occupying an hour and a half, and I will then follow for half an hour. We will alternate in like manner in each successive place.

Very respectfully, your obedient servant,

S. A. DOUGLAS

With the following communication from Lincoln, arrangements for the formal debates were completed.

HON. S. A. DOUGLAS: SPRINGFIELD,

DEAR SIR   July 31, 1858

Yours of yesterday, naming places, times, and terms, for joint discussions between us, was received this morning. Although, by the terms, as you propose, you take *four* openings and closes to my *three*, I accede, and thus close the arrangement. I direct this to you at Hillsboro; and shall try to have both your letter and this, appear in the *Journal* and *Register* of Monday morning. Your Obt. Servt.

A. LINCOLN—

Douglas' progress from Bement to Paris, where he was to speak on Saturday, July 31, furnishes a good example of the hardships of political campaigning in 1858. By the time he reached Bement on the late afternoon of Thursday, July 29, he had made a speech of two hours' duration and had traveled eight miles by carriage. At 1:30 a.m. on Friday, July 30, he took a Great Western (Wabash) train for Tolono, twenty miles to the northeast. There he remained until afternoon, when he boarded a southbound Illinois Central train for Mattoon, twenty-three miles distant. At Mattoon the people demanded a speech. Douglas obliged, stopping only in time to reach the St. Louis, Alton and Terre Haute (Big Four) station by 10:40 p.m., when the eastbound train for Paris was due to arrive. But the train was five hours late. To quote the correspondent of the Times:[4]

---

[4] Letter from Paris, July 31, in Chicago *Times*, August 6.

The long, long weary hours we spent in waiting for it will not soon be forgotten by any of the gentlemen who were applying their ears to the rails during the first two hours, "to *see if they could hear it coming,*" and fancying in every noise that broke the stillness of the night that the notice to put on the brakes was being given by the engineer at some station above us. One by one the watchers, their patience completely exhausted, threw themselves down on the platform, and accommodating themselves to circumstances, made a bed out of the hard boards. Your correspondent, among others, selected a soft board, and without the drapery of his couch about him, laid down to pleasant dreams, not at all disturbed by the heavy dew which fell, or the evolutions of an amateur militia company. We ought to have been in Paris at midnight, and the people there had made every preparation to receive Senator Douglas in a becoming manner, and waited for the train until about 3 o'clock, when fearing that the health of the music might be endangered by the dampness of the morning air, they had reluctantly retired, leaving a guard of honor in charge of the guns to give notice of his arrival. We reached Paris about 6 o'clock in the morning, and Senator Douglas was welcomed with a salute of thirty-two guns. Flags were flying in all directions, and as we drove to the hotel, people at their doors and windows and in the streets, in various styles of *dishabille,* evinced their pleasure at seeing us.

Douglas had spent thirty-eight hours, including necessary stop-over time, to cover a total distance of eighty-seven miles. Today the same trip would be made by automobile in two hours or less.

From Paris, Douglas moved across the state to the old Whig territory east of Alton and Edwardsville. On August 2 he made the first appearance of his life in Hillsboro. The Times *correspondent described an idyllic setting:*[5]

The meeting today was held in the Montgomery county fair grounds, a good stage was erected, numerous seats placed around it, and the noble old trees which towered overhead shaded those present from the rays of the sun, and contributed with a pleasant breeze stirring to make the people comfortable. Here there was room for all. A lady could sit down without first having to gather her hoops beneath her, and a gentleman had plenty of standing or leaning room without encroaching on the comfort of those around him. I suppose there were from eight to ten thousand people present, a large proportion of whom were ladies. The number of babies

[5] Issue of August 2.

on all hands spoke well for the flourishing condition of the county, and the increasing growth and strength of the Democratic party in this section.

August 4th found the Senator at Greenville in Bond County, where he spoke in the afternoon. In meeting his engagements in this part of the state the railroads were of little use. The Times *commented:*[6]

Senator Douglas is taxing his strength severely, but it does not seem to impair his health. He talked two hours today, and speaks tomorrow at Highland, on Friday at Edwardsville, and on Saturday at Winchester, and in the interval of time between these addresses, travels over one hundred and fifty miles mostly by stage. He leaves Greenville tomorrow before sunrise, and drives to Highland. The success of a great cause is worth more than ordinary exercise.

At Winchester, on August 7, Douglas was in the town to which he had come in the fall of 1833, a penniless young man hoping to find a place as a teacher. In his opening remarks he expressed his affection for Winchester and its people.[7]

Ladies and Gentlemen, Fellow-Citizens:

To say that I am profoundly impressed with the keenest gratitude for the kind and cordial welcome you have given me in the eloquent and too partial remarks which have been addressed to me, is but a feeble expression of the emotions of my heart. There is no spot in this vast globe which fills me with such emotions as when I come to this place and recognize the faces of my old and good friends who now surround me and bid me welcome. Twenty-five years ago I entered this town on foot, with my coat upon my arm, without an acquaintance in a thousand miles, and without knowing where I could get money to pay a week's board. Here I made the first six dollars I ever earned in my life, and obtained the first regular occupation that I ever pursued. For the first time in my life I then felt that the responsibilities of manhood were upon me, although I was under age, for I had none to advise with and knew no one upon whom I had a right to call for assistance or for friendship. Here I found the then settlers of the country my friends—my first start in life was taken here, not only as a private citizen, but my first election to public office by the people was conferred upon me by those

[6] Letter from Greenville, August 4, in Chicago *Times*, August 7.

[7] Chicago *Times*, August 12, 1858.

whom I am now addressing and by their fathers. A quarter of a century has passed, and that penniless boy stands before you with his heart full and gushing with the sentiments which such associations and recollections necessarily inspire.

Douglas pushed north to Beardstown on the Illinois River. The town offered the kind of welcome that had already become characteristic of the campaign. The Times *reported:*[8]

BEARDSTOWN, Aug. 11, 1858

The meeting here today, in favor of Senator Douglas, was the largest which ever assembled here or at any place in Cass county. During the whole day, notwithstanding the intense heat of the weather, delegations from every section of this and the surrounding counties continued to pour in until the town was actually overflowing with people.

Senator Douglas, after speaking at Pittsfield, took a private conveyance over to Naples, a small town on the Illinois river, where he took passage early this morning, in the steamboat *Sam Young*, for Beardstown, accompanied by a large number of friends. When the boat came in sight of the town, a gun stationed on the shore spoke out a welcome, and the swaying to and fro of the immense throng which lined the river front showed that expectation was on the tip-toe. Ten minutes served to bring the boat to her dock, during which, the noise of the gun, the music of the bands, the hurras of the multitude, the pushing and squeezing in the crowd to get a good position to see, and the general liveliness and activity manifested by everybody, contributed to make up a scene which it was pleasant to stand at a distance and behold, but rather too exciting to take part in during such hot weather.

The arrangements for the reception of Senator Douglas were capital. The City Guard and Independent Guard, two fine military organizations, were drawn up in open column on both sides of the landing, thus preventing the crowd from rushing upon Mr. Douglas as he passed from the boat to a carriage. As he left the boat, and was recognized by the people, a shout arose which awoke the echoes of the Illinois, and as he passed along the line, the troops presented arms, and cried welcome, whilst those who were outside made frantic efforts to break through the line in order to get near him, and screamed themselves hoarse in very joy that he was at last among them. Having taken a seat in one of the carriages which the committee had in readiness, he was escorted by the two companies,

[8] Issue of August 17.

and by a large number of citizens in carriages and on horseback to the National Hotel, where quarters had been provided for him.

The speaking was not to take place until 2 o'clock, and the three or four hours which intervened between his arrival and that time, Senator Douglas spent in receiving his friends. About 12 o'clock, a delegation from Virginia township, numbering about six hundred people, arrived. A large open car, drawn by six horses, in which were seated thirty-two young ladies, dressed in white, and each bearing a banner upon which was inscribed the name of one of the states, was a striking feature of the display this delegation made. Other flags and banners were carried by this delegation, it being headed by a horseman bearing a large and beautifully worked banner, with the word "DOUGLAS" upon it, and the band wagon following bearing a transparency, with the inscription, "STEPHEN A. DOUGLAS, the Champion of the Right, the Constitution, the Union as it is, and fidelity to correct principles."

The delegation from Chandlerville carried a painting representing one of Lincoln's illustrations, in which he referred to Douglas as a caged and toothless lion, and himself as a living dog.[9] The picture represented the lion full of strength brushing the dog, which, by the way, bore Lincoln's favorite name, "Spot,"[10] away with his tail, and under it was the inscription, "The lion is alive, the dog is dead." This caused much merriment wherever it went.

In his speech at Beardstown, Douglas rebuked Lincoln harshly for the charge of conspiracy which he had first made in the "House Divided" speech and had repeated in subsequent addresses. The reaction of the audience gave the Times *correspondent an opportunity to portray Douglas as a man of magnanimity and good manners. The reporter wrote:*

A little occurrence during the meeting furnishes further evidence of the disposition of Senator Douglas to treat Mr. Lincoln friendly and kindly. At the conclusion of his speech, after the crowd had expressed their satisfaction and approval of what they had heard in three times three cheers, someone thought it necessary that an expression of disapprobation and dislike for Mr. Lincoln and his sentiments should be made, and accordingly proposed three groans for Lincoln, which were about being given when Senator Douglas called

[9] See the "House Divided" speech, pp. 6–7.

[10] An allusion to the resolutions which Lincoln, as a member of Congress, had introduced in an effort to force the President to admit that Mexico rather than the United States had jurisdiction over the "spot" where the first blood of the Mexican War had been shed.

upon those present to remember that Democrats never forgot that they were gentlemen, and that such conduct would be improper, which immediately put a stop to it.

So far, only Douglas had been in the field. On August 12 Lincoln took to the stump. By scheduling his first meeting for Beardstown he had something approaching the advantage of the closing speaker in a debate. With Lincoln went Horace White, who would report the progress of the challenger for the Press and Tribune *of Chicago. White's account follows:*[11]

BEARDSTOWN, ILL., Aug. 12, 1858

"Old Abe" has finally got on his high-heeled shoes. He has just finished speaking to an enormous crowd from this and the adjoining counties of Schuyler and Morgan. His speech was just two hours in length, and I but repeat the opinion of his entire audience when I say that it far exceeds in power, and energy, and vehemence any of Mr. Lincoln's previous efforts in this campaign, and that it dwarfed the Douglas harangue of yesterday into *nothing.* A dozen men have remarked in my hearing since the conclusion of the speech, that it is no wonder Douglas refused to stand in the way of Lincoln's logic more than seven times in three months.

Mr. Lincoln arrived in our city this morning, on board the steamer *Sam Gaty* from Naples. A procession of three or four hundred citizens went down to the landing to meet and escort him to the National Hotel. The valorous Democracy had taken the precaution, after using the corporation cannon all day yesterday, *to fill it up with pounded brick,* so that the Republicans couldn't have the use of it today. The stratagem succeeded finely—the gun wouldn't go off. Nevertheless we had two fine bands of music, two military companies—the "Beardstown City Guards" and the "Independents"— and a cavalcade of forty horsemen to supply the deficiency and add to the *eclat* of the reception. As Mr. Lincoln stepped from the boat, three rousing cheers went up for "Old Abe." He then entered a carriage and the procession moved up to and around the public square and thence to the National Hotel, where three more hearty cheers were given by the assembled multitude. At ten o'clock the Schuyler County delegation came in—*three hundred strong!* No one had expected more than fifty or sixty, although ample notice had been given of our meeting. From ten o'clock until noon the farmers kept pouring in from the country, and two fine companies came in from Morgan County. There was less noise, less liquor and fewer

[11] In issue of August 17.

street fights today than yesterday, but the enthusiasm was far greater.

Between one and two o'clock the crowd collected in the public square to hear Lincoln's first speech in the regular campaign. The marshal of the day estimated the number present at 3,000. There could not have been less than 2,500 at the very least calculation. At precisely two o'clock the escorting procession moved from the hotel to the square, when three tremendous cheers were given for Abraham Lincoln. The reception speech was made by Mr. Rich, one of the veteran Whigs of Cass County. He alluded in a happy manner to the battles fought in the old times when Henry Clay was the idol of the Whigs and Abraham Lincoln his representative man in Illinois; and he now welcomed the speaker in behalf of Cass County, and particularly in behalf of those sterling friends with whom he did battle for the principles taught by Clay, and Webster, and John Quincy Adams. . . .

It would be needless for me to go through with Mr. Lincoln's argument, though I am persuaded it would make the most formidable document of the campaign. . . .

When Mr. Lincoln had concluded, three cheers were again given, and repeated and re-repeated, after which the audience dispersed.

After Beardstown, both contestants moved upriver to Havana, where Douglas spoke on the 13th and Lincoln a day later. The rival newspapermen reported the meetings of their respective favorites, but time permitted them to attend and describe the rallies of the opposition. Their accounts are striking examples of the biased journalism in which all indulged. Witness the Press and Tribune *story of Douglas at Havana.*[12]

HAVANA, ILL., Aug. 13, 1858

The Pro-Slavery ringleader of the North-West has visited us and made a speech, which has cruelly disappointed his friends, and lost him a hundred votes in Mason County, at the very least. A considerable majority of these new-created enemies will vote the Republican ticket this fall—the balance have slumped over to Buchanan and the National Democracy. My candid opinion is that Mr. Douglas can do nothing so *certain* to elect Abe Lincoln to the Senate, as to deliver the speech which he gave us today, in every county seat in the State. If I might prescribe a judicious course for the Little Giant, for the balance of the campaign, I should just tell him to *be sick.* . . .

It would be difficult for me to give an adequate idea of the

[12] Issue of August 20.

littleness, meanness and foulness of Douglas' harangue here today. It was the universal remark that Murray McConnell must have written the speech. You have heard of Murray, of course. He is the greatest blackguard of Illinois—the old original Jacob in the dialect of fishwomen.[13] He has blackguarded all over Mason County a thousand times; consequently when we want to say that anybody has especially disgraced himself in a public speech, we say that he has played Murray McConnell. Douglas has played Murray McConnell today, the way Hamlet's players out-Heroded Herod. For instance, he called Lincoln a liar, a coward(!), a wretch and a sneak, and he called Trumbull a sneak, a wretch and a coward and a liar. Murray would have used more than half these epithets. He (Douglas) returned to his vomit half a dozen times with a new volley of barroom phrases for Lincoln and Trumbull. The only solution of his extraordinary conduct given by his friends would not be creditable for a reputation for sobriety. A considerable number of Old Line Whigs whom I have met today have said they were disposed to think favorably of Mr. Douglas, but they never did and never would vote for a *Short-Boy*.[14]

A curious and unexpected feature of Douglas' speech today is that he had spent almost the whole of his time in *defending himself*. Starting out with the declaration that he would not allow himself to be drawn from the real issues of the campaign, viz: negro equality and amalgamation, to defend himself against the assaults of his enemies—he immediately went to chewing on Lincoln's speech before the Republican State Convention, and he chewed on it for a whole hour, like a criminal under an indictment. Then he strove to set up a defence against Trumbull's charge of his complicity in an attempt to have a constitution framed for Kansas, in 1856, without being submitted to the people. The chief point in his defence here, it must be admitted, was his calling Senator T. a liar and a wretch and a vagabond, and applying to him all the other choice resources of the Douglas vocabulary.

In the "attacking" part of the speech I heard nothing but negro equality and amalgamation—amalgamation and negro equality—with a slight tincture of blackguardism against the Declaration of Independence. These themes he pursued till his audience was wholly nauseated. During this section of the harangue an old Democrat came up to me and asked what I thought of the speech? "Superlative

---

[13] A prominent Democrat of Jacksonville, Illinois, serving, in 1858, as Fifth Auditor of the Treasury by appointment of President Pierce.

[14] "Short Boys. A gang of New York rowdies." John Russell Bartlett, *Dictionary of Americanisms* (Second Edition, Boston, 1859).

nonsense and Dead-Rabbitism," I replied. "Give me your hand on that, old boy," was the rejoinder; "a man who can stand there and argue an hour against things that nobody ever advocated, don't get my vote, if his name is Douglas."

. . . The audience today might have numbered 1,500 at a liberal estimate, including women and children—and I know that one-half of them were staunch Republicans. When the whistle of the steamer *Editor*, bringing Lincoln to town, was heard, nearly one-half of the crowd broke away and ran to the levee. When Douglas had finished, there was a dead silence for about two minutes, when a man with a mottled face came forward and proposed three cheers for Stephen A. Douglas. They were responded to by about thirty men near the platform. And so ended one of the rankest humbugs that ever visited the old County of Mason.

Lincoln fared no better in the Times.[15]

HAVANA, ILL., Aug. 14

Our little city, which has been in a state of unusual political excitement since the commencement of the Senatorial contest, was in a vortex of excitement yesterday when Senator Douglas addressed the people, which has not yet entirely subsided, Mr. Lincoln being here today. I have just returned from hearing Lincoln, and propose to give you an account of his doings. . . .

I was at the landing when the *Sam Gaty*, on which he came up the Illinois River, arrived.[16] There were not fifty people down to receive him beside the Guards, who, having turned out the day before for Douglas, did the handsome thing by extending the same courtesy to him, and the river banks, which yesterday were so crowded that standing room could barely be found, today looked bare and deserted. As Lincoln was about leaving the boat, the American flag was run up on board, but, as if indignant at being raised in honor of such a man, it displayed itself at mast head Union Jack down, and this little circumstance, together with his forgetting his carpet bag and umbrella, and being obliged to go back for them, seemed to affect Lincoln so much that it was with difficulty that the committee could convey him ashore over the plank, which in fact they did not succeed in doing until a gentleman relieved him of his umbrella, which he manifested a determination to carry between his legs, and which it was with the

---

[15] August 20.

[16] The *Editor*, according to the *Press and Tribune*. The reader may take his choice.

greatest difficulty he could be extricated from.[17] Do you know that
it is my firm belief that Lincoln, among his other weaknesses, nour-
ishes that of omens, and that that flag worried him. The procession
which met him at the boat, including the soldiers, did not number
one hundred and fifty, and at the meeting there were not 1,800
people present from actual count.

Lincoln is failing rapidly, but he has lost none of his awkwardness.
He is all legs and arms, and his constant efforts to hide the extreme
length of these members by keeping them twisted up when not in
use, makes his movements very kinky and uncertain. His gestures
when speaking, are positively painful, and while listening to him
we are constantly uncomfortable, because you cannot divest yourself of the idea that he is suffering from an attack brought on by
an imprudent indulgence in unripe fruit. The speech, today, was in
many respects like his Chicago speech. He is still on the defensive,
and still clings to negro equality, though I think his friends, during
the week or two they have had him on hand up in Springfield, have
bleached him a little. He did not request us to swallow the negro
entire, but diluted the dose, no doubt thinking that down in this
more southerly climate there were weaker stomachs than you possess in Chicago. He confessed that the negro was the subject of his
thoughts by day, and that the Declaration of Independence having
declared their equality, he was at a loss to know what to do with
them, and where to put them, that they might exercise it. He admitted that they were not physically equal to the white race, but
thought they were equal under the law, and that it was our duty
to bring them to a state of social equality with ourselves. Having
thus discoursed, what do you suppose he next attempted? To defend the administration and President Buchanan! He wished the
people to understand that President Buchanan had never fought the
right of the people of Kansas to form their own constitution, but
had only, as a matter of fact, contended that the Lecompton constitution had been made by the people. Any one who said otherwise
of the President, wronged him. . . .

He was going on defending the administration, when Dr. Foster,
the rankest Abolitionist in our city, who acted as marshal of the
day, pulled him pretty roughly by the coat tail, and asked him
whether he had forgotten what he had told him about what Douglas
had said of Trumbull? "No," answered Lincoln nervously, "I am
coming to it." "Well, be careful now," said Foster, "I wouldn't say
much more in that strain, but speak out for Trumbull."

[17] The reader is respectfully urged to reread this sentence. If not unique in
English prose, it must be very nearly so.

... All Mr. Lincoln could say in defense was that he did not know whether the charges against Douglas were true or not, but that his knowledge of Trumbull led him to believe that he would not say anything that he could not prove, and he would leave the matter with him. You should have seen the blank faces among the Republicans at this moment, and heard the jeers and derisions of the Democrats. An indignant Democrat declared that Trumbull was a cheat and a liar, and that Lincoln knew it, and was no better, which called forth a proposition "to put him out," but it was not deemed expedient under the circumstances to attempt it. Did you ever see a sick dog, with his tail between his legs, and looking as mournful as if he had no friends to mourn for him after his death, and was obliged to act a part of the funeral ceremony himself before giving up life, well that is just the appearance of Abe Lincoln and the other "living dogs" in this region. They will kill Lincoln before they make him Senator if they keeping loading him as they have done. They have obliged him to carry the negro on his back, a load, which, judging from his Springfield speech, he willingly consented to bear (not expecting it to be so hot in Illinois this summer); but now they order him to take Trumbull up too, and carry him about the State and protect him. Have not his party friends given him a nice family to nurse?

At Bath, where Lincoln spoke on August 16, he found himself in something of the same position Douglas had been in at Winchester. Lincoln, too, spoke with nostalgia.

In commencing his speech today, in a grove adjoining Bath, where a large and most respectable audience greeted him, Mr. Lincoln said he had many things since coming into Mason County to remind him that he had ceased to be a young man. Among the old men, he had met more than half a dozen who were in the same company with him 27 years ago in the Black Hawk war—a war which truly was not a very extensive one, or calculated to make great heroes of men engaged in it. But here are these old men now, some of them on the stand with him; and on this very spot, 22 years ago, he (Mr. L.) had with his own hands staked out the first plat of this town of Bath, then a wooded wilderness. But what more reminded him of his advancing age, was the number of young men around him, now, and for years past, voters, who were the sons of his friends of early years, and who are now of the age he was when he first knew their fathers. Here at least he expected to be heard with candor and respectful attention—and he was so heard, throughout an address of more than two hours' duration.[18]

Lewistown, county seat of Fulton County, outdid itself for the Republican candidate.[19]

LEWISTOWN, FULTON COUNTY, ILL., Aug. 17

The pageant which announced the arrival of Abraham Lincoln, "Senator from Illinois," in the County of Fulton, was a magnificent and imposing affair. Thirty-two guns were fired at sunrise, and banners were hung from the court house, the Bliss Hotel, and across the principal streets. At nine o'clock a cavalcade of one hundred horsemen, preceded by the Canton Brass Band, assembled in front of the public square and gave three mighty cheers for Lincoln—after which they formed a procession and started down the Havana road to meet the escort which was bringing our candidate over from Bath. All along the road the procession was swelled by volunteers who mounted their horses and joined in the cavalcade. About two miles out of town they met the delegation from Bath, when the marshal of the day ordered a halt, and three tremendous cheers were given by a spontaneous impulse. A brief and happy reception speech was then made by George Phelps, Esq., in behalf of the Republicans and Old Line Whigs of Fulton. Mr. Lincoln alighted and made a response which was received with loud cheers; after which the procession opened, and the Canton Band and the carriage conveying Mr. L. passed through its entire length. Shortly after 10 o'clock the companies arrived in town and deployed in front of the court house, where the multitude again gave expression to their enthusiasm by continued cheers. A general adjournment was then effected for dinner—the hotels in the place being obliged to keep their tables set from ten till one o'clock.

Considerably before two, the whole space in front of the court house, extending the length of an entire block, was filled with people. Nearly all the towns in the county were represented, and I met several hard-working Republicans from McDonough, Schuyler and Mason.

At two o'clock, Judge Kellogg introduced Mr. Lincoln, who was again greeted with vociferous applause. After the noise had subsided, he commenced and delivered the ablest, and, as I think, the most powerful argument ever heard in old Fulton. The speech was

[18] Chicago *Press and Tribune*, August 21, 1858.

[19] Chicago *Press and Tribune*, August 21, 1858.

two hours and a half long, yet there seemed to me to be more listeners at the conclusion than at the beginning.

Perhaps it was the warmth of Lewistown's welcome, perhaps it was one of those rare inspirations that come to a speaker on the spur of the moment. Whatever the cause, Lincoln delivered a eulogy of the Declaration of Independence that stands as one of the high points of the campaign.[20]

The Declaration of Independence

The Declaration of Independence was formed by the representatives of American liberty from thirteen states of the confederacy —twelve of which were slaveholding communities. We need not discuss the way or the reason of their becoming slaveholding communities. It is sufficient for our purpose that *all of them* greatly deplored the evil and that they placed a provision in the Constitution which they supposed would gradually remove the disease by cutting off its source. This was the abolition of the slave trade. So general was conviction—the public determination—to abolish the African slave trade, that the provision which I have referred to as being placed in the Constitution, declared that it should *not* be abolished prior to the year 1808. A constitutional provision was necessary to prevent the people, through Congress, from putting a stop to the traffic immediately at the close of the war. Now, if slavery had been a good thing, would the Fathers of the Republic have taken a step calculated to diminish its beneficent influences among themselves, and snatch the boon wholly from their posterity? These communities, by their representatives in old Independence Hall, said to the whole world of men: "We hold these truths to be self evident: that all men are created equal; that they are endowed by their Creator with certain unalienable rights; that among these are life, liberty and the pursuit of happiness." This was their majestic interpretation of the economy of the Universe. This was their lofty, and wise, and noble understanding of the justice of the Creator to His creatures. [Applause.] Yes, gentlemen, to *all* His creatures, to the whole great family of man. In their enlightened belief, nothing stamped with the divine image and likeness was sent into the world to be trodden on, and degraded, and imbruted by its fellows. They grasped not only the whole race of man then living, but they reached forward and seized upon the farthest posterity. They erected a beacon to guide their children and their children's children, and the countless

[20] *Ibid.*

myriads who should inhabit the earth in other ages. Wise statesmen as they were, they knew the tendency of prosperity to breed tyrants, and so they established these great self-evident truths, that when in the distant future some man, some faction, some interest, should set up the doctrine that none but rich men, or none but white men, were entitled to life, liberty and the pursuit of happiness, their posterity might look up again to the Declaration of Independence and take courage to renew the battle which their fathers began—so that truth, and justice, and mercy, and all the humane and Christian virtues might not be extinguished from the land; so that no man would hereafter dare to limit and circumscribe the great principles on which the temple of liberty was being built. [Loud cheers.]

Now, my countrymen (Mr. Lincoln continued with great earnestness,) if you have been taught doctrines conflicting with the great landmarks of the Declaration of Independence; if you have listened to suggestions which would take away from its grandeur, and mutilate the fair symmetry of its proportions; if you have been inclined to believe that all men are *not* created equal in those inalienable rights enumerated by our chart of liberty, let me entreat you to come back. Return to the fountain whose waters spring close by the blood of the Revolution. Think nothing of me—take no thought for the political fate of any man whomsoever—but come back to the truths that are in the Declaration of Independence. You may do anything with me you choose, if you will but heed these sacred principles. You may not only defeat me for the Senate, but you may take me and put me to death. While pretending no indifference to earthly honors, I *do claim* to be actuated in this contest by something higher than an anxiety for office. I charge you to drop every paltry and insignificant thought for any man's success. It is nothing; I am nothing; Judge Douglas is nothing. *But do not destroy that immortal emblem of humanity—the Declaration of American Independence.*

CHAPTER FOUR

THE OTTAWA DEBATE

"From sunrise till high noon on Saturday [August 21]," the Press and Tribune *reported,*[1] *"Ottawa was deluged in dust. The first of the seven great debates which Douglas had consented to hold with Lincoln, had started La Salle, Will, Kendall, Grundy, Kankakee, Cook and other surrounding counties, in unwonted commotion. Before breakfast Ottawa was beleaguered with a multiplying host from all points of the compass. At eight o'clock the streets and avenues leading from the country were so enveloped with dust that the town resembled a vast smoke house. Teams, trains and processions poured in from every direction like an army with banners. National flags, mottoes and devices fluttered and stared from every street corner. Military companies and bands of music monopolized the thoroughfares around the court house and the public square. Two brass twelve pounders banged away in the centre of the city and drowned the hubbub of the multitude with their own higher capacities for hubbub. Vanity Fair never boiled with madder enthusiasm."*

Both candidates arrived in Ottawa about noon, Lincoln coming by train from Morris, where he had spent the preceding night, and Douglas traveling by carriage from Peru. A cheering crowd escorted Lincoln from the Rock Island Railroad station to the home of Ottawa's mayor, Joseph O. Glover; a welcoming procession greeted Douglas on the road west of the town and accompanied him to the Geiger House.

The Press and Tribune *report continues: "At one o'clock the crowd commenced pouring into the public square. The rush was literally tremendous. The speaking stand had been foolishly left unguarded, and was so crowded with people, before the officers of the day arrived, that half an hour was consumed in a battle to make room for the speakers and reporters. Even then the accommodations were of the most wretched character. Two or three times the surge*

---

[1] Weekly issue, August 26.

*of people on the platform nearly drove the reporters off, and half
a dozen clowns on the roof broke through some of the boards and
let them down on the heads of the reception committees. The whole
number of persons present could not have been less than twelve
thousand."*

*At 2:30, with the sun scorching the standing spectators, Douglas
opened the debate.*

Douglas' Opening Speech

Ladies and gentlemen:

I appear before you to-day for the purpose of discussing the leading political topics which now agitate the public mind. By an
arrangement between Mr. Lincoln and myself, we are present here
to-day for the purpose of having a joint discussion as the representatives of the two great political parties of the state and Union, upon
the principles in issue between these parties and this vast concourse
of people, shows the deep feeling which pervades the public mind
in regard to the questions dividing us.

Prior to 1854 this country was divided into two great political
parties, known as the Whig and Democratic parties. Both were
national and patriotic, advocating principles that were universal in
their application. An Old Line Whig could proclaim his principles
in Louisiana and Massachusetts alike. Whig principles had no
boundary section line, they were not limited by the Ohio river, nor
by the Potomac, nor by the line of the free and slave states, but
applied and were proclaimed wherever the Constitution ruled or
the American flag waved over the American soil. ("Hear him," and
three cheers.) So it was, and so it is with the great Democratic
party, which, from the days of Jefferson until this period, has proven
itself to be the historic party of this nation. While the Whig and
Democratic parties differed in regard to a bank, the tariff, distribution, the specie circular and the sub-treasury, they agreed on the
great slavery question which now agitates the Union. I say that the
Whig party and the Democratic party agreed on this slavery question while they differed on those matters of expediency to which I
have referred. The Whig party and the Democratic party jointly
adopted the compromise measures of 1850 as the basis of a proper
and just solution of this slavery question in all its forms. Clay was
the great leader, with Webster on his right and Cass on his left, and

sustained by the patriots in the Whig and Democratic ranks, who had devised and enacted the compromise measures of 1850.

In 1851, the Whig party and the Democratic party united in Illinois in adopting resolutions endorsing and approving the principles of the compromise measures of 1850, as the proper adjustment of that question. In 1852, when the Whig party assembled in convention at Baltimore for the purpose of nominating a candidate for the presidency, the first thing it did was to declare the compromise measures of 1850, in substance and in principle, a suitable adjustment of that question. (Here the speaker was interrupted by loud and long continued applause.) My friends, silence will be more acceptable to me in the discussion of these questions than applause. I desire to address myself to your judgment, your understanding, and your consciences, and not to your passions or your enthusiasm. When the Democratic convention assembled in Baltimore in the same year, for the purpose of nominating a Democratic candidate for the presidency, it also adopted the compromise measures of 1850 as the basis of Democratic action. Thus you see that up to 1853-'54, the Whig party and the Democratic party both stood on the same platform with regard to the slavery question. That platform was the right of the people of each state and each territory to decide their local and domestic institutions for themselves, subject only to the federal Constitution.

During the session of Congress of 1853-'54, I introduced into the Senate of the United States a bill to organize the territories of Kansas and Nebraska on that principle which had been adopted in the compromise measures of 1850, approved by the Whig party and the Democratic party in Illinois in 1851, and endorsed by the Whig party and the Democratic party in national convention in 1852. In order that there might be no misunderstanding in relation to the principle involved in the Kansas and Nebraska Bill, I put forth the true intent and meaning of the act in these words: "It is the true intent and meaning of this act not to legislate slavery into any state or territory, or to exclude it therefrom, but to leave the people thereof perfectly free to form and regulate their domestic institutions in their own way, subject only to the federal constitution." Thus, you see, that up to 1854, when the Kansas and Nebraska Bill was brought into Congress for the purpose of carrying out the principles which both parties had up to that time endorsed and approved, there had been no division in this country in regard to that principle except the opposition of the Abolitionists. In the House of Representatives of the Illinois legislature, upon a resolution asserting that principle, every Whig and every Democrat in the House voted in the affirmative, and only four men voted against it, and those four were old line Abolitionists. (Cheers.)

In 1854, Mr. Abraham Lincoln and Mr. Trumbull entered into an arrangement, one with the other, and each with his respective friends, to dissolve the old Whig party on the one hand, and to dissolve the old Democratic party on the other, and to connect the members of both into an Abolition party under the name and disguise of a Republican party. (Laughter and cheers, "hurrah for Douglas.") The terms of that arrangement between Mr. Lincoln and Mr. Trumbull have been published to the world by Mr. Lincoln's special friend, James H. Matheny, Esq., and they were that Lincoln should have Shields' place in the U.S. Senate, which was then about to become vacant, and that Trumbull should have my seat when my term expired. (Great laughter.) Lincoln went to work to abolitionize the Old Whig party all over the state, pretending that he was then as good a Whig as ever; (laughter) and Trumbull went to work in his part of the state preaching abolitionism in its milder and lighter form, and trying to abolitionize the Democratic party, and bring old Democrats handcuffed and bound hand and foot into the abolition camp. ("Good," "hurrah for Douglas," and cheers.) In pursuance of the arrangement, the parties met at Springfield in October, 1854, and proclaimed their new platform. Lincoln was to bring into the abolition camp the Old Line Whigs, and transfer them over to Giddings, Chase, Ford, Douglass and Parson Lovejoy,[2] who were ready to receive them and christen them in their new faith. (Laughter and cheers.) They laid down on that occasion a platform for their new Republican party, which was to be thus constructed. I have the resolutions of their state convention then held, which was the first mass state convention ever held in Illinois by the Black Republican party, and I now hold them in my hands and will read a part of them, and cause the others to be printed. Here is the most important and material resolution of this abolition platform.

1. *Resolved*, That we believe this truth to be self-evident, that when parties become subversive of the ends for which they are established, or incapable of restoring the government to the true principles of the Constitution, it is the right and duty of the people to dissolve the political bands by which they may have been connected therewith, and to organize new parties upon such principles and with such views as the circumstances and exigencies of the nation may demand.

2. *Resolved*, That the times imperatively demand the reorganization of

[2] Joshua R. Giddings, Congressman from Ohio; Salmon P. Chase, Governor of Ohio; Thomas H. Ford, Ohio Abolitionist; Frederick Douglass, Negro journalist and lecturer; Owen Lovejoy, Illinois Congressman. All five were either Abolitionists or radical opponents of slavery.

parties, and repudiating all previous party attachments, names and pre-dilections, we unite ourselves together in defence of the liberty and Consti-tution of the country, and will hereafter co-operate as the Republican party, pledged to the accomplishment of the following purposes: to bring the ad-ministration of the government back to the control of first principles; to restore Nebraska and Kansas to the position of free territories; that, as the Constitution of the United States, vests in the states, and not in Congress, the power to legislate for the extradition of fugitives from labor, to repeal and entirely abrogate the fugitive slave law; to restrict slavery to those states in which it exists; to prohibit the admission of any more slave states into the Union; to abolish slavery in the District of Columbia; to exclude slavery from all the territories over which the general government has ex-clusive jurisdiction; and to resist the acquirements of any more territories unless the practice of slavery therein forever shall have been prohibited.

3. *Resolved*, That in furtherance of these principles we will use such constitutional and lawful means as shall seem best adapted to their accom-plishment, and that we will support no man for office, under the general or state government, who is not positively and fully committed to the sup-port of these principles, and whose personal character and conduct is not a guaranty that he is reliable, and who shall not have abjured old party allegiance and ties.

(The resolutions, as they were read, were cheered throughout.) Now, gentlemen, your Black Republicans have cheered every one of those propositions, ("good and cheers,") and yet I venture to say that you cannot get Mr. Lincoln to come out and say that he is now in favor of each one of them. (Laughter and applause. "Hit him again.") That these propositions, one and all, constitute the plat-form of the Black Republican party of this day, I have no doubt, ("good") and when you were not aware for what purpose I was reading them, your Black Republicans cheered them as good Black Republican doctrines. ("That's it," etc.) My object in reading these resolutions, was to put the question to Abraham Lincoln this day, whether he now stands and will stand by each article in that creed and carry it out. ("Good." "Hit him again.") I desire to know wheth-er Mr. Lincoln to-day stands as he did in 1854, in favor of the un-conditional repeal of the fugitive slave law. I desire him to answer whether he stands pledged to-day, as he did in 1854, against the admission of any more slave states into the Union, even if the people want them. I want to know whether he stands pledged against the admission of a new state into the Union with such a constitution as the people of that state may see fit to make. ("That's it;" "put it at him.") I want to know whether he stands to-day pledged to the abo-lition of slavery in the District of Columbia. I desire him to answer whether he stands pledged to the prohibition of the slave trade be-tween the different states. ("He does.") I desire to know whether he stands pledged to prohibit slavery in all the territories of the United

States, north as well as south of the Missouri Compromise line, ("Kansas too.") I desire him to answer whether he is opposed to the acquisition of any more territory unless slavery is first prohibited therein. I want his answer to these questions. Your affirmative cheers in favor of this abolition platform is not satisfactory. I ask Abraham Lincoln to answer these questions, in order that when I trot him down to lower Egypt I may put the same questions to him. (Enthusiastic aplause.) My principles are the same everywhere. (Cheers, and "hark.") I can proclaim them alike in the North, the South, the East, and the West. My principles will apply wherever the Constitution prevails and the American flag waves. ("Good," and applause.) I desire to know whether Mr. Lincoln's principles will bear transplanting from Ottawa to Jonesboro? I put these questions to him to-day distinctly, and ask an answer. I have a right to an answer ("that's so," "he can't dodge you," etc.), for I quote from the platform of the Republican party, made by himself and others at the time that party was formed, and the bargain made by Lincoln to dissolve and kill the old Whig party, and transfer its members, bound hand and foot, to the Abolition party, under the direction of Giddings and Fred Douglass. (Cheers.) In the remarks I have made on this platform, and the position of Mr. Lincoln upon it, I mean nothing personally disrespectful or unkind to that gentleman. I have known him for nearly twenty-five years. There were many points of sympathy between us when we first got acquainted. We were both comparatively boys, and both struggling with poverty in a strange land. I was a school-teacher in the town of Winchester, and he a flourishing grocery-keeper in the town of Salem. (Applause and laughter.) He was more successful in his occupation than I was in mine, and hence more fortunate in this world's goods. Lincoln is one of those peculiar men who perform with admirable skill everything which they undertake. I made as good a school-teacher as I could and when a cabinet maker I made a good bedstead and tables, although my old boss said I succeeded better with bureaus and secretaries than anything else; (cheers,) but I believe that Lincoln was always more successful in business than I, for his business enabled him to get into the legislature. I met him there, however, and had a sympathy with him, because of the up hill struggle we both had in life. He was then just as good at telling an anecdote as now. ("No doubt.") He could beat any of the boys wrestling, or running a foot race, in pitching quoits or tossing a copper, could ruin more liquor than all the boys of the town together, (uproarious laughter,) and the dignity and impartiality with which he presided at a horse race or fist fight, excited the admiration and won the praise of everybody that was present and participated. (Renewed laughter.) I sympathized with him, because he was struggling with difficulties and so was I. Mr. Lincoln served with me in the legislature in 1836, when we both retired, and he subsided, or became submerged, and he was lost sight of as a public man for some years. In 1846, when Wilmot introduced his celebrated proviso, and the abolition tornado swept over the country, Lincoln again turned up as a member of Congress from the Sangamon district. I was then in the Senate of the United States, and was glad to welcome my old friend and companion. Whilst in Congress, he distinguished himself by his opposition to the Mexican war, taking the side of the common enemy against his own country; ("that's true,") and when he returned home he found that the indignation of the people followed him everywhere, and he was again submerged or obliged to retire into private life, forgotten by his former friends. ("And will be again.") He came up again in 1854, just in time to make this Abolition or Black Republican platform, in company with Giddings, Lovejoy, Chase, and Fred Douglass for the Republican party to stand upon. (Laughter, "Hit him again," &c.) Trumbull, too, was one of our own contemporaries. He was born and raised in old Connecticut, was bred a federalist, but removing to Georgia, turned nullifier when nullification was popular, and as soon as he disposed of his clocks and wound up his business, migrated to Illinois, (laughter,) turned politician and lawyer here, and made his appearance in 1841, as a member of the legislature. He became noted as the author of the scheme to repudiate a large portion of the state debt of Illinois, which, if successful, would have brought infamy and disgrace upon the fair escutcheon of our glorious state. The odium attached to that measure consigned him to oblivion for a time. I helped to do it. I walked into a public meeting in the hall of the House of Representatives and replied to his repudiating speeches, and resolutions were carried over his head denouncing repudiation, and asserting the moral and legal obligation of Illinois to pay every dollar of the debt she owed and every bond that bore her seal. ("Good," and cheers.) Trumbull's malignity has followed me since I thus defeated his infamous scheme.

These two men having formed this combination to abolitionize the old Whig party and the old Democratic party, and put themselves into the Senate of the United States, in pursuance of their bargain, are now carrying out that arrangement. Matheny states that Trumbull broke faith; that the bargain was that Lincoln should be the Senator in Shields' place, and Trumbull was to wait for mine; (laughter and cheers,) and the story goes, that Trumbull cheated Lincoln, having control of four or five abolitionized Democrats who were holding over in the Senate; he would not let them vote for Lincoln, and which obliged the rest of the Abolitionists to support him in order to secure an Abolition Senator. There are a number of authorities for the truth of this besides Matheny, and I suppose that even Mr. Lincoln will not deny it. (Applause and laughter.)

Mr. Lincoln demands that he shall have the place intended for Trumbull, as Trumbull cheated him and got his, and Trumbull is stumping the state traducing me for the purpose of securing that position for Lincoln, in order to quiet him. ("Lincoln can never get it, &c.") It was in consequence of this arrangement that the Republican Convention was empanelled to instruct for Lincoln and nobody else, and it was on this account that they passed resolutions that he was their first, their last, and their only choice. Archy Williams was nowhere, Browning was nobody, Wentworth was not to be considered, they had no man in the Republican party for the place except Lincoln, for the reason that he demanded that they should carry out the arrangement. ("Hit him again.")

Having formed this new party for the benefit of deserters from Whiggery, and deserters from Democracy, and having laid down the abolition platform which I have read, Lincoln now takes his stand and proclaims his abolition doctrines. Let me read a part of them. In his speech at Springfield to the convention which nominated him for the Senate, he said:

In my opinion it will not cease until a crisis shall have been reached and passed. "A house divided against itself cannot stand." I believe this government *cannot endure permanently half slave and half free.* I do not expect the Union to be dissolved—I do not expect the house to fall—*but I do expect it will cease to be divided.* It will become all one thing, or all the other. Either the opponents of slavery *will arrest the further spread of it,* and place it where the public mind shall rest in the belief *that it is in the course of ultimate extinction;* or its advocates *will push it forward till it shall become alike lawful in all the states*—old as well as new, North as well as South.

("Good," "good," and cheers.)

I am delighted to hear you Black Republicans say "good." (Laughter and cheers.) I have no doubt that doctrine expresses your sentiments ("hit them again," "that's it,") and I will prove to you now, if you will listen to me, that it is revolutionary and destructive of the existence of this government. ("Hurrah for Douglas," "good," and cheers.) Mr. Lincoln, in the extract from which I have read, says that this government cannot endure permanently in the same condition in which it was made by its framers—divided into free and slave states. He says that it has existed for about seventy years thus divided, and yet he tells you that it cannot endure permanently on the same principles and in the same relative condition in which our fathers made it. ("Neither can it.") Why can it not exist divided into free and slave states? Washington, Jefferson, Franklin, Madison, Hamilton, Jay, and the great men of that day, made this government divided into free states and slave states, and left each state perfectly free to do as it pleased on the subject of slavery. ("Right, right.") Why can it not exist on the same principles on which our fathers made it? ("It can.") They knew when they framed the Constitution that in a country as wide and broad as this, with such a variety of climate, production and interest, the people necessarily required different laws and institutions in different localities. They knew that the laws and regulations which would suit the granite hills of New Hampshire would be unsuited to the rice plantations of South Carolina, ("right, right,") and they, therefore, provided that each state should retain its own legislature, and its own sovereignty with the full and complete power to do as it pleased within its own limits, in all that was local and not national. (Applause.) One of the reserved rights of the states, was the right to regulate the relations between master and servant, on the slavery question. At the time the Constitution was formed, there were thirteen states in the Union, twelve of which were slaveholding states and one a free state. Suppose this doctrine of uniformity preached by Mr. Lincoln, that the states should all be free or all be slave had prevailed and what would have been the result? Of course, the twelve slaveholding states would have overruled the one free state, and slavery would have been fastened by a constitutional provision on every inch of the American Republic, instead of being left as our fathers wisely left it, to each state to decide for itself. ("Good, good," and three cheers for Douglas.) Here I assert that uniformity in the local laws and institutions of the different states is neither possible or desirable. If uniformity had been adopted when the government was established, it must inevitably have been the uniformity of slavery everywhere, or else the uniformity of negro citizenship and negro equality everywhere.

We are told by Lincoln that he is utterly opposed to the Dred Scott decision, and will not submit to it, for the reason that he says it deprives the negro of the rights and privileges of citizenship. (Laughter and applause.) That is the first and main reason which he assigns for his warfare on the Supreme Court of the United States and its decision. I ask you, are you in favor of conferring

upon the negro the rights and privileges of citizenship? ("No, no.")
Do you desire to strike out of our state constitution that clause
which keeps slaves and free negroes out of the state, and allow the
free negroes to flow in, ("never,") and cover your prairies with
black settlements? Do you desire to turn this beautiful state into a
free negro colony, ("no, no,") in order that when Missouri abolishes
slavery she can send one hundred thousand emancipated slaves into
Illinois, to become citizens and voters, on an equality with yourselves? ("Never," "no.") If you desire negro citizenship, if you desire to allow them to come into the state and settle with the white
man, if you desire them to vote on an equality with yourselves, and
to make them eligible to office, to serve on juries, and to adjudge
your rights, then support Mr. Lincoln and the Black Republican
party, who are in favor of the citizenship of the negro. ("Never,
never.") For one, I am opposed to negro citizenship in any and
every form. (Cheers.) I believe this government was made on the
white basis. ("Good.") I believe it was made by white men, for the
benefit of white men and their posterity for ever, and I am in favor
of confining citizenship to white men, men of European birth and
descent, instead of conferring it upon negroes, Indians and other
inferior races. ("Good for you." "Douglas forever.")

Mr. Lincoln, following the example and lead of all the little
Abolition orators, who go around and lecture in the basements of
schools and churches, reads from the Declaration of Independence,
that all men were created equal, and then asks how can you deprive
a negro of that equality which God and the Declaration of Independence awards to him. He and they maintain that negro equality
is guaranteed by the laws of God, and that it is asserted in the
Declaration of Independence. If they think so, of course they have
a right to say so, and so vote. I do not question Mr. Lincoln's conscientious belief that the negro was made his equal, and hence is
his brother, (laughter,) but for my own part, I do not regard the
negro as my equal, and positively deny that he is my brother or any
kin to me whatever. ("Never." "Hit him again," and cheers.) Lincoln
has evidently learned by heart Parson Lovejoy's catechism. (Laughter and applause.) He can repeat it as well as Farnsworth,[3] and he
is worthy of a medal from father Giddings and Fred Douglass for
his abolitionism. (Laughter.) He holds that the negro was born his
equal and yours, and that he was endowed with equality by the
Almighty, and that no human law can deprive him of these rights
which were guaranteed to him by the Supreme Ruler of the uni-

---

[3] John F. Farnsworth of Chicago, Congressman from Illinois.

verse. Now, I do not believe that the Almighty ever intended the negro to be the equal of the white man. ("Never, never.") If he did, he has been a long time demonstrating the fact. (Cheers.) For thousands of years the negro has been a race upon the earth, and during all that time, in all latitudes and climates, wherever he has wandered or been taken, he has been inferior to the race which he has there met. He belongs to an inferior race, and must always occupy an inferior position. ("Good," "that's so," &c.) I do not hold that because the negro is our inferior that therefore he ought to be a slave. By no means can such a conclusion be drawn from what I have said. On the contrary, I hold that humanity and Christianity both require that the negro shall have and enjoy every right, every privilege, and every immunity consistent with the safety of the society in which he lives. ("That's so.") On that point, I presume, there can be no diversity of opinion. You and I are bound to extend to our inferior and dependent being every right, every privilege, every facility and immunity consistent with the public good. The question then arises what rights and privileges are consistent with the public good. This is a question which each state and each territory must decide for itself—Illinois has decided it for herself. We have provided that the negro shall not be a slave, and we have also provided that he shall not be a citizen, but protect him in his civil rights, in his life, his person and his property, only depriving him of all political rights whatsoever, and refusing to put him on an equality with the white man. ("Good.") That policy of Illinois is satisfactory to the Democratic party and to me, and if it were to the Republicans, there would then be no question upon the subject; but the Republicans say that he ought to be made a citizen, and when he becomes a citizen he becomes your equal, with all your rights and privileges. ("He never shall.") They assert the Dred Scott decision to be monstrous because it denies that the negro is or can be a citizen under the Constitution. Now, I hold that Illinois had a right to abolish and prohibit slavery as she did, and I hold that Kentucky has the same right to continue and protect slavery that Illinois had to abolish it. I hold that New York had as much right to abolish slavery as Virginia has to continue it, and that each and every state of this Union is a sovereign power, with the right to do as it pleases upon this question of slavery, and upon all its domestic institutions. Slavery is not the only question which comes up in this controversy. There is a far more important one to you, and that is, what shall be done with the free negro? We have settled the slavery question as far as we are concerned; we have prohibited it in Illinois forever, and in doing so, I think we have done wisely, and there is no man in the state who would be more strenuous in his opposition to the introduction of slavery than I would; (cheers) but when we settled it for ourselves, we exhausted all our power over that subject. We have done our whole duty, and can do no more. We must leave each and every other state to decide for itself the same question. In relation to the policy to be pursued towards the free negroes, we have said that they shall not vote; whilst Maine, on the other hand, has said that they shall vote. Maine is a sovereign state, and has the power to regulate the qualifications of voters within her limits. I would never consent to confer the right of voting and of citizenship upon a negro, but still I am not going to quarrel with Maine for differing from me in opinion. Let Maine take care of her own negroes and fix the qualifications of her own voters to suit herself, without interfering with Illinois, and Illinois will not interfere with Maine. So with the state of New York. She allows the negro to vote provided he owns two hundred and fifty dollars worth of property, but not otherwise. While I would not make any distinction whatever between a negro who held property and one who did not; yet if the sovereign state of New York chooses to make that distinction it is her business and not mine, and I will not quarrel with her for it. She can do as she pleases on this question if she minds her own business, and we will do the same thing. Now, my friends, if we will only act conscientiously and rigidly upon this great principle of popular sovereignty which guarantees to each state and territory the right to do as it pleases on all things local and domestic instead of Congress interfering, we will continue at peace one with another. Why should Illinois be at war with Missouri, or Kentucky with Ohio, or Virginia with New York, merely because their institutions differ? Our fathers intended that our institutions should differ. They knew that the North and the South having different climates, productions and interests, required different institutions. This doctrine of Mr. Lincoln's of uniformity among the institutions of the different states is a new doctrine, never dreamed of by Washington, Madison, or the framers of this government. Mr. Lincoln and the Republican party set themselves up as wiser than these men who made this government, which has flourished for seventy years under the principle of popular sovereignty, recognizing the right of each state to do as it pleased. Under that principle, we have grown from a nation of three or four millions to a nation of about thirty millions of people; we have crossed the Allegheny mountains and filled up the whole North West, turning the prairie into a garden, and building up churches and schools, thus spreading civilization and Christianity where before there was nothing but savage-barbarism. Under that principle we have become from a feeble nation, the most powerful on the face of the earth, and if we only adhere to that principle, we can go forward increasing in territory, in power, in strength and in glory until the Republic of America shall be the North Star that shall guide the friends of freedom throughout the civilized world. ("Long may you live," and great applause.) And why can we not adhere to the great principle of self-government, upon which our institutions were originally based. ("We can.") I believe that this new doctrine preached by Mr. Lincoln and his party will dissolve the Union if it succeeds. They are trying to array all the Northern states in one body against the South, to excite a sectional war between the free states and the slave states, in order that the one or the other may be driven to the wall.

I am told that my time is out. Mr. Lincoln will now address you for an hour and a half, and I will then occupy a half hour in replying to him. (Three times three cheers were here given for Douglas.)

Lincoln rose to long-sustained applause. Minutes passed before he could make himself heard.

Lincoln's Reply

My Fellow Citizens:

When a man hears himself somewhat misrepresented, it provokes him—at least, I find it so with myself; but when the misrepresentation becomes very gross and palpable, it is more apt to amuse him. [Laughter.] The first thing I see fit to notice, is the fact that Judge Douglas alleges, after running through the history of the old Democratic and the old Whig parties, that Judge Trumbull and myself made an arrangement in 1854, by which I was to have the place of Gen. Shields in the United States Senate, and Judge Trumbull was to have the place of Judge Douglas. Now all I have to say upon that subject is, that I think no man—not even Judge Douglas—can prove it, *because it is not true.* [Cheers.] I have no doubt he is "*conscientious*" in saying it. [Laughter.] As to those resolutions that he took such a length of time to read, as being the platform of the Republican party in 1854, I say I never had anything to do with them, and I think Trumbull never had. [Renewed laughter.] Judge Douglas cannot show that either one of us ever did have any thing to do with them. I believe *this* is true about those resolutions: There was a call for a convention to form a Republican party at Springfield, and I think that my friend Mr. Lovejoy, who is here upon this stand, had a hand in it. I think this is true, and I think if he will remember accurately, he will be able to recollect that he tried to get me into it, and I would not go in. [Cheers and laughter.] I believe it is also true, that I went away from Springfield when the convention was in session, to attend court in Tazewell County. It is true they did place my name, though without authority, upon the committee, and afterwards wrote me to attend the meeting of the committee, but I refused to do so, and I never had anything to do with that organization. This is the plain truth about all that matter of the resolutions.

Now, about this story that Judge Douglas tells of Trumbull bargaining to sell out the old Democratic party, and Lincoln agreeing to sell out the old Whig party, I have the means of *knowing* about that; [laughter] Judge Douglas cannot have; and I know there is no substance to it whatever. [Applause.] Yet I have no doubt he is "*conscientious*" about it. [Laughter.] I know that after Mr. Lovejoy got into the legislature that winter, he complained of me that I had told all the old Whigs in his district that the old Whig party was good enough for them, and some of them voted against him because I told them so. Now I have no means of totally disproving such charges as this which the Judge makes. A man cannot prove a negative, but he has a right to claim that when a man makes an affirmative charge, he must offer some proof to show the truth of what he says. I certainly cannot introduce testimony to show the negative about things, but I have a right to claim that if a man says he *knows* a thing, then he must show *how* he knows it. I always have a right to claim this, and it is not satisfactory to me that he may be "conscientious" on the subject. [Cheers and Laughter.]

Now gentlemen, I hate to waste my time on such things, but in regard to that general abolition tilt that Judge Douglas makes, when he says that I was engaged at that time in selling out and abolitionizing the old Whig party—I hope you will permit me to read a part of a printed speech that I made then at Peoria, which will show altogether a different view of the position I took in that contest of 1854.

VOICE—Put on your specs.

MR. LINCOLN—Yes, sir, I am obliged to do so. I am no longer a young man. [Laughter.]

This is the *repeal* of the Missouri Compromise.[4] The foregoing history may not be precisely accurate in every particular; but I am sure it is suffi-

[4] In his scrapbook of the Debates, Lincoln made the following marginal note at this point: "This extract from Mr. Lincoln's Peoria Speech of 1854, was read by him in the Ottawa debate, but was not reported fully or accurately in either the Times or Press & Tribune. It is inserted now as necessary to a complete report of the debate."

ciently so, for all the uses I shall attempt to make of it, and in it, we have before us, the chief materials enabling us to correctly judge whether the repeal of the Missouri Compromise is right or wrong.

I think, and shall try to show, that it is wrong; wrong in its direct effect, letting slavery into Kansas and Nebraska—and wrong in its prospective principle, allowing it to spread to every other part of the wide world, where men can be found inclined to take it.

This *declared* indifference, but as I must think, covert *real* zeal for the spread of slavery, I can not but hate. I hate it because of the monstrous injustice of slavery itself. I hate it because it deprives our republican example of its just influence in the world—enables the enemies of free institutions, with plausibility, to taunt us as hypocrites—causes the real friends of freedom to doubt our sincerity, and especially because it forces so many really good men amongst ourselves into an open war with the very fundamental principles of civil liberty—criticising the Declaration of Independence, and insisting that there is no right principle of action but *self-interest*.

Before proceeding, let me say I think I have no prejudice against the Southern people. They are just what we would be in their situation. If slavery did not now exist amongst them, they would not introduce it. If it did now exist amongst us, we should not instantly give it up. This I believe of the masses North and South. Doubtless there are individuals, on both sides, who would not hold slaves under any circumstances; and others who would gladly introduce slavery anew, if it were out of existence. We know that some Southern men do free their slaves, go north, and become tip-top Abolitionists; while some Northern ones go south, and become most cruel slave-masters.

When Southern people tell us they are no more responsible for the origin of slavery, than we; I acknowledge the fact. When it is said that the institution exists, and that it is very difficult to get rid of it, in any satisfactory way, I can understand and appreciate the saying. I surely will not blame them for not doing what I should not know how to do myself. If all earthly power were given me, I should not know what to do, as to the existing institution. My first impulse would be to free all the slaves, and send them to Liberia,—to their own native land. But a moment's reflection would convince me, that whatever of high hope, (as I think there is) there may be in this, in the long run, its sudden execution is impossible. If they were all landed there in a day, they would all perish in the next ten days; and there are not surplus shipping and surplus money enough in the world to carry them there in many times ten days. What then? Free them all, and keep them among us as underlings? Is it quite certain that this betters their condition? I think I would not hold one in slavery, at any rate; yet the point is not clear enough to me to denounce people upon. What next? Free them, and make them politically and socially, our equals? My own feelings will not admit of this; and if mine would, we well know that those of the great mass of white people will not. Whether this feeling accords with justice and sound judgment, is not the sole question, if indeed, it is any part of it. A universal feeling, whether well or ill-founded, can not be safely disregarded. We can not, then, make them equals. It does seem to me that systems of gradual emancipation might be adopted; but for their tardiness in this, I will not undertake to judge our brethren of the South.

When they remind us of their constitutional rights, I acknowledge them, not grudgingly, but fully, and fairly; and I would give them any legislation for the reclaiming of their fugitives, which should not, in its stringency, be more likely to carry a free man into slavery, than our ordinary criminal laws are to hang an innocent one.

But all this, to my judgment, furnishes no more excuse for permitting slavery to go into our own free territory, than it would for reviving the African slave trade by law. The law which forbids the bringing of slaves *from* Africa; and that which has so long forbid the taking them *to* Nebraska, can hardly be distinguished on any moral principle; and the repeal of the former could find quite as plausible excuses as that of the latter.

I have reason to know that Judge Douglas *knows* that I said this. I think he has the answer here to one of the questions he put to me. I do not mean to allow him to catechise me unless he pays back for it in kind. I will not answer questions one after another unless he reciprocates, but as he made this inquiry and I have answered it before, he has got it without my getting anything in return. He has got my answer on the fugitive slave law.

Now gentlemen, I don't want to read at any greater length, but this is the true complexion of all I have ever said in regard to the institution of slavery and the black race. This is the whole of it, and anything that argues me into his idea of perfect social and political equality with the negro, is but a specious and fantastic arrangement of words, by which a man can prove a horse chestnut to be a chestnut horse. [Laughter.] I will say here, while upon this subject, that I have no purpose directly or indirectly to interfere with the institution of slavery in the states where it exists. I believe I have no lawful right to do so, and I have no inclination to do so. I have no purpose to introduce political and social equality between the white and the black races. There is a physical difference between the two, which in my judgment will probably forever forbid their living together upon the footing of perfect equality, and inasmuch as it becomes a necessity that there must be a difference, I, as well as Judge Douglas, am in favor of the race to which I belong, having the superior position. I have never said anything to the contrary, but I hold that notwithstanding all this, there is no reason in the world why the negro is not entitled to all the natural rights enumerated in the Declaration of Independence, the right to life, liberty and the pursuit of happiness. [Loud cheers.] I hold that he is as much entitled to these as the white man. I agree with Judge Douglas he is not my equal in many respects—certainly not in color, perhaps not in moral or intellectual endowment. But in the right to eat the bread, without leave of anybody else, which his own hand earns, *he is my equal and the equal of Judge Douglas, and the equal of every living man.* [Great applause.]

Now I pass on to consider one or two more of these little follies. The Judge is woefully at fault about his early friend Lincoln being a "grocery keeper."[5] [Laughter.] I don't know as it would be a great sin, if I had been, but he is mistaken. Lincoln never kept a grocery anywhere in the world. [Laughter.] It is true that Lincoln did work the latter part of one winter in a small still house, up at the head of a hollow. [Roars of laughter.] And so I think my friend, the Judge, is equally at fault when he charges me at the time when I was in Congress of having opposed our soldiers who were fighting in the Mexican war. The Judge did not make his charge very distinctly but I can tell you what he can prove by referring to the record. You remember I was an old Whig, and whenever the Democratic party tried to get me to vote that the war had been righteously begun by the President, I would not do it. But whenever they asked for any money, or land warrants, or anything to pay the soldiers there, during all that time, I gave the same votes that Judge Douglas did. [Loud applause.] You can think as you please as to whether that was consistent. Such is the truth; and the Judge has the right to make all he can out of it. But when he, by a general charge, conveys the idea that I withheld supplies from the soldiers who were fighting in the Mexican war, or did anything else to hinder the soldiers, he is, to say the least, grossly and altogether mistaken, as a consultation of the records will prove to him.

As I have not used up so much of my time as I had supposed, I will dwell a little longer upon one or two of these minor topics upon with the Judge has spoken. He has read from my speech in Springfield, in which I say that "a house divided against itself cannot stand." Does the Judge say it *can* stand? [Laughter.] I don't know whether he does or not. The Judge does not seem to be attending to me just now, but I would like to know if it is his opinion that a house divided against itself *can stand*. If he does, then there is a question of veracity, not between him and me, but between the Judge and an authority of a somewhat higher character. [Laughter and applause.]

Now, my friends, I ask your attention to this matter for the purpose of saying something seriously. I know that the Judge may readily enough agree with me that the maxim which was put forth by the Saviour is true, but he may allege that I misapply it; and the Judge has a right to urge that, in my application, I do misapply it, and then I have a right to show that I do *not* misapply it. When he undertakes to say that because I think this nation, so far as the

---

[5] In 1858, "grocery" was synonymous with "tavern," or "saloon."

question of slavery is concerned, will all become one thing or all the other, I am in favor of bringing about a dead uniformity in the various states, in all their institutions, he argues erroneously. The great variety of the local institutions in the states, springing from differences in the soil, differences in the face of the country, and in the climate, are bonds of union. They do not make "a house divided against itself," but they make a house united. If they produce in one section of the country what is called for by the wants of another section, and this other section can supply the wants of the first, they are not matters of discord but bonds of union, true bonds of union. But can this question of slavery be considered as among *these* varieties in the institutions of the country? I leave it to you to say whether, in the history of our government, this institution of slavery has not always failed to be a bond of union, and, on the contrary, been an apple of discord and an element of division in the house. [Cries of "Yes, yes," and applause.] I ask you to consider whether, so long as the moral constitution of men's minds shall continue to be the same, after this generation and assemblage shall sink into the grave, and another race shall arise, with the same moral and intellectual development we have—whether, if that institution is standing in the same irritating position in which it now is, it will not continue an element of division? [Cries of "Yes, yes."] If so, then I have a right to say that in regard to this question, the Union is a house divided against itself, and when the Judge reminds me that I have often said to him that the institution of slavery has existed for eighty years in some states, and yet it does not exist in some others, I agree to the fact, and I account for it by looking at the position in which our fathers originally placed it—restricting it from the new territories where it had not gone, and legislating to cut off its source by the abrogation of the slave trade, thus putting the seal of legislation *against its spread.* The public mind *did* rest in the belief that it was in the course of ultimate extinction. [Cries of "Yes, yes."] But lately, I think—and in this I charge nothing on the Judge's motives—lately, I think, that he, and those acting with him, have placed that institution on a new basis, which looks to the *perpetuity and nationalization of slavery.* [Loud cheers.] And while it is placed upon this new basis, I say, and I have said, that I believe we shall not have peace upon the question until the opponents of slavery arrest the further spread of it, and place it where the public mind shall rest in the belief that it is in the course of ultimate extinction; or, on the other hand, that its advocates will push it forward until it shall become alike lawful in all the states, old as well as new, North as well as South. Now, I believe if we would arrest the spread, and place it where Washington, and Jefferson, and Madison placed it, it *would be* in the course of ultimate extinction, and the public mind *would*, as for eighty years past, believe that it was in the course of ultimate extinction. The crisis would be past and the institution might be let alone for a hundred years, if it should live so long, in the states where it exists, yet it would be going out of existence in the way best for both the black and the white races. [Great cheering.]

A Voice—Then do you repudiate popular sovereignty?

Mr. Lincoln—Well, then, let us talk about popular sovereignty! [Laughter.] What is popular sovereignty? [Cries of "A humbug," "a humbug."] Is it the right of the people to have slavery or not have it, as they see fit, in the territories? I will state—and I have an able man to watch me—my understanding is that popular sovereignty, as now applied to the question of slavery, does allow the people of a territory to have slavery if they want to, but does not allow them *not* to have it if they *do not* want it. [Applause and laughter.] I do not mean that if this vast concourse of people were in a territory of the United States, any one of them would be obliged to have a slave if he did not want one; but I do say that, as I understand the Dred Scott decision, if any one man wants slaves, all the rest have no way of keeping that one man from holding them.

When I made my speech at Springfield, of which the Judge complains, and from which he quotes, I really was not thinking of the things which he ascribes to me at all. I had no thought in the world that I was doing anything to bring about a war between the free and slave states. I had no thought in the world that I was doing anything to bring about a political and social equality of the black and white races. It never occurred to me that I was doing anything or favoring anything to reduce to a dead uniformity all the local institutions of the various states. But I must say, in all fairness to him, if he thinks I am doing something which leads to these bad results, it is none the better that I did not mean it. It is just as fatal to the country, if I have any influence in producing it, whether I intend it or not. But can it be true, that placing this institution upon the original basis—the basis upon which our fathers placed it—can have any tendency to set the Northern and the Southern states at war with one another, or that it can have any tendency to make the people of Vermont raise sugar cane, because they raise it in Louisiana, or that it can compel the people of Illinois to cut pine logs on the Grand Prairie, where they will not grow, because they cut pine logs in Maine, where they do grow? [Laughter.] The Judge says this is a new principle started in regard to this question. Does the Judge claim that he is working on the plan of the founders of government? I think he says in some of his speeches—indeed I have one here now—that he saw evidence of a policy to allow slavery to be south of a certain line, while north of it it should be excluded, and he saw an indisposition on the part of the country to stand upon that policy, and therefore he set about studying the subject upon *original principles,* and upon *original principles* he got up the Nebraska Bill! I am fighting it upon these "original principles"— fighting it in the Jeffersonian, Washingtonian, and Madisonian fashion. [Laughter and applause.]

Now my friends I wish you to attend for a little while to one or two other things in that Springfield speech. My main object was to show, so far as my humble ability was capable of showing to the people of this country, what I believed was the truth—that there was a *tendency,* if not a conspiracy among those who have engineered this slavery question for the last four or five years, to make slavery perpetual and universal in this nation. Having made that speech principally for that object, after arranging the evidences that I thought tended to prove my proposition, I concluded with this bit of comment:

We cannot absolutely know that these exact adaptations are the result of pre-concert, but when we see a lot of framed timbers, different portions of which we know have been gotten out at different times and places, and by different workmen—Stephen, Franklin, Roger and James, for instance— and when we see these timbers joined together, and see they exactly make the frame of a house or a mill, all the tenons and mortices exactly fitting and all the lengths and proportions of the different pieces exactly adapted to their respective places and not a piece too many or too few—not omitting even the scaffolding—or if a single piece be lacking we see the place in the frame exactly fitted and prepared yet to bring such piece in—in such a case we feel it impossible not to believe that Stephen and Franklin, and Roger and James, all understood one another from the beginning, and all worked upon a common plan or draft drawn before the first blow was struck. [Great cheers.]

When my friend, Judge Douglas, came to Chicago, on the 9th of July, this speech having been delivered on the 16th of June, he made an harangue there, in which he took hold of this speech of mine, showing that he had carefully read it; and while he paid no attention to *this* matter at all, but complimented me as being a "kind, amiable, and intelligent gentleman," notwithstanding I had said this; he goes on and eliminates, or draws out, from my speech this tendency of mine to set the states at war with one another, to make all the institutions uniform, and set the niggers and white people to marrying together. [Laughter.] Then, as the Judge had complimented me with these pleasant titles, (I must confess to my weakness,) I was a little "taken," [laughter] for it came from a great man. I was not very much accustomed to flattery, and it came the sweeter to me. I was rather like the Hoosier, with the gingerbread, when he said he reckoned he loved it better than any other man, and got less of it. [Roars of laughter.] As the Judge had so flattered me, I could not make up my mind that he meant to deal unfairly with me; so I went to work to show him that he misunderstood the whole scope of my speech, and that I really never intended to set the people at war with one another. As an illustration, the next time I met him, which was at Springfield, I used this expression, that I claimed no right under the Constitution, nor had I any inclination, to enter into the slave states and interfere with the institution of slavery. He says upon that: Lincoln will not enter into the slave states, but will go to the banks of the Ohio, on this side, and shoot over! [Laughter.] He runs on, step by step, in the horse-chestnut style of argument, until in the Springfield speech, he says, "Unless he shall be successful in firing his batteries until he shall have extinguished slavery in all the states, the Union shall be dissolved." Now I don't think that was exactly the way to treat a kind, amiable, intelligent gentleman. [Roars of laughter.] I know if I had asked the Judge to show when or where it was I had said that, if I didn't succeed in firing into the slave states until slavery should be extinguished, the Union should be dissolved, he could not have shown it. I understand what he would do. He would say, "I don't mean to quote from you, but this was the *result* of what you say." But I have the right to ask, and I do ask now, Did you not put it in such a form that an ordinary reader or listener would take it as an expression *from me?* [Laughter.]

In a speech at Springfield, on the night of the 17th, I thought I might as well attend to my own business a little, and I recalled his attention as well as I could to this charge of conspiracy to nationalize slavery. I called his attention to the fact that he had acknowledged, in my hearing twice, that he had carefully read the speech, and, in the language of the lawyers, as he had twice read the speech, and still had put in no plea or answer, I took a default on him. I insisted that I had a right then to renew that charge of conspiracy. Ten days afterwards, I met the Judge at Clinton—that is to say, I was on the ground, but not in the discussion—and heard him make a speech. Then he comes in with his plea to this charge, for the first time, and his plea when put in, as well as I can recollect it, amounted to this: that he never had any talk with Judge Taney or the President of the United States with regard to the Dred Scott decision before it was made. I (Lincoln) ought to know that the man who makes a charge without knowing it to be true, falsifies as much as he who knowingly tells a falsehood; and lastly, that he would pronounce the whole thing a falsehood; but he would make no personal application of the charge of falsehood, not because of any regard for the "kind, amiable, intelligent gentleman," but because of his own personal self-respect! [Roars of laughter.] I have understood since then, (but [turning to Judge Douglas] will not hold the Judge to it if he is not willing) that he has broken through the "self-respect," and has got to saying the thing *out*. The Judge nods to me that it is so. [Laughter.] It is fortunate for me that I can keep as good-humored as I do, when the Judge acknowledges that he has been trying to make a question of veracity with me. I know the Judge is a great man, while I am only a small man, but *I feel that I have got him.* [Tremendous cheering.] I demur to that plea. I waive all objections that it was not filed till after default was taken, and demur to it upon the merits. What if Judge Douglas never did talk with Chief Justice Taney and the President, before the Dred Scott decision was made, does it follow that he could not have had as perfect an understanding without talking, as with it? I am not disposed to stand upon my legal advantage. I am disposed to take his denial as being like an answer in chancery, that he neither had any knowledge, information or belief in the existence of such a conspiracy. I am disposed to take his answer as being as broad as though he had put it in these words. And now, I ask, even if he has done so, have not I a right to *prove it on him*, and to offer the evidence of more than two witnesses, by whom to prove it; and if the evidence proves the existence of the conspiracy, does his broad answer denying all knowledge, information, or belief, disturb the fact? It can only show that he was *used* by conspirators, and was not a *leader* of them. [Vociferous cheering.]

Now in regard to his reminding me of the moral rule that persons who tell what they do not know to be true, falsify as much as those who knowingly tell falsehoods. I remember the rule, and it must be borne in mind that in what I have read to you, I do not say that I *know* such a conspiracy to exist. To that, I reply *I believe it.* If the Judge says that I do *not* believe it, then *he* says what *he* does not know, and falls within his own rule, that he who asserts a thing which he does not know to be true, falsifies as much as he who knowingly tells a falsehood. I want to call your attention to a little discussion on that branch of the case, and the evidence which brought my mind to the conclusion which I expressed as my *belief*. If, in arraying that evidence, I had stated anything which was false or erroneous, it needed but that Judge Douglas should point it out, and I would have taken it back with all the kindness in the world. I do not deal in that way. If I have brought forward anything not a fact, if he will point it out, it will not even ruffle me to take it back. But if he will not point out anything erroneous in the evidence, is it not rather for him to show, by a comparison of the evidence that I have *reasoned* falsely, than to call the "kind, amiable, intelligent gentleman," a liar? [Cheers and laughter.] If I have reasoned to a false conclusion, it is the vocation of an able debater to show by argument that I have wandered to an erroneous conclusion. I want to ask your attention to a portion of the Nebraska Bill, which Judge Douglas has quoted: "It being the true intent and meaning of this act, not to legislate slavery into any territory or state, nor to exclude it therefrom, but to leave the people thereof perfectly free to form and regulate their domestic institutions in their own way, subject only to the Constitution of the United States." Thereupon Judge Douglas and others began to argue in favor of "Popular Sovereignty"—the right of the people to have slaves if they wanted them, and to exclude slavery if they did not want them. "But," said, in substance, a Senator from Ohio, (Mr. Chase, I believe,) "we more than suspect that you do not mean to allow the people to exclude slavery if they wish to, and if you do mean it, accept an amendment which I propose expressly authorizing the people to exclude slavery." I believe I have the amendment here before me, which was offered, and under which the people of the territory, through their proper representatives, might if they saw fit, prohibit the existence of slavery therein. And now I state it as a *fact*, to be taken back if there is any mistake about it, that Judge Douglas and those acting with him, *voted that amendment down.* [Tremendous applause.] I now think that those men who voted it down, had a *real reason* for doing so. They know what that reason was. It looks to us, since we have seen the Dred Scott decision pronounced holding that "under the Constitution" the people cannot exclude slavery—I say it looks to outsiders, poor, simple, "amiable, intelligent gentlemen," [great laughter,] as though the niche was left as a place to put that Dred Scott decision in—[laughter and cheers]—a niche which would have been spoiled by adopting the amendment. And now, I say again, if *this* was not the reason, it will avail the Judge much more to calmly and good-humoredly point out to these people what that *other* reason was for voting the amendment down, than, swelling himself up, to vociferate that he may be provoked to call somebody a liar. [Tremendous applause.]

Again: there is in that same quotation from the Nebraska Bill this clause—"It being the true intent and meaning of this bill not to legislate slavery into any territory or *state*." I have always been puzzled to know what business the word "state" had in that connection. Judge Douglas knows. *He put it there.* He knows what he put it there for. We outsiders cannot say what he put it there for. The law they were passing was not about states, and was not making provisions for states. What was it placed there for? After seeing the Dred Scott decision, which holds that the people cannot exclude slavery from a *territory*, if another Dred Scott decision shall come, holding that they cannot exclude it from a *state*, we shall discover that when the word was originally put there, it was in view of something which was to come in due time, we shall see that it was the *other half* of something. [Applause.] I now say again, if there is any different reason for putting it there, Judge Douglas, in a good-humored way, without calling anybody a liar, *can tell what the reason was.* [Renewed cheers.]

When the Judge spoke at Clinton, he came very near making a charge of falsehood against me. He used, as I found it printed in a newspaper, which I remember was very nearly like the real speech, the following language:

I did not answer the charge [of conspiracy] before, for the reason that I did not suppose there was a man in America with a heart so corrupt as to believe such a charge could be true. I have too much respect for Mr. Lincoln to suppose he is serious in making the charge.

I confess this is rather a curious view, that out of respect for me he should consider I was making what I deemed rather a grave charge in fun. [Laughter.] I confess it strikes me rather strangely. But I let it pass. As the Judge did not for a moment believe that there was a man in America whose heart was so "corrupt" as to make such a charge, and as he places me among the "men in America" who have hearts base enough to make such a charge, I hope he will excuse me if I hunt out another charge very like this; and if it should turn out that in hunting I should find that other, and it should turn out to be Judge Douglas himself who made it, I hope he will reconsider this question of the deep corruption of heart he has thought fit to ascribe to me. [Great applause and laughter.] In Judge Douglas' speech of March 22d, 1858, which I hold in my hand, he says:

In this connection there is another topic to which I desire to allude. I seldom refer to the course of newspapers, or notice the articles which they publish in regard to myself; but the course of the Washington *Union* has been so extraordinary, for the last two or three months, that I think it well enough to make some allusion to it. It has read me out of the Democratic party every other day, at least for two or three months, and keeps reading me out, (laughter;) and, as if it had not succeeded still continues to read me out, using such terms as "traitor," "renegade," "deserter," and other kind and polite epithets of that nature. Sir, I have no vindication to make of my democracy against the Washington *Union,* or any other newspapers. I am willing to allow my history and action for the last twenty years to speak for themselves as to my political principles, and my fidelity to political obligations. The Washington *Union* has a personal grievance. When its editor was nominated for Public Printer I declined to vote for him, and stated that at some time I might give my reasons for doing so. Since I declined to give that vote, this scurrilous abuse, these vindictive and constant attacks have been repeated almost daily on me. Will my friend from Michigan read the article to which I allude.

This is a part of the speech. You must excuse me from reading the entire article of the Washington *Union,* as Mr. Stuart read it for Mr. Douglas. The Judge goes on and sums up, as I think correctly:

Mr. President, you here find several distinct propositions advanced boldly by the Washington *Union* editorially and apparently *authoritatively,* and every man who questions any of them is denounced as an Abolitionist, a Free-Soiler, a fanatic. The propositions are, first, that the primary object of all government at its original institution is the protection of person and property; second, that the Constitution of the United States declares that the citizens of each state shall be entitled to all the privileges and immunities of citizens in the several states; and that, therefore, thirdly, all state laws, whether organic or otherwise, which prohibit the citizens of one state from settling in another with their slave property, and especially declaring it forfeited, are direct violations of the original intention of the government and Constitution of the United States; and fourth, that the emancipation of the slaves of the northern states was a gross outrage on the rights of property, inasmuch as it was involuntarily done on the part of the owner.

Remember that this article was published in the *Union* on the 17th of November, and on the 18th appeared the first article giving the adhesion of the *Union* to the Lecompton constitution. It was in these words:

"KANSAS AND HER CONSTITUTION.—The vexed question is settled. The problem is solved. The dread point of danger is passed. All serious trouble to Kansas affairs is over and gone."

And a column, nearly of the same sort. Then, when you come to look into the Lecompton constitution, you find the same doctrine incorporated in it which was put forth editorially in the *Union.* What is it?

"ARTICLE 7, *Section 1.* The right of property is before and higher than any constitutional sanction; and the right of the owner of a slave to such slave and its increase is the same and as inviolable as the right of the owner of any property whatever."

Then in the schedule is a provision that the constitution may be amended after 1864 by a two-thirds vote.

"But no alteration shall be made to affect the right of property in the ownership of slaves."

It will be seen by these clauses in the Lecompton constitution that they are identical in spirit with this *authoritative* article in the Washington *Union* of the day previous to its indorsement of this constitution.

I pass over some portions of the speech, and I hope that any one who feels interested in this matter will read the entire section of the speech, and see whether I do the Judge injustice. He proceeds:

> When I saw that article in the *Union* of the 17th of November, followed by the glorification of the Lecompton constitution on the 18th of November, and this clause in the constitution asserting the doctrine that a state has no right to prohibit slavery within its limits, I saw that there was a *fatal blow* being struck at the sovereignty of the states of this Union.

I stop the quotation there, again requesting that it may all be read. I have read all of the portion I desire to comment upon. What is this charge that the Judge thinks I must have a very corrupt heart to make? It was a purpose on the part of certain high functionaries to make it impossible for the people of one state to prohibit the people of any other state from entering it with their "property," so called, and making it a slave state. In other words, it was a charge implying a design to make the institution of slavery national. And now I ask your attention to what Judge Douglas has himself done here. I know he made that part of the speech as a reason why he had refused to vote for a certain man for public printer, but when we get at it, the charge itself is the very one I made against him, that he thinks I am so corrupt for uttering. Now whom does he make that charge against? Does he make it against that newspaper editor merely? No; he says it is identical in spirit with the Lecompton constitution, and so the framers of that constitution are brought in with the editor of the newspaper in that "fatal blow being struck." He did not call it a "conspiracy." In his language it is a "fatal blow being struck." And if the words carry the meaning better when changed from a "conspiracy" into a "fatal blow being struck," I will change *my* expression and call it "fatal blow being struck." [Cheers and laughter.] We see the charge made not merely against the editor of the *Union* but all the framers of the Lecompton constitution; and not only so, but the article was an *authoritative* article. By whose authority? Is there any question but he means it was by the authority of the President, and his Cabinet—the administration?

Is there any sort of question but he means to make that charge? Then there are the editors of the *Union*, the framers of the Lecompton constitution, the President of the United States and his Cabinet, and all the supporters of the Lecompton constitution in Congress and out of Congress, who are all involved in this "fatal blow being struck." I commend to Judge Douglas' consideration the question of *how corrupt a man's heart must be to make such a charge!* [Vociferous cheering.]

Now my friends, I have but one branch of the subject, in the little time I have left, to which to call your attention, and as I shall come to a close at the end of that branch, it is probable that I shall not occupy quite all the time allotted to me. Although on these questions I would like to talk twice as long as I have, I could not enter upon another head and discuss it properly without running over my time. I ask the attention of the people here assembled and elsewhere, to the course that Judge Douglas is pursuing every day as bearing upon this question of making slavery national. Not going back to the records but taking the speeches he makes, the speeches he made yesterday and day before and makes constantly all over the country—I ask your attention to them. In the first place what is necessary to make the institution national? Not war. There is no danger that the people of Kentucky will shoulder the muskets and with a young nigger stuck on every bayonet march into Illinois and force them upon us. There is no danger of our going over there and making war upon them. Then what is necessary for the nationalization of slavery? It is simply the next Dred Scot decision. It is merely for the Supreme Court to decide that no state under the Constitution can exclude it, just as they have already decided that under the Constitution neither Congress nor the territorial legislature can do it. When that is decided and acquiesced in, the whole thing is done. This being true, and this being the way as I think that slavery is to be made national, let us consider what Judge Douglas is doing every day to that end. In the first place, let us see what influence he is exerting on public sentiment. In this and like communities, public sentiment is everything. With public sentiment, nothing can fail; without it nothing can succeed. Consequently he who moulds public sentiment, goes deeper than he who enacts statutes or pronounces decisions. He makes statutes and decisions possible or impossible to be executed. This must be borne in mind, as also the additional fact that Judge Douglas is a man of vast influence, so great that it is enough for many men to profess to believe anything, when they once find out that Judge Douglas professes to believe it. Consider also the attitude he occupies at the head of a large party—a party which he claims has a majority of all the voters in the country. This man sticks to a decision which forbids the people of a territory from excluding slavery, and he does so not because he says it is right in itself—he does not give any opinion on that—but because it has been *decided by the Court,* and being decided by the Court, he is, and you are bound to take it in your political action as *law*—not that he judges at all of its merits, but because a decision of the Court is to him a *"Thus saith the Lord."* [Applause.] He places it on that

ground alone, and you will bear in mind that thus committing himself unreservedly to this decision, *commits him to the next one* just
as firmly as to this. He did not commit himself on account of the
merit or demerit of the decision, but it is a *Thus saith the Lord*. The
next decision, as much as this, will be a *thus saith the Lord*. There
is nothing that can divert or turn him away from this decision. It is
nothing that I point out to him that his great prototype, Gen. Jackson, did not believe in the binding force of decisions. It is nothing to
him that Jefferson did not so believe. I have said that I have often
heard him approve of Jackson's course in disregarding the decision
of the Supreme Court pronouncing a national bank constitutional.
He says, I did not hear him say so. He denies the accuracy of my
recollection. I say he ought to know better than I, but I will make
no question about this thing, though it still seems to me that I heard
him say it twenty times. [Applause and laughter.] I will tell him
though, that he now claims to stand on the Cincinnati platform,
which affirms that Congress *cannot* charter a national bank, in the
teeth of that old standing decision that Congress *can* charter a bank.
[Loud applause.] And I remind him of another piece of history on
the question of respect for judicial decisions, and it is a piece of
Illinois history, belonging to a time when the large party to which
Judge Douglas belonged, were displeased with a decision of the
Supreme Court of Illinois, because they had decided that a Governor
could not remove a Secretary of State. You will find the whole story
in Ford's *History of Illinois,* and I know that Judge Douglas will not
deny that he was then in favor of overslaughing that decision by
the mode of adding five new judges, so as to vote down the four old
ones. Not only so, but it ended in *the Judge's sitting down on that
very bench as one of the five new Judges to break down the four
old ones.* [Cheers and laughter.] It was in this way precisely that
he got his title of Judge. Now, when the Judge tells me that men
appointed conditionally to sit as members of a court, will have to
be catechised beforehand upon some subject, I say "You know
Judge; you have tried it." [Laughter.] When he says a court of this
kind will lose the confidence of all men, will be prostituted and
disgraced by such a proceeding, I say, "You know best, Judge; you
have been through the mill." [Great laughter.] But I cannot shake
Judge Douglas' teeth loose from the Dred Scott decision. Like some
obstinate animal (I mean no disrespect,) that will hang on when
he has once got his teeth fixed, you may cut off a leg, or you may
tear away an arm, still he 'will not relax his hold. And so I may
point out to the Judge, and say that he is bespattered all over, from

the beginning of his political life to the present time, with attacks upon judicial decisions—I may cut off limb after limb of his public record, and strive to wrench him from a single dictum of the Court —yet I cannot divert him from it. He hangs to the last, to the Dred Scott decision. [Loud cheers.] These things show there is a purpose *strong as death and eternity* for which he adheres to this decision, and for which he will adhere to *all other decisions* of the same Court. [Vociferous applause.]

A HIBERNIAN—Give us something besides Dred Scott.

MR. LINCOLN—Yes; no doubt you want to hear something that don't hurt. [Laughter and applause.] Now, having spoken of the Dred Scott decision, one more word and I am done. Henry Clay, my beau ideal of a statesman, the man for whom I fought all my humble life—Henry Clay once said of a class of men who would repress all tendencies to liberty and ultimate emancipation, that they must, if they would do this, go back to the era of our independence, and muzzle the cannon which thunders its annual joyous return; they must blow out the moral lights around us; they must penetrate the human soul, and eradicate there the love of liberty; and then and not till then, could they perpetuate slavery in this country! [Loud cheers.] To my thinking, Judge Douglas is, by his example and vast influence, doing that very thing in this community, [cheers,] when he says that the negro has nothing in the Declaration of Independence. Henry Clay plainly understood the contrary. Judge Douglas is going back to the era of our Revolution, and to the extent of his ability, muzzling the cannon which thunders its annual joyous return. When he invites any people willing to have slavery, to establish it, he is blowing out the moral lights around us. [Cheers.] When he says he "cares not whether slavery is voted down or voted up,"—that it is a sacred right of self-government—he is in my judgment penetrating the human soul and eradicating the light of reason and the love of liberty in this American people. [Enthusiastic and continued applause.] And now I will only say that when, by all these means and appliances, Judge Douglas shall succeed in bringing public sentiment to an exact accordance with his own views—when these vast assemblages shall echo back all these sentiments—when they shall come to repeat his views and to avow his principles, and to say all that he says on these mighty questions— then it needs only the formality of the second Dred Scott decision, which he endorses in advance, to make slavery alike lawful in all the states—old as well as new, North as well as South.

My friends, that ends the chapter. The Judge can take his half-hour.

Douglas' Rejoinder

Fellow citizens:

I will now occupy the half-hour allotted to me in replying to Mr. Lincoln. The first point to which I will call your attention is, as to what I said about the organization of the Republican party in 1854, and the platform that was formed on the 5th of October, of that year, and I will then put the question to Mr. Lincoln whether or not he approves of each article in that platform ("he answered that already"), and ask for a specific answer. ("He has answered." "You cannot make him answer," &c.) I did not charge him with being a member of the committee which reported that platform. ("Yes, you did.") I charged that that platform was the platform of the Republican party adopted by them. The fact that it was the platform of the Republican party is not denied, but Mr. Lincoln now says, that although his name was on the committee which reported it, that he does not think he was there, but thinks he was in Tazewell, holding court. ("He said he was there.") Gentlemen, I ask your silence, and no interruption. Now, I want to remind Mr. Lincoln that he was at Springfield, when that convention was held, and those resolutions adopted. ("You can't do it." "He wasn't there," &c.)

[Mr. Glover, chairman of the Republican committee—I hope no Republican will interrupt Mr. Douglas. The masses listened to Mr. Lincoln attentively, and as respectable men we ought now to hear Mr. Douglas, and without interruption.] ("Good.")

Mr. Douglas, resuming—The point I am going to remind Mr. Lincoln of is this: that after I had made my speech in 1854, during the fair, he gave me notice that he was going to reply to me the next day. I was sick at the time, but I staid over in Springfield to hear his reply and to reply to him. On that day this very convention, the resolutions adopted by which I have read, was to meet in the Senate chamber. He spoke in the hall of the House; and when he got through his speech—my recollection is distinct, and I shall never forget it—Mr. Codding[6] walked in as I took the stand to reply, and gave notice that the Republican State Convention would meet instantly in the Senate chamber, and called upon the Republicans to retire there and go into this very convention, instead of remaining and listening to me. (Three cheers for Douglas.)

Mr. Lincoln, interrupting, excitedly and angrily—Judge, add that

---

[6] Ichabod Codding, Congregational minister, Abolitionist, lecturer on temperance and other subjects beloved of the radicals of the time.

I went along with them. (This interruption was made in a pitiful, mean, sneaking way, as Lincoln floundered around the stand.)

MR. DOUGLAS—Gentlemen, Mr. Lincoln tells me to add that he went along with them to the Senate chamber. I will not add that, because I do not know whether he did or not.

MR. LINCOLN, again interrupting—I know he did not.

[Two of the Republican committee here seized Mr. Lincoln, and by a sudden jerk caused him to disappear from the front of the stand, one of them saying quite audibly, "What are you making such a fuss for. Douglas didn't interrupt you, and can't you see that the people don't like it."]

MR. DOUGLAS—I do not know whether he knows it or not, that is not the point, and I will yet bring him to on the question.

In the first place—Mr. Lincoln was selected by the very men who made the Republican organization, on that day to reply to me. He spoke for them and for that party, and he was the leader of the party; and on the very day he made his speech in reply to me preaching up this same doctrine of negro equality, under the Declaration of Independence, this Republican party met in convention. (Three cheers for Douglas.) Another evidence that he was acting in concert with them is to be found in the fact that that convention waited an hour after its time of meeting to hear Lincoln's speech, and Codding, one of their leading men marched in the moment Lincoln got through, and gave notice that they did not want to hear me and would proceed with the business of the convention. ("Strike him again,"—three cheers, etc.) Still another fact. I have here a newspaper printed at Springfield, Mr. Lincoln's own town, in October, 1854, a few days afterwards, publishing these resolutions, charging Mr. Lincoln with entertaining these sentiments, and trying to prove that they were also the sentiments of Mr. Yates, then candidate for Congress. This has been published on Mr. Lincoln over and over again, and never before has he denied it. (Three cheers.)

But my friends, this denial of his that he did not act on the committee is a miserable quibble to avoid the main issue, (applause) ("That's so,") which is that this Republican platform declares in favor of the unconditional repeal of the fugitive slave law. Has Lincoln answered whether he endorsed that or not? ("No, no.") I called his attention to it when I first addressed you and asked him for an answer and I then predicted that he would not answer. ("Bravo," "glorious" and cheers.) How does he answer? Why that he was not on the committee that wrote the resolutions. (Laughter.) I then repeated the next proposition contained in the resolutions, which was to restrict slavery in those states in which it exists and asked him whether he endorsed it. Does he answer yes, or no? He says in reply, "I was not on the committee at the time; I was up in Tazewell." The next question I put to him was, whether he was in favor of prohibiting the admission of any more slave states into the Union. I put the question to him distinctly, whether, if the people of the territory, when they had sufficient population to make a state, should form their constitution recognizing slavery, he would vote for or against its admission. ("That's it.") He is a candidate for the United States Senate, and it is possible, if he should be elected, that he would have to vote directly on that question. ("He never will.") I asked him to answer me and you whether he would vote to admit a state into the Union, with slavery or without it, as its own people might choose. ("Hear him," "That's the doctrine," and applause.) He did not answer that question. ("He never will.") He dodges that question also, under the cover that he was not on the committee at the time, that he was not present when the platform was made. I want to know if he should happen to be in the Senate when a state applied for admission, with a constitution acceptable to her own people, he would vote to admit that state, if slavery was one of its institutions. ("That's the question.") He avoids the answer.

MR. LINCOLN—interrupting the third time excitedly, "No, Judge" —(Mr. Lincoln again disappeared suddenly aided by a pull from behind.)

MR. DOUGLAS. It is true he gives the Abolitionists to understand by a hint that he would not vote to admit such a state. And why? He goes on to say that the man who would talk about giving each state the right to have slavery, or not, as it pleased, was akin to the man who would muzzle the guns which thundered forth the annual joyous return of the day of our independence. (Great laughter.) He says that that kind of talk is casting a blight on the glory of this country. What is the meaning of that? That he is not in favor of each state having the right to do as it pleases on the slavery question? ("Stick it to him," "don't spare him," and applause.) I will put the question to him again and again, and I intend to force it out of him. (Immense applause.)

Then again, this platform which was made at Springfield by his own party, when he was its acknowledged head, provides that Republicans will insist on the abolition of slavery in the District of Columbia, and I asked Lincoln specifically whether he agreed with them in that? Did you get an answer? ("No, no.") He is afraid to answer it. ("We will not vote for him.") He knows I will trot him down to Egypt.[7] (Laughter and cheers.) I intend to make him

[7] The southernmost quarter of Illinois.

answer there, ("that's right,") or I will show the people of Illinois that he does not intend to answer these questions. ("Keep him to the point," "give us more," etc.) The convention to which I have been alluding goes a little further, and pledges itself to exclude slavery from all the territories over which the general government has exclusive jurisdiction north of 36 deg. 30 min., as well as south. Now I want to know whether he approves that provision. ("He'll never answer" and cheers.) I want him to answer, and when he does, I want to know his opinion on another point, which is, whether he will redeem the pledge of this platform and resist the acquirement of any more territory unless slavery therein shall be forever prohibited. I want him to answer this last question. Each of the questions I have put to him are practical questions, questions based upon the fundamental principles of the Black Republican party, and I want to know whether he is the first, last and only choice of a party with whom he does not agree in principle. (Great applause.) ("Rake him down.") He does not deny but that that principle was unanimously adopted by the Republican party; he does not deny that the whole Republican party is pledged to it; he does not deny that a man who is not faithful to it is faithless to the Republican party, and now I want to know whether that party is unanimously in favor of a man who does not adopt that creed and agree with them in their principles: I want to know whether the man who does not agree with them, and who is afraid to avow his differences and who dodges the issue, is the first, last and only choice of the Republican party. (Cheers.)

A VOICE.—"How about the conspiracy?"

MR. DOUGLAS—Never mind, I will come to that soon enough. ("Bravo, Judge," "hurra," three cheers for Douglas.) But the platform which I have read to you not only lays down these principles but it adds:

> Resolved, That in furtherance of these principles we will use such constitutional and lawful means as shall seem best adapted to their accomplishment, and that we will support no man for office, under the general or state government, who is not positively and fully committed to the support of these principles, and whose personal character and conduct is not a guarantee that he is reliable, and who shall not have abjured old party allegiance and ties.

("Good," "you have him," &c.)

The Black Republican party stands pledged that they will never support Lincoln until he has pledged himself to that platform, (tremendous applause, men throwing up their hats, and shouting, "you've got him,") but he cannot devise his answer; he has not made up his mind, whether he will or not. (Great laughter.) He talked about everything else he could think of to occupy his hour and a half, and when he could not think of anything more to say, without an excuse for refusing to answer these questions, he sat down long before his time was out. (Cheers.)

In relation to Mr. Lincoln's charge of conspiracy against me, I have a word to say. In his speech to-day he quotes a playful part of his speech at Springfield, about Stephen, and James, and Franklin, and Roger, and says that I did not take exception to it. I did not answer it, and he repeats it again. I did not take exception to this figure of his. He has a right to be as playful as he pleases in throwing his arguments together, and I will not object; but I did take objection to his second Springfield speech, in which he stated that he intended his first speech a charge of corruption or conspiracy against the Supreme Court of the United States, President Pierce, President Buchanan, and myself. That gave the offensive character to the charge. He then said that when he made it he did not know whether it was true or not (laughter), but inasmuch as Judge Douglas had not denied it, although he had replied to the other parts of his speech three times, he repeated it as a charge of conspiracy against me, thus charging me with moral turpitude. When he put it in that form I did say that inasmuch as he repeated the charge simply because I had not denied it, I would deprive him of the opportunity of ever repeating it again, by declaring that it was in all its bearings an infamous lie. [Three cheers for Douglas.] He says he will repeat it until I answer his folly, and nonsense about Stephen, and Franklin, and Roger, and Bob, and James.

He studied that out, prepared that one sentence with the greatest care, committed it to memory, and put it in his first Springfield speech, and now he carries that speech around and reads that sentence to show how pretty it is. (Laughter.) His vanity is wounded because I will not go into that beautiful figure of his about the building of a house. (Renewed laughter.) All I have to say is, that I am not green enough to let him make a charge which he acknowledges he does not know to be true, and then take up my time in answering it, when I know it to be false and nobody else knows it to be true. (Cheers.)

I have not brought a charge of moral turpitude against him. When he, or any other man, brings one against me, instead of disproving it I will say that it is a lie, and let him prove it if he can. (Enthusiastic applause.)

I have lived twenty-five years in Illinois. I have served you with all the fidelity and ability which I possess, ("That's so," "good," and cheers,) and Mr. Lincoln is at liberty to attack my public action, my votes, and my conduct; but when he dares to attack my moral integrity, by a charge of conspiracy between myself, Chief Justice Taney, and the Supreme Court and two Presidents of the United States, I will repel it. ("Three cheers for Douglas.")

Mr. Lincoln has not character enough for integrity and truth merely on his own *ipse dixit* to arraign President Buchanan, President Pierce, and nine judges of the Supreme Court, not one of whom would be complimented by being put on an equality with him. ("Hit him again, three cheers" &c.) There is an unpardonable presumption in a man putting himself up before thousands of people, and pretending that his *ipse dixit,* without proof, without fact and without truth, is enough to bring down and destroy the purest and best of living men. ("Hear him," "Three cheers.")

Fellow-citizens, my time is fast expiring; I must pass on. Mr. Lincoln wants to know why I voted against Mr. Chase's amendment to the Nebraska Bill. I will tell him. In the first place, the bill already conferred all the power which Congress had, by giving the people the whole power over the subject. Chase offered a proviso that they might abolish slavery, which by implication would convey the idea that they could prohibit by not introducing that institution. Gen. Cass[8] asked him to modify his amendment, so as to provide that the people might either prohibit or introduce slavery, and thus make it fair and equal. Chase refused to so modify his proviso, and then Gen. Cass and all the rest of us, voted it down. (Immense cheering.) These facts appear on the journals and debates of Congress, where Mr. Lincoln found the charge, and if he had told the whole truth, there would have been no necessity for me to occupy your time in explaining the matter. (Laughter and applause.)

Mr. Lincoln wants to know why the word "state," as well as "territory," was put into the Nebraska Bill! I will tell him. It was put there to meet just such false arguments as he has been adducing. (Laughter.) That first, not only the people of the territories should do as they pleased, but that when they come to be admitted as states, they should come into the Union with or without slavery, as the people determined. I meant to knock in the head this abolition doctrine of Mr. Lincoln's, that there shall be no more slave states, even if the people want them. (Tremendous applause.) And it does not do for him to say, or for any other Black Republican to say, that there is nobody in favor of the doctrine of no more slave states, and that nobody wants to interfere with the right of the people to

---

[8] Lewis Cass, U.S. Senator from Michigan in 1854. Salmon P. Chase, Governor of Ohio in 1858, had served in the U.S. Senate from 1849 to 1855.

do as they please. What was the origin of the Missouri difficulty and the Missouri Compromise? The people of Missouri formed a constitution as a slave state, and asked admission into the Union, but the Free Soil party of the North being in a majority, refused to admit her because she had slavery as one of her institutions. Hence this first slavery agitation arose upon a state and not upon a territory, and yet Mr. Lincoln does not know why the word state was placed in the Kansas-Nebraska Bill. (Great laughter and applause.) The whole abolition agitation arose on that doctrine of prohibiting a state from coming in with slavery or not, as it pleased, and that same doctrine is here in this Republican platform of 1854; it has never been repealed; and every Black Republican stands pledged by that platform, never to vote for any man who is not in favor of it. Yet Mr. Lincoln does not know that there is a man in the world who is in favor of preventing a state from coming in as it pleases, notwithstanding. The Springfield platform says that they, the Republican party, will not allow a state to come in under such circumstances. He is an ignorant man. (Cheers.)

Now you see that upon these very points I am as far from bringing Mr. Lincoln up to the line as I ever was before. He does not want to avow his principles. I do want to avow mine, as clear as sunlight in mid-day. (Cheers and applause.) Democracy is founded upon the eternal principle of right. ("That is the talk.") The plainer these principles are avowed before the people, the stronger will be the support which they will receive. I only wish I had the power to make them so clear that they would shine in the heavens for every man, woman, and child to read. (Loud cheering.) The first of those principles that I would proclaim would be in opposition to Mr. Lincoln's doctrine of uniformity between the different states, and I would declare instead the sovereign right of each state to decide the slavery question as well as all other domestic questions for themselves, without interference from any other state or power whatsoever. ("Hurrah for Douglas.")

When that principle is recognized you will have peace and harmony and fraternal feeling between all the states of this Union; until you do recognize that doctrine there will be sectional warfare agitating and distracting the country. What does Mr. Lincoln propose? He says that the Union cannot exist divided into free and slave states. If it cannot endure thus divided, then he must strive to make them all free or all slave, which will inevitably bring about a dissolution of the Union. (Cries of "he can't do it.")

Gentlemen, I am told that my time is out and I am obliged to stop. (Three times three cheers were here given for Senator Douglas.)

CHAPTER FIVE

THE FREEPORT DEBATE

With the Freeport debate set for August 27, both Lincoln and Douglas remained in western and northwestern Illinois. On August 23 Lincoln spoke at Henry; on the 25th he addressed meetings at Augusta and Macomb. Douglas filled only one major engagement: a Democratic rally at Galena on the 25th. The Little Giant was having trouble with his voice. "Senator Douglas spoke for two hours and a quarter with great apparent ease," the Times *commented,[1] "although for the past few days he has been suffering from a severe bronchial affection from which he has not yet entirely recovered."*

On the night of August 26 Douglas proceeded by train from Galena to Freeport. The Times *described the reception accorded him:[2]*

As he stepped upon the platform, he was greeted with tremendous shouts and cheers. A grand salute was fired at the same time, which, as it resounded through the city, gave notice to the people that the champion of popular rights had arrived, and thousands of persons flocked from the hotels and from all parts of the city, swelling the assemblage to not less than five thousand persons. A procession was formed, and, with not less than a thousand torches, music, the cheers of the people, and the thunders of the cannon, Judge Douglas was escorted to the Brewster House. When the head of the procession reached the hotel, the ranks opened, and the carriage containing the people's guest drove up to the door. At this moment the scene was the grandest ever beheld in Freeport. The whole area of the streets in the vicinity of the hotel was densely packed; a few squares off, the cannon was belching forth its notes of welcome; a thousand torches blazed with brilliancy; the crowd cheered lustily, and from windows, balconies, house-tops, etc., there were to be seen the smiling faces and waving handkerchiefs of ladies.

Lincoln, who had spent the night of August 26 at Amboy, reached Freeport on a twelve-car special train at 10:00 the following morn-

---

[1] August 28.   [2] August 29.

ing. A cold day, with cloudy skies that dripped rain during the morning, did not dampen the enthusiasm of the thousands who had invaded the city for the second debate. The warmth of the welcome attested the fact that Lincoln was in Republican territory. According to the Press and Tribune:[3]

Some two thousand citizens of Freeport and vicinity had assembled to escort him to the Brewster House. Six deafening cheers were given as our next Senator stepped from the cars; after which the whole company formed in procession and escorted him around the principal streets to the elegant hotel. Here the reception speech was delivered by Hon. Thomas J. Turner—to which Mr. Lincoln responded in a few appropriate remarks. Half an hour later a train of eight cars arrived from Galena. Another procession was formed, preceded by a banner on which was inscribed:

THE GALENA LINCOLN CLUB

The delegation marched to the Brewster House and gave three rousing cheers for Abraham Lincoln. Mr. L. appeared on the balcony and returned his thanks amid a storm of applause. But the special train on the Galena road from Rockford, Marengo and Belvidere, eclipsed the whole—*consisting of sixteen cars and over a thousand persons.* They also marched to the Brewster House with a national flag bearing the words:

WINNEBAGO COUNTY
FOR
"OLD ABE"

Mr. Lincoln was again called out and received with loud cheers...

At two o'clock the people rushed to the grove, a couple of squares in the rear of the Brewster House. The crowd was about one-third larger than that at Ottawa. It formed a vast circle around a pyramid of lumber in the centre, which had been erected for the speakers and reporters.

Here Lincoln had the opening. After a short introduction by Thomas J. Turner, the Republican contender rose to speak.

Lincoln's Opening Speech

Ladies and Gentlemen:

On Saturday last, Judge Douglas and myself first met in public discussion. He spoke one hour, I an hour-and-a-half, and he replied

[3] August 30, 1858.

for half an hour. The order is now reversed. I am to speak an hour, he an hour-and-a-half, and then I am to reply for half an hour. I propose to devote myself during the first hour to the scope of what was brought within the range of his half-hour speech at Ottawa. Of course there was brought within the scope in that half-hour's speech something of his own opening speech. In the course of that opening argument Judge Douglas proposed to me seven distinct interrogatories. In my speech of an hour and a half, I attended to some other parts of his speech, and incidentally, as I thought, answered one of the interrogatories then. I then distinctly intimated to him that I would answer the rest of his interrogatories on condition only that he should agree to answer as many for me. He made no intimation at the time of the proposition, nor did he in his reply allude at all to that suggestion of mine. I do him no injustice in saying that he occupied at least half of his reply in dealing with me as though I had *refused* to answer his interrogatories. I now propose that I will answer any of the interrogatories, upon condition that he will answer questions from me not exceeding the same number. I give him an opportunity to respond. The Judge remains silent. I now say to you that I will answer his interrogatories, whether he answers mine or not; [applause] and that after I have done so, I shall propound mine to him. [Applause.]

[Owing to the press of people against the platform, our reporter did not reach the stand until Mr. Lincoln had spoken to this point. The previous remarks were taken by a gentleman in Freeport, who has politely furnished them to us.]

I have supposed myself, since the organization of the Republican party at Bloomington, in May, 1856, bound as a party man by the platforms of the party, then and since. If in any interrogatories which I shall answer I go beyond the scope of what is within these platforms it will be perceived that no one is responsible but myself.

Having said thus much, I will take up the Judge's interrogatories as I find them printed in the Chicago *Times*, and answer them *seriatim*. In order that there may be no mistake about it, I have copied the interrogatories in writing, and also my answers to them. The first one of these interrogatories is in these words:

Question 1. "I desire to know whether Lincoln to-day stands, as he did in 1854, in favor of the unconditional repeal of the fugitive slave law?"

Answer. I do not now, nor ever did, stand in favor of the unconditional repeal of the fugitive slave law. [Cries of "Good," "Good."]

Q. 2. "I desire him to answer whether he stands pledged today, as he did in 1854, against the admission of any more slave states into the Union, even if the people want them?"

A. I do not now, nor ever did, stand pledged against the admission of any more slave states into the Union.

Q. 3. "I want to know whether he stands pledged against the admission of a new state into the Union with such a constitution as the people of that state may see fit to make."

A. I do not stand pledged against the admission of a new state into the Union, with such a constitution as the people of that state may see fit to make. [Cries of "good," "good."]

Q. 4. "I want to know whether he stands to-day pledged to the abolition of slavery in the District of Columbia?"

A. I do not stand to-day pledged to the abolition of slavery in the District of Columbia.

Q. 5. "I desire him to answer whether he stands pledged to the prohibition of the slave trade between the different states?"

A. I do not stand pledged to the prohibition of the slave trade between the different states.

Q. 6. "I desire to know whether he stands pledged to prohibit slavery in all the territories of the United States, north as well as south of the Missouri Compromise line."

A. I am impliedly, if not expressly, pledged to a belief in the *right* and *duty* of Congress to prohibit slavery in all the United States territories. [Great applause.]

Q. 7. "I desire him to answer whether he is opposed to the acquisition of any new territory unless slavery is first prohibited therein."

A. I am not generally opposed to honest acquisition of territory; and, in any given case, I would or would not oppose such acquisition, accordingly as I might think such acquisition would or would not aggravate the slavery question among ourselves. [Cries of "good, good."]

Now, my friends, it will be perceived upon an examination of these questions and answers, that so far I have only answered that I was not *pledged* to this, that or the other. The Judge has not framed his interrogatories to ask me anything more than this, and I have answered in strict accordance with the interrogatories, and have answered truly that I am not *pledged* at all upon any of the points to which I have answered. But I am not disposed to hang upon the exact form of his interrogatory. I am rather disposed to take up at least some of these questions, and state what I really think upon them.

As to the first one, in regard to the fugitive slave law, I have never hesitated to say, and I do not now hesitate to say, that I think, under the Constitution of the United States, the people of the southern states are entitled to a congressional fugitive slave law. Having said that, I have had nothing to say in regard to the existing fugitive slave law further than that I think it should have been framed so as to be free from some of the objections that pertain to it, without lessening its efficiency. And inasmuch as we are not now in an agitation in regard to an alteration or modification of that law, I would not be the man to introduce it as a new subject of agitation upon the general question of slavery.

In regard to the other question of whether I am pledged to the admission of any more slave states into the Union, I state to you very frankly that I would be exceedingly sorry ever to be put in a position of having to pass upon that question. I should be exceedingly glad to know that there would never be another slave state admitted into the Union; [applause]; but I must add, that if slavery shall be kept out of the territories during the territorial existence of any one given territory, and then the people shall, having a fair chance and a clear field, when they come to adopt the constitution, do such an extraordinary thing as to adopt a slave constitution, uninfluenced by the actual presence of the institution among them, I see no alternative, if we own the country, but to admit them into the Union. [Applause.]

The third interrogatory is answered by the answer to the second, it being, as I conceive, the same as the second.

The fourth one is in regard to the abolition of slavery in the District of Columbia. In relation to that, I have my mind very distinctly made up. I should be exceedingly glad to see slavery abolished in the District of Columbia. [Cries of "good, good."] I believe that Congress possesses the constitutional power to abolish it. Yet as a member of Congress, I should not with my present views, be in favor of *endeavoring* to abolish slavery in the District of Columbia, unless it would be upon these conditions. *First,* that the abolition should be gradual. *Second,* that it should be on a vote of the majority of qualified voters in the District, and *third,* that compensation should be made to unwilling owners. With these three conditions, I confess I would be exceedingly glad to see.Congress abolish slavery in the District of Columbia, and, in the language of Henry Clay, "sweep from our Capital that foul blot upon our nation." [Loud applause.]

In regard to the fifth interrogatory, I must say here, that as to the question of the abolition of the slave trade between the different states, I can truly answer, as I have, that I am *pledged* to nothing about it. It is a subject to which I have not given that mature consideration that would make me feel authorized to state a position so as to hold myself entirely bound by it. In other words, that question has never been prominently enough before me to induce me to investigate whether we really have the constitutional power to do it. I could investigate it if I had sufficient time, to bring myself to a conclusion upon that subject, but I have not done so, and I say so frankly to you here, and to Judge Douglas. I must say, however, that if I should be of opinion that Congress does possess the constitutional power to abolish the slave trade among the different states, I should still not be in favor of the exercise of that power unless upon some conservative principle as I conceive it, akin to what I have said in relation to the abolition of slavery in the District of Columbia.

My answer as to whether I desire that slavery should be prohibited in all the territories of the United States is full and explicit within itself, and cannot be made clearer by any comments of mine. So I suppose in regard to the question whether I am opposed to the acquisition of any more territory unless slavery is first prohibited therein, my answer is such that I could add nothing by way of illustration, or making myself better understood, than the answer which I have placed in writing.

Now in all this, the Judge has me and he has me on the record. I suppose he had flattered himself that I was really entertaining one set of opinions for one place and another set for another place— that I was afraid to say at one place what I uttered at another. What I am saying here I suppose I say to a vast audience as strongly tending to Abolitionism as any audience in the state of Illinois, and I believe I am saying that which, if it would be offensive to any persons and render them enemies to myself, would be offensive to persons in this audience.

I now proceed to propound to the Judge the interrogatories, so far as I have framed them. I will bring forward a new installment when I get them ready. [Laughter.] I will bring them forward now, only reaching to number four.

The first one is—

Question 1. If the people of Kansas shall, by means entirely unobjectionable in all other respects, adopt a state constitution, and ask admission into the Union under it, *before* they have the requisite number of inhabitants according to the English Bill—some ninety-three thousand—will you vote to admit them? [Applause.]

Q. 2. Can the people of a United States territory, in any lawful way, against the wish of any citizen of the United States, exclude slavery from its limits prior to the formation of a state constitution? [Renewed applause.]

Q. 3. If the Supreme Court of the United States shall decide that states can not exclude slavery from their limits, are you in favor of acquiescing in, adopting and following such decision as a rule of political action? [Loud applause.]

Q. 4. Are you in favor of acquiring additional territory, in disregard of how such acquisition may affect the nation on the slavery question? [Cries of "good," "good."]

As introductory to these interrogatories which Judge Douglas propounded to me at Ottawa, he read a set of resolutions which he said Judge Trumbull and myself had participated in adopting, in the first Republican State Convention held at Springfield, in October, 1854. He insisted that I and Judge Trumbull, and perhaps, the entire Republican party were responsible for the doctrines contained in the set of resolutions which he read, and I understand that it was from that set of resolutions that he deduced the interrogatories which he propounded to me, using these resolutions as a sort of authority for propounding those questions to me. Now I say here to-day that I do not answer his interrogatories because of their springing at all from that set of resolutions which he read. I answered them because Judge Douglas thought fit to ask them. [Applause.] I do not now, nor never did recognize any responsibility upon myself in that set of resolutions. When I replied to him on that occasion, I assured him that I never had anything to do with them. I repeat here to-day, that I never in any possible form had anything to do with that set of resolutions. It turns out, I believe, that those resolutions were never passed in any convention held in Springfield. [Cheers and Laughter.] It turns out that they were never passed at any convention or any public meeting that I had any part in. I believe it turns out in addition to all this, that there was not, in the fall of 1854, any convention holding a session in Springfield, calling itself a Republican State Convention; yet it is true there was a convention, or assemblage of men calling themselves a convention, at Springfield, that did pass *some* resolutions. But so little did I really know of the proceedings of that convention, or what set of resolutions they had passed, though having a general knowledge that there had been such an assemblage of men there, that when Judge Douglas read the resolutions, I really did not know but they had been the resolutions passed then and there. I did not question that they were the resolutions adopted. For I could not bring myself to suppose that Judge Douglas could say what he did upon this subject without *knowing* that it was true. [Cheers and laughter.] I contented myself, on that occasion, with denying, as I truly could, all connection with them, not denying or affirming whether they were passed at Springfield. Now it turns out that he had got hold of some resolutions passed at some convention or public meeting in Kane County. [Renewed laughter.] I wish to say here that I don't conceive that in any fair and just mind this discovery relieves me at all. I had just as much to do with the convention in Kane County as that in Springfield. I am just as much responsible for the resolutions at Kane County as those at Springfield, the amount of the responsibility being exactly nothing in either case; no more than there would be in regard to a set of resolutions passed in the moon. [Laughter and loud cheers.]

I allude to this extraordinary matter in this canvass for some further purpose than anything yet advanced. Judge Douglas did not make his statement upon that occasion as matters that he believed to be true, but he stated them roundly as *being true,* in such form as to pledge his veracity for their truth. When the whole matter turns out as it does, and when we consider who Judge Douglas is— that he is a distinguished Senator of the United States—that he has served nearly twelve years as such—that his character is not at all limited as an ordinary Senator of the United States, but that his name has become of world-wide renown—it is *most extraordinary* that he should so far forget all the suggestions of justice to an adversary, or of prudence to himself, as to venture upon the assertion of that which the slightest investigation would have shown him to be wholly false. [Cheers.] I can only account for his having done so upon the supposition that that evil genius which has attended him through his life, giving to him an apparent astonishing prosperity, such as to lead very many good men to doubt there being any advantage in virtue over vice—[Cheers and laughter] I say I can only account for it on the supposition that that evil genius has at last made up its mind to forsake him. [Continued cheers and laughter.]

And I may add that another extraordinary feature of the Judge's conduct in this canvass—made more extraordinary by this incident— is that he is in the habit, in almost all the speeches he makes, of charging falsehood upon his adversaries—myself and others. I now ask whether he is able to find in anything that Judge Trumbull, for instance, has said, or in anything that I have said, a justification at all compared with what we have, in this instance, for that sort of vulgarity. [Cries of "good," "good," "good."]

I have been in the habit of charging as a matter of belief on my part, that, in the introduction of the Nebraska Bill into Congress, there was a conspiracy to make slavery perpetual and national. I have arranged from time to time the evidence which establishes and proves the truth of this charge. I recurred to this charge at Ottawa. I shall not now have time to dwell upon it at very great length, but inasmuch as Judge Douglas in his reply of half an hour, made some points upon me in relation to it, I propose noticing a few of them.

The Judge insists that, in the first speech I made, in which I very distinctly made that charge, he thought for a good while I was in fun! that I was playful—that I was not sincere about it—and that he only grew angry and somewhat excited when he found that I insisted upon it as a matter of earnestness. He says he characterised it as a falsehood as far as I implicated his *moral character* in that transaction. Well, I did not know, till he presented that view that I had implicated his moral character. He is very much in the habit, when he argues me up into a position I never thought of occupying, of very cosily saying he has no doubt Lincoln is "conscientious" in saying so. He should remember that I did not know but what *he* WAS ALTOGETHER "CONSCIENTIOUS" in that matter. [Great laughter.] I can conceive it possible for men to conspire to do a good thing, and I really find nothing in Judge Douglas' course or arguments that is contrary to or inconsistent with his belief of a conspiracy to nationalize and spread slavery as being a good and blessed thing, [continued laughter,] and so I hope he will understand that I do not at all question but that in all this matter he is entirely "conscientious." [More laughter and cheers.]

But to draw your attention to one of the points I made in this case, beginning at the beginning. When the Nebraska Bill was introduced, or a short time afterwards, by an amendment I believe, it was provided that it must be considered "the true intent and meaning of this act not to legislative slavery into any state or territory, or to exclude it therefrom, but to leave the people thereof perfectly free to form and regulate their own domestic institutions in their own way, subject only to the Constitution of the United States." I have called his attention to the fact that when he and some others began arguing that they were giving an increased degree of liberty to the people in the territories over and above what they formerly had on the question of slavery, a question was raised whether the law was enacted to give such unconditional liberty to the people, and to test the sincerity of this mode of argument, Mr. Chase, of Ohio, introduced an amendment, in which he made the law—if the amendment were adopted—expressly declare that the people of the territory should have the power to exclude slavery if they saw fit. I have asked attention also to the fact that Judge

Douglas and those who acted with him, voted that amendment down, notwithstanding it expressed exactly the thing they said was the true intent and meaning of the law. I have called attention to the fact that in subsequent times, a decision of the Supreme Court has been made in which it has been declared that a territorial legislature has no constitutional right to exclude slavery. And I have argued and said that for men who did intend that the people of the territory should have the right to exclude slavery absolutely and unconditionally, the voting down of Chase's amendment is wholly inexplicable. It is a puzzle—a riddle. But I have said that with men who did look forward to such a decision, or who had it in contemplation, that such a decision of the Supreme Court would or might be made, the voting down of that amendment would be perfectly rational and intelligible. It would keep Congress from coming in collision with the decision when it was made. Anybody can conceive that if there was an intention or expectation that such a decision was to follow, it would not be a very desirable party attitude to get into for the Supreme Court—all or nearly all its members belonging to the same party—to decide one way, when the party in Congress had decided the other way. Hence it would be very rational for men expecting such a decision, to keep the niche in that law clear for it. After pointing this out, I tell Judge Douglas that it looks to me as though here was the reason why Chase's amendment was voted down. I tell him that as he did it, and knows why he did it, if it was done for a reason different from this, *he knows what that reason was, and can tell us what it was.* I tell him, also, it will be vastly more satisfactory to the country, for him to give some other plausible, intelligible reason *why* it was voted down than to stand upon his dignity and call people liars. [Loud cheers.] Well, on Saturday he did make his answer, and what do you think it was? He says if I had only taken upon myself to tell the whole truth about that amendment of Chase's no explanation would have been necessary on his part—or words to that effect. Now, I say here, that I am quite unconscious of having suppressed anything material to the case, and I am very frank to admit if there is any sound reason other than that which appeared to me material, it is quite fair for him to present it. What reason does he propose? That when Chase came forward with his amendment expressly authorizing the people to exclude slavery from the limits of every territory, Gen. Cass proposed to Chase, if he (Chase) would add to his amendment that the people should have the power to *introduce* or exclude, they would let it go. (This is substantially all of his reply.) And because Chase would not do that, they voted his amendment down. Well, it turns out, I believe, upon examination, that General Cass took some part in the little running debate upon that amendment, and then ran away *and did not vote on it at all.* [Laughter.] Is not that the fact? So confident, as I think, was Gen. Cass, that there was a snake somewhere about, he chose to run away from the whole thing. This is an inference I draw from the fact that though he took part in the debate, his name does not appear in the ayes and noes. But does Judge Douglas' reply amount to a satisfactory answer? [Cries of "yes," "yes," and "no," "no."] There is some little difference of opinion here. [Laughter.] But I ask attention to a few more views bearing on the question of whether it amounts to a satisfactory answer. The men, who were determined that that amendment should not get into the bill and spoil the place where the Dred Scott decision was to come in, sought an excuse to get rid of it somewhere. One of these ways—one of these excuses—was to ask Chase to add to his proposed amendment a provision that the people might *introduce* slavery if they wanted to. They very well knew Chase would do no such thing—that Mr. Chase was one of the men differing from them on the broad principle of his insisting that freedom was *better* than slavery—a man who would not consent to enact a law, penned with his own hand, by which he was made to recognize slavery on the one hand and liberty on the other as *precisely equal;* and when they insisted on his doing this, they very well knew they insisted on that which he would not for a moment think of doing, and that they were only bluffing him. I believe (I have not, since he made his answer, had a chance to examine the journals or *Congressional Globe,* and therefore speak from memory)—I believe the state of the bill at that time, according to parliamentary rules, was such that no member could propose an additional amendment to Chase's amendment. I rather think this is the truth—the Judge shakes his head. Very well. I would like to know, then, *if they wanted Chase's amendment fixed over, why somebody else could not have offered to do it?* If they wanted it amended, why did they not offer the amendment? Why did they stand there taunting and quibbling at Chase? [Laughter.] Why did they not *put it in themselves?* But to put it on the other ground; suppose that there was such an amendment offered, and Chase's was an amendment to an amendment; until one is disposed of by parliamentary law, you cannot pile another on. Then all these gentlemen had to do was to vote Chase's on, and then in the amended form in which the whole stood, add their own amendment to it if they wanted it put in that shape. This was all they were obliged to do, and the ayes and noes show that there were 36 who voted it down, against 10 who voted in favor of it. The 36 held entire sway and control. They could in some form or other have put that bill in the exact shape they wanted. If there was a rule preventing their amending it at the time, they could pass that, and then Chase's amendment being merged, put it in the shape they wanted. They did not choose to do so, but they went into a quibble with Chase to get him to add what they knew he would not add, and because he would not, they stand upon that flimsy pretext for voting down what they argued was the meaning and intent of their own bill. They left room thereby for this Dred Scott decision, which goes very far to make slavery national throughout the United States.

I pass one or two points I have because my time will very soon expire, but I must be allowed to say that Judge Douglas recurs again, as he did upon one or two other occasions, [to] the enormity of Lincoln—an insignificant individual like Lincoln—upon his *ipse dixit* charging a conspiracy upon a large number of members of Congress, the Supreme Court and two Presidents, to nationalize slavery. I want to say that, in the first place, I have made no charge of this sort upon my *ipse dixit*. I have only arrayed the evidence tending to prove it, and presented it to the understanding of others, saying what I think it proves, but giving you the means of judging whether it proves it or not. This is precisely what I have done. I have not placed it upon my *ipse dixit* at all. On this occasion, I wish to recall his attention to a piece of evidence which I brought forward at Ottawa on Saturday, showing that he had made substantially the *same charge* against substantially the *same persons*, excluding his dear self from the category. I ask him to give some attention to the evidence which I brought forward, that he himself had discovered a "fatal blow being struck" against the right of the people to exclude slavery from their limits, which fatal blow he assumed as in evidence in an article in the Washington *Union*, published "by authority." I ask by whose authority? He discovers a similar or identical provision in the Lecompton constitution. Made by whom? The framers of that constitution. Advocated by whom? By all the members of the party in the nation, who advocated the introduction of Kansas into the Union under the Lecompton constitution.

I have asked his attention to the evidence that he arrayed to prove that such a fatal blow was being struck, and to the facts which he brought forward in support of that charge—being identical with the one which he thinks so villainous in me. He pointed it not at a newspaper editor merely, but at the President and his Cabinet and the members of Congress advocating the Lecompton constitution and those framing that instrument. I must again be permitted to remind him, that although my *ipse dixit* may not be as great as his, yet it somewhat reduces the force of his calling my attention to the *enormity* of my making a like charge against him. [Loud applause.]

Go on, Judge Douglas.

Douglas' Reply

Ladies and Gentlemen:

The silence with which you have listened to Mr. Lincoln during his hour is creditable to this vast audience, composed of men of various political parties. Nothing is more honorable to any large mass of people assembled for the purpose of a fair discussion, than that kind and respectful attention that is yielded not only to your political friends, but to those who are opposed to you in politics.

I am glad that at last I have brought Mr. Lincoln to the conclusion that he had better define his position on certain political questions to which I called his attention at Ottawa. He there showed no disposition, no inclination to answer them. I did not present idle questions for him to answer merely for my gratification. I laid the foundation for those interrogatories by showing that they constituted the platform of the party whose nominee he is for the Senate. I did not presume that I had the right to catechise him as I saw proper, unless I showed that his party, or a majority of it, stood upon the platform and were in favor of the propositions upon which my questions were based. I desired simply to know, inasmuch as he had been nominated as the first, last, and only choice of his party, whether he concurred in the platform which that party had adopted for its government. In a few moments I will proceed to review the answers which he has given to these interrogatories; but in order to relieve his anxiety I will first respond to those which he has presented to me. Mark you, he has not presented interrogatories which have ever received the sanction of the party with which I am acting, and hence he has no other foundation for them than his own curiosity. ("That's a fact.")

First, he desires to know if the people of Kansas shall form a constitution by means entirely proper and unobjectionable and ask admission into the Union as a state, before they have the requisite population for a member of Congress, whether I will vote for that admission. Well, now, I regret exceedingly that he did not answer that interrogatory himself before he put it to me, in order that we might understand, and not be left to infer, on which side he is. ("Good, good.") Mr. Trumbull, during the last session of Congress, voted from the beginning to the end against the admission of Oregon, although a free state, because she had not the requisite population for a member of Congress. ("That's it.") Mr. Trumbull would not consent, under any circumstances, to let a state, free or slave, come into the Union until it had the requisite population. As Mr. Trumbull is in the field, fighting for Mr. Lincoln, I would like to have Mr. Lincoln answer his own question and tell me whether he is fighting Trumbull on that issue or not. ("Good, put it to him," and cheers.) But I will answer his question. In reference to Kansas; it is my opinion, that as she has population enough to constitute a slave state, she has people enough for a free state. (Cheers.) I will not make Kansas an exceptional case to the other states of the Union. ("Sound," and "hear, hear.") I hold it to be a sound rule of universal application to require a territory to contain the requisite population for a member of Congress, before it is admitted as a state into the Union. I made that proposition in the Senate in 1856, and I renewed it during the last session, in a bill providing that no territory of the United States should form a constitution and apply for admission until it had the requisite population. On another occasion I proposed that neither Kansas, or any other territory, should be admitted until it had the requisite population. Congress did not adopt any of my propositions containing this general rule, but did make an exception of Kansas. I will stand by that exception. (Cheers.) Either Kansas must come in as a free state, with whatever population she may have, or the rule must be applied to all the other territories alike. (Cheers.) I therefore answer at once, that it having been decided that Kansas has people enough for a slave state, I hold that she has enough for a free state. ("Good," and applause.) I hope Mr. Lincoln is satisfied with my answer; ("he ought to be," and cheers,) and now I would like to get his answer to his own interrogatory—whether or not he will vote to admit Kansas before she has the requisite population. ("Hit him again.") I want to know whether he will vote to admit Oregon before that territory has the requisite population. Mr. Trumbull will not, and the same reason that commits Mr. Trumbull against the admission of Oregon, commits him against Kansas, even if she should apply for admission as a free state. ("You've got him," and cheers.) If there is any sincerity, any truth in the argument of Mr. Trumbull in the Senate against the admission of Oregon because she had not 93,420 people, although her population was larger than that of Kansas, he stands pledged against the admission of both Oregon and Kansas until they have 93,420 inhabitants. I would like Mr. Lincoln to answer this question. I would like him to take his own medicine. (Laughter.) If he differs with Mr. Trumbull, let him answer his argument against the admission of Oregon, instead of poking questions at me. ("Right, good, good," laughter and cheers.)

The next question propounded to me by Mr. Lincoln is, can the people of a territory in any lawful way against the wishes of any citizen of the United States; exclude slavery from their limits prior to the formation of a state constitution? I answer emphatically, as Mr. Lincoln has heard me answer a hundred times from every stump in Illinois, that in my opinion the people of a territory can, by lawful means, exclude slavery from their limits prior to the formation of a state constitution. (Enthusiastic applause.) Mr. Lincoln knew that I had answered that question over and over again. He heard me argue the Nebraska Bill on that principle all over the state in 1854, in 1855 and in 1856, and he has no excuse for pretending to be in doubt as to my position on that question. It matters not what way the Supreme Court may hereafter decide as to the abstract question whether slavery may or may not go into a territory under the Constitution, the people have the lawful means to introduce it or exclude it as they please, for the reason that slavery cannot exist a day or an hour anywhere, unless it is supported by local police regulations. ("Right, right.") Those police regulations can only be established by the local legislature, and if the people are opposed to slavery they will elect representatives to that body who will by unfriendly legislation effectually prevent the introduction of it into their midst. If, on the contrary, they are for it, their legislation will favor its extension. Hence, no matter what the decision of the Supreme Court may be on that abstract question, still the right of the people to make a slave territory or a free territory is perfect and complete under the Nebraska Bill. I hope Mr. Lincoln deems my answer satisfactory on that point.

[Deacon Bross spoke.][4]

In this connection, I will notice the charge which he has introduced in relation to Mr. Chase's amendment. I thought that I had chased that amendment out of Mr. Lincoln's brain at Ottawa; (laughter) but it seems that it still haunts his imagination, and he is not yet satisfied. I had supposed that he would be ashamed to

---

[4] William Bross, one of the proprietors of the Chicago *Press and Tribune.* Lincoln, in his debates scrapbook, deleted this and subsequent references to Bross. They are supplied here from the Chicago *Times'* report of the Freeport debate.

press that question further. He is a lawyer, and has been a member of Congress, and has occupied his time and amused you by telling you about parliamentary proceedings. He ought to have known better than to try to palm off his miserable impositions upon this intelligent audience. ("Good," and cheers.) The Nebraska Bill provided that the legislative power, and authority of the said territory, should extend to all rightful subjects of legislation consistent with the organic act and the Constitution of the United States. It did not make any exception as to slavery, but gave all the power that it was possible for Congress to give, without violating the Constitution to the territorial legislature, with no exception or limitation on the subject of slavery at all. The language of that bill which I have quoted, gave the full power and the full authority over the subject of slavery, affirmatively and negatively, to introduce it or exclude it, so far as the Constitution of the United States would permit. What more could Mr. Chase give by his amendment? Nothing. He offered his amendment for the identical purpose for which Mr. Lincoln is using it, to enable demagogues in the country to try and deceive the people. ("Good, hit him again," and cheers.)

[Deacon Bross spoke.]

His amendment was to this effect. It provided that the legislature should have the power to exclude slavery; and General Cass suggested, "why not give the power to introduce as well as exclude?" The answer was, they have the power already in the bill to do both. Chase was afraid his amendment would be adopted if he put the alternative proposition and so make it fair both ways, but would not yield. He offered it for the purpose of having it rejected. He offered it, as he has himself avowed over and over again, simply to make capital out of it for the stump. He expected that it would be capital for small politicians in the country, and that they would make an effort to deceive the people with it, and he was not mistaken, for Lincoln is carrying out the plan admirably. ("Good, good.") Lincoln knows that the Nebraska Bill, without Chase's amendment, gave all the power which the Constitution would permit. Could Congress confer any more? ("No, no.") Could Congress go beyond the Constitution of the country? We gave all, a full grant, with no exception in regard to slavery one way or the other. We left that question as we left all others, to be decided by the people for themselves, just as they pleased. I will not occupy my time on this question. I have argued it before all over Illinois. I have argued it in this beautiful city of Freeport; I have argued it in the North, the South, the East and the West, avowing the same sentiments and the same principles. I have not been afraid to avow my sentiments up here for fear I would be trotted down into Egypt. (Cheers and laughter.)

The third question which Mr. Lincoln presented is, if the Supreme Court of the United States shall decide that a state of this Union cannot exclude slavery from its own limits will I submit to it? I am amazed that Lincoln should ask such a question. ("A school boy knows better.") Yes, a school boy does know better. Mr. Lincoln's object is to cast an imputation upon the Supreme Court. He knows that there never was but one man in America, claiming any degree of intelligence or decency, who ever for a moment pretended such a thing. It is true that the Washington *Union,* in an article published on the 17th of last December, did put forth that doctrine, and I denounced the article on the floor of the Senate, in a speech which Mr. Lincoln now pretends was against the President. The *Union* had claimed that slavery had a right to go into the free states, and that any provision in the Constitution or laws of the free states to the contrary were null and void. I denounced it in the Senate, as I said before, and I was the first man who did. Lincoln's friends, Trumbull, and Seward, and Hale, and Wilson, and the whole Black Republican side of the Senate were silent. They left it to me to denounce it. (Cheers.) And what was the reply made to me on that occasion? Mr. Toombs, of Georgia, got up and undertook to lecture me on the ground that I ought not to have deemed the article worthy of notice, and ought not to have replied to it; that there was not one man, woman or child south of the Potomac, in any slave state, who did not repudiate any such pretension. Mr. Lincoln knows that that reply was made on the spot, and yet now he asks this question. He might as well ask me, suppose Mr. Lincoln should steal a horse would I sanction it; (laughter,) and it would be as genteel in me to ask him, in the event he stole a horse, what ought to be done with him. He casts an imputation upon the Supreme Court of the United States by supposing that they would violate the Constitution of the United States. I tell him that such a thing is not possible. (Cheers.) It would be an act of moral treason that no man on the bench could ever descend to. Mr. Lincoln himself would never in his partisan feelings so far forget what was right as to be guilty of such an act. ("Good, good.")

The fourth question of Mr. Lincoln is, are you in favor of acquiring additional territory in disregard as to how such acquisition may effect the Union on the slavery question. This question is very ingeniously and cunningly put.

[Deacon Bross here spoke, *sotto voce,*—the reporter understanding him to say, "Now we've got him."]

The Black Republican creed lays it down expressly, that under no circumstances shall we acquire any more territory unless slavery is first prohibited in the country. I ask Mr. Lincoln whether he is in favor of that proposition. Are you (addressing Mr. Lincoln) opposed to the acquisition of any more territory, under any circumstances, unless slavery is prohibited in it? That he does not like to answer. When I ask him whether he stands up to that article in the platform of his party, he turns, Yankee-fashion, and without answering it, asks me whether I am in favor of acquiring territory without regard to how it may affect the Union on the slavery question. ("Good.") I answer that whenever it becomes necessary, in our growth and progress to acquire more territory, that I am in favor of it, without reference to the question of slavery, and when we have acquired it, I will leave the people free to do as they please, either to make it slave or free territory, as they prefer. [Here Deacon Bross spoke, the reporter believes that he said, "That's bold." It was said solemnly.] It is idle to tell me or you that we have territory enough. Our fathers supposed that we had enough when our territory extended to the Mississippi River, but a few years' growth and expansion satisfied them that we needed more, and the Louisiana territory, from the west branch of the Mississippi, to the British possessions, was acquired. Then we acquired Oregon, then California and New Mexico. We have enough now for the present, but this is a young and a growing nation. It swarms as often as a hive of bees, and as new swarms are turned out each year, there must be hives in which they can gather and make their honey. ("Good.") In less than fifteen years, if the same progress that has distinguished this country for the last fifteen years continues, every foot of vacant land between this and the Pacific Ocean, owned by the United States, will be occupied. Will you not continue to increase at the end of fifteen years as well as now? I tell you, increase, and multiply, and expand, is the law of this nation's existence. ("Good.") You cannot limit this great republic by mere boundary lines, saying, "thus far shalt thou go, and no further." Any one of you gentlemen might as well say to a son twelve years old that he is big enough, and must not grow any larger, and in order to prevent his growth put a hoop around him to keep him to his present size. What would be the result? Either the hoop must burst and be rent asunder, or the child must die. So it would be with this great nation. With our natural increase, growing with a rapidity unknown in any other part of the globe, with the tide of emigration that is fleeing from despotism in the old world to seek a refuge in our own, there is a constant torrent pouring into this country that requires more land, more territory upon which to settle, and just as fast as our interests and our destiny require additional territory in the north, in the south, or on the islands of the ocean, I am for it, and when we acquire it will leave the people, according to the Nebraska Bill, free to do as they please on the subject of slavery and every other question. ("Good, good," "hurra for Douglas.")

I trust now that Mr. Lincoln will deem himself answered on his four points. He racked his brain so much in devising these four questions that he exhausted himself, and had not strength enough to invent the others. (Laughter.) As soon as he is able to hold a council with his advisers, Lovejoy, Farnsworth, and Fred. Douglass, he will frame and propound others. ("Good, good," &c. Renewed laughter, in which Mr. Lincoln feebly joined, saying that he hoped with their aid to get seven questions, the number asked him by Judge Douglas, and so make *conclusions* even.) You Black Republicans who say good, I have no doubt think that they are all good men. ("White, white.") I have reason to recollect that some people in this country think that Fred. Douglass is a very good man. The last time I came here to make a speech, while talking from the stand to you people of Freeport, as I am doing to-day, I saw a carriage and a magnificent one it was, drive up and take a position on the outside of the crowd; a beautiful young lady was sitting on the box seat, whilst Fred. Douglass and her mother reclined inside, and the owner of the carriage acted as driver. (Laughter, cheers, cries of "right, what have you to say against it," &c.) I saw this in your own town. ("What of it.") All I have to say of it is this, that if you, Black Republicans, think that the negro ought to be on a social equality with your wives and daughters, and ride in a carriage with your wife, whilst you drive the team, you have a perfect right to do so. ("Good, good," and cheers, mingled with hooting and cries of "white, white.") I am told that one of Fred. Douglass' kinsmen, another rich black negro, is now traveling in this part of the state making speeches for his friend Lincoln as the champion of black men. ("White men, white men," and "what have you got to say against it," "that's right," &c.) All I have to say on that subject is that those of you who believe that the negro is your equal and ought to be on an equality with you socially, politically, and legally, have a right to entertain those opinions, and of course will vote for Mr. Lincoln. ("Down with the negro," "no, no," &c.)

I have a word to say on Mr. Lincoln's answer to the interrogatories contained in my speech at Ottawa, and which he has pretended to reply to here to-day. Mr. Lincoln makes a great parade of the fact that I quoted a platform as having been adopted by the

Black Republican party at Springfield in 1854, which, it turns out, was adopted at another place. Mr. Lincoln loses sight of the thing itself in his ecstasies over the mistake I made in stating the place where it was done. He thinks that that platform was not adopted on the right "spot."

When I put the direct questions to Mr. Lincoln to ascertain whether he now stands pledged to that creed—to the unconditional repeal of the fugitive slave law, a refusal to admit any more slave states into the Union even if the people want them, a determination to apply the Wilmot Proviso not only to all the territory we now have, but all that we may hereafter acquire, he refused to answer, and his followers say, in excuse, that the resolutions upon which I based my interrogatories were not adopted at the *"right spot."* (Laughter and applause.) Lincoln and his political friends are great on *"spots."* (Renewed laughter.) In Congress, as a representative of this state, he declared the Mexican war to be unjust and infamous, and would not support it, or acknowledge his own country to be right in the contest, because he said that American blood was not shed on American soil in the *"right spot."* ("Lay on to him.") And now he cannot answer the questions I put to him at Ottawa because the resolutions I read were not adopted at the *"right spot."* It may be possible that I was led into error as to the *spot* on which the resolutions I then read were proclaimed, but I was not, and am not in error as to the fact of their forming the basis of the creed of the Republican party when that party was first organized. [Cheers.] I will state to you the evidence I had, and upon which I relied for my statement that the resolutions in question were adopted at Springfield on the 5th of October, 1854. Although I was aware that such resolutions had been passed in this district, and nearly all the northern congressional districts and county conventions, I had not noticed whether or not they had been adopted by any state convention. In 1856, a debate arose in Congress between Major Thomas L. Harris, of the Springfield district, and Mr. Norton, of the Joliet district, on political matters connected with our state, in the course of which Major Harris quoted those resolutions as having been passed by the first Republican State Convention that ever assembled in Illinois. I knew that Major Harris was remarkable for his accuracy, that he was a very conscientious and sincere man, and I also noticed that Norton did not question the accuracy of this statement. I therefore took it for granted that it was so, and the other day when I concluded to use the resolutions at Ottawa, I wrote to Charles H. Lanphier, editor of the *State Register,* at Springfield, calling his attention to them, telling him that I had been informed that Major Harris was lying sick at Springfield, and desiring him to call upon him and ascertain all the facts concerning the resolutions, the time and the place where they were adopted. In reply Mr. Lanphier sent me two copies of his paper, which I have here. The first is a copy of the *State Register,* published at Springfield, Mr. Lincoln's own town, on the 16th of October 1854, only eleven days after the adjournment of the convention, from which I desire to read the following:

> During the late discussions in this city, Lincoln made a speech, to which Judge Douglas replied. In Lincoln's speech he took the broad ground that, according to the Declaration of Independence, the whites and blacks are equal. From this he drew the conclusion, which he several times repeated, that the white man had no right to pass laws for the government of the black man without the nigger's consent. This speech of Lincoln's was heard and applauded by all the Abolitionists assembled in Springfield. So soon as Mr. Lincoln was done speaking, Mr. Codding arose and requested all the delegates to the Black Republican convention to withdraw into the senate chamber. They did so, and after long deliberation, they laid down the following abolition platform as the platform on which they stood. We call the particular attention of all our readers to it.

Then follows the identical platform, word for word, which I read at Ottawa. (Cheers.) Now, that was published in Mr. Lincoln's own town, eleven days after the convention was held, and it has remained on record up to this day never contradicted.

When I quoted the resolutions at Ottawa and questioned Mr. Lincoln in relation to them, he said that his name was on the committee that reported them, but he did not serve, nor did he think he served, because he was, or thought he was, in Tazewell county at the time the convention was in session. He did not deny that the resolutions were passed by the Springfield convention. He did not know better, and evidently thought that they were, but afterwards his friends declared that they had discovered that they varied in some respects from the resolutions passed by that convention. I have shown you that I had good evidence for believing that the resolutions had been passed at Springfield. Mr. Lincoln ought to have known better; but not a word is said about his ignorance on the subject, whilst I, notwithstanding the circumstances, am accused of forgery.

Now, I will show you that if I have made a mistake as to the place where these resolutions were adopted—and when I get down to Springfield I will investigate the matter and see whether or not I have—that the principles they enunciate were adopted as the Black Republican platform ("white, white,") in the various counties and congressional districts throughout the north end of the state in 1854. This platform was adopted in nearly every county that gave a Black Republican majority for the legislature in that year, and here is a man (pointing to Mr. Denio,[5] who sat on the stand near Deacon Bross,) who knows as well as any living man that it was the creed of the Black Republican party at that time. I would be willing to call Denio as a witness, or any other honest man belonging to that party. I will now read the resolutions adopted at the Rockford Convention on the 30th of August, 1854, which nominated Washburne for Congress. You elected him on the following platform:

Resolved, That the continued and increasing aggressions of slavery in our country are destructive of the best rights of a free people, and that such aggressions cannot be successfully resisted without the united political action of all good men.

Resolved, That the citizens of the United States hold in their hands peaceful, constitutional, and efficient remedy against the encroachments of the slave power, the ballot box, and, if that remedy is boldly and wisely applied, the principles of liberty and eternal justice will be established.

Resolved, That we accept this issue forced upon us by the slave power, and, in defense of freedom, will co-operate and be known as Republicans, pledged to the accomplishment of the following purposes:

To bring the administration of the government back to the control of first principles; to restore Kansas and Nebraska to the position of free Territories; to repeal and entirely abrogate the fugitive slave law; to restrict slavery to those states in which it exists; to prohibit the admission of any more slave states into the Union; to exclude slavery from all the territories over which the general government has exclusive jurisdiction, and to resist the acquisition of any more territories unless the introduction of slavery therein forever shall have been prohibited.

Resolved, That in furtherance of these principles we will use such constitutional and lawful means as shall seem best adapted to their accomplishment, and that we will support no man for office under the general or state government who is not positively committed to the support of these principles and whose personal character and conduct is not a guaranty that he is reliable and shall abjure all party allegiance and ties.

Resolved, That we cordially invite persons of all former political parties whatever in favor of the object expressed in the above resolutions to unite with us in carrying them into effect.

[Senator Douglas was frequently interrupted in reading these resolutions by loud cries of "Good, good," "that's the doctrine," and vociferous applause.]

Well, you think that is a very good platform, do you not? ("Yes, yes, all right," and cheers.) If you do, if you approve it now, and think it is all right, you will not join with those men who say that I libel you by calling these your principles, will you? ("Good, good,

[5] Cyrenius B. Denio, who represented Jo Daviess County in the state legislature.

hit him again," and great laughter and cheers.) Now, Mr. Lincoln complains; Mr. Lincoln charges that I did you and him injustice by saying that this was the platform of your party. (Renewed laughter.) I am told that Washburne made a speech in Galena last night in which he abused me awfully for bringing to light this platform on which he was elected to Congress. He thought that you had forgotten it, as he and Mr. Lincoln desire to. (Laughter.) He did not deny but that you had adopted it, and that he had subscribed to and was pledged to it, but he did not think it was fair to call it up and remind the people that it was their platform.

[Here Deacon Bross spoke.]

But I am glad to find that you are more honest in your abolitionism than your leaders, by avowing that it is your platform, and right in your opinion. (Laughter, "you have them, good, good.")

In the adoption of that platform, you not only declared that you would resist the admission of any more slave states, and work for the repeal of the fugitive slave law, but you pledged yourselves not to vote for any man for state or federal offices who was not committed to these principles. ("Exactly so." "Exactly so!" Cheers.) You were thus committed. Similar resolutions to those were adopted in your county convention here, and now with your admissions that they are your platform and embody your sentiments now as they did then, what do you think of Mr. Lincoln, your candidate for the U.S. Senate, who is attempting to dodge the responsibility of this platform, because it was not adopted in the right spot? (Shouts of laughter, "hurra for Douglas," &c.) I thought that it was adopted in Springfield, but it turns out it was not, that it was adopted at Rockford and in the various counties which comprise this congressional district. When I get into the next district, I will show that the same platform was adopted there, and so on through the state, until I nail the responsibility of it upon the back of the Black Republican party throughout the state. ("White, white," three cheers for Douglas.)

(A Voice—"Couldn't you modify and call it brown?" Laughter.)

Mr. Douglas—Not a bit. I thought that you were becoming a little brown when your members in Congress voted for the Crittenden-Montgomery bill, but since you have backed out from that position and gone back to Abolitionism, you are black, and not brown. (Shouts of laughter, and a voice, "Can't you ask him another question.")

Gentlemen, I have shown you what your platform was in 1854. You still adhere to it. The same platform was adopted by nearly all the counties where the Black Republican party had a majority in

1854. I wish now to call your attention to the action of your representatives in the legislature when they assembled together at Springfield. In the first place you must remember that this was the organization of a new party. It is so declared in the resolutions themselves which say that you are going to dissolve all old party ties and call the new party Republican. The old Whig party was to have its throat cut from ear to ear, and the Democratic party was to be annihilated and blotted out of existence, whilst in lieu of these parties the Black Republican party was to be organized on this Abolition platform. You know who the chief leaders were in breaking up and destroying these two great parties. Lincoln on the one hand and Trumbull on the other, being disappointed politicians, (laughter,) and having retired or been driven to obscurity by an outraged constituency because of their political sins, formed a scheme to abolitionize the two parties and lead the Old Line Whigs and Old Line Democrats captive, bound hand and foot into the Abolition camp. Giddings, Chase, Fred. Douglass and Lovejoy were here to christen them whenever they were brought in. (Great laughter.) Lincoln went to work to dissolve the Old Line Whig party. Clay was dead, and although the sod was not yet green on his grave, this man undertook to bring into disrepute those great compromise measures of 1850, with which Clay and Webster were identified. Up to 1854 the old Whig party and the Democratic party had stood on a common platform so far as this slavery question was concerned. You Whigs and we Democrats differed about the bank, the tariff, distribution, the specie circular and the sub-treasury, but we agreed on this slavery question and the true mode of preserving the peace and harmony of the Union. The compromise measures of 1850 were introduced by Clay, were defended by Webster, and supported by Cass, and were approved by Fillmore, and sanctioned by the national men of both parties. They constituted a common plank upon which both Whigs and Democrats stood. In 1852 the Whig party in its last national convention at Baltimore endorsed and approved these measures of Clay, and so did the national convention of the Democratic party held that same year. Thus the Old Line Whigs and the Old Line Democrats stood pledged to the great principle of self-government, which guarantees to the people of each territory the right to decide the slavery question for themselves. In 1854 after the death of Clay and Webster, Mr. Lincoln on the part of the Whigs undertook to abolitionize the Whig party, by dissolving it, transferring the members into the Abolition camp and making them train under Giddings, Fred. Douglass, Lovejoy, Chase, Farnsworth, and other Abolition leaders. Trumbull undertook to dissolve the

Democratic party by taking old Democrats into the Abolition camp. Mr. Lincoln was aided in his efforts by many leading Whigs throughout the state, your member of Congress, Mr. Washburne, being one of the most active. ("Good fellow.") Trumbull was aided by many renegades from the Democratic party, among whom were John Wentworth, (laughter,) Tom Turner and others with whom you are familiar.

MR. TURNER, who was one of the moderators, here interposed and said that he had drawn the resolutions which Senator Douglas had read.

MR. DOUGLAS—Yes, and Turner says that he drew these resolutions. ("Hurra for Turner." "Hurra for Douglas.") That is right, give Turner cheers for drawing the resolutions if you approve them. If he drew those resolutions he will not deny that they are the creed of the Black Republican party.

MR. TURNER—They are our creed exactly. (Cheers)

MR. DOUGLAS—And yet Lincoln denies that he stands on them. ("Good, good," and laughter.) Mr. Turner says that the creed of the Black Republican party is the admission of no more slave states, and yet Mr. Lincoln declares that he would not like to be placed in a position where he would have to vote for them. All I have to say to friend Lincoln is, that I do not think there is much danger of his being placed in such a position. (More laughter.) As Mr. Lincoln would be very sorry to be placed in such an embarrassing position as to be obliged to vote on the admission of any more slave states, I propose, out of mere kindness, to relieve him from any such necessity. (Renewed laughter and cheers.)

When the bargain between Lincoln and Trumbull was completed for abolitionizing the Whig and Democratic parties, they "spread" over the state, Lincoln still pretending to be an Old Line Whig in order to "rope in" the Whigs, and Trumbull pretending to be as good a Democrat as he ever was in order to coax the Democrats over into the Abolition ranks. ("That's exactly what we want.") They played the part that "decoy ducks" play down on the Potomac River. In that part of the country they make artificial ducks and put them on the water in places where the wild ducks are to be found for the purpose of decoying them. Well, Lincoln and Trumbull played the part of these "decoy ducks" and deceived enough Old Line Whigs and Old Line Democrats to elect a Black Republican legislature. When that legislature met, the first thing it did was to elect a Speaker of the House the very man who is now boasting that he wrote the Abolition platform on which Lincoln will not stand. ("Good," "hit him again," and cheers.) I want to know of Mr.

Turner whether or not, when he was elected he was a good embodiment of Republican principles?

MR. TURNER—I hope I was then and am now.

MR. DOUGLAS—He answers that he hopes he was then and is now.
He wrote that Black Republican platform, and is satisfied with it
now. ("Hurrah for Turner," "good," &c.) I admire and acknowledge Turner's honesty. Every man of you know that what he says
about these resolutions being the platform of the Black Republican
party is true, and you also know that each one of these men who
are shuffling and trying to deny it are only trying to cheat the people
out of their votes for the purpose of deceiving them still more after
the election. ("Good," and cheers.) I propose to trace this thing a
little further, in order that you can see what additional evidence
there is to fasten this revolutionary platform upon the Black Republican party. When the legislature assembled, there was an United
States Senator to elect in the place of Gen. Shields, and before they
proceeded to ballot, Lovejoy insisted on laying down certain principles by which to govern the party. It has been published to the
world and satisfactorily proven that there was at the time the alliance was made between Trumbull and Lincoln to abolitionize the
two parties, an agreement that Lincoln should take Shields' place
in the United States Senate, and Trumbull should have mine so soon
as they could conveniently get rid of me. When Lincoln was beaten
for Shields' place in a manner I will refer to in a few minutes, he
felt very sore and restive; his friends grumbled, and some of them
came out and charged that the most infamous treachery had been
practised against him; that the bargain was that Lincoln was to
have had Shields' place, and Trumbull was to have waited for mine,
but that Trumbull having the control of a few abolitionized Democrats, he prevented them from voting for Lincoln, thus keeping
him within a few votes of an election until he succeeded in forcing
the party to drop him and elect Trumbull. Well, Trumbull having
cheated Lincoln, his friends made a fuss, and in order to keep them
and Lincoln quiet, the party were obliged to come forward, in advance, at the last state election, and make a pledge that they would
go for Lincoln and nobody else. Lincoln could not be silenced in
any other way.

Now, there are a great many Black Republicans of you who do
not know this thing was done. ("White, white," and great clamor.)
I wish to remind you that while Mr. Lincoln was speaking there
was not a Democrat vulgar and black-guard enough to interrupt
him. (Great applause and cries of "hurrah for Douglas.") But I
know that the shoe is pinching you. I am clinching Lincoln now and

you are scared to death for the result. (Cheers.) I have seen this thing before. I have seen men make appointments for joint discussions, and the moment their man has been heard, try to interrupt and prevent a fair hearing of the other side. I have seen your mobs before, and defy your wrath. (Tremendous applause.) My friends, do not cheer, for I need my whole time. The object of the opposition is to occupy my attention in order to prevent me from giving the whole evidence and nailing this double dealing on the Black Republican party. As I have before said, Lovejoy demanded a declaration of principles on the part of the Black Republicans of the legislature before going into an election for United States Senator. He offered the following preamble and resolutions which I hold in my hand:

Whereas, human slavery is a violation of the principles of natural and revealed rights; and whereas, the fathers of the Revolution, fully imbued with the spirit of these principles, declared freedom to be the inalienable birthright of all men; and whereas, the preamble to the Constitution of the United States avers that that instrument was ordained to establish justice, and secure the blessings of liberty to ourselves and our posterity; and whereas, in furtherance of the above principles, slavery was forever prohibited in the old Northwest Territory, and more recently in all that territory lying west and north of the state of Missouri, by the act of the federal government; and whereas, the repeal of the prohibition, last referred to, was contrary to the wishes of the people of Illinois, a violation of an implied compact, long deemed and held sacred by the citizens of the United States, and a wide departure from the uniform action of the general government in relation to the extension of slavery; therefore,

Resolved, by the House of Representatives, the Senate concurring therein, That our Senators in Congress be instructed, and our Representatives requested, to introduce, if not otherwise introduced, and to vote for a bill to restore such prohibition to the aforesaid territories, and also to extend a similar prohibition to all territory which now belongs to the United States, or which may hereafter come under their jurisdiction.

Resolved, That our Senators in Congress be instructed, and our Representatives requested, to vote against the admission of any state into the Union, the constitution of which does not prohibit slavery, whether the territory out of which such state may have been formed shall have been acquired by conquest, treaty, purchase, or from original territory of the United States.

Resolved, That our Senators in Congress be instructed and our Representatives requested to introduce and vote for a bill to repeal an act entitled "an act respecting fugitives from justice and persons escaping from the service of their masters"; and, failing in that, for such a modification of it as shall secure the right of *habeas corpus* and trial by jury before the regularly-constituted authorities of the state, to all persons claimed as owing service or labor.

(Cries of "good," "good," and cheers.) Yes, you say "good," "good," and I have no doubt you think so. Those resolutions were introduced by Mr. Lovejoy immediately preceding the election of Senator. They declared first, that the Wilmot Proviso must be applied to all territory north of 36 deg., 30 min. Secondly, that it must be applied to all territory south of 36 deg., 30 min. Thirdly, that it must be applied to all the territory now owned by the United States, and finally, that it must be applied to all territory hereafter to be acquired by the United States. The next resolution declares that no more slave states shall be admitted into this Union under any circumstances whatever, no matter whether they are formed out of territory now owned by us or that we may hereafter acquire, by treaty, by Congress, or in any manner whatever. (A VOICE, "That is right.") You say that is right. We will see in a moment. The next resolution demands the unconditional repeal of the fugitive slave law, although its unconditional repeal would leave no provision for carrying out that clause of the Constitution of the United States which guarantees the surrender of fugitives. If they could not get an unconditional repeal, they demanded that that law should be so modified as to make it as nearly useless as possible. Now I want to show you who voted for these resolutions. When the vote was taken on the first resolution it was decided in the affirmative—yeas 41, nays 32. You will find that this is a strict party vote, between the Democrats, on the one hand, and the Black Republicans, on the other. (Cries, of "white, white," and clamor.) I know your name, and always call things by their right name. The point I wish to call your attention to, is this: that these resolutions were adopted on the 7th day of February, and that on the 8th they went into an election for a U.S. Senator, and on that day every man who voted for these resolutions, with but two exceptions, voted for Lincoln for the U.S. Senate. (Cries of "good, good," and "give us their names.") I will read the names over to you if you want them, but I believe your object is to occupy my time. (Cries of "that is it.")

On the next resolution, the vote stood—yeas 33, nays 40, and on the third resolution—yeas 35, nays 47. I wish to impress it upon you, that every man who voted for those resolutions, with but two exceptions, voted on the next day for Lincoln, for U.S. Senator. Bear in mind that the members who thus voted for Lincoln were elected to the legislature, pledged to vote for no man for office under the state or federal government who was not committed to this Black Republican platform. (Cries of "white, white," and "good for you.") They were all so pledged. Mr. Turner, who stands by me, and who then represented you, and who says that he wrote those resolutions, voted for Lincoln, when he was pledged not to do so unless Lincoln was committed in favor of those resolutions. I now ask Mr. Turner, (turning to Turner) did you violate your pledge in voting for Mr. Lincoln, or did he commit himself to your platform before you cast your vote for him? (Mr. Lincoln here started forward, and grasping Mr. Turner, shook him nervously, and said, "Don't answer, Turner, you have no right to answer.")

I could go through the whole list of names here and show you that all the Black Republicans in the legislature, ("white, white,") who voted for Mr. Lincoln, had voted on the day previous for these resolutions. For instance, here are the names of Sargent and Little of Jo Daviess and Carroll; Thomas J. Turner, of Stephenson; Lawrence, of Boone and McHenry; Swan, of Lake; Pinckney, of Ogle county, and Lyman, of Winnebago. Thus you see every member from your congressional district voted for Mr. Lincoln, and they were pledged not to vote for him unless he was committed to the doctrine of no more slave states, the prohibition of slavery in the territories, and the repeal of the fugitive slave law. Mr. Lincoln tells you to-day that he is not pledged to any such doctrine. Either Mr. Lincoln was then committed to those propositions, or Mr. Turner violated his pledges to you when he voted for him. Either Lincoln was pledged to each one of those propositions, or else every Black Republican—(cries of "white, white,")—representative from this congressional district violated his pledge of honor to his constituents by voting for him. I ask you which horn of the dilemma will you take? Will you hold Lincoln up to the platform of his party, or will you accuse every representative you had in the legislature of violating his pledge of honor to his constituents. (VOICES; "we go for Turner," "we go for Lincoln," "hurrah for Douglas," "hurrah for Turner.") There is no escape for you. Either Mr. Lincoln was committed to those propositions, or your members violated their faith. Take either horn of the dilemma you choose. There is no dodging the question, I want Lincoln's answer. He says he was not pledged to repeal the fugitive slave law, that he does not quite like to do it; he will not introduce a law to repeal it, but thinks there ought to be some law; he does not tell what it ought to be; upon the whole, he is altogether undecided, and don't know what to think or to do. That is the substance of his answer upon the repeal of the fugitive slave law. I put the question to him distinctly, whether he endorsed that part of the Black Republican platform which calls for the entire abrogation and repeal of the fugitive slave law. He answers no! that he does not endorse that, but he does not tell what he is for, or what he will vote for. His answer is, in fact, no answer at all. Why cannot he speak out and say what he is for and what he will do? (Cries of "that's right.")

In regard to there being no more slave states, he is not pledged to that. He would not like, he says, to be put in a position where he would have to vote one way or another upon that question. I pray you do not put him in a position that would embarrass him so much. (Laughter.) Gentlemen, if he goes to the Senate, he may be put in that position, and then which way will he vote?

[A Voice—"How will you vote?"]

MR. DOUGLAS—I will vote for the admission of just such a state as by the form of their constitution the people show they want; if they want slavery, they shall have it; if they prohibit slavery, it shall be prohibited. They can form their institutions to please themselves, subject only to the Constitution; and I for one stand ready to receive them into the Union. ("Three cheers for Douglas.") Why cannot your Black Republican candidates talk out as plain as that when they are questioned? (Cries of "good, good.")

[Here Deacon Bross spoke.]

I do not want to cheat any man out of his vote. No man is deceived in regard to my principles if I have the power to express myself in terms explicit enough to convey my ideas.

Mr. Lincoln made a speech when he was nominated for the U.S. Senate which covers all these abolition platforms. He there lays down a proposition so broad in its Abolitionism as to cover the whole ground.

In my opinion it (the slavery agitation) will not cease until a crisis shall have been reached and passed. "A house divided against itself cannot stand." I believe this government cannot endure permanently half slave and half free. I do not expect the house to fall—but I do expect it will cease to be divided. It will become all one thing or all the other. Either the opponents of slavery will arrest the further spread of it, and place it where the public mind shall rest in the belief that it is in the course of ultimate extinction, or its advocates will push it forward till it shall become alike lawful in all the states—old as well as new, North as well as South.

There you find that Mr. Lincoln lays down the doctrine that this Union cannot endure divided as our Fathers made it, with free and slave states. He says they must all become one thing, or all the other; that they must be all free or slave, or else the Union cannot continue to exist. It being his opinion that to admit any more slave states, to continue to divide the Union into free and slave states, will dissolve it. I want to know of Mr. Lincoln whether he will vote for the admission of another slave state. (Cries of "Bring him out.")

He tells you the Union cannot exist unless the states are all free or all slave; he tells you that he is opposed to making them all slave, and hence he is for making them all free, in order that the Union may exist; and yet he will not say that he will not vote against the admission of another slave state, knowing that the Union must be dissolved if he votes for it. (Great laughter.) I ask you if that is fair dealing? The true intent and inevitable conclusion to be drawn from his first Springfield speech is, that he is opposed to the admission of any more slave states under any circumstance. If he is so opposed why not say so? If he believes this Union cannot endure divided into free and slave states, that they must all become free in order to save the Union, he is bound, as an honest man, to vote against any more slave states. If he believes it he is bound to do it. Show me that it is my duty in order to save the Union to do a particular act, and I will do it if the Constitution does not prohibit it. (Applause.) I am not for the dissolution of the Union under any circumstances. (Renewed applause.) I will pursue no course of conduct that will give just cause for the dissolution of the Union. The hope of the friends of freedom throughout the world rests upon the perpetuity of this Union. The down-trodden and oppressed people who are suffering under European despotism all look with hope and anxiety to the American Union as the only resting place and permanent home of freedom and self-government.

Mr. Lincoln says that he believes that this Union cannot continue to endure with slave states in it, and yet he will not tell you distinctly whether he will vote for or against the admission of any more slave states, but says he would not like to be put to the test. (Laughter.) I do not think he will be put to the test. (Renewed laughter.) I do not think that the people of Illinois desire a man to represent them who would not like to be put to the test on the performance of a high constitutional duty. (Cries of "good.") I will retire in shame from the Senate of the United States when I am not willing to be put to the test in the performance of my duty. I have been put to severe tests. ("That is so.") I have stood by my principles in fair weather and in foul, in the sunshine and in the rain. I have defended the great principles of self-government here among you when Northern sentiment ran in a torrent against me. (A Voice,—"that is so,") and I have defended that same great principle when Southern sentiment came down like an avalanche upon me. I was not afraid of any test they put to me. I knew I was right —I knew my principles were sound—I knew that the people would see in the end that I had done right, and I knew that the God of Heaven would smile upon me if I was faithful in the performance of my duty. (Cries of "good," cheers and laughter.)

Mr. Lincoln makes a charge of corruption against the Supreme Court of the United States, and two Presidents of the United States, and attempts to bolster it up by saying that I did the same against the Washington *Union*. Suppose I did make that charge of corruption against the Washington *Union*, when it was true, does that justify him in making a false charge against me and others? That is the question I would put. He says that at the time the Nebraska Bill was introduced, and before it was passed there was a conspiracy between the Judges of the Supreme Court, President Pierce, President Buchanan and myself by that bill, and the decision of the court to break down the barrier and establish slavery all over the Union. Does he not know that that charge is historically false as against President Buchanan? He knows that Mr. Buchanan was at that time in England, representing this country with distinguished ability at the Court of St. James, that he was there for a long time before and did not return for a year or more after. He knows that to be true, and that fact proves his charge to be false as against Mr. Buchanan. (Cheers.) Then again, I wish to call his attention to the fact that at the time the Nebraska Bill was passed the Dred Scott case was not before the Supreme Court at all; it was not upon the docket of the Supreme Court; it had not been brought there, and the Judges in all probability, knew nothing of it. Thus the history of the country proves the charge to be false as against them. As to President Pierce, his character as a man of integrity and honor is enough to vindicate him from such a charge, (laughter and applause,) and as to myself, I pronounce the charge an infamous lie, whenever and wherever made, and by whomsoever made. I am willing that Mr. Lincoln should go and rake up every public act of mine, every measure I have introduced, report I have made, speech delivered, and criticise them, but when he charges upon me a corrupt conspiracy for the purpose of perverting the institutions of the country, I brand it as it deserves. I say the history of the country proves it to be false, and that it could not have been possible at the time. But now he tries to protect himself in this charge, because I made a charge against the Washington *Union*. My speech in the Senate against the Washington *Union* was made because it advocated a revolutionary doctrine, by declaring that the free states had not the right to prohibit slavery within their own limits. Because I made that charge against the Washington *Union*, Mr. Lincoln says it was a charge against Mr. Buchanan. Suppose it was; is Mr. Lincoln the peculiar defender of Mr. Buchanan? Is he so interested in the federal administration, and so bound to it, that he must jump to the rescue and defend it from every attack that I may make against it? (Great laughter and cheers.) I understand the whole thing. The Washington *Union*, under that most corrupt of all men, Cornelius

Wendell, is advocating Mr. Lincoln's claim to the Senate. Wendell was the printer of the last Black Republican House of Representatives; he was a candidate before the present Democratic House, but was ignominiously kicked out, and then he took the money which he had made out of the public printing by means of the Black Republicans, bought the Washington *Union*, and is now publishing it in the name of the Democratic party, and advocating Mr. Lincoln's election to the Senate. Mr. Lincoln therefore considers any attack upon Wendell and his corrupt gang as a personal attack upon him. (Immense cheering and laughter.) This only proves what I have charged, that there is an alliance between Lincoln and his supporters and the federal office-holders of this state, and presidential aspirants out of it, to break me down at home.

[A VOICE—"That is impossible," and cheering.]

Mr. Lincoln feels bound to come in to the rescue of the Washington *Union*. In that speech which I delivered in answer to the Washington *Union*, I made it distinctly against the *Union*, and against the *Union* alone. I did not choose to go beyond that. If I have occasion to attack the President's conduct, I will do it in language that will not be misunderstood. When I differed with the President, I spoke out so that you all heard me. ("That you did," and cheers.) That question passed away; it resulted in the triumph of my principle by allowing the people to do as they please, and there is an end of the controversy. ("Hear, hear.") Whenever the great principle of self-government—the right of the people to make their own constitution, and come into the Union with slavery, or without it, as they see proper—shall again arise, you will find me standing firm in defence of that principle, and fighting whoever fights it. ("Right, right." "Good, good," and cheers.) If Mr. Buchanan stands, as I doubt not he will, by the recommendation contained in his message, that hereafter all state constitutions ought to be submitted to the people before the admission of the state into the Union, he will find me standing by him firmly, shoulder to shoulder, in carrying it out. I know Mr. Lincoln's object, he wants to divide the Democratic party, in order that he may defeat me and get to the Senate.

Lincoln's Rejoinder

My friends, it will readily occur to you that I cannot in half an hour notice all the things that so able a man as Judge Douglas can say in an hour and a half, and I hope, therefore, if there be anything that he has said upon which you would like to hear something from me, but which I omit to comment upon, you will bear in mind that it would be expecting an impossibility for me to go over his whole ground. I can but take up some of the points that he has dwelt upon, and employ my half-hour specially on them.

The first thing I have to say to you is a word in regard to Judge Douglas' declaration about the "vulgarity and blackguardism" in the audience—that no such thing, as he says, was shown by any Democrat while I was speaking. Now, I only wish, by way of reply on this subject, to say that while *I* was speaking *I* used no "vulgarity or blackguardism" towards any Democrat. [Great laughter and applause.]

Now, my friends, I come to all this long portion of the Judge's speech—perhaps half of it—which he has devoted to the various resolutions and platforms that have been adopted in the different counties in the different congressional districts, and in the Illinois legislature—which he supposes are at variance with the positions I have assumed before you to-day. It is true that many of these resolutions are variance with the positions I have here assumed. All I have to ask is that we talk reasonably and rationally about it. I happen to know, the Judge's opinion to the contrary notwithstanding, that I have never tried to conceal my opinions, nor tried to deceive any one in reference to them. He may go and examine all the members who voted for me for United States Senator in 1855, after the election of 1854. They were pledged to certain things here at home, and were determined to have pledges from me, and if he will find any of these persons who will tell him anything inconsistent with what I say now, I will resign, or rather retire from the race, and give him no more trouble. [Applause.] The plain truth is this: At the introduction of the Nebraska policy, we believed there was a new era being introduced in the history of the Republic, which tended to the spread and perpetuation of slavery. But in our opposition to that measure we did not agree with one another in everything. The people in the north end of the state were for stronger measures of opposition than we of the central and southern portions of the state, but we were all opposed to the Nebraska doctrine. We had that one feeling and that one sentiment in common. You at the north end met in your conventions and passed your resolutions. We in the middle of the state and further south did not hold such conventions and pass the same resolutions, although we had in general a common view and a common sentiment. So that these meetings which the Judge has alluded to, and the resolutions he has read from were local and did not spread over the whole state. We at last met together in 1856 from all parts of the state, and we agreed upon a common platform. You, who held more extreme notions either yielded those notions, or if not wholly yielding them, agreed to yield them practically, for the sake of embodying the opposition to the measures which the opposite party were pushing forward at that time. We met you then, and if there was anything yielded, it was for practical purposes. We agreed then upon a platform for the party throughout the entire state of Illinois, and now we are all bound as a party, *to that platform.* And I say here to you, if any one expects of me—in the case of my election—that I will do anything not signified by our Republican platform and my answers here to-day, I tell you very frankly that person will be deceived. I do not ask for the vote of any one who supposes that I have secret purposes or pledges that I dare not speak out. Cannot the Judge be satisfied? If he fears, in the unfortunate case of my election, [laughter] that my going to Washington will enable me to advocate sentiments contrary to those which I expressed when you voted for and elected me, I assure him that his fears are wholly needless and groundless. Is the Judge really afraid of any such thing? [Laughter.] I'll tell you what he is afraid of. *He is afraid we'll all pull together.* [Applause, and cries of "we will, we will."] This is what alarms him more than anything else. [Laughter.] For my part, I do hope that all of us, entertaining a common sentiment in opposition to what appears to us a design to nationalize and perpetuate slavery, will waive minor differences on questions which either belong to the dead past or the distant future, and all pull together in this struggle. What are your sentiments? ["We will, we will," and loud cheers.] If it be true, that on the ground which I occupy—ground which I occupy as frankly and boldly as Judge Douglas does his—my views, though partly coinciding with yours, are not as perfectly in accordance with your feelings as his are, I do say to you in all candor, Go for him and not for me. I hope to deal in all things fairly with Judge Douglas, and with the people of the state, in this contest. And if I should never be elected to any office, I trust I may go down with no stain of falsehood upon my reputation,—notwithstanding the hard opinions Judge Douglas chooses to entertain of me. [Laughter.]

The Judge has again addressed himself to the abolition tendencies of a speech of mine, made at Springfield in June last. I have so often tried to answer what he is always saying on that melancholy theme, that I almost turn with disgust from the discussion—from the repetition of an answer to it. I trust that nearly all of this intelligent audience have read that speech. ["We have; we have."] If you have, I may venture to leave it to you to inspect it closely, and see whether it contains any of those "bugaboos" which frighten Judge Douglas. [Laughter.]

The Judge complains that I did not fully answer his questions. If I have the sense to comprehend and answer those questions, I have done so fairly. If it can be pointed out to me how I can more fully and fairly answer him, I aver I have not the sense to see how it is to be done. He says I do not declare I would in any event vote for the admission of a slave state into the Union. If I have been fairly reported he will see that I did give an explicit answer to his interrogatories. I did not merely say that I would dislike to be put to the test; but I said clearly, if I were put to the test, and a territory from which slavery had been excluded should present herself with a state constitution sanctioning slavery—a most extraordinary thing and wholly unlikely ever to happen—I did not see how I could avoid voting for her admission. But he refuses to understand that I said so, and he wants this audience to understand that I did not say so. Yet it will be so reported in the printed speech that he cannot help seeing it.

He says if I should vote for the admission of a slave state I would be voting for a dissolution of the Union, because I hold that the Union can not permanently exist half slave and half free. I repeat that I do not believe this government *can* endure permanently half slave and half free, yet I do not admit, nor does it at all follow, that the admission of a single slave state will permanently fix the character and establish this as a universal slave nation. The Judge is very happy indeed at working up these quibbles. [Laughter and cheers.] Before leaving the subject of answering questions I aver as my confident belief, when you come to see our speeches in print, that you will find every question which he has asked me more fairly and boldly and fully answered than he has answered those which I put to him. Is not that so? [Cries of "yes, yes."] The two speeches may be placed side by side; and I will venture to leave it to impartial judges whether his questions have not been more directly and circumstantially answered than mine.

Judge Douglas says he made a charge upon the editor of the Washington *Union, alone,* of entertaining a purpose to rob the states of their power to exclude slavery from their limits. I undertake to say, and I make the direct issue, that he did *not* make his charge against the editor of the *Union* alone. [Applause.] I will undertake to prove by the record here, that he made that charge against more and higher dignitaries than the editor of the Washington *Union*. I am quite aware that he was shirking and dodging around the form in which he put it, but I can make it manifest that he leveled his "fatal blow" against more persons than this Washington editor. Will he dodge it now by alleging that I am trying to defend Mr. Buchanan against the charge? Not at all. Am I not making the same charge myself? [Laughter and applause.] I am trying to show that you, Judge Douglas, are a witness on my side. [Renewed laughter.] I am not defending Buchanan, and I will tell Judge Douglas that in my opinion, when he made that charge, he had an eye farther North than he has to-day. He was then fighting against people who called him a Black Republican and an Abolitionist. It is mixed all through his speech, and it is tolerably manifest that his eye was a great deal farther north than it is to-day. [Cheers and laughter.] The Judge says that though he made this charge Toombs got up and declared there was not a man in the United States, except the editor of the *Union,* who was in favor of the doctrines put forth in that article. And thereupon, I understand that the Judge withdrew the charge. Although he had taken extracts from the newspaper, and then from the Lecompton constitution, to show the existence of a conspiracy to bring about a "fatal blow," by which the states were to be deprived of the right of excluding slavery, it all went to pot as soon as Toombs got up and told him it was not true. [Laughter.] It reminds me of the story that John Phoenix, the California railroad surveyor, tells. He says they started out from the Plaza to the Mission of Dolores. They had two ways of determining distances. One was by a chain and pins taken over the ground. The other was by a "go-it-ometer"—an invention of his own—a three-legged instrument, with which he computed a series of triangles between the points. At night he turned to the chain-man to ascertain what distance they had come, and found that by some mistake he had merely dragged the chain over the ground without keeping any record. By the "go-it-ometer" he found he had made ten miles. Being skeptical about this, he asked a drayman who was passing how far it was to the plaza. The drayman replied it was just half a mile, and the surveyor put it down in his book—just as Judge Douglas says, after he had made his calculations and computations, he took Toombs' statement. [Great laughter.] I have no doubt that after Judge Douglas had made his charge, he was as easily satisfied about its truth as the surveyor was of the drayman's statement of the distance to the Plaza. [Renewed laughter.] Yet it is a fact that the man who put forth all that matter which Douglas deemed a "fatal blow" at state sovereignty, was elected by the Democrats as public printer.

Now, gentlemen, you may take Judge Douglas' speech of March 22d, 1858, beginning about the middle of page 21, and reading to the bottom of page 24, and you will find the evidence on which I say that he did not make his charge against the editor of the *Union* alone. I cannot stop to read it, but I will give it to the reporters. Judge Douglas said:

Mr. President, you here find several distinct propositions advanced boldly by the Washington *Union* editorially and apparently *authoritatively*, and every man who questions any of them is denounced as an abolitionist, a Free-Soiler, a fanatic. The propositions are, first, that the primary object of all government at its original institution is the protection of persons and property; second, that the Constitution of the United States declares that the citizens of each state shall be entitled to all the privileges and immunities of citizens in the several states; and that, therefore, thirdly, all state laws, whether organic or otherwise, which prohibit the citizens of one state from settling in another with their slave property, and especially declaring it forfeited, are direct violations of the original intention of the government and Constitution of the United States; and fourth, that the emancipation of the slaves of the Northern states was a gross outrage on the rights of property, inasmuch as it was involuntarily done on the part of the owner.

Remember that this article was published in the *Union* on the 17th of November, and on the 18th appeared the first article giving the adhesion of the *Union* to the Lecompton constitution. It was in these words:

"KANSAS AND HER CONSTITUTION.—The vexed question is settled. The problem is solved. The dread point of danger is passed. All serious trouble to Kansas affairs is over and gone."

And a column, nearly, of the same sort. Then, when you come to look into the Lecompton constitution, you find the same doctrine incorporated in it which was put forth editorially in the *Union*. What is it?

"ARTICLE 7. *Section* 1. The right of property is before and higher than any constitutional sanction; and the right of the owner of a slave to such slave and its increase is the same and as inviolable as the right of the owner of any property whatever."

Then in the schedule is a provision that the constitution may be amended after 1864 by a two-thirds vote.

"But no alteration shall be made to affect the right of property in the ownership of slaves."

It will be seen by these clauses in the Lecompton constitution that they are identical in spirit with this *authoritative* article in the Washington *Union* of the day previous to its indorsement of this constitution.

When I saw that article in the *Union* of the 17th of November, followed by the glorification of the Lecompton constitution on the 18th of November, and this clause in the constitution asserting the doctrine that a state has no right to prohibit slavery within its limits, I saw that there was a *fatal blow* being struck at the sovereignty of the states of this union.

Here he says, "Mr. President, you here find several distinct propositions advanced boldly, and apparently *authoritatively*." By whose authority, Judge Douglas? [Great cheers and laughter.] Again, he says in another place, "It will be seen by these clauses in the Lecompton constitution, that they are identical in spirit with this *authoritative* article." *By whose authority?* [Renewed cheers.] Who do you mean to say authorized the publication of these articles? He knows that the Washington *Union* is considered the organ of the administration. *I* demand of Judge Douglas *by whose authority* he meant to say those articles were published, if not by the authority of the President of the United States and his Cabinet? I defy him to show whom he referred to, if not to these high functionaries in the federal government. More than this, he says the articles in that paper and the provisions of the Lecompton constitution are "identical," and being identical, he argues that the authors are co-operating and conspiring together. He does not use the word "conspiring," but what other construction can you put upon it? He winds up with this:

> When I saw that article in the *Union* of the 17th of November, followed by the glorification of the Lecompton constitution on the 18th of November, and this clause in the constitution asserting the doctrine that a state has no right to prohibit slavery within its limits, I saw that there was a *fatal blow* being struck at the sovereignty of the states of this Union.

I ask him if all this fuss was made over the editor of this newspaper. [Laughter.] It would be a terribly *"fatal blow"* indeed which a single man could strike, when no President, no Cabinet officer, no member of Congress, was giving strength and efficiency to the movement. Out of respect to Judge Douglas' good sense I must believe he didn't manufacture his idea of the "fatal" character of that blow out of such a miserable scapegrace as he represents that editor to be. But the Judge's eye is farther south now. [Laughter and cheers.] Then, it was very peculiarly and decidedly north. His hope rested on the idea of visiting the great "Black Republican" party, and making it the tail of his new kite. [Great laughter.] He knows he was then expecting from day to day to turn Republican and place himself at the head [of] our organization. He has found that these despised "Black Republicans" estimate him by a standard which he has taught them none too well. Hence he is crawling back into his old camp, and you will find him eventually installed in full fellowship among those whom he was then battling, and with whom he now pretends to be at such fearful variance. [Loud applause and cries of "go on, go on."] I cannot, gentlemen, my time has expired.

CHAPTER SIX

THE CAMPAIGN PROGRESSES

With more than two weeks between the Freeport debate and the one scheduled for Jonesboro on September 15, the two candidates had time for intensive campaigning. Both men concentrated on the central third of the state, the old Whig counties whose voters would decide the election. The last day of August found Lincoln at Carlinville, where the Press and Tribune *reporter noted that Lincoln's second Freeport question, and Douglas' answer, were already having an effect.*[1]

Mr. Lincoln arrived here this morning and was warmly greeted by a host of personal friends. His speech at Freeport had not only disarmed the Democracy and hushed up their clamor about "Abolitionism," but, in the adroitness of his cornering Douglas on the Dred Scott decision, had stunned the blackguards who pretend to regard that decision as the great judicial illumination of the age. Douglas' answer to Mr. Lincoln's question amounts to nothing more nor less than *Mob Law* to keep slavery out of the territories, and the Dred Scotties cannot help seeing it. What sort of "police regulations" enable old McGee, of Ruffian notoriety, to hold slaves in Kansas? According to Douglas, he holds them simply because his neighbors don't club him and his niggers out of the territory! Hurrah for popular sovereignty and mob law! Hit him again.

Mr. Lincoln spoke from three o'clock till five this afternoon in the grove just south of the town. The audience numbered about one thousand. His remarks were an earnest and profound exhortation against the extension of slavery, free from declamation, rant or vulgarity. He was listened to with increasing attention from first to last, and when he had finished three rousing cheers went up for "our next Senator."

Douglas stopped at Joliet to address a large rally before proceeding to the central part of the state. Although the region was strongly

[1] Letter from Carlinville, August 31, in *Press and Tribune*, September 3.

anti-slavery, he went out of his way to attack two prominent Repub-
licans with Abolitionist leanings: John F. Farnsworth, member of
Congress from the Chicago district, and Owen Lovejoy of Princeton,
brother of the martyred Elijah P. Lovejoy, former Congregational
minister and, since 1856, member of Congress from the Ottawa
district. The Times *reported Douglas' strictures.*[2]

Senator Douglas . . . showed up the position of direct hostility
occupied by Farnsworth and Lovejoy to Lincoln, and that whilst
the former are asking to be re-elected to Congress on their pledge
to high Heaven that they would let their right arm wither sooner
than vote for the admission of a slave state; and that if the people
of a territory were "to do such an extraordinary thing as to adopt
a slave constitution, uninfluenced by the presence of the actual
institution among them, I (Lincoln) see no alternative, if we own
the country, but to admit them into the Union." How, asked Mr.
Douglas of the Black Republicans, can you expose yourselves to the
ridicule and contempt of mankind by professing to be fighting for
principle, and yet supporting Mr. Lincoln with one set of principles,
and Lovejoy and Farnsworth with another?

The Times *reporter, on his own account, took after Lovejoy.*[3]

Parson Lovejoy was on the stand during the meeting. With his
characteristic impudence he presented himself at the door leading
into the court house and thence through to the stand, which was
erected against the north side of the building, and when told by the
chairman of the committee that none but the speaker, the committee,
and the reporters were permitted on the stand, he still persisted in
pushing his way on, and took a seat directly in front of the audience.
Here he sat with his hat on, surrounded by gentlemen, who, out of
respect for the ladies at least, had removed their castors, and whenever he could get an opportunity would interrupt Senator Douglas
by some remark, or addressing himself to the crowd would say, "I
only ask a half-hour to answer him." At last the patience of all hands
having become exhausted by his frequent interruptions and his
angry and excited manner, Senator Douglas turned and administered
a personal rebuke to him which will never be forgotten by those
who heard it. It could not have been more direct or more severe, and
the poor, negro-stealing, contemptible wretch, completely thrown
off his guard, or unable to call up sufficient impudence to brazen

[2] Letter from Joliet, September 1, in Chicago *Times,* September 2.
[3] *Ibid.*

the thing out coolly, was the picture of misery as he sat there and heard his true character as a clerical slanderer and falsifier given to him. Parson Lovejoy will be more careful in the future how he thrusts himself forward. True, he was prepared for emergencies, and no doubt expected that he would be able to excite the crowd to such a degree as to bring an attack on him, or intended to show them that he was prepared for such a thing, for he held in his hand a large knife, with a dirk blade, and people looked on him in perfect astonishment that he should thus make so public display of such a desperate weapon.

At Pontiac, on September 2, Douglas introduced a new feature: a question-and-answer period at the conclusion of his set speech. The Times' *report reveals Douglas' adroitness in the technique of the stump.*[4]

Senator Douglas spoke for nearly three hours. . . . At the conclusion of his speech, it having been intimated that there were those present who desired to put questions to him, he intimated his readiness, if there was anyone who did not understand the principles he advocated and the position he occupied, to explain to them fully and fairly in answer to respectful questions which might be put to him. A man here called out, "They say you have turned your coat half a dozen times; we would like to know about that."

Senator Douglas in reply said that before answering that, he was disposed to act as Dr. Franklin, who, when he was Minister to Paris had a question put to him by the Academy of Science, why it was that in a pitcher so full of water that it would not hold another drop, a fish could be placed without making it run over. The doctor before answering, tried the experiment, and when he placed the fish in found that it did overrun, so that it was unnecessary to answer the question. (Great applause.)

"Thus when you say that I have changed my coat, I would like you to tell me when, and where, and how. Never having changed my coat, your question, like the question put to Dr. Franklin, is no question at all. (Applause.) I can prove by every old line Whig and Democrat in Illinois, that for twenty-five years I have fought the Whig party as fairly, as boldly, and as fearlessly as any other man in the state. Is that not so? ('Yes, yes, you always did.') And I have stood by the Democratic party equally as well. (Cheers.) The old Whig party has been betrayed by the corrupt coalition which I have already explained to you, into Abolitionism, and now

[4] Issue of September 5.

[179]

Old Line Whigs are joining the Democratic party and making common cause with us against this sectional, Abolition party. (Renewed applause.)

"I would like to know when and where I have changed my principles. If you mean with regard to the doctrine of popular sovereignty, I am prepared to compare records with any living man on that subject. In 1854, when I brought forward the Nebraska Bill, asserting the right of the people of each state and territory to decide the question of slavery for themselves, I could travel from Boston to Chicago by the light of my own effigy at night, and could see it dangling from the limbs of the trees in the day time. I think you will all bear me testimony that I did not wink, or dodge, or yield a hair's breadth when the torrent of Northern fanaticism was threatening to overwhelm me. (Cries of 'that's so,' and great applause.) And you will also bear testimony that during last winter when this same great principle of popular sovereignty was assailed from the South, that I then fought its enemies as boldly, without yielding to the torrent of Southern indignation and Southern fanaticism. (Renewed applause.) I stand by my principles and follow them to their logical conclusion, and I will not depart from them either to the right or the left to flatter one section or the other. My plan is to do justice to the South, and justice to the North, justice to everybody, and to avoid courting the popular breeze, or wavering in order to follow the popular sentiment. ('That's true,' 'good,' &c.) I would be willing to throw open my whole political life and compare records with any man of my age who has been in public life as long. (Cheers.) By this I do not pretend that I have been, or am any more consistent than any other man, but I do insist that I have acted honestly and faithfully in my political course. ('That you have,' and applause.)"

The question was here asked:

"Do you believe in the right of the state of Illinois to give up a fugitive slave?"

MR. DOUGLAS—"I will answer you upon that point. I hold that by the Constitution of the United States a fugitive from labor is required to be delivered up, and I hold that Congress is the proper legislative body to pass laws for that purpose. I hold further, that it is the duty of every member of Congress to vote for a law which will be efficient in securing the rendition of fugitives. I believe the present law to be tolerably efficient, but if it should not prove sufficiently so I would make another. (Cheers.) So long as I am your representative and take an oath to support the Constitution of the

United States, I will do all in my power to carry it out in good faith. ('That's right,' and intense enthusiasm.) I want to know whether your candidate would vote in favor of rendering up a fugitive slave?"

THE QUESTIONER—"I am a radical Abolitionist and have no candidate." (Laughter and cries of 'Don't Abe suit you?' 'What's wrong with him?')

MR. DOUGLAS—"I wish to say a word about that. I admire your candor in saying that you are a radical Abolitionist. For that reason you would not surrender a fugitive slave, and yet you will vote for Mr. Lincoln, who says that he will, and support his election to the United States Senate."

THE QUESTIONER (fervently)—"No, never!"

MR. DOUGLAS—"Then you are a more honest man than I thought you were." (Great laughter and cheers.)

From Pontiac, Douglas proceeded to Lincoln, the Logan County town which had been named for his rival when it was founded in 1853. There the Democratic candidate had to resort to the unusual expedient of speaking in a circus tent—a performance which the Republicans found vastly amusing. The Times *reported the meeting.*[5]

Not less than six thousand people were present at the meeting. It was intended that the speaking should be from the court house, where a commodious stand had been erected, and seats arranged capable of seating three thousand people, but owing to the wind, a perfect gale blowing at the time, and preventing a speaker from making himself heard, it was found necessary to hold the meeting in the large circus tent of Spalding & Rogers, which they generously tendered for that purpose. I was told by one of the gentlemen connected with the establishment that the tent seated fifteen hundred and was capable of holding, sitting and standing, four thousand people. The seats were filled almost exclusively by the ladies, and when every inch of standing room inside was occupied, and there were still large numbers trying to crowd in, it was found necessary to remove one side of the tent, in order to give the two or three thousand outside an opportunity to hear.

The tent afforded good shelter from the wind, and in it Senator Douglas was able to make himself heard to the extreme limits of the vast throng, thus gratifying and satisfying those who had come great distances to hear him. He spoke nearly three hours, with great vigor

[5] Letter from Lincoln, September 3, in Chicago *Times,* September 7.

and eloquence, and there could not have been a better feeling exhibited than was shown by the thousands who listened to him.

The Times *correspondent made his account of the meeting at Lincoln the vehicle for an allusion to a rumored propensity of the Republican candidate.*

I had a pleasant little chat with a Black Republican in Bloomington the other night, who was endeavoring to explain to me Abe's peculiar points. He admitted that he had not done well either in Ottawa or Freeport, but said that it was altogether owing to his unfortunate style. I frankly owned that from the talk about the man, I had expected to find Mr. Lincoln much more able than he had yet shown himself to be, and that I had been greatly disappointed in him. His friend acknowledged that he was not calculated to make much of an impression under any of the circumstances which I had heard him in large crowds with ladies present; "but," said he, "get old Abe before a town-meeting, where every once in awhile he can get off a smutty joke and raise a laugh, he'll take the crowd, and there's no man can beat him." I was satisfied. If Mr. Lincoln's popularity consists in smutty jokes, his friends have much to be proud of.

From Carlinville, Lincoln had gone north to Clinton, where he spoke on September 2, and then to Bloomington for a meeting two days later. On the 6th he was at Monticello for the second time during the campaign. There the Republicans staged a typical rally, extravagantly reported, as usual, by the Press and Tribune.[6]

This is the day that Hon. A. Lincoln had appointed to address the people of Piatt County. At an early hour the "country folk" began to flock into town in every conceivable mode of transit, and as early as 9 o'clock the town was literally alive with the sturdy yeomanry of Piatt County.

At 10 o'clock, the delegation from the adjoining county of Champaign reached the town and was met and preceded through the principal streets by a deputation of the Piatt boys and girls, each of the former of whom bore an American flag, and the latter representing and bearing the names of all the states. The Champaign delegation presented a lively appearance. It was at least 700 strong, had two bands of music and banners almost innumerable. I give you some of the devices:

[6] Letter from Monticello, September 6, in *Press and Tribune,* September 9.

CHAMPAIGN FOR OLD ABE IS *REAL* PAIN
FOR DUG

DOUGLAS' SEVEN CARDINAL PRINCIPLES:—
FIVE LOAVES AND TWO SMALL FISHES

DOUGLAS' POLITICAL HISTORY IN THREE
SHORT WORDS: "HURRAH FOR *ME!*"

—Then there was one with a picture of an Old Buck at full run with poor little Dug in vain pursuit, frantically exclaiming, "Don't leave me, Buck!—Abe wants *my place.* I'm for the English Bill now!" and many others of the same sort. The procession—a very long and fine one—after parading the streets marched out to the Bement road one mile, where they met Mr. Lincoln attended by a delegation of 800 persons who had come from Decatur by a special train, and the procession thus augmented returned through town to an adjacent grove, where dinner was to be served and the speaking to take place.

Mr. Lincoln's progress through the town was indeed a triumphal one. Cheer after cheer rent the air from the vast multitude which thronged the streets as he was perceived in the procession. While dinner was preparing, Mr. Weldon made an address of over an hour long, which was well received. At dinner it was found that although an immense quantity of victuals was provided, yet there was scarcely half enough for the assemblage. Everybody was astonished at the turn-out. . . .

After dinner Lincoln was introduced to the immense concourse by Thos. Milligan, Esq., and was received by a storm of cheers. He addressed the people for nearly three hours, and I never heard him make a finer speech except at Ottawa when he skinned Dug. The enthusiasm was overwhelming, and his conclusion was a strain of sublime eloquence which would have done credit to Clay or Webster in their palmiest days. Two years ago the American party was against us here, and Lincoln tells with irresistible humor of his reception when his procession consisted of one man carrying a large flag, and himself and his audience consisted of 30 persons. But all is changed now. The Americans, Old Line Whigs and Republicans are firmly united, and all efforts to distract them—and such efforts are not wanting—will be utterly in vain.

While Lincoln spoke at Monticello, Douglas addressed a Democratic rally at Jacksonville, where he had resided for some years after his brief stay in Winchester. B. F. Bristow welcomed the home-town boy who had made good.[7]

Honored and Respected Sir:

Permit me, on behalf of your fellow-citizens of "Old Morgan," to bid you welcome. Yes, welcome, thrice welcome, is the swelling emotion which now with gushing fullness throbs and beats in ten thousand hearts. Our happiness in meeting you here today differs in some respects from that with which you have been greeted by your fellow-citizens in other sections of our country. We receive you as "old friends" to the cherished home of your younger days. We receive you as one of our children; one whose brilliant career in life dates its starting point in Jacksonville. You came among us, sir, the poor schoolmaster, and you have been the architect of your own fortunes. In you we recognize a happy illustration of the glorious quality of our beloved institutions. You have made your way in life by self-exertion, unaided by exclusive privileges, or by the trappings of wealth and power. Under our constitution and laws you have been permitted to develop your great faculties unobstructed by legal impediments. We have watched your rapid rise and progress with feelings of thrilling interest; from the time you represented our county in the state legislature up to the present moment, we have been constant witnesses of your conflicts and your triumphs, and we are proud today in recognizing in you the embodiment of a principle which is wholly American, a principle with which you have become so intimately identified as to constitute a part of your being, a principle recognizing a man's right to self-government, a principle based upon a patriotism which is as broad as our glorious Union, not hemmed in by state or geographical lines, nor regulated or passed by local politics, a principle that knows no North, no South, no East, no West, but only knows them as one country—one and inseparable. In your conflicts in battling for this undying principle, calumny and detraction have in vain emptied all their vials upon your head; so fierce and so malignant has been the attack of your enemies that many of your friends have quailed with fear. But amid the roar of Kansas shriekers and the thunder of Lecompton

---

[7] Letter from Jacksonville, September 7, in Chicago *Times*, September 10.

hirelings, you have advanced undaunted. And, now how changed, consternation and dismay fill the souls of your enemies, you have outlived malice and envy.

Yes, sir, we are glad today that your life has been spared to prove to the world that your ambition was no more than a holy aspiration to make your country the greatest, most powerful, and the freest on earth.

> He who ascends the mountain top, shall find
> Its lofty peaks most wrapped in clouds and snow;
> He who surpasses or subdues mankind,
> Must look down on the hate of those below;
> Round him are icy, rocky, and loudly blow
> Contending tempests on his naked head,
> And thus reward the toils to which these summits led.

In the name of your fellow-citizens of old Morgan, I again bid you a hearty welcome.

Douglas responded to Bristow's tribute, and then spoke for almost three hours. "After the speech," the Times *reported, "Senator Douglas received and shook hands with an immense number of people. Several young men, who years ago were his pupils when he was teaching school, made themselves known, and the meeting was a most pleasant and interesting one."*

After the Monticello rally Lincoln traveled southeast to Paris. In describing the meeting there the Press and Tribune *correspondent lampooned Usher F. Linder, an old Whig friend of Lincoln's who had recently gone over to the Democracy, and drew an altogether different picture of Owen Lovejoy from the one sketched by the* Times *at Joliet.[8]*

PARIS, EDGAR Co., ILL., Sept. 8, 1858

It is confidently asserted down this way that our neighbor, Hon. Usher F. Linder, has received a touching epistle from Massa Douglas, running something in this wise: *"For God's sake,* Linder, come up into the northern part of the State and help me. Every bull-dog in the state is after me"—or something equivalent to this, indicating rather a feverish state of mind on the part of the man who lately bragged about having *thirty* majority in the next legislature. But you may tell Massa Douglas that Hon. U. F. Linder has got more than his hands full if he takes care of a couple of counties on the Wabash which embrace the aggregate of his influence. It would

[8] Chicago *Press and Tribune,* September 11.

hardly seem possible for a man who acquired so extensive a notoriety in connection with the Alton mob which finished its barbarian proceedings with the murder of Lovejoy,[9] to make many votes in the counties of Winnebago, Kane, Cook, Bureau; nor do I think it was wholly judicious in Douglas to send for a man with that kind of a record.

The audience which assembled in this place yesterday to hear Hon. Abraham Lincoln was larger by five hundred persons than that which came together last month to make the Douglas "demonstration." In this estimate I exclude the Indiana contribution which constituted so distinguished a part of the Douglas crowd—seven carloads having come over from Indianapolis and Terre Haute on that occasion. Omitting these non-voters, you can find plenty of men here to make affirmation that our doings yesterday eclipsed the "Dimmecratic" performance in numbers, enthusiasm and everything else.

Old Abe arrived in Paris on the 3 o'clock train from the west—having been detained several hours at Tolono and Mattoon, where the people gave him public receptions and literally compelled him to speak. Hon. Owen Lovejoy and Hon. James Miller, our State Treasurer, had arrived rather unexpectedly on the morning train, and were heartily welcomed. It was amusing, I assure you, to witness the curiosity, not unmixed with terror, with which Mr. Lovejoy was regarded by some of our oldest and most respectable citizens. Evidently many of them expected to find him wearing horns and a tail. In the absence of Mr. Lincoln, he was urgently called for and finally took the stand. He had spoken about half an hour when the procession from the depot arrived at the grove with Old Abe, who was greeted with three rousing cheers. The effect of Mr. Lovejoy's speech will be referred to again—doubtless to the entire satisfaction of Douglas, Linder & Co.

Mr. Lincoln spoke for two hours with unusual power and effect. It has been repeatedly remarked to me since the adjournment of the exercises, that "it was the clearest argument ever delivered in Edgar County."

. . . When Mr. Lincoln had concluded (at five o'clock) and after three loud cheers had been given for him, and three for the Republican ticket, it was proposed that the audience adjourn till evening and listen to Mr. Lovejoy and Mr. Oglesby at the court house. This motion was promptly negatived by the whole crowd, who insisted

[9] Elijah P. Lovejoy, older brother of Owen Lovejoy. In 1837 Elijah P. Lovejoy was killed by a mob at Alton, Illinois, as the result of his persistent efforts to publish an anti-slavery newspaper.

that Lovejoy should occupy the remaining hour till tea time, and "pitch in right smart." I venture the assertion that no equal number of persons could be found within a hundred miles of Chicago who would come forward more eagerly to hear Owen Lovejoy than did Republicans, Americans and Democrats in Edgar County, yesterday. They had got a taste of that which was good, and they were bound to have more before the first mouthful got cold. Mr. Lovejoy spoke until six o'clock, amid frequent and continued applause. "If that's what they call Abolitionism, I'm an Abolitionist," has been the constant remark of both Republicans and Old Line Whigs, since the conclusion of the exercises. Indeed, so much pleased was the entire community, that Mr. Lovejoy was again called out in the evening, and spoke nearly half an hour at the court house. A delegation of Americans from Grandview started for home about seven o'clock, shouting for Lincoln and Oglesby. I inquired of one of them, a rigid Fillmore man, what he had to say against Lovejoy now. "One of the best speeches that ever came out of a man's mouth," was the reply. "No more *Abolition* than I've believed in all my life."

On September 8 and 9 Douglas took a brief respite and visited the Missouri state fair at St. Louis. On the 10th he spoke at Belleville, Illinois. That evening "For God's Sake" Linder—already so nicknamed by the Republicans—drew favorable notice from the Times. The Democratic reporter, however, was more facile at invective than at praise. In the best partisan fashion of the day he flayed the Buchanan Democrats, represented by former Governor John Reynolds, and the hirelings of the Press and Tribune.[10]

There is an obscure little sheet published in town called the *Star of Egypt*, the especial organ of Gov. Reynolds, who, by the way, spent today out of town. It is not worth mentioning except to state that it is under the control of a man by the name of Hughes, who is trying to get the postoffice at this place, and is using the "Old Ranger," now declared by everybody to be in his dotage, to secure that end. The Danites in St. Clair County are composed of a poor, weak, palsied old man, tottering on the verge of the grave, with hardly strength enough to utter the blasphemy his tongue frames, and the other an arrant knave, who has cheated everybody in Belleville, and is despised by every one who knows him. They publish the *Star of Egypt* between them for gratuitous circulation.

There is a poor, mean, pitiful, sneaking cur, on the mink-skin order, named Davidson, traveling around and attending our meet-

[10] Letter from Belleville, September 10, in Chicago *Times*, September 15.

ings for the *Press and Tribune*. Today he had the impudence to offer to betray Deacon Bross and serve in the Democratic ranks, for a consideration in hand paid. What a mercenary crew the *Press and Tribune* attaches are. From the deacon to the lowest liar on the staff they are always in the market, and ready to sell themselves. The monkey to whom I now allude is constantly in company with a quack medicine doctor, who cures corns, bunions, &c., and I learn has secured a share in his business by being connected with the *Press and Tribune*. This partnership even extends to the doctor's wife, and the party being as thick as three in a bed, and bringing another *ism* into long *Abe*'s platform—that of "free love."

CHAPTER SEVEN

THE JONESBORO DEBATE

The day of the third joint debate (September 15) had now ap- proached. The Press and Tribune *set the stage with an unaccus- tomed minimum of partisanship.*[1]

Until ten o'clock . . . the only evidence of the third great debate, in old Jonesboro, was a procession calling itself the Johnson County delegation, consisting of two yoke of steers and a banner inscribed "Stephen A. Douglas," turned bottom upwards. Nothing else un- usual transpired during the forenoon until the arrival of two special trains—one from Centralia and the other from Cairo—which came in about the same time. The former consisted of four cars filled with attendants on the state fair. The latter brought Mr. Douglas, his brass cannon and a band of music from some unknown point, and five or six carloads of passengers from Cairo, Mound City, Kentucky and Missouri. Arrived at Anna (Jonesboro station) three cheers were *not* given—in default of which the faithful brass cannon banged away spitefully. Mr. Douglas entered a carriage in a quiet and orderly manner, and was driven over to old Jonesboro, about a mile distant. Mr. Lincoln had arrived in town on the evening of the preceding day.

Shortly before two o'clock the people entered the fair grounds, a little north of the town, where the speaking stand had been erected. The inevitable brass cannon was there before them, filling the yard with a loud noise and a bad smell. Several banners were brought up on the Douglas train from Cairo, and distributed around the stand —the principal one inscribed with a paraphrase from Holy Writ:

> MY SON, IF BOLTERS ENTICE THEE,
> CONSENT THOU NOT

This was claimed by the Buchanan men as having been stolen from them at a recent county convention.

[1] September 17.

The entire audience on the ground numbered between fourteen and fifteen hundred by actual count. To those who do not know the location of Jonesboro it will be sufficient to say that it is the county seat of Union Co., thirty-three miles north of Cairo, and about three hundred and fifty miles south of Chicago. It is very pleasantly and healthfully situated among the hills towards the confluence of the Ohio and Mississippi rivers, and is about 400 feet above the high water mark.[2]

"The brass cannon was subdued with difficulty," the Press and Tribune *commented tartly, "and Mr. Douglas was introduced to the audience by Col. Hecker, Jr."*

Douglas' Opening Speech

Ladies and Gentlemen:

I appear before you to-day in pursuance of a previous notice, and have made arrangements with Mr. Lincoln to divide time and discuss with him the leading political topics that now agitate the country.

Prior to 1854 this country was divided into two great political parties known as Whig and Democratic. These parties differed from each other on certain questions which were then deemed to be important to the best interests of the republic. Whigs and Democrats differed about a bank, the tariff, distribution, the specie circular and the sub-treasury. On those issues we went before the country and discussed the principles, objects and measures of the two great parties. Each of the parties could proclaim its principles in Louisiana as well as in Massachusetts, in Kentucky as well as in Illinois. Since that period, a great revolution has taken place in the formation of parties, by which they now seem to be divided by a geographical line, a large party in the North being arrayed under the abolition or republican banner in hostility to the Southern states, Southern people, and Southern institutions. It becomes important for us to inquire how this transformation of parties has occurred, made from

---

[2] Horace White, who wrote these paragraphs, recalled later: "The audience . . . was small, not more than 1,000 or 1,500, and nearly all Democrats. . . . The country people came into the little town with ox teams mostly, and a very stunted breed of oxen, too. Their wagons were old-fashioned, and looked as though they were ready to fall in pieces." In Herndon and Weik, *Abraham Lincoln* (New York, 1892), II, 118.

those of national principles to geographical factions. You remember that in 1850, this country was agitated from its centre to its circumference about this slavery question, it became necessary for the leaders of the great Whig party and the leaders of the great Democratic party to postpone, for the time being, their particular disputes and unite first to save the Union before they should quarrel as to the mode in which it was to be governed. During the Congress of 1849, '50, Henry Clay was the leader of the Union men, supported by Cass and Webster and the leaders of the democracy and the leaders of the Whigs, in opposition to Northern Abolitionists or Southern disunionists. That great contest of 1850 resulted in the establishment of the compromise measures of that year, which measures rested on the great principle that the people of each state and each territory of this Union ought to be permitted to regulate their own domestic institutions in their own way subject to no other limitation than that which the federal Constitution imposes.

I now wish to ask you whether that principle was right or wrong which guaranteed to every state and every community the right to form and regulate their domestic institutions to suit themselves. These measures were adopted, as I have previously said, by the joint action of the Union Whigs and Union Democrats, in opposition to Northern Abolitionists and Southern disunionists. In 1852, when the Whig party assembled at Baltimore, in national convention for the last time, they adopted the principle of the compromise measures of 1850 as their rule of party action in the future. One month thereafter the Democrats assembled at the same place to nominate a candidate for the Presidency, and declared the same great principle as the rule of action by which the Democracy would be governed. The presidential election of 1852 was fought on that basis. It is true that the Whigs claimed special merit for the adoption of those measures, because they asserted that their great Clay originated them, their God-like Webster defended them, and their Fillmore signed the bill making them the law of the land; but on the other hand the Democrats claimed special credit for the Democracy, upon the ground that we gave twice as many votes in both Houses of Congress for the passage of these measures as the Whig party.

Thus you see that in the presidential election of 1852, the Whigs were pledged by their platform and their candidate to the principle of the compromise measures of 1850, and the Democracy were likewise pledged by our principles, our platform, and our candidate to the same line of policy, to preserve peace and quiet between the different sections of this Union. Since that period the Whig party has been transformed into a sectional party, under the name of the Republican party, whilst the Democratic party continues the same national party it was at that day. All sectional men, all men of Abolition sentiments and principles, no matter whether they were old Abolitionists or had been Whigs or Democrats, rally under the sectional Republican banner, and consequently all national men, all Union loving men, whether Whigs, Democrats, or by whatever name they have been known, ought to rally under the stars and stripes in defence of the Constitution, as our fathers made it, and of the Union as it existed under the Constitution.

How has this departure from the faith of the Democracy and the faith of the Whig party been accomplished? In 1854, certain restless, ambitious, and disappointed politicians throughout the land took advantage of the temporary excitement created by the Nebraska Bill to try and dissolve the old Whig party and the old Democratic party, to abolitionize their members and lead them, bound hand and foot, captives into the abolition camp. In the state of New York a convention was held by some of these men and a platform adopted, every plank of which was as black as night, each one relating to the negro, and not one referring to the interests of the white man. That example was followed throughout the Northern states, the effect being made to combine all the free states in hostile array against the slave states. The men who thus thought that they could build up a great sectional party, and through its organization control the political destinies of this country, based all their hopes on the single fact that the North was the stronger division of the nation, and hence, if the North could be combined against the South, a sure victory awaited their efforts. I am doing no more than justice to the truth of history when I say that in this state Abraham Lincoln, on behalf of the Whigs, and Lyman Trumbull, on behalf of the Democrats, were the leaders who undertook to perform this grand scheme of abolitionizing the two parties to which they belonged. They had a private arrangement as to what should be the political destiny of each of the contracting parties before they went into the operation. The arrangement was that Mr. Lincoln was to take the old line Whigs with him, claiming that he was still as good a Whig as ever, over to the Abolitionists, and Mr. Trumbull was to run for Congress in the Belleville district, and, claiming to be a good Democrat, coax the old Democrats into the abolition camp, and when, by the joint efforts of the abolitionized Whigs, the abolitionized Democrats, and the old line Abolition and Free Soil party of this state, they should secure a majority in the legislature. Lincoln was then to be made United States Senator in Shields' place, Trumbull remaining in Congress until I should be accommodating enough to die or resign, and give him a chance to follow Lincoln. (Laughter, applause, and cries of "don't die.") That was a very nice little bargain so far as Lincoln and Trumbull were concerned, if it had been carried out in good faith, and friend Lincoln had attained to senatorial dignity according to the contract. They went into the contest in every part of the state, calling upon all disappointed politicians to join in the crusade against the Democracy, and appealed to the prevailing sentiments and prejudices in all the northern counties of the state. In three congressional districts in the north end of the state they adopted, as the platform of this new party thus formed by Lincoln and Trumbull in the connection with the Abolitionists, all of those principles which aimed at a warfare on the part of the North against the South. They declared in that platform that the Wilmot proviso was to be applied to all the territories of the United States, north as well as south of 36 deg. 30 min., and not only to all the territory we then had, but all that we might hereafter acquire; that hereafter no more slave states should be admitted into this Union, even if the people of such state desired slavery; that the fugitive slave law should be absolutely and unconditionally repealed; that slavery should be abolished in the District of Columbia; that the slave trade should be abolished between the different states, and, in fact, every article in their creed related to this slavery question, and pointed to a Northern geographical party in hostility to the Southern states of this Union. Such were their principles in northern Illinois. A little further south they became bleached and grew paler just in proportion as public sentiment moderated and changed in this direction. They were Republicans or Abolitionists in the north, anti-Nebraska men down about Springfield, and in this neighborhood they contented themselves with talking about the inexpediency of the repeal of the Missouri Compromise. (Shouts of laughter.) In the extreme northern counties they brought out men to canvass the state whose complexion suited their political creed, and hence Fred Douglass, the negro, was to be found there, following General Cass, and attempting to speak on behalf of Lincoln, Trumbull and abolitionism against that illustrious Senator. (Renewed laughter.) Why, they brought Fred Douglass to Freeport when I was addressing a meeting there in a carriage driven by the white owner, the negro sitting inside with the white lady and her daughter. ("Shame.") When I got through canvassing the northern counties that year and progressed as far south as Springfield, I was met and opposed in discussion by Lincoln, Lovejoy, Trumbull, and Sidney Breese, who were on one side. (Laughter.) Father Giddings, the high priest of Abolitionism, had just been there, and Chase came about the time I left. ("Why didn't you shoot him?") I did take a running shot at them, but as I was single-handed against the white, black and mixed drove, I had to use a short gun and fire into the crowd instead of taking them off singly with a rifle. (Great laughter and cheers.) Trumbull had for his lieutenants, in aiding him to abolitionize the Democracy, such men as John Wentworth, of Chicago, Gov. Reynolds, of Belleville, Sidney Breese, of Carlisle, and John Dougherty, of Union, ("good," "good," "give it to them," &c.,) each of whom modified his opinions to suit the particular locality he was in. Dougherty, for instance, would not go much further than to talk about the inexpediency of the Nebraska Bill, whilst his allies at Chicago, advocated negro citizenship and negro equality, putting the white man and the negro on the same basis under the law. ("Never, never.") Now these men, four years ago, were engaged in a conspiracy to break down the Democracy; to-day they are again acting together for the same purposes. They do not hoist the same flag; they do not own the same principles, or profess the same faith; but conceal their union for the sake of policy. In the northern counties, you find that all the conventions are called in the name of the Black Republican party; at Springfield, they dare not call a Republican convention, but invite all the enemies of the Democracy to unite, and when they get down into Egypt, Trumbull issues notices calling upon the *"free democracy"* to assemble and hear him speak. I have one of the handbills calling a Trumbull meeting at Waterloo the other day, which I received there, which is in the following language:

A meeting of the Free Democracy will take place in Waterloo, on Monday, Sept. 13th inst., whereat Hon. Lyman Trumbull, Hon. Jehu Baker and others will address the people upon the different political topics of the day. Members of all parties are cordially invited to be present, and hear and determine for themselves.

THE MONROE FREE DEMOCRACY

What is that name of "Free Democrats" put forth for unless to deceive the people, and make them believe that Trumbull and his followers are not the same party as that which raises the black flag of Abolitionism in the northern part of this state, and makes war upon the Democratic party throughout the state. When I put that question to them at Waterloo on Saturday last, one of them rose and stated that they had changed their name for political effect in order to get votes. There was a candid admission. Their object in changing their party organization and principles in different localities was avowed to be an attempt to cheat and deceive some portion of the people until after the election. Why cannot a political party that is conscious of the rectitude of its purposes and the soundness of its principles declare them every where alike. I would disdain to hold any political principles that I could not avow in the same terms in Kentucky that I declared in Illinois, in Charleston as well as in Chicago, in New Orleans as well as in New York. (Cheers.) So long as we live under a constitution common to all the states, our political faith ought to be as broad, as liberal, and just as that constitution itself, and should be proclaimed alike in every portion of the Union. ("Hear, hear.") But it is apparent that our opponents find it necessary, for partizan effect, to change their colors in different counties in order to catch the popular breeze, and hope with these discordant materials combined together to secure a majority in the legislature for the purpose of putting down the Democratic party. This combination did succeed in 1854 so far as to elect a majority of their confederates to the legislature, and the first important act which they performed was to elect a Senator in the place of the eminent and gallant Senator Shields. His term expired in the United States Senate at that time, and he had to be crushed by the abolition coalition for the simple reason that he would not join in their conspiracy to wage war against one-half of the Union. That was the only objection to Gen. Shields. He had served the people of the state with ability in the legislature, he had served you with fidelity and ability as auditor, he had performed his duties to the satisfaction of the whole country as head of the Land Department at Washington, he had covered the state and the Union with immortal glory on the bloody fields of Mexico in defence of the honor of our flag, and yet he had to be stricken down by this unholy combination. And for what cause? Merely because he would not join a combination of one-half of the states to make war upon the other half, after having poured out his heart's blood for all the states in the Union. Trumbull was put in his place by Abolitionism. How did Trumbull get there? Before the Abolitionists would consent to go into an election for United States Senator they required all the members of this new combination to show their hands upon this question of abolitionism. Lovejoy, one of their high priests, brought in resolutions defining the abolition creed, and required them to commit themselves on it by their votes—yea or nay. In that creed, as laid down by Lovejoy, they declared first, that the Wilmot proviso must be put on all the territories of the United States north as well as south of 36 deg. 30 min., and that no more territory should ever be acquired unless slavery was at first prohibited therein; second, that no more states should ever be received into the Union unless slavery was first prohibited, by constitutional provision, in such states; third, that the fugitive slave law must be immediately repealed, or, failing in that, then such amendments were to be made to it as would render it useless and inefficient for the objects for which it was passed, &c. The next day after these resolutions were offered they were voted upon, part of them carried, and the others defeated, the same men who voted for them, with only two exceptions, voting soon after for Abraham Lincoln as their candidate for the United States Senate. He came within one or two votes of being elected, but he could not quite get the number required, for the simple reason that his friend Trumbull, who was a party to the bargain by which Lincoln was to take Shields' place, controlled a few abolitionized Democrats in the legislature, and would not allow them all to vote for him, thus wronging Lincoln by permitting him on each ballot to be almost elected, but not quite, until he forced them to drop Lincoln and elect him (Trumbull), in order to unite the party. (Immense laughter.) Thus you find, that although the legislature was carried that year by the bargain between Trumbull, Lincoln, and the Abolitionists, and the union of these discordant elements in one harmonious party; yet Trumbull violated his pledge, and played a Yankee trick on Lincoln when they came to divide the spoils. (Laughter and cheers. Mr. Lincoln greatly agitated, his face buried in his hands.) Perhaps you would like a little evidence on this point. If you would, I will call Col. Jas. H. Matheny, of Springfield, to the stand, Mr. Lincoln's especial confidential friend for the last twenty years, and see what he will say upon the subject of this bargain. Matheny is now the Black Republican or Abolition candidate for Congress in the Springfield district against the gallant Col. Harris, and is making speeches all over that part of the state against me and in favor of Lincoln, in concert with Trumbull. He ought to be a good witness, and I will read an extract from a speech which he made in 1856, when he was mad because his friend Lincoln had been cheated. It is one of numerous speeches of the same tenor that were made about that time, exposing this bargain between Lincoln, Trumbull, and the Abolitionists. Matheny then said:

The Whigs, Abolitionists, Know Nothings, and renegade Democrats made a solemn compact for the purpose of carrying this state against the Democracy, on this plan: 1st. That they would all combine and elect Mr. Trumbull to Congress, and thereby carry his district for the legislature, in order to throw all the strength that could be obtained into that body against the Democrats. 2d. That when the legislature should meet, the officers of that body, such as speaker, clerks, doorkeepers, &c., would be given to the Abolitionists; and 3d, That the Whigs were to have the United States

Senator. That, accordingly, in good faith, Trumbull was elected to Congress, and his district carried for the legislature, and, when it convened, the Abolitionists got all the officers of that body, and thus far the "bond" was fairly executed. The Whigs, on their part, demanded the election of Abraham Lincoln to the United States Senate, that the bond might be fulfilled, the other parties to the contract having already secured to themselves all that was called for. But, in the most perfidious manner, they refused to elect Mr. Lincoln; and the mean, low-lived, sneaking Trumbull succeeded, by pledging all that was required by any party, in thrusting Lincoln aside and foisting himself, an excrescence from the rotten bowels of the Democracy, into the United States Senate; and thus it has ever been, that an *honest* man makes a bad bargain when he conspires or contracts with rogues.

Matheny thought that his friend Lincoln made a bad bargain when he conspired and contracted with such rogues as Trumbull and his abolition associates in that campaign. (Great cheers and laughter; Lincoln looking very miserable.) Lincoln was shoved off the track, and he and his friends all at once began to mope, became sour and mad, (laughter,) and disposed to tell, but dare not; (shouts of laughter;) and thus they stood for a long time until the Abolitionists coaxed and flattered him back by their assurances that he should certainly be a Senator in Douglas' place. (Roars of laughter, Lincoln looking as if he had not a friend on earth, although Herr Kriesman whispered "never mind" into his ear.) In that way the Abolitionists have been enabled to hold Lincoln to the alliance up to this time, and now they have brought him into a fight against me, and he is to see if he is again to be cheated by them. Lincoln this time though required more of them than a promise, and holds their bond, if not security, that Lovejoy shall not cheat him as Trumbull did. (Renewed shouts of laughter.)

When the Republican convention assembled at Springfield in June last for the purpose of nominating state officers only, the Abolitionists could not get Lincoln and his friends into it until they would pledge themselves that Lincoln should be their candidate for the Senate; and you will find, in proof of this, that that convention passed a resolution unanimously declaring that Abraham Lincoln was the "first, last and only choice" of the Republicans for United States Senator. He was not willing to have it understood that he was merely their first choice, or their last choice, but their *only* choice. The Black Republican party had nobody else. Browning was nowhere, Gov. Bissell was of no account, Archie Williams was not to be taken into consideration, John Wentworth was not worth mentioning, John M. Palmer was degraded, and their party presented the extraordinary spectacle of having but one—the first, last, and only choice for the Senate. (Laughter.) Suppose Lincoln should die, what a horrible condition the Republican party would be in. (A groan from Lincoln, and great laughter.) They would have nobody left. They have no other choice, and it was necessary for them to put themselves before the world in this ludicrous, ridiculous attitude of having no other choice in order to quiet Lincoln's suspicions, and assure him that he was not to be cheated by Lovejoy, and the trickery by which Trumbull out-generalled him. Well, gentlemen, I think they will have a nice time of it before they get through. I do not intend to give them any chance to cheat Lincoln at all this time. (Cheers.) I intend to relieve him and them from all anxiety upon that subject, and spare them the mortification of more exposures of contracts violated, and the pledged honor of rogues forfeited. (Great applause.)

But I wish to invite your attention to the chief points at issue between Mr. Lincoln and myself in this discussion. Mr. Lincoln, knowing that he was to be the candidate of his party on account of the arrangement of which I have already spoken, knowing that he was to receive the nomination of the convention for the United States Senate, had his speech, accepting that nomination, all written and committed to memory, ready to be delivered the moment the nomination was announced. Accordingly, when it was made he was in readiness, and delivered his speech, a portion of which I will read, in order that I may state his political principles fairly, by repeating them in his own language.

We are now far into the fifth year since a policy was instituted for the avowed object, and with the confident promise of putting an end to slavery agitation; under the operation of that policy, that agitation had not only not ceased, but had constantly augmented. I believe it will not cease until a crisis shall have been reached and passed. A house divided against itself cannot stand. I believe this government cannot endure permanently half slave and half free. I do not expect the Union to be dissolved. I do not expect the house to fall, but I do expect it will cease to be divided. It will become all one thing or all the other. Either, the opponents of slavery will arrest the spread of it and place it where the public mind shall rest in the belief that it is in the course of ultimate extinction, or its advocates will push it forward until it shall become alike lawful in all the States North as well as South.

There you have Mr. Lincoln's first and main proposition, upon which he bases his claims, stated in his own language. He tells you that this Republic cannot endure permanently divided into slave and free states, as our fathers made it. He says that they must all become free or all become slave, that they must all be one thing or all be the other, or this government cannot last. Why can it not last if we will execute the government in the same spirit and upon the same principles upon which it is founded. Lincoln, by his proposition, says to the South, "If you desire to maintain your institutions as they are now, you must not be satisfied with minding your own business, but you must invade Illinois and all the other Northern states, establish slavery in them and make it universal;" and in the same language he says to the North, "you must not be content with regulating your own affairs and minding your own business, but if you desire to maintain your freedom you must invade the Southern states, abolish slavery there and everywhere, in order to have the states all one thing or all the other." I say that this is the inevitable and irresistible result of Mr. Lincoln's argument inviting a warfare between the North and the South, to be carried on with ruthless vengeance, until the one section or the other shall be driven to the wall and become the victim of the rapacity of the other. What good would follow such a system of warfare? Suppose the North should succeed in conquering the South, how much would she be the gainer, or suppose the South should conquer the North, could the Union be preserved in that way? Is this sectional warfare to be waged between Northern states and Southern states until they all shall become uniform in their local and domestic institutions merely because Mr. Lincoln says that a house divided against itself cannot stand, and pretends that this scriptural quotation, this language of our Lord and Master, is applicable to the American Union and the American Constitution? Washington and his compeers in the convention that framed the Constitution, made this government divided into free and slave states. It was composed then of thirteen sovereign and independent states, each having sovereign authority over its local and domestic institutions, and all bound together by the federal Constitution. Mr. Lincoln likens that bond of the federal Constitution joining free and slave states together to a house divided against itself, and says that it is contrary to the law of God and cannot stand. When did he learn, and by what authority does he proclaim, that this government is contrary to the law of God, and cannot stand? It has stood thus divided into free and slave states from its organization up to this day. During that period we have increased from four millions to thirty millions of people; we have extended our territory from the Mississippi to the Pacific Ocean; we have acquired the Floridas and Texas and other territory sufficient to double our geographical extent; we have increased in population, in wealth, and in power beyond any example on earth; we have risen from a weak and feeble power to become the terror and admiration of the civilized world; and all this has been done under a constitution which Mr. Lincoln, in substance, says is in violation of the law of God, and under a union divided into free and slave states, which Mr. Lincoln thinks, because of such division, cannot stand. Surely, Mr. Lincoln is a wiser man than those who framed the government. Washington did not believe, nor did his compatriots, that the local laws and domestic institutions that were well adapted to the green mountains of Vermont were suited to the rice plantations of South Carolina; they did not believe at that day that in a republic so broad and expanded as this, containing such a variety of climate, soil and interest, that uniformity in the local laws and domestic institutions were either desirable or possible. They believed then as our experience has proved to us now, that each locality, having different interests, a different climate and different surroundings, required different local laws; local policy and local institutions adapted to the wants of that locality. Thus our government was formed on the principle of diversity in the local institutions and laws and not on that of uniformity.

As my time flies, I can only glance at these points and not present them as fully as I would wish, because I desire to bring all the points in controversy between the two parties before you in order to have Mr. Lincoln's reply. He makes war on the decision of the Supreme Court in the case known as the Dred Scott case. I wish to say to you, fellow-citizens, that I have no war to make on that decision, or any other ever rendered by the Supreme Court. I am content to take that decision as it stands delivered by the highest judicial tribunal on earth, a tribunal established by the Constitution of the United States for that purpose, and hence that decision becomes the law of the land, binding on you, on me, and on every other good citizen, whether we like it or not. Hence I do not choose to go into an argument to prove, before this audience, whether or not Chief Justice Taney understood the law better than Abraham Lincoln. (Laughter.)

Mr. Lincoln objects to that decision, first and mainly because it deprives the negro of the rights of citizenship. I am as much opposed to his reason for that objection as I am to the objection itself. I hold that a negro is not and never ought to be a citizen of the United States. ("Good, good," and tremendous cheers.) I hold that this government was made on the white basis, by white men, for the benefit of white men and their posterity forever, and should be administered by white men and none others. I do not believe that the Almighty made the negro capable of self-government. I am aware that all the abolition lecturers that you find traveling about through the country are in the habit of reading the Declaration of Independence to prove that all men were created equal and endowed by their Creator with certain inalienable rights, among which are life, liberty, and the pursuit of happiness. Mr. Lincoln is very much in the habit of following in the track of Lovejoy in this particular, by reading that part of the Declaration of Independence to prove that the negro was endowed by the Almighty with the inalienable right of equality with white men. Now, I say to you, my fellow-citizens, that in my opinion the signers of the Declaration had no reference to the negro whatever when they declared all men to be created equal. They desired to express by that phrase, white men, men of European birth and European descent, and had no reference either to the negro, the savage Indians, the Fejee, the Malay, or any other inferior and degraded race, when they spoke of the equality of men. One great evidence that such was their understanding, is to be found in the fact that at that time every one of the thirteen colonies was a slaveholding colony, every signer of the Declaration represented a slave-holding constituency, and we know that no one of them emancipated his slaves, much less offered citizenship to them when they signed the Declaration, and yet, if they had intended to declare that the negro was the equal of the white man, and entitled by divine right to an equality with him, they were bound, as honest men, that day and hour to have put their negroes on an equality with themselves. (Cheers.) Instead of doing so, with uplifted eyes to Heaven they implored the Divine blessing upon them, during the seven years' bloody war they had to fight to maintain that Declaration, never dreaming that they were violating divine law by still holding the negroes in bondage and depriving them of equality.

My friends, I am in favor of preserving this government as our fathers made it. It does not follow by any means that because a negro is not your equal or mine that hence he must necesarily be a slave. On the contrary, it does follow that we ought to extend to the negro every right, every privilege, every immunity which he is capable of enjoying consistent with the good of society. When you ask me what these rights are, what their nature and extent is, I tell you that that is a question which each state of this Union must decide for itself. Illinois has already decided the question. We have decided that the negro must not be a slave within our limits, but we have also decided that the negro shall not be a citizen within our limits; that he shall not vote, hold office, or exercise any political rights. I maintain that Illinois, as a sovereign state, has a right thus to fix her policy with reference to the relation between the white man and the negro; but while we had the right to decide the question for ourselves we must recognize the same right in

Kentucky and in every other state to make the same decision, or a different one. Having decided our own policy with reference to the black race, we must leave Kentucky and Missouri and every other state perfectly free to make just such a decision as they see proper on that question.

Kentucky has decided that question for herself. She has said that within her limits a negro shall not exercise any political rights, and she has also said that a portion of the negroes under the laws of that state shall be slaves. She had as much right to adopt that as her policy as we had to adopt the contrary as our policy. New York has decided that in that state a negro may vote if he has $250 of property, and if he owns that much he may vote upon an equality with the white man. I, for one, am utterly opposed to negro suffrage anywhere and under any circumstances; yet, inasmuch as the Supreme Court have decided in the celebrated Dred Scott case that a state has a right to confer the privilege of voting upon free negroes, I am not going to make war upon New York because she has adopted a policy repugnant to my feelings. ("That's good.") But New York must mind her own business, and keep her negro suffrage to herself and not attempt to force it upon us. (Great applause.)

In the state of Maine they have decided that a negro may vote and hold office on an equality with a white man. I had occasion to say to the Senators from Maine in a discussion last session, that if they thought that the white people within the limits of their state were no better than negroes, I would not quarrel with them for it, but they must not say that my white constituents of Illinois were no better than negroes, or we would be sure to quarrel. (Cheers.)

The Dred Scott decision covers the whole question, and declares that each state has the right to settle this question of suffrage for itself, and all questions as to the relations between the white man and the negro. Judge Taney expressly lays down the doctrine. I receive it as law, and I say that while those states are adopting regulations on that subject disgusting and abhorrent, according to my views, I will not make war on them if they will mind their own business and let us alone. ("Bravo," and cheers.)

I now come back to the question, why cannot this Union exist forever divided into free and slave states as our fathers made it? It can thus exist if each state will carry out the principles upon which our institutions were founded, to wit: the right of each state to do as it pleases, without meddling with its neighbors. Just act upon that great principle, and this Union will not only live forever, but it will extend and expand until it covers the whole continent, and make this confederacy one grand ocean-bound republic. We must bear in mind that we are yet a young nation growing with a rapidity unequalled in the history of the world, that our national increase is great, and that the emigration from the old world is increasing, requiring us to expand and acquire new territory from time to time in order to give our people land to live upon. If we live upon the principle of state rights and state sovereignty, each state regulating its own affairs and minding its own business, we can go on and extend indefinitely, just as fast and as far as we need the territory. The time may come, indeed has now come, when our interests would be advanced by the acquisition of the island of Cuba. (Terrific applause.) When we get Cuba we must take it as we find it, leaving the people to decide the question of slavery for themselves, without interference on the part of the federal government, or of any state of this Union. So, when it becomes necessary to acquire any portion of Mexico or Canada, or of this continent or the adjoining islands, we must take them as we find them, leaving the people free to do as they please, to have slavery or not, as they choose. I never have inquired and never will inquire whether a new state applying for admission has slavery or not for one of her institutions. If the constitution that is presented be the act and deed of the people and embodies their will, and they have the requisite population, I will admit them with slavery or without it just as the people shall determine. ("That's good." "That's right," and cheers.) My objection to the Lecompton constitution did not consist in the fact that it made Kansas a slave state. I would have been as much opposed to its admission under such a constitution as a free state as I was opposed to its admission under it as a slave state. I hold that that was a question which that people had a right to decide for themselves, and that no power on earth ought to have interfered with that decision. In my opinion, the Lecompton constitution was not the act and deed of the people of Kansas, and did not embody their will, and the recent election in that territory, at which it was voted down by nearly ten to one, shows conclusively that I was right in saying when the constitution was presented, that it was not the act and deed of the people, and did not embody their will.

If we wish to preserve our institutions in their purity, and transmit them unimpaired to our latest posterity, we must preserve with religious good faith that great principle of self-government which guarantees to each and every state, old and new, the right to make just such constitutions as they deserve, and come into the Union with their own constitution and not one palmed upon them. (Cheers.) Whenever you sanction the doctrine that Congress may crowd a constitution down the throats of an unwilling people against their consent, you will subvert the great fundamental principle upon which all our free institutions rest. In the future I have no fear that the attempt will ever be made. President Buchanan declared in his annual message, that hereafter the rule adopted in the Minnesota case, requiring a constitution to be submitted to the people, should be followed in all future cases, and if he stands by that recommendation there will be no division in the Democratic party on that principle in the future. Hence, the great mission of the Democracy is to unite the fraternal feeling of the whole country, restore peace and quiet by teaching each state to mind its own business, and regulate its own domestic affairs, and all to unite carrying out the Constitution as our fathers made it, and thus to preserve the Union and render it perpetual in all time to come. Why should we not act as our fathers who made the government? There was no sectional strife in Washington's army. They were all brethren of a common confederacy, they fought under a common flag that they might bestow upon their posterity a common destiny, and to this end they poured out their blood in common streams and shared in some instances a common grave. (Three hearty cheers for Douglas.)

Lincoln's Reply

Ladies and Gentlemen:

There is very much in the principles that Judge Douglas has here enunciated that I most cordially approve, and over which I shall have no controversy with him. In so far as he has insisted that all the states have the right to do exactly as they please about all their domestic relations, including that of slavery, I agree entirely with him. He places me wrong in spite of all I can tell him, though I repeat it again and again, insisting that I have no difference with him upon this subject. I have made a great many speeches, some of which have been printed, and it will be utterly impossible for him to find anything that I have ever put in print contrary to what I now say upon this subject. I hold myself under constitutional obligations to allow the people in all the states without interference, direct or indirect, to do exactly as they please, and I deny that I have any inclination to interfere with them, even if there were no such constitutional obligation. I can say again that I am placed improperly—altogether improperly in spite of all I can say—when it is insisted that I entertain any other view or purposes in regard to that matter.

While I am upon this subject, I will make some answers briefly to certain propositions that Judge Douglas has put. He says, "Why can't this Union endure permanently, half slave and half free?" I have said that I supposed it could not, and I will try, before this new audience, to give briefly some of the reasons for entertaining that opinion. Another form of his question is, "Why can't we let it stand as our fathers placed it?" That is the exact difficulty between us, I say that Judge Douglas and his friends have changed them from the position in which our fathers originally placed it. I say in the way our fathers originally left the slavery question, the institution was in the course of ultimate extinction, and the public mind rested in the belief that it *was* in the course of ultimate extinction. I say when this government was first established it was the policy of its founders to prohibit the spread of slavery into the new territories of the United States, where it had not existed. But Judge Douglas and his friends have broken up that policy and placed it upon a new basis by which it is to become national and perpetual. All I have asked or desired anywhere is that it should be placed back again upon the basis that the fathers of our government originally placed it upon. I have no doubt that it *would* become extinct, for all time to come, if we but re-adopted the policy of the fathers by restricting it to the limits it has already covered—restricting it from the new territories.

I do not wish to dwell at great length on this branch of the subject at this time, but allow me to repeat one thing that I have stated before. Brooks, the man who assaulted Senator Sumner on the floor of the Senate, and who was complimented with dinners and silver pitchers, and gold-headed canes, and a good many other things for that feat, in one of his speeches declared that when this government was originally established nobody expected that the institution of slavery would last until this day. That was but the opinion of one man, but it was such an opinion as we can never get from Judge Douglas or anybody in favor of slavery in the North at all. You *can* sometimes get it from a Southern man. He said at the same time that the framers of our government did not have the knowledge that experience has taught us—that experience and the invention of the cotton-gin have taught us that the perpetuation of slavery is a necessity. He insisted, therefore, upon its being changed from the basis upon which the fathers of the government left it to the basis of its perpetuation and nationalization.

I insist that this is the difference between Judge Douglas and myself—that Judge Douglas is helping that change along. I insist upon this government being placed where our fathers originally placed it.

I remember Judge Douglas once said that he saw the evidences on the statute books of Congress, of a policy in the origin of government to divide slavery and freedom by a geographical line—that he saw an indisposition to maintain that policy, and therefore he set about studying up a way to settle the institution on the right basis—the basis which he thought it ought to have been placed upon at first; and in that speech he confesses that he seeks to place it not upon the basis that the fathers placed it upon, but upon one gotten up on "original principles." When he asks me why we cannot get along with it in the attitude where our fathers placed it he had better clear up the evidences that he has himself changed it from that basis; that he has himself been chiefly instrumental in changing the policy of the fathers. [Applause.] Any one who will read his speech of the 22d of last March, will see that he there makes an open confession, showing that he set about fixing the institution upon an altogether different set of principles. I think I have fully answered him when he asks me why we cannot let it alone upon the basis where our fathers left it, by showing that has himself changed the whole policy of the government in that regard.

Now, fellow citizens, in regard to this matter about a contract that was made between Judge Trumbull and myself, and all that long portion of Judge Douglas' speech on this subject—I wish simply to say what I have said to him before, that he cannot know whether it is true or not, and I *do know* that there is not a word of truth in it. [Applause.] And I have told him so before. [Continued applause. "That's right." "Hit him again."] I don't want any harsh language indulged in, but I do not know how to deal with this persistent insisting on a story that I know to be utterly without truth. It used to be a fashion amongst men that when a charge was made some sort of proof was brought forward to establish it, and if no proof was found to exist, the charge was dropped. I don't know how to meet this kind of an argument. I don't want to have a fight with Judge Douglas, and I have no way of making an argument up into the consistency of a corn-cob and stopping his mouth with it. [Laughter and applause.] All I can do is, good-humoredly to say that from the beginning to the end of all that story about a bargain between Judge Trumbull and myself, *there is not a word of truth in it.* [Applause.] I can only ask him to show some sort of evidence of the truth of his story. He brings forward here and reads from what he contends is a speech by James H. Matheny charging such a bargain between Trumbull and myself. My own opinion is that

Matheny did do some such immoral thing as to tell a story that he knew nothing about. I believe he did. I contradicted it instantly and it has been contradicted by Judge Trumbull, while nobody has produced any proof, because there is none. Now whether the speech which the Judge brings forward here is really the one Matheny made I do not know, and I hope the Judge will pardon me for doubting the genuineness of this document since his production of those Springfield resolutions at Ottawa. [Laughter and cheers.] I do not wish to dwell at any great length upon this matter. I can say nothing when a long story like this is told except it is not true, and demand that he who insists upon it shall produce some proof. That is all any man can do, and I leave it in that way for I know of no other way of dealing with it.

The Judge has gone over a long account of the old Whig and Democratic parties, and it connects itself with this charge against Trumbull and myself. He says that they agreed upon a compromise in regard to the slavery question in 1850; that in a national Democratic convention resolutions were passed to abide by that compromise as a finality upon the slavery question. He also says that the Whig party in national convention agreed to abide by and regard as a finality, the compromise of 1850. I understand the Judge to be altogether right about that; I understand that part of the history of the country as stated by him to be correct. I recollect that I, as a member of that party, acquiesced in that compromise. I recollect in the presidential election which followed, when we had General Scott up for the Presidency, Judge Douglas was around berating us Whigs as Abolitionists, precisely as he does to-day—not a bit of difference. I have often heard him. We could do nothing when the old Whig party was alive that was not Abolitionism, but it has got an extremely good name since it has passed away. [Laughter.]

When that compromise was made it did not repeal the old Missouri Compromise. It left a region of United States territory half as large as the present territory of the United States, north of the line of 36° 30′ in which slavery was prohibited by act of Congress. This compromise did not repeal that one. It did not affect or propose to repeal it. But at last it became Judge Douglas' duty, as he thought (and I find no fault with him) as Chairman of the Committee on Territories, to bring in a bill for the organization of a territorial government—first of one, then of two territories north of that line. When he did so it ended in his inserting a provision substantially repealing the Missouri Compromise. That was because the Compromise of 1850 *had not* repealed it. And now I ask why he could not have let that compromise alone? We were quiet from the agitation of the slavery question. We were making no fuss about it. All had acquiesced in the compromise measures of 1850. We never had been seriously disturbed by any abolition agitation before that period. When he came to form governments for the territories north of the line of 36° 30', why could he not have let that matter stand as it was standing? [Applause.] Was it necessary to the organization of a territory? Not at all. Iowa lay north of the line and had been organized as a territory and had come into the Union as a state without disturbing that compromise. There was no sort of necessity for destroying it to organize these territories. But gentlemen, it would take up all my time to meet all the little quibbling arguments of Judge Douglas to show that the Missouri Compromise was repealed by the Compromise of 1850. My own opinion is that a careful investigation of all the arguments to sustain the position that that compromise was virtually repealed by the Compromise of 1850 would show that they are the merest fallacies. I have the report that Judge Douglas first brought into Congress at the time of the introduction of the Nebraska Bill, which in its original form *did not* repeal the Missouri Compromise, and he there expressly stated that he had forborne to do so *because it had not been done by the Compromise of 1850.* I close this part of the discussion on my part by asking him the question again "Why when we had peace under the Missouri Compromise could you not have let it alone?"

In complaining of what I said in my speech at Springfield in which he says I accepted my nomination for the senatorship, (where by the way he is at fault, for if he will examine it he will find no acceptance in it;) he again quotes that portion in which I said that "a house divided against itself cannot stand." Let me say a word in regard to that matter.

He tries to persuade us that there must be a variety in the different institutions of the states of the Union; that that variety necessarily proceeds from the variety of soil, climate, of the face of the country and the difference in the natural features of the states. I agree to all that. Have these very matters ever produced any difficulty amongst us? Not at all. Have we ever had any quarrel over the fact that they have laws in Louisiana designed to regulate the commerce that springs from the production of sugar? Or because we have a different class relative to the production of flour in this state? Have they produced any differences? Not at all. They are the very cements of this Union. They don't make the house a house divided against itself. They are the props that hold up the house and sustain the Union.

But has it been so with this element of slavery? Have we not always had quarrels and difficulties over it? And when will we cease to have quarrels over it? Like causes produce like effects. It is worth while to observe that we have generally had comparative peace upon the slavery question and that there has been no cause for alarm until it was excited by the effort to spread it into new territory. Whenever it has been limited to its present bounds and there has been no effort to spread it, there has been peace. All the trouble and convulsion has proceeded from efforts to spread it over more territory. It was thus at the date of the Missouri Compromise. It was so again with the annexation of Texas; so with the territory acquired by the Mexican war, and it is so now. Whenever there has been an effort to spread it there has been agitation and resistance. Now I appeal to this audience, (very few of whom are my political friends,) as national men, whether we have reason to expect that the agitation in regard to this subject will cease while the causes that tend to reproduce agitation are actively at work? Will not the same cause that produced agitation in 1820 when the Missouri Compromise was formed—that which produced the agitation upon the annexation of Texas and at other times—work out the same results always? Do you think that the nature of man will be changed—that the same causes that produced agitation at one time will not have the same effect at another?

This has been the result so far as my observation of the slavery question and my reading in history extends. What right have we then to hope that the trouble will cease—that the agitation will come to an end—until it shall either be placed back where it originally stood and where the fathers originally placed it, or on the other hand until it shall entirely master all opposition. This is the view I entertain, and this is the reason I entertained it, as Judge Douglas has read from my Springfield speech.

Now, my friends, there is one other thing that I feel myself under some sort of obligation to mention. Judge Douglas has here to-day—in a very rambling way, I was about saying—spoken of the platforms for which he seeks to hold me responsible. He says, "Why can't you come out and make an open avowal of principles in all places alike?" and he reads from an advertisement that he says was used to notify the people of a speech to be made by Judge Trumbull at Waterloo. In commenting on it he desires to know whether we cannot speak frankly and manfully as he and his friends do! How, I ask, do his friends speak out their own sentiments? A convention of his party in this State met on the 21st of April, at Springfield, and passed a set of resolutions which they proclaim to the country as their platform. This does constitute their platform, and it is because Judge Douglas claims it is his platform—that there are his principles and purposes—that he has a right to declare he speaks his sentiments "frankly and manfully." On the 9th of June, Col. John Dougherty, Gov. Reynolds and others, calling themselves National Democrats, met in Springfield and adopted a set of resolutions which are as easily understood, as plain and as definite in stating to the country and to the world what they believed in and would stand upon, as Judge Douglas' platform. Now, what is the reason, that Judge Douglas is not willing that Col. Dougherty and Gov. Reynolds should stand upon their own written and printed platform as well as he upon his? Why must he look farther than their platform when he claims himself to stand by his platform?

Again, in reference to our platform: On the 16th of June the Republicans had their convention and published their platform, which is as clear and distinct as Judge Douglas'. In it they spoke their principles as plainly and as definitely to the world. What is the reason that Judge Douglas is not willing I should stand upon that platform? Why must he go around hunting for some one who is supporting me, or has supported me at some time in his life, and who has said something at some time contrary to that platform? Does the Judge regard that rule as a good one? If it turn out that the rule is a good one for me—that I am responsible for any and every opinion that any man has expressed who is my friend—then it is a good rule for him. I ask, is it not as good a rule for him as it is for me? In my opinion, it is not a good rule for either of us. Do you think differently, Judge?

MR. DOUGLAS—I do not.

MR. LINCOLN—Judge Douglas says he does not think differently. I am glad of it. Then can he tell me why he is looking up resolutions of five or six years ago, and insisting that they were my platform, notwithstanding my protest that they are not, and never were my platform, and my pointing out the platform of the state convention which he delights to say nominated me for the Senate? I cannot see what he means by parading these resolutions, if it is not to hold me responsible for them in some way. If he says to me here, that he does not hold the rule to be good, one way or the other, I do not comprehend how he could answer me more fully if he answered me at greater length. I will therefore put in as my answer to the resolutions that he has hunted up against me, what I, as a lawyer, would call a good plea to a bad declaration. [Laughter.] I understand that it is a maxim of law, that a poor plea may be a good plea to a bad declaration. I think that the opinions the Judge brings from those who support me, yet differ from me, is a bad declaration against me; but if I can bring the same things against him, I am putting in a good plea to that kind of declaration, and now I propose to try it.

At Freeport Judge Douglas occupied a large part of his time in producing resolutions and documents of various sorts, as I understood to make me somehow responsible for them; and I propose now doing a little of the same sort of thing for him. In 1850 a very clever gentleman by the name of Thompson Campbell, a personal friend of Judge Douglas and myself, a political friend of Judge Douglas and opponent of mine, was a candidate for Congress in the Galena District. He was interrogated as to his views on this same slavery question. I have here before me the interrogatories and Campbell's answers to them. I will read them:

INTERROGATORIES

1st. Will you, if elected, vote for and cordially support a bill prohibiting slavery in the territories of the United States?

2d. Will you vote for and support a bill abolishing slavery in the District of Columbia?

3d. Will you oppose the admission of any slave states which may be formed out of Texas or the territories?

4th. Will you vote for and advocate the repeal of the fugitive slave law passed at the recent session of Congress?

5th. Will you advocate and vote for the election of a Speaker of the House of Representatives who shall be willing to organize the committees of that House, so as to give the free states their just influence in the business of legislation?

6th. What are your views not only as to the constitutional right of Congress to prohibit the slave trade between the states, but also as to the expediency of exercising that right immediately?

CAMPBELL'S REPLY

To the first and second interrogatories, I answer unequivocally in the affirmative.

To the third interrogatory I reply, that I am opposed to the admission of any more slave states into the Union, that may be formed out of Texan or any other territory.

To the fourth and fifth interrogatories I unhesitatingly answer in the affirmative.

To the sixth interrogatory I reply, that so long as the slave states continue to treat slaves as articles of commerce, the constitution confers power on Congress to pass laws regulating that peculiar COMMERCE, and that the protection of human rights imperatively demands the interposition of every constitutional means to prevent this most inhuman and iniquitous traffic.

T. CAMPBELL

[211]

I want to say here that Thompson Campbell was elected to Congress on that platform as the Democratic candidate in the Galena district, against Martin P. Sweet.

JUDGE DOUGLAS—Give me the date of the letter.

MR. LINCOLN—The time Campbell ran was in 1850. I have not the exact date here. It was some time in 1850 that these interrogatories were put and the answer given. Campbell was elected to Congress, and served out his term. I think a second election came up before he served out his term and he was not re-elected. Whether defeated or not nominated, I do not know. [Mr. Campbell was nominated for re-election by the Democratic party, by acclamation.] At the end of his term his very good friend, Judge Douglas, got him a high office from President Pierce, and sent him off to California. Is not that the fact? Just at the end of his term in Congress it appears that our mutual friend Judge Douglas got our mutual friend Campbell a good office, and sent him to California upon it. And not only so, but on the 27th of last month when Judge Douglas and myself spoke at Freeport in joint discussion, there was his same friend Campbell, come all the way from California, to help the Judge beat me; and there was poor Martin P. Sweet standing on the platform, trying to help poor me to be elected. [Laughter.] That is true of one of Judge Douglas' friends.

So again, in that same race of 1850, there was a congressional convention assembled at Joliet, and it nominated R. S. Molony, for Congress, and unanimously adopted the following resolutions:

Resolved, That we are uncompromisingly opposed to the extension of slavery; and while we would not make such opposition a ground of interference with the interests of the states where it exists, yet we moderately but firmly insist that it is the duty of Congress to oppose its extension into territory now free, by all means compatible with the obligations of the Constitution, and with good faith to our sister states; that these principles were recognized by the Ordinance of 1787, which received the sanction of Thomas Jefferson, who is acknowledged by all to be the great oracle and expounder of our faith.

Subsequently the same interrogatories were propounded to Dr. Molony which had been addressed to Campbell, as above, with the exception of the 6th respecting the inter-state slave trade, to which Dr. Molony, the Democratic nominee for Congress, replied as follows:

I received the written interrogatories this day, and as you will see by the La Salle *Democrat* and Ottawa *Free Trader*, I took at Peru on the 5th and at Ottawa on the 7th the affirmative side of interrogatories 1st and 2d, and in relation to the admission of any more slave states from free territory, my position taken at these meetings as correctly reported in said papers was

[212]

emphatically and *distinctly* opposed to it. In relation to the admission of any more slave states from Texas whether I shall go against it or not will depend upon the opinion that I may hereafter form of the true meaning and nature of the resolutions of annexation. If, by said resolutions, the honor and good faith of the nation is pledged to admit more slave states from Texas when she (Texas) may apply for the admission of such state then I should, if in Congress, vote for their admission. But if not so PLEDGED and bound by sacred contract, then a bill for the admission of more slave states from Texas would *never* receive my vote.

To your 4th interrogatory I answer *most decidedly* in the affirmative, and for reasons set forth in my reported remarks at Ottawa last Monday.

To your 5th interrogatory I also reply in the affirmative *most cordially*, and that I will use my utmost exertions to secure the nomination and election of a man who will accomplish the objects of said interrogatories. I most cordially approve of the resolutions adopted at the union meeting held at Princeton on the 27th September ult. Yours, &c.,

R. S. MOLONY

All I have to say in regard to Dr. Molony, is that he was the regularly nominated Democratic candidate for Congress in his district—was elected at that time, at the end of his term was appointed to a land office at Danville. (I never heard anything of Judge Douglas' instrumentality in this.) He held this office a considerable time, and when we were at Freeport the other day, there were hand bills scattered about notifying the public that after our debate was over, R. S. Molony would make a Democratic speech in favor of Judge Douglas. That is all I know of my own personal knowledge. It is added here to this resolution, and truly I believe that—

"Among those who participated in the Joliet convention, and who supported its nominee, with his platform as laid down in the resolution of the convention and in his reply as above given, we call at random the following names, all of which are recognized at this day as leading Democrats:

"COOK COUNTY—E. B. Williams, Charles McDonell, Arno Voss, Thomas Hoyne, Isaac Cook."

I reckon we ought to except Cook. [Laughter.]

"F. C. Sherman."

"WILL—Joel A. Matteson, S. W. Bowen."

"KANE—B. F. Hall, G. W. Renwick, A. M. Herrington, Elijah Wilcox."

"McHENRY—W. M. Jackson, Enos W. Smith, Neil Donnelly."

"LaSALLE—John Hise, William Reddick."

William Reddick! another one of Judge Douglas' friends that stood on the stand with him at Ottawa, at the time the Judge says my knees trembled so that I had to be carried away. [Laughter.] The names are all here:

"DuPage—Nathan Allen."

"DeKalb—Z. B. Mayo."

Here is another set of resolutions which I think are apposite to the matter in hand.

On the 28th of February of the same year, a Democratic district convention was held at Naperville, to nominate a candidate for circuit judge. Among the delegates were Bowen and Kelly, of Will; Captain Naper, H. H. Cody, Nathan Allen, of DuPage; W. M. Jackson, J. M. Strode, P. W. Platt and Enos W. Smith, of McHenry; J. Horsman and others, of Winnebago. Col. Strode presided over the convention. The following resolutions were unanimously adopted— the first on motion of P. W. Platt, the second on motion of William M. Jackson.

Resolved, That this convention is in favor of the Wilmot Proviso, both in principle and practice, and that we know of no good reason why any person should oppose the largest latitude in Free Soil, Free Territory and Free Speech.

Resolved, That in the opinion of this convention the time has arrived when all men should be free, white as well at others.

Judge Douglas—What is the date of those resolutions?

Mr. Lincoln—I understand it was in 1850, but I do not know it. I do not state a thing and say I know it, when I do not. But I have the highest belief that this is so. I know of no way to arrive at the conclusion that there is an error in it. I mean to put a case no stronger than the truth will allow. But what I was going to comment upon is an extract from a newspaper in DeKalb County, and it strikes me as being rather singular, I confess, under the circumstances. There is a Judge Mayo in that county, who is a candidate for the legislature, for the purpose, if he secures his election, of helping to re-elect Judge Douglas. He is the editor of a newspaper [DeKalb County Sentinel], and in that paper I find the extract I am going to read. It is part of an editorial article in which he was electioneering as fiercely as he could for Judge Douglas and against me. It was a curious thing, I think, to be in such a paper. I will agree to that, and the Judge may make the most of it:

Our education has been such, that we have ever been rather in favor of the equality of the blacks; that is, that they should enjoy all the privileges of the whites where they reside. We are aware that this is not a very popular doctrine. We have had many a confab with some who are now strong "Republicans," we taking the broad ground of equality and they the opposite ground.

We were brought up in a state where blacks were voters, and we do not know of any inconvenience resulting from it, though perhaps it would not work as well where the blacks are more numerous. We have no doubt of the right of the whites to guard against such an evil, if it is one. Our opinion is that it would be best for all concerned to have the colored population in a state by themselves. [In this I agree with him]; but if within the jurisdiction of the United States, *we say by all means they should have the right to have their Senators and Representatives in Congress, and to vote for President.* With us "worth makes the man and want of it the fellow." We have seen many a "nigger" that we thought more of than some white man.

That is one of Judge Douglas' friends. Now I do not want to leave myself in an attitude where I can be misrepresented, so I will say I do not think the Judge is responsible for this article; but he is quite as responsible for it, as I would be if one of my friends had said it. I think that is fair enough. [Cheers.]

I have here also a set of resolutions passed by a Democratic state convention in Judge Douglas' own good old state of Vermont, that I think ought to be good for him too:

Resolved, That liberty is a right inherent and inalienable in man, and that herein *all men are equal.*

Resolved, That we claim no authority in the federal government to abolish slavery in the several states, but we do claim for it constitutional power perpetually to prohibit the introduction of slavery into territory now free, and abolish it wherever, under the jurisdiction of Congress it exists.

Resolved, That this power ought immediately to be exercised in prohibiting the introduction and existence of slavery in New Mexico and California, in abolishing slavery and the slave trade in the District of Columbia, on the high seas, and wherever else, under the Constitution, it can be reached.

Resolved, That no more slave states should be admitted into the Federal Union.

Resolved, That the government ought to return to its ancient policy, not to extend, nationalize or encourage, but to limit, localize and discourage slavery.

At Freeport I answered several interrogatories that had been propounded to me by Judge Douglas at the Ottawa meeting. The Judge has yet not seen fit to find any fault with the position that I took in regard to those seven interrogatories, which were certainly broad enough, in all conscience, to cover the entire ground. In my answers, which have been printed, and all have had the opportunity of seeing, I take the ground that those who elect me must expect that I will do nothing which is not in accordance with those answers. I have some right to assert that Judge Douglas has no fault to find with them. But he chooses to still try to thrust me upon different ground without paying any attention to my answers, the obtaining of which from me cost him so much trouble and concern. At the same time, I propounded four interrogatories to him, claiming it as a right that he should answer as many interrogatories for me as I did for him, and I would reserve myself for a future installment when I got them ready. The Judge in answering me upon that occasion, put in what I suppose he intends as answers to all four of my interrogatories. The first one of these interrogatories I have before me, and it is in these words:

Question 1. If the people of Kansas shall, by means entirely unobjectionable in all other respects, adopt a state constitution, and ask admission into the Union under it, *before* they have the requisite number of inhabitants according to the English Bill—some ninety-three thousand—will you vote to admit them?

As I read the Judge's answer in the newspaper, and as I remember it as pronounced at the time, he does not give any answer which is equivalent to yes or no—I will or I won't. He answers at very considerable length, rather quarreling with me for asking the question, and insisting that Judge Trumbull had done something that I ought to say something about; and finally getting out such statements as induce me to infer that he means to be understood he will, in that supposed case, vote for the admission of Kansas. I only bring this forward now for the purpose of saying that if he chooses to put a different construction upon his answer he may do it. But if he does not, I shall from this time forward assume that he will vote for the admission of Kansas in disregard of the English bill. He has the right to remove any misunderstanding I may have. I only mention it now that I may hereafter assume this to be the true construction of his answer, if he does not now choose to correct me.

The second interrogatory that I propounded to him, was this:

Q. 2 Can the people of a United States territory, in any lawful way, against the wish of any citizen of the United States, exclude slavery from its limits prior to the formation of a state constitution?

To this Judge Douglas answered that they can lawfully exclude slavery from the territory prior to the formation of a constitution. He goes on to tell us how it can be done. As I understand him, he holds that it can be done by the territorial legislature refusing to make any enactments for the protection of slavery in the territory, and especially by adopting unfriendly legislation to it. For the sake of clearness I state it again; that they can exclude slavery from the territory, 1st, by withholding what he assumes to be an indispensable assistance to it in the way of legislation; and 2d, by unfriendly legislation. If I rightly understand him, I wish to ask your attention for a while to his position.

In the first place, the Supreme Court of the United States has decided that any congressional prohibition of slavery in the territories is unconstitutional—that they have reached this proposition as a conclusion from their former proposition that the Constitution of the United States expressly recognizes property in slaves, and from that other constitutional provision that no person shall be deprived of property without due process of law. Hence they reach the conclusion that as the Constitution of the United States expressly recognizes property in slaves, and prohibits any person from being deprived of property without due process of law, to pass an act of Congress by which a man who owned a slave on one side of a line would be deprived of him if he took him on the other side, is depriving him of that property without due process of law. That I understand to be the decision of the Supreme Court. I understand also that Judge Douglas adheres most firmly to that decision; and the difficulty is, how is it possible for any power to exclude slavery from the territory unless in violation of that decision? That is the difficulty.

In the Senate of the United States, in 1856, Judge Trumbull in a speech, substantially if not directly, put the same interrogatory to Judge Douglas, as to whether the people of a territory had the lawful power to exclude slavery prior to the formation of a constitution? Judge Douglas then answered at considerable length, and his answer will be found in the *Congressional Globe*, under date of June 9th, 1856. The Judge said that whether the people could exclude slavery prior to the formation of a constitution or not *was a question to be decided by the Supreme Court*. He put that proposition, as will be seen by the *Congressional Globe*, in a variety of forms, all running to the same thing in substance—that it was a question for the Supreme Court. I maintain that when he says, after the Supreme Court have decided the question, that the people may yet exclude slavery by any means whatever, he does virtually say, that it is *not* a question for the Supreme Court. [Applause.] He shifts his ground. I appeal to you whether he did not say it was a question for the Supreme Court. Has not the Supreme Court decided that question? When he now says the people *may* exclude slavery, does he not make it a question for the people? Does he not virtually shift his ground and say that it is *not* a question for the Court, but for the people? This is a very simple proposition—a very plain and naked one. It seems to me that there is no difficulty in deciding it. In a variety of ways he said that it was a question for the Supreme Court. He did not stop then to tell us that whatever the Supreme Court decides the people can by withholding necessary "police regulations" keep slavery out. He did not make any such answer. I

submit to you now, whether the new state of the case has not induced the Judge to sheer away from his original ground. [Ap-
plause.] Would not this be the impression of every fair-minded
man?

I hold that the proposition that slavery cannot enter a new country without police regulations is historically false. It is not true at
all. I hold that the history of this country shows that the institution
of slavery was originally planted upon this continent *without* these
"police regulations" which the Judge now thinks necessary for the
actual establishment of it. Not only so, but is there not another fact—
how came this Dred Scott decision to be made? It was made upon
the case of a negro being taken and actually held in slavery in Minnesota Territory, claiming his freedom because the act of Congress
prohibited his being so held there. *Will the Judge pretend that Dred
Scott was not held there without police regulations?* There is at
least one matter of record as to his having been held in slavery in
the territory, not only without police regulations, but in the teeth of
congressional legislation supposed to be valid at the time. This
shows that there is vigor enough in slavery to plant itself in a new
country even against unfriendly legislation. It takes not only law
but the *enforcement* of law to keep it out. That is the history of this
country upon the subject.

I wish to ask one other question. It being understood that the
Constitution of the United States guarantees property in slaves in
the territories, if there is any infringement of the right of that property, would not the United States courts, organized for the government of the territory, apply such remedy as might be necessary in
that case? It is a maxim held by the courts, that there is no wrong
without its remedy; and the courts have a remedy for whatever is
acknowledged and treated as a wrong.

Again: I will ask you my friends, if you were elected members of
the legislature, what would be the first thing you would have to do
before entering upon your duties? *Swear to support the Constitution
of the United States.* Suppose you believe, as Judge Douglas does,
that the Constitution of the United States guarantees to your neighbor the right to hold slaves in that territory—that they are his
property—how can you clear your oaths unless you give him such
legislation as is necessary to enable him to enjoy that property?
What do you understand by supporting the constitution of a state
or of the United States? Is it not to give such constitutional helps to
the rights established by that constitution as may be practically
needed? Can you, if you swear to support the constitution, and believe that the constitution establishes a right, clear your oath, with-

out giving it support? Do you support the constitution if, knowing or believing there is a right established under it which needs specific legislation, you withhold that legislation? Do you not violate and disregard your oath? I can conceive of nothing plainer in the world. There can be nothing in the words "support the constitution," if you may run counter to it by refusing support to any right established under the constitution. And what I say here will hold with still more force against the Judge's doctrine of "unfriendly legislation." How could you, having sworn to support the constitution, and believing it guaranteed the right to hold slaves in the territories, assist in legislation *intended* to defeat that right? That would be violating your own view of the constitution. Not only so, but if you were to do so, how long would it take the courts to hold your votes unconstitutional and void? Not a moment.

Lastly I would ask—is not Congress, itself, under obligation to give legislative support to any right that is established under the United States Constitution? I repeat the question—is not Congress, itself, bound to give legislative support to any right that is established in the United States Constitution? A member of Congress swears to support the Constitution of the United States, and if he sees a right established by that Constitution which needs specific legislative protection, can he clear his oath without giving that protection? Let me ask you why many of us who are opposed to slavery upon principle give our acquiescence to a fugitive slave law? Why do we hold ourselves under obligations to pass such a law, and abide by it when it is passed? Because the Constitution makes provision that the owners of slaves shall have the right to reclaim them. It gives the right to reclaim slaves, and that right is, as Judge Douglas says, a barren right, unless there is legislation that will enforce it.

The mere declaration "No person held to service or labor in one state under the laws thereof, escaping into another, shall in consequence of any law or regulation therein be discharged from such service or labor, but shall be delivered up on claim of the party to whom such service or labor may be due" is powerless without specific legislation to enforce it. Now on what ground would a member of Congress who is opposed to slavery in the abstract vote for a fugitive law, as I would deem it my duty to do? Because there is a constitutional right which needs legislation to enforce it. And although it is distasteful to me, I have sworn to support the Constitution, and having so sworn I cannot conceive that I do support it if I withheld from that right any necessary legislation to make it practical. And if that is true in regard to a fugitive slave law, is the right to have fugitive slaves reclaimed any better fixed in the Constitution than the right to hold slaves in the territories? For this decision is a just exposition of the Constitution as Judge Douglas thinks. Is the one right any better than the other? Is there any man who while a member of Congress would give support to the one any more than the other? If I wished to refuse to give legislative support to slave property in the territories, if a member of Congress, I could not do it holding the view that the Constitution establishes that right. If I did it at all, it would be because I deny that this decision properly construes the Constitution. But if I acknowledge with Judge Douglas that this decision properly construes the Constitution, I cannot conceive that I would be less than a perjured man if I should refuse in Congress to give such protection to that property as in its nature it needed.

At the end of what I have said here I propose to give the Judge my fifth interrogatory which he may take and answer at his leisure. My fifth interrogatory is this: If the slaveholding citizens of a United States territory should need and demand congressional legislation for the protection of their slave property in such territory, would you, as a member of Congress, vote for or against such legislation?

JUDGE DOUGLAS—Will you repeat that? I want to answer that question.

MR. LINCOLN—If the slaveholding citizens of a United States territory should need and demand congressional legislation for the protection of their slave property in such territory, would you, as a member of Congress vote for or against such legislation?

I am aware that in some of the speeches Judge Douglas has made, he has spoken as if he did not know or think that the Supreme Court had decided that a territorial legislature cannot exclude slavery. Precisely what the Judge would say upon the subject—whether he would say definitely that he does not understand they have so decided, or whether he would say he does understand that the Court have so decided, I do not know; but I know that in his speech at Springfield he spoke of it as a thing they had not decided yet; and in his answer to me at Freeport, he spoke of it so far again as I can comprehend it, as a thing that had not yet been decided. Now I hold that if the Judge does entertain that view I think he is not mistaken in so far as it can be said that the Court has not decided anything save the mere question of jurisdiction. I know the legal arguments that can be made—that after a court has decided that it cannot take jurisdiction of a case, it then has decided all that is before it, and that is the end of it. A plausible argument can be made in favor of that proposition, but I know that Judge Douglas has said in one of his speeches that the court went forward *like honest men as they were* and decided all the points in the case. If any points are really extrajudicially decided because not necessarily before them, then this one as to the power of the territorial legislature to exclude slavery is one of them, as also the one that the Missouri Compromise was null and void. They are both extra-judicial or neither is according as the Court held that they had no jurisdiction in the case between the parties, because of want of capacity of one party to maintain a suit in that Court. I want, if I have sufficient time, to show that the Court did *pass its opinion,* but that is the only thing actually done in the case. If they did not decide, they showed what they were ready to decide whenever the matter was before them. What is that opinion? After having argued that Congress had no power to pass a law excluding slavery from a United States territory, they then used language to this effect:—that inasmuch as Congress itself could not exercise such a power, it followed as a matter of course that it could not authorize a territorial government to exercise it, for the territorial legislature can do no more than Congress could do. Thus it expressed its opinion emphatically against the power of a territorial legislature to exclude slavery, leaving us in just as little doubt on that point as upon any other point they really decided.

Now, my fellow citizens, I will detain you only a little while longer. My time is very nearly out. I find a report of a speech made by Judge Douglas at Joliet, since we last met at Freeport—published I believe in the *Missouri Republican*—on the 9th of this month, in which Judge Douglas says:

You know at Ottawa, I read this platform, and asked him if he concurred in each and all of the principles set forth in it. He would not answer these questions. At last I said frankly, I wish you to answer them, because when I get them up here where the color of your principles is a little darker than in Egypt, I intend to trot you down to Jonesboro. The very notice that I was going to take him down to Egypt made him tremble in the knees so that he had to be carried from the platform. He laid up seven days, and in the meantime held a consultation with his political physicians, they had Lovejoy and Farnsworth and all the leaders of the Abolition party, they consulted it all over, and at last Lincoln came to the conclusion that he would answer, so he came up to Freeport last Friday.

Now that statement altogether furnishes a subject for philosophical contemplation. [Laughter.] I have been treating it in that way, and I have really come to the conclusion that I can explain it in no other way than by believing the Judge is crazy. [Renewed laughter.] If he was in his right mind, I cannot conceive how he would have risked disgusting the four or five thousand of his own friends who stood there, and knew, as to my having been carried from the platform, that there was not a word of truth in it.

JUDGE DOUGLAS—Didn't they carry you off?

MR. LINCOLN—There; that question illustrates the character of this man Douglas, exactly. He smiles now and says, "Didn't they carry you off?" But he says then, *"He had to be carried off;"* and he said it to convince the country that he had so completely broken me down by his speech that I had to be carried away. Now he seeks to dodge it, and asks, "Didn't they carry you off?" Yes, they did. *But, Judge Douglas, why didn't you tell the truth?* [Great laughter and cheers.] I would like to know why you didn't tell the truth about it. [Continued laughter.] And then again, "He laid up seven days." He puts this in print for the people of the country to read as a serious document. I think if he had been in his sober senses he would not have risked that barefacedness in the presence of thousands of his own friends, who knew that I made speeches within six of the seven days at Henry, Marshall County; Augusta, Hancock County, and Macomb, McDonough County, including all the necessary travel to meet him again at Freeport at the end of the six days. Now, I say, there is no charitable way to look at that statement, except to conclude that he is actually crazy. [Laughter.] There is another thing in that statement that alarmed me very greatly as he states it, that he was going to "trot me down to Egypt." Thereby he would have you to infer that I would not come to Egypt unless he forced me— that I could not be got here, unless he, giant-like, had hauled me down here. [Laughter.] That statement he makes, too, in the teeth of the knowledge that I had made the stipulation to come down here, *and that he himself had been very reluctant to enter into the stipulation.* [Cheers and laughter.] More than all this, Judge Douglas, when he made that statement must have been crazy, and wholly out of his sober senses, or else he would have known that when he got me down here—that promise—that windy promise—of his powers to annihilate me, wouldn't amount to anything. Now, how little do I look like being carried away trembling? Let the Judge go on, and after he is done with his half hour, I want you all, if I can't go home myself, to let me stay and rot here; and if anything happens to the Judge, if I cannot carry him to the hotel and put him to bed, let me stay here and rot. [Great laughter.] I say, then, there is something *extraordinary* in this statement? I ask you if you know any other living man who would make such a statement? [Cries of "No," "no." "Yes," "yes."] I will ask my friend Casey, over there, if he would do such a thing? [Casey dropped his head and said nothing.] Would he send that out and have his men take it as the truth? Did the Judge talk of trotting me down to Egypt to scare me to death? Why, I know this people better than he does. I was raised just a little east of here. I am a part of this people. But the Judge was raised further north, and perhaps he has some horrid idea of what this people might be induced to do. [Roars of laughter and cheers.] But really I have talked about this matter perhaps longer than I ought, for it is no great thing, and yet the smallest are often the most difficult things to deal with. The Judge has set about seriously trying to make the impression that when we meet at different places I am literally in his clutches—that I am a poor, helpless, decrepit mouse, and that I can do nothing at all. This is one of the ways he has taken to create that impression. I don't know any other way to meet it, except this. I don't want to quarrel with him—to call him a liar—but when I come square up to him I don't know what else to call him, if I must tell the truth out. [Cheers and laughter.] I want to be at peace, and reserve all my fighting powers for necessary occasions. My time, now, is very nearly out, and I give up the trifle that is left to the Judge to let him set my knees trembling again, if he can.

Douglas' Rejoinder

My friends, while I am very grateful to you for the enthusiasm which you show for me, I will say in all candor, that your quietness will be much more agreeable than your applause, inasmuch as you deprive me of some part of my time whenever you cheer. ("All right," "go ahead," "we won't interrupt," &c.)

I will commence where Mr. Lincoln left off, and make a remark upon this serious complaint of his about my speech at Joliet. I did say there in a playful manner that when I put these questions to Mr. Lincoln at Ottawa he failed to answer, and that he trembled and had to be carried off the stand, and required seven days to get up his reply. (Laughter.) That he did not walk off from that stand he will not deny. That when the crowd went away from the stand with me, a few persons carried him home on their shoulders and laid him down, he will admit. (Shouts of laughter.) I wish to say to you that whenever I degrade my friends and myself by allowing them to carry me on their backs along through the public streets when I am able to walk I am willing to be deemed crazy. ("All right, Douglas," laughter and applause. Lincoln chewing his nails in a rage in a back corner.) I did not say whether I beat him or he beat me in the argument. It is true I put these questions to him, and I put them not as

mere idle questions, but showed that I based them upon the creed
of the Black Republican party as declared by their conventions in
that portion of the state which he depends upon to elect him, and
desired to know whether he endorsed that creed. He would not
answer. When I reminded him that I intended bringing him into
Egypt and renewing my questions if he refused to answer, he then
consulted and did get up his answers one week after,—answers
which I may refer to in a few minutes and show you how equivocal
they are. My object was to make him avow whether or not he stood
by the platform of his party; the resolutions I then read, and upon
which I based my questions, had been adopted by his party in the
Galena congressional district, and the Chicago and Bloomington
congressional districts, composing a large majority of the counties in
this state that give Republican or Abolition majorities. Mr. Lincoln
cannot and will not deny that the doctrines laid down in these resolutions were in substance put forth in Lovejoy's resolutions which
were voted for by a majority of his party, some of them, if not all,
receiving the support of every man of his party. Hence, I laid a
foundation for my questions to him before I asked him whether that
was or was not the platform of his party. He says that he answered
my questions. One of them was whether he would vote to admit any
more slave states into the Union. The creed of the Republican party
as set forth in the resolutions of their various conventions was that
they would under no circumstances vote to admit another slave
state. It was put forth in the Lovejoy resolutions in the legislature,
it was put forth and passed in a majority of all the counties of this
state which give Abolition or Republican majorities, or elect members to the legislature of that school of politics. I had a right to
know whether he would vote for or against the admission of another
slave state in the event the people wanted it. He first answered that
he was not pledged on the subject, and then said, "In regard to the
other question of whether I am pledged to the admission of any
more slave states into the Union, I state to you very frankly that I
would be exceedingly sorry ever to be put in the position of having
to pass on that question. ("No doubt," and laughter. Mr. Lincoln
looks savagely into the crowd for the man who said "no doubt.") I
should be exceedingly glad to know that there would never be another slave state admitted into the Union; but I must add that if
slavery shall be kept out of the territories during the territorial existence of any one given territory, and then the people, having a fair
chance and clean field when they come to adopt a constitution, do
such an extraordinary thing as adopt a slave constitution, uninfluenced by the actual presence of the institution among them, I see

no alternative, if we own the country, but to admit them into the Union."

Now analyze that answer. In the first place he says he would be exceedingly sorry to be put in a position where he would have to vote on the question of the admission of a slave state. Why is he a candidate for the Senate if he would be sorry to be put in that position? I trust the people of Illinois will not put him in a position which he would be so sorry to occupy. ("There's no danger," &c.) The next position he takes is that he would be glad to know that there would never be another slave state, yet, in certain contingencies, he might have to vote for one. What is that contingency? "If Congress keeps slavery out by law while it is a territory, and then the people should have a fair chance and should adopt slavery, uninfluenced by the presence of the institution," he supposes he would have to admit the state. Suppose Congress should not keep slavery out during their territorial existence, then how would he vote when the people applied for admission into the Union with a slave constitution? That he does not answer, and that is the condition of every territory we have now got. Slavery is not kept out of Kansas by act of Congress, and when I put the question to Mr. Lincoln whether he will vote for the admission with or without slavery, as her people may desire, he will not answer, and you have not got an answer from him. In Nebraska slavery is not prohibited by act of Congress, but the people are allowed, under the Nebraska Bill, to do as they please on the subject; and when I ask him whether he will vote to admit Nebraska with a slave constitution if her people desire it, he will not answer. So with New Mexico, Washington territory, Arizona, and the four new states to be admitted from Texas. You cannot get an answer from him to these questions. His answer only applies to a given case, to a condition—things which he knows do not exist in any one territory in the Union. He tries to give you to understand that he would allow the people to do as they please, and yet he dodges the question as to every territory in the Union. I now ask why cannot Mr. Lincoln answer to each of these territories? He has not done it, and he will not do it. The Abolitionists up north understand that this answer is made with a view of not committing himself on any one territory now in existence. It is so understood there, and you cannot expect an answer from him on a case that applies to any one territory, or applies to the new states which by compact we are pledged to admit out of Texas, when they have the requisite population and desire admission. I submit to you whether he has made a frank answer, so that you can tell how he would vote in any one of these cases. "He would be sorry to be put in the position." Why would he be sorry to be put in this position if his duty required him to give the vote? If the people of a territory ought to be permitted to come into the Union as a state, with slavery or without it, as they pleased, why not give the vote admitting them cheerfully? If in his opinion they ought not to come in with slavery, even if they wanted to, why not say that he would cheerfully vote against their admission? His intimation is that conscience would not let him vote "No," and he would be sorry to do that which his conscience would compel him to do as an honest man. (Laughter and cheers.)

In regard to the contract or bargain between Trumbull, the Abolitionists and him, which he denies, I wish to say that the charge can be proved by notorious historical facts. Trumbull, Lovejoy, Giddings, Fred Douglass, Hale, and Banks, were traveling the state at that time making speeches on the same side and in the same cause with him. He contents himself with the simple denial that no such thing occurred. Does he deny that he, and Trumbull, and Breese, and Giddings, and Chase, and Fred Douglass, and Lovejoy, and all those Abolitionists and deserters from the Democratic party, did make speeches all over this state in the same common cause? Does he deny that Jim Matheny was then and is now his confidential friend, and does he deny that Matheny made the charge of the bargain and fraud in his own language, as I have read it from his printed speech. Matheny spoke of his own personal knowledge of that bargain existing between Lincoln, Trumbull, and the Abolitionists. He still remains Lincoln's confidential friend, and is now a candidate for Congress, and is canvassing the Springfield district for Lincoln. I assert that I can prove the charge to be true in detail if I can ever get it where I can summon and compel the attendance of witnesses. I have the statement of another man to the same effect as that made by Matheny, which I am not permitted to use yet, but Jim Matheny is a good witness on that point, and the history of the country is conclusive upon it. That Lincoln up to that time had been a Whig, and then undertook to abolitionize the Whigs and bring them into the Abolition camp, is beyond denial; that Trumbull up to that time had been a Democrat, and deserted, and undertook to abolitionize the Democracy, and take them into the Abolition camp, is beyond denial; that they are both now active, leading, distinguished members of this Abolition Republican party, in full communion, is a fact that cannot be questioned or denied.

But Lincoln is not willing to be responsible for the creed of his party. He complains because I hold him responsible, and in order to avoid the issue, he attempts to show that individuals in the Democratic party, many years ago, expressed abolition sentiments. It is true that Tom Campbell, when a candidate for Congress in 1850, published the letter which Lincoln read. When I asked Lincoln for the date of that letter he could not give it. The date of the letter has been suppressed by other speakers who have used it, though I take it for granted that Lincoln did not know the date. If he will take the trouble to examine, he will find that the letter was published only two days before the election, and was never seen until after it, except in one county. Tom Campbell would have been beat to death by the Democratic party if that letter had been made public in his district. As to Molony, it is true he uttered sentiments of the kind referred to by Mr. Lincoln, and the best Democrats would not vote for him for that reason. I returned from Washington after the passage of the compromise measures in 1850, and when I found Molony running under John Wentworth's tutelage, and on his platform, I denounced him, and declared that he was no Democrat. In my speech at Chicago, just before the election that year, I went before the infuriated people of that city and vindicated the compromise measures of 1850. Remember the city council had passed resolutions nullifying acts of Congress and instructing the police to withhold their assistance from the execution of the laws, and as I was the only man in the city of Chicago who was responsible for the passage of the compromise measures, I went before the crowd, justified each and every one of those measures, and let it be said to the eternal honor of the people of Chicago, that when they were convinced by my exposition of those measures that they were right and they had done wrong in opposing them, they repealed their nullifying resolutions and declared that they would acquiesce in and support the laws of the land. These facts are well known, and Mr. Lincoln can only get up individual instances, dating back to 1849, '50, which are contradicted by the whole tenor of the Democratic creed.

But Mr. Lincoln does not want to be held responsible for the Black Republican doctrine of no more slave states. Farnsworth is the candidate of his party to-day in the Chicago district, and he made a speech in the last Congress in which he called upon God to palsy his right arm if he ever voted for the admission of another slave state, whether the people wanted it or not. Lovejoy is making speeches all over the state for Lincoln now, and taking ground against any more slave states. Washburne, the Black Republican candidate for Congress in the Galena district, is making speeches in favor of this same Abolition platform declaring no more slave states. Why are men running for Congress in the northern districts, and taking that Abolition platform for their guide, when Mr.

Lincoln does not want to be held to it down here in Egypt and in the centre of the state, and objects to it so as to get votes here. ("He can't get any.") Let me tell Mr. Lincoln that his party in the northern part of the state hold to that Abolition platform, and that if they do not in the south and in the centre they present the extraordinary spectacle of a house divided against itself, and hence cannot stand. ("Hurra.") I now bring down upon him the vengeance of his own scriptural quotation, and give it a more appropriate application than he did, when I say to him that his party, abolition in one end of the state and opposed to it in the other, is a house divided against itself, and cannot stand, and ought not to stand, for it attempts to cheat the American people out of their votes by disguising its sentiments. (Cheers.)

Mr. Lincoln attempts to cover up and get over his Abolitionism by telling you that he was raised a little east of you, (laughter,) beyond the Wabash in Indiana, and he thinks that makes a mighty sound and good man of him on all these questions. I do not know that the place where a man is born or raised has much to do with his political principles. The worst Abolitionists I have ever known in Illinois have been men who have sold their slaves in Alabama and Kentucky, and have come here and turned Abolitionists whilst spending the money got for the negroes they sold, ("that's so," and laughter,) and I do not know that an Abolitionist from Indiana or Kentucky ought to have any more credit because he was born and raised among slaveholders. ("Not a bit," "not as much," &c.) I do not know that a native of Kentucky is more excusable because raised among slaves, his father and mother having owned slaves, he comes to Illinois, turns Abolitionist, and slanders the graves of his father and mother, and breathes curses upon the institutions under which he was born, and his father and mother bred. True, I was not born out west here. I was born away down in Yankee land, ("good,") I was born in a valley in Vermont ("all right,") with the high mountains around me. I love the old green mountains and valleys of Vermont, where I was born, and where I played in my childhood. I went up to visit them some seven or eight years ago, for the first time for twenty odd years. When I got there they treated me very kindly. They invited me to the commencement of their college, placed me on the seats with their distinguished guests, and conferred upon me the degree of LL.D. in latin, (doctor of laws,) the same as they did on old Hickory, at Cambridge, many years ago, and I give you my word and honor I understood just as much of the latin as he did. (Laughter.) When they got through conferring the honorary degree, they called upon me for a speech, and I got up with my heart full and swelling with gratitude for their kindness, and I said to them, "My friends, Vermont is the most glorious spot on the face of this globe for a man to be born in, *provided* he emigrates when he is very young." (Uproarious shouts of laughter.)

I emigrated when I was very young. I came out here when I was a boy, and I found my mind liberalized, and my opinions enlarged when I got on these broad prairies, with only the Heavens to bound my vision, instead of having them circumscribed by the little narrow ridges that surrounded the valley where I was born. But, I discard all flings of the land where a man was born. I wish to be judged by my principles, by those great public measures and constitutional principles upon which the peace, the happiness and the perpetuity of this republic now rest.

Mr. Lincoln has framed another question, propounded it to me, and desired my answer. As I have said before, I did not put a question to him that I did not first lay a foundation for by showing that it was a part of the platform of the party whose votes he is now seeking, adopted in a majority of the countries where he now hopes to get a majority, and supported by the candidates of his party now running in those counties. But I will answer his question. It is as follows: "If the slaveholding citizens of a United States territory should need and demand congressional legislation for the protection of their slave property in such territory, would you, as a member of Congress, vote for or against such legislation?" I answer him that it is a fundamental article in the Democratic creed that there should be non-interference and non-intervention by Congress with slavery in the states or territories. (Immense cheering.) Mr. Lincoln could have found an answer to his question in the Cincinnati platform, if he had desired it. (Renewed applause.) The Democratic party have always stood by that great principle of non-interference and non-intervention by Congress with slavery in the states and territories alike, and I stand on that platform now. (Cheer after cheer was here given for Douglas.)

Now I desire to call your attention to the fact that Lincoln did not define his own position in his own question. ("He can't, it's too far south," and laughter.) How does he stand on that question? He put the question to me at Freeport whether or not I would vote to admit Kansas into the Union before she had 93,420 inhabitants. I answered him at once that it having been decided that Kansas had now population enough for a slave state, she had population enough for a free state. ("Good; that's it," and cheers.)

I answered the question unequivocally, and then I asked him

whether he would vote for or against the admission of Kansas before she had 93,420 inhabitants, and he would [not] answer me. Today he has called attention to the fact that in his opinion my answer on that question was not quite plain enough, and yet he has not answered it himself. (Great laughter.) He now puts a question in relation [to] congressional interference in the territories to me. I answer him direct, and yet he has not answered the question himself. I ask you whether a man has any right, in common decency, to put questions in these public discussions, to his opponent, which he will not answer himself, when they are pressed home to him. I have asked him three times, whether he would vote to admit Kansas whenever the people applied with a constitution of their own making and their own adoption, under circumstances that were fair, just and unexceptionable, but I cannot get an answer from him. Nor will he answer the question which he put to me, and which I have just answered in relation to congressional interference in the territories, by making a slave code there.

It is time that he goes on to answer the question by arguing that under the decision of the Supreme Court it is the duty of a man to vote for a slave code in the territories. He says that it is his duty, under the decision that the court has made, and if he believes in that decision he would be a perjured man if he did not give the vote. I want to know whether he is not bound to a decision which is contrary to his opinions just as much as to one in accordance with his opinions. ("Certainly.") If the decision of the Supreme Court, the tribunal created by the Constitution to decide the question, is final and binding, is he not bound by it just as strongly as if he was for it instead of against it originally. Is every man in this land allowed to resist decisions he does not like, and only support those that meet his approval? What are important courts worth unless their decisions are binding on all good citizens? It is the fundamental principle of the judiciary that its decisions are final. It is created for that purpose so that when you cannot agree among yourselves on a disputed point you appeal to the judicial tribunal which steps in and decides for you, and that decision is then binding on every good citizen. It is the law of the land just as much with Mr. Lincoln against it as for it. And yet he says that if that decision is binding he is a perjured man if he does not vote for a slave code in the different territories of this Union. Well, if you (turning to Mr. Lincoln) are not going to resist the decision, if you obey it, and do not intend to array mob law against the constituted authorities, then, according to your own statement, you will be a perjured man if you do not vote to establish slavery in these territories. My doctrine is, that even taking Mr. Lincoln's view that the decision recognizes the right of a man to carry his slaves into the territories of the United States, if he pleases, yet after he gets there he needs affirmative law to make that right of any value. The same doctrine not only applies to slave property, but all other kinds of property. Chief Justice Taney places it upon the ground that slave property is on an equal footing with other property. Suppose one of your merchants should move to Kansas and open a liquor store; he has a right to take groceries and liquors there, but the mode of selling them, and the circumstances under which they shall be sold, and all the remedies must be prescribed by local legislation, and if that is unfriendly it will drive him out just as effectually as if there was a constitutional provision against the sale of liquor. So the absence of local legislation to encourage and support slave property in a territory excludes it practically just as effectually as if there was a positive constitutional provision against it. Hence, I assert that under the Dred Scott decision you cannot maintain slavery a day in a territory where there is an unwilling people and unfriendly legislation. If the people are opposed to it, our right is a barren, worthless, useless right, and if they are for it, they will support and encourage it. We come right back, therefore, to the practical question, if the people of a territory want slavery they will have it, and if they do not want it you cannot force it on them. And this is the practical question, the great principle upon which our institutions rest. ("That's the doctrine.") I am willing to take the decision of the Supreme Court as it was pronounced by that august tribunal without stopping to inquire whether I would have decided that way or not. I have had many a decision made against me on questions of law which I did not like, but I was bound by them just as much as if I had had a hand in making them, and approved them. Did you ever see a lawyer or a client lose his case that he approved the decision of the court. They always think the decision unjust when it is given against them. In a government of laws like ours we must sustain the Constitution as our fathers made it, and maintain the rights of the states as they are guaranteed under the Constitution, and then we will have peace and harmony between the different states and sections of this glorious Union. (Prolonged cheering.)

CHAPTER EIGHT

THE CHARLESTON DEBATE

*Douglas took advantage of the three days between the Jonesboro
and Charleston debates by attending rallies at Benton and Centralia;
Lincoln contented himself with visiting the Illinois State Fair, held
that year at Centralia.*

*Saturday, September 18, found Charleston crowded. The Times
reported:[1]*

From twelve to fifteen thousand were present. The Democracy
were out in their strength and struck terror into the hearts of their
enemies. Things were so arranged that Senator Douglas should be
received at Mattoon on his arrival from lower Egypt, by the delegations from the eastern part of Coles and escorted down to Charleston, ten miles distant. Accordingly, on Saturday morning at 3 o'clock,
when he reached Mattoon, his friends were waiting for him; and
he was welcomed with a salute and escorted to the house of a friend,
which was brilliantly illuminated. At eight o'clock the various delegations formed in procession and waited upon him to attend him
down to Charleston. Before starting, Col. Cunningham, in behalf
of his fellow citizens, welcomed Senator Douglas to Coles County
in a beautiful address, in the course of which he called his attention
to a part of the procession, consisting of thirty-two young ladies on
horseback, representing the federal Union, sixteen of whom carried
the national colors waving from ash sticks, and the other sixteen
carrying the same colors on hickory sticks, thus furnishing a beautiful illustration of the union between the Whigs and Democrats
when our country was endangered by the agitation of sectional men
in 1850, and emblematic of the union which now exists between the
national men of these two parties to defeat and crush out Abolitionism. Senator Douglas made a happy and appropriate response, and
the line of march was then taken up for Charleston. It was a glorious sight to see the long line of teams filled with men, women and

[1] September 21.

[232]

children, extending across the prairie as far as the eye could reach, the flags gaily flying in the morning breeze, and the brass instruments of the numerous bands gleaming in the sun. At every house and every cross-road the procession received accessions, until when entering Charleston, it was nearly two miles long. On the outskirts of the town it was met by the citizens of Charleston and the delegations from the western part of Coles and the adjoining counties, who carried several large and splendid banners, upon one of which appeared, "Edgar county good for five hundred majority for the Little Giant," and on another, "This government was made for white men—Douglas for life." Passing through the streets of Charleston, the procession halted in front of the Union Hotel, which was almost hid by banners and flags, and here Senator Douglas was welcomed to Charleston by Hon. O. B. Ficklin in a most eloquent and telling speech, to which he responded. The Black Republicans had stationed a band at the opposite corner, and when Mr. Ficklin commenced his address the musicians were ordered to play, which they did, preventing the people from hearing what was going on; but this little piece of malicious fun was soon stopped, and it was with the greatest difficulty that the enraged crowd could be prevented from visiting upon the offenders a severe mark of their anger.

On the size of the crowd the Press and Tribune *agreed, although its appraisal of popular preference naturally differed from that of the rival journal.*[2]

On Friday evening the hotels in the town were already crowded to excess, and the streets were hung with national flags, banners, and all manner of artistic devices which could be pressed into political service. Early on Saturday morning the town began to fill up with delegations and teams from the adjoining precincts and the surrounding counties. A special train from Indiana brought eleven car loads of interested lookers-on from that state. People came on horseback and muleback, in wagons, in freight trains and on foot— some with badges and some with banners, some with their dinners and some without. At ten o'clock the streets and sidewalks around the public square were almost impassable, and those who essayed out-doors anywhere in the vicinity were well nigh stifled with dust for their pains. The chief decoration of the day was a gigantic banner, eighty feet long, hung across the street from the court house to a high building on the west side of the street. On one side was inscribed:

[2] September 21.

COLES COUNTY
FOUR HUNDRED MAJORITY FOR LINCOLN

On the reverse was a painting of "Old Abe 30 Years Ago," driving three yoke of oxen, attached to a yawl-like Kentucky wagon. This was flanked by two magnificent specimens of the stars and stripes.

Mr. Lincoln and Mr. Douglas both passed the previous night in Mattoon. Two processions were started from that thriving town on Saturday morning, to escort the speakers to Charleston. About half past ten another long and imposing procession of carriages, horsemen, bands of music, and conspicuous above all, a mammoth car covered with white muslin and silk and decorated with wild flowers, bearing a huge inscription, "LINCOLN, OGLESBY, MARSHALL AND CRADDOCK," and carrying thirty-two young ladies with banners inscribed with names of the states of the confederacy—moved out of Charleston to meet Mr. Lincoln. About an hour afterwards the two Republican processions returned together. They constituted without question the most formidable array of the campaign. Innumerable banners fluttered in the wind farther than the eye could reach through the cloud of dust that accompanied them. As they entered the town the procession was a mile in length. As compared with it, the Douglas escort was a very puny affair. The car provided for the thirty-two ladies on that side of the house, somehow contained only fifteen, and a majority of these were under eight years of age—suggesting the idea of their being territories rather than states.

Upon reaching Charleston, Lincoln was welcomed by H. P. H. Bromwell. The Republican candidate responded felicitously.[3]

"Fellow citizens: I have not been accustomed to these demonstrations and popular gatherings in my journeyings through our state heretofore. I accept them, and I particularly accept this as a testimonial, not to myself, but to the cause and the principles which your favor has caused me to represent in this contest. I thank you most sincerely for this flattering reception, for the kind welcome your speaker has uttered, and [turning to the car conveying the young ladies] for this beautiful basket of flowers. [Loud cheers.] I can now only express my thanks for this fine demonstration, and say that I will more fully address you and discuss the issues involved in the present struggle, at another hour."

Lincoln took the stand at 2:45, to be greeted with "vociferous and protracted applause."

[3] *Ibid.*

Lincoln's Opening Speech

Ladies and Gentlemen:

It will be very difficult for an audience so large as this to hear distinctly what a speaker says, and consequently it is important that as profound silence be preserved as possible.

While I was at the hotel to-day an elderly gentleman called upon me to know whether I was really in favor of producing a perfect equality between the negroes and white people. [Great laughter.] While I had not proposed to myself on this occasion to say much on that subject, yet as the question was asked me I thought I would occupy perhaps five minutes in saying something in regard to it. I will say then that I am not, nor ever have been in favor of bringing about in any way the social and political equality of the white and black races, [applause]—that I am not nor ever have been in favor of making voters or jurors of negroes, nor of qualifying them to hold office, nor to intermarry with white people; and I will say in addition to this that there is a physical difference between the white and black races which I believe will for ever forbid the two races living together on terms of social and political equality. And inasmuch as they cannot so live, while they do remain together there must be the position of superior and inferior, and I as much as any other man am in favor of having the superior position assigned to the white race. I say upon this occasion I do not perceive that because the white man is to have the superior position the negro should be denied everything. I do not understand that because I do not want a negro woman for a slave I must necessarily want her for a wife. [Cheers and laughter.] My understanding is that I can just let her alone. I am now in my fiftieth year, and I certainly never have had a black woman for either a slave or a wife. So it seems to me quite possible for us to get along without making either slaves or wives of negroes. I will add to this that I have never seen to my knowledge a man, woman or child who was in favor of producing a perfect equality, social and political, between negroes and white men. I recollect of but one distinguished instance that I ever heard of so frequently as to be entirely satisfied of its correctness—and that is the case of Judge Douglas' old friend Col. Richard M. Johnson.[4] [Laughter.] I will also add to the remarks I have made, (for I am

---

[4] According to Thomas P. Abernethy in the *Dictionary of American Biography*, Richard M. Johnson, Vice-President of the United States, 1837–41, "never married, but had two daughters by Julia Chinn, a mulatto who came to him in the distribution of his father's estate."

not going to enter at large upon this subject,) that I have never had the least apprehension that I or my friends would marry negroes if there was no law to keep them from it, [laughter] but as Judge Douglas and his friends seem to be in great apprehension that they might, if there were no law to keep them from it, [roars of laughter] I give him the most solemn pledge that I will to the very last stand by the law of this state, which forbids the marrying of white people with negroes. [Continued laughter and applause.] I will add one further word, which is this, that I do not understand there is any place where an alteration of the social and political relations of the negro and the white man can be made except in the state legislature —not in the Congress of the United States—and as I do not really apprehend the approach of any such thing myself, and as Judge Douglas seems to be in constant horror that some such danger is rapidly approaching, I propose as the best means to prevent it that the Judge be kept at home and placed in the state legislature to fight the measure. [Uproarious laughter and applause.] I do not propose dwelling longer at this time on this subject.

When Judge Trumbull, our other Senator in Congress, returned to Illinois in the month of August, he made a speech at Chicago in which he made what may be called *a charge* against Judge Douglas, which I understand proved to be very offensive to him. The Judge was at that time out upon one of his speaking tours through the country, and when the news of it reached him, as I am informed, he denounced Judge Trumbull in rather harsh terms for having said what he did in regard to that matter. I was traveling at that time and speaking at the same places with Judge Douglas on subsequent days, and when I heard of what Judge Trumbull had said of Douglas and what Douglas had said back again, I felt that I was in a position where I could not remain entirely silent in regard to the matter. Consequently upon two or three occasions I alluded to it, and alluded to it in no other wise than to say that in regard to the charge brought by Trumbull against Douglas, I *personally* knew nothing and sought to say nothing about it—that I did personally know Judge Trumbull—that I believed him to be a man of veracity —that I believed him to be a man of capacity sufficient to know very well whether an assertion he was making as a conclusion drawn from a set of facts, was true or false; and as a conclusion of my own from that, I stated it as my belief, if Trumbull should ever be called upon he would prove everything he had said. I said this upon two or three occasions. Upon a subsequent occasion, Judge Trumbull spoke again before an audience at Alton, and upon that occasion not only repeated his charge against Douglas, but arrayed the evidence he relied upon to substantiate it. This speech was published at length; and subsequently at Jacksonville Judge Douglas alluded to the matter. In the course of his speech, and near the close of it, he stated in regard to myself what I will now read: "Judge Douglas proceeded to remark that he should not hereafter occupy his time in refuting such charges made by Trumbull, but that Lincoln having indorsed the character of Trumbull for veracity, he should hold him (Lincoln) responsible for the slanders." I have done simply what I have told you, to subject me to this invitation to notice the charge. I now wish to say that it had not originally been my purpose to discuss that matter at all. But inasmuch as it seems to be the wish of Judge Douglas to hold me responsible for it, then for once in my life I will play General Jackson and to the just extent I take the responsibility. [Great applause and cries of "good, good," "hurrah for Lincoln," etc.]

I wish to say at the beginning that I will hand to the reporters that portion of Judge Trumbull's Alton speech which was devoted to this matter, and also that portion of Judge Douglas' speech made at Jacksonville in answer to it. I shall thereby furnish the readers of this debate with the complete discussion between Trumbull and Douglas. I cannot now read them, for the reason that it would take half of my first hour to do so. I can only make some comments upon them. Trumbull's charge is in the following words: "Now, the charge is, that there was a plot entered into to have a constitution formed for Kansas and put in force without giving the people an opportunity to vote upon it, and that Mr. Douglas was in the plot." I will state, without quoting further, for all will have an opportunity of reading it hereafter, that Judge Trumbull brings forward what he regards as sufficient evidence to substantiate this charge.

[The extracts handed to our reporter by Mr. Lincoln are quite too lengthy to appear in this number of the PRESS AND TRIBUNE. Judge Trumbull's speech at Alton has already had a place in our columns, and Senator Douglas's remarks at Jacksonville are faithfully repeated in his portion of this (Charleston) debate.]

It will be perceived Judge Trumbull shows that Senator Bigler,[5] upon the floor of the Senate, had declared there had been a conference among the Senators, in which conference it was determined to have an enabling act passed for the people of Kansas to form a constitution under,[6] and in this conference it was agreed among

[5] William Bigler, Senator from Pennsylvania, 1856–61. He supported Buchanan in the Kansas imbroglio.

[6] The Toombs Bill. This measure provided for a fair registration of *bona fide* Kansas voters and for the election of delegates to a convention which should

them that it was best not to have a provision for submitting the constitution to a vote of the people after it should be formed. He then brings forward to show, and showing, as he deemed, that Judge Douglas reported the bill back to the Senate with that clause stricken out. He then shows that there was a new clause inserted into the bill, which would in its nature *prevent* a reference of the constitution back for a vote of the people—if, indeed, upon a mere silence in the law, it could be assumed that they had the right to vote upon it. These are the general statements that he has made.

I propose to examine the points in Judge Douglas' speech, in which he attempts to answer that speech of Judge Trumbull's. When you come to examine Judge Douglas' speech, you will find that the first point he makes is—"Suppose it were true that there was such a change in the bill, and that I struck it out—is that a proof of a plot to force a constitution upon them against their will?" His striking out such a provision, if there was such a one in the bill, he argues does not establish the proof that it was stricken out for the purpose of robbing the people of that right. I would say, in the first place, that that would be a *most manifest* reason for it. It is true, as Judge Douglas states, that many territorial bills have passed without having such a provision in them. I believe it is true, though I am not certain, that in some instances, constitutions framed under such bills have been submitted to a vote of the people, with the law silent upon the subject, but it does not appear that they once had their enabling acts framed with an express provision *for* submitting the constitution to be framed, to a vote of the people, and then that they were stricken out when Congress did not mean to alter the effect of the law. That there have been bills which never had the provision in, I do not question; but when was that provision taken out of one that it was in? More especially does this evidence tend to prove the proposition that Trumbull advanced, when we remember that the provision was stricken out of the bill almost simultaneously with the time that Bigler says there was a conference among certain Senators, and in which it was agreed that a bill should be passed leaving that out. Judge Douglas, in answering Trumbull, omits to attend to the testimony of Bigler, that there was a meeting in which it was agreed they should so frame the bill that there should be no submission of the constitution to a vote of the people. The Judge does not notice this part of it. If you take this as one piece of evi-

---

frame a constitution for the prospective state. The Senate passed the bill July 2, 1856. The House, with a Republican majority, refused to consider it, party leaders taking the position that under the bill Kansas could conceivably enter the Union as a slave state.

dence, and then ascertain that simultaneously Judge Douglas struck out a provision that did require it to be submitted, and put the two together, I think it will make a pretty fair show of proof that Judge Douglas did, as Trumbull says, enter into a plot to put in force a constitution for Kansas without giving the people any opportunity of voting upon it.

But I must hurry on. The next proposition that Judge Douglas puts is this: "But upon examination it turns out that the Toombs bill never did contain a clause requiring the constitution to be submitted." This is a mere question of fact, and can be determined by evidence. I only want to ask this question—Why did not Judge Douglas say that these words were not stricken out of the Toombs bill, or this bill from which it is alleged the provision was stricken out—a bill which goes by the name of Toombs, because he originally brought it forward? I ask why, if the Judge wanted to make a direct issue with Trumbull, did he not take the exact proposition Trumbull made in his speech, and say it was not stricken out? Trumbull has given the exact words that he says were in the Toombs bill, and he alleges that when the bill came back, they were stricken out. Judge Douglas does not say that the words which Trumbull says were stricken out, were not so stricken out, but he says there was no provision in the Toombs bill to submit the constitution to a vote of the people. We see at once that he is merely making an issue upon the meaning of the words. He has not undertaken to say that Trumbull tells a lie about these words being stricken out; but he is really, when pushed up to it, only taking an issue upon the meaning of the words. Now, then, if there be any issue upon the meaning of the words, or if there be upon the question of fact as to whether these words were stricken out, I have before me what I suppose to be a genuine copy of the Toombs bill, in which it can be shown that the words Trumbull says were in it, were, in fact, originally there. If there be any dispute upon the fact, I have got the documents here to show they were there. If there be any controversy upon the sense of the words—whether these words which were stricken out really constituted a provision for submitting the matter to a vote of the people, as that is a matter of argument, I think I may as well use Trumbull's own argument. He says that the proposition is in these words:

That the following propositions be and the same are hereby offered to the said convention of the people of Kansas when formed, for their free acceptance or rejection; which, if accepted by the convention *and ratified by the people at the election for the adoption of the constitution,* shall be obligatory upon the United States and the said state of Kansas.

Now, Trumbull alleges that these last words were stricken out of the bill when it came back, and he says this was a provision for submitting the constitution to a vote of the people, and his argument is this: "Would it have been possible to ratify the land propositions at the election for the adoption of the constitution, unless such an election was to be held?" [Applause and laughter.] That is Trumbull's argument. Now Judge Douglas does not meet the charge at all, but he stands up and says there was no such proposition in that bill for submitting the constitution to be framed to a vote of the people. Trumbull admits that the language is not a direct provision for submitting it, but it is a provision necessarily implied from another provision. He asks you how it is possible to ratify the land proposition at the election for the adoption of the constitution, if there was no election to be held for the adoption of the constitution. And he goes on to show that it is not any less a law because the provision is put in that indirect shape than it would be if it was put directly. But I presume I have said enough to draw attention to this point, and I pass it by also.

Another one of the points that Judge Douglas makes upon Trumbull, and at very great length, is, that Trumbull, while the bill was pending, said in a speech in the Senate that he supposed the constitution to be made would have to be submitted to the people. He asks, if Trumbull thought so then, what ground is there for anybody thinking otherwise now? Fellow citizens, this much may be said in reply: That bill had been in the hands of a party to which Trumbull did not belong. It had been in the hands of the committee at the head of which Judge Douglas stood. Trumbull perhaps had a printed copy of the original Toombs bill. I have not the evidence on that point, except a sort of inference I draw from the general course of business there. What alterations, or what provisions in the way of altering, were going on in committee, Trumbull had no means of knowing, until the altered bill was reported back. Soon afterwards, when it was reported back, there was a discussion over it, and perhaps Trumbull in reading it hastily in the altered form did not perceive all the bearings of the alterations. He was hastily borne into the debate, and it does not follow that because there was something in it Trumbull did not perceive, that something did not exist. More than this, is it true that what Trumbull did can have any effect on what Douglas did? [Applause.] Suppose Trumbull had been in the plot with these other men, would that let Douglas out of it? [Applause and laughter.] Would it exonerate Douglas that Trumbull didn't then perceive he was in the plot? He also asks the question: Why didn't Trumbull propose to

amend the bill if he thought it needed any amendment? Why, I
believe that everything Judge Trumbull had proposed, particularly
in connection with this question of Kansas and Nebraska, since he
had been on the floor of the Senate, had been promptly voted down
by Judge Douglas and his friends. He had no promise that an
amendment offered by him to anything on this subject would receive the slightest consideration. Judge Trumbull did bring to the
notice of the Senate at that time the fact that there was no provision for submitting the constitution about to be made for the
people of Kansas, to a vote of the people. I believe I may venture
to say that Judge Douglas made some reply to this speech of Judge
Trumbull's, *but he never noticed that part of it at all.* And so the
thing passed by. I think, then, the fact that Judge Trumbull offered
no amendment, does not throw much blame upon him; and if it did,
it does not reach the question of fact *as to what Judge Douglas was
doing.* [Applause.] I repeat that if Trumbull had himself been in the
plot, it would not at all relieve the others who were in it from
blame. If I should be indicted for murder, and upon the trial it
should be discovered that I had been implicated in that murder,
but that the prosecuting witness was guilty too, that would not at all
touch the question of my crime. It would be no relief to my neck
that they discovered this other man who charged the crime upon me
to be guilty too.

Another one of the points Judge Douglas makes upon Judge
Trumbull is, that when he spoke in Chicago he made his charge to
rest upon the fact that the bill had the provision in it for submitting
the constitution to a vote of the people, when it went into his
(Judge Douglas') hands, that it was missing when he reported it
to the Senate, and that in a public speech he had subsequently said
the alteration in the bill was made while it was in committee, and
that they were made in consultation between him (Judge Douglas)
and Toombs. And Judge Douglas goes on to comment upon the fact
of Trumbull's adducing in his Alton speech the proposition that the
bill not only came back with that proposition stricken out, but with
another clause and another provision in it, saying that "until the
complete execution of this act there shall be no election in said
territory,"—which Trumbull argued was not only taking the provision for submitting to a vote of the people out of the bill, but was
adding an affirmative one, in that it prevented the people from
exercising the right under a bill that was merely silent on the question. Now in regard to what he says, that Trumbull shifts the issue
—that he shifts his ground—and I believe he uses the term, that "it
being proven false, he has changed ground"—I call upon all of you,

when you come to examine that portion of Trumbull's speech, (for it will make a part of mine,) to examine whether Trumbull has shifted his ground or not. I say he did not shift his ground, but that he brought forward his original charge and the evidence to sustain it yet more fully, but precisely as he originally made it. Then, in addition thereto, he brought in a new piece of evidence. He shifted no ground. He brought no new piece of evidence inconsistent with his former testimony, but he brought a new piece, tending, as he thought, and as I think, to prove his proposition. To illustrate: A man brings an accusation against another, and on trial the man making the charge introduces A and B to prove the accusation. At a second trial he introduces the same witnesses, who tell the same story as before, and a third witness, who tells the same thing, and in addition, gives further testimony corroborative of the charge. So with Trumbull. There was no shifting of ground, nor inconsistency of testimony between the new piece of evidence and what he originally introduced.

But Judge Douglas says that he himself moved to strike out that last provision of the bill, and that on his motion it was stricken out and a substitute inserted. That I presume is the truth. I presume it is true that that last proposition was stricken out by Judge Douglas. Trumbull has not said it was not. Trumbull has himself said that it was so stricken out. He says: "I am speaking of the bill as Judge Douglas reported it back. It was amended somewhat in the Senate before it passed, but I am speaking of it as he brought it back." Now when Judge Douglas parades the fact that the provision was stricken out of the bill when it came back, he asserts nothing contrary to what Trumbull alleges. Trumbull has only said that he originally put it in—not that he did not strike it out. Trumbull says it was not in the bill when it went to the committee. When it came back it was in, and Judge Douglas said the alterations were made by him in consultation with Toombs. Trumbull alleges therefore as his conclusion that Judge Douglas put it in. Then if Douglas wants to contradict Trumbull and call him a liar, let him say he did not put it in, and not that he didn't take it out again. It is said that a bear is sometimes hard enough pushed to drop a cub, and so I presume it was in this case. [Loud applause.] I presume the truth is that Douglas put it in and afterwards took it out. [Laughter and cheers.] That I take it is the truth about it. Judge Trumbull says one thing; Douglas says another thing, and the two don't contradict one another at all. The question is, what did he put it in for? In the first place what did he take the other provision out of the bill for?

—the provision which Trumbull argued was necessary for submitting the constitution to a vote of the people? What did he take that out for, and having taken it out, what did he put this in for? I say that in the run of things it is not unlikely forces conspire, to render it vastly expedient for Judge Douglas to take that latter clause out again. The question that Trumbull has made is that Judge Douglas put it in, and he don't meet Trumbull at all unless he denies that.

In the clause of Judge Douglas' speech upon this subject he uses this language towards Judge Trumbull. He says: "He forges his evidence from beginning to end, and by falsifying the record he endeavors to bolster up his false charge." Well, that is a pretty serious statement. Trumbull forges his evidence from beginning to end. Now upon my own authority I say that it is not true. [Great cheers and laughter.] What is a forgery? Consider the evidence that Trumbull has brought forward. When you come to read the speech, as you will be able to, examine whether the evidence is a forgery from beginning to end. He had the bill or document in his hand like that [holding up a paper]. He says that is a copy of the Toombs bill— the amendment offered by Toombs. He says that is a copy of the bill as it was introduced and went into Judge Douglas' hands. Now, does Judge Douglas say that is a forgery? That is one thing Trumbull brought forward. Judge Douglas says he forged it from beginning to end! That is the "beginning," we will say. Does Douglas say that is a forgery? Let him say it to-day and we will have a subsequent examination upon this subject. [Loud applause.] Trumbull then holds up another document like this and says that is an exact copy of the bill as it came back in the amended form out of Judge Douglas' hands. Does Judge Douglas say that is a forgery? Does he say it in his general sweeping charge? Does he say so now? If he does not, then take this Toombs bill and the bill in the amended form and it only needs to compare them to see that the provision is in the one and not in the other; it leaves the inference inevitable that it was taken out. [Applause.]

But while I am dealing with this question let us see what Trumbull's other evidence is. One other piece of evidence I will read. Trumbull says there are in this original Toombs bill these words: "That the following propositions be, and the same are hereby offered to the said convention of the people of Kansas, when formed, for their free acceptance or rejection; which, if accepted by the convention and ratified by the people at the election for the adoption of the constitution, shall be obligatory upon the United States and the said state of Kansas." Now, if it is said that this is a forgery, we will open the paper here and see whether it is or not. Again, Trumbull says as he goes along, that Mr. Bigler made the following statement in his place in the Senate, December 9, 1857.

I was present when that subject was discussed by Senators before the bill was introduced, and the question was raised and discussed, whether the constitution, when formed, should be submitted to a vote of the people. It was held by those most intelligent on the subject, that in view of all the difficulties surrounding that territory, the danger of any experiment at that time of a popular vote, it would be better there should be no such provision in the Toombs bill; and it was my understanding, in all the intercourse I had, that the convention would make a constitution, and send it here without submitting it to the popular vote.

Then Trumbull follows on: "In speaking of this meeting again on the 21st December, 1857, (*Congressional Globe*, same vol., page 113,) Senator Bigler said:

Nothing was further from my mind than to allude to any social or confidential interview. The meeting was not of that character. Indeed, it was semi-official and called to promote the public good. My recollection was clear that I left the conference under the impression that it had been deemed best to adopt measures to admit Kansas as a state through the agency of one popular election, and that for delegates to this convention. This impression was stronger because I thought the spirit of the bill infringed upon the doctrine of non-intervention, to which I had great aversion; but with the hope of accomplishing a great good, and as no movement had been made in that direction in the Territory, I waived this objection, and concluded to support the measure. I have a few items of testimony as to the correctness of these impressions, and with their submission I shall be content. I have before me the bill reported by the Senator from Illinois on the 7th of March, 1856, providing for the admission of Kansas as a state, the third section of which reads as follows:

"That the following propositions be, and the same are hereby offered to the said convention of the people of Kansas, when formed, for their free acceptance or rejection; which if accepted by the convention and ratified by the people at the election for the adoption of the constitution, shall be obligatory upon the United States and the said state of Kansas."

The bill read in his place by the Senator from Georgia, on the 25th of June, and referred to Committee on Territories, contained the same section, word for word. Both these bills were under consideration at the conference referred to; but, Sir, when the Senator from Illinois reported the Toombs bill to the Senate with amendments, the next morning it did not contain that portion of the third section which indicated to the convention that the constitution should be approved by the people. The words "AND RATIFIED BY THE PEOPLE AT THE ELECTION FOR THE ADOPTION OF THE CONSTITUTION," had been stricken out.

Now these things Trumbull says were stated by Bigler upon the floor of the Senate on certain days, and that they are recorded in the "Congressional Globe" on certain pages. Does Judge Douglas say this is a forgery? Does he say there is no such thing in the "Congressional Globe?" What does he mean when he says Judge Trumbull forges his evidence from beginning to end? So again he says in another place, that Judge Douglas, in his speech Dec. 9, 1857, ("Congressional Globe," part 1, page 15) stated:

That during the last session of Congress I [Mr. Douglas] reported a bill from the Committee on Territories, to authorize the people of Kansas to assemble and form a constitution for themselves. Subsequently the Senator from Georgia [Mr. Toombs] brought forward a substitute for my bill, which, *after having been modified by him and myself in consultation,* was passed by the Senate.

Now Trumbull says this is a quotation from a speech of Douglas, and is recorded in the "Congressional Globe." Is *it* a forgery? Is it there or not? It may not be there, but I want the Judge to take these pieces of evidences, and distinctly say they are forgeries if he dare do it. [Great applause.]

A Voice—"He will."

Mr. Lincoln—Well, sir, you had better not commit him. [Cheers and laughter.] He gives other quotations—another from Judge Douglas. He says:

I will ask the Senator to show me an intimation, from any one member of the Senate, in the whole debate on the Toombs bill, and in the Union, from any quarter, that the constitution was not to be submitted to the people. I will venture to say that on all sides of the chamber it was so understood at the time. If the opponents of the bill had understood it was not, they would have made the point on it; and if they had made it, we should certainly have yielded to it; and put in the clause. That is a discovery made since the President found out that it was not safe to take it for granted that that would be done, which ought in fairness to have been done.

Judge Trumbull says Douglas made that speech and it is recorded. Does Judge Douglas say it is a forgery and was not true? Trumbull says somewhere, and I propose to skip it, but it will be found by any one who will read this debate, that he did distinctly bring it to the notice of those who were engineering the bill, that it lacked that provision, and then he goes on to give another quotation from Judge Douglas, where Judge Trumbull uses this language:

Judge Douglas, however, on the same day and in the same debate, probably recollecting or being reminded of the fact that I had objected to the Toombs bill when pending that it did not provide for a submission of the constitution to the people, made another statement, which is to be found in the same volume of the *Globe*, page 22, in which he says:

"That the bill was silent on this subject was true, and my attention was called to that about the time it was passed; and I took the fair construction to be, that powers not delegated were reserved, and that of course the constitution would be submitted to the people."

Whether this statement is consistent with the statement just before made, that had the point been made it would have been yielded to, or that it was a new discovery, you will determine.

So I say, I do not know whether Judge Douglas will dispute this, and yet maintain his position that Trumbull's evidence "was forged from beginning to end." I will remark that I have not got these Congressional Globes with me. They are large books and difficult to carry about, and if Judge Douglas shall say that on these points where Trumbull has quoted from them, there are no such passages there, I shall not be able to prove they are there upon this occasion, but I will have another chance. Whenever he points out the forgery and says, "I declare that this particular thing which Trumbull has uttered is not found where he says it is," then my attention will be drawn to that, and I will arm myself for the contest—stating now that I have not the slightest doubt on earth that I will find every quotation just where Trumbull says it is. Then the question is, how can Douglas call that a forgery? How can he make out that it is a forgery? What is a forgery? It is the bringing forward something in writing or in print purporting to be of certain effect when it is altogether untrue. If you come forward with my note for one hundred dollars when I have never given such a note, there is a forgery. If you come forward with a letter purporting to be written by me which I never wrote, there is another forgery. If you produce anything in writing or print saying it is so and so, the document not being genuine, a forgery has been committed. How do you make this a forgery when every piece of evidence is genuine? If Judge Douglas does say these documents and quotations are false and forged he has a full right to do so, but until he does it specifically we don't know how to get at him. If he does say they are false and forged, I will then look further into it, and I presume I can procure the certificates of the proper officers that they are genuine copies. I have no doubt each of these extracts will be found exactly where Trumbull says it is. Then I leave it to you if Judge Douglas, in making his sweeping charge that Judge Trumbull's evidence is forged from beginning to end, at all meets the case—if that is the way to get at the facts. I repeat again, if he will point out which one is a forgery, I will carefully examine it, and if it proves that any one of them is really a forgery it will not be me who will hold to it any longer. I have always wanted to deal with every one I meet candidly and honestly. If I have made any assertion not warranted by facts, and it is pointed out to me, I will withdraw it cheerfully. But I do not choose to see Judge Trumbull calumniated, and the evidence he has brought forward branded in general terms, "a forgery from beginning to end." This is not the legal way of meeting a charge, and I submit to all intelligent persons, both friends of Judge Douglas and of myself, whether it is.

Now coming back—how much time have I left?

THE MODERATOR—Three minutes.

MR. LINCOLN—The point upon Judge Douglas is this. The bill that went into his hands had the provision in it for a submission of the constitution to the people; and I say its language amounts to an express provision for a submission, and that he took the provision out. He says it was known that the bill was silent in this particular; *but I say, Judge Douglas, it was not silent when you got it.* [Great applause.] It was vocal with the declaration when you got it, for a submission of the constitution to the people. And now, my direct question to Judge Douglas is, to answer why, if he deemed the bill silent on this point, he found it necessary to strike out those particular harmless words. If he had found the bill silent and without this provision, he might say what he does now. If he supposed it was implied that the constitution would be submitted to a vote of the people, how could these two lines so encumber the statute as to make it necessary to strike them out? How could he infer that a submission was still implied, after its express provision had been stricken from the bill? I find the bill vocal with the provision, while he silenced it. He took it out, and although he took out the other provision preventing a submission to a vote of the people, I ask, *why did you first put it in?* I ask him whether he took the original provision out, which Trumbull alleges was in the bill? If he admits that he did take it, *I ask him what he did it for?* It looks to us as if he had altered the bill. If it looks differently to him—if he has a different reason for his action from the one we assign him—he can tell it. I insist upon knowing why he made the bill silent upon that point when it was vocal before he put his hands upon it.

I was told, before my last paragraph, that my time was within three minutes of being out. I presume it is expired now. I therefore close. [Three tremendous cheers were given as Mr. Lincoln retired.]

Douglas' Reply

Ladies and Gentlemen:

I had supposed that we assembled here to-day for the purpose of a joint discussion between Mr. Lincoln and myself upon the political questions that now agitate the whole country. The rule of such discussions is, that the opening speaker shall touch upon all the points he intends to discuss in order that his opponent, in reply, shall have the opportunity of answering them. Let me ask you what questions of public policy relating to the welfare of this state or the Union, has Mr. Lincoln discussed before you? ("None, none," and great applause.) Gentlemen, allow me to suggest that silence is the best compliment you can pay me. I need my whole time, and your cheering only occupies it. Mr. Lincoln simply contented himself at the outset by saying, that he was not in favor of social and political equality between the white man and the negro, and did not desire the law so changed as to make the latter voters or eligible to office. I am glad that I have at last succeeded in getting an answer out of him upon this question of negro citizenship and eligibility to office, for I have been trying to bring him to the point on it ever since this canvass commenced.

I will now call your attention to the question which Mr. Lincoln has occupied his entire time in discussing. He spent his whole hour in retailing a charge made by Senator Trumbull against me. The circumstances out of which that charge was manufactured, occurred prior to the last presidential election, over two years ago. If the charge was true, why did Trumbull [not] make it in 1856, when I was discussing the questions of that day all over this state with Lincoln and him, and when it was pertinent to the then issue. He was then as silent as the grave on the subject. If that charge was true, the time to have brought it forward was the canvas of 1856, the year when the Toombs bill passed the Senate. When the facts were fresh in the public mind, when the Kansas question was the paramount question of the day, and when such a charge would have had a material bearing on the election. Why did he and Lincoln remain silent then, knowing that such a charge could be made and proven if true? Were they not false to you and false to the country in going through that entire campaign, concealing their knowledge of this enormous conspiracy which, Mr. Trumbull says, he then knew and would not tell? (Laughter.) Mr. Lincoln intimates in his speech, a good reason why Mr. Trumbull would not tell, for, he says, that it might be true, as I proved that it was at Jacksonville, that Trumbull was also in the plot, yet that the fact of Trumbull's being in the plot would not in any way relieve me. He illustrates this argument by supposing himself on trial for murder, and says that it would be no extenuating circumstance if, on his trial, another man was found to be a party to his crime. Well, if Trumbull was in the plot, and concealed it in order to escape the odium which would have fallen upon himself, I ask you whether you can believe him now when he turns state's evidence, and avows his own infamy in order to implicate me. ("He is a liar, and a traitor. We couldn't believe Lyman Trumbull under oath," &c.) I am amazed that Mr. Lincoln should now come forward and endorse that charge, occupying his whole hour in reading Mr. Trumbull's speech in support of it. Why, I ask, does not Mr. Lincoln make a speech of his own instead of taking up his time reading Trumbull's speech at Alton? (Cheers.) I supposed that Mr. Lincoln was capable of making a public speech on his own account, or I should not have accepted the banter from him for a joint discussion. (Cheers and voices: "How about the charges?") Do not trouble yourselves, I am going to make my speech in my own way, and I trust as the Democrats listened patiently and respectfully to Mr. Lincoln, that his friends will not interrupt me when I am answering him. When Mr. Trumbull returned from the East, the first thing he did when he landed at Chicago was to make a speech wholly devoted to assaults upon my public character and public action. Up to that time I had never alluded to his course in Congress, or to him directly or indirectly, and hence his assaults upon me were entirely without provocation and without excuse. Since then he has been traveling from one end of the state to the other repeating his vile charge. I propose now to read it in his own language:

Now, fellow citizens, I make the distinct charge, that there was a preconcerted arrangement and plot entered into by the very men who now claim credit for opposing a constitution formed and put in force without giving the people any opportunity to pass upon it. This, my friends, is a serious charge, but I charge it to-night that the very men who traverse the country under banners proclaiming popular sovereignty, by design concocted a bill on purpose to force a constitution upon that people.

In answer to someone in the crowd, who asked him a question, Trumbull said:

And you want to satisfy yourself that he was in the plot to force a constitution upon that people? I will satisfy you. I will cram the truth down any honest man's throat until he cannot deny it. And to the man who does deny it, I will cram the lie down his throat till he shall cry enough. (Voices, "shameful," "that's decency for you," &c.)

It is preposterous—it is the most damnable effrontery that man ever put on, to conceal a scheme to defraud and cheat the people out of their rights and then claim credit for it.

That is the polite language Senator Trumbull applied to me, his colleague, when I was two hundred miles off. ("That's like him.") Why did he not speak out as boldly in the Senate of the United States, and cram the lie down my throat when I denied the charge, first made by Bigler, and made him take it back. You all recollect how Bigler assaulted me when I was engaged in a hand to hand fight, resisting a scheme to force a constitution on the people of Kansas against their will. He then attacked me with this charge; but I proved its utter falsity; nailed the slander to the counter, and made him take the back track. There is not an honest man in America who read that debate who will pretend that the charge is true. ("Hurra for Douglas.") Trumbull was then present in the Senate, face to face with me, and why did he not then rise and repeat the charge, and say he would cram the lie down my throat. ("He was afraid.") I tell you that Trumbull then knew it was a lie. He knew that Toombs denied that there ever was a clause in the bill he brought forward calling for and requiring a submission of the Kansas constitution to the people. I will tell you what the facts of the case were. I introduced a bill to authorize the people of Kansas to form a constitution, and come into the Union as a state whenever they should have the requisite population for a member of Congress, and Mr. Toombs proposed a substitute, authorizing the people of Kansas, with their then population of only 25,000, to form a constitution, and come in at once. The question at issue was, whether we would admit Kansas with a population of 25,000, or, make her wait until she had the ratio entitling her to a representative in Congress, which was 93,420. That was the point of dispute in the Committee of Territories, to which both my bill and Mr. Toombs' substitute had been referred. I was overruled by a majority of the committee, my proposition rejected, and Mr. Toombs' proposition to admit Kansas then, with her population of 25,000, adopted. Accordingly, a bill to carry out his idea of immediate admission was reported as a substitute for mine—the only points at issue being, as I have already said, the question of population, and the adoption of safeguards against frauds at the election. Trumbull knew this— the whole Senate knew it—and hence he was silent at that time. He waited until I became engaged in this canvass, and finding that I was showing up Lincoln's Abolitionism and negro equality doctrines (cheers), that I was driving Lincoln to the wall, and white men would not support his rank Abolitionism, he came back from the East and trumped up a system of charges against me, hoping that I would be compelled to occupy my entire time in defending myself, so that I would not be able to show up the enormity of the principles of the Abolitionists. Now, the only reason, and the true reason, why Mr. Lincoln has occupied the whole of his first hour in this issue between Trumbull and myself is, to conceal from this vast audience the real questions which divide the two great parties. ("That's it"; and cheers.)

[250]

I am not going to allow them to waste much of my time with these personal matters. I have lived in this state twenty-five years, most of that time have been in public life, and my record is open to you all. If that record is not enough to vindicate me from these petty, malicious assaults, I despise ever to be elected to office by slandering my opponents and traducing other men. (Cheers.) Mr. Lincoln asks you to elect him to the United States Senate to-day solely because he and Trumbull can slander me. Has he given any other reason? ("No, no.") Has he avowed what he was desirous to do in Congress on any one question? ("No, no.") He desires to ride into office not upon his own merits, not upon the merits and soundness of his principles, but upon his success in fastening a stale old slander upon me. ("That's the truth." "Hear, hear.")

I wish you to bear in mind that up to the time of the introduction of the Toombs bill, and after its introduction, there had never been an act of Congress for the admission of a new state which contained a clause requiring its constitution to be submitted to the people. The general rule made the law silent on the subject, taking it for granted that the people would demand and compel a popular vote on the ratification of their constitution. Such was the general rule under Washington, Jefferson, Madison, Jackson and Polk, under the Whig Presidents and the Democratic Presidents from the beginning of the government down, and nobody dreamed that an effort would ever be made to abuse the power thus confided to the people of a territory. For this reason our attention was not called to the fact of whether there was or was not a clause in the Toombs bill compelling submission, but it was taken for granted that the constitution would be submitted to the people whether the law compelled it or not.

Now, I will read from the report made by me as Chairman of the Committee on Territories at the time I reported back the Toombs substitution to the Senate. It contained several things which I had voted against in committee, but had been overruled by a majority of the members, and it was my duty as chairman of the committee to report the bill back as it was agreed upon by them. The main point upon which I had been overruled was the question of population. In my report accompanying the Toombs bill, I said:

In the opinion of your committee, whenever a constitution shall be formed in any territory, preparatory to its admission into the Union as a state, justice, the genius of our institutions, the whole theory of our republican system imperatively demand that the voice of the people shall be fairly expressed, and their will embodied in that fundamental law, without fraud, or violence, or intimidation, or any other improper or unlawful influence, and subject to no other restrictions than those imposed by the Constitution of the United States. (Cheers.)

There you find that we took it for granted that the constitution was to be submitted to the people whether the bill was silent on the subject or not. Suppose I had reported it so, following the example of Washington, Adams, Jefferson, Madison, Monroe, Adams, Jackson, Van Buren, Harrison, Tyler, Polk, Taylor, Fillmore, and Pierce, would that fact have been evidence of a conspiracy to force a constitution upon the people of Kansas against their will? (A unanimous "No!") If the charge which Mr. Lincoln makes be true against me, it is true against Zachary Taylor, Millard Fillmore, and every Whig President as well as every Democratic President, and against Henry Clay, who, in the Senate or the House, for forty years advocated bills similar to the one I reported, no one of them containing a clause compelling the submission of the constitution to the people. Are Mr. Lincoln and Mr. Trumbull prepared to charge upon all those eminent men from the beginning of the government down to the present day, that the absence of a provision compelling submission, in the various bills passed by them authorizing the people of territories to form state constitutions, is evidence of a corrupt design on their part to force a constitution upon an unwilling people? ("We'll skin them if they dare to.")

I ask you to reflect on these things, for I tell you that there is a conspiracy to carry this election for the Black Republicans by slander, and not by fair means. Mr. Lincoln's speech this day is conclusive evidence of the fact. He has devoted his entire time to an issue between Mr. Trumbull and myself, and has not uttered a word about the politics of the day. Are you going to elect Mr. Trumbull's colleague upon an issue between Mr. Trumbull and me? (Laughter, and "No, no!") I thought I was running against Abraham Lincoln, that he claimed to be my opponent, had challenged me to a discussion of the public questions of the day with him, and was discussing these questions with me; but it turns out that his only hope is to ride into office on Trumbull's back, who will carry him by falsehood. (Cheers.)

Permit me to pursue this subject a little further. An examination of the record proves that Trumbull's charge—that the Toombs bill originally contained a clause requiring the constitution to be submitted to the people—*is false*. The printed copy of the bill which Mr. Lincoln held up before you, and which he pretends contains such a clause, merely contains a clause requiring a submission of the land grant, and *there is no clause in it requiring a submission*

[252]

of the constitution. Mr. Lincoln can not find such a clause in it. My report shows that we took it for granted that the people would require a submission of the constitution, and secure it for themselves. There never was a clause in the Toombs bill requiring the constitution to be submitted; Trumbull knew it at the time, and his speech made on the night of its passage discloses the fact that he knew it was silent on the subject. Lincoln pretends, and tells you that Trumbull has not changed his evidence in support of his charge since he made his speech in Chicago. Let us see. The Chicago TIMES took up Trumbull's Chicago speech, compared it with the official records of Congress, and proved that speech to be false in its charge that the original Toombs bill required a submission of the constitution to the people. Trumbull then saw that he was caught—and his falsehood exposed—and he went to Alton, and, under the very walls of the penitentiary, (laughter,) made a new speech, in which he predicated his assault upon me in the allegation that I had caused to be voted into the Toombs bill a clause which prohibited the convention from submitting the constitution to the people, and quoted what he pretended was the clause. Now, has not Mr. Trumbull entirely changed the evidence on which he bases his charge? ("Yes, yes!" "Lincoln's as big a liar as Trumbull," &c.) The clause which he quoted in his Alton speech (which he has published and circulated broadcast over the state) as having been put into the Toombs bill by me is in the following words:

And until the complete execution of this act, no other election shall be held in said territory.

Trumbull says that the object of that amendment was to prevent the convention from submitting the constitution to a vote of the people.

Now, I will show you that when Trumbull made that statement at Alton he knew it to be untrue. I read from Trumbull's speech in the Senate on the Toombs bill on the night of its passage. He then said:

There is nothing said in this bill, so far as I have discovered, about submitting the constitution which is to be formed, to the people for their sanction or rejection. Perhaps the convention will have the right to submit it, if it should think proper, but it is certainly not compelled to do so according to the provisions of the bill.

Thus you see that Trumbull, when the bill was on its passage in the Senate, said that it was silent on the subject of submission, and that there was nothing in the bill one way or the other on it. In his Alton speech he says that there was a clause in the bill preventing its submission to the people, and that I had it voted in as an amendment. Thus I convict him of falsehood and slander by quoting from him on the passage of the Toombs' bill in the Senate of the United States, his own speech, made on the night of July 2, 1856, and reported in the *Congressional Globe* for the 1st session 34th Congress, Vol. 33. What will you think of a man who makes a false charge and falsifies the records to prove it? I will now show you that the clause which Trumbull says was put in the bill on my motion, was never put in at all by me, but was stricken out on my motion and another substituted in its place. I call your attention to the same volume of the *Congressional Globe* to which I have already referred, page 795, where you will find the following in the report of the proceedings of the Senate:

MR. DOUGLAS—I have an amendment to offer from the committee on territories. On page 8, section 11, strike out the words "until the complete execution of this act no other election shall be held in said territory," and insert the amendment which I hold in my hand.

You see from this that I moved to strike out the very words that Trumbull says I put in. The Committee on Territories overruled me in committee and put the clause in, but as soon as I got the bill back into the Senate I moved to strike it out and put another clause in its place. On the same page you will find that my amendment was agreed to *unanimously*. I then offered another amendment, recognizing the right of the people of Kansas under the Toombs bill, to order just such elections as they saw proper. You can find it on page 796 of the same volume. I will read it.

MR. DOUGLAS—I have another amendment to offer from the committee, to follow the amendment which has been adopted. The bill reads now, "And until the complete execution of this act, no other election shall be held in said territory." It has been suggested that it should be modified in this way, "And to avoid conflict in the complete execution of this act, all other elections in said territory are hereby postponed until such time as said convention shall appoint," so that they can appoint the day in the event that there should be a failure to come into the Union.

The amendment was *unanimously* agreed to—clearly and distinctly recognizing the right of the convention to order just as many elections as they saw proper in the execution of the act. Trumbull concealed in his Alton speech the fact that the clause he quoted had been stricken out in my motion, and the other fact that this other clause was put in the bill on my motion, and made the false charge that I incorporated into the bill a clause preventing submission, in the face of the fact, that on my motion, the bill was so amended before it passed as to recognize in express words the right and duty of submission.

On this record that I have produced before you, I repeat my charge that Trumbull did falsify the public records of the country, in order to make his charge against me, ("it's plain," and tremendous applause,) and I tell Mr. Abraham Lincoln that if he will examine these records, he will then know that what I state is true. Mr. Lincoln has this day endorsed Mr. Trumbull's veracity after he had my word for it that that veracity was proved to be violated and forfeited by the public records. It will not do for Mr. Lincoln in parading his calumnies against me to put Mr. Trumbull between him and the odium and responsibility which justly attaches to such calumnies. I tell him that I am as ready to persecute the endorser as the maker of a forged note. (Cheers.) I regret the necessity of occupying my time with these petty personal matters. It is unbecoming the dignity of a canvass for an office of the character for which we are candidates. When I commenced the canvass at Chicago, I spoke of Mr. Lincoln in terms of kindness as an old friend—I said that he was a good citizen, of unblemished character, against whom I had nothing to say. I repeated these complimentary remarks about him in my successive speeches, until he became the endorser for these and other slanders against me. If there is anything personally disagreeable, uncourteous, or disreputable in these personalities, the sole responsibility rests on Mr. Lincoln, Mr. Trumbull and their backers.

I will show you another charge made by Mr. Lincoln against me, as an offset to his determination of willingness to take back anything that is incorrect, and to correct any false statement he may have made. He has several times charged that the Supreme Court, President Pierce, President Buchanan and myself, at the time I introduced the Nebraska Bill in January, 1854, at Washington, entered into a conspiracy to establish slavery all over this country. I branded this charge as a falsehood, and then he repeated it, asked me to analyze its truth and answer it. I told him, "Mr. Lincoln, I know what you are after—you want to occupy my time in personal matters, to prevent me from showing up the revolutionary principles which the Abolition party—whose candidate you are—have proclaimed to the world." But he asked me to analyze his proof, and I did so. I called his attention to the fact that at the time the Nebraska Bill was introduced, there was no such case as the Dred Scott case pending in the Supreme Court, nor was it brought there for years afterwards, and hence that it was impossible there could have been any such conspiracy between the Judges of the Supreme Court and the other parties involved. I proved by the record that the charge was false, and what did he answer? Did he take it back

like an honest man and say that he had been mistaken? No, he repeated the charge, and said, that although there was no such case
pending that year, that there was an understanding between the
Democratic owners of Dred Scott and the Judges of the Supreme
Court and other parties involved that the case should be brought up.
I then demanded to know who these Democratic owners of Dred
Scott were. He could not or would not tell; he did not know. In
truth, there were no Democratic owners of Dred Scott on the face
of the land. (Laughter.) Dred Scott was owned at that time by the
Rev. Dr. Chaffee, an Abolition member of Congress from Springfield, Massachusetts, and his wife, (immense laughter and applause,)
and Mr. Lincoln ought to have known that Dred Scott was so
owned, for the reason that as soon as the decision was announced
by the court, Dr. Chaffee and his wife executed a deed emancipating
him, and put that deed on record. (Cheers.) It was a matter of
public record, therefore, that at the time the case was taken to the
Supreme Court, Dred Scott was owned by an Abolition member of
Congress, a friend of Lincoln's, and a leading man of his party,
while the defence was conducted by Abolition lawyers—and thus
the Abolitionists managed both sides of the case. I have exposed
these facts to Mr. Lincoln, and yet he will not withdraw his charge
of conspiracy. I now submit to you whether you can place any
confidence in a man who continues to make a charge when its utter
falsity is proven by the public records. I will state another fact to
show how utterly reckless and unscrupulous this charge against the
Supreme Court, President Pierce, President Buchanan and myself is.
Lincoln says that President Buchanan was in the conspiracy at
Washington in the winter of 1854, when the Nebraska Bill was
introduced. The history of this country shows that James Buchanan
was at that time representing this country at the Court of St. James,
Great Britain, with distinguished ability and usefulness, that he had
not been in the United States for nearly a year previous, and that
he did not return until about three years after. (Cheers.) Yet Mr.
Lincoln keeps repeating this charge of conspiracy against Mr.
Buchanan, when the public records prove it to be untrue. Having
proved it to be false as far as the Supreme Court and President
Buchanan are concerned, I drop it, leaving the public to say whether
I, by myself, without their concurrence, could have gone into a conspiracy with them. (Laughter and cheers.) My friends, you see that
the object clearly is to conduct the canvass on personal matters, and
hunt me down with charges that are proven to be false by the
public records of the country. I am willing to throw open my whole
public and private life to the inspection of any man, or all men who

desire to investigate it. Having resided among you twenty-five years, during nearly the whole of which time a public man, exposed to more assaults, perhaps more abuse than any man living of my age, or who ever did live, and having survived it all and still commanded your confidence, I am willing to trust to your knowledge of me and my public conduct without making any more defence against these assaults. (Great cheering.)

Fellow-citizens, I came here for the purpose of discussing the leading political topics which now agitate the country. I have no charges to make against Mr. Lincoln, none against Mr. Trumbull, and none against any man who is a candidate, except in repelling their assaults upon me. If Mr. Lincoln is a man of bad character, I leave you to find it out; if his votes in the past are not satisfactory, I leave others to ascertain the fact; if his course on the Mexican war was not in accordance with your notions of patriotism and fidelity to our own country as against a public enemy, I leave you to ascertain the fact. I have no assaults to make upon him except to trace his course on the questions that now divide the country and engross so much of the people's attention.

You know that prior to 1854 this country was divided into two great political parties, one the Whig, the other the Democratic. I, as a Democrat for twenty years prior to that time, had been in public discussions in this state as an advocate of Democratic principles, and I can appeal with confidence to every Old Line Whig within the hearing of my voice to bear testimony that during all that period I fought you Whigs like a man on every question that separated the two parties. I had the highest respect for Henry Clay as a gallant party leader, as an eminent statesman, and as one of the bright ornaments of this country; but I conscientiously believed that the Democratic party was right on the questions which separated the Democrats from the Whigs. The man does not live who can say that I ever personally assailed Henry Clay or Daniel Webster, or any one of the leaders of that great party, whilst I combatted with all my energy the measures they advocated. What did we differ about in those days? Did Whigs and Democrats differ about this slavery question. On the contrary, did we not, in 1850, unite to a man in favor of that system of compromise measures which Mr. Clay introduced, Webster defended, Cass supported, and Fillmore approved and made the law of the land by his signature. While we agreed on those compromise measures we differed about a bank, the tariff, distribution, the specie circular, the sub-treasury, and other questions of that description. Now let me ask you which one of those questions on which Whigs and Democrats then differed now remains to divide two great parties. Every one of those questions which divide Whigs and Democrats has passed away, the country has out-grown them, they have passed into history. Hence it is immaterial whether you were right or I was right on the bank, the sub-treasury, and other questions, because they no longer continue living issues. What then has taken the place of those questions about which we once differed? The slavery question has now become the leading and controlling issue; that question on which you and I agreed, on which the Whigs and Democrats united, has now become the leading issue between the national Democracy on the one side, and the Republican or Abolition party on the other.

Just recollect for a moment the memorable contest of 1850, when this country was agitated from its centre to its circumference by the slavery agitation. All eyes in this nation were then turned to the three great lights that survived the days of the Revolution. They looked to Clay, then in retirement at Ashland, and to Webster and Cass in the United States Senate. Clay had retired to Ashland, having, as he supposed, performed his mission on earth, and was preparing himself for a better sphere of existence in another world. In that retirement he heard the discordant, harsh and grating sounds of sectional strife and disunion, and he aroused and came forth and resumed his seat in the Senate, that great theatre of his great deeds. From the moment that Clay arrived among us he became the leader of all the Union men whether Whigs or Democrats. For nine months we each assembled, each day, in the council chamber, Clay in the chair, with Cass upon his right hand and Webster upon his left, and the Democrats and Whigs gathered around, forgetting differences, and only animated by one common, patriotic sentiment to devise means and measures by which we could defeat the mad and revolutionary scheme of the northern Abolitionists and southern disunionists. (Cheers.) We did devise those means. Clay brought them forward, Cass advocated them, the Union Democrats and Union Whigs voted for them, Fillmore signed them, and they gave peace and quiet to the country. Those compromise measures of 1850 were founded upon the great fundamental principle that the people of each state and each territory ought to be left free to form and regulate their own domestic institutions in their own way subject only to the federal Constitution. (Cheers. "Hear, hear.") I will ask every old line Democrat and every Old Line Whig within the hearing of my voice, if I have not truly stated the issues as they then presented themselves to the country. You recollect that the Abolitionists raised a howl of indignation and cried for vengeance and the destruction of Democrats and Whigs both, who supported those compromise measures of 1850. When I returned home to Chicago, I found the citizens inflamed and infuriated against the authors of those great measures. Being the only man in that city who was held responsible for affirmative votes on all those measures, I came forward and addressed the assembled inhabitants, defended each and every one of Clay's compromise measures as they passed the Senate and the House and were approved by President Fillmore. Previous to that time, the city council had passed resolutions nullifying the act of Congress and instructing the police to withhold all assistance from its execution; but the people of Chicago listened to my defense, and like candid, frank, conscientious men, when they became convinced that they had done an injustice to Clay, Webster, Cass, and all of us who had supported those measures, they repealed their nullifying resolutions and declared that the laws should be executed and the supremacy of the Constitution maintained. Let it always be recorded in history to the immortal honor of the people of Chicago, that they returned to their duty when they found that they were wrong, and did justice to those whom they had blamed and abused unjustly. When the legislature of this state assembled that year, they proceeded to pass resolutions approving the compromise measures of 1850. When the Whig party assembled in 1852 at Baltimore in national convention for the last time, to nominate Scott for the Presidency, they adopted as a part of their platform the compromise measures of 1850 as the cardinal plank upon which every Whig would stand and by which 'he would regulate his future conduct. When the Democratic party assembled at the same place one month after to nominate General Pierce, we adopted the same platform so far as those compromise measures were concerned, agreeing that we would stand by those glorious measures as a cardinal article in the Democratic faith. Thus you see that in 1852 all the old Whigs and all the old Democrats stood on a common plank so far as this slavery question was concerned, differing on other questions.

Now, let me ask how is it, that since that time so many of you Whigs have wandered from the true path marked out by Clay and carried out broad and wide by the great Webster? How is it that so many old line Democrats have abandoned the old faith of their party and joined with Abolitionism and Freesoilism to overturn the platform of the old Democrats, and the platform of the old Whigs? You cannot deny that since 1854, there has been a great revolution on this one question. How has it been brought about? I answer, that no sooner was the sod grown green over the grave of the immortal Clay, no sooner was the rose planted on the tomb of the Godlike Webster, than many of the leaders of the Whig party, such as

Seward, of New York and his followers, led off and attempted to abolitionize the Whig party, and transfer all your old Whigs bound hand and foot into the Abolition camp. Seizing hold of the temporary excitement produced in this country by the introduction of the Nebraska Bill, the disappointed politicians in the Democratic party, united with the disappointed politicians in the Whig party, and endeavored to form a new party composed of all the Abolitionists. of abolitionized Democrats and abolitionized Whigs, banded together in an Abolition platform.

And who led the crusade against national principles in this state? I answer, Abraham Lincoln on behalf of the Whigs, and Lyman Trumbull on behalf of the Democrats, formed a scheme by which they would abolitionize the two great parties in this state on condition that Lincoln should be sent to the United States Senate in place of Gen. Shields, and that Trumbull should go to Congress from the Belleville district, until I would be accommodating enough either to die or resign for his benefit, and then he was to go to the Senate in my place. You all remember that during the year 1854 these two worthy gentlemen, Mr. Lincoln and Mr. Trumbull, one an Old Line Whig and the other an Old Line Democrat, were hunting in partnership to elect a legislature against the Democratic party. I canvassed the state that year from the time I returned home until the election came off, and spoke in every county that I could reach during that period. In the northern part of the state I found Lincoln's ally, in the person of FRED. DOUGLASS, THE NEGRO, preaching Abolition doctrines, while Lincoln was discussing the same principles down here, and Trumbull, a little farther down, was advocating the election of members to the legislature who would act in concert with Lincoln's and Fred. Douglass' friends. I witnessed an effort made at Chicago by Lincoln's then associates, and now supporters, to put Fred. Douglass, the negro, on the stand at a Democratic meeting to reply to the illustrious Gen. Cass when he was addressing the people there. ("Shame on them.") They had the same negro hunting me down, and they now have a negro traversing the northern counties of the state, and speaking in behalf of Lincoln. ("Hit him again"; "he's a disgrace to the white people," &c.) Lincoln knows that when we were at Freeport in joint discussion, there was a distinguished colored friend of his there then who was on the stump for him, (shouts of laughter,) and who made a speech there the night before we spoke, and another the night after, a short distance from Freeport, in favor of Lincoln, and in order to show how much interest the colored brethren felt in the success of their brother Abe. (Renewed laughter.) I have with me here, and would read if it would not occupy too much of my time, a speech made by Fred. Douglass in Poughkeepsie, N.Y., a short time since to a large convention, in which he conjures all the friends of negro equality and negro citizenship to rally as one man around Abraham Lincoln, the perfect embodiment of their principles, and by all means to defeat Stephen A. Douglas. ("It can't be done," &c.) Thus you find that this Republican party in the northern part of the state had colored gentlemen for their advocates in 1854, in company with Lincoln and Trumbull, as they have now. When in October, 1854, I went down to Springfield to attend the state fair, I found the leaders of this party all assembled together under the title of an anti-Nebraska meeting. It was Black Republicans up north, and anti-Nebraska at Springfield. I found Lovejoy, a high priest of Abolitionism, and Lincoln one of the leaders who was towing the old line Whigs into the Abolition camp, and Trumbull, Sidney Breese, and Gov. Reynolds, all making speeches against the Democratic party and myself, at the same place and in the same cause. ("They're all birds of a feather, shun them.") The same men who are now fighting the Democratic party and the regular Democratic nominees in this state were fighting us then. They did not then acknowledge that they had become Abolitionists, and many of them deny it now. Breese, Dougherty, and Reynolds were then fighting the Democracy under the title of anti-Nebraska men, and now they are fighting the Democracy under the pretence that they are *simon pure* Democrats. (Laughter.) Saying that they are authorized to have every office-holder in Illinois beheaded who prefers the election of Douglas to that of Lincoln, or the success of the Democratic ticket in preference to the Abolition ticket for members of Congress, state officers, members of the legislature, or any office in the state. They canvassed the state against us in 1854, as they are doing now, owning different names and different principles in different localities, but having a common object in view, viz: the defeat of all men holding national principles in opposition to this sectional Abolition party. They carried the legislature in 1854, and when it assembled in Springfield they proceeded to elect a United States Senator, all voting for Lincoln with one or two exceptions, which exceptions prevented them from quite electing him. And why should they not elect him? Had not Trumbull agreed that Lincoln should have Shields' place? Had not the Abolitionists agreed to it? Was it not the solemn compact, the condition on which Lincoln agreed to abolitionize the old Whigs that he should be Senator? Still, Trumbull having control of a few abolitionized Democrats, would not allow them all to vote for Lincoln on any one ballot, and thus kept him for some time within one or two votes of an election until he worried out Lincoln's friends, and compelled them to drop him and elect Trumbull in violation of the bargain. (Cheers.) I desire to read you a piece of testimony in confirmation of the notoriously public facts which I have stated to you. Col. Jas. H. Matheny, of Springfield, is and for twenty years has been the confidential personal and political friend and manager of Mr. Lincoln. Matheny is this very day the candidate of the Republican or Abolition party for Congress against the gallant Major Thos. L. Harris, in the Springfield district, and is making speeches for Lincoln and against me. I will read you the testimony of Matheny about this bargain between Lincoln and Trumbull when they undertook to abolitionize Whigs and Democrats only four years ago. Matheny being mad at Trumbull for having played a Yankee trick on Lincoln, exposed the bargain in a public speech two years ago, and I will read the published report of that speech, the correctness of which Mr. Lincoln will not deny:

The Whigs, Abolitionists, Know Nothings, and renegade Democrats, made a solemn compact for the purpose of carrying this state against the Democracy on this plan: 1st, That they would all combine and elect Mr. Trumbull to Congress, and thereby carry his district for the legislature, in order to throw all the strength that could be obtained into that body against the Democrats. 2d. That when the legislature should meet, the officers of that body, such as speaker, clerks, doorkeepers, &c, would be given to the Abolitionists; and 3d, That the Whigs were to have the United States Senator. Thus, accordingly, in good faith, Trumbull was elected to Congress, and his district carried for the legislature, and when it convened the Abolitionists got all the officers of that body, and thus far the "bond" was fairly executed. The Whigs, on their part, demanded the election of Abraham Lincoln to the United States Senate, that the bond might be fulfilled, the other parties to the contract having already secured to themselves all that was called for. But, in the most perfidious manner, they refused to elect Mr. Lincoln; and the mean, low-lived, sneaking Trumbull succeeded by pleading all that was required by any party, in thrusting Lincoln aside and foisting himself, an excresence from the rotten bowels of the Democracy into the United States Senate: and thus it has ever been, that an *honest* man makes a bad bargain when he conspires or contracts with rogues.

Lincoln's confidential friend, Matheny, thought that Lincoln made a bad bargain when he conspired with such rogues as Trumbull and the Abolitionists. (Great laughter.) I would like to know whether Lincoln had as high an opinion of Trumbull's veracity when the latter agreed to support him for the Senate, and then cheated him as he does now, (renewed laughter,) when Trumbull comes forward and makes charges against me. You could not then prove Trumbull an honest man either by Lincoln, by Matheny, or by any of Lincoln's friends. They charged everywhere that Trumbull had cheated them out of the bargain, and Lincoln found sure enough that it was a *bad bargain* to contract and conspire with rogues. (Laughter.)

And now I will explain to you what has been a mystery all over the state and Union, the reason why Lincoln was nominated for the United States Senate by the Black Republican convention. You know it has never been usual for any party, or any convention to nominate a candidate for United States Senator. Probably this was the first time that such a thing was ever done. The Black Republican convention had not been called for that purpose, but to nominate a state ticket, and every man was surprised and many disgusted when Lincoln was nominated. Archie Williams thought he was entitled to it. Browning knew that he deserved it, Wentworth was certain that he would get it, Peck had hopes, Judd felt sure that he was the man, and Palmer had claims and had made arrangements to secure it; but to their utter amazement, Lincoln was nominated by the convention, (laughter,) and not only that, but he received the nomination unanimously, by a resolution declaring that Abraham Lincoln was "the first, last, and only choice" of the Republican party. How did this occur? Why, because they could not get Lincoln's friends to make another bargain with "rogues," (laughter,) unless the whole party would come up as one man and pledge their honor that they would stand by Lincoln first, last and all the time, and that he should not be cheated by Lovejoy this time, as he was by Trumbull before. Thus, by passing this resolution, the Abolitionists are all for him, Lovejoy and Farnsworth are canvassing for him, Giddings is ready to come here in his behalf, and the negro speakers are already on the stump for him, and he is sure not to be cheated this time. He would not go into the arrangement until he got their bond for it, and Trumbull is compelled now to take the stump, get up false charges against me, and travel all over the state to try and elect Lincoln, in order to keep Lincoln's friends quiet about the bargain in which Trumbull cheated them four years ago. You see, now, why it is that Lincoln and Trumbull are so mighty fond of each other. (Tremendous laughter.) They have entered into a conspiracy to break me down by these assaults on my public character, in order to draw my attention from a fair exposure of the mode in which they attempted to abolitionize the old Whig and the old Democratic parties and lead them captive into the Abolition camp. ("That's so," and "hear, hear.") Do you not all remember that Lincoln went around here four years ago making speeches to you, and telling you that you should all go for the Abolition ticket, and swearing that he was as good a Whig as he ever was; (laughter;) and that Trumbull went all over the state making pledges to the old Democrats, and trying to coax them into the Abolition camp, swearing by his Maker, with the uplifted hand, that he was still a Democrat, always intended to be, and that never would he desert the Democratic party. (Laughter.) He got your votes to elect an Abolition legislature, which passed Abolition resolutions, attempted to pass Abolition laws, and sustained Abolitionists for office, state and national. Now, the same game is attempted to be played over again. Then Lincoln and Trumbull made captives of the old Whigs and old Democrats and carried them into the Abolition camp where Father Giddings, the high priest of Abolitionism, received and christened them in the dark cause just as fast as they were brought in. ("Hear, hear.") Giddings found the converts so numerous that he had to have assistance, and he sent for John P. Hale, N. P. Banks, Chase, and other Abolitionists, and they came on, and with Lovejoy and Fred. Douglass, the negro, helped to baptize these new converts as Lincoln, Trumbull, Breese, Reynolds, and Dougherty could capture them and bring them within the Abolition clutch. Gentlemen, they are now around making the same kind of speeches. Trumbull was down in Monroe County the other day assailing me and making a speech in favor of Lincoln, and I will show you under what notice his meeting was called. You see these people are Black Republicans or Abolitionists up north, while at Springfield to-day, they dare not call their convention "Republican," but are obliged to say "a convention of all men opposed to the Democratic party," and in Monroe County and lower Egypt Trumbull advertises their meetings as follows:

A meeting of the Free Democracy will take place at Waterloo, on Monday, September 12th inst., whereat Hon. Lyman Trumbull, Hon. Jehu Baker, and others, will address the people upon the different political topics of the day. Members of all parties are cordially invited to be present, and hear and determine for themselves.

September 9, 1858   THE FREE DEMOCRACY

Did you ever before hear of this new party called the "Free Democracy?"

What object have these Black Republicans in changing their name in every county? ("To cheat people.") They have one name in the north, another in the centre, and another in the south. When I used to practice law before my distinguished judicial friend, whom I recognize in the crowd before me, if a man was charged with horse stealing and the proof showed that he went by one name in Stephenson County, another in Sangamon, a third in Monroe, and a fourth in Randolph, we thought that the fact of his changing his name so often to avoid detection, was pretty strong evidence of his guilt.

I would like to know why it is that this great free soil abolition party is not willing to avow the same name in all parts of the state? ("They dare not.") If this party believes that its course is just, why does it not avow the same principle in the North, and in the South, in the East and in the West, wherever the American flag waves over American soil. (Cheers.)

A VOICE—The party does not call itself Black Republican in the North.

MR. DOUGLAS—Sir, if you will get a copy of the paper published at Waukegan, fifty miles from Chicago, which advocates the election of Mr. Lincoln, and has his name flying at its mast-head, you will find that it declares that "this paper is devoted to the cause of *Black Republicanism*. ("Good," "hit him again," and cheers.) I had a copy of it and intended to bring it down here into Egypt to let you see what name the party rallied under up in the northern part of the state, and to convince you that their principles are as different in the two sections of the state as is their name. I am sorry that I have mislaid it and have not got it here. Their principles in the north are jet black, (laughter,) in the centre they are in color a decent mulatto, (renewed laughter,) and in lower Egypt they are almost white. (Shouts of laughter.) Why, I admired many of the white sentiments contained in Lincoln's speech at Jonesboro, and could not help but contrast them with the speeches of the same distinguished orator made in the northern part of the state. Down here he denies that the Black Republican party is opposed to the admission of any more slave states, under any circumstances, and says that they are willing to allow the people of each state when it wants to come into the Union, to do just as it pleases on the question of slavery. In the north, you find Lovejoy, their candidate for Congress in the Bloomington district, Farnsworth, their candidate in the Chicago district, and Washburne, their candidate in the Galena district, all declaring that never will they consent, under any circumstances, to admit another slave state, even if the people want it. ("That's so.") Thus, while they avow one set of principles up there, they avow another and entirely different set down here. And here let me recall to Mr. Lincoln the scriptural quotation which he has applied to the federal government, that a house divided against itself cannot stand, and ask him how does he expect this Abolition party to stand when in one-half of the state it advocates a set of principles which it has repudiated in the other half. (Laughter and applause.)

I am told that I have but eight minutes more. I would like to talk to you an hour and a half longer, but I will make the best use I can of the remaining eight minutes. Mr. Lincoln said in his first remarks that he was not in favor of the social and political equality of the negro with the white man. Everywhere up north he has declared that he was not in favor of the social and political equality of the negro, but he would not say whether or not he was opposed to negroes voting and negro citizenship. I want to know whether he is for or against negro citizenship? He declared his utter opposition to the Dred Scott decision, and advanced as a reason that the court had decided that it was not possible for a negro to be a citizen under the Constitution of the United States. If he is opposed to the Dred Scott decision for that reason he must be in favor of conferring the right and privilege of citizenship upon the negro! I have been trying to get an answer from him on that point, but have never yet obtained one, and I will show you why. In every speech he made in the north he quoted the Declaration of Independence to prove that all men were created equal, and insisted that the phrase "all men," included the negro as well as the white man, and that the equality rested upon Divine law. Here is what he said on that point:

I should like to know if, taking this old Declaration of Independence, which declares that all men are equal upon principle, and making exceptions to it where will it stop. If one man says it does not mean a negro, why may not another say it does not mean some other man? If that declaration is not the truth let us get the statute book in which we find it and tear it out!

Lincoln maintains there that the Declaration of Independence asserts that the negro is equal to the white man, and that under Divine law, and if he believes so it was rational for him to advocate negro citizenship, which, when allowed, puts the negro on an equality under the law. ("No negro equality for us"; "down with Lincoln.") I say to you in all frankness, gentlemen, that in my opinion a negro is not a citizen, cannot be, and ought not to be, under the Constitution of the United States. ("That's the doctrine.") I will not even qualify my opinion to meet the declaration of one of the Judges of the Supreme Court in the Dred Scott case, "that a negro descended from African parents, who was imported into this country as a slave, is not a citizen, and cannot be." I say that this government was established on the white basis. It was made by white men, for the benefit of white men and their posterity forever, and never should be administered by any except white men. (Cheers.) I declare that a negro ought not to be a citizen, whether his parents were imported into this country as slaves or not, or whether or not he was born here. It does not depend upon the place a negro's parents were born, or whether they were slaves or not, but upon the fact that he is a negro, belonging to a race incapable of self government, and for that reason ought not to be on an equality with white men. (Immense applause.)

My friends, I am sorry that I have not time to pursue this argument further, as I might have done but for the fact that Mr. Lincoln compelled me to occupy a portion of my time in repelling those gross slanders and falsehoods that Trumbull has invented against me and put in circulation. In conclusion, let me ask you why should this government be divided by a geographical line—arraying all men North in one great hostile party against all men South? Mr. Lincoln tells you, in his speech at Springfield, "that a house divided against itself cannot stand; that this government, divided into free and slave states, cannot endure permanently; that they must either be all free or all slave; all one thing or all the other." Why cannot this government endure divided into free and slave states, as our fathers made it? When this government was established by Washington, Jefferson, Madison, Jay, Hamilton, Franklin, and the other sages and patriots of that day, it was composed of free states and slave states, bound together by one common constitution. We have existed and prospered from that day to this thus divided, and have increased with a rapidity never before equalled in wealth, the extension of territory, and all the elements of power and greatness, until we have become the first nation on the face of the globe. Why can we not thus continue to prosper? We can if we will live up to and execute the government upon those principles upon which our fathers established it. During the whole period of our existence Divine Providence has smiled upon us, and showered upon our nation richer and more abundant blessings than have ever been conferred upon any other.

Senator Douglas' time here expired, and he stopped on the minute, amidst deafening applause.

Lincoln's Rejoinder

Fellow Citizens:

It follows as a matter of course that a half-hour answer to a speech of an hour-and-a-half can be but a very hurried one. I shall only be able to touch upon a few of the points suggested by Judge Douglas, and give them a brief attention, while I shall have to totally omit others for the want of time.

Judge Douglas has said to you that he has not been able to get from me an answer to the question whether I am in favor of negro citizenship. So far as I know, the Judge never asked me the question before. [Applause.] He shall have no occasion to ever ask it again, for I tell him very frankly that I am not in favor of negro citizenship. [Renewed applause.] This furnishes me an occasion for saying a few words upon the subject. I mentioned in a certain speech of mine which has been printed, that the Supreme Court had decided that a negro could not possibly be made a citizen, and without saying what was my ground of complaint in regard to that, or whether I had any ground of complaint, Judge Douglas has from that thing manufactured nearly every thing that he ever says about my disposition to produce an equality between the negroes and the white people. [Laughter and applause.] If any one will read my speech, he will find I mentioned that as one of the points decided in the course of the Supreme Court opinions, but I did not state what objection I had to it. But Judge Douglas tells the people what my objection was when I did not tell them myself. [Loud applause and laughter.] Now my opinion is that the different states have the power to make a negro a citizen under the Constitution of the United States if they choose. The Dred Scott decision decides that they have not that power. If the state of Illinois had that power I should be opposed to the exercise of it. [Cries of "good," "good," and applause.] That is all I have to say about it.

Judge Douglas has told me that he heard my speeches north and my speeches south—that he had heard me at Ottawa and at Freeport in the north, and recently at Jonesboro in the south, and there was a very different cast of sentiment in the speeches made at the different points. I will not charge upon Judge Douglas that he wilfully misrepresents me, but I call upon every fair-minded man to take these speeches and read them, *and I dare him to point out any difference between my printed speeches north and south.* [Great cheering.] While I am here perhaps I ought to say a word, if I have the time, in regard to the latter portion of the Judge's speech, which was a sort of declamation in reference to my having said I entertained the belief that this government would not endure, half slave and half free. I have said so and I did not say it without what seemed to me to be good reasons. It perhaps would require more time than I have now to set forth these reasons in detail; but let me ask you a few questions. Have we ever had any peace on this slavery question? ["No, no."] When are we to have peace upon it if it is kept in the position it now occupies? ["Never."] How are we ever to have peace upon it? That is an important question. To be sure if we will all stop and allow Judge Douglas and his friends to march on in their present career until they plant the institution all over the nation, here and wherever else our flag waves, and we acquiesce in it, there will be peace. But let me ask Judge Douglas how he is going to get the people to do that? [Applause.] They have been wrangling over this question for at least forty years. This was the cause of the agitation resulting in the Missouri Compromise—this produced the troubles at the annexation of Texas, in the acquisition of the territory acquired in the Mexican war. Again, this was the trouble which was quieted by the Compromise of 1850, when it was settled "*forever*," as both the great political parties declared in their national conventions. That "forever" turned out to be just four years, [laughter] *when Judge Douglas himself re-opened it.* [Immense applause, cries of "hit him again," &c.] When is it likely to come to an end? He introduced the Nebraska Bill in 1854 to put *another end* to the slavery agitation. He promised that it would finish it all up immediately, and he has never made a speech since until he got into a quarrel with the President about the Lecompton constitution, in which he has not declared that we are *just at the end* of the slavery agitation. But in one speech, I think last winter, he did say that he didn't quite see when the end of the slavery agitation would come. [Laughter and cheers.] Now he tells us again that it is all over, and the people of Kansas have voted down the Lecompton constitution. How is it over? That was only one of the attempts at putting an end to the slavery agitation—one of these "final settlements." [Renewed laughter.] Is Kansas in the Union? Has she formed a constitution that she is likely to come in under? Is not the slavery agitation still an open question in that territory? Has the voting down of that constitution put an end to all the trouble? Is that more likely to settle it than every one of these previous attempts to settle the slavery agitation. [Cries of "No," "No."] Now, at this day in the history of the world we can no more foretell where the end of this slavery agitation will be than we can see the end of the world itself. The Nebraska-Kansas Bill was introduced four years and a half ago, and if the agitation is ever to come to an end, we may say we are four years and a half nearer the end. So, too, we can say we are four years and a half nearer the end of the world; and we can just as clearly see the end of the world as we can see the end of this agitation. [Applause.] The Kansas settlement did not conclude it. If Kansas should sink to-day, and leave a great vacant space in the earth's surface, this vexed question would still be among us. I say, then, there is no way of putting an end to the slavery agitation amongst us but to put it back upon the basis where our fathers placed it, [applause] no way but to keep it out of our new territories [renewed applause]—to restrict it forever to the old states where it now exists. [Tremendous and prolonged cheering; cries of "That's the doctrine," "Good," "Good," &c.] Then the public mind *will* rest in the belief that it is in the course of ultimate extinction. That is one way of putting an end to the slavery agitation. [Applause.]

The other way is for us to surrender and let Judge Douglas and his friends have their way and plant slavery over all the states—cease speaking of it as in any way a wrong—regard slavery as one of the common matters of property, and speak of negroes as we do of our horses and cattle. But while it drives on in its state of progress as it is now driving, and as it has driven for the last five years, I have ventured the opinion, and I say to-day, that we will have no end to the slavery agitation until it takes one turn or the other. [Applause.] I do not mean that when it takes a turn towards ulti-mate extinction it will be in a day, nor in a year, nor in two years. I do not suppose that in the most peaceful way ultimate extinction would occur in less than a hundred years at the least; but that it will occur in the best way for both races in God's own good time, I have no doubt. [Applause.] But, my friends, I have used up more of my time than I intended on this point.

Now, in regard to this matter about Trumbull and myself having made a bargain to sell out the entire Whig and Democratic parties in 1854—Judge Douglas brings forward no evidence to sustain his charge, except the speech Matheny is said to have made in 1856, in which he told a cock-and-bull story of that sort, upon the same moral principles that Judge Douglas tells it here to-day. [Loud ap-plause.] This is the simple truth. I do not care greatly for the story, but this is the truth of it, and I have twice told Judge Douglas to his face, that from beginning to end there is not one word of truth in it. [Thunders of applause.] I have called upon him for the proof, and he does not at all meet me as Trumbull met him upon that of which we were just talking, by producing the record. He didn't bring the record, because there was no record for him to bring. [Cheers and laughter.] When he asks if I am ready to indorse Trum-bull's veracity after he has broken a bargain with me, I reply that if Trumbull *had* broken a bargain with me, I would not be likely to indorse his veracity [laughter and applause]; but I am ready to indorse his veracity because *neither in that thing, nor in any other, in all the years that I have known Lyman Trumbull, have I known him to fail of his word or tell a falsehood, large or small.* [Great cheering.] It is for that reason that I indorse Lyman Trumbull.

MR. JAMES BROWN—(*Douglas postmaster*).—What does Ford's history say about him?

MR. LINCOLN—Some gentleman asks me what Ford's History says about him. My own recollection is, that Ford speaks of Trumbull in very disrespectful terms in several portions of his book, *and that he talks a great deal worse of Judge Douglas.* [Roars of laughter and applause.] I refer you, sir, to the history for examination. [Cheers.]

Judge Douglas complains, at considerable length, about a disposition on the part of Trumbull and myself to attack him personally. I want to attend to that suggestion a moment. I don't want to be unjustly accused of dealing illiberally or unfairly with an adversary, either in court, or in a political canvass, or anywhere else. I would despise myself if I supposed myself ready to deal less liberally with an adversary than I was willing to be treated myself. Judge Douglas, in a general way, without putting it in a direct shape, revives the old charge against me, in reference to the Mexican war. He does not take the responsibility of putting it in a very definite form, but makes a general reference to it. That charge is more than ten years old. He complains of Trumbull and myself, because he says we bring charges against him one or two years old. He knows, too, that in regard to the Mexican war story, the more respectable papers of his own party throughout the state have been compelled to take it back and acknowledge that it was a lie. [Continued and vociferous applause.]

Here Mr. Lincoln turned to the crowd on the platform, and selecting Hon. Orlando B. Ficklin, led him forward and said:

I do not mean to do anything with Mr. Ficklin except to present his face and tell you that *he personally knows it to be a lie!* He was a member of Congress at the only time I was in Congress, and he (Ficklin) knows that whenever there was an attempt to procure a vote of mine which would indorse the origin and justice of the war, I refused to give such indorsement, and voted against it; but I never voted against the supplies for the army, and he knows, as well as Judge Douglas, that whenever a dollar was asked by way of compensation or otherwise, for the benefit of the soldiers, *I gave all the votes that Ficklin or Douglas did, and perhaps more.* [Loud applause.]

Mr. FICKLIN—My friends, I wish to say this in reference to the matter. Mr. Lincoln and myself are just as good personal friends as Judge Douglas and myself. In reference to this Mexican war, my recollection is that when Ashmun's resolution (amendment) was offered by Mr. Ashmun of Massachusetts, in which he declared that the Mexican war was unnecessarily and unconstitutionally commenced by the President—my recollection is that Mr. Lincoln voted for that resolution.

Mr. LINCOLN—That is the truth. Now you all remember that was a resolution censuring the President for the manner in which the war was *begun*. You know they have charged that I voted against the supplies, by which I starved the soldiers who were out fighting the battles of their country. I say that Ficklin knows it is false. When that charge was brought forward by the Chicago *Times*, the Springfield *Register* (Douglas organ) reminded the *Times* that the charge really applied to John Henry; and I do know that John Henry *is now making speeches and fiercely battling for Judge Douglas*. [Loud applause.] If the Judge now says that he offers this as a sort of a set-off to what I said to-day in reference to Trumbull's charge, then I remind him that he made this charge before I said a word about Trumbull's. He brought this forward at Ottawa, the first time we met face to face; and in the opening speech that Judge Douglas made, he attacked me in regard to a matter ten years old. Isn't he a pretty man to be whining about people making charges against him only *two* years old. [Cheers.]

The Judge thinks it is altogether wrong that I should have dwelt upon this charge of Trumbull's at all. I gave the apology for doing so in my opening speech. Perhaps it didn't fix your attention. I said that when Judge Douglas was speaking at places where I spoke on the succeeding day, he used very harsh language about this charge. Two or three times afterwards I said I had confidence in Judge Trumbull's veracity and intelligence; and my own opinion was, from what I knew of the character of Judge Trumbull, that he would vindicate his position, and prove whatever he had stated to be true. This I repeated two or three times; and then I dropped it, without saying anything more on the subject for weeks—perhaps a month. I passed it by without noticing it at all till I found at Jacksonville, Judge Douglas, in the plenitude of his power, is not willing to answer Trumbull and let me alone; but he comes out there and uses this language: "He should not hereafter occupy his time in refuting such charges made by Trumbull, but that Lincoln, having indorsed the character of Trumbull for veracity, he should hold him (Lincoln) responsible for the slanders." What was Lincoln to do? [Laughter.] Did he not do right, when he had the fit opportunity of meeting Judge Douglas here, to tell him he was ready for the responsibility? [Enthusiastic cheering, "good, good. Hurrah for Lincoln!"] I ask a candid audience whether in doing thus Judge Douglas was not the assailant rather than I? ["Yes, yes, Hit him again!"] Here I meet him face to face and say I am ready to take the responsibility so far as it rests upon me.

Having done so, I ask the attention of this audience to the question whether I have succeeded in sustaining the charge ["yes," "yes"], and whether Judge Douglas has at all succeeded in rebutting it? [Loud cries of "no, no."] You all heard me call upon him to say *which of these pieces of evidence was a forgery?* Does he say that what I present here as a copy of the original Toombs bill is a forgery? ["No," "no."] Does he say that what I present as a copy of the bill reported by himself is a forgery? ["No," "no," "no."] Or what is presented as a transcript from the *Globe*, of the quotations from Bigler's speech is a forgery? ["No," "no," "no."] Does he say the quotations from his own speech are forgeries? ["No," "no," "no."] Does he say this transcript from Trumbull's speech is a forgery? [Loud cries of "no, no." "He didn't deny one of them."] *I would then like to know how it comes about, that when each piece of a story is true, the whole story turns out false?* [Great cheers and laughter.] I take it these people have some sense; they see plainly that Judge Douglas is playing cuttlefish, [laughter] a small species of fish that has no mode of defending itself when pursued except by throwing out a black fluid, which makes the water so dark the enemy cannot see it and thus it escapes. [Roars of laughter.] Ain't the Judge playing the cuttlefish? ["Yes, yes," and cheers.]

Now I would ask very special attention to the consideration of Judge Douglas' speech at Jacksonville; and when you shall read his speech of to-day, I ask you to watch closely and see which of these pieces of testimony, every one of which he says is a forgery, he has shown to be such. *Not one of them has he shown to be a forgery.* Then I ask the original question, if each of the pieces of testimony is true, *how it is possible that the whole is a falsehood?* [Loud and continued cheers.]

In regard to Trumbull's charge that he (Douglas) inserted a provision into the bill to prevent the constitution being submitted to the people, what was his answer? He comes here and reads from the *Congressional Globe* to show that on his motion that provision was struck out of the bill. Why, Trumbull has not said it was not stricken out, but Trumbull says he (Douglas) put it in, and it is no answer to the charge to say he afterwards took it out. Both are perhaps true. It was in regard to that thing precisely that I told him he had dropped the cub. [Roars of laughter.] Trumbull shows you that by his introducing the bill it was his cub. [Laughter.] It is no answer to that assertion to call Trumbull a liar merely because he did not specially say Douglas struck it out. Suppose that were the case, does it answer Trumbull? [No, no.] I assert that you (pointing to an individual,) are here to-day, and you undertake to prove me a liar by showing that you were in Mattoon yesterday. [Laughter.] I say that you took your hat off your head, and you prove me a liar by putting it on your head. [Roars of laughter.] That is the whole force of Douglas' argument.

Now, I want to come back to my original question. Trumbull says that Judge Douglas had a bill with a provision in it for submitting a constitution to be made to a vote of the people of Kansas. Does Judge Douglas deny that fact? [Cries of "no, no."] Does he deny that the provision which Trumbull reads was put in that bill? ["No, no."] Then Trumbull says he struck it out. Does he dare to deny that? ["No, no, no."] He does not, and I have the right to repeat the question—*why, Judge Douglas took it out?* [Immense applause.] Bigler has said there was a combination of certain Senators, among whom he did not include Judge Douglas, by which it was agreed that the Kansas bill should have a clause in it not to have the con-stitution formed under it submitted to a vote of the people. He did not say that Douglas was among them, but we prove by another source that about the same time Douglas comes into the Senate *with that provision stricken out of the bill.* Although Bigler cannot say they were all working in concert, yet it looks very much as if the thing was agreed upon and done with a mutual understanding after the conference; and while we do not know that it was absolutely so, yet it looks so probable that we have a right to call upon the man who knows the true reason why it was done, *to tell what the true reason was.* [Great cheers.] When he will not tell what the true reason was, he stands in the attitude of an accused thief who has stolen goods in his possession, and when called to account, refuses to tell where he got them. [Immense applause.] Not only is this the evidence, but when he comes in with the bill having the provision stricken out, he tells us in a speech, not then but since, that these alterations and modifications in the bill *had been made by* HIM, *in consultation with Toombs, the originator of the bill.* He tells us the same to-day. He says there were certain modifications made in the bill in committee that he did not vote for. I ask you to remember while certain amendments were made which he disapproved of, but which a majority of the committee voted in, he has himself told us that in this particular *the alterations and modifications were made by him upon consultation with Toombs.* [Enthusiastic cheering.] We have his own word that these alterations were made *by him* and not by the committee. ["That's so," "good, good."] Now, I ask what is the reason Judge Douglas is so chary about coming to the exact ques-tion? What is the reason he will not tell you anything about HOW it was made, BY WHOM it was made, or that he remembers it being made at all? Why does he stand playing upon the meaning of words, and quibbling around the edges of the evidence? If he can explain all this, but leaves it unexplained, I have a right to infer that Judge Douglas understood it was the purpose of his party, in engineering that bill through, to make a constitution and have Kansas come into the Union with that constitution, *without its being submitted to a vote of the people.* ["That's it."] If he will explain his action on this question, by giving a *better reason* for the facts that happened, than he has done, it will be satisfactory. But until he does that—until he gives a better or more plausible reason than he has offered against the evidence in the case—*I suggest to him it will not avail him at all that he swells himself up, takes on dignity, and calls people liars.* [Great applause and laughter.] Why, sir, there is not a word in Trumbull's speech that depends on Trumbull's veracity at all. He has only arrayed the evidence and told you what follows as a matter of reasoning. There is not a statement in the whole speech that depends on Trumbull's word. If you have ever studied geometry, you remember that by a course of reasoning Euclid proves that all the angles in a triangle are equal to two right angles. Euclid has shown you how to work it out. Now, if you undertake to disprove that proposition, and to show that it is erroneous, would you prove it to be false by calling Euclid a liar? [Roars of laughter and enthusiastic cheers.] They tell me that my time is out, and therefore I close.

CHAPTER NINE

TOUCHES OF TEMPER

*So far, the campaign had been good-natured. The newspapers
wrote as if their political opponents were scoundrels, but that was
the accepted practice. The crowds had behaved well. But on September 20, at Sullivan, an incident occurred which might have ended
in a brawl. The* Times—*and Douglas—made the most of it.*[1]

SULLIVAN, Sept. 20, 1858

. . . Senator Douglas, this morning, left Mattoon, under the escort
of a large company of citizens of Coles and Moultrie counties. Safely
arriving at the open prairie, which stands a little way off from this
town, he was met by an immense concourse of persons, certainly to
the number of two thousand, mounted on horses, and in vehicles of
various kinds. These formed in procession, and escorted him to
town, where he was received with every evidence of hearty welcome.

When I reached this place, I was astonished to find that Lincoln
had an appointment for the same time and place. I was much astonished that he should endeavor to impose himself upon a Democratic
audience in quite so bold a manner. I rather doubted, the more
especially as I remembered his apologies to Mr. Douglas, made on
his way from Bement to Monticello, on the 29th day of July last,
for following him instead of marking out an independent line of
canvass for himself. My doubts were soon put an end to, however,
for, happening in the Judge's room at the hotel, I was, as were also
the following named gentlemen, to wit: Messrs. Bushrod W. Henry,
John Guin, Carn Knight and John Y. Hill, a witness to the following
occurrence:

A young man entering the room was introduced as George Lynn,
Jr. That gentleman at once stated that he was the bearer of a message from his friend Mr. Lincoln, at the same time he placed into
the hands of Mr. Douglas a note, written in pencil, the chirography

[1] Letter from Sullivan, September 20, in Chicago *Times*, September 24.

being unmistakably that of Abraham Lincoln, of which the following is an exact copy:

"Understanding that Judge Douglas would speak before dinner, I announced that I would address our friends at Freeland's Grove at 2 p.m. As he does not begin till 1 o'clock, if he will announce the fact, so that I can understand it, I will postpone to 3 o'clock. (Signed) A. LINCOLN."

As he delivered the note, Mr. Lynn repeated its substance by word of mouth, whereupon Mr. Douglas at once requested him to notify Lincoln that he would make the announcement as was asked, thus accepting the proposition. Mr. Lynn then retired.

Shortly after, Mr. Douglas was escorted to the speaker's stand, erected in the court house square, around which he found an immense gathering of people, extending clear back to the court house on the one side and some hundreds of people being on the street at the rear of the stand. When the hearty cheers which greeted his appearance had subsided, Mr. John R. Eden proceeded in behalf of the Democracy to deliver to him an address of welcome. . . .

Mr. Douglas then proceeded to speak. Before entering upon his speech, however, he made the announcement stipulated for by Mr. Lincoln, thus fulfilling his part of a contract unjustly demanded by his opponent, for that gentleman had, according to the code of ethics under which I was tutored, certainly no right to attempt to rob Douglas of his audience which his friends had provided together by announcement made six weeks since. . . .

Mr. Douglas then proceeded to a careful review of the revolutionary tendencies of the doctrines, the enunciation of which have rendered Lincoln a worthy member of the Abolition party, and the fervent belief of which has fitted him to become the first, last, and only choice of the Lovejoy, Farnsworth, Abolition, Black Republican party. . . .

The speaker then paid his respects to the speech of Mr. Trumbull, summing up in a few words his proof of the falsity of the charge therein contained. He then made another new point for Lincoln to weep over, as relating to the action of that gentleman in connection with the Mexican war. He said that Lincoln had been the means, in his closing speech, of rivetting a charge on himself by accusing him (speaker) of announcing a charge which he had never made. . . .

At this juncture one of the fellows who was acting as marshal for the Black Republican crew, rode up to the edge of the crowd, blue sash and all, and called out that Lincoln was waiting to be escorted by his friends to the grove. One square off the Indiana band of music, imported at unheard of expense, was blowing their mightiest to drown the voice of the Senator. A few persons with blue badges, inscribed "A. Lincoln," marched out of the crowd. When these had left, Mr. Douglas was about to proceed, when the band marched on, followed by the few who were going to listen to the "tall sucker." He was however stopped by his friends remarking, that the procession, if such it could be called, had faced in a direction opposite to the Abolitionist stand, with the evident intention of forcing a way through the Democratic meeting.

Lincoln, as I am informed by a dozen men, was at this time in the procession. The blacks then advanced round the square, taking all its sides, until they came to where the street was blocked by a portion of the Democratic crowd. On arriving upon the confines of which, the band being in advance, was attempted to be driven through. A general melee seemed to be inevitable, but Mr. Douglas, leaving the stand, urged his audience to be patient. Blows were struck on both sides. [The] wagon was turned out of the road, and the band will probably return to Indiana with a lively remembrance of the agile manner in which they vacated their article; Lincoln, in his buggy, took the back track, went and laid by until three o'clock so as not appear to have encouraged such a dastardly outrage by his presence; the footmen of the crowd got through with great difficulty, and the remainder of the few buggies wheeled about. . .

When order was restored, and that was not many minutes after the dastards left, Mr. Douglas proceeded to speak of the matter. He said:

"Ladies and Gentlemen: Now that this unpleasant scene which has disturbed our meeting somewhat has passed by, it is well that I should call your attention to the facts of the case, so that there can be no dispute about the truth of it in the future.

"You all know that in the month of July I made an appointment to speak today, and the gentleman who brought the notice of that appointment to you is now by my side. Some weeks after that appointment had been made and published in the newspapers, Mr. Lincoln made an appointment here for the same day. On Saturday last, Mr. Lincoln approached me at the stand in Charleston, and stated that he regretted that we had an appointment in collision, that he did not know of my appointment when he made his, but inasmuch as they had come on the same day, that he would not speak until I was through, and would not come to listen to me, and hence would not reply to me, but would make his speech after I got through the same as if he was speaking to a different audience.

"Today one of his friends, named George Lynn, Jr., came to my room at the hotel with this memorandum, which I will read, and a verbal message.

[Mr. Douglas here read the letter published above.]

"Mr. Lincoln's friend brought me that written proposition, that he would postpone his meeting until 3 o'clock if I would announce from this stand the fact that I accepted the proposition. I call upon you thousands now, to bear testimony, that before I uttered one word of my speech, I did, in a distinct and loud tone of voice, announce that I had been requested by Mr. Lincoln to give notice that he would speak at Freeland's Grove—that his meeting was postponed until 3 o'clock. Hence I complied with this compact on my part, as I can prove by you thousands here assembled. I call your attention to this fact, that at twenty-five minutes past 2 o'clock he, with his friends and a band of music, drove round the stand and came right up within forty feet of where I am now speaking, driving in the midst of some of my friends, beating their drum so as to break up this meeting. (Loud cries of 'You are right,' &c.) They drove right up here, and undertook to fight their way through those who, attending this meeting, stood upon the street, coming in a direction the opposite from their stand, that they might do it. (Cries of 'That is so.') Their stand was on the north side of the town, they started from the north, drove up on the south side, and came down on the east, in order to get on this side, going three squares out of their way in order to get to our meeting to break it up."

MR. THORNTON—"Will any gentleman who saw Lincoln announce the fact?"

A VOICE—"He was in, but turned round and went back."

MR. DOUGLAS—"I do not know whether he was in the procession, but a gentleman at my side says that he was in the procession up to the time when a fight seemed likely to ensue, when he turned round and went in the other direction. I do not of my own knowledge know whether he was in the procession or not; but the fact that that procession organized and drove up here to break up this meeting, in violation of the written agreement which I hold in my hand, signed and written by Mr. Lincoln, no honest man will deny. Hence, I say, that this disturbance is in violation of Mr. Lincoln's word to me at Charleston, on Saturday—it is in violation of his written agreement here today, which writing I have in my hand—it was a deliberate attempt on the part of his friends to break up a Democratic meeting, it was started at the very time when I was making a point on Mr. Lincoln, from which all his friends shrunk in despair, and it was begun suddenly, in order to break off the chain of my argument. It was evidently a preconcerted plan, and therefore I say that I am warranted, under this state of facts, in charging that Mr. Lincoln, as well as his friends, has been a party this day to break up this meeting, in order to prevent me from exposing his alliance with the Abolitionists, and repelling the false charges which he made against me at Charleston, and to which I had no opportunity to reply at that place." (Cries of "That is so," "Hit him again," &c.)

The Judge then continued his remarks to the full conclusion of his speech, and was succeeded on the stand by Mr. Thornton, of Shelbyville, who, as an Old Line Whig, refuses to be abolitionized.

The immediate response of the Press and Tribune *was an editorial denying that Douglas had published notice of the Sullivan meeting, as he had claimed.*[2] *The editorial concluded:*

The balance of the *Times'* story undoubtedly contains as much truth as this. Its correspondent is the same low-lived fellow who mutilates Lincoln's speeches into suitable shape for the readers of the *Times,* and he is believed just so far as the affidavits of respectable men will interfere to sustain his assertions.

But the Press and Tribune *editors seem to have felt that something more was needed to keep the Democrats from making too much political hay from the Sullivan encounter. Their regular correspondent had not been present, so a special report was called for, and published in the issue of October 1.*

SULLIVAN, MOULTRIE Co., Sept. 20, 1858

Having been a resident of this place twelve years, and believing this to have been the most memorable day of the whole twelve, I take the liberty of sending you in brief the particulars of our two political demonstrations, and the events growing out of the same which were not wholly in accordance with programme. Hon. S. A. Douglas made an appointment to speak here a short time since, but caused it to be published only in a local paper in this place. Mr. Lincoln seeing there was no appointment for Douglas in the Chicago *Times* or *State Register,* and not being aware of his hocus-pocus arrangement at this place, announced that he would speak at "Sullivan, Monday, September 20th," and caused it to be so published in his regular list of appointments. Mr. Douglas' appointment was at ten o'clock. Consequently Mr. Lincoln's friends fixed his hour at two, so that the people might have the opportunity of hearing

[2] Issue of September 25.

both. No sooner did the Douglas men learn of this arrangement than they persuaded Mr. Douglas to postpone his hour to *one o'clock,* thinking to get the crowd around him and keep them so they could not hear Mr. Lincoln.

Accordingly at one o'clock Douglas took the stand and commenced. I shall not attempt to tell what he said, farther than that I listened to him fifty minutes, and heard him vociferate "Black Republican" twenty-one times, and "Abolitionist" or "Abolitionism" thirty-four times. The balance was a dish of foolish and harmless blackguardism.

At two o'clock the Republican band started for the grove where Mr. Lincoln was to speak. The crowd began at once to disperse, and being more than half Lincoln men, the Little Giant began to beg them not to leave him all alone. His appeal to our charity had no perceptible effect; so his friends thought they would adopt more potent measures. The first man who jumped into the street to stop the crowd is notorious in our community for two events. The first is that he tried his hand, a short time ago, at whipping his wife. In this he was successful—turning the poor woman into the street with her eyes discolored, and her person otherwise badly bruised. He afterwards bragged of the exploit. The other distinguishing performance of this character was his getting himself appointed a deputy officer to acquire the shelter of the law in shooting one of his neighbors, with whom he had had a fight in which he did not triumph as gloriously as when he fought his wife. This man and a few more of his political faith and social standing undertook to stop the crowd. The Lincoln boys knocked down three or four of them and the rest took to their heels.

We then passed on to the grove and heard Old Abe make one of his most telling speeches. His audience was much larger than the Douglas crowd and his speech infinitely superior in logic, manner and morals.

OLD PICK

The campaign continued at full speed. After Sullivan, Douglas spoke at Danville, to be followed by Lincoln the next day. On September 23 Douglas addressed a large meeting at Urbana. Lincoln, scheduled to speak there on the 24th, arrived while the Democratic rally was in progress. The Times *account contains a description of the two small towns that would become famous as the seat of the University of Illinois, and also a caricature of Lincoln farfetched even by the prevailing standards of journalism.*[3]

[3] In issue of September 26.

Urbana, the county seat of Champaign, and the centre of one of the finest tracts of prairie land in Illinois, had its greatest political celebration today. Senator Douglas' appointment brought in an immense crowd, and from early dawn until meridian there was a perfect jam of vehicles in the streets—the old farmers, with their wives, sons and daughters in their holiday attire, appearing in great force. At half-past two o'clock the procession was formed, the prominent and most beautiful part of which were thirty-two young ladies on horseback, representing the thirty-two states of the Union, and after marching through New Urbana and Old Urbana, they proceeded to the fair ground, where the speaking was to take place.

You may not understand the terms "New Urbana" and "Old Urbana," and I will therefore make a short digression to explain. The original Urbana has been settled for some twelve or fourteen years, those who commenced it having selected the ridge which here divides the waters of the Mississippi from those of the Ohio River, for the site of the town. When the Illinois Central Railroad was built, the town was left about a mile to the east of the road, and the inhabitants, with the usual enterprise and energy which characterize the people of the Sucker State, not being able to bring the mountain to them, went to the mountain, and laid the foundation of a new town on the railroad, which they called New Urbana,[4] to distinguish it from the old town. The Illinois Central road have built here a large freight and engine depot, which has made the place one of considerable importance, and the population is now upwards of two thousand, equal to that of the old town, which can be seen slumbering off on the ridge. . . .

But to return. The procession having reached the fair ground, the ladies seated and the gentlemen comfortably situated, the meeting was organized and Senator Douglas commenced his speech. He spoke for over two hours to one of the most attentive audiences he has yet had, and the entrance of Lincoln into the fair ground with a band of music, which he now *carries* with him (perhaps to show that he is not weak in the knees), and with which he had hurriedly followed Senator Douglas from Sullivan, caused no disturbance or interruption whatever. Lincoln's band proceeded to one corner of the grounds and played for some time, the intervals between their pieces being filled by the pop-corn man, corn doctor, and other

---

[4] Now Champaign. The University of Illinois was not founded until 1868. Though officially located in Urbana, it sprawls over into Champaign, now contiguous.

pedlars, who are Lincoln's most intimate friends, and who, on this occasion, surrounded him, yelled their wares to draw a crowd, and then when the band struck up with the impudent familiarity for which this class is distinguished, introduced their customers to Lincoln, selling a paper of pop-corn, or a bottle of the corn extractor, and an introduction to their distinguished friend cheap as dirt. They had poor success, however, in their efforts to draw off what Lincoln at Sullivan called the "country bumpkins," and at last gave up, Lincoln being escorted by the corn doctor to visit a new humbug who has made his appearance on the scene, and who swallows any quantity of swords and digests them to amuse his audience. Lincoln was much interested in his new acquaintance, who gave him a private exhibition, and was curious to know whether the "broad" sword was not the most terrible and deadly weapon, inasmuch as small swords were so easily swallowed and evidently harmless. The professor replied in the affirmative, giving Lincoln an affecting story of the death of his brother in an attempt to handle one of the latter. Lincoln then displayed his muscle, and announced to the professor his intention to hereafter carry a "broad" sword always about his person, and to lop off the head of any man who should ever again, as at Sullivan, pitch the leader of his band out of a wagon, and invited the professor to accompany him and stand by him in the next trial of the kind. This the professor promised to do, and they then embraced and parted, not, however, before the professor had told Lincoln that he was his friend in principle, as he was of partly negro extraction himself. Lincoln ordered his band into their wagon, and, with the pop-corn man, proceeded to hunt up the Democratic marshal, to whom he apologized for having made so much noise, stating that he thought the speaking was over when he entered the grounds, and then requested him to announce from the stand, after Senator Douglas had concluded, that he (Lincoln) would address "sich" of the crowd as would like "ter hear him" next day. This announcement was made in plain English and not in the slang of the Black Republican chief.

Between September 24 and October 7, the date of the fifth joint debate, Douglas attended rallies at Onarga, Kankakee, Hennepin, Henry, Metamora, Pekin, Oquawka, and Monmouth; Lincoln's schedule took him from Urbana to Jacksonville, Winchester, Pittsfield, Metamora, and Pekin. Everywhere the meetings followed the established pattern: salutes, marching bands, processions, florid addresses of welcome by local dignitaries. The Press and Tribune, *in*

an editorial which can be taken very nearly at face value,[5] marveled
at the efforts of the contesting parties and the public interest.

Our readers in the northern part of the state where the Democracy entertain no suspicion of strength, and hence make no battle
against the overwhelming Republican host, can have no adequate
idea of the fierceness and intensity of the conflict waging in the
central and southern counties. The great battle ground lies between
the parallel of Peoria and the parallel of Alton. North of this field
the only ground which Douglasites claim to be debatable is the
senatorial district of Jo Daviess and Stephenson and the representative district comprising the south half of Cook County. In both
these localities they have been regularly and uniformly beaten since
the passage of the Nebraska Bill—the majorities being larger or
smaller just in the proportion it was presumed would be more or
less distasteful to Stephen A. Douglas. South of the broad area
constituting the ground of our tournament, we have the never failing
county of St. Clair with her two representatives, and one or two
other localities which will give the public more definite information
of their latitude after the first of November. Thus we of the north
have comparatively little of the frenzy which characterizes the contest in the wide belt whose boundaries include the cities of Peoria
and Alton.

It may be safely alleged that American politics have never developed so close and heated a campaign as the one now in progress
within this parallelogram. Every inch of ground presumed to be
doubtful, is contested with the energy of desperation. The eyes of
the Union are riveted on the combatants, to the exclusion of all
other objects of political interest, for all perceive that the history
of the Republic is shaping itself around the Illinois battle field. In
the momentousness of the event, the fate of Mr. Douglas' personal
self is of trifling consequence. To him it is everything, and everything else is nothing. To the world, the triumph of free principles
or the ascendancy of the dogmas of Dred Scott, are the vital and
absorbing elements of our conflict. Whichever way the beam shall
fall (so it is held abroad) that way will the nation incline in 1860.
Let the Republicans, Americans, Whigs, and all who would bring
back the country to the policy of the founders of our government,
and place Abraham Lincoln in the Senate of the United States, work
on with this sense of responsibility upon them—that they are making
the history of their country for many years to come.

[5] October 1.

CHAPTER TEN

THE GALESBURG DEBATE

Fall had come to north-central Illinois by October 7. Rain had pelted Galesburg on the day and night before, and what one of the reporters called "an Arctic frost, accompanied by a sour northwest wind," put teeth to chattering. Nevertheless, the audience outnumbered by two or three thousand the attendance at any of the four earlier debates.

Shortly after ten o'clock Douglas arrived by train from Monmouth. The welcoming delegation included three military companies and a group of students from Lombard University, who presented a banner inscribed, "From the Democracy of Lombard University to Stephen A. Douglas." Lincoln traveled the nine miles from Knoxville by buggy. A cavalcade of a hundred riders, women as well as men, met him on the road and escorted him to the home of Henry R. Sanderson, where the Republican students of Lombard presented a testimonial banner.

The debate began at two-thirty. A stand had been erected on the east side of the Knox College building, but the chill wind continued and often kept the speakers from being heard. Nevertheless, the audience remained to the end.

Douglas spoke first.

Douglas' Opening Speech

Ladies and Gentlemen:

Four years ago I appeared before the people of Knox County for the purpose of defending my political action upon the compromise measures of 1850 and the passage of the Kansas-Nebraska Bill. Those of you before me, who were present then, will remember that I vindicated myself for supporting those two measures by the fact that they rested upon the great fundamental principle that the people of each state and each territory of this Union have the right, and ought to be permitted to exercise the right of regulating their own domestic concerns in their own way, subject to no other limitation or restriction than that which the Constitution of the United States imposes upon them. I then called upon the people of Illinois to decide whether that principle of self-government was right or wrong. If it was, and is right, then the compromise measures of 1850 were right, and, consequently, the Kansas and Nebraska Bill, based upon the same principle, must necessarily have been right. ("That's so," and cheers.)

The Kansas and Nebraska Bill declared, in so many words, that it was the true intent and meaning of the act not to legislate slavery into any state or territory, nor to exclude it therefrom, but to leave the people thereof perfectly free to form and regulate their domestic institutions in their own way, subject only to the Constitution of the United States. For the last four years I have devoted all my energies, in private and public, to commend that principle to the American people. Whatever else may be said in condemnation or support of my political course, I apprehend that no honest man will doubt the fidelity with which, under all circumstances, I have stood by it.

During the last year a question arose in the Congress of the United States whether or not that principle would be violated by the admission of Kansas into the Union under the Lecompton constitution. In my opinion, the attempt to force Kansas in under that constitution was a gross violation of the principle enunciated in the compromise measures of 1850, and Kansas and Nebraska Bill of 1854, and therefore I led off in the fight against the Lecompton constitution and conducted it until the effort to carry that constitution through Congress was abandoned. And I can appeal to all men, friends and foes, Democrats and Republicans, Northern men, Southern men, that during the whole of that fight I carried the banner of popular sovereignty aloft, and never allowed it to trail in the dust, or lowered my flag until victory perched upon our arms. (Cheers!) When the Lecompton constitution was defeated, the question arose in the minds of those who had advocated it what they should next resort to in order to carry out their views. They devised a measure known as the English Bill, and granted a general amnesty and political pardon to all men who had fought against the Lecompton constitution, provided they would support that bill. I for one did not choose to accept the pardon or to avail myself of the amnesty granted on that condition. The fact that the supporters of Lecompton were willing to forgive all differences of opinion at that time in the event those who opposed it favored the English Bill, was an admission that they did not think that opposition to Lecompton impaired a man's standing in the Democratic party. Now the question arises, what was that English Bill which certain men are now attempting to make a test of political orthodoxy in this country? It provided, in substance, that the Lecompton constitution should be sent back to the people of Kansas for their adoption or rejection, at an election which was held in August last, and in case they refused admission under it that Kansas should be kept out of the Union until she had 93,420 inhabitants. I was in favor of sending the constitution back in order to enable the people to say whether or not it was their act and deed, and embodied their will; but the other proposition, that if they refused to come into the Union under it, they should be kept out until they had double or treble the population they then had, I never would sanction by my vote. The reason why I could not sanction it is to be found in the fact that by the English Bill, if the people of Kansas had only agreed to become a slaveholding state under the Lecompton constitution, they could have done so with 35,000 people, but if they insisted on being a free state, as they had a right to do, then they were to be punished by being kept out of the Union until they had nearly three times that population. I then said in my place in the Senate, as I now say to you, that whenever Kansas has population enough for a slave state she has population enough for a free state. ("That's it," and cheers.) I have never yet given a vote, and I never intend to record one making an odious and unjust distinction between the different states of this Union. (Applause.) I hold it to be a fundamental principle in our republican form of government that all the states of this Union, old and new, free and slave, stand on an exact equality. Equality among the different states is a cardinal principle on which all our institutions rest. Wherever, therefore, you make a discrimination, saying to a slave state that it shall be admitted with 35,000 inhabitants, and to a free state that it shall not be admitted until it has 93,000 or 100,000 inhabitants, you are throwing the whole weight of the federal government into the scale in favor of one class of states against the other. Nor would I on the other hand any sooner sanction the doctrine that a free state could be admitted into the Union with 35,000 people, while a slave state was kept out until it had 93,000. I have always declared in the Senate my willingness, and I am willing now to adopt the rule, that no territory shall ever become a state until it has the requisite population for a member of Congress, according to the then existing ratio. But while I have always been, and am now willing to adopt that general rule, I was not willing and would not consent to make an exception of Kansas, as a punishment for her obstinacy, in demanding the right to do as she pleased in the formation of her constitution. It is proper that I should remark here, that my opposition to the Lecompton constitution did not rest upon the peculiar position taken by Kansas on the subject of slavery. I held then, and hold now, that if the people of Kansas want a slave state, it is their right to make one and be received into the Union under it; if, on the contrary, they want a free state, it is their right to have it, and no man should ever oppose their admission because they ask it under the one or the other. I hold to that great principle of self-government which asserts the right of every people to decide for themselves the nature and character of the domestic institutions and fundamental law under which they are to live.

The effort has been and is now being made in this state by certain postmasters and other federal office holders, to make a test of faith on the support of the English Bill. These men are now making speeches all over the state against me and in favor of Lincoln, either directly or indirectly, because I would not sanction a discrimination between slave and free states by voting for the English Bill. But while that bill is made a test in Illinois for the purpose of breaking up the Democratic organization in this state, how is it in the other states? Go to Indiana, and there you find English himself, the author of the English Bill, who is a candidate for re-election to Congress, has been forced by public opinion to abandon his own darling project, and to give a promise that he will vote for the admission of Kansas at once, whenever she forms a constitution in pursuance of law, and ratifies it by a majority vote of her people. Not only is this the case with English himself, but I am informed that every Democratic candidate for Congress in Indiana takes that same ground. Pass to Ohio, and there you find that Groesbeck, and Pendleton, and Cox, and all the other anti-Lecompton men who stood shoulder to shoulder with me against the Lecompton constitution, but voted for the English Bill, now repudiate it and take the same ground that I do on that question. So it is with the Joneses and others of Pennsylvania, and so it is with every other Lecompton Democrat in the free states. They now abandon even the English Bill, and come back to the true platform which I proclaimed at the time in the Senate, and upon which the Democracy of Illinois now stand. And yet, notwithstanding the fact, that every Lecompton and anti-Lecompton Democrat in the free states has abandoned the English Bill, you are told that it is to be made a test upon me, while the power and patronage of the government are all exerted to elect men to Congress in the other states who occupy the same position with reference to it that I do. It seems that my political offence consists in the fact that I first did not vote for the English Bill, and thus pledge myself to keep Kansas out of the Union until she has a population of 93,420, and then return home, violate that pledge, repudiate the bill, and take the opposite ground. If I had done this, perhaps the administration would now be advocating my re-election, as it is that of the others who have pursued this course. I did not choose to give that pledge, for the reason that I did not intend to carry out that principle. I never will consent, for the sake of conciliating the frowns of power, to pledge myself to do that which I do not intend to perform. I now submit the question to you as my constituency, whether I was not right, first, in resisting the adoption of the Lecompton constitution; and secondly, in resisting the English Bill. (An universal "Yes," from the crowd.) I repeat, that I opposed the Lecompton constitution because it was not the act and deed of the people of Kansas, and did not embody their will. I denied the right of any power on earth under our system of government to force a constitution on an unwilling people. ("Hear, hear"; "that's the doctrine," and cheers.) There was a time when some men could pretend to believe that the Lecompton constitution embodied the will of the people of Kansas, but that time has passed. The question was referred to the people of Kansas under the English Bill last August, and then, at a fair election, they rejected the Lecompton constitution by a vote of from eight to ten against it to one in its favor. Since it has been voted down by so overwhelming a majority, no man can pretend that it was the act and deed of that people. ("That's so"; and cheers.) I submit the question to you whether or not if it had not been for me that constitution would have been crammed down the throats of the people of Kansas against their consent. ("It would, it would." "Hurra for Douglas"; "three cheers for Douglas," &c.) While at least ninety-nine out of every hundred people here present agree that I was right in defeating that project, yet my enemies use the fact that I did defeat it by doing right, to break me down and put another man in the U.S. Senate in my place. ("No, no, you'll be returned"; three cheers, &c.) The very men who acknowledge that I was right in defeating Lecompton, now form an alliance with federal office holders, professed Lecompton men, to defeat me, because I did right. ("It can't be done.") My political opponent, Mr. Lincoln, has no hope on earth, and has never dreamed that he had a chance of success, were it not for the aid he is receiving from federal office holders, who are using their influence and the patronage of the government against me in revenge for my having defeated the Lecompton constitution. ("Hear him"; and applause.) What do you Republicans think of a political organization that will try to make an unholy and unnatural combination with its professed foes to beat a man merely because he has done right? ("Shame on it.") You know such is the fact with regard to your own party. You know that the axe of decapitation is suspended over every man in office in Illinois, and the terror of proscription is threatened every Democrat by the present administration unless he supports the Republican ticket in preference to my Democratic associates and myself. ("The people are with you." "Let them threaten," &c.) I could find an instance in the postmaster of the city of Galesburg, and in every other postmaster in this vicinity, all of whom have been stricken down simply because they discharged the duties of their offices honestly, and supported the regular Democratic ticket in this state in the right. The Republican party is availing itself of every unworthy means in the present contest to carry the election, because its leaders know that if they let this chance slip they will never have another, and their hopes of making this a Republican state will be blasted forever.

Now, let me ask you whether the country has any interest in sustaining this organization known as the Republican party? That party is unlike all other political organizations in this country. All other parties have been national in their character—have avowed their principles alike in the slave and the free states, in Kentucky as well as in Illinois, in Louisiana as well as in Massachusetts. Such was the case with the old Whig party, and such was and is the case with the Democratic party. Whigs and Democrats could proclaim their principles boldly and fearlessly in the north and in the south, in the east and in the west, wherever the Constitution ruled and the American flag waved over American soil.

But now you have a sectional organization, a party which appeals to the Northern section of the Union against the Southern, a party which appeals to Northern passion, Northern pride, Northern ambition, and Northern prejudices, against Southern people, the Southern states and Southern institutions. The leaders of that party hope that they will be able to unite the Northern states in one great sectional party, and inasmuch as the North is the strongest section, that they will thus be enabled to out vote, conquer, govern, and control the South. Hence you find that they now make speeches advocating principles and measures which cannot be defended in any slave-holding state of this Union. Is there a Republican residing in Galesburg who can travel into Kentucky and carry his principles with him across the Ohio? ("No.") What Republican from Massachusetts can visit the Old Dominion without leaving his principles behind him when he crosses Mason and Dixon's line? Permit me to say to you in perfect good humor, but in all sincerity, that no political creed is sound which cannot be proclaimed fearlessly in every state of this Union where the federal Constitution is not the supreme law of the land. ("That's so," and cheers.) Not only is this Republican party unable to proclaim its principles alike in the North and in the South, in the free states and in the slave states, but it cannot even proclaim them in the same forms and give them the same strength and meaning in all parts of the same state. My friend Lincoln finds its extremely difficult to manage a debate in the centre part of the state, where there is a mixture of men from the North and the South. In the extreme northern part of Illinois he can proclaim as bold and radical Abolitionism as ever Giddings, Lovejoy, or Garrison enunciated, but when he gets down a little further south he claims that he is an Old Line Whig, (great laughter,) a disciple of Henry Clay, ("Singleton says he defeated Clay's nomination for the Presidency," and cries of "that's so,") and declares that he still adheres to the Old Line Whig creed, and has nothing whatever to do with Abolitionism, or negro equality, or negro citizenship. ("Hurrah for Douglas.") I once before hinted this of Mr. Lincoln in a public speech, and at Charleston he defied me to show that there was any difference between his speeches in the north and in the south, and that they were not in strict harmony. I will now call your attention to two of them, and you can then say whether you would be apt to believe that the same man ever uttered both. (Laughter and cheers.) In a speech in reply to me at Chicago in July last, Mr. Lincoln, in speaking of the equality of the negro with the white man used the following language:

I should like to know, if taking this old Declaration of Independence, which declares that all men are equal upon principle, and making exceptions to it, where will it stop? If one man says it does not mean a negro, why may not another man say it does not mean another man? (Laughter.) If the Declaration is not the truth, let us get the statute book in which we find it and tear it out. Who is so bold as to do it? If it is not true, let us tear it out.

You find that Mr. Lincoln there proposed that if the doctrine of the Declaration of Independence, declaring all men to be born equal, did not include the negro and put him on an equality with the white man, that we should take the statute book and tear it out. (Laughter and cheers.) He there took the ground that the negro race is included in the Declaration of Independence as the equal of the white race, and that there could be no such thing as a distinction in the races, making one superior and the other inferior. I read now from the same speech:

My friends, [he says,] I have detained you about as long as I desire to do, and I have only to say let us discard all this quibbling about this man and the other man—this race and that race, and the other race being inferior and therefore they must be placed in an inferior position, discarding our standard that we have left us. Let us discard all these things, and unite as one people throughout this land, until we shall once more stand up declaring that all men are created equal.

("That's right," &c.)

Yes, I have no doubt that you think it is right, but the Lincoln men down in Coles, Tazewell and Sangamon counties *do not* think it is right. (Immense applause and laughter. "Hit him again," &c.) In the conclusion of the same speech, talking to the Chicago Abolitionists, he said: "I leave you, hoping that the lamp of liberty will burn in your bosoms until there shall no longer be a doubt that all men are created free and equal." ("Good," "good," "shame," &c.) Well, you say good to that, and you are going to vote for Lincoln because he holds that doctrine. ("That's so.") I will not blame you for supporting him on that ground, but I will show you in immediate contrast with that doctrine, what Mr. Lincoln said down in Egypt in order to get votes in that locality where they do not hold to such a doctrine. In a joint discussion between Mr. Lincoln and myself, at Charleston, I think, on the 18th of last month, Mr. Lincoln referring to this subject used the following language:

I will say then, that I am not nor ever have been in favor of bringing about in any way, the social and political equality of the white and black races; that I am not nor ever have been in favor of making voters of the free negroes, or jurors, or qualifying them to hold office, or having them to marry with white people. I will say in addition, that there is a physical difference between the white and black races, which, I suppose, will forever forbid the two races living together upon terms of social and political equality, and inasmuch as they cannot so live, that while they do remain together, there must be the position of superior and inferior, that I as much as any other white man am in favor of the superior position being assigned to the white man.

("Good for Lincoln.")

Fellow-citizens, here you find men hurrahing for Lincoln and saying that he did right, when in one part of the state he stood up for negro equality, and in another part for political effect, discarded the doctrine and declared that there always must be a superior and inferior race. ("They're not men. Put them out," &c.) Abolitionists up north are expected and required to vote for Lincoln because he goes for the equality of the races, holding that by the Declaration of Independence the white man and the negro were created equal and endowed by the Divine law with that equality, and down south

he tells the old Whigs, the Kentuckians, Virginians, and Tennesseeans, that there is a physical difference in the races, making one
superior and the other inferior, and that he is in favor of maintaining the superiority of the white race over the negro. Now, how can
you reconcile those two positions of Mr. Lincoln? He is to be voted
for in the south as a pro-slavery man, and he is to be voted for in
the north as an Abolitionist. ("Give it to him." "Hit him again.")
Up here he thinks it is all nonsense to talk about a difference between the races, and says that we must "discard all quibbling about
this race and that race and the other race being inferior, and therefore they must be placed in an inferior position." Down south he
makes this "quibble" about this race and that race and the other
race being inferior as the creed of his party, and declares that the
negro can never be elevated to the position of the white man. You
find that his political meetings are called by different names in different counties in the state. Here they are called Republican meetings, but in old Tazewell, where Lincoln made a speech last Tuesday, he did not address a *Republican* meeting, but "a grand rally
of the *Lincoln men*." (Great laughter.) There are very few Republicans there, because Tazewell County is filled with old Virginians
and Kentuckians, all of whom are Whigs or Democrats, and if Mr.
Lincoln had called an Abolition or Republican meeting there, he
would not get many votes. (Laugher.) Go down into Egypt and you
find that he and his party are operating under an alias there, which
his friend Trumbull has given them, in order that they may cheat
the people. When I was down in Monroe County a few weeks ago
addressing the people, I saw handbills posted announcing that Mr.
Trumbull was going to speak in behalf of Lincoln, and what do you
think the name of his party was there? Why the *"Free Democracy."*
(Great laughter.) Mr. Trumbull and Mr. Jehu Baker were announced to address the Free Democracy of Monroe County, and
the bill was signed "Many Free Democrats." The reason that Lincoln and his party adopted the name of "Free Democracy" down
there was because Monroe County has always been an old fashioned
Democratic county, and hence it was necessary to make the people
believe that they were Democrats, sympathized with them, and
were fighting for Lincoln as Democrats. ("That's it," &c.) Come up
to Springfield, where Lincoln now lives and always has lived, and
you find that the convention of his party which assembled to nominate candidates for legislature, who are expected to vote for him
if elected, dare not adopt the name of Republican, but assembled
under the title of "all opposed to the Democracy." (Laughter and
cheers.) Thus you find that Mr. Lincoln's creed cannot travel

through even one half of the counties of this state, but that it changes its hues and becomes lighter and lighter, as it travels from the extreme north, until it is nearly white, when it reaches the extreme south end of the state. ("That's so, it's true," etc.) I ask you, my friends, why cannot Republicans avow their principles alike everywhere? I would despise myself if I thought that I was procuring your votes by concealing my opinions, and by avowing one set of principles in one part of the state, and a different set in another part. If I do not truly and honorably represent your feelings and principles, then I ought not to be your Senator; and I will never conceal my opinions, or modify or change them a hair's breadth in order to get votes. I tell you that this Chicago doctrine of Lincoln's—declaring that the negro and the white man are made equal by the Declaration of Independence and by Divine Providence—is a monstrous heresy. ("That's so," and terrific applause.) The signers of the Declaration of Independence never dreamed of the negro when they were writing that document. They referred to white men, to men of European birth and European descent, when they declared the equality of all men. I see a gentleman there in the crowd shaking his head. Let me remind him that when Thomas Jefferson wrote that document he was the owner, and so continued until his death, of a large number of slaves. Did he intend to say in that Declaration that his negro slaves, which he held and treated as property, were created his equals by Divine law, and that he was violating the law of God every day of his life by holding them as slaves? ("No, no.") It must be borne in mind that when that Declaration was put forth every one of the thirteen colonies were slaveholding colonies, and every man who signed that instrument represented a slaveholding constituency. Recollect, also, that no one of them emancipated his slaves, much less put them on an equality with himself, after he signed the Declaration. On the contrary, they all continued to hold their negroes as slaves during the Revolutionary war. Now, do you believe—are you willing to have it said—that every man who signed the Declaration of Independence declared the negro his equal, and then was hypocrite enough to continue to hold him as a slave, in violation of what he believed to be the divine law? ("No, no,") And yet when you say that the Declaration of Independence includes the negro, you charge the signers of it with hypocrisy.

I say to you, frankly, that in my opinion this government was made by our fathers on the white basis. It was made by white men for the benefit of white men and their posterity forever, and was intended to be administered by white men in all time to come. ("That's so," and cheers.) But while I hold that under our constitution and political system the negro is not a citizen, cannot be a citizen, and ought not to be a citizen, it does not follow by any means that he should be a slave. On the contrary it does follow that the negro, as an inferior race, ought to possess every right, every privilege, every immunity which he can safely exercise consistent with the safety of the society in which he lives. ("That's so," and cheers.) Humanity requires, and Christianity commands that you shall extend to every inferior being, and every dependent being, all the privileges, immunities and advantages which can be granted to them consistent with the safety of society. If you ask me the nature and extent of these privileges, I answer that that is a question which the people of each state must decide for themselves. ("That's it.") Illinois has decided that question for herself. We have said that in this state the negro shall not be a slave, nor shall he be a citizen. Kentucky holds a different doctrine. New York holds one different from either, and Maine one different from all. Virginia, in her policy on this question, differs in many respects from the others, and so on, until there is hardly two states whose policy is exactly alike in regard to the relation of the white man and the negro. Nor can you reconcile them and make them alike. Each state must do as it pleases. Illinois had as much right to adopt the policy which we have on that subject as Kentucky had to adopt a different policy. The great principle of this government is that each state has the right to do as it pleases on all these questions, and no other state, or power on earth has the right to interfere with us, or complain of us merely because our system differs from theirs. In the compromise measures of 1850, Mr. Clay declared that this great principle ought to exist in the territories as well as in the states, and I reasserted his doctrine in the Kansas and Nebraska Bill in 1854.

But Mr. Lincoln cannot be made to understand, and those who are determined to vote for him, no matter whether he is a pro-slavery man in the south and a negro equality advocate in the north, cannot be made to understand how it is that in a territory the people can do as they please on the slavery question under the Dred Scott decision. Let us see whether I cannot explain it to the satisfaction of all impartial men. Chief Justice Taney has said in his opinion in the Dred Scott case, that a negro slave being property, stands on an equal footing with other property, and that the owner may carry them into United States territory the same as he does other property. ("That's so.") Suppose any two of you, neighbors, should conclude to go to Kansas, one carrying $100,000 worth of negro slaves and the other $100,000 worth of mixed merchandise, including quantities of liquors. You both agree that under that decision you may carry your property to Kansas, but when you get it there, the merchant who is possessed of the liquors is met by the Maine liquor law, which prohibits the sale or use of his property, and the owner of the slaves is met by equally unfriendly legislation, which makes his property worthless after he gets it there. What is the right to carry your property into the territory worth to either, when unfriendly legislation in the territory renders it worthless after you get it there? The slaveholder when he gets his slaves there finds that there is no local law to protect him in holding them, no slave code, no police regulation maintaining and supporting him in his right, and he discovers at once that the absence of such friendly legislation excludes his property from the territory, just as irresistibly as if there was a positive constitutional prohibition excluding it. Thus you find it is with any kind of property in a territory, it depends for its protection on the local and municipal law. If the people of a territory want slavery, they make friendly legislation to introduce it, but if they do not want it, they withhold all protection from it, and then it cannot exist there. Such was the view taken on the subject by different Southern men when the Nebraska Bill passed. See the speech of Mr. Orr, of South Carolina, the present Speaker of the House of Representatives of Congress made at that time, and there you will find this whole doctrine argued out at full length. Read the speeches of other Southern congressmen, Senators and Representatives, made in 1854, and you will find that they took the same view of the subject as Mr. Orr—that slavery could never be forced on a people who did not want it. I hold that in this country there is no power on the face of the globe that can force any institution on an unwilling people. The great fundamental principle of our government is that the people of each state and each territory shall be left perfectly free to decide for themselves what shall be the nature and character of their institutions. When this government was made, it was based on that principle. At the time of its formation there were twelve slaveholding states and one free state in this Union. Suppose this doctrine of Mr. Lincoln and the Republicans, of uniformity of the laws of all the states on the subject of slavery, had prevailed; suppose Mr. Lincoln himself had been a member of the convention which framed the Constitution, and that he had risen in that august body, and addressing the father of his country, had said as he did in Springfield:

A house divided against itself cannot stand. I believe this government cannot endure permanently half slave and half free. I do not expect the

Union to be dissolved—I do not expect the house to fall, but I do expect it will cease to be divided. It will become all one thing or all the other.

What do you think would have been the result? ("Hurrah for Douglas.") Suppose he had made that convention believe that doctrine and they had acted upon it, what do you think would have been the result? Do you believe that the one free state would have outvoted the twelve slaveholding states, and thus abolished slavery? ("No! no!" and cheers.) On the contrary, would not the twelve slaveholding states have outvoted the one free state, and under his doctrine have fastened slavery by an irrevocable constitutional provision upon every inch of the American Republic? Thus you see that the doctrine he now advocates, if proclaimed at the beginning of the government, would have established slavery everywhere throughout the American continent, and are you willing, now that we have the majority section, to exercise a power which we never would have submitted to when we were in the minority? ("No, no," and great applause.) If the Southern states had attempted to control our institutions, and make the states all slave when they had the power, I ask would you have submitted to it? If you would not, are you willing now that we have become the strongest under that great principle of self-government that allows each state to do as it pleases —to attempt to control the Southern institutions? ("No, no.") Then, my friends, I say to you that there is but one path of peace in this republic, and that is to administer this government as our fathers made it, divided into free and slave states, allowing each state to decide for itself whether it wants slavery or not. If Illinois will settle the slavery question for herself, mind her own business and let her neighbors alone, we will be at peace with Kentucky, and every other Southern state. If every other state in the Union will do the same there will be peace between the North and the South, and in the whole Union.

I am told that my time has expired. (Nine cheers for Douglas.)

Lincoln's Reply

My Fellow Citizens:

A very large portion of the speech which Judge Douglas has addressed to you has previously been delivered and put in print. [Laughter.] I do not mean that for a hit upon the Judge at all. [Renewed laughter.] If I had not been interrupted, I was going to say that such an answer as I was able to make to a very large portion of it, had already been more than once made and published. There has been an opportunity afforded to the public to see our respective views upon the topics discussed in a large portion of the speech which he has just delivered. I make these remarks for the purpose of excusing myself for not passing over the entire ground that the Judge has traversed. I however desire to take up some of the points that he has attended to, and ask your attention to them, and I shall follow him backwards upon some notes which I have taken, reversing the order by beginning where he concluded.

The Judge has alluded to the Declaration of Independence, and insisted that negroes are not included in that Declaration; and that it is a slander upon the framers of that instrument, to suppose that negroes were meant therein; and he asks you: Is it possible to believe that Mr. Jefferson, who penned the immortal paper, could have supposed himself applying the language of that instrument to the negro race, and yet hold a portion of that race in slavery? Would he not at once have freed them? I only have to remark upon this part of the Judge's speech, (and that, too, very briefly, for I shall not detain myself, or you, upon that point for any great length of time,) that I believe the entire records of the world, from the date of the Declaration of Independence up to within three years ago, may be searched in vain for one single affirmation, from one single man, that the negro was not included in the Declaration of Independence. I think I may defy Judge Douglas to show that he ever said so, that Washington ever said so, that any President ever said so, that any member of Congress ever said so, or that any living man upon the whole earth ever said so, until the necessities of the present policy of the Democratic party, in regard to slavery, had to invent that affirmation. [Tremendous applause.] And I will remind Judge Douglas and this audience, that while Mr. Jefferson was the owner of slaves, as undoubtedly he was, in speaking upon this very subject, he used the strong language that "he trembled for his country when he remembered that God was just;" and I will offer the highest premium in my power to Judge Douglas if he will show that he, in all his life, ever uttered a sentiment at all akin to that of Jefferson. [Great applause and cries of "Hit him again," "good," "good."]

The next thing to which I will ask your attention is the Judge's comments upon the fact, as he assumes it to be, that we cannot call our public meetings as Republican meetings; and he instances Tazewell County as one of the places where the friends of Lincoln have called a public meeting and have not dared to name it a Republican meeting. He instances Monroe County as another where Judge Trumbull and Jehu Baker addressed the persons whom the Judge assumes to be the friends of Lincoln, calling them the "Free Democracy." I have the honor to inform Judge Douglas that he spoke in that very county of Tazewell last Saturday, and I was there on Tuesday last, and when he spoke there he spoke under a call not venturing to use the word "Democrat." [Cheers and laughter.] (Turning to Judge Douglas.) What do you think of this? [Immense applause and roars of laughter.]

So again, there is another thing to which I would ask the Judge's attention upon this subject. In the contest of 1856 his party delighted to call themselves together as the "National Democracy," but now, if there should be a notice put up anywhere for a meeting of the "National Democracy," Judge Douglas and his friends would not come. [Laughter.] They would not suppose themselves invited. [Renewed laughter and cheers.] They would understand that it was a call for those hateful postmasters whom he talks about. [Uproarious laughter.]

Now a few words in regard to these extracts from speeches of mine, which Judge Douglas has read to you, and which he supposes are in very great contrast to each other. Those speeches have been before the public for a considerable time, and if they have any inconsistency in them, if there is any conflict in them the public have been able to detect it. When the Judge says, in speaking on this subject, that I make speeches of one sort for the people of the northern end of the state, and of a different sort for the southern people, he assumes that I do not understand that my speeches will be put in print and read north and south. I knew all the while that the speech that I made at Chicago and the one I made at Jonesboro and the one at Charleston, would all be put in print and all the reading and intelligent men in the community would see them and know all about my opinions. And I have not supposed, and do not now suppose, that there is any conflict whatever between them. ["They are all good speeches!" "Hurrah for Lincoln!"] But the Judge will have it that if we do not confess that there is a sort of inequality between the white and black races, which justifies us in making them slaves, we must, then, insist that there is a degree of equality that requires us to make them our wives. [Loud applause, and cries, "Give it to him;" "Hit him again."] Now, I have all the while taken a broad distinction in regard to that matter; and that is all there is in these different speeches which he arrays here, and the entire reading of either of the speeches will show that that distinction was made. Perhaps by taking two parts of the same speech, he could have got up as much of a conflict as the one he has found. I have all the while maintained, that in so far as it should be insisted that there was an equality between the white and black races that should produce a perfect social and political equality, it was an impossibility. This you have seen in my printed speeches, and with it I have said, that in their right to "life, liberty and the pursuit of happiness," as proclaimed in that old Declaration, the inferior races are our equals. [Long-continued cheering.] And these declarations I have constantly made in reference to the abstract moral question, to contemplate and consider when we are legislating about any new country which is not already cursed with the actual presence of the evil—slavery. I have never manifested any impatience with the necessities that spring from the actual presence of black people amongst us, and the actual existence of slavery amongst us where it does already exist; but I have insisted that, in legislating for new countries, where it does not exist, there is no just rule other than that of moral and abstract right! With reference to those new countries, those maxims as to the right of a people to "life, liberty and the pursuit of happiness," were the just rules to be constantly referred to. There is no misunderstanding this, except by men interested to misunderstand it. [Applause.] I take it that I have to address an intelligent and reading community, who will peruse what I say, weigh it, and then judge whether I advance improper or unsound views, or whether I advance hypocritical, and deceptive, and contrary views in different portions of the country. I believe myself to be guilty of no such thing as the latter, though, of course, I cannot claim that I am entirely free from all error in the opinions I advance.

The Judge has also detained us a while in regard to the distinction between his party and our party. His he assumes to be a national party—ours, a sectional one. He does this in asking the question whether this country has any interest in the maintenance of the Republican party? He assumes that our party is altogether sectional —that the party to which he adheres is national; and the argument is, that no party can be a rightful party—can be based upon rightful principles—unless it can announce its principles everywhere. I presume that Judge Douglas could not go into Russia and announce the doctrine of our national democracy; he could not denounce the doctrine of kings, and emperors, and monarchies, in Russia; and it may be true of this country, that in some places we may not be able to proclaim a doctrine as clearly true as the truth of democracy, because there is a section so directly opposed to it that they will not tolerate us in doing so. Is it the true test of the soundness of a doctrine, that in some places people won't let you proclaim it? ["No, no, no."] Is that the way to test the truth of any doctrine? ["No, no, no."] Why, I understood that at one time the people of Chicago would not let Judge Douglas preach a certain favorite doctrine of his. [Laughter and cheers.] I commend to his consideration the question, whether he takes that as a test of the unsoundness of what he wanted to preach. [Loud cheers.]

There is another thing to which I wish to ask attention for a little while on this occasion. What has always been the evidence brought forward to prove that the Republican party is a sectional party? The main one was that in the southern portion of the Union the people did not let the Republicans proclaim their doctrine amongst them. That has been the main evidence brought forward—that they had no supporters, or substantially none, in the slave states. The South have not taken hold of our principles as we announce them; nor does Judge Douglas now grapple with those principles. We have a Republican state platform, laid down in Springfield in June last, stating our position all the way through the questions before the country. We are now far advanced in this canvass. Judge Douglas and I have made perhaps forty speeches apiece, and we have now for the fifth time met face to face in debate, and up to this day I have not found either Judge Douglas or any friend of his taking hold of the Republican platform or laying his finger upon anything in it that is wrong. [Cheers.] I ask you all to recollect that. Judge Douglas turns away from the platform of principles to the fact that he can find people somewhere who will not allow us to announce those principles. [Applause.] If he had great confidence that our principles were wrong, he would take hold of them and demonstrate them to be wrong. But he does not do so. The only evidence he has of their being wrong is in the fact that there are people who won't allow us to preach them. I ask again, is that the way to test the soundness of a doctrine? [Cries of "No," "No."]

I ask his attention also to the fact that by the rule of nationality he is himself fast becoming sectional. [Great cheers and laughter.] I ask his attention to the fact that his speeches would not go as current now south of the Ohio River as they have formerly gone there. [Loud cheers.] I ask his attention to the fact that he felicitates himself to-day that all the Democrats of the free states are agreeing with him, [applause,] while he omits to tell us that the Democrats of any slave state agree with him. If he has not thought of this, I commend to his consideration the evidence in his own declaration, on this day, of his becoming sectional too. [Immense cheering.] I see it rapidly approaching. Whatever may be the result of this ephemeral contest between Judge Douglas and myself, I see the day rapidly approaching when his pill of sectionalism, which he has been thrusting down the throats of Republicans for years past, will be crowded down his own throat. [Tremendous applause.]

Now in regard to what Judge Douglas said (in the beginning of his speech) about the Compromise of 1850, containing the principle of the Nebraska Bill, although I have often presented my views upon that subject, yet as I have not done so in this canvass, I will, if you please, detain you a little with them. I have always maintained, so far as I was able, that there was nothing of the principle of the Nebraska Bill in the Compromise of 1850 at all—nothing whatever. Where can you find the principle of the Nebraska Bill in that compromise? If anywhere, in the two pieces of the compromise organizing the territories of New Mexico and Utah. It was expressly provided in these two acts, that, when they came to be admitted into the Union, they should be admitted with or without slavery, as they should choose, by their own constitutions. Nothing was said in either of those acts as to what was to be done in relation to slavery during the territorial existence of those territories, while Henry Clay constantly made the declaration, (Judge Douglas recognizing him as a leader) that, in his opinion, the old Mexican laws would control that question during the territorial existence, and that these old Mexican laws excluded slavery. How can that be used as a principle for declaring that during the territorial existence as well as at the time of framing the constitution, the people, if you please, might have slaves if they wanted them? I am not discussing the question whether it is right or wrong; but how are the New Mexican and Utah laws patterns for the Nebraska Bill? I maintain that the organization of Utah and New Mexico *did not* establish a general principle at all. It had no feature of establishing a general principle. The acts to which I have referred were a part of a general system of compromises. They did not lay down what was proposed as a regular policy for the territories; only an agreement in this particular case to do in that way, because other things were done that were to be a compensation for it. They were allowed to come in in that shape, because in another way it was paid for—considering that as a part of that system of measures called the Compromise of 1850, which finally included half a dozen acts. It included the admission of California as a free state, which was kept out of the Union for half a year because it had formed a free constitution. It included the settlement of the boundary of Texas, which had been undefined before, which was in itself a slavery question; for, if you pushed the line farther west, you made Texas larger, and made more slave territory; while, if you drew the line towards the east, you narrowed the boundary and diminished the domain of slavery, and by so much increased free territory. It included the abolition of the slave trade in the District of Columbia. It included the passage of a new fugitive slave law. All these things were put together, and though passed in separate acts, were nevertheless in legislation, (as the speeches at the time will show,) made to depend upon each other. Each got votes, with the understanding that the other measures were to pass, and by this system of compromise, in that series of measures, those two bills—the New Mexico and Utah bills—were passed; and I say for that reason they could not be taken as models, framed upon their own intrinsic principle, for all future territories. And I have the evidence of this in the fact that Judge Douglas, a year afterwards, or more than a year afterwards, perhaps, when he first introduced bills for the purpose of framing new territories, did not attempt to follow these bills of New Mexico and Utah; and even when he introduced this Nebraska Bill, I think you will discover that he did not exactly follow them. But I do not wish to dwell at great length upon this branch of the discussion. My own opinion is, that a thorough investigation will show most plainly that the New Mexico and Utah bills were part of a system of compromise, and not designed as patterns for future territorial legislation; and that this Nebraska Bill did not follow them as a pattern at all.

The Judge tells, in proceeding, that he is opposed to making any odious distinctions between free and slave states. I am altogether unaware that the Republicans are in favor of making any odious distinctions between the free and slave states. But there still is a difference, I think, between Judge Douglas and the Republicans in this. I suppose that the real difference between Judge Douglas and his friends, and the Republicans on the contrary, is that the Judge is not in favor of making any difference between slavery and liberty —that he is in favor of eradicating, of pressing out of view, the questions of preference in this country for free over slave institutions; and consequently every sentiment he utters discards the idea that there is any wrong in slavery. Everything that emanates from him or his coadjutors in their course of policy, carefully excludes the thought that there is anything wrong in slavery. All their arguments, if you will consider them, will be seen to exclude the thought that there is anything whatever wrong in slavery. If you will take the Judge's speeches, and select the short and pointed sentences expressed by him—as his declaration that he "don't care whether slavery is voted up or down"—you will see at once that this is perfectly logical, if you do not admit that slavery is wrong. If you do admit that it is wrong, Judge Douglas cannot logically say that he don't care whether a wrong is voted up or voted down. Judge Douglas declares that if any community want slavery they have a right to have it. He can say that logically, if he says that there is no wrong in slavery; but if you admit that there is a wrong in it, he cannot logically say that anybody has a right to do wrong. He insists that, upon the score of equality, the owners of slaves and owners of property—of horses and every other sort of property—should be alike and hold them alike in a new territory. That is perfectly logical, if the two species of property are alike and are equally founded in right. But if you admit that one of them is wrong, you cannot institute any equality between right and wrong. And from this difference of sentiment—the belief on the part of one that the institution is wrong, and a policy springing from that belief which looks to the arrest of the enlargement of that wrong; and this other sentiment, that it is no wrong, and a policy sprung from that sentiment which will tolerate no idea of preventing that wrong from growing larger, and looks to there never being an end of it through all the existence of things,—arises the real difference between Judge Douglas and his friends, on the one hand, and the Republicans on the other. Now, I confess myself as belonging to that class in the country who contemplate slavery as a moral, social and political evil, having due regard for its actual existence amongst us and the difficulties of getting rid of it in any satisfactory way, and to all the constitutional obligations which have been thrown about it; but, nevertheless, desire a policy that looks to the prevention of it as a wrong, and looks hopefully to the time when as a wrong it may come to an end. [Great applause.]

Judge Douglas has again, for, I believe, the fifth time, if not the seventh, in my presence, reiterated his charge of a conspiracy or combination between the National Democrats and Republicans. What evidence Judge Douglas has upon this subject I know not, inasmuch as he never favors us with any. [Laughter and cheers.] I have said upon a former occasion, and I do not choose to suppress it now, that I have no objection to the division in the Judge's party. [Cheers.] He got it up himself. It was all his and their work. He had, I think, a great deal more to do with the steps that led to the Lecompton constitution than Mr. Buchanan had [applause]; though at last, when they reached it, they quarrelled over it, and their friends divided upon it. [Applause.] I am very free to confess to Judge Douglas that I have no objection to the division, [loud applause and laughter]; but I defy the Judge to show any evidence that I have in any way promoted that division, unless he insists on being a witness himself in merely saying so. [Laughter.] I can give all fair friends of Judge Douglas here to understand exactly the view that Republicans take in regard to that division. Don't you remember how two years ago the opponents of the Democratic party were divided between Fremont and Fillmore? I guess you do. ["Yes, sir, we remember it mighty well."] Any Democrat who remembers that division, will remember also that he was at the time very glad of it, [laughter,] and then he will be able to see all there is between the National Democrats and the Republicans. What we now think of the two divisions of Democrats, you then thought of the Fremont and Fillmore divisions. [Great cheers.] That is all there is of it.

But, if the Judge continues to put forward the declaration that there is an unholy and unnatural alliance between the Republicans and the National Democrats, I now want to enter my protest against receiving him as an entirely competent witness upon that subject. [Loud cheers.] I want to call to the Judge's attention an attack he made upon me in the first one of these debates, at Ottawa, on the 21st of August. In order to fix extreme Abolitionism upon me, Judge Douglas read a set of resolutions which he declared had been passed by a Republican state convention, in Oct., 1854, at Springfield, Illinois, and he declared I had taken part in that convention. It turned out that although a few men calling themselves an Anti-Nebraska state convention had sat at Springfield about that time, yet neither did I take any part in it, nor did it pass the resolutions or any such resolutions as Judge Douglas read. [Great applause.] So apparent had it become that the resolutions which he read had not been passed at Springfield at all, nor by a state convention in which I had taken part, that seven days afterwards, at Freeport, Judge Douglas declared that he had been misled by Charles H. Lanphier, editor of the *State Register*, and Thomas L. Harris, member of Congress in that district, and he promised in that speech that when he went to Springfield he would investigate the matter. Since then Judge Douglas has been to Springfield, and I presume has made the investigation; but a month has passed since he has been there, and so far as I know, he has made no report of the result of his investigation. [Great applause.] I have waited as I think sufficient time for the report of that investigation, and I have some curiosity to see and hear it. [Applause.] A fraud—an absolute forgery was committed, and the perpetration of it was traced to the three—Lanphier, Harris and Douglas. [Applause and laughter.] Whether it can be narrowed in any way so as to exonerate any one of them, is what Judge Douglas' report would probably show. [Applause and laughter.]

It is true that the set of resolutions read by Judge Douglas were published in the *Illinois State Register* on the 16th Oct., 1854, as being the resolutions of an Anti-Nebraska convention, which had sat in that same month of October, at Springfield. But it is also true that the publication in the *Register* was a forgery then, [cheers], and the question is still behind, which of the three, if not all of them, committed that forgery? [Great applause.] The idea that it was done by mistake, is absurd. The article in the *Illinois State Register* contains part of the real proceedings of that Springfield convention, showing that the writer of the article had the real proceedings before him, and purposely threw out the genuine resolutions passed by the convention, and fraudulently substituted the others. Lanphier then, as now, was the editor of the *Register*, so that there seems to be but little room for his escape. But then it is to be borne in mind that Lanphier had less interest in the object of that forgery than either of the other two. [Cheers.] The main object of that forgery at that time was to beat Yates and elect Harris to Congress, and that object was known to be exceedingly dear to Judge Douglas at that time. [Laughter.] Harris and Douglas were both in Springfield when the convention was in session, and although they both left before the fraud appeared in the *Register*, subsequent events show that they both had their eyes fixed upon that convention.

The fraud having been apparently successful upon the occasion, both Harris and Douglas have more than once since then been attempting to put it to new uses. As the fisherman's wife, whose drowned husband was brought home with his body full of eels, said when she was asked, "What was to be done with him?" *Take the eels out and set him again*," [great laughter;] so Harris and Douglas have shown a disposition to take the eels out of that stale fraud by which they gained Harris' election, and set the fraud again more than once. [Tremendous cheering and laughter.] On the 9th of July, 1856, Douglas attempted a repetition of it upon Trumbull on the floor of the Senate of the United States, as will appear from the appendix of the *Congressional Globe* of that date.

On the 9th of August Harris attempted it again upon Norton in the House of Representatives, as will appear by the same documents —the appendix to the *Congressional Globe* of that date. On the 21st of August last all three—Lanphier, Douglas and Harris—re-attempted it upon me at Ottawa. [Tremendous applause.] It has been clung to and played out again and again as an exceedingly high trump by this blessed trio. [Roars of laughter and tumultuous applause, "Give it to him," &c.] And now that it has been discovered publicly to be a fraud, we find that Judge Douglas manifests no surprise at it at all. [Laughter, "That's it," "Hit him again."] He makes no complaint of Lanphier who must have known it to be a fraud from the beginning.

He, Lanphier and Harris are just as cozy now, and just as active in the concoction of new schemes as they were before the general discovery of this fraud. Now all this is very natural if they are all alike guilty in that fraud, [laughter and cheers,] and it is very unnatural if any one of them is innocent. [Great laughter, "Hit him again," "Hurrah for Lincoln."] Lanphier perhaps insists that the rule of honor among thieves does not quite require him to take all upon himself, [laughter,] and consequently my friend Judge Douglas finds it difficult to make a satisfactory report upon his investigation. [Laughter and applause.] But meanwhile the three are agreed that each is *"a most honorable man."* [Cheers and explosions of laughter.]

Judge Douglas requires an indorsement of his truth and honor by a re-election to the United States Senate, and he makes and reports against me and against Judge Trumbull day after day charges which we know to be utterly untrue, without for a moment seeming to think that this one unexplained fraud, which he promised to investigate, will be the least drawback to his claim to belief. Harris ditto. He asks a re-election to the lower House of Congress without seeming to remember at all that he is involved in this dishonorable fraud! The *Illinois State Register,* edited by Lanphier, then, as now, the central organ of both Harris and Douglas, continues to din the public ear with this assertion without seeming ·to suspect that these assertions are at all lacking in title to belief.

After all, the question still recurs upon us, how did that fraud originally get into the *State Register?* Lanphier then as now was the editor of that paper. Lanphier knows. Lanphier cannot be ignorant of how and by whom it was originally concocted. Can he be induced to tell, or if he has told, can Judge Douglas be induced to tell how it originally was concocted? It may be true that Lanphier insists that the two men for whose benefit it was originally devised, shall at least bear their share of it! How that is, I do not know, and while it remains unexplained I hope to be pardoned if I insist that the mere fact of Judge Douglas making charges against Trumbull and myself is not quite sufficient evidence to establish them! [Great cheering. "Hit him again." "Give it to him," &c.]

While we were at Freeport, in one of these joint discussions, I answered certain interrogatories which Judge Douglas had propounded to me, and there in turn propounded some to him, which he in a sort of way answered. The third one of these interrogatories I have with me and wish now to make some comments upon it. It was in these words: "If the Supreme Court of the United States shall decide that the states cannot exclude slavery from their limits, are you in favor of acquiescing in, adhering to and following such decision, as a rule of political action?"

To this interrogatory Judge Douglas made no answer in any just sense of the word. He contented himself with sneering at the thought that it was possible for the Supreme Court ever to make such a decision. He sneered at me for propounding the interrogatory. I had not propounded it without some reflection, and I wish now to address to this audience some remarks upon it.

In the second clause of the sixth article, I believe it is of the Constitution of the United States, we find the following language: "This Constitution and the laws of the United States which shall be made in pursuance thereof; and all treaties made or which shall be made under the authority of the United States, shall be the supreme law of the land; and the judges in every state shall be bound thereby anything in the constitution or laws of any state to the contrary notwithstanding."

The essence of the Dred Scott case is compressed into the sentence which I will now read: "Now, as we have already said in an earlier part of this opinion, upon a different point, the right of property in a slave is distinctly and expressly affirmed in the Constitution." I repeat it, *"The right of property in a slave is distinctly and expressly affirmed in the Constitution!"* What is to be *"affirmed"* in the Constitution? Made firm in the Constitution—so made that it cannot be separated from the Constitution without breaking the Constitution—durable as the Constitution, and part of the Constitution. Now, remembering the provision of the Constitution which I have read, affirming that that instrument is the supreme law of the land; that the Judges of every state shall be bound by it, any law or constitution of any state to the contrary notwithstanding; that the right of property in a slave is affirmed in that Constitution, is made, formed into and cannot be separated from it without breaking it; durable as the instrument; part of the instrument;—what follows as a short and even syllogistic argument from it? I think it follows, and I submit to the consideration of men capable of arguing, whether as I state it in syllogistic form the argument has any fault in it:

Nothing in the constitution or laws of any state can destroy a right distinctly and expressly affirmed in the Constitution of the United States.

The right of property in a slave is distinctly and expressly affirmed in the Constitution of the United States;

Therefore, nothing in the Constitution or laws of any state can destroy the right of property in a slave.

I believe that no fault can be pointed out in that argument; assuming the truth of the premises, the conclusion, so far as I have capacity at all to understand it, follows inevitably. There is a fault in it as I think, but the fault is not in the reasoning; but the falsehood in fact is a fault of the premises. I believe that the right of property in a slave *is not* distinctly and expressly affirmed in the Constitution, and Judge Douglas thinks it *is*. I believe that the Supreme Court and the advocates of that decision may search in vain for the place in the Constitution where the right of property in a slave is distinctly and expressly affirmed. I say, therefore, that I think one of the premises is not true in fact. But it is true with Judge Douglas. It is true with the Supreme Court who pronounced it. They are estopped from denying it, and being estopped from denying it, the conclusion follows that the Constitution of the United States being the supreme law, no constitution or law can interfere with it. It being affirmed in the decision that the right of property in a slave is distinctly and expressly affirmed in the Constitution, the conclusion inevitably follows that no state law or constitution can destroy that right. I then say to Judge Douglas and to all others, that I think it will take a better answer than a sneer to show that those who have said that the right of property in a slave is distinctly and expressly affirmed in the Constitution, are not prepared to show that no constitution or law can destroy that right. I say I believe it will take a far better argument than a mere sneer to show to the minds of intelligent men that whoever has so said, is not prepared, whenever public sentiment is so far advanced as to justify it, to say the other. ["That's so."] This is but an opinion, and the opinion of one very humble man; but it is my opinion that the Dred Scott decision, as it is, never would have been made in its present form if the party that made it had not been sustained previously by the elections. My own opinion is, that the new Dred Scott decision, deciding against the right of the people of the states to exclude slavery, will never be made, if that party is not sustained by the elections. [Cries of "Yes, yes."] I believe, further, that it is just as sure to be made as to-morrow is to come, if that party shall be sustained. ["We won't sustain it, never, never."] I have said, upon a former occasion, and I repeat it now, that the course of argument that Judge Douglas makes use of upon this subject, (I charge not his motives in this), is preparing the public mind for that new Dred Scott decision. I have asked him again to point out to me the reasons for his firm adherence to the Dred Scott decision as it is. I have turned his attention to the fact that General Jackson differed with him in regard to the political obligation of a Supreme Court decision. I have asked his attention to the fact that Jefferson differed with him in regard to the political obligation of a Supreme Court decision. Jefferson said, that "Judges are as honest as other men, and not more so." And he said, substantially, that "whenever a free people should give up in absolute submission to any department of government, retaining for themselves no appeal from it, their liberties were gone." I have asked his attention to the fact that the Cincinnati platform, upon which he says he stands, disregards a time-honored decision of the Supreme Court, in denying the power of Congress to establish a national bank. I have asked his attention to the fact that he himself was one of the most active instruments at one time in breaking down the Supreme Court of the state of Illinois, because it had made a decision distasteful to him—a struggle ending in the remarkable circumstance of his sitting down as one of the new Judges who were to overslaugh that decision—[loud applause]—getting his title of Judge in that very way. [Tremendous applause and laughter.]

So far in this controversy I can get no answer at all from Judge Douglas upon these subjects. Not one can I get from him, except that he swells himself up and says, "All of us who stand by the decision of the Supreme Court are the friends of the Constitution; all you fellows that dare question it in any way, are the enemies of the Constitution." [Continued laughter and cheers.] Now, in this very devoted adherence to this decision, in opposition to all the great political leaders whom he has recognized as leaders—in opposition to his former self and history, there is something very marked. And the manner in which he adheres to it—not as being right upon the merits, as he conceives (because he did not discuss that at all), but as being absolutely obligatory upon every one simply because of the source from whence it comes—as that which no man can gainsay, whatever it may be,—this is another marked feature of his adherence to that decision. It marks it in this respect, that it commits him to the next decision, whenever it comes, as being as obligatory as this one, since he does not investigate it, and won't inquire whether this opinion is right or wrong. So he takes the next one without inquiring whether *it* is right or wrong. [Applause.] He teaches men this doctrine, and in so doing prepares the public mind to take the next decision when it comes, without any inquiry. In this I think I argue fairly (without questioning motives at all) that Judge Douglas is most ingeniously and powerfully preparing the public mind to take that decision when it comes; and not only so, but he is doing it in various other ways. In these general maxims about liberty—in his assertions that he "don't care whether slavery is voted up or voted down;" that "whoever wants slavery has a right to have it;" that "upon principles of equality it should be allowed to go everywhere;"

that "there is no inconsistency between free and slave institutions." In this he is also preparing (whether purposely or not), the way for making the institution of slavery national! [Cries of "Yes," "Yes," "That's so."] I repeat again, for I wish no misunderstanding, that I do not charge that he means it so; but I call upon your minds to inquire, if you were going to get the best instrument you could, and then set it to work in the most ingenious way, to prepare the public mind for this movement, operating in the free states, where there is now an abhorrence of the institution of slavery, could you find an instrument so capable of doing it as Judge Douglas? or one employed in so apt a way to do it? [Great cheering. Cries of "Hit him again," "That's the doctrine."]

I have said once before, and I will repeat it now, that Mr. Clay, when he was once answering an objection to the Colonization Society, that it had a tendency to the ultimate emancipation of the slaves, said that "those who would repress all tendencies to liberty and ultimate emancipation must do more than put down the benevolent efforts of the Colonization Society—they must go back to the era of our liberty and independence, and muzzle the cannon that thunders its annual joyous return—they must blot out the moral lights around us—they must penetrate the human soul, and eradicate the light of reason and the love of liberty!" And I do think—I repeat, though I said it on a former occasion—that Judge Douglas, and whoever like him teaches that the negro has no share, humble though it may be, in the Declaration of Independence, is going back to the era of our liberty and independence, and, so far as in him lies, muzzling the cannon that thunders its annual joyous return; ["That's so"] that he is blowing out the moral lights around us, when he contends that whoever wants slaves has a right to hold them; that he is penetrating, so far as lies in his power, the human soul, and eradicating the light of reason and the love of liberty, when he is in every possible way preparing the public mind, by his vast influence, for making the institution of slavery perpetual and national. [Great applause, and cries of "Hurrah for Lincoln," "That's the true doctrine."]

There is, my friends, only one other point to which I will call your attention for the remaining time that I have left me, and perhaps I shall not occupy the entire time that I have, as that one point may not take me clear through it.

Among the interrogatories that Judge Douglas propounded to me at Freeport, there was one in about this language: "Are you opposed to the acquisition of any further territory to the United States, unless slavery shall first be prohibited therein?" I answered as I thought, in this way, that I am not generally opposed to the acquisition of additional territory, and that I would support a proposition for the acquisition of additional territory, according as my supporting it was or was not calculated to aggravate this slavery question amongst us. I then proposed to Judge Douglas another interrogatory, which was correlative to that: "Are you in favor of acquiring additional territory in disregard of how it may affect us upon the slavery question?" Judge Douglas answered, that is, in his own way he answered it. [Laughter.] I believe that, although he took a good many words to answer it, it was a little more fully answered than any other. The substance of his answer was, that this country would continue to expand—that it would need additional territory—that it was as absurd to suppose that we could continue upon our present territory, enlarging in population as we are, as it would be to hoop a boy twelve years of age, and expect him to grow to man's size without bursting the hoops. [Laughter.] I believe it was something like that. Consequently he was in favor of the acquisition of further territory, as fast as we might need it, in disregard of how it might affect the slavery question. I do not say this as giving his exact language, but he said so substantially, and he would leave the question of slavery where the territory was acquired, to be settled by the people of the acquired territory. ["That's the doctrine."] May be it is; let us consider that for a while. This will probably, in the run of things, become one of the concrete manifestations of this slavery question. If Judge Douglas' policy upon this question succeeds, and gets fairly settled down, until all opposition is crushed out, the next thing will be a grab for the territory of poor Mexico, an invasion of the rich lands of South America, then the adjoining islands will follow, each one of which promises additional slave fields. And this question is to be left to the people of those countries for settlement. When we shall get Mexico, I don't know whether the Judge will be in favor of the Mexican people that we get with it settling that question for themselves and all others; because we know the Judge has a great horror for mongrels, [laughter,] and I understand that the people of Mexico are most decidedly a race of mongrels. [Renewed laughter.] I understand that there is not more than one person there out of eight who is pure white, and I suppose from the Judge's previous declaration that when we get Mexico or any considerable portion of it, that he will be in favor of these mongrels settling the question, which would bring him somewhat into collision with his horror of an inferior race.

It is to be remembered, though, that this power of acquiring additional territory is a power confided to the President and Senate of the United States. It is a power not under the control of the Representatives of the people any further than they, the President and the Senate can be considered the representatives of the people. Let me illustrate that by a case we have in our history. When we acquired the territory from Mexico in the Mexican war, the House of Representatives, composed of the immediate representatives of the people all the time insisted that the territory thus to be acquired should be brought up upon condition that slavery should be forever prohibited therein, upon terms and in the language that slavery had been prohibited from coming into this country. That was insisted upon constantly, and never failed to call forth an assurance that any territory thus acquired should have that prohibition in it, so far as the House of Representatives was concerned. But at last the President and Senate acquired the territory without asking the House of Representatives anything about it, and took it without that prohibition. They have the power of acquiring territory without the immediate representatives of the people being called upon to say anything about it, and thus furnishing a very apt and powerful means of bringing new territory into the Union, and when it is once brought into the country, involving us anew in this slavery agitation. It is, therefore, as I think, a very important question for the consideration of the American people, whether the policy of bringing in additional territory, without considering at all how it will operate upon the safety of the Union in reference to this one great disturbing element in our national politics, shall be adopted as the policy of the country. You will bear in mind that it is to be acquired, according to the Judge's view, as fast at it is needed, and the indefinite part of this proposition is that we have only Judge Douglas and his class of men to decide how fast it is needed. We have no clear and certain way of determining or demonstrating how fast territory is needed by the necessities of the country. Whoever wants to go out filibustering, then, thinks that more territory is needed. Whoever wants wider slave fields, feels sure that some additional territory is needed as slave territory. Then it is as easy to show the necessity of additional slave territory as it is to assert anything that is incapable of absolute demonstration. Whatever motive a man or set of men may have for making annexation of property or territory, it is very easy to assert, but much less easy to disprove, that it is necessary for the wants of the country.

And now it only remains for me to say that I think it is a very grave question for the people of this Union to consider whether, in view of the fact that this slavery question has been the only one that has ever endangered our republican institutions—the only one

that has ever threatened or menaced a dissolution of the Union—
that has ever disturbed us in such a way as to make us fear for the
perpetuity of our liberty—in view of these facts, I think it is an
exceedingly interesting and important question for this people to
consider, whether we shall engage in the policy of acquiring additional territory, discarding altogether from our consideration, while
obtaining new territory, the question how it may affect us in regard
to this the only endangering element to our liberties and national
greatness. The Judge's view has been expressed. I, in my answer to
his question, have expressed mine. I think it will become an important and practical question. Our views are before the public. I am
willing and anxious that they should consider them fully—that they
should turn it about and consider the importance of the question,
and arrive at a just conclusion as to whether it is or is not wise in
the people of this Union, in the acquisition of new territory, to consider whether it will add to the disturbance that is existing amongst
us—whether it will add to the one only danger that has ever threatened the perpetuity of the Union or our own liberties. I think it is
extremely important that they shall decide, and rightly decide that
question before entering upon that policy.

And now, my friends, having said the little I wish to say upon
this head, whether I have occupied the whole of the remnant of my
time or not, I believe I could not enter upon any new topic so as
to treat it fully without transcending my time, which I would not
for a moment think of doing. I give way to Judge Douglas.

Three tremendous cheers for Lincoln from the whole vast audience were given with great enthusiasm, as their favorite retired.

Douglas' Rejoinder

Gentlemen:

The highest compliment you can pay me during the brief half
hour that I have to conclude is by observing a strict silence. I desire
to be heard rather than to be applauded. ("Good.")

The first criticism that Mr. Lincoln makes on my speech was that
it was in substance what I have said everywhere else in the state
where I have addressed the people. I wish I could say the same of
his speech. ("Good;" "you have him," and applause.) Why, the
reason I complain of him is because he makes one speech north and
another south. ("That's so.") Because he has one set of sentiments
for the Abolition counties and another set for the counties opposed

to Abolitionism. ("Hit him over the knuckles.") My point of complaint against him is that I cannot induce him to hold up the same standard, to carry the same flag in all parts of the state. He does not pretend, and no other man will, that I have one set of principles for Galesburg and another for Charleston. ("No, no.") He does not pretend that I hold to one doctrine in Chicago and to an opposite one in Jonesboro. I have proved that he has a different set of principles for each of these localities. All I asked of him was that he should deliver the speech that he has made here to-day in Coles County instead of in old Knox. It would have settled the question between us in that doubtful county. Here I understand him to re-affirm the doctrine of negro equality, and to assert that by the Declaration of Independence the negro is declared equal to the white man. He tells you to-day that the negro was included in the Declaration of Independence when it asserted that all men were created equal. ("We believe it.") Very well. (Here an uproar arose, persons in various parts of the crowd indulging in cat calls, groans, cheers, and other noises, preventing the speaker from proceeding.)

Mr. Douglas—Gentlemen, I ask you to remember that Mr. Lincoln was listened to respectfully, and I have the right to insist that I shall not be interrupted during my reply.

Mr. Lincoln—I hope that silence will be preserved.

Mr. Douglas—Mr. Lincoln asserts to-day as he did at Chicago, that the negro was included in that clause of the Declaration of Independence which says that all men were created equal and endowed by the Creator with certain inalienable rights, among which are life, liberty and the pursuit of happiness. ("Ain't that so?") If the negro was made his equal and mine, if that equality was established by Divine law, and was the negro's inalienable right, how came he to say at Charleston to the Kentuckians residing in that section of our state, that the negro was physically inferior to the white man, belonged to an inferior race, and he was for keeping him always in that inferior condition? ("Good.") I wish you to bear these things in mind. At Charleston he said that the negro belonged to an inferior race, and that he was for keeping him in that inferior condition. There he gave the people to understand that there was no moral question involved, because the inferiority being established, it was only a question of degree and not a question of right; here, to-day, instead of making it a question of degree, he makes it a moral question, says that it is a great crime to hold the negro in that inferior condition. ("He's right.") Is he right now or was he right in Charleston? ("Both.") He is right then, sir, in your estimation, not because he is consistent, but because he can trim his principles any way in any section, so as to secure votes. All I desire of him is that he will declare the same principles in the south that he does in the north.

But did you notice how he answered my position that a man should hold the same doctrines throughout the length and breadth of this republic? He said, "Would Judge Douglas go to Russia and proclaim the same principles he does here?" I would remind him that Russia is not under the American Constitution. ("Good," and laughter.) If Russia was a part of the American republic, under our federal Constitution, and I was sworn to support that Constitution, I would maintain the same doctrine in Russia that I do in Illinois. (Cheers.) The slaveholding states are governed by the same federal Constitution as ourselves, and hence a man's principles, in order to be in harmony with the Constitution, must be the same in the South as they are in the North, the same in the free states as they are in the slave states. Whenever a man advocates one set of principles in one section, and another set in another section, his opinions are in violation of the spirit of the Constitution which he has sworn to support. ("That's so.") When Mr. Lincoln went to Congress in 1847, and laying his hand upon the holy evangelists, made a solemn vow in the presence of high Heaven that he would be faithful to the Constitution,—what did he mean? the Constitution as he expounds it in Galesburg, or the Constitution as he expounds it in Charleston? (Cheers.)

Mr. Lincoln has devoted considerable time to the circumstance that at Ottawa I read a series of resolutions as having been adopted at Springfield, in this state, on the 4th or 5th of October, 1854, which happened not to have been adopted there. He has used hard names; has dared to talk about fraud, (laughter), about forgery, and has insinuated that there was a conspiracy between Mr. Lanphier, Mr. Harris, and myself to perpetuate a forgery. (Renewed laughter.) Now, bear in mind that he does not deny that these resolutions were adopted in a majority of all the Republican counties of this state in that year; he does not deny that they were declared to be the platform of this Republican party in the first congressional district, in the second, in the third, and in many counties of the fourth, and that they thus became the platform of his party in a majority of the counties upon which he now relies for support; he does not deny the truthfulness of the resolutions, but takes exceptions to the *spot* on which they were adopted. He takes to himself great merit because he thinks they were not adopted on the right spot for me to use them against him, just as he was very severe in Congress upon the government of his country when he thought that he had dis-

covered that the Mexican war was not begun in the right *spot*, and
was therefore unjust. (Renewed laughter.) He tries very hard to
make out that there is something very extraordinary in the place
where the thing was done, and not in the thing itself. I never believed before that Abraham Lincoln would be guilty of what he has
done this day in regard to those resolutions. In the first place, the
moment it was intimated to me that they had been adopted at
Aurora and Rockford instead of Springfield, I did not wait for him
to call my attention to the fact, but led off and explained in my first
meeting after the Ottawa debate, what the mistake was, and how
it had been made. ("That's so.") I supposed that for an honest man,
conscious of his own rectitude, that explanation would be sufficient.
I did not wait for him, after the mistake was made, to call my attention to it, but frankly explained it at once as an honest man would.
(Cheers.) I also gave the authority on which I had stated that these
resolutions were adopted by the Springfield Republican convention.
That I had seen them quoted by Major Harris in a debate in Congress, as having been adopted by the first Republican state convention in Illinois, and that I had written to him and asked him for
the authority as to the time and place of their adoption; that Major
Harris being extremely ill, Charles H. Lanphier had written to me
for him, that they were adopted at Springfield, on the 5th of October, 1854, and had sent me a copy of the Springfield paper containing them. I read them from the newspaper just as Mr. Lincoln reads
the proceedings of meetings held years ago from the newspapers.
After giving that explanation, I did not think there was an honest
man in the state of Illinois who doubted that I had been led into the
error, if it was such, innocently, in the way I detailed; and I will
now say that I do not now believe that there is an honest man on
the face of the globe who will not regard with abhorrence and disgust Mr. Lincoln's insinuations of my complicity in that forgery, if
it was a forgery. (Cheers.) Does Mr. Lincoln wish to push these
things to the point of personal difficulties here? I commenced this
contest by treating him courteously and kindly; I always spoke of
him in words of respect, and in return he has sought, and is now
seeking, to divert public attention from the enormity of his revolutionary principles by impeaching men's sincerity and integrity, and
inviting personal quarrels. ("Give it to him," and cheers.)

I desired to conduct this contest with him like a gentleman, but
I spurn the insinuation of complicity and fraud made upon the
simple circumstance of an editor of a newspaper having made a
mistake as to place where a thing was done, but not as to the thing
itself. These resolutions were the platform of this Republican party

of Mr. Lincoln's of that year. They were adopted in a majority of the Republican counties in the state; and when I asked him at Ottawa whether they formed the platform upon which he stood, he did not answer, and I could not get an answer out of him. He then thought, as I thought, that those resolutions were adopted at the Springfield convention, but excused himself by saying that he was not there when they were adopted, but had gone to Tazewell court in order to avoid being present at the convention. He saw them published as having been adopted at Springfield, and so did I, and he knew that if there was a mistake in regard to them, that I had nothing under heaven to do with it. Besides, you find that in all these northern counties where the Republican candidates are running pledged to him, that the conventions which nominated them adopted that identical platform. One cardinal point in that platform which he shrinks from is this—that there shall be no more slave states admitted into the Union, even if the people want them. Lovejoy stands pledged against the admission of any more slave states. ("Right, so do we.") So do you, you say. Farnsworth stands pledged against the admission of any more slave states. ("Most right.") Washburne stands pledged the same way. ("Good, good.") The candidate for the legislature who is running on Lincoln's ticket in Henderson and Warren, stands committed by his vote in the legislature to the same thing, and I am informed, but do not know of the fact, that your candidate here is also so pledged. ("Hurrah for him," "good.") Now, you Republicans all hurrah for him, and for the doctrine of "no more slave states," and yet Lincoln tells you that his conscience will not permit him to sanction that doctrine. (Immense applause.) And complains because the resolutions I read at Ottawa made him as a member of the party, responsible for sanctioning the doctrine of no more slave states. You are one way, you confess, and he is or pretends to be the other, and yet you are both governed by *principle* in supporting one another. If it be true, as I have shown it is, that the whole Republican party in the northern part of the state stands committed to the doctrine of no more slave states, and that this same doctrine is repudiated by the Republicans in the other part of the state, I wonder whether Mr. Lincoln and his party do not present the case which he cited from the Scriptures, of a house divided against itself which cannot stand! (Tremendous shouts of applause.) I desire to know what are Mr. Lincoln's principles and the principles of his party? I hold, and the party with which I am identified hold, that the people of each state, old and new, have the right to decide the slavery question for themselves, ("That's it," "Right," and immense applause,) and when I used the remark that I did not care whether slavery was voted up or down, I used it in the connection that I was for allowing Kansas to do just as she pleased on the slavery question. I said that I did not care whether they voted slavery up or down, because they had the right to do as they pleased on the question, and therefore my action would not be controlled by any such consideration. ("That's the doctrine.") Why cannot Abraham Lincoln, and the party with which he acts, speak out their principles so that they may be understood? Why do they claim to be one thing in one part of the state and another in the other part? Whenever I allude to the Abolition doctrines, which he considers a slander to be charged with being in favor of, you all endorse them, and hurrah for them, not knowing that your candidate is ashamed to acknowledge them. ("You have them;" and cheers.)

I have a few words to say upon the Dred Scott decision, which has troubled the brain of Mr. Lincoln so much. (Laughter.) He insists that that decision would carry slavery into the free states, notwithstanding that the decision says directly the opposite; and goes into a long argument to make you believe that I am in favor of, and would sanction the doctrine that would allow slaves to be brought here and held as slaves contrary to our constitution and laws. Mr. Lincoln knew better when he asserted this; he knew that one newspaper, and so far as is within my knowledge, but one ever asserted that doctrine, and that I was the first man in either House of Congress that read that article in debate, and denounced it on the floor of the Senate as revolutionary. When the Washington *Union*, on the 17th of last November published an article to that effect, I branded it at once, and denounced it, and hence the *Union* has been pursuing me ever since. Mr. Toombs, of Georgia, replied to me, and said that there was not a man in any of the slave states south of the Potomac River that held any such doctrine. Mr. Lincoln knows that there is not a member of the Supreme Court who holds that doctrine; he knows that every one of them, as shown by their opinions, holds the reverse. Why this attempt, then, to bring the Supreme Court into disrepute among the people? It looks as if there was an effort being made to destroy public confidence in the highest judicial tribunal on earth. Suppose he succeeds in destroying public confidence in the court, so that the people will not respect its decisions, but will feel at liberty to disregard them, and resist the laws of the land, what will he have gained? He will have changed the government from one of laws into that of a mob, in which the strong arm of violence will be substituted for the decisions of the courts of justice. ("That's so.") He complains because I did not go into an argument reviewing Chief Justice Taney's opinion, and the other opinions of the different judges, to determine whether their reasoning is right or wrong on the questions of law. What use would that be? He wants to take an appeal from the Supreme Court to this meeting to determine whether the questions of law were decided properly. He is going to appeal from the Supreme Court of the United States to every town meeting in the hope that he can excite a prejudice against that court, and on the wave of that prejudice ride into the Senate of the United States, when he could not get there on his own principles, or his own merits. (Laughter and cheers; "hit him again.") Suppose he should succeed in getting into the Senate of the United States, what then will he have to do with the decision of the Supreme Court in the Dred Scott case? Can he reverse that decision when he gets there? Can he act upon it? Has the Senate any right to reverse it or revise it? He will not pretend that it has. Then why drag the matter into this contest, unless for the purpose of making a false issue, by which he can direct public attention from the real issue?

He has cited General Jackson in justification of the war he is making on the decision of the court. Mr. Lincoln misunderstands the history of the country, if he believes there is any parallel in the two cases. It is true that the Supreme Court once decided that if a bank of the United States was a necessary fiscal agent of the government, it was constitutional, and if not, that it was unconstitutional, and also, that whether or not it was necessary for that purpose, was a political question for Congress and not a judicial one for the courts to determine. Hence the court would not determine the bank unconstitutional. Jackson respected the decision, obeyed the law, executed it and carried it into effect during its existence; ("that's so,") but after the charter of the bank expired and a proposition was made to create a new bank, General Jackson said, "It is unnecessary, and improper, and therefore, I am against it on constitutional grounds as well as those of expediency." Is Congress bound to pass every act that is constitutional? Why, there are a thousand things that are constitutional, but yet are inexpedient and unnecessary, and you surely would not vote for them merely because you had the right to? And because General Jackson would not do a thing which he had a right to do, but did not deem expedient or proper, Mr. Lincoln is going to justify himself in doing that which he has no right to do. (Laughter.) I ask him, whether he is not bound to respect and obey the decisions of the Supreme Court as well as me? The Constitution has created that court to decide all constitutional questions in the last resort, and when such decisions have been made, they become the law of the land, ("that's so,") and you, and he, and myself, and every other good citizen are bound by them. Yet, he argues that I am bound by their decisions and he is not. He says that their decisions are binding on Democrats, but not on Republicans. (Laughter and applause.) Are not Republicans bound by the laws of the land, as well as Democrats? And when the court has fixed the construction of the Constitution on the validity of a given law, is not their decision binding upon Republicans as well as upon Democrats? ("It ought to be.") Is it possible that you Republicans have the right to raise your mobs and oppose the laws of the land and the constituted authorities, and yet hold us Democrats bound to obey them? My time is within half a minute of expiring, and all I have to say is, that I stand by the laws of the land. ("That's it"; "hurrah for Douglas.") I stand by the Constitution as our fathers made it, by the laws as they are enacted, and by the decisions of the court upon all points within their jurisdiction as they are pronounced by the highest tribunal on earth; and any man who resists these must resort to mob law and violence to overturn the government of laws.

CHAPTER ELEVEN

THE QUINCY DEBATE

Although there were only six days between the fifth and sixth debates, neither candidate could afford to rest. On October 8, the day after Galesburg, Lincoln addressed a rally at Toulon; Douglas proceeded to Macomb where he spoke on the 9th, while Lincoln expounded Republican principles at Oquawka and Burlington, Iowa. A heavy rain on Sunday, October 10, turned the roads of western Illinois into continuous mud holes and left a legacy of dark, cold clouds, but the weather did not deter crowds from gathering on the 11th to hear Lincoln at Monmouth and Douglas at Carthage.

Douglas spent October 12, the day before the debate, at Augusta, where he spoke in the afternoon and then boarded a train for Quincy. Apparently Lincoln rested during the day, and spent the night at Macomb so that he could arrive at Quincy in good time the following morning.

The Times *reported Douglas' reception at Quincy.*[1]

Senator Douglas had been stopping for a brief time at Augusta, when he left on Tuesday evening, for Quincy, in the cars of the Chicago and Quincy railroad. At Camp Point, on the route—a small town of about one thousand inhabitants—the Senator was met by a great cavalcade of military, bands of music, and citizens gathered from that and the adjacent towns. In front of the station house a splendid bonfire was flaming, and hundreds of torches were carried in the streets. Every house in the town was illuminated—presenting, altogether, one of the finest spectacles witnessed during this splendid campaign. The train having a few minutes to spare, short speeches were made by Senator Douglas, I. N. Morris, and Major Roosevelt. The last named gentleman is candidate for the legislature in Hancock County.

The Senator arrived in Quincy at 9 o'clock and 30 minutes, where he was received by one of the most extensive and brilliant torchlight processions ever witnessed. On either side of the immense pro-

[1] October 15, 1858.

[322]

cession by which Senator Douglas was escorted to his hotel—the Quincy House—stood in line hundreds of men holding up to view appropriate and gorgeous transparencies. The evening reception was complete in all respects, and brilliant beyond description.

The Press and Tribune, *with equal fervor, recorded Lincoln's appearance on the scene.*[1]

A clear sky and altogether an admirable day, after a series of cold, dismal storms, was accorded to the sixth public debate between Lincoln and Douglas at Quincy. . . . The crowd was very large, and although less in number than at the Galesburg debate, the excitement and enthusiasm on both sides were more marked and vociferous.

The hubbub commenced about nine o'clock, shortly before the arrival of a long special train from Macomb and the intermediate stations on which Mr. Lincoln was expected. An immense procession was formed . . . to receive the Republican champion. About half-past nine the booming of cannon announced the arrival of the train, and a tumultuous rush was made for the depot. Six rousing cheers were given as Mr. Lincoln stepped from the cars; after which the procession marched . . . through several streets to the front of the court house. The entire line was half an hour in passing the corner of Third and Jersey streets. The principal device in the train was a model ship on wheels, drawn by four horses, and labelled "CONSTITUTION." It was filled with sailors and the helm was managed by a *live coon.* A suitable contrast to this was one of the contrivances in the Douglas procession. As though not sufficiently insulting to the Old Line Whigs in the general run of their banners and mottoes, a dead coon was borne aloft suspended by the tail, from the principal Dred Scott wagon.

Mr. Lincoln was finally escorted to the residence of O. H. Browning, Esq., and after giving him three cheers which were heard all over the city, the multitude dispersed for dinner. . . .

Among the listeners to the debate were a boat load of passengers from Keokuk, Iowa, and another from Hannibal, Missouri.

The speaking commenced at half-past two o'clock, in Washington Square. A serious accident occurred shortly before the arrival of the speakers, caused by the giving away of a part of the railing around the platform. Twelve or fifteen persons were precipitated backwards to the ground, accompanied in their fall by a heavy wooden bench. Three persons were severely bruised, though not dangerously injured.

[1] October 15.

Lincoln's Opening Speech

Ladies and Gentlemen:

I have had no immediate conference with Judge Douglas, but I will venture to say he and I will perfectly agree that your entire silence both when I speak and when he speaks will be most agreeable to us.

In the month of May, 1856, the elements in the state of Illinois, which have since been consolidated into the Republican party, assembled together in a state convention at Bloomington. They adopted at that time what, in political language, is called a platform. In June of the same year, the elements of the Republican party in the nation assembled together in a national convention at Philadelphia. They adopted what is called the national platform. In June, 1858—the present year—the Republicans of Illinois re-assembled at Springfield, in state convention, and adopted again their platform, as I suppose not differing in any essential particular from either of the former ones, but perhaps adding something in relation to the new developments of political progress in the country.

The convention that assembled in June last did me the honor, if it be one, and I esteem it such, to nominate me as their candidate for the United States Senate. I have supposed that in entering upon this canvass I stood generally upon these platforms. We are now met together on the 13th of October of the same year, only four months from the adoption of the last platform, and I am unaware that in this canvass, from the beginning until to-day, any one of our adversaries has taken hold of our platforms or laid his finger upon anything that he calls wrong in them.

In the very first one of these joint discussions between Senator Douglas and myself, Senator Douglas, without alluding at all to these platforms, or any one of them, of which I have spoken, attempted to hold me responsible for a set of resolutions passed long before the meeting of either one of these conventions of which I have spoken. And as a ground for holding me responsible for these resolutions, he assumed that they had been passed at a state convention of the Republican party, and that I took part in that convention. It was discovered afterwards that this was erroneous, that the resolutions which he endeavored to hold me responsible for, had not been passed by any state convention anywhere—had not been passed at Springfield, where he supposed they had, or assumed that they had, and that they had been passed in no convention in which I had taken part. The Judge, nevertheless, was not willing to give up

the point that he was endeavoring to make upon me, and he therefore thought to still hold me to the point that he was endeavoring
to make, by showing that the resolutions that he read, had been
passed at a local convention in the northern part of the state, although it was not a local convention that embraced my residence
at all, nor one that reached, as I suppose, nearer than 150 to 200
miles of where I was when it met, nor one in which I took any part
at all. He also introduced other resolutions passed at other meetings,
and by combining the whole, although they were all antecedent to
the two state conventions, and the one national convention I have
mentioned, still he insisted and now insists, as I understand, that I
am in some way responsible for them.

At Jonesboro, on our third meeting, I insisted to the Judge that
I was in no way rightfully held responsible for the proceedings of
this local meeting or convention in which I had taken no part, and
in which I was in no way embraced; but I insisted to him that if he
thought I was responsible for every man or every set of men everywhere, who happen to be my friends, the rule ought to work both
ways, and he ought to be responsible for the acts and resolutions of
all men or sets of men who were or are now his supporters and
friends, ["good, good,"] and gave him a pretty long string of resolutions, passed by men who are now his friends, and announcing doctrines for which he does not desire to be held responsible.

This still does not satisfy Judge Douglas. He still adheres to his
proposition, that I am responsible for what some of my friends in
different parts of the state have done; but that he is not responsible
for what his have done. At least so I understand him. But in addition
to that, the Judge at our meeting in Galesburg, last week, undertakes to establish that I am guilty of a species of double-dealing
with the public—that I make speeches of a certain sort in the north,
among the Abolitionists, which I would not make in the south, and
that I make speeches of a certain sort in the south which I would
not make in the north. I apprehend in the course I have marked out
for myself that I shall not have to dwell at very great length upon
this subject.

As this was done in the Judge's opening speech at Galesburg, I
had an opportunity, as I had the middle speech then, of saying
something in answer to it. He brought forward a quotation or two
from a speech of mine delivered at Chicago, and then to contrast
with it he brought forward an extract from a speech of mine at
Charleston, in which he insisted that I was greatly inconsistent, and
insisted that his conclusion followed that I was playing a double
part, and speaking in one region one way and in another region

another way. I have not time now to dwell on this as long as I would like, and I wish only now to re-quote that portion of my speech at Charleston which the Judge quoted, and then make some comments upon it. This he quotes from me as being delivered at Charleston, and I believe correctly: "I will say, then, that I am not, nor ever have been, in favor of bringing about in any way the social and political equality of the white and black races—that I am not nor ever have been in favor of making voters or jurors of negroes, nor of qualifying them to hold office, nor to intermarry with white people; and I will say in addition to this that there is a physical difference between the white and black races which will ever forbid the two races living together on terms of social and political equality. And inasmuch as they cannot so live, while they do remain together, there must be the position of superior and inferior. I am as much as any other man in favor of having the superior position assigned to the white race." ["Good," "Good," and loud cheers.] This, I believe, is the entire quotation from the Charleston speech as the Judge made it. His comments are as follows:

Yes, here you find men who hurrah for Lincoln, and say he is right when he discards all distinction between races, or when he declares that he discards the doctrine that there is such a thing as a superior and inferior race; and Abolutionists are required and expected to vote for Mr. Lincoln because he goes for the equality of the races, holding that in the Declaration of Independence the white man and the negro were declared equal, and endowed by Divine law with equality. And down south with the Old Line Whigs, with the Kentuckians, the Virginians, and the Tennesseeans, he tells you that there is a physical difference between the races, making the one superior, the other inferior, and he is in favor of maintaining the superiority of the white race over the negro.

Those are the Judge's comments. Now I wish to show you, that a month, or only lacking three days of a month, before I made the speech at Charleston, which the Judge quotes from, he had himself heard me say substantially the same thing. It was in our first meeting, at Ottawa—and I will say a word about where it was and the atmosphere it was in, after a while—but, at our first meeting, at Ottawa, I read an extract from an old speech of mine, made nearly four years ago, not merely to show my sentiments, but to show that my sentiments were long entertained and openly expressed; in which extract I expressly declared that my own feelings would not admit a social and political equality between the white and black races, and that even if my own feelings would admit of it, I still knew that the public sentiment of the country would not, and that such a thing was an utter impossibility, or substantially that. That extract from my old speech the reporters, by some sort of accident, passed over, and it was not reported. I lay no blame upon anybody. I suppose they thought that I would hand it over to them, and dropped reporting while I was reading it, but afterwards went away without getting it from me. At the end of that quotation from my old speech, which I read at Ottawa, I made the comments which were reported at that time, and which I will now read, and ask you to notice how very nearly they are the same as Judge Douglas says were delivered by me down in Egypt. After reading I added these words: "Now, gentlemen, I don't want to read at any great length, but this is the true complexion of all I have ever said in regard to the institution of slavery or the black race, and this is the whole of it; and anything that argues me into his idea of perfect social and political equality with the negro is but a specious and fantastical arrangement of words by which a man can prove a horse-chestnut to be a chestnut horse. I will say here, while upon this subject, that I have no purpose directly or indirectly to interfere with the institution in the states where it exists. I believe I have no right to do so. I have no inclination to do so. I have no purpose to introduce political and social equality between the white and black races. There is a physical difference between the two, which, in my judgment, will probably forever forbid their living together on the footing of perfect equality, and inasmuch as it becomes a necessity that there must be a difference, I as well as Judge Douglas am in favor of the race to which I belong having the superior position." [Cheers, "That's the doctrine."] "I have never said anything to the contrary, but I hold that, notwithstanding all this, there is no reason in the world why the negro is not entitled to all the rights enumerated in the Declaration of Independence—the right of life, liberty and the pursuit of happiness. I hold that he is as much entitled to these as the white man. I agree with Judge Douglas that he is not my equal in many respects, certainly not in color—perhaps not in intellectual and moral endowments; but in the right to eat the bread without leave of anybody else which his own hand earns, he is my equal and the equal of Judge Douglas, and the equal of every other man." [Loud cheers.]

I have chiefly introduced this for the purpose of meeting the Judge's charge that the quotation he took from my Charleston speech was what I would say down south among the Kentuckians, the Virginians, &c., but would not say in the regions in which was supposed to be more of the Abolition element. I now make this comment: That speech from which I have now read the quotation, and which is there given correctly, perhaps too much so for good taste, was made away up north in the Abolition district of this state *par excellence*—in the Lovejoy district—in the personal presence of Lovejoy, for he was on the stand with us when I made it. It had been made and put in print in that region only three days less than a month before the speech made at Charleston, the like of which Judge Douglas thinks I would not make where there was any Abolition element. I only refer to this matter to say that I am altogether unconscious of having attempted any double dealing anywhere—that upon one occasion I may say one thing and leave other things unsaid, and *vice versa;* but that I have said anything on one occasion that is inconsistent with what I have said elsewhere, I deny—at least I deny it so far as the intention is concerned. I find that I have devoted to this topic a larger portion of my time than I had intended. I wished to show, but I will pass it upon this occasion, that in the sentiment I have occasionally advanced upon the Declaration of Independence, I am entirely borne out by the sentiments advanced by our old Whig leader, Henry Clay, and I have the book here to show it from; but because I have already occupied more time than I intended to do on that topic, I pass over it.

At Galesburg, I tried to show that by the Dred Scott decision, pushed to its legitimate consequences, slavery would be established in all the states as well as in the territories. I did this because, upon a former occasion, I had asked Judge Douglas whether, if the Supreme Court should make a decision declaring that the states had not the power to exclude slavery from their limits, he would adopt and follow that decision as a rule of political action; and because he had not directly answered that question, but had merely contented himself with sneering at it, I again introduced it, and tried to show that the conclusion that I stated followed inevitably and logically from the proposition already decided by the court. Judge Douglas had the privilege of replying to me at Galesburg, and again he gave me no direct answer as to whether he would or would not sustain such a decision if made. I give him this third chance to say yes or no. He is not obliged to do either—probably he will not do either—[laughter] but I give him the third chance. I tried to show then that this result—this conclusion inevitably followed from the point already decided by the court. The Judge, in his reply, again sneers at the thought of the court making any such decision, and in the course of his remarks upon this subject, uses the language which I will now read. Speaking of me, the Judge says:

"He goes on and insists that the Dred Scott decision would carry slavery into the free states, notwithstanding the decision itself says the contrary." And he adds: "Mr. Lincoln knows that there is no member of the Supreme Court that holds that doctrine. He knows that every one of them in their opinions held the reverse."

I especially introduce this subject again for the purpose of saying that I have the Dred Scott decision here, and I will thank Judge Douglas to lay his finger upon the place in the entire opinions of the court where any one of them "says the contrary." It is very hard to affirm a negative with entire confidence. I say, however, that I have examined that decision with a good deal of care, as a lawyer examines a decision, and so far as I have been able to do so, the Court has no where in its opinions said that the states have the power to exclude slavery, nor have they used other language substantially that. I also say, so far as I can find, not one of the concurring Judges has said that the states can exclude slavery, nor said anything that was substantially that. The nearest approach that any one of them has made to it, so far as I can find, was by Judge Nelson, and the approach he made to it was exactly, in substance, the Nebraska Bill —that the states had the exclusive power over the question of slavery, so far as they are not limited by the Constitution of the United States. I asked the question, therefore, if the non-concurring Judges, McLean or Curtis, had asked to get an express declaration that the states could absolutely exclude slavery from their limits, what reason have we to believe that it would not have been voted down by the majority of the Judges, just as Chase's amendment was voted down by Judge Douglas and his compeers when it was offered to the Nebraska Bill. [Cheers.]

Also at Galesburg, I said something in regard to those Springfield resolutions that Judge Douglas had attempted to use upon me at Ottawa, and commented at some length upon the fact that they were, as presented, not genuine. Judge Douglas in his reply to me seemed to be somewhat exasperated. He said he would never have believed that Abraham Lincoln, as he kindly called me, would have attempted such a thing as I had attempted upon that occasion; and among other expressions which he used toward me, was that I dared to say forgery—that I had *dared* to say forgery [turning to Judge Douglas]. Yes, Judge, I did dare to say forgery. [Loud applause.] But in this political canvass, the Judge ought to remember that I was not the first who *dared* to say forgery. At Jacksonville Judge Douglas made a speech in answer to something said by Judge Trumbull, and at the close of what he said upon that subject, he *dared* to say that Trumbull had forged his evidence. He said, too, that he should not concern himself with Trumbull any more, but thereafter he should hold Lincoln responsible for the slanders upon him. [Laughter.] When I met him at Charleston after that, although

I think that I should not have noticed the subject if he had not said he would hold me responsible for it, I spread out before him the statements of the evidence that Judge Trumbull had used, and I asked Judge Douglas, piece by piece, to put his finger upon one piece of all that evidence that he would say was a forgery! When I went through with each and every piece, Judge Douglas did not *dare* then to say that any piece of it was a forgery. [Laughter, and cries of "good, good."] So it seems that there are some things that Judge Douglas dares to do, and some that he dares not to do. [Great applause and laughter.]

A VOICE—It's the same thing with you.

MR. LINCOLN—Yes, sir, it's the same thing with me. I do dare to say forgery, when it's true, and I don't dare to say forgery when it's false. [Thunders of applause. Cries of "Hit him again," "Give it to him, Lincoln."] Now, I will say here to this audience and to Judge Douglas, I have not dared to say he committed a forgery, and I never shall until I know it; but I did dare to say—just to suggest to the Judge—that a forgery had been committed, which by his own showing had been traced to him and two of his friends. [Roars of laughter and loud cheers.] I dared to suggest to him that he had expressly promised in one of his public speeches to investigate that matter, and I dared to suggest to him that there was an implied promise that when he investigated it he would make known the result. I dared to suggest to the Judge that he could not expect to be quite clear of suspicion of that fraud, for since the time that promise was made he had been with those friends, and had not kept his promise in regard to the investigation and the report upon it. [Loud laughter. Cries of "Good, good," "Hit him hard."] I am not a very daring man, [laughter] but I dared that much, Judge, and I am not much scared about it yet. [Uproarious laughter and applause.] When the Judge says he wouldn't have believed of Abraham Lincoln that he would have made such an attempt as that, he reminds me of the fact that he entered upon this canvass with the purpose to treat me courteously; that touched me somewhat. [Great laughter.] It sets me to thinking. I was aware, when it was first agreed that Judge Douglas and I were to have these seven joint discussions, that they were the successive acts of a drama—perhaps I should say, to be enacted not merely in the face of audiences like this, but in the face of the nation, and to some extent, by my relation to him, and not from anything in myself, in the face of the world; and I am anxious that they should be conducted with dignity and in the good temper which would be befitting the vast audience before which it was conducted. But when Judge Douglas got home from Washington and made his first speech in Chicago, the evening afterwards I made some sort of a reply to it. His second speech was made at Bloomington, in which, he commented upon my speech at Chicago, and said that I had used language ingeniously contrived to conceal my intentions, or words to that effect. Now, I understand that this is an imputation upon my veracity and my candor. I do not know what the Judge understood by it; but in our first discussion at Ottawa, he led off by charging a bargain, somewhat corrupt in its character, upon Trumbull and myself—that we had entered into a bargain, one of the terms of which was that Trumbull was to abolitionize the old Democratic party, and I (Lincoln) was to abolitionize the old Whig party—I pretending to be as good an Old Line Whig as ever. Judge Douglas may not understand that he implicated my truthfulness and my honor, when he said I was doing one thing and pretending another; and I misunderstood him if he thought he was treating me in a dignified way, as a man of honor and truth, as he now claims he was disposed to treat me. Even after that time, at Galesburg, when he brings forward an extract from a speech made at Chicago, and an extract from a speech made at Charleston, to prove that I was trying to play a double part—that I was trying to cheat the public, and get votes upon one set of principles at one place and upon another set of principles at another place—I do not understand but what he impeaches my honor, my veracity and my candor, and because *he* does this, I do not understand that I am bound, if I see a truthful ground for it, to keep my hands off of him. As soon as I learned that Judge Douglas was disposed to treat me in this way, I signified in one of my speeches that I should be driven to draw upon whatever of humble resources I might have—to adopt a new course with him. I was not entirely sure that I should be able to hold my own with him, but I at least had the purpose made to do as well as I could upon him; and now I say that I will not be the first to cry "hold." I think it originated with the Judge, and when he quits, I probably will. [Roars of laughter.] But I shall not ask any favors at all. He asks me, or he asks the audience, if I wish to push this matter to the point of personal difficulty. I tell him, no. He did not make a mistake, in one of his early speeches, when he called me an "amiable" man, though perhaps he did when he called me an "intelligent" man. [Laughter.] It really hurts me very much to suppose that I have wronged anybody on earth. I again tell him, no! I very much prefer, when this canvass shall be over, however it may result, that we at least part without any bitter recollections of personal difficulties.

The Judge, in his concluding speech at Galesburg, says that I was pushing this matter to a personal difficulty, to avoid the responsibility for the enormity of my principles. I say to the Judge and to this audience now, that I will again state our principles as well as I hastily can in all their enormity, and if the Judge hereafter chooses to confine himself to a war upon these principles, he will probably not find me departing from the same course.

We have in this nation this element of domestic slavery. It is a matter of absolute certainty that it is a disturbing element. It is the opinion of all the great men who have expressed an opinion upon it, that it is a dangerous element. We keep up a controversy in regard to it. That controversy necessarily springs from difference of opinion, and if we can learn exactly—can reduce to the lowest elements—what that difference of opinion is, we perhaps shall be better prepared for discussing the different systems of policy that we would propose in regard to that disturbing element. I suggest that the difference of opinion, reduced to its lowest terms, is no other than the difference between the men who think slavery a wrong and those who do not think it wrong. The Republican party think it wrong—we think it is a moral, a social and a political wrong. We think it is a wrong not confining itself merely to the persons or the states where it exists, but that it is a wrong in its tendency, to say the least, that extends itself to the existence of the whole nation. Because we think it wrong, we propose a course of policy that shall deal with it as a wrong. We deal with it as with any other wrong, in so far as we can prevent its growing any larger, and so deal with it that in the run of time there may be some promise of an end to it. We have a due regard to the actual presence of it amongst us and the difficulties of getting rid of it in any satisfactory way, and all the constitutional obligations thrown about it. I suppose that in reference both to its actual existence in the nation, and to our constitutional obligations, we have no right at all to disturb it in the states where it exists, and we profess that we have no more inclination to disturb it than we have the right to do it. We go further than that; we don't propose to disturb it where, in one instance, we think the Constitution would permit us. We think the Constitution would permit us to disturb it in the District of Columbia. Still we do not propose to do that, unless it should be in terms which I don't suppose the nation is very likely soon to agree to—the terms of making the emancipation gradual and compensating the unwilling owners. Where we suppose we have the constitutional right, we restrain ourselves in reference to the actual existence of the institution and the difficulties thrown about it. We also oppose it as an evil so far as it seeks to spread itself. We insist on the policy that shall restrict it to its present limits. We don't suppose that in doing this we violate anything due to the actual presence of the institution, or anything due to the constitutional guarantees thrown around it.

We oppose the Dred Scott decision in a certain way, upon which I ought perhaps to address you a few words. We do not propose that when Dred Scott has been decided to be a slave by the court, we, as a mob, will decide him to be free. We do not propose that, when any other one, or one thousand, shall be decided by that court to be slaves, we will in any violent way disturb the rights of property thus settled; but we nevertheless do oppose that decision as a political rule which shall be binding on the voter, to vote for nobody who thinks it wrong, which shall be binding on the members of Congress or the President to favor no measure that does not actually concur with the principles of that decision. We do not propose to be bound by it as a political rule in that way, because we think it lays the foundation not merely of enlarging and spreading out what we consider an evil, but it lays the foundation for spreading that evil into the states themselves. We propose so resisting it as to have it reversed if we can, and a new judicial rule established upon this subject.

I will add this, that if there be any man who does not believe that slavery is wrong in the three aspects which I have mentioned, or in any one of them, that man is misplaced, and ought to leave us. While, on the other hand, if there be any man in the Republican party who is impatient over the necessity springing from its actual presence, and is impatient of the constitutional guarantees thrown around it, and would act in disregard of these, he too is misplaced standing with us. He will find his place somewhere else; for we have a due regard, so far as we are capable of understanding them, for all these things. This, gentlemen, as well as I can give it, is a plain statement of our principles in all their enormity.

I will say now that there is a sentiment in the country contrary to me—a sentiment which holds that slavery is not wrong, and therefore it goes for policy that does not propose dealing with it as a wrong. That policy is the Democratic policy, and that sentiment is the Democratic sentiment. If there be a doubt in the mind of any one of this vast audience that this is really the central idea of the Democratic party, in relation to this subject, I ask him to bear with me while I state a few things tending, as I think, to prove that proposition. In the first place, the leading man—I think I may do my friend Judge Douglas the honor of calling him such—advocating the present Democratic policy, never himself says it is wrong. He has the high distinction, so far as I know, of never having said slavery is either right or wrong. [Laughter.] Almost everybody else says one or the other, but the Judge never does. If there be a man in the Democratic party who thinks it is wrong, and yet clings to that party, I suggest to him in the first place that his leader don't talk as he does, for he never says that it is wrong. In the second place, I suggest to him that if he will examine the policy proposed to be carried forward, he will find that he carefully excludes the idea that there is anything wrong in it. If you will examine the arguments that are made on it, you will find that every one carefully excludes the idea that there is anything wrong in slavery. Perhaps that Democrat who says he is as much opposed to slavery as I am, will tell me that I am wrong about this. I wish him to examine his own course in regard to this matter a moment, and then see if his opinion will not be changed a little. You say it is wrong; but don't you constantly object to anybody else saying so? Do you not constantly argue that this is not the right place to oppose it? You say it must not be opposed in the free states, because slavery is not here; it must not be opposed in the slave states, because it is there; it must not be opposed in politics, because that will make a fuss; it must not be opposed in the pulpit, because it is not religion. [Loud cheers.] Then where is the place to oppose it? There is no suitable place to oppose it. There is no place in the country to oppose this evil overspreading the continent, which you say yourself is coming. Frank Blair and Gratz Brown tried to get up a system of gradual emancipation in Missouri, had an election in August and got beat, and you, Mr. Democrat, threw up your hat, and halloed "hurrah for Democracy." [Enthusiastic cheers.] So I say again that in regard to the arguments that are made, when Judge Douglas says he "don't care whether slavery is voted up or voted down," whether he means that as an individual expression of sentiment, or only as a sort of statement of his views on national policy, it is alike true to say that he can thus argue logically if he don't see anything wrong in it; but he cannot say so logically if he admits that slavery is wrong. He cannot say that he would as soon see a wrong voted up as voted down. When Judge Douglas says that whoever, or whatever community, wants slaves, they have a right to have them, he is perfectly logical if there is nothing wrong in the institution; but if you admit that it is wrong, he cannot logically say that anybody has a right to do wrong. When he says that slave property and horse and hog property are alike to be allowed to go into the territories, upon the principles of equality, he is reasoning truly, if there is no difference between them as property; but if the one is property, held rightfully, and the other is wrong, then there is no equality between the right and wrong; so that, turn it in any way you can, in all the arguments sustaining the Democratic policy, and in that policy itself, there is a careful, studied exclusion of the idea that there is anything wrong in slavery. Let us understand this. I am not, just here, trying to prove that we are right and they are wrong. I have been stating where we and they stand, and trying to show what is the real difference between us; and I now say that whenever we can get the question distinctly stated—can get all these men who believe that slavery is in some of these respects wrong, to stand and act with us in treating it as a wrong—then, and not till then, I think we will in some way come to an end of this slavery agitation. [Prolonged cheers.]

Douglas' Reply

Ladies and Gentlemen:

Permit me to say that unless silence is observed it will be impossible for me to be heard by this immense crowd, and my friends can confer no higher favor upon me than by omitting all expressions of applause or approbation. ("We cannot help it, Douglas," &c.) I desire to be heard rather than to be applauded. I wish to address myself to your reason, your judgment, your sense of justice, and not to your passions.

I regret that Mr. Lincoln should have deemed it proper for him to again indulge in gross personalities and base insinuations in regard to the Springfield resolutions. It has imposed upon me the necessity of using some portion of my time for the purpose of calling to your attention to the facts of the case, and it will then be for you to say what you think of a man who can predicate such a charge upon the circumstances he has this. I had seen the platform adopted by a Republican congressional convention held in Aurora, the second congressional district, in September, 1854, published as purporting to be the platform of the Republican party. That platform declared that the Republican party was pledged never to admit another slave state into the union, and also that it pledged to prohibit slavery in all the territories of the United States, not only all that we then had, but all that we should thereafter acquire, and to repeal unconditionally the fugitive slave law, abolish slavery in the District of Columbia, and prohibit the slave trade between the different states. These and other articles against slavery were contained in this platform, and unanimously adopted by the Republican congressional convention in that district. I had also seen that the Republican congressional conventions at Rockford, in the first district, and at Bloomington, in the third, had adopted the same platform that year, nearly word for word, and had declared it to be the platform of the Republican party. I had noticed that Major Thomas L. Harris, a member of Congress from the Springfield district, had referred to that platform in a speech in Congress as having been adopted by the first Republican state convention which assembled in Illinois. When I had occasion to use the fact in this canvass, I wrote to Major Harris to know on what day that convention was held, and to ask him to send me its proceedings. He being sick, Charles H. Lanphier answered my letter by sending me the published proceedings of the convention held at Springfield on the 5th of October, 1854, as they appeared in the report of the *State Register*. I read those resolutions from that newspaper the same as any of you would refer back and quote any fact from the files of a newspaper which had published it. Mr. Lincoln pretends that after I had so quoted those resolutions he discovered that they had never been adopted at Springfield. He does not deny their adoption by the Republican party at Aurora, at Bloomington, and at Rockford, and by nearly all the Republican county conventions in northern Illinois where his party is in a majority, but merely because they were not adopted on the *"spot"* on which I said they were, he chooses to quibble about the place rather than meet and discuss the merits of the resolutions themselves. I stated when I quoted them that I did so from the *State Register*. I gave my authority. Lincoln believed at the time, as he has since admitted, that they had been adopted at Springfield, as published. Does he believe now, that I did not tell the truth when I quoted those resolutions? He knows, in his heart, that I quoted them in good faith, believing, at the time, that they had been adopted at Springfield. I would consider myself an infamous wretch, if, under such circumstances, I could charge any man with being a party to a trick or a fraud. (Great applause.) And I will tell him, too, that it will not do to charge a forgery on Charles H. Lanphier or Thomas L. Harris. No man on earth, who knows them, and knows Lincoln, would take his oath against their word. (Cheers.) There are not two men in the state of Illinois, who have higher characters for truth, for integrity, for moral character, and for elevation of tone, as gentlemen, than Mr. Lanphier and Mr. Harris. Any man who attempts to make such charges as Mr. Lincoln has indulged in against them, only proclaims himself a slanderer. (Vociferous applause.)

I will now show you that I stated with entire fairness, as soon as it was made known to me, that there was a mistake about the spot where the resolutions had been adopted, although their truthfulness, as a declaration of the principles of the Republican party, had not, and could not be questioned. I did not wait for Lincoln to point out the mistake; but the moment I discovered it, I made a speech, and published it to the world, correcting the error. I corrected it myself, as a gentleman, and an honest man, and as I always feel proud to do when I have made a mistake. I wish Mr. Lincoln could show that he has acted with equal fairness, and truthfulness, when I have convinced him that he has been mistaken. ("Hit him again," and cheers.) I will give you an illustration to show you how he acts in a similar case: In a speech at Springfield, he charged Chief Justice Taney, and his associates, President Pierce, President Buchanan, and myself, with having entered into a conspiracy at the time the Nebraska Bill was introduced, by which the Dred Scott decision was to be made by the Supreme Court, in order to carry slavery everywhere under the Constitution. I called his attention to the fact, that at the time alluded to, to wit: the introduction of the Nebraska Bill, it was not possible that such a conspiracy could have been entered into, for the reason that the Dred Scott case had never been taken before the Supreme Court, and was not taken before it for a year after; and I asked him to take back that charge. Did he do it? ("No.") I showed him that it was impossible that the charge could be true, I proved it by the record, and I then called upon him to retract his false charge. What was his answer? Instead of coming out like an honest man and doing so, he reiterated the charge, and said that if the case had not gone up to the Supreme Court from the courts of Missouri at the time he charged that the Judges of the Supreme Court entered into the conspiracy, yet, that there was an understanding with the Democratic owners of Dred Scott, that they would take it up. I have since asked him who the Democratic owners of Dred Scott were, but he could not tell, and why? Because there were no such Democratic owners in existence. Dred Scott at the time was owned by the Rev. Dr. Chaffee, an Abolition member of Congress, of Springfield, Massachusetts, in right of his wife. He was owned by one of Lincoln's friends, and not by Democrats at all; (immense cheers, "give it to him," &c.) his case was conducted in court by Abolition lawyers, so that both the prosecution and the defense were in the hands of the Abolition political friends of Mr. Lincoln. (Renewed cheering.) Notwithstanding I thus proved by the record that his charge against the Supreme Court was false, instead of taking it back, he resorted to another false charge to sustain the infamy of it. (Cheers.) He also charged President Buchanan with having been a party to the conspiracy. I directed his attention to the fact that the charge could not possibly be true, for the reason that at the time specified, Mr. Buchanan was not in America, but was three thousand miles off, representing the United States at the Court of St. James, and had been there for a year previous, and did not return until three years afterwards. Yet, I never could get Mr. Lincoln to take back his false charge, although I have called upon him over and over again. He refuses to do it, and either remains silent, or, resorts to other tricks to try and palm his slander off on the country. (Cheers.) Therein you will find the difference between Mr. Lincoln and myself. When I make a mistake, as an honest man, I correct it without being asked to do so, but when he makes a false charge he sticks to it, and never corrects it. ("Don't spare him," and cheers.) One word more in regard to these resolutions: I quoted them at Ottawa merely to ask Mr. Lincoln whether he stood on that platform. That was the purpose for which I quoted them. I did not think that I had a right to put idle questions to him, and I first laid a foundation for my questions by showing that the principles which I wished him either to affirm or deny had been adopted by some portion of his friends, at least, as their creed. Hence I read the resolutions, and put the questions to him, and he refused to answer them. (Laughter, "he was afraid," &c.) Subsequently, one week afterwards, he did answer a part of them, but the others he has not answered up to this day. ("No, and never will," "never can," and cheers.) My friends, if you are my friends, you will be silent, instead of interrupting me by your applause. ("We can't help it.")

Now, let me call your attention for a moment to the answers which Mr. Lincoln made at Freeport to the questions which I propounded him at Ottawa, based upon the platform adopted by a majority of the Abolition counties of the state, which now as then supported him. In answer to my question whether he endorsed the Black Republican principle of "no more slave states," he answered that he was not pledged against the admission of any more slave states, but that he would be very sorry if he should ever be placed in a position where he would have to vote on the question; that he would rejoice to know that no more slave states would be admitted into the Union; "but," he added, "if slavery shall be kept out of the territories during the territorial existence of any one given territory, and then the people shall, having a fair chance and a clear field when they come to adopt the constitution, do such an extraordinary thing as to adopt a slave constitution, uninfluenced by the actual presence of the institution among them, I see no alternative, if we own the country, but to admit them into the Union." The point I wish him to answer is this: Suppose Congress should not prohibit slavery in the territory, and it applied for admission with a constitution recognizing slavery, then how would he vote? His answer at Freeport does not apply to any territory in America. I ask you, (turning to Lincoln,) will you vote to admit Kansas into the Union, with just such a constitution as her people want, with slavery or without as they shall determine? He will not answer. ("He's afraid," and cheers.) I have put that question to him time and time again, and have not been able to get an answer out of him. I ask you again, Lincoln, will you vote to admit New Mexico when she has the requisite population with such a constitution as her people adopt, either recognizing slavery or not as they shall determine? He will not answer. I put the same question to him in reference to Oregon and the new states to be carved out of Texas, in pursuance of the contract between Texas and the United States, and he will not answer. He will not answer these questions in reference to any territory now in existence; but says, that if Congress should prohibit slavery in a territory, and when its people asked for admission as a state, they should adopt slavery as one of their institutions, that he supposes he would have to let it come in. (Laughter.) I submit to you whether that answer of his to my question does not justify me in saying that he has a fertile genius in devising language to conceal his thoughts. ("Good for you," "hurrah for Douglas," &c.) I ask you whether there is an intelligent man in America who does not believe, that that answer was made for the purpose of concealing what he intended to do. ("No, no," and cheers.) He wished to make the Old Line Whigs believe that he would stand by the compromise measures of 1850, which declared that the states might come into the Union with slavery, or without as they pleased, while Lovejoy and his Abolition allies up north, explained to the Abolitionists, that in taking this ground he preached good Abolition doctrine, because his proviso would not apply to any territory in America, and therefore there was no chance of his being governed by it. It would have been quite easy for him to have said, that he would let the people of a state do just as they pleased, if he desired to convey such an idea. Why did he not do it? ("He was afraid to.") He would not answer my question directly, because up north, the Abolition creed declares that there shall be no more slave states, while down south, in Adams County, in Coles, and in Sangamon, he and his friends are afraid to advance that doctrine. Therefore, he gives an evasive and equivocal answer, to be construed one way in the south and another way in the north, which, when analyzed, it is apparent is not an answer at all with reference to any territory now in existence. ("Hit him on the woolly side," "Hurrah for Douglas," &c.)

Mr. Lincoln complains that, in my speech the other day at Galesburg, I read an extract from a speech delivered by him at Chicago, and then another from his speech at Charleston, and compared them, thus showing the people that he had one set of principles in one part of the state and another in the other part. And how does he answer that charge? Why, he quotes from his Charleston speech as I quoted from it, and then quotes another extract from a speech which he made at another place, which he says is the same as the extract from his speech at Charleston; but he does not quote the extract from his Chicago speech, upon which I convicted him of double dealing. (Cheers.) I quoted from his Chicago speech to prove that he held one set of principles up north among the Abolitionists, and from his Charleston speech to prove that he held another set down at Charleston and in southern Illinois. In his answer to this charge, he ignores entirely his Chicago speech, and merely argues that he said the same thing which he said at Charleston at another place. If he did, it follows that he has twice, instead of once, held one creed in one part of the state and a different creed in another part. ("He can't get out of it," and cheers.) Up at Chicago, in the opening of the campaign, he reviewed my reception speech, and undertook to answer my argument attacking his favorite doctrine of negro equality. I had shown that it was a falsification of the Declaration of Independence to pretend that that instrument applied to and included negroes in the clause declaring that all men were created equal. What was Lincoln's reply? I will read from his Chicago speech, and the one which he did not quote, and dare not quote, in this part of the State. ("Good," "hear, hear," &c.) He said:

I should like to know, if taking this old Declaration of Independence, which declares that all men are equal upon principle, and making exceptions to it, where will it stop? If one man says it does not mean a negro, why may not another man say it does not mean another man? If that declaration is not the truth, let us get the statute book in which we find it and tear it out!

There you find that Mr. Lincoln told the Abolitionists of Chicago that if the Declaration of Independence did not declare that the negro was created by the Almighty the equal of the white man, that you ought to take that instrument and tear out the clause which says that all men were created equal. ("Hurrah for Douglas.") But let me call your attention to another part of the same speech. You know that in his Charleston speech, an extract from which he has read, he declared that the negro belongs to an inferior race; is physically inferior to the white man, and should always be kept in an inferior position. I will now read to you what he said at Chicago on that point. In concluding his speech at that place, he remarked:

My friends, I have detained you about as long as I desire to do, and I have only to say let us discard all this quibbling about this man and the other man—this race and that race and the other race being inferior, and therefore they must be placed in an inferior position, discarding our standard that we have left us. Let us discard all these things, and unite as one people throughout this land until we shall once more stand up declaring that all men are created equal.

Thus you see, that when addressing the Chicago Abolitionists he declared that all distinctions of race must be discarded and blotted out, because the negro stood on an equal footing with the white man; that if one man said the Declaration of Independence did not mean a negro when it declared all men are created equal, that another man would say that it did not mean another man; and hence we ought to discard all differences between the negro race and all other races, and declare them all created equal. Did old Giddings, when he came down among you four years ago, preach more radical Abolitionism than that? ("No, never.") Did Lovejoy, or Lloyd Garrison, or Wendell Phillips, or Fred. Douglass, ever take higher Abolition grounds than that? Lincoln told you that I had charged him with getting up these personal attacks to conceal the enormity of his principles, and then commenced talking about something else, omitting to quote this part of his Chicago speech which contained the enormity of his principles to which I alluded. He knew that I alluded to his negro-equality doctrines when I spoke of the enormity of his principles, yet he did not find it convenient to answer on that point. Having shown you what he said in his Chicago speech in reference to negroes being created equal to white men, and about discarding all distinctions between the two races, I will again read to you what he said at Charleston:

I will say then, that I am not nor ever have been in favor of bringing about in any way, the social and political equality of the white and black races; that I am not nor ever have been in favor of making voters of the free negroes, or jurors, or qualifying them to hold office, or having them to marry with white people. I will say in addition, that there is a physical difference between the white and black races, which, I suppose, will forever forbid the two races living together upon terms of social and political equality, and inasmuch as they cannot so live, that while they do remain together, there must be the position of superior and inferior, that I as much as any other man am in favor of the superior position being assigned to the white man.

A VOICE—That's the doctrine.

MR. DOUGLAS—Yes, sir, that is good doctrine, but Mr. Lincoln is afraid to advocate it in the latitude of Chicago, where he hopes to get his votes. (Cheers.) It is good doctrine in the anti-Abolition counties for him, and his Chicago speech is good doctrine in the Abolition counties. I assert, on the authority of these two speeches of Mr. Lincoln, that he holds one set of principles in the Abolition counties, and a different and contradictory set in the other counties. ("That's so," and cheers.) I do not question that he said at Ottawa what he quoted, but that only convicts him further, by proving that he has twice contradicted himself instead of once. ("Good," and applause.) Let me ask him why he cannot avow his principles the same in the north as in the south—the same in every county, if he has a conviction that they are just? But I forgot—he would not be a Republican if his principles would apply alike to every part of the country. The party to which he belongs is bounded and limited by geographical lines. With their principles they cannot even cross the Mississippi River on your ferry boats. (Immense applause.) They cannot cross over the Ohio into Kentucky. Lincoln himself cannot visit the land of his fathers, the scenes of his childhood, the graves of his ancestors, and carry his Abolition principles, as he declared them at Chicago, with him. ("Hit him again," and cheers.)

This Republican organization appeals to the North against the South; it appeals to Northern passion, Northern prejudice, and Northern ambition, against Southern people, Southern states, and Southern institutions, and its only hope of success is by that appeal. Mr. Lincoln goes on to justify himself in making a war upon slavery, upon the ground that Frank Blair and Gratz Brown did not succeed in their warfare upon the institution in Missouri. (Laughter.) Frank Blair was elected to Congress in 1856, from the state of Missouri as a Buchanan Democrat, and he turned Fremonter after the people elected him, thus belonging to one party before his election, and another afterwards. ("Treachery never succeeds.") What right then had he to expect, after having thus cheated his constituency, that they would support him at another election? ("None." "Hurrah for Douglas," &c.) Mr. Lincoln thinks that it is his duty to preach a crusade in the free states, against slavery, because it is a crime, as he believes, and ought to be extinguished; and because the people of the slave states will never abolish it. How is he going to abolish it? Down in the southern part of the state he takes the ground openly that he will not interfere with slavery where it exists, and says that he is not now and never was in favor of interfering with slavery where it exists in the states. Well, if he is not in favor of that, how does he expect to bring slavery in a course of ultimate extinction? ("Hit him again.") How can he extinguish it in Kentucky, in Virginia, in all the slave states by his policy, if he will not pursue a policy which will interfere with it in the states where it exists? ("That's so.") In his speech at Springfield before the Abolition or Republican convention, he declared his hostility to any more slave states in this language:

Under the operation of that policy the agitation has not only not ceased, but has constantly augmented. In my opinion it will not cease until a crisis shall have been reached and passed. "A house divided against itself cannot stand." I believe this government cannot endure permanently half slave and half free. I do not expect the Union to be dissolved—I do not expect the house to fall—but I do expect it will cease to be divided. It will become all one thing or all the other. Either the opponents of slavery will arrest the further spread of it, and place it where the public mind shall rest in the belief that it is in the course of ultimate extinction; or, its advocates will push it forward until it shall become alike lawful in all the states—old as well as new, North as well as South.

Mr. Lincoln there told his Abolition friends that this government could not endure permanently, divided into free and slave states as our fathers made it, and that it must become all free or all slave, otherwise, that the government could not exist. How then does Lincoln propose to save the Union, unless by compelling all the states to become free, so that the house shall not be divided against itself? He intends making them all free; he will preserve the Union in that way, and yet, he is not going to interfere with slavery anywhere it now exists. How is he going to bring it about? Why, he will agitate, he will induce the North to agitate until the South shall be worried out, and forced to abolish slavery. Let us examine the policy by which that is to be done. He first tells you that he would prohibit slavery everywhere in the territories. He would thus confine slavery within its present limits. When he thus gets it confined, and surrounded, so that it cannot spread, the natural laws of increase will go on until the negroes will be so plenty that they cannot live on the soil. He will hem them in until starvation seizes them, and by starving them to death, he will put slavery in the course of ultimate extinction. If he is not going to interfere with slavery in the states, but intends to interfere and prohibit it in the territories, and thus smother slavery out, it naturally follows, that he can extinguish it only by extinguishing the negro race, for his policy would drive them to starvation. This is the humane and Christian remedy that he proposes for the great crime of slavery.

He tells you that I will not argue the question whether slavery is right or wrong. I tell you why I will not do it. I hold that under the

Constitution of the United States, each state of this Union has a right to do as it pleases on the subject of slavery. In Illinois we have exercised that sovereign right by prohibiting slavery within our own limits. I approve of that line of policy. We have performed our whole duty in Illinois. We have gone as far as we have a right to go under the Constitution of our common country. It is none of our business whether slavery exists in Missouri or not. Missouri is a sovereign state of this Union, and has the same right to decide the slavery question for herself that Illinois has to decide it for herself. ("Good.") Hence I do not choose to occupy the time allotted to me in discussing a question that we have no right to act upon. ("Right.") I thought that you desired to hear us upon those questions coming within our constitutional power of action. Lincoln will not discuss these. What one question has he discussed that comes within the power or calls for the action or interference of an United States Senator? He is going to discuss the rightfulness of slavery when Congress cannot act upon it either way. He wishes to discuss the merits of the Dred Scott decision when under the Constitution, a Senator has no right to interfere with the decision of judicial tribunals. He wants your exclusive attention to two questions that he has no power to act upon; to two questions that he could not vote upon if he was in Congress, to two questions that are not practical, in order to conceal your attention from other questions which he might be required to vote upon should he ever become a member of Congress. He tells you that he does not like the Dred Scott decision. Suppose he does not, how is he going to help himself? He says that he will reverse it. How will he reverse it? I know of but one mode of reversing judicial decisions, and that is by appealing from the inferior to the superior court. But I have never yet learned how or where an appeal could be taken from the Supreme Court of the United States! The Dred Scott decision was pronounced by the highest tribunal on earth. From that decision there is no appeal this side of Heaven. Yet, Mr. Lincoln says he is going to reverse that decision. By what tribunal will he reverse it? Will he appeal to a mob? Does he intend to appeal to violence, to lynch law? Will he stir up strife and rebellion in the land and overthrow the court by violence? He does not deign to tell you how he will reverse the Dred Scott decision, but keeps appealing each day from the Supreme Court of the United States to political meetings in the country. (Laughter.) He wants me to argue with you the merits of each point of that decision before this political meeting. I say to you, with all due respect, that I choose to abide by the decisions of the Supreme Court as they are pronounced. It is not for me to inquire after a decision is made whether I like it in all the points or not. When I used to practice law with Lincoln, I never knew him to be beat in a case that he did not get mad at the judge and talk about appealing; (laughter,) and when I got beat I generally thought the court was wrong, but I never dreamed of going out of the court house and making a stump speech to the people against the judge, merely because I had found out that I did not know the law as well as he did. (Great laughter.) If the decision did not suit me, I appealed until I got to the Supreme Court, and then if that court, the highest tribunal in the world, decided against me, I was satisfied, because it is the duty of every law-abiding man to obey the constitutions, the laws, and the constituted authorities. He who attempts to stir up odium and rebellion in the country against the constituted authorities, is stimulating the passions of men to resort to violence and to mobs instead of to the law. Hence, I tell you that I take the decisions of the Supreme Court as the law of the land, and I intend to obey them as such.

But, Mr. Lincoln says that I will not answer his question as to what I would do in the event of the court making so ridiculous a decision as he imagines they would by deciding that the free state of Illinois could not prohibit slavery within her own limits. I told him at Freeport why I would not answer such a question. I told him that there was not a man possessing any brains in America, lawyer or not, who ever dreamed that such a thing could be done. ("Right.") I told him then, as I say now, that by all the principles set forth in the Dred Scott decision, it is impossible. I told him then, as I do now, that it is an insult to men's understanding, and a gross calumny on the court, to presume in advance that it was going to degrade itself so low as to make a decision known to be in direct violation of the Constitution.

A Voice—The same thing was said about the Dred Scott decision before it passed.

Mr. Douglas—Perhaps you think that the Court did the same thing in reference to the Dred Scott decision: I have heard a man talk that way before. The principles contained in the Dred Scott decision had been affirmed previously in various other decisions. What court or judge ever held that a negro was a citizen? (Laughter.) The state courts had decided that question over and over again, and the Dred Scott decision on that point only affirmed what every court in the land knew to be the law.

But, I will not be drawn off into an argument upon the merits of the Dred Scott decision. It is enough for me to know that the Constitution of the United States created the Supreme Court for the pur-

[345]

pose of deciding all disputed questions touching the true construction of that instrument, and when such decisions are pronounced, they are the law of the land, binding on every good citizen. Mr. Lincoln has a very convenient mode of arguing upon the subject. He holds that because he is a Republican that he is not bound by the decisions of the Court, but that I being a Democrat am so bound. (Laughter and cheers.) It may be that Republicans do not hold themselves bound by the laws of the land and the Constitution of the country as expounded by the courts; it may be an article in the Republican creed that men who do not like a decision, have a right to rebel against it; but when Mr. Lincoln preaches that doctrine, I think he will find some honest Republican—some law-abiding man in that party—who will repudiate such a monstrous doctrine. The decision in the Dred Scott case is binding on every American citizen alike; and yet Mr. Lincoln argues that the Republicans are not bound by it, because they are opposed to it, (laughter,) whilst Democrats are bound by it, because we will not resist it. A Democrat cannot resist the constituted authorities of this country. ("Good.") A Democrat is a law-abiding man, a Democrat stands by the Constitution and the laws, and relies upon liberty as protected by law, and not upon mob or political violence.

I have never yet been able to make Mr. Lincoln understand, or can I make any man who is determined to support him, right or wrong, understand how it is that under the Dred Scott decision the people of a territory, as well as a state, can have slavery or not, just as they please. I believe that I can explain that proposition to all constitution-loving, law-abiding men in a way that they cannot fail to understand it. Chief Justice Taney, in his opinion in the Dred Scott case, said that slaves being property, the owner of them has a right to take them into a territory the same as he would any other property; in other words, that slave property, so far as the right to enter a territory is concerned, stands on the same footing with other property. Suppose we grant that proposition. Then any man has a right to go to Kansas and take his property with him, but when he gets there he must rely upon the local law to protect his property, whatever it may be. ("That's so.") In order to illustrate this, imagine that three of you conclude to go to Kansas. One takes $10,000 worth of slaves, another $10,000 worth of liquors, and the third $10,000 worth of dry goods. When the man who owns the dry goods arrives out there and commences selling them, he finds that he is stopped and prohibited from selling until he gets a license, which will destroy all the profits he can make on his goods to pay for. When the man with the liquors gets there and tries to sell he finds a Maine liquor law in force which prevents him. Now, of what use is his right to go there with his property unless he is protected in the enjoyment of that right after he gets there? ("That's it.") The man who goes there with his slaves finds that there is no law to protect him when he arrives there. He has no remedy if his slaves run away to another country: there is no slave code or police regulations, and the absence of them excludes his slaves from the territory just as effectually and as positively as a constitutional prohibition could.

Such was the understanding when the Kansas and Nebraska Bill was pending in Congress. Read the speech of Speaker Orr, of South Carolina, in the House of Representatives, in 1856, on the Kansas question, and you will find that he takes the ground that while the owner of a slave has a right to go into a territory, and carry his slaves with him, that he cannot hold them one day or hour unless there is a slave code to protect him. He tells you that slavery would not exist a day in South Carolina, or any other state, unless there was a friendly people and friendly legislation. Read the speeches of that giant in intellect, Alexander H. Stephens, of Georgia, and you will find them to the same effect. Read the speeches of Sam Smith, of Tennessee, and of all Southern men, and you will find that they all understood this doctrine then as we understand it now. Mr. Lincoln cannot be made to understand it, however. Down at Jonesboro, he went on to argue that if it be the law that a man has a right to take his slaves into territory of the United States under the Constitution, that then a member of Congress was perjured if he did not vote for a slave code. I ask him whether the decision of the Supreme Court is not binding upon him as well as on me? If so, and he holds that he would be perjured if he did not vote for a slave code under it, I ask him whether, if elected to Congress, he will so vote? I have a right to his answer, and I will tell you why. He put that question to me down in Egypt, and did it with an air of triumph. This was about the form of it: "In the event of a slaveholding citizen of one of the territories should need and demand a slave code to protect his slaves, will you vote for it?" I answered him that a fundamental article in the Democratic creed, as put forth in the Nebraska Bill and the Cincinnati platform, was non-intervention by Congress with slavery in the states and territories, ("Good," "That's the doctrine," and cheers,) and hence, that I would not vote in Congress for any code of laws either for or against slavery in any territory. I will leave the people perfectly free to decide that question for themselves. (Cheers.)

Mr. Lincoln and the Washington *Union* both think this a monstrous bad doctrine. Neither Mr. Lincoln or the Washington *Union* like my Freeport speech on that subject. The *Union*, in a late number, has been reading me out of the Democratic party because I hold that the people of a territory, like those of a state, have the right to have slavery or not, as they please. It has devoted three and a half columns to prove certain propositions, one of which I will read. It says:

We propose to show that Judge Douglas' action in 1850 and 1854 was taken with especial reference to the announcement of doctrine and programme which was made at Freeport. The declaration at Freeport was, that "in his opinion the people can, by lawful means, exclude slavery from a territory before it comes in as a state;" and he declared that his competitor had "heard him argue the Nebraska Bill on that principle all over Illinois in 1854, 1855, and 1856, and had no excuse to pretend to have any doubt upon that subject."

The Washington *Union* there charges me with the monstrous crime of now proclaiming on the stump the same doctrine that I carried out in 1850, by supporting Clay's compromise measures. The *Union* also charges that I am now proclaiming the same doctrine that I did in 1854 in support of the Kansas and Nebraska Bill. It is shocked that I should now stand where I stood in 1850, when I was supported by Clay, Webster, Cass and the great men of that day, and where I stood in 1854, and in 1856, when Mr. Buchanan was elected President. It goes on to prove and succeeds in proving from my speeches in Congress on Clay's compromise measures, that I held the same doctrines at that time that I do now, and then proves that by the Kansas and Nebraska Bill I advanced the same doctrine that I now advance. It remarks:

So much for the course taken by Judge Douglas on the compromises of 1850. The record shows, beyond the possibility of cavil or dispute, that he expressly intended in those bills to give the territorial legislatures power to exclude slavery. How stands his record in the memorable session of 1854 with reference to the Kansas-Nebraska Bill itself? We shall not overhaul the votes that were given on that notable measure. Our space will not afford it. We have his own words, however, delivered in his speech closing the great debate on that bill on the night of March 3, 1854, to show that *he meant* to do in 1854 precisely what *he had meant* to do in 1850. The Kansas-Nebraska Bill being upon its passage, he said:

It then quotes my remarks upon the passage of the bill as follows:

The principle which we propose to carry into effect by this bill is this: That Congress shall neither legislate slavery into any territory or state nor out of the same; but the people shall be left free to regulate their domestic concerns in their own way, subject only to the Constitution of the United States. In order to carry this principle into practical operation, it becomes necessary to remove whatever legal obstacles might be found in the way of its free exercise. It is only for the purpose of carrying out this great fundamental principle of self-government that the bill renders the eighth section of the Missouri act inoperative and void.

Now, let me ask, will those Senators who have arraigned me, or any one of them, have the assurance to rise in his place and declare that this great principle was never thought of or advocated as applicable to territorial bills, in 1850; that, from that session until the present, nobody ever thought of incorporating this principle in all new territorial organizations, &c., &c. I will begin with the compromises of 1850. Any Senator who will take the trouble to examine our journals will find that on the 25th of March of that year I reported from the committee on territories two bills, including the following measures: the admission of California, a territorial government for Utah, a territorial government for New Mexico and the adjustment of the Texas boundary. These bills proposed to leave the people of Utah and New Mexico free to decide the slavery question for themselves, *in the precise language of the Nebraska Bill* now under discussion. A few weeks afterwards the Committee of Thirteen took those bills and put a wafer between them and reported them back to the Senate as one bill, with some slight amendments. *One of these amendments was, that the territorial legislatures should not legislate upon the subject of African slavery. I objected to this provision,* upon the ground that it subverted the great principle of self-government, *upon which the bill had been originally framed by the territorial committee.* On the first trial the Senate refused to strike it out, but subsequently did so, upon full debate, in order to establish that principle as the rule of action in territorial organizations.

The *Union* comments thus upon my speech on that occasion:

Thus it is seen that, in framing the Nebraska-Kansas Bill, Judge Douglas framed it in the terms and upon the model of those of Utah and New Mexico, and that in the debate he took pains expressly to revive the recollection of the voting which had taken place upon amendments affecting the powers of the territorial legislatures over the subject of slavery in the bills of 1850, in order to give the same meaning, force, and effect to the Nebraska-Kansas Bill on this subject as had been given to those of Utah and New Mexico.

The Union proves the following propositions: First, that I sustained Clay's compromise measures on the ground that they established the principle of self-government in the territories. Secondly, that I brought in the Kansas and Nebraska Bill founded upon the same principles as Clay's compromise measures of 1850; and thirdly, that my Freeport speech is in exact accordance with those principles. And what do you think is the imputation that the *Union* casts upon me for all this? It says that my Freeport speech is not Democratic, and that I was not a Democrat in 1854 or in 1850! Now, is not that funny? (Great laughter and cheers.) Think that the author of the Kansas and Nebraska Bill was not a Democrat when he introduced it. The *Union* says I was not a sound Democrat in 1850, nor in 1854, nor in 1856, nor am I in 1858 because I have always taken and now occupy the ground that the people of a territory, like those of a state, have the right to decide for themselves whether slavery shall or shall not exist in a territory. I wish to cite for the benefit of the Washington *Union* and the followers of that sheet, one authority on that point, and I hope the authority will be deemed satisfactory to that class of politicians. I will read from Mr. Buchanan's letter accepting the nomination of the Democratic convention for the Presidency. You know that Mr. Buchanan, after he was nominated, declared to the Keystone Club, in a public speech, that he was no longer James Buchanan, but the embodiment of the Democratic platform. In his letter to the committee which informed him of his nomination, accepting it he defined the meaning of the Kansas and Nebraska Bill and the Cincinnati platform in these words:

The recent legislation of Congress respecting domestic slavery, derived as it has been from the original and pure fountain of legitimate political power, the will of the majority, promises ere long to allay the dangerous excitment. This legislation is founded upon principles as ancient as free government itself, and in accordance with them has simply declared that the people of a territory like those of a state shall decide for themselves whether slavery shall or shall not exist within their limits.

Thus you see that James Buchanan accepted the nomination at Cincinnati, on the condition that the people of a territory, like those of a state, should be left to decide for themselves whether slavery should, or should not exist within their limits. I sustained James Buchanan for the Presidency on that platform, as adopted at Cincinnati, and expounded by himself. He was elected President on that platform, and now we are told by the Washington *Union* that no man is a true Democrat who stands on the platform on which Mr. Buchanan was nominated, and which he has explained and expounded himself. (Laughter.) We are told that a man is not a Democrat who stands by Clay, Webster, and Cass, and the compromise measures of 1850, and the Kansas and Nebraska Bill of 1854. Whether a man be a Democrat or not on that platform, I intend to stand there as long as I have life. ("Stick to it," and cheers.) I intend to cling firmly to that great principle which declares the right of each state and each territory to settle the question of slavery, and every other domestic question for themselves. I hold that if they want a slave state they have a right under the Constitution of the United States to make it so, and if they want a free state, it is their right to have it. But the *Union*, in advocating the claims of Lincoln over me to the Senate, lays down two unpardonable heresies which it says I advocate. The first, is the right of the people of a territory, the same as a state, to decide for themselves the question whether slavery shall exist within their limits, in the language of Mr.

Buchanan; and the second is, that a constitution shall be submitted to the people of a territory for its adoption or rejection before their admission as a state under it. It so happens that Mr. Buchanan is pledged to both these heresies, for supporting which the Washington *Union* has read me out of the Democratic church. In his annual message he said that he trusted that the example of the Minnesota case would be followed in all future cases, requiring a submission of the constitution; and in his letter of acceptance, he said that the people of a territory, the same as a state, had the right to decide for themselves whether slavery should exist within their limits. Thus you find that this little corrupt gang who control the *Union,* and wish to elect Lincoln in preference to me—because, as they say, of these two heresies which I support—denounce President Buchanan when they denounce me, if he stands now by the principles upon which he was elected. Will they pretend that he does not now stand by the principles on which he was elected? Do they hold that he has abandoned the Kansas-Nebraska Bill, the Cincinnati platform, and his own letter accepting his nomination, all of which declare the right of the people of a territory, the same as a state, to decide the slavery question for themselves? I will not believe that he has betrayed or intends to betray the platform which elected him ("good"); but if he does, I will not follow him. ("Good again.") I will stand by that great principle, no matter who may desert it. I intend to stand by it for the purpose of preserving peace between the North and the South, the free and the slave states. ("Hurrah for Douglas.") If each state will only agree to mind its own business, and let its neighbors alone, there will be peace forever between us. We in Illinois tried slavery when a territory, and found it was not good for us in this climate and with our surroundings, and hence we abolished it. We then adopted a free state constitution, as we had a right to do. In this state we have declared that a negro shall not be a citizen ("all right"), and we have also declared that he shall not be a slave. We had a right to adopt that policy. Missouri has just as good a right to adopt the other policy. ("That's it.") I am now speaking of rights under the Constitution, and not of moral or religious rights. I do not discuss the morals of the people of Missouri, but let them settle that matter for themselves. I hold that the people of the slaveholding states are civilized men as well as ourselves, that they bear consciences as well as we, and that they are accountable to God and their posterity and not to us. It is for them to decide therefore the moral and religious right of the slavery question for themselves within their own limits. I assert that they had as much right under the Constitution to adopt the system of policy which they have as we had to adopt ours. So it is with every other state in this Union. Let each state stand firmly by that great constitutional right, let each state mind its own business and let its neighbors alone, and there will be no trouble on this question. If we will stand by that principle, then Mr. Lincoln will find that this republic can exist forever divided into free and slave states, as our fathers made it and the people of each state have decided. Stand by that great principle and we can go on as we have done, increasing in wealth, in population, in power, and in all the elements of greatness, until we shall be the admiration and terror of the world. We can go on and enlarge as our population increases, and we require more room, until we make this continent one ocean-bound republic. Under that principle the United States can perform that great mission, that destiny which Providence has marked out for us. Under that principle we can receive with entire safety that stream of intelligence which is constantly flowing from the Old World to the New, filling up our prairies, clearing our wildernesses and building cities, towns, railroads and other internal improvements, and thus make this the asylum of the oppressed of the whole earth. We have this great mission to perform, and it can only be performed by adhering faithfully to that principle of self-government on which our institutions were all established. I repeat that the principle is the right of each state, each territory, to decide this slavery question for itself, to have slavery or not, as it chooses, and it does not become Mr. Lincoln, or anybody else, to tell the people of Kentucky that they have no consciences, that they are living in a state of iniquity, and that they are cherishing an institution to their bosoms in violation of the law of God. Better for him to adopt the doctrine of "judge not lest ye be judged." ("Good," and applause.) Let him perform his own duty at home, and he will have a better fate in the future. I think there are objects of charity enough in the free states to excite the sympathies and open the pockets of all the benevolence we have amongst us, without going abroad in search of negroes, of whose condition we know nothing. We have enough objects of charity at home, and it is our duty to take care of our own poor, and our own suffering, before we go abroad to intermeddle with other people's business.

My friends, I am told that my time is within two minutes of expiring. I have omitted many topics that I would like to have discussed before you at length. There were many points touched by Mr. Lincoln that I have not been able to take up for the want of time. I have hurried over each subject that I have discussed as rapidly as possible so as to omit but few, but one hour and a half is not time sufficient for a man to discuss at length one half of the great questions which are now dividing the public mind.

In conclusion, I desire to return to you my grateful acknowledgements for the kindness and the courtesy with which you have listened to me. It is something remarkable that in an audience as vast as this, composed of men of opposite politics and views, with their passions highly excited, there should be so much courtesy, kindness and respect exhibited not only towards one another, but towards the speakers, and I feel that it is due to you that I should thus express my gratitude for the kindness with which you have treated me. (Nine cheers were here given for Douglas.)

Lincoln's Rejoinder

My Friends:

Since Judge Douglas has said to you in his conclusion that he had not time in an hour and a half to answer all I had said in an hour, it follows of course that I will not be able to answer in half an hour all that he said in an hour and a half. [Cheers and laughter.]

I wish to return Judge Douglas my profound thanks for his public annunciation here to-day, to be put on record, that his system of policy in regard to the institution of slavery *contemplates that it shall last forever.* [Great cheers, and cries of "Hit him again."] We are getting a little nearer the true issue of this controversy, and I am profoundly grateful for this one sentence. Judge Douglas asks you "why cannot the institution of slavery, or rather, why cannot the nation, part slave and part free, continue as our fathers made it *forever?*" In the first place, I insist that our fathers *did not* make this nation half slave and half free, or part slave and part free. [Applause, and "That's so."] I insist that they found the institution of slavery existing here. They did not make it so, but they left it so because they knew of no way to get rid of it at that time. ["Good," "Good," "That's true."] When Judge Douglas undertakes to say that as a matter of choice the fathers of the government made this nation part slave and part free, *he assumes what is historically a falsehood.* [Long continued applause.] More than that; when the fathers of the government cut off the source of slavery by the abolition of the slave trade, and adopted a system of restricting it from the new territories where it had not existed, I maintain that they placed it where they understood, and all sensible men understood, it was in the course of ultimate extinction ["that's so"]; and when Judge

Douglas asks me why it cannot continue as our fathers made it, I ask him why he and his friends could not let it remain as our fathers made it? [Tremendous cheering.]

It is precisely all I ask of him in relation to the institution of slavery, that it shall be placed upon the basis that our fathers placed it upon. Mr. Brooks, of South Carolina, once said, and truly said, that when this government was established, no one expected the institution of slavery to last until this day; and that the men who formed this government were wiser and better men than the men of these days; but the men of these days had experience which the fathers had not, and that experience had taught them the invention of the cotton gin, and this had made the perpetuation of the institution of slavery a necessity in this country. Judge Douglas could not let it stand upon the basis upon which our fathers placed it, but removed it and *put it upon the cotton gin basis.* [Roars of laughter and enthusiastic applause.] It is a question, therefore, for him and his friends to answer—why they could not let it remain where the fathers of the government originally placed it. [Cheers, and cries of "Hurrah for Lincoln!" "Good!" "Good!"]

I hope nobody has understood me as trying to sustain the doctrine that we have a right to quarrel with Kentucky, or Virginia, or any of the slave states, about the institution of slavery—thus giving the Judge an opportunity to make himself eloquent and valiant against us in fighting for their rights. I expressly declared in my opening speech, that I had neither the inclination to exercise, nor the belief in the existence of the right to interfere with the states of Kentucky or Virginia in doing as they pleased with slavery or any other existing institution. [Loud applause.] Then what becomes of all his eloquence in behalf of the rights of states, which are assailed by no living man? [Applause. "He knows it's all humbuggery."]

But I have to hurry on, for I have but a half hour. The Judge has informed me, or informed this audience, that the Washington *Union* is laboring for my election to the United States Senate. [Cheers and laughter.] That is news to me—not very ungrateful news either. [Turning to Mr. W. H. Carlin, who was on the stand]—I hope that Carlin will be elected to the State Senate and will vote for me. [Mr. Carlin shook his head.] Carlin don't fall in, I perceive, and I suppose he will not do much for me [laughter], but I am glad of all the support I can get anywhere, if I can get it without practicing any deception to obtain it. In respect to this large portion of Judge Douglas' speech, in which he tries to show that in the controversy between himself and the administration party he is in the right, I do not feel myself at all competent or inclined to answer him. I say to him, "Give it to them [laughter]—give it to them just all you can" [renewed laughter and cheers]—and, on the other hand, I say to Carlin, and Jake Davis, and to this man Wagley[2] up here in Hancock, "Give it to Douglas [roars of laughter]—just pour it into him." [Cheers and laughter—"Good for you," "Hurrah for Lincoln!"]

Now in regard to this matter of the Dred Scott decision, I wish to say a word or two. After all, the Judge will not say whether, if a decision is made holding that the people of the *states* cannot exclude slavery, he will support it or not. He obstinately refuses to say what he will do in that case. The Judges of the Supreme Court as obstinately refused to say what they would do on this subject. Before this I reminded him that at Galesburg he had said the Judges had expressly declared the contrary, and you remember that in my opening speech I told him I had the book containing that decision here, and I would thank him to lay his finger on the place where any such thing was said. He has occupied his hour and a half, and he has not ventured to try to sustain his assertion. [Loud cheers.] *He never will.* [Renewed cheers.] But he is desirous of knowing how we are going to reverse the Dred Scott decision. Judge Douglas ought to know how. Did not he and his political friends find a way to reverse the decision of that same Court in favor of the constitutionality of the national bank? [Cheers and laughter.] Didn't they find a way to do it so effectually that they have reversed it as completely as any decision ever was reversed—so far as its practical operation is concerned? [Cheers, and cries of "good," "good."] And let me ask you, didn't Judge Douglas find a way to reverse the decision of our Supreme Court, when it decided that Carlin's father—old Governor Carlin—had not the constitutional power to remove a Secretary of State? [Great cheering and laughter.] Did he not appeal to the "MOBS" as he calls them? Did he not make speeches in the lobby to show how villainous that decision was, and how it ought to be overthrown? Did he not succeed too in getting an act passed by the legislature to have it overthrown? And didn't he himself sit down on that bench as one of the five added judges, who were to overslaugh the four old ones—getting his name of "Judge" in that way and no other? [Thundering cheers and laughter.] If there is a villainy in using disrespect or making opposition to Supreme Court decisions, I commend it to Judge Douglas' earnest consideration. [Cheers and laughter.] I know of no man in the state of Illinois who ought to know so well about *how much* villainy it takes to oppose a decision of the Supreme Court, as our honorable friend, Stephen A. Douglas. [Long continued applause.]

---

[2] Carlin, Davis, and Wagley were all candidates for the legislature.

Judge Douglas also makes the declaration that I say the Democrats are bound by the Dred Scott decision while the Republicans are not. In the sense in which he argues, I never said it; but I will tell you what I have said and what I do not hesitate to repeat today. I have said that as the Democrats believe that decision to be correct and that the extension of slavery is affirmed in the national constitution, they are bound to support it as such; and I will tell you here that General Jackson once said each man was bound to support the Constitution "as he understood it." Now, Judge Douglas understands the Constitution according to the Dred Scott decision, and he is bound to support it as he understands it. [Cheers.] I understand it another way, and therefore I am bound to support it in the way in which I understand it. [Prolonged applause.] And as Judge Douglas believes that decision to be correct, I will remake that argument if I have time to do so. Let me talk to some gentleman down there among you who looks me in the face. We will say you are a member of the territorial legislature, and like Judge Douglas, you believe that the right to take and hold slaves there is a constitutional right. The first thing you do is to *swear you will support the Constitution* and all rights guaranteed therein; that you will, whenever your neighbor needs your legislation to support his constitutional rights, not withhold that legislation. If you withhold that necessary legislation for the support of the Constitution and constitutional rights, do you not commit perjury? [Cries of "Yes."] I ask every sensible man, if that is not so? ["Yes, yes"—"That's a fact."] That is undoubtedly just so, say what you please. Now that is precisely what Judge Douglas says, that this is a constitutional right. Does the Judge mean to say that the territorial legislature in legislating may be withholding necessary laws, or by passing unfriendly laws, *nullify that constitutional right?* Does he mean to say that? Does he mean to ignore the proposition so long known and well established in the law, that what you cannot do directly, you cannot do indirectly? Does he mean that? The truth about the matter is this: Judge Douglas has sung paeans to his "popular sovereignty" doctrine until his Supreme Court cooperating with him has *squatted* his squatter sovereignty out. [Uproarious laughter and applause.] But he will keep up this species of humbuggery about squatter sovereignty. He has at last invented this sort of *do nothing sovereignty*—[renewed laughter]— that the people may exclude slavery by a sort of "sovereignty" that is exercised by doing nothing at all. [Continued laughter.] Is not that running his popular sovereignty down awfully? [Laughter.] Has it not got down as thin as the homoeopathic soup that was made by boiling the shadow of a pigeon that had starved to death? [Roars of laughter and cheering.] But at last, when it is brought to the test of close reasoning, there is not even that thin decoction of it left. It is a presumption impossible in the domain of thought. It is precisely no other than the putting of that most unphilosophical proposition, that two bodies may occupy the same space at the same time. The Dred Scot decision covers the whole ground, and while it occupies it, there is no room even for the shadow of a starved pigeon to occupy the same ground. [Great cheering and laughter.]

A VOICE, on the platform—"Your time is almost out." [Loud cries of "Go on, go on"—"We'll listen all day."]

Well, I'll talk to you a little longer. Judge Douglas, in reply to what I have said about having upon a previous occasion made the speech at Ottawa as the one he took an extract from, at Charleston, says it only shows that I practiced the deception twice. Now, my friends, are any of you obtuse enough to swallow that? ["No, no, we're not such fools."] Judge Douglas had said I had made a speech at Charleston that I would not make up north, and I turned around and answered him by showing I *had* made that same speech up north—had made it at Ottawa—made it in his hearing—made it in *the* Abolition district—in Lovejoy's district—in the personal presence of Lovejoy himself—in the same atmosphere exactly in which I had made my Chicago speech of which he complains so much.

Now, in relation to my not having said anything about the quotation from the Chicago speech: He thinks that is a terrible subject for me to handle. Why, gentlemen, I can show you that the substance of the Chicago speech I delivered two years ago in "Egypt," as he calls it. It was down at Springfield. That speech is here in this book, and I could turn to it and read it to you but for the lack of time. I have not now the time to read it. ["Read it, read it, read it."] No, gentlemen, I am obliged to use discretion in disposing most advantageously of my brief time. The Judge has taken great exception to my adopting the heretical statement in the Declaration of Independence, that "all men are created equal," and he has a great deal to say about negro equality. I want to say that in sometimes alluding to the Declaration of Independence, I have only uttered the sentiments that Henry Clay used to hold. Allow me to occupy your time a moment with what he said. Mr. Clay was at one time called upon in Indiana, and in a way that I suppose was very insulting, to liberate his slaves, and he made a written reply to that application, and one portion of it is in these words:

What is the *foundation* of this appeal to me in Indiana, to liberate the slaves under my care in Kentucky? It is a general declaration in the act announcing to the world the independence of the thirteen American colonies, that *"men are created equal."* Now, as an abstract principle, *there is no doubt of the truth of that declaration,* and it is desirable in the *original construction* of society, and in organized societies, to keep it in view as a great fundamental principle.

[Loud cheers. "Hurrah for Clay."] When I sometimes, in relation to the organization of new societies in new countries, where the soil is clean and clear, insisted that we should keep that principle in view, Judge Douglas will have it that I want a negro wife. [Great laughter.] He never can be brought to understand that there is any middle ground on this subject. I have lived until my fiftieth year, and have never had a negro woman either for a slave or a wife, [cheers] and I think I can live fifty centuries, for that matter, without having had one for either. [Cheers and laughter.] I maintain that you may take Judge Douglas' quotations from my Chicago speech, and from my Charleston speech, and the Galesburg speech, —in his speech of to-day, and compare them over, and I am willing to trust them with you upon his proposition that they show rascality or double dealing. I deny that they do. [Great applause.]

The Judge does not seem at all disposed to have peace, but I find he is disposed to have a personal warfare with me. He says that my oath would not be taken against the bare word of Charles H. Lanphier or Thomas L. Harris. Well, that is altogether a matter of opinion. [Laughter.] It is certainly not for me to vaunt my word against oaths of these gentlemen, but I will tell Judge Douglas again the facts upon which I *"dared"* to say they proved a forgery. I pointed out at Galesburg that the publication of these resolutions in the *Illinois State Register* could not have been the result of accident, as the proceedings of that meeting bore unmistakable evidence of being done by a man who *knew* it was a forgery; that it was a publication partly taken from the real proceedings of the convention, and partly from the proceedings of a convention at another place; which showed that he had the real proceedings before him, and taking one part of the resolutions, he threw out another part and substituted false and fraudulent ones in their stead. I pointed that out to him, and also that his friend Lanphier, who was editor of the *Register* at that time and now is, must have known how it was done. Now whether *he* did it or got some friend to do it for him, I could not tell, but he certainly knew all about it. I pointed out to Judge Douglas that in his Freeport speech he had promised to *investigate* that matter. Does he now say he did not make that promise? ["No," "No."] I have a right to ask *why he did not keep it?* [Tremendous applause.] I call upon him to tell here to-day why he did not keep that promise. That fraud has been traced up so that it lies between him, Harris and Lanphier. There is little room for escape for Lanphier. [Laughter.] Lanphier is doing the Judge good service, and Douglas desires his word to be taken for the truth. He desires Lanphier to be taken as authority in what he states in his newspaper. He desires Harris to be taken as a man of vast credibility, and when this thing lies among them, they will not press it to show where the guilt really belongs. Now, as he has said that he would investigate it, and implied that he would tell us the result of his investigation, I demand of him to tell why he did not investigate it, if he did not; and if he did, *why he won't tell the result.* [Great cheers.] I call upon him for that.

This is the third time that Judge Douglas has assumed that he learned about these resolutions by Harris' attempting to use them against Norton on the floor of Congress. I tell Judge Douglas the public records of the country show that *he* himself attempted it upon Trumbull a month before Harris tried them on Norton [great applause]—that Harris had the opportunity of *learning it from him,* rather than he from Harris. I now ask his attention to that part of the record on the case. My friends, I am not disposed to detain you longer in regard to that matter.

I am told that I still have five minutes left. There is another matter I wish to call attention to. He says, when he discovered there was a mistake in that case, he came forward magnanimously, without my calling his attention to it, and explained it. I will tell you how he became so magnanimous. When the newspapers of our side had discovered and published it, and put it beyond his power to deny it, then he came forward and made a virtue of necessity by acknowledging it. [Great applause.] Now he argues that all the point there was in those resolutions, although never passed at Springfield, is retained by their being passed at other localities. Is that true? He said I had a hand in passing them, in his opening speech—that I was in the convention and helped to pass them. Do the resolutions touch me at all? It strikes me there is some difference between holding a man responsible for an act which he *has not* done, and holding him responsible for an act that he *has* done. You will judge whether there is any difference in the *"spots."* [Laughter and cheers.] And he has taken credit for great magnanimity in coming forward and acknowledging what is proved on him beyond even the capacity of Judge Douglas to deny, and he has more capacity in that way than any other living man. [Laughter and cheers.]

Then he wants to know why I won't withdraw the charge in regard to a conspiracy to make slavery national, as he has withdrawn the one he made. May it please his worship, I will withdraw it *when it is proven false on me as that was proved false on him.* [Shouts of applause and laughter.] I will add a little more than that. I will withdraw it whenever a reasonable man shall be brought to believe that the charge is not true. [Renewed applause.] I have asked Judge Douglas' attention to certain matters of fact tending to prove the charge of a conspiracy to nationalize slavery, and he says he convinces me that this is all untrue because Buchanan was not in the country at that time, and because the Dred Scott case had not then got into the Supreme Court; and he says that I say the *Democratic* owners of Dred Scott got up the case. I never did say that. [Applause.] I defy Judge Douglas to show that I ever said so *for I never uttered it.* [One of Mr. Douglas' reporters gesticulated affirmatively at Mr. Lincoln.] I don't care if your hireling does say I did, I tell you myself that *I never said the "Democratic" owners of Dred Scott got up the case.* [Tremendous enthusiasm.] I have never pretended to know whether Dred Scott's owners were Democrats or Abolitionists, or Free Soilers or Border Ruffians. I have said that there is evidence about the case tending to show that it was a made up case, for the purpose of getting that decision. I have said that that evidence was very strong in the fact that when Dred Scott was declared to be a slave, the owner of him made him free, showing that he had had the case tried and the question settled for such use as could be made of that decision; he cared nothing about the property thus declared to be his by that decision. [Enthusiastic applause.] But my time is out and I can say no more.

CHAPTER TWELVE

THE ALTON DEBATE

Both Lincoln and Douglas stayed in Quincy after the debate. The following day they embarked together on the river packet, "City of Louisiana," arriving at Alton on the early morning of October 15.

The day was a special one for Lincoln. Mrs. Lincoln came down on an excursion train from Springfield. The train also carried the Springfield Cadets, of which Lincoln's oldest son Robert was a member.

Neither Times *nor* Press and Tribune *gave much space to the preliminaries of the debate. The* Times *reporter indulged in a personal attack on Lincoln who, he alleged, "seated himself where his motions could not be observed by the Senator, and, whenever a point was made against him, would shake his head at the crowd, intimating that it was not true, and that they could place no reliance on what was said."[1] The* Press and Tribune *contented itself with two factual paragraphs.[2]*

The final passage-at-arms between Lincoln and Douglas came off at Alton . . . two days subsequently to the Quincy debate. The speakers, accompanied by a few friends, took passage on the fine steamer *City of Louisiana,* at Quincy on Thursday—reaching Alton at 5 o'clock Friday morning.

There was very little excitement manifest in the city during the forenoon, beyond the constant arrival of people from the country and the neighboring towns. A train of eight or ten cars came down from Springfield, Carlinville, and other stations on the Alton and Chicago Railroad; and the steamer *White Cloud* brought up a full load from St. Louis. The whole number in attendance upon the discussion was probably between four and five thousand. By mutual agreement the friends of the respective candidates made no processions or other demonstrations of enthusiasm. The debate passed off

[1] October 17.

[2] October 18.

with rather less than the ordinary amount of applause, but with unusually close attention on the part of the audience. The speaking commenced at 2 o'clock p.m., at the south front of the new city hall.

As Douglas took the stand to make the opening speech, Thomas M. Hope, a Buchanan Democrat, called out a question.

DR. HOPE—Judge, before you commence speaking, allow me to ask you a question.

SENATOR DOUGLAS—If you will not occupy too much of my time.

DR. HOPE—Only an instant.

SENATOR DOUGLAS—What is your question?

DR. HOPE—Do you believe that the territorial legislatures ought to pass laws to protect slavery in the territories?

SENATOR DOUGLAS—You will get an answer in the course of my remarks. (Applause.)

Douglas' Opening Speech

Ladies and Gentlemen:

It is now nearly four months since the canvass between Mr. Lincoln and myself commenced. On the 16th of June the Republican convention assembled at Springfield and nominated Mr. Lincoln as their candidate for the U.S. Senate, and he, on that occasion, delivered a speech in which he laid down what he understood to be the Republican creed and the platform on which he proposed to stand during the contest. The principal points in that speech of Mr. Lincoln's were: First, that this government could not endure permanently divided into free and slave states, as our fathers made it; that they must all become free or all become slave; all become one thing or all become the other, otherwise this Union could not continue to exist. I give you his opinions almost in the identical language he used. His second proposition was a crusade against the Supreme Court of the United States because of the Dred Scott decision; urging as an especial reason for his opposition to that decision that it deprived the negroes of the rights and benefits of that clause in the Constitution of the United States which guarantees to the citizens of each state, all the rights, privileges, and immunities of the citizens of the several states. On the 10th of July I returned home, and delivered a speech to the people of Chicago, in which· I announced it to be my purpose to appeal to the people of Illinois to sustain the course I had pursued in Congress. In that speech I joined issue with Mr. Lincoln on the points which he had presented. Thus there was an issue clear and distinct made up between us on these two propositions laid down in the speech of Mr. Lincoln at Springfield, and controverted by me in my reply to him at Chicago. On the next day, the 11th of July,[3] Mr. Lincoln replied to me at Chicago, explaining at some length, and re-affirming the positions which he had taken in his Springfield speech. In that Chicago speech he even went further than he had before, and uttered sentiments in regard to the negro being on an equality with the white man. ("That's so.") He adopted in support of this position the argument which Lovejoy and Codding, and other Abolition lecturers had made familiar in the northern and central portions of the State, to wit: that the Declaration of Independence having declared all men free and equal, by Divine law, also that negro equality was an inalienable right, of which they could not be deprived. He insisted, in that speech, that the Declaration of Independence included the negro in the clause asserting that all men were created equal, and went so far as to say that if one man was allowed to take the position, that it did not include the negro, others might take the position that it did not include other men. He said that all these distinctions between this man and that man, this race and the other race, must be discarded, and we must all stand by the Declaration of Independence, declaring that all men were created equal.

The issue thus being made up between Mr. Lincoln and myself on three points, we went before the people of the state. During the following seven weeks, between the Chicago speeches and our first meeting at Ottawa, he and I addressed large assemblages of the people in many of the central counties. In my speeches I confined myself closely to those three positions which he had taken controverting his proposition that this Union could not exist as our fathers made it, divided into free and slave states, controverting his proposition of a crusade against the Supreme Court because of the Dred Scott decision, and controverting his proposition that the Declaration of Independence included and meant the negroes as well as the white men, when it declared all men to be created equal. (Cheers for Douglas.) I supposed at that time that these propositions constituted a distinct issue between us, and that the opposite positions we had taken upon them we would be willing to be held to in every part of the state. I never intended to waver one hair's breadth from that issue either in the north or the south, or wherever I should

[3] Douglas had forgotten the exact dates. He had returned to Chicago and spoken there on July 9; Lincoln had replied on July 10.

address the people of Illinois. I hold that when the time arrives that I cannot proclaim my political creed in the same terms not only in the northern but the southern part of Illinois, not only in the Northern but the Southern states, and wherever the American flag waves over American soil, that then there must be something wrong in that creed. ("Good, good," and cheers.) So long as we live under a common constitution, so long as we live in a confederacy of sovereign and equal states, joined together as one for certain purposes, that any political creed is radically wrong which cannot be proclaimed in every state, and every section of that Union alike. I took up Mr. Lincoln's three propositions in my several speeches, analyzed them, and pointed out what I believed to be the radical errors contained in them. First, in regard to his doctrine that this government was in violation of the law of God which says, that a house divided against itself cannot stand, I repudiated it as a slander upon the immortal framers of our Constitution. I then said, have often repeated, and now again assert, that in my opinion this government can endure forever, ("good") divided into free and slave states as our fathers made it,—each state having the right to prohibit, abolish or sustain slavery just as it pleases. ("Good," "right," and cheers.) This government was made upon the great basis of the sovereignty of the states, the right of each state to regulate its own domestic institutions to suit itself, and that right was conferred with understanding and expectation that inasmuch as each locality had separate interests, each locality must have different and distinct local and domestic institutions, corresponding to its wants and interests. Our fathers knew when they made the government, that the laws and institutions which were well adapted to the green mountains of Vermont, were unsuited to the rice plantations of South Carolina. They knew then, as well as we know now, that the laws and institutions which would be well adapted to the beautiful prairies of Illinois would not be suited to the mining regions of California. They knew that in a Republic as broad as this, having such a variety of soil, climate and interest, there must necessarily be a corresponding variety of local laws—the policy and institutions of each state adapted to its condition and wants. For this reason this Union was established on the right of each state to do as it pleased on the question of slavery, and every other question; and the various states were not allowed to complain of, much less interfere, with the policy of their neighbors. ("That's good doctrine," "that's the doctrine," and cheers.)

Suppose the doctrine advocated by Mr. Lincoln and the Abolitionists of this day had prevailed when the Constitution was made, what would have been the result? Imagine for a moment that Mr. Lincoln had been a member of the convention that framed the Constitution of the United States, and that when its members were about to sign that wonderful document, he had arisen in that convention as he did at Springfield this summer, and addressing himself to the President, had said "a house divided against itself cannot stand; (laughter) this government divided into free and slave states cannot endure, they must all be free or all be slave, they must all be one thing or all the other, otherwise, it is a violation of the law of God, and cannot continue to exist;"—suppose Mr. Lincoln had convinced that body of sages, that that doctrine was sound, what would have been the result? Remember that the Union was then composed of thirteen states, twelve of which were slaveholding and one free. Do you think that the one free state would have outvoted the twelve slaveholding states, and thus have secured the abolition of slavery? ("No, no.") On the other hand, would not the twelve slaveholding states have outvoted the one free state, and thus have fastened slavery, by a constitutional provision, on every foot of the American Republic forever? You see that if this Abolition doctrine of Mr. Lincoln had prevailed when the government was made, it would have established slavery as a permanent institution, in all the states whether they wanted it or not, and the question for us to determine in Illinois now as one of the free states is, whether or not we are willing, having become the majority section, to enforce a doctrine on the minority, which we would have resisted with our heart's blood had it been attempted on us when we were in a minority. ("We never will," "good, good," and cheers.) How has the South lost her power as the majority section in this Union, and how have the free states gained it, except under the operation of that principle which declares the right of the people of each state and each territory to form and regulate their domestic institutions in their own way. It was under that principle that slavery was abolished in New Hampshire, Rhode Island, Connecticut, New York, New Jersey, and Pennsylvania; it was under that principle that one half of the slaveholding states became free; it was under that principle that the number of free states increased until from being one out of twelve states, we have grown to be the majority of states of the whole Union, with the power to control the House of Representatives and Senate, and the power, consequently, to elect a President by Northern votes without the aid of a Southern state. Having obtained this power under the operation of that great principle, are you now prepared to abandon the principle and declare that merely because we have the power you will wage a war against

THE LINCOLN-DOUGLAS DEBATES

the Southern states and their institutions until you force them to abolish slavery everywhere. ("No, never," and great applause.)

After having pressed these arguments home on Mr. Lincoln for seven weeks, publishing a number of my speeches, we met at Ottawa in joint discussion, and he then began to crawfish a little, and let himself down. (Immense applause.) I there propounded certain questions to him. Amongst others, I asked him whether he would vote for the admission of any more slave states in the event the people wanted them. He would not answer. (Applause and laughter.) I then told him that if he did not answer the question there I would renew it at Freeport, and would then trot him down into Egypt and again put it to him. (Cheers.) Well, at Freeport, knowing that the next joint discussion took place in Egypt, and being in dread of it, he did answer my question in regard to no more slave states in a mode which he hoped would be satisfactory to me, and accomplish the object he had in view. I will show you what his answer was. After saying that he was not pledged to the Republican doctrine of "no more slave states," he declared

I state to you freely, frankly, that I should be exceedingly sorry to ever be put in the position of having to pass upon that question. I should be exceedingly glad to know that there never would be another slave state admitted into this Union.

Here, permit me to remark, that I do not think the people will ever force him into a position against his will. (Great laughter and applause.) He went on to say:

But I must add in regard to this, that if slavery shall be kept out of the territory during the territorial existence of any given territory and then the people should, having a fair chance and clear field when they come to adopt a constitution, if they should do the extraordinary thing of adopting a slave constitution, uninfluenced by the actual presence of the institution among them, I see no alternative if we own the country, but we must admit it into the Union.

That answer Mr. Lincoln supposed would satisfy the Old Line Whigs, composed of Kentuckians and Virginias, down in the southern part of the state. Now, what does it amount to? I desired to know whether he would vote to allow Kansas to come into the Union with slavery or not as her people desired. He would not answer; but in a round about way said that if slavery should be kept out of a territory during the whole of its territorial existence, and then the people, when they adopted a state constitution, asked admission as a slave state, he supposed he would have to let the state come in. The case I put to him was an entirely different one. I desired to know whether he would vote to admit a state if Congress had not prohibited slavery in it during its territorial existence, as Congress never pretended to do under Clay's compromise measures of 1850. He would not answer, and I have not yet been able to get an answer from him. (Laughter, "he'll answer this time," "he's afraid to answer," etc.) I have asked him whether he would vote to admit Nebraska if her people asked to come in as a state with a constitution recognizing slavery, and he refused to answer. ("Put him through," "give it to him," and cheers.) I have put the question to him with reference to New Mexico, and he has not uttered a word in answer. I have enumerated the territories, one after another, putting the same question to him with reference to each, and he has not said, and will not say, whether, if elected to Congress, he will vote to admit any territory now in existence with such a constitution as her people may adopt. He invents a case which does not exist, and cannot exist under this government, and answers it; but he will not answer the question I put to him in connection with any of the territories now in existence. ("Hurrah for Douglas," "three cheers for Douglas.") The contract we entered into with Texas when she entered the Union obliges us to allow four states to be formed out of the old state, and admitted with or without slavery as the respective inhabitants of each may determine. I have asked Mr. Lincoln three times in our joint discussions whether he would vote to redeem that pledge, and he has never yet answered. He is as silent as the grave on the subject. (Laughter, "Lincoln must answer," "he will," &c.) He would rather answer as to a state of the case which will never arise than commit himself by telling what he would do in a case which would come up for his action soon after his election to Congress. ("He'll never have to act on any question," and laughter.) Why can he not say whether he is willing to allow the people of each state to have slavery or not as they please, and to come into the Union when they have the requisite population as a slave or a free State as they decide? I have no trouble in answering the question. I have said everywhere, and now repeat it to you, that if the people of Kansas want a slave state they have a right, under the Constitution of the United States, to form such a state, and I will let them come into the Union with slavery or without, as they determine. ("That's right," "good," "hurrah for Douglas all the time," and cheers.) If the people of any other territory desire slavery let them have it. If they do not want it let them prohibit it. It is their business not mine. ("That's the doctrine.") It is none of your business in Missouri whether Kansas shall adopt slavery or reject it. It is the business of her people and none of yours. The people of Kansas has as much right to decide that question for themselves as you have in Missouri to decide it for yourselves, or we in Illinois to decide it for ourselves. ("That's what we believe," "We stand by that," and cheers.)

And here I may repeat what I have said in every speech I have made in Illinois, that I fought the Lecompton constitution to its death, not because of the slavery clause in it, but because it was not the act and deed of the people of Kansas. I said then in Congress, and I say now, that if the people of Kansas want a slave state, they have a right to have it. If they wanted the Lecompton constitution, they had a right to have it. I was opposed to that constitution because I did not believe that it was the act and deed of the people, but on the contrary, the act of a small, pitiful minority acting in the name of the majority. When at last it was determined to send that constitution back to the people, and accordingly, in August last, the question of admission under it was submitted to a popular vote, the citizens rejected it by nearly ten to one, thus showing conclusively, that I was right when I said that the Lecompton constitution was not the act and deed of the people of Kansas, and did not embody their will. (Cheers.)

I hold that there is no power on earth, under our system of government, which has the right to force a constitution upon an unwilling people. ("That's so.") Suppose there had been a majority of ten to one in favor of slavery in Kansas, and suppose there had been an Abolition President, and an Abolition administration, and by some means the Abolitionists succeeded in forcing an Abolition constitution on those slaveholding people, would the people of the South have submitted to that act for one instant. ("No, no.") Well, if you of the South would not have submitted to it a day, how can you, as fair, honorable and honest men insist on putting a slave constitution on a people who desire a free state. ("That's so," and cheers.) Your safety and ours depend upon both of us acting in good faith, and living up to that great principle which asserts the right of every people to form and regulate their domestic institutions to suit themselves, subject only to the Constitution of the United States. ("That's the doctrine," and immense applause.)

Most of the men who denounced my course on the Lecompton question, objected to it not because I was not right, but because they thought it expedient at that time, for the sake of keeping the party together, to do wrong. (Cheers.) I never knew the Democratic party to violate any one of its principles out of policy or expediency, that it did not pay the debt with sorrow. There is no safety or success for our party unless we always do right, and trust the consequences to God and the people. I chose not to depart from principle for the sake of expediency in the Lecompton question, and I never intend to do it on that or any other question. (Good.)

But I am told that I would have been all right if I had only voted for the English Bill after Lecompton was killed. (Laughter and cheers.) You know a general pardon was granted to all political offenders on the Lecompton question, provided they would only vote for the English Bill. I did not accept the benefits of that pardon, for the reason that I had been right in the course I had pursued, and hence did not require any forgiveness. Let us see how the result has been worked out. English brought in his bill referring the Lecompton constitution back to the people, with the provision that if it was rejected Kansas should be kept out of the Union until she had the full ratio of population required for a member of Congress, thus in effect declaring that if the people of Kansas would only consent to come into the Union under the Lecompton constitution, and have a slave state when they did not want it, they should be admitted with a population of 35,000, but that if they were so obstinate as to insist upon having just such a constitution as they thought best, and to desire admission as a free state, then they should be kept out until they had 93,420 inhabitants. I then said, and I now repeat to you, that whenever Kansas has people enough for a slave state she has people enough for a free state. ("That's the doctrine all over," "Hurrah for Douglas.") I was and am willing to adopt the rule that no state shall ever come into the Union until she has the full ratio of population for a member of Congress, provided that rule is made uniform. I made that proposition in the Senate last winter, but a majority of the Senators would not agree to it; and I then said to them if you will not adopt the general rule I will not consent to make an exception of Kansas.

I hold that it is a violation of the fundamental principles of this government to throw the weight of federal power into the scale, either in favor of the free or the slave states. Equality among all the states of this Union is a fundamental principle in our political system. We have no more right to throw the weight of the federal government into the scale in favor of the slaveholding than the free states, and last of all should our friends in the South consent for a moment that Congress should withhold its powers either way when they know that there is a majority against them in both Houses of Congress.

Fellow citizens, how have the supporters of the English Bill stood up to their pledges not to admit Kansas until she obtained a population of 93,420 in the event she rejected the Lecompton constitution? How? The newspapers inform us that English himself, whilst conducting his canvass for re-election, and in order to secure it, pledged himself to his constituents that if returned he would disregard his own bill and vote to admit Kansas into the Union with such population as she might have when she made application. (Laughter and applause.) We are informed that every Democratic candidate for Congress in all the states where elections have recently been held, was pledged against the English Bill, with perhaps one or two exceptions. Now, if I had only done as these anti-Lecompton men who voted for the English Bill in Congress, pledging themselves to refuse to admit Kansas if she refused to become a slave state until she had a population of 93,420, and then returned to their people, forfeited their pledge, and made a new pledge to admit Kansas at any time she applied, without regard to population, I would have had no trouble. You saw the whole power and patronage of the federal government wielded in Indiana, Ohio, and Pennsylvania to re-elect anti-Lecompton men to Congress who voted against Lecompton, then voted for the English Bill, and then denounced the English Bill, and pledged themselves to their people to disregard it. ("Good.") My sin consists in not having given a pledge, and then in not having afterwards forfeited it. For that reason, in this state, every postmaster, every route agent, every collector of the ports, and every federal office holder, forfeits his head the moment he expresses a preference for the Democratic candidates against Lincoln and his Abolition associates. ("That's so," and cheers.) A Democratic administration which we helped to bring into power, deems it consistent with its fidelity to principle and its regard to duty, to wield its power in this state in behalf of the Republican Abolition candidates in every county and every congressional district against the Democratic party. All I have to say in reference to the matter is, that if that administration have not regard enough for principle, if they are not sufficiently attached to the creed of the Democratic party to bury forever their personal hostilities in order to succeed in carrying out our glorious principles, I have. ("Good, good," and cheers.) I have no personal difficulties with Mr. Buchanan or his cabinet. He chose to make certain recommendations to Congress as he had a right to do on the Lecompton question. I could not vote in favor of them. I had as much right to judge for myself how I should vote as he had how he should recommend. He undertook to say to me, if you do not vote as I tell you, I will take off the heads of your friends. (Laughter.) I replied to him, "you did not elect me, I represent Illinois and I am accountable to Illinois, as my constituency, and to God, but not to the

President or to any other power on earth." ("Good, good," and vociferous applause.)

And now this warfare is made on me because I would not surrender my connections of duty, because I would not abandon my constituency, and receive the orders of the executive authorities how I should vote in the Senate of the United States. ("Never do it," "three cheers," &c.) I hold that an attempt to control the Senate on the part of the executive is subversive of the principles of our constitution. ("That's right.") The executive department is independent of the Senate, and the Senate is independent of the President. In matters of legislation the President has a veto on the action of the Senate, and in appointments and treaties the Senate has a veto on the President. He has no more right to tell me how I shall vote on his appointments than I have to tell him whether he shall veto or approve a bill that the Senate has passed. Whenever you recognize the right of the executive to say to a Senator, "do this, or I will take off the heads of your friends," you convert this government from a republic into a despotism. ("Hear, hear," and cheers.) Whenever you recognize the right of a President to say to a member of Congress, "vote as I tell you, or I will bring a power to bear against you at home which will crush you," you destroy the independence of the representative, and convert him into a tool of executive power. ("That's so," and applause.) I resisted this invasion of the constitutional rights of a Senator, and I intend to resist it as long as I have a voice to speak, or a vote to give. Yet, Mr. Buchanan cannot provoke me to abandon one iota of Democratic principles out of revenge or hostility to his course. ("Good, good, three cheers for Douglas.") I stand by the platform of the Democratic party, and by its organization, and support its nominees. If there are any who choose to bolt, the fact only shows that they are not as good Democrats as I am. ("That's so," "good," and applause.)

My friends, there never was a time when it was as important for the Democratic party, for all national men, to rally and stand together as it is to-day. We find all sectional men giving up past differences and continuing the one question of slavery, and when we find sectional men thus uniting, we should unite to resist them and their treasonable designs. Such was the case in 1850, when Clay left the quiet and peace of his home, and again entered upon public life to quell agitation and restore peace to a distracted Union. Then we Democrats, with Cass at our head, welcomed Henry Clay, whom the whole nation regarded as having been preserved by God for the times. He became our leader in that great fight, and we rallied around him the same as the Whigs rallied around Old Hickory in

1832, to put down nullification. (Cheers.) Thus you see that whilst Whigs and Democrats fought fearlessly in old times about banks, the tariff, distribution, the specie circular, and the sub-treasury, all united as a band of brothers when the peace, harmony, or integrity of the Union was imperiled. (Tremendous applause.) It was so in 1850, when Abolitionism had even so far divided this country, North and South, as to endanger the peace of the Union; Whigs and Democrats united in establishing the compromise measures of that year, and restoring tranquillity and good feeling. These measures passed on the joint action of the two parties. They rested on the great principle that the people of each state and each territory should be left perfectly free to form and regulate their domestic institutions to suit themselves. You Whigs and we Democrats justified them in that principle. In 1854, when it became necessary to organize the territories of Kansas and Nebraska, I brought forward the bill on the same principle. In the Kansas-Nebraska Bill you find it declared to be the true intent and meaning of the act not to legislate slavery into any state or territory, nor to exclude it therefrom, but to leave the people thereof perfectly free to form and regulate their domestic institutions in their own way. ("That's so," and cheers.) I stand on that same platform in 1858 that I did in 1850, 1854, and 1856. The Washington *Union*, pretending to be the organ of the administration, in the number of the 5th of this month, devotes three columns and a half to establish these propositions: First, that Douglas, in his Freeport speech, held the same doctrine that he did in his Nebraska Bill in 1854; second, that in 1854 Douglas justified the Nebraska Bill upon the ground that it was based upon the same principle as Clay's compromise measures of 1850. The *Union* thus proved that Douglas was the same in 1858 that he was in 1856, 1854, and 1850, and consequently argued that he was never a Democrat. (Great laughter.) Is it not funny that I was never a Democrat? (Renewed laughter.) There is no pretence that I have changed a hair's breadth. The *Union* proves by my speeches that I explained the compromise measures of 1850 just as I do now, and that I explained the Kansas and Nebraska Bill in 1854 just as I did in my Freeport speech, and yet says that I am not a Democrat, and cannot be trusted, because I have not changed during the whole of that time. It has occurred to me that in 1854 the author of the Kansas and Nebraska Bill was considered a pretty good Democrat. (Cheers.) It has occurred to me that in 1856, when I was exerting every nerve and every energy for James Buchanan, standing on the same platform then that I do now, that I was a pretty good Democrat. (Renewed applause.) They now tell me that I am not a Democrat, because I assert that the people of a territory, as well as those of a state, have the right to decide for themselves whether slavery can or can not exist in such territory. Let me read what James Buchanan said on that point when he accepted the Democratic nomination for the Presidency in 1856. In his letter of acceptance, he used the following language:

The recent legislation of Congress respecting domestic slavery, derived as it has been from the original and pure fountain of legitimate political power, the will of the majority, promises ere long to allay the dangerous excitement. This legislation is founded upon principles as ancient as free government itself, and in accordance with them has simply declared that the people of a territory like those of a state, shall decide for themselves WHETHER SLAVERY SHALL OR SHALL NOT EXIST WITHIN THEIR LIMITS.

Dr. Hope will there find my answer to the question he propounded to me before I commenced speaking. (Vociferous shouts of applause.) Of course no man will consider it an answer, who is outside of the Democratic organization, bolts Democratic nominations, and indirectly aids to put Abolitionists into power over Democrats. But whether Dr. Hope considers it an answer or not, every fair minded man will see that James Buchanan has answered the question, and has asserted that the people of a territory, like those of a state, shall decide for themselves whether slavery shall or shall not exist within their limits. I answer specifically if you want a further answer, and say that while under the decision of the Supreme Court, as recorded in the opinion of Chief Justice Taney, slaves are property like all other property and can be carried into territory of the United States the same as any other description of property, yet when you get them there they are subject to the local law of the territory just like all other property. You will find in a recent speech delivered by that able and eloquent statesman, Hon. Jefferson Davis, at Bangor, Maine, that he took the same view of this subject that I did in my Freeport speech. He there said:

If the inhabitants of any territory should refuse to enact such laws and police regulations as would give security to their property or to his, it would be rendered more or less valueless in proportion to the difficulties of holding it without such protection. In the case of property in the labor of man, or what is usually called slave property, the insecurity would be so great that the owner could not ordinarily retain it. Therefore, though the right would remain, the remedy being withheld, it would follow that the owner would be practically debarred, by the circumstances of the case, from taking slave property into a territory where the sense of the inhabitants was opposed to its introduction. So much for the oft repeated fallacy of forcing slavery upon any community.

You will also find that the distinguished Speaker of the present House of Representatives, Hon. Jas. L. Orr, construed the Kansas and Nebraska Bill in this same way in 1856, and also that great intellect of the South, Alex. H. Stephens, put the same construction upon it in Congress that I did in my Freeport speech. The whole South are rallying to the support of the doctrine that if the people of a territory want slavery they have a right to have it, and if they do not want it that no power on earth can force it upon them. I hold that there is no principle on earth more sacred to all the friends of freedom than that which says that no institution, no law, no constitution, should be forced on an unwilling people contrary to their wishes; and I assert that the Kansas and Nebraska Bill contains that principle. It is the great principle contained in that bill. It is the principle on which James Buchanan was made President. Without that principle he never would have been made President of the United States. I will never violate or abandon that doctrine if I have to stand alone. ("Hurrah for Douglas.") I have resisted the blandishments and threats of power on the one side, and seduction on the other, and have stood immovably for that principle, fighting for it when assailed by Northern mobs, or threatened by Southern hostility. ("That's the truth," and cheers.) I have defended it against the North and the South, and I will defend it against whoever assails it, and I will follow it wherever its logical conclusions lead me. ("So will we all," "hurrah for Douglas.") I say to you that there is but one hope, one safety for this country, and that is to stand immovably by that principle which declares the right of each state and each territory to decide these questions for themselves. ("Hear him, hear him.") This government was founded on that principle, and must be administered in the same sense in which it was founded.

But the Abolition party really think that under the Declaration of Independence the negro is equal to the white man, and that negro equality is an inalienable right conferred by the Almighty, and hence, that all human laws in violation of it are null and void. With such men it is no use for me to argue. I hold that the signers of the Declaration of Independence had no reference to negroes at all when they declared all men to be created equal. They did not mean negro, nor the savage Indians, nor the Fejee Islanders, nor any other barbarous race. They were speaking of white men. ("It's so," "it's so," and cheers.) They alluded to men of European birth and European descent—to white men, and to none others, when they declared that doctrine. ("That's the truth.") I hold that this government was established on the white basis. It was established by white men for the benefit of white men and their posterity forever, and should be administered by white men, and none others.

But it does not follow, by any means, that merely because the negro is not a citizen, and merely because he is not our equal, that, therefore, he should be a slave. On the contrary, it does follow, that we ought to extend to the negro race, and to all other dependent races all the rights, all the privileges, and all the immunities which they can exercise consistently with the safety of society. Humanity requires that we should give them all these privileges; Christianity commands that we should extend those privileges to them. The question then arises what are those privileges, and what is the nature and extent of them. My answer is that that is a question which each state must answer for itself. We in Illinois have decided it for ourselves. We tried slavery, kept it up for twelve years, and finding that it was not profitable we abolished it for that reason, and became a free state. We adopted in its stead the policy that a negro in this state shall not be a slave and shall not be a citizen. We have a right to adopt that policy. For my part I think it is a wise and sound policy for us. You in Missouri must judge for yourselves whether it is a wise policy for you. If you choose to follow our example, very good; if you reject it, still well, it is your business, not ours. So with Kentucky. Let Kentucky adopt a policy to suit herself. If we do not like it we will keep away from it, and if she does not like ours let her stay at home, mind her own business and let us alone. If the people of all the states will act on that great principle, and each state mind its own business, attend to its own affairs, take care of its own negroes and not meddle with its neighbors, then there will be peace between the North and the South, the East and the West, throughout the whole Union. (Cheers.) Why can we not thus have peace? Why should we thus allow a sectional party to agitate this country, to array the North against the South, and convert us into enemies instead of friends, merely that a few ambitious men may ride into power on a sectional hobby? How long is it since these ambitious Northern men wished for a sectional organization? Did any one of them dream of a sectional party as long as the North was the weaker section and the South the stronger? Then all were opposed to sectional parties; but the moment the North obtained the majority in the House and Senate by the admission of California, and could elect a President without the aid of Southern votes, that moment ambitious Northern men formed a scheme to excite the North against the South, and make the people be governed in their votes by geographical lines, thinking that the North, being the stronger section, would outvote the South, and consequently they, the leaders, would ride into office on a sectional hobby. I am told that my hour is out. It was very short.

Lincoln's Reply

Ladies and Gentlemen:

I have been somewhat, in my own mind, complimented by a large portion of Judge Douglas' speech—I mean that portion which he devotes to the controversy between himself and the present administration. [Cheers and laughter.] This is the seventh time Judge Douglas and myself have met in these joint discussions, and he has been gradually improving in regard to his war with the administration. [Laughter, "That's so."] At Quincy, day before yesterday, he was a little more severe upon the administration than I had heard him upon any former occasion, and I took pains to compliment him for it. I then told him to "Give it to them with all the power he had;" and as some of them were present I told them I would be very much obliged if they would *give it to him* in about the same way. [Uproarious laughter and cheers.] I take it he has now vastly improved upon the attack he made then upon the administration. I flatter myself he has really taken my advice on this subject. All I can say now is to recommend to him and to them what I then commended—to prosecute the war against one another in the most vigorous manner. I say to them again—"Go it, husband!—Go it, bear!" [Great laughter.]

There is one other thing I will mention before I leave this branch of the discussion—although I do not consider it much of my business, any way. I refer to that part of the Judge's remarks where he undertakes to involve Mr. Buchanan in an inconsistency. He reads something from Mr. Buchanan, from which he undertakes to involve him in an inconsistency; and he gets something of a cheer for having done so. I would only remind the Judge that while he is very valiantly fighting for the Nebraska Bill and the repeal of the Missouri Compromise, it has been but a little while since he was the *valiant advocate* of the Missouri Compromise. [Cheers.] I want to know if Buchanan has not as much right to be inconsistent as Douglas has? [Loud applause and laughter; "Good, good!" "Hurrah for Lincoln!"] Has Douglas the *exclusive right,* in this country, of being *on all sides of all questions?* Is nobody allowed that high privilege but himself? Is he to have an entire *monopoly* on that subject? [Great laughter.]

So far as Judge Douglas addressed his speech to me, or so far as it was about me, it is my business to pay some attention to it. I have heard the Judge state two or three times what he has stated to-day—that in a speech which I made at Springfield, Illinois, I had in a very especial manner, complained that the Supreme Court in the Dred Scott case had decided that a negro could never be a citizen of the United States. I have omitted by some accident heretofore to analyze this statement, and it is required of me to notice it now. In point of fact it is *untrue*. I never have complained *especially* of the Dred Scott decision because it held that a negro could not be a citizen, and the Judge is always wrong when he says I ever did so complain of it. I have the speech here, and I will thank him or any of his friends to show where I said that a negro should be a citizen, and complained especially of the Dred Scott decision because it declared he could not be one. I have done no such thing, and Judge Douglas' so persistently insisting that I have done so, has strongly impressed me with the belief of a pre-determination on his part to misrepresent me. He could not get his foundation for insisting that I was in favor of this negro equality anywhere else as well as he could by assuming that untrue proposition. Let me tell this audience what is true in regard to that matter; and the means by which they may correct me if I do not tell them truly is by a recurrence to the speech itself. I spoke of the Dred Scott decision in my Springfield speech, and I was then endeavoring to prove that the Dred Scott decision was a portion of a system or scheme to make slavery national in this country. I pointed out what things had been decided by the court. I mentioned as a fact that they had decided that a negro could not be a citizen—that they had done so, as I supposed, to deprive the negro, under all circumstances, of the remotest possibility of every becoming a citizen and claiming the rights of a citizen of the United States under a certain clause of the Constitution. I stated that, without making any complaint of it at all. I then went on and stated the other points decided in the case, namely: that the bringing of a negro into the state of Illinois and holding him in slavery for two years here was a matter in regard to which they would not decide whether it made him free or not; that they decided the further point that taking him into a United States territory where slavery was prohibited by act of Congress, did not make him free because that act of Congress as they held was unconstitutional. I mentioned these three things as making up the points decided in that case. I mentioned them in a lump taken in connection with the introduction of the Nebraska Bill, and the amendment of Chase, offered at the time, declaratory of the right of the people of the territories to *exclude slavery*, which was voted down by the friends of the bill. I mentioned all these things together, as evidence tending to prove a combination and conspiracy to make the institution of slavery national. In that connection and in that way I mentioned the decision on the point that a negro could not be a citizen, and in no other connection.

Out of this, Judge Douglas builds up his beautiful fabrication—of my purpose to introduce a perfect, social, and political equality between the white and black races. His assertion that I made an "especial objection" (that is his exact language) to the decision on this account, is untrue in point of fact.

Now, while I am upon this subject, and as Henry Clay has been alluded to, I desire to place myself, in connection with Mr. Clay, as nearly right before this people as may be. I am quite aware what the Judge's object is here by all these allusions. He knows that we are before an audience, having strong sympathies southward by relationship, place of birth, and so on. He desires to place me in an extremely Abolition attitude. He read upon a former occasion, and alludes without reading to-day, to a portion of a speech which I delivered in Chicago. In his quotations from that speech as he has made them upon former occasions, the extracts were taken in such a way, as I suppose, brings them within the definition of what is called *garbling*—taking portions of a speech which, when taken by themselves, do not present the entire sense of the speaker as expressed at the time. I propose, therefore, out of that same speech, to show how one portion of it which he skipped over (taking an extract before and an extract after) will give a different idea and the true idea I intended to convey. It will take me some little time to read it, but I believe I will occupy the time in that way.

You have heard him frequently allude to my controversy with him in regard to the Declaration of Independence. I confess that I have had a struggle with Judge Douglas on that matter, and I will try briefly to place myself right in regard to it on this occasion. I said—and it is between the extracts Judge Douglas has taken from this speech, and put in his published speeches—:

It may be argued that there are certain conditions that make necessities and impose them upon us, and to the extent that a necessity is imposed upon a man he must submit to it. I think that was the condition in which we found ourselves when we established this government. We had slaves among us, we could not get our constitution unless we permitted them to remain in slavery, we could not secure the good we did secure if we grasped for more; and having by necessity submitted to that much, it does not destroy the principle that is the charter of our liberties. Let that charter remain as our standard.

Now I have upon all occasions declared as strongly as Judge Douglas against the disposition to interfere with the existing institution of slavery. You hear me read it from the same speech from which he takes garbled extracts for the purpose of proving upon me a disposition to interfere with the institution of slavery, and establish a perfect social and political equality between negroes and white people.

Allow me while upon this subject briefly to present one other extract from a speech of mine, more than a year ago, at Springfield, in discussing this very same question, soon after Judge Douglas took his ground that negroes were not included in the Declaration of Independence:

I think the authors of that notable instrument intended to include *all* men, but they did not mean to declare all men equal *in all respects*. They did not mean to say all men were equal in color, size, intellect, moral development or social capacity. They defined with tolerable distinctness in what they did consider all men created equal—equal in certain inalienable rights, among which are life, liberty and the pursuit of happiness. This they said, and this they meant. They did not mean to assert the obvious untruth, that all were then actually enjoying that equality, nor yet, that they were about to confer it immediately upon them. In fact they had no power to confer such a boon. They meant simply to declare the *right* so that the *enforcement* of it might follow as fast as circumstances should permit.

They meant to set up a standard maxim for free society which should be familiar to all: constantly looked to, constantly labored for, and even though never perfectly attained, constantly approximated and thereby constantly spreading and deepening its influence and augmenting the happiness and value of life to all people, of all colors, everywhere.

There again are the sentiments I have expressed in regard to the Declaration of Independence upon a former occasion—sentiments which have been put in print and read wherever anybody cared to know what so humble an individual as myself chose to say in regard to it.

At Galesburg the other day, I said in answer to Judge Douglas, that three years ago there never had been a man, so far as I knew or believed, in the whole world, who had said that the Declaration of Independence did not include negroes in the term "all men." I re-assert it to-day. I assert that Judge Douglas and all his friends may search the whole records of the country, and it will be a matter of great astonishment to me if they shall be able to find that one human being three years ago had ever uttered the astounding sentiment that the term "all men" in the Declaration did not include the negro. Do not let me be misunderstood. I know that more than three years ago there were men who, finding this assertion constantly in the way of their schemes to bring about the ascendancy and perpetuation of slavery, *denied the truth of it*. I know that Mr. Calhoun and all the politicians of his school denied the truth of the Declaration. I know that it ran along in the mouths of some Southern men for a period of years, ending at last in that shameful though rather forcible declaration of Pettit of Indiana, upon the floor of the United States Senate, that the Declaration of Independence was in that respect "a self-evident lie," rather than a self-evident truth. But I say, with a perfect knowledge of all this hawking at the Declaration without directly attacking it, that three years ago there never had lived a man who had ventured to assail it in the sneaking way of pretending to believe it and then asserting it did not include the negro. [Cheers.] I believe the first man who ever said it was Chief Justice Taney in the Dred Scott case, and the next to him was our friend Stephen A. Douglas. [Cheers and laughter.] And now it has become the catch-word of the entire party. I would like to call upon his friends everywhere to consider how they have come in so short a time to view this matter in a way so entirely different from their former belief? to ask whether they are not being borne along by an irresistible current—whither, they know not? [Great applause.]

In answer to my proposition at Galesburg last week, I see that some man in Chicago has got up a letter addressed to the Chicago *Times,* to show as he professes that somebody *had* said so before; and he signs himself "An Old Line Whig," if I remember correctly. In the first place I would say he *was not* an Old Line Whig. I am somewhat acquainted with Old Line Whigs. I was with the Old Line Whigs from the origin to the end of that party; I became pretty well acquainted with them, and I know they always had some sense, whatever else you could ascribe to them. [Great laughter.] I know there never was one who had not more sense than to try to show by the evidence he produces that some man had, prior to the time I named, said that negroes were not included in the term "all men" in the Declaration of Independence. What is the evidence he produces? I will bring forward *his* evidence and let you see what *he* offers by way of showing that somebody more than three years ago had said negroes were not included in the Declaration. He brings forward part of a speech from Henry Clay—*the* part of *the* speech of Henry Clay which I used to bring forward to prove precisely the contrary. [Laughter.] I guess we are surrounded to some extent to-day, by the old friends of Mr. Clay, and they will be glad to hear anything from that authority. While he was in Indiana a man presented him a petition to liberate his negroes, and he, (Mr. Clay) made a speech in answer to it, which I suppose he carefully wrote out himself and caused to be published. I have before me an extract from that speech which constitutes the evidence this pretended "Old Line Whig" at Chicago brought forward to show that Mr. Clay didn't suppose the negro was included in the Declaration of Independence. Hear what Mr. Clay said:

And what is the foundation of this appeal to me in Indiana, to liberate the slaves under my care in Kentucky? It is a general declaration in the act announcing to the world the independence of the thirteen American colonies, that all men are created equal. Now, as an abstract principle, *there is no doubt of the truth of that declaration;* and it is desirable *in the original construction of society, and in organized societies,* to keep it in view as a great fundamental principle. But, then, I apprehend that in no society that ever did exist, or ever shall be formed, was or can the equality asserted among the members of the human race be practically enforced and carried out. There are portions, large portions, women, minors, insane, culprits, transient sojourners, that will always probably remain subject to the government of another portion of the community.

That declaration whatever may be the extent of its import, was made by the delegations of the thirteen states. In most of them slavery existed, and had long existed, and was established by law. It was introduced and forced upon the colonies by the paramount law of England. Do you believe, that in making that Declaration the states that concurred in it intended that it should be tortured into a virtual emancipation of all the slaves within their respective limits? Would Virginia and other Southern states have ever united in a declaration which was to be interpreted into an abolition of slavery among them? Did any one of the thirteen colonies entertain such a design or expectation? To impute such a secret and unavowed purpose would be to charge a political fraud upon the noblest band of patriots that ever assembled in council; a fraud upon the confederacy of the Revolution; a fraud upon the union of those states whose constitution not only recognized the lawfulness of slavery, but permitted the importation of slaves from Africa until the year 1808.

This is the entire quotation brought forward to prove that somebody previous to three years ago had said the negro was not included in the term "all men" in the Declaration. How does it do so? In what way has it a tendency to prove that? Mr. Clay says *it is true as an abstract principle* that all men are created equal, but that we cannot practically apply it in all cases. He illustrates this by bringing forward the cases of females, minors and insane persons with whom it cannot be enforced; but he says it is true as an abstract principle in the organization of society as well as in organized society, and it should be kept in view as a fundamental principle. Let me read a few words more before I add some comments of my own. Mr. Clay says a little further on:

I desire no concealment of my opinions in regard to the institution of slavery. I look upon it as a great evil; and deeply lament that we have derived it from the parental government; and from our ancestors. But here they are and the question is, how can they be best dealt with? If a state of nature existed and we were about to lay the foundations of society, *no man would be more strongly opposed that I should be, to incorporating the institution of slavery among its elements.*

Now here in this same book—in this same speech—is this same extract brought forward to prove that Mr. Clay held that the negro was not included in the Declaration of Independence—no such statement on his part, but the declaration *that it is a great fundamental truth,* which should be constantly kept in view in the organization of society and in societies already organized. But if I say a word about it—if I attempt, as Mr. Clay said all good men ought to do, to keep it in view—if, in this "organized society," I ask to have the public eye turned upon it—if I ask, in relation to the organization of new territories that the public eye should be turned upon it—forthwith I am villified as you hear me to-day. What have I done, that I have not the license of Henry Clay's illustrious example here in doing? Have I done aught that I have not his authority for, while maintaining that in organizing new territories and societies this fundamental principle should be regarded, and in organized society holding it up to the public view and recognizing what *he* recognized as the great principle of free government? [Great applause, and cries of "Hurrah for Lincoln."]

And when this new principle—this new proposition that no human being ever thought of three years ago,—is brought forward, *I combat* it as having an evil tendency, if not an evil design; I combat it as having a tendency to dehumanize the negro—to take away from him the right of ever striving to be a man. I combat it as being one of the thousand things constantly done in these days to prepare the public mind to make property, and nothing but property of the *negro in all the states of this Union.* [Tremendous applause. "Hurrah for Lincoln." "Hurrah for Trumbull."]

But there is a point that I wish before leaving this part of the discussion to ask attention to. I have read, and I repeat the words of Henry Clay:

I desire no concealment of my opinions in regard to the institution of slavery. I look upon it as a great evil and deeply lament that we have derived it from the parental government, and from our ancestors. I wish every slave in the United States was in the country of his ancestors. But here they are; the question is how they can best be dealt with? If a state of nature existed and we were about to lay the foundation of society, no man would be more strongly opposed than I should be to incorporate the institution of slavery among its elements.

The principle upon which I have insisted in this canvass, is in relation to laying the foundations of new societies. I have never sought to apply these principles to the old states for the purpose of abolishing slavery in those states. It is nothing but a miserable perversion of what I *have* said, to assume that I have declared Missouri, or any other slave state shall emancipate her slaves. I have proposed no such thing. But when Mr. Clay says that in laying the foundations of societies in our territories where it does not exist he would be opposed to the introduction of slavery as an element, I insist that we have *his warrant*—his license for insisting upon the exclusion of that element, which he declared in such strong and emphatic language *was most hateful to him*. [Loud applause.]

Judge Douglas has again referred to a Springfield speech in which I said "a house divided against itself cannot stand." The Judge has so often made the entire quotation from that speech that I can make it from memory. I used this language:

We are now far into the fifth year since a policy was initiated with the avowed object and confident promise of putting an end to the slavery agitation. Under the operation of this policy, that agitation has not only not ceased but has constantly augmented. In my opinion it will not cease until a crisis shall have been reached and passed. "A house divided against itself cannot stand." I believe this government cannot endure permanently half slave and half free. I do not expect the house to fall—but I do expect it will cease to be divided. It will become all one thing, or all the other. Either the opponents of slavery will arrest the further spread of it, and place it where the public mind shall rest in the belief that it is in the course of ultimate extinction, or its adocates will push it forward till it shall become alike lawful in all the states—old as well as new, North as well as South.

That extract and the sentiments expressed in it, have been extremely offensive to Judge Douglas. He has warred upon them as Satan does upon the Bible. [Laughter.] His perversions upon it are endless. Here now are my views upon it in brief.

I said we were now far into the fifth year since a policy was initiated with the avowed object and confident promise of putting an end to the slavery agitation. Is it not so? When that Nebraska Bill was brought forward four years ago last January, was it not for the "avowed object" of putting an end to the slavery agitation? We were to have no more agitation in Congress; it was all to be banished to the territories. By the way, I will remark here that, as Judge Douglas is very fond of complimenting Mr. Crittenden in these days, Mr. Crittenden has said there was a falsehood in that whole business, for there was *no slavery agitation at that time to allay*. We were for a little while *quiet* on the troublesome thing and that very allaying plaster of Judge Douglas', stirred it up again. [Applause and laughter.] But was it not understood or intimated with the "confident promise" of putting an end to the slavery agitation. Surely it was. In every speech you heard Judge Douglas make, until he got into this "imbroglio," as they call it, with the administration about the Lecompton constitution, every speech on that Nebraska Bill was full of his felicitations that we were *just at the end* of the slavery agitation. The last tip of the last joint of the old serpent's tail was just drawing out of view. [Cheers and laughter.] But has it proved so? I have asserted that under that policy that agitation "has not only not ceased, but has constantly augmented." When was there ever a greater agitation in Congress than last winter? When was it as great in the country as to-day?

There was a collateral object in the introduction of that Nebraska policy which was to clothe the people of the territories with a superior degree of self-government, beyond what they had ever had before. The first object and the main one of conferring upon the people a higher degree of "self government," is a question of fact to be determined by you in answer to a single question. Have you ever heard or known of a people any where on earth who had as little to do, as, in the first instance of its use, the people of Kansas had with this same right of "self-government"? [Loud applause.] In its main policy, and in its collateral object, *it has been nothing but a living, creeping lie from the time of its introduction, till today.* [Loud cheers.]

I have intimated that I thought the agitation would not cease until a crisis should have been reached and passed. I have stated in what way I thought it would be reached and passed. I have said that it might go one way or the other. We might, by arresting the further spread of it and placing it where the fathers originally placed it, put it where the public mind should rest in the belief that it was in the course of ultimate extinction. Thus the agitation may cease. It may be pushed forward until it shall become alike lawful in all the states, old as well as new, North as well as South. I have said, and I repeat, my wish is that the further spread of it may be arrested, and that it may be placed where the public mind shall rest in the belief that it is in the course of ultimate extinction. [Great applause.] I have expressed that as my wish. I entertain the opinion upon evidence sufficient to my mind, that the fathers of this government placed that institution where the public mind *did* rest in the belief that it was in the course of ultimate extinction. Let me ask why they made provision that the source of slavery—the African slave trade—should be cut off at the end of twenty years? Why did they make provision that in all the new territory we owned at that time slavery should be forever inhibited? Why stop its spread in one direction and cut off its source in another, if they did not look to its being placed in the course of ultimate extinction?

Again; the institution of slavery is only mentioned in the Constitution of the United States two or three times, and in neither of these cases does the word "slavery" or "negro race" occur; but covert language is used each time, and for a purpose full of significance. What is the language in regard to the prohibition of the African slave trade? It runs in about this way: "The migration or importation of such persons as any of the states now existing shall think proper to admit, shall not be prohibited by the Congress prior to the year one thousand eight hundred and eight."

The next allusion in the Constitution to the question of slavery and the black race, is on the subject of the basis of representation, and there the language used is, "Representatives and direct taxes shall be apportioned among the several states which may be included within this Union, according to their respective numbers, which shall be determined by adding to the whole number of free persons, including those bound to service for a term of years, and excluding Indians not taxed—three-fifths of all other persons."

It says "persons," not slaves, not negroes; but this "three-fifths" can be applied to no other class among us than the negroes.

Lastly, in the provision for the reclamation of fugitive slaves it is said: "No person held to service or labor in one state under the laws thereof escaping into another, shall in consequence of any law or regulation therein, be discharged from such service or labor, but shall be delivered up, on claim of the party to whom such service or labor may be due." There again there is no mention of the word "negro" or of slavery. In all three of these places, being the only allusions to slavery in the instrument, covert language is used. Language is used not suggesting that slavery existed or that the black race were among us. And I understand the contemporaneous history of those times to be that covert language was used with a purpose, and that purpose was that in our Constitution, which it was hoped and is still hoped will endure forever—when it should be read by intelligent and patriotic men, after the institution of slavery had passed from among us—there should be nothing on the face of the great charter of liberty suggesting that such a thing as negro slavery had ever existed among us. [Enthusiastic applause.] This is part of the evidence that the fathers of the government expected and intended the institution of slavery to come to an end. They expected and intended that it should be in the course of ultimate extinction. And when I say that I desire to see the further spread of it arrested I only say I desire to see that done which the fathers have first done. When I say I desire to see it placed where the public mind will rest in the belief that it is in the course of ultimate extinction, I only say I desire to see it placed where they placed it. It is not true that our fathers, as Judge Douglas assumes, made this government part slave and part free. Understand the sense in which he puts it. He assumes that slavery is a rightful thing within itself,—was introduced by the framers of the Constitution. The exact truth is, that they found the institution existing among us, and they left it as they found it. But in making the government they left this institution with many clear marks of disapprobation upon it. They found slavery among them and they left it among them because of the difficulty—the absolute impossibility of its immediate removal. And when Judge Douglas asks me why we cannot let it remain part slave and part free as the fathers of the government made [it], he asks a question based upon an assumption which is itself a falsehood; and I turn upon him and ask him the question, when the policy that the fathers of the government had adopted in relation to this element among us was the best policy in the world—the only wise policy—the only policy that we can ever safely continue upon—that will ever give us peace unless this dangerous element masters us all and becomes a national institution—*I turn upon him and ask him why he could not let it alone?* [Great and prolonged cheering.] I turn and ask him why he was driven to the necessity of introducing a *new policy* in regard to it? He has himself said he introduced a new policy. He said so in his speech on the 22d of March of the present year, 1858. I ask him why he could not let it remain where our fathers placed it? I ask too of Judge Douglas and his friends why we shall not again place this institution upon the basis on which the fathers left it? I ask you when he infers that I am in favor of setting the free and slave states at war, when the institution was placed in that attitude by those who made the Constitution, *did they make any war?* ["No;" "no;" and cheers.] If we had no war out of it when thus placed, wherein is the ground of belief that we shall have war out of it if we return to that policy? Have we had any peace upon this matter springing from any other basis? ["No, no."] I maintain that we have not. I have proposed nothing more than a return to the policy of the fathers.

I confess, when I propose a certain measure of policy, it is not enough for me that I do not intend anything evil in the result, but it is incumbent on me to show that it has not a *tendency* to that result. I have met Judge Douglas in that point of view. I have not only made the declaration that I do not *mean* to produce a conflict between the states, but I have tried to show by fair reasoning, and I think I have shown to the minds of fair men, that I propose nothing but what has a most peaceful tendency. The quotation that I happened to make in that Springfield speech, that "a house divided against itself cannot stand," and which has proved so offensive to the Judge, was part and parcel of the same thing. He tries to show

[386]

that variety in the domestic institutions of the different states is necessary and indispensable. I do not dispute it. I have no controversy with Judge Douglas about that. I shall very readily agree with him that it would be foolish for us to insist upon having a cranberry law here, in Illinois, where we have no cranberries, because they have a cranberry law in Indiana, where they have cranberries. [Laughter, "good, good."] I should insist that it would be exceedingly wrong in us to deny to Virginia the right to enact oyster laws where they have oysters, because we want no such laws here. [Renewed laughter.] I understand, I hope, quite as well as Judge Douglas or anybody else, that the variety in the soil and climate and face of the country, and consequent variety in the industrial pursuits and productions of a country, require systems of law conforming to this variety in the natural features of the country. I understand quite as well as Judge Douglas, that if we here raise a barrel of flour more than we want, and the Louisianians raise a barrel of sugar more than they want, it is of mutual advantage to exchange. That produces commerce, brings us together, and makes us better friends. We like one another the more for it. And I understand as well as Judge Douglas, or anybody else, that these mutual accommodations are the cements which bind together the different parts of this Union—that instead of being a thing to "divide the house"—figuratively expressing the Union,—they tend to sustain it; they are the props of the house tending always to hold it up.

But when I have admitted all this, I ask if there is any parallel between these things and this institution of slavery? I do not see that there is any parallel at all between them. Consider it. When have we had any difficulty or quarrel amongst ourselves about the cranberry laws of Indiana, or the oyster laws of Virginia, or the pine lumber laws of Maine, or the fact that Louisiana produces sugar, and Illinois flour? When have we had any quarrels over these things? When have we had perfect peace in regard to this thing which I say is an element of discord in this Union? We have sometimes had peace, but when was it? It was when the institution of slavery remained quiet where it was. We have had difficulty and turmoil whenever it has made a struggle to spread itself where it was not. I ask then, if experience does not speak in thunder tones, telling us that the policy which has given peace to the country heretofore, being returned to, gives the greatest promise of peace again. ["Yes;" "yes."] You may say and Judge Douglas has intimated the same thing, that all this difficulty in regard to the institution of slavery is the mere agitation of office seekers and ambitious Northern politicians. He thinks we want to get "his place," I suppose. [Cheers and laughter.] I agree that there are office seekers amongst us. The Bible says somewhere that we are desperately selfish. I think we would have discovered that fact without the Bible. I do not claim that I am any less so than the average of men, but I do claim that I am not more selfish than Judge Douglas. [Roars of laughter and applause.]

But is it true that all the difficulty and agitation we have in regard to this institution of slavery springs from office seeking—from the mere ambition of politicians? Is that the truth? How many times have we had danger from this question? Go back to the day of the Missouri Compromise. Go back to the Nullification question, at the bottom of which lay this same slavery question. Go back to the time of the annexation of Texas. Go back to the troubles that led to the Compromise of 1850. You will find that every time, with the single exception of the Nullification question, they sprung from an endeavor to spread this institution. There never was a party in the history of this country, and there probably never will be of sufficient strength to disturb the general peace of the country. Parties themselves may be divided and quarrel on minor questions, yet it extends not beyond the parties themselves. But does *not* this question make a disturbance outside of political circles? Does it not enter into the churches and rend them asunder? What divided the great Methodist Church into two parts, North and South? What has raised this constant disturbance in every Presbyterian General Assembly that meets? What disturbed the Unitarian Church in this very city two years ago? What has jarred and shaken the great American Tract Society recently, not yet splitting it, but sure to divide it in the end. Is it not this same mighty, deep seated power that somehow operates on the minds of men, exciting and stirring them up in every avenue of society—in politics, in religion, in literature, in morals, in all the manifold relations of life? [Applause.] Is this the work of politicians? Is that irresistible power which for fifty years has shaken the government and agitated the people to be stilled and subdued by pretending that it is an exceedingly simple thing, and we ought not to talk about it? [Great cheers and laughter.] If you will get everybody else to stop talking about it, I assure I will quit before they have half done so. [Renewed laughter.] But where is the philosophy or statesmanship which assumes that you can quiet that disturbing element in our society which has disturbed us for more than half a century, which has been the only serious danger that has threatened our institutions—I say, where is the philosophy or the statesmanship based on the assumption that we are to quit talking about it [applause], and that the public mind is all at once to cease being agitated by it? Yet this is the policy here in the North that Douglas is advocating—that we are to care nothing about it! I ask you if it is not a false philosophy? Is it not a false statesmanship that undertakes to build up a system of policy upon the basis of caring nothing about *the very thing that every body does care the most about?* ["Yes, yes," and applause]—a thing which all experience has shown we care a very great deal about? [Laughter and applause.]

The Judge alludes very often in the course of his remarks to the exclusive right which the states have to decide the whole thing for themselves. I agree with him very readily that the different states have that right. He is but fighting a man of straw when he assumes that I am contending against the right of the states to do as they please about it. Our controversy with him is in regard to the new territories. We agree that when the states come in as states they have the right and the power to do as they please. We have no power as citizens of the free states or in our federal capacity as members of the federal Union through the general government, to disturb slavery in the states where it exists. We profess constantly that we have no more inclination than belief in the power of the government to disturb it; yet we are driven constantly to defend ourselves from the assumption that we are warring upon the rights of the *states*. What I insist upon is, that the new territories shall be kept free from it while in the territorial condition. Judge Douglas assumes that we have no interest in them—that we have no right whatever to interfere. I think we have some interest. I think that as white men we have. Do we not wish for an outlet for our surplus population, if I may so express myself? Do we not feel an interest in getting to that outlet with such institutions as we would like to have prevail there? If *you* go to the territory opposed to slavery and another man comes upon the same ground with his slave, upon the assumption that the things are equal, it turns out that he has the equal right all his way and you have no part of it your way. If he goes in and makes it a slave territory, and by consequence a slave state, is it not time that those who desire to have it a free state were on equal ground. Let me suggest it in a different way. How many Democrats are there about here ["a thousand"] who have left slave states and come into the free state of Illinois to get rid of the institution of slavery. [Another voice—"a thousand and one."] I reckon there are a thousand and one. [Laughter.] I will ask you, if the policy you are now advocating had prevailed when this country was in a territorial condition, where would you have gone to get rid of it? [Applause.] Where would you have found your free state or territory to go to? And when hereafter, for any cause, the people in this place shall desire to find new homes, if they wish to be rid of the institution, where will they find the place to go? [Loud cheers.]

Now irrespective of the moral aspect of this question as to whether there is a right or wrong in enslaving a negro, I am still in favor of our new territories being in such a condition that white men may find a home—may find some spot where they can better their condition—where they can settle upon new soil and better their condition in life. [Great and continued cheering.] I am in favor of this not merely, (I must say it here as I have elsewhere,) for our own people who are born amongst us, but as an outlet for *free white people everywhere*, the world over—in which Hans and Baptiste and Patrick, and all other men from all the world, may find new homes and better their conditions in life. [Loud and long continued applause.]

I have stated upon former occasions, and I may as well state again, what I understand to be the real issue in this controversy between Judge Douglas and myself. On the point of my wanting to make war between the free and the slave states, there has been no issue between us. So, too, when he assumes that I am in favor of introducing a perfect social and political equality between the white and black races. These are false issues, upon which Judge Douglas has tried to force the controversy. There is no foundation in truth for the charge that I maintain either of these propositions. The real issue in this controversy—the one pressing upon every mind—is the sentiment on the part of one class that looks upon the institution of slavery *as a wrong*, and of another class that *does not* look upon it as a wrong. The sentiment that contemplates the institution of slavery in this country as a wrong is the sentiment of the Republican party. It is the sentiment around which all their actions—all their arguments circle—from which all their propositions radiate. They look upon it as being a moral, social and political wrong; and while they contemplate it as such, they nevertheless have due regard for its actual existence among us, and the difficulties of getting rid of it in any satisfactory way and to all the constitutional obligations thrown about it. Yet having a due regard for these, they desire a policy in regard to it that looks to its not creating any more danger. They insist that it should as far as may be, *be treated* as a wrong, and one of the methods of treating it as a wrong is to *make provision that it shall grow no larger*. [Loud applause.] They also desire a policy that looks to a peaceful end of slavery at sometime, as being wrong. These are the views they entertain in regard to it as I under-

stand them; and all their sentiments—all their arguments and propositions are brought within this range. I have said and I repeat it
here, that if there be a man amongst us who does not think that
the institution of slavery is wrong in any one of the aspects of which
I have spoken, he is misplaced and ought not to be with us. And
if there be a man amongst us who is so impatient of it as a wrong
as to disregard its actual presence among us and the difficulty of
getting rid of it suddenly in a satisfactory way, and to disregard the
constitutional obligations thrown about it, that man is misplaced if
he is on our platform. We disclaim sympathy with him in practical
action. He is not placed properly with us.

On this subject of treating it as a wrong, and limiting its spread,
let me say a word. Has any thing ever threatened the existence of
this Union save and except this very institution of slavery? What is
it that we hold most dear amongst us? Our own liberty and prosperity. What has ever threatened our liberty and prosperity save and
except this institution of slavery? If this is true, how do you propose
to improve the condition of things by enlarging slavery—by spreading it out and making it bigger? You may have a wen or a cancer
upon your person and not be able to cut it out lest you bleed to
death; but surely it is no way to cure it, to engraft it and spread it
over your whole body. That is no proper way of treating what you
regard a wrong. You see this peaceful way of dealing with it as a
wrong—restricting the spread of it, and not allowing it to go into
new countries where it has not already existed. That is the peaceful
way, the old-fashioned way, the way in which the fathers themselves
set us the example.

On the other hand, I have said there is a sentiment which treats
it as *not* being wrong. That is the Democratic sentiment of this day.
I do not mean to say that every man who stands within that range
positively asserts that it is right. That class will include all who positively assert that it is right, and all who like Judge Douglas treat
it as indifferent and do not say it is either right or wrong. These two
classes of men fall within the general class of those who do not look
upon it as a wrong. And if there be among you anybody who supposes that he as a Democrat, can consider himself "as much opposed
to slavery as anybody," I would like to reason with him. You never
treat it as a wrong. What other thing that you consider as a wrong,
do you deal with as you deal with that? Perhaps you *say* it is wrong,
*but your leader never does, and you quarrel with anybody who says
it is wrong.* Although you pretend to say so yourself you can find
no fit place to deal with it as a wrong. You must not say anything
about it in the free states, *because it is not here.* You must not say

anything about it in the slave states, *because it is there.* You must not say anything about it in the pulpit, because that is religion and has nothing to do with it. You must not say anything about it in politics, *because that will disturb the security of "my place."* [Shouts of laughter and cheers.] There is no place to talk about [it] as being a wrong, although you say yourself it *is* a wrong. But finally you will screw yourself up to the belief that if the people of the slave states should adopt a system of gradual emancipation on the slavery question, you would be in favor of it. You would be in favor of it. You say that is getting it in the right place, and you would be glad to see it succeed. But you are deceiving yourself. You all know that Frank Blair and Gratz Brown, down there in St. Louis, undertook to introduce that system in Missouri. They fought as valiantly as they could for the system of gradual emancipation which you pretend you would be glad to see succeed. Now I will bring you to the test. After a hard fight they were beaten, and when the news came over here you threw up your hats and *hurrahed for Democracy.* [Great applause and laughter.] More than that, take all the argument made in favor of the system you have proposed, and it carefully excludes the idea that there is anything wrong in the institution of slavery. The arguments to sustain that policy carefully excluded it. Even here to-day you heard Judge Douglas quarrel with me because I uttered a wish that it might sometime come to an end. Although Henry Clay could say he wished every slave in the United States was in the country of his ancestors, I am denounced by those pretending to respect Henry Clay for uttering a wish that it might sometime, in some peaceful way, come to an end. The Democratic policy in regard to that institution will not tolerate the merest breath, the slightest hint, of the least degree of wrong about it. Try it by some of Judge Douglas' arguments. He says he "don't care whether it is voted up or voted down" in the territories. I do not care myself in dealing with that expression, whether it is intended to be expressive of his individual sentiments on the subject, or only of the national policy he desires to have established. It is alike valuable for my purpose. Any man can say that who does not see anything wrong in slavery, but no man can logically say it who does see a wrong in it; because no man can logically say he don't care whether a wrong is voted up or voted down. He may say he don't care whether an indifferent thing is voted up or down, but he must logically have a choice between a right thing and a wrong thing. He contends that whatever community wants slaves has a right to have them. So they have if it is not a wrong. But if it is a wrong, he cannot say people have a right to do wrong. He says that upon the score of equality, slaves should be allowed to go in a new territory, like other property. This is strictly logical if there is no difference between it and other property. If it and other property are equal, his argument is entirely logical. But if you insist that one is wrong and the other right, there is no use to institute a comparison between right and wrong. You may turn over everything in the Democratic policy from beginning to end, whether in the shape it takes on the statute book, in the shape it takes in the Dred Scott decision, in the shape it takes in conversation or the shape it takes in short maxim-like arguments—it everywhere carefully excludes the idea that there is anything wrong in it.

That is the real issue. That is the issue that will continue in this country when these poor tongues of Judge Douglas and myself shall be silent. It is the eternal struggle beween these two principles—right and wrong—throughout the world. They are the two principles that have stood face to face from the beginning of time; and will ever continue to struggle. The one is the common right of humanity and the other the divine right of kings. It is the same principle in whatever shape it develops itself. It is the same spirit that says, "You work and toil and earn bread, and I'll eat it." [Loud applause.] No matter in what shape it comes, whether from the mouth of a king who seeks to bestride the people of his own nation and live by the fruit of their labor, or from one race of men as an apology for enslaving another race, it is the same tyrannical principal. I was glad to express my gratitude at Quincy, and I re-express it here to Judge Douglas—*that he looks to no end of the institution of slavery.* That will help the people to see where the struggle really is. It will hereafter place with us all men who really do wish the wrong may have an end. And whenever we can get rid of the fog which obscures the real question—when we can get Judge Douglas and his friends to avow a policy looking to its perpetuation—we can get out from among them that class of men and bring them to the side of those who treat it as a wrong. Then there will soon be an end of it, and that end will be its "ultimate extinction." Whenever the issue can be distinctly made, and all extraneous matter thrown out so that men can fairly see the real difference between the parties, this controversy will soon be settled, and it will be done peaceably too. There will be no war, no violence. It will be placed again where the wisest and best men of the world, placed it. Brooks of South Carolina once declared that when this Constitution was framed, its framers did not look to the institution existing until this day. When he said this, I think he stated a fact that is fully borne out by the history of the times. But he also said they were better and wiser men than the men of these days; yet the men of these days had experience which they had not, and by the invention of the cotton gin it became a necessity in this country that slavery should be perpetual. I now say that willingly or unwillingly, purposely or without purpose, Judge Douglas has been the most prominent instrument in changing the position of the institution of slavery which the fathers of the government expected to come to an end ere this—*and putting it upon Brooks' cotton gin basis*, [great applause,]—placing it where he openly confesses he has no desire there shall ever be an end of it. [Renewed applause.]

I understand I have ten minutes yet. I will employ it in saying something about this argument Judge Douglas uses, while he sustains the Dred Scot decision, that the people of the territories can still somehow exclude slavery. The first thing I ask attention to is the fact that Judge Douglas constantly said, before the decision, that whether they could or not, *was a question for the Supreme Court*. [Cheers.] But after the Court has made the decision he virtually says it is *not* a question for the Supreme Court, but for the people. [Renewed applause.] And how is it he tells us they can exclude it? He says it needs "police regulations," and that admits of "unfriendly legislation." Although it is a right established by the Constitution of the United States to take a slave into a territory of the United States and hold him as property, yet unless the territorial legislature will give friendly legislation, and, more especially, if they adopt unfriendly legislation, they can practically exclude him. Now, without meeting this proposition as a matter of fact, I pass to consider the real constitutional obligation. Let me take the gentleman who looks me in the face before me, and let us suppose that he is a member of the territorial legislature. The first thing he will do will be to swear that he will support the Constitution of the United States. His neighbor by his side in the territory has slaves and needs territorial legislation to enable him to enjoy that constitutional right. Can he withhold the legislation which his neighbor needs for the enjoyment of a right which is fixed in his favor in the Constitution of the United States which he has sworn to support? Can he withhold it without violating his oath? And more especially, can he pass unfriendly legislation to violate his oath? Why this is a *monstrous* sort of talk about the Constitution of the United States! [Great applause.] *There has never been as outlandish or lawless a doctrine from the mouth of any respectable man on earth.* [Tremendous cheers.] I do not believe it is a constitutional right to hold slaves in a territory of the United States. I believe the decision was improperly made and I go for reversing it. Judge Douglas is furious

against those who go for reversing a decision. But he is for legislating it out of all force while the law itself stands. I repeat that
there has never been so monstrous a doctrine uttered from the
mouth of a respectable man. [Loud cheers.]

I suppose most of us, (I know it of myself,) believe that the
people of the Southern states are entitled to a congressional fugitive
slave law—that it is a right fixed in the Constitution. But it cannot
be made available to them without congressional legislation. In the
Judge's language, it is a "barren right" which needs legislation before it can become efficient and valuable to the persons to whom
it is guaranteed. And as the right is constitutional I agree that the
legislation shall be granted to it—and that not that we like the institution of slavery. We profess to have no taste for running and catch-
ing niggers—at least I profess no taste for that job at all. Why then
do I yield support to a fugitive slave law? Because I do not understand that the Constitution, which guarantees that right, can be
supported without it. And if I believed that the right to hold a slave
in a territory was equally fixed in the Constitution with the right
to reclaim fugitives, I should be bound to give it the legislation
necessary to support it. I say that no man can deny his obligation
to give the necessary legislation to support slavery in a territory,
who believes it is a constitutional right to have it there. No man
can, who does not give the Abolitionist an argument to deny the
obligation enjoined by the Constitution to enact a fugitive slave law.
Try it now. It is the strongest Abolition argument ever made. I say
if that Dred Scot decision is correct then the right to hold slaves in
a territory is equally a constitutional right with the right of a slaveholder to have his runaway returned. No one can show the distinction between them. The one is express, so that we cannot deny it.
The other is construed to be in the Constitution, so that he who
believes the decision to be correct believes in the right. And the
man who argues that by unfriendly legislation, in spite of that constitutional right, slavery may be driven from the territories, cannot
avoid furnishing an argument by which Abolitionists may deny the
obligation to return fugitives, and claim the power to pass laws
unfriendly to the right of the slaveholder to reclaim his fugitive.
I do not know how such an argument may strike a popular assembly
like this, but I defy anybody to go before a body of men whose
minds are educated to estimating evidence and reasoning, and show
that there is an iota of difference between the constitutional right
to reclaim a fugitive, and the constitutional right to hold a slave,
in a territory, provided this Dred Scott decision is correct. [Cheers.]
I defy any man to make an argument that will justify unfriendly

legislation to deprive a slaveholder of his right to hold his slave in a territory, that will not equally, in all its length, breadth and thickness furnish an argument for nullifying the fugitive slave law. Why there is not such an Abolitionist in the nation as Douglas, after all. [Loud and enthusiastic applause.]

Douglas' Rejoinder

Mr. Lincoln has concluded his remarks by saying that there is not such an Abolitionist as I am in all America. (Laughter.) If he could make the Abolitionists of Illinois believe that, he would not have much show for the Senate. (Great laughter and applause.) Let him make the Abolitionists believe the truth of that statement and his political back is broken. (Renewed laughter.)

His first criticism upon me is the expression of his hope that the war of the administration will be prosecuted against me and the Democratic party of his state with vigor. He wants that war prosecuted with vigor; I have no doubt of it. His hopes of success, and the hopes of his party depend solely upon it. They have no chance of destroying the Democracy of this state except by the aid of federal patronage. ("That's a fact," "good," and cheers.) He has all the federal office-holders here as his allies, ("That's so,") running separate tickets against the Democracy to divide the party although the leaders all intend to vote directly the Abolition ticket, and only leave the green-horns to vote this separate ticket who refuse to go into the Abolition camp. (Laughter and cheers.) There is something really refreshing in the thought that Mr. Lincoln is in favor of prosecuting one war vigorously. (Roars of laughter.) It is the first war I ever knew him to be in favor of prosecuting. (Renewed laughter.) It is the first war that I ever knew him to believe to be just or constitutional. (Laughter and cheers.) When the Mexican war [was] being waged, and the American army was surrounded by the enemy in Mexico, he thought that war was unconstitutional, unnecessary and unjust. ("That's so," "you've got him," "he voted against it," &c.) He thought it was not commenced on the right *spot*. (Laughter.)

When I made an incidental allusion of that kind in the joint discussion over at Charleston some weeks ago, Lincoln, in replying, said that I, Douglas, had charged him with voting against supplies for the Mexican war, and then he reared up, full length, and swore that he never voted against the supplies—that it was a slander—and caught hold of Ficklin, who sat on the stand, and said, "Here,

Ficklin, tell the people that it is a lie." (Laughter and cheers.) Well, Ficklin, who had served in Congress with him, stood up and told them all that he recollected about it. It was that when George Ashmun, of Massachusetts, brought forward a resolution declaring the war unconstitutional, unnecessary, and unjust, that Lincoln had voted for it. "Yes," said Lincoln, "I did." Thus he confessed that he voted that the war was wrong, that our country was in the wrong, and consequently that the Mexicans were in the right; but charged that I had slandered him by saying that he voted against the supplies. I never charged him with voting against the supplies in my life, because I knew that he was not in Congress when they were voted. (Tremendous shouts of laughter.) The war was commenced on the 13th day of May, 1846, and on that day we appropriated in Congress ten millions of dollars and fifty thousand men to prosecute it. During the same session we voted more men and more money, and at the next session we voted more men and more money, so that by the time Mr. Lincoln entered Congress we had enough men and enough money to carry on the war, and had no occasion to vote any more. (Laughter and cheers.) When he got into the House, being opposed to the war, and not being able to stop the supplies, because they had all gone forward, all he could do was to follow the lead of Corwin, and prove that the war was not begun on the right spot, and that it was unconstitutional, unnecessary, and wrong. Remember, too, that this he did after the war had been begun. It is one thing to be opposed to the declaration of a war, another and very different thing to take sides with the enemy against your own country after the war has been commenced. ("Good," and cheers.) Our army was in Mexico at the time, many battles had been fought; our citizens, who were defending the honor of their country's flag, were surrounded by the daggers, the guns and the poison of the enemy. Then it was that Corwin made his speech in which he declared that the American soldiers ought to be welcomed by the Mexicans with bloody hands and hospitable graves; then it was that Ashmun and Lincoln voted in the House of Representatives that the war was unconstitutional and unjust; and Ashmun's resolution, Corwin's speech, and Lincoln's vote were sent to Mexico and read at the head of the Mexican army, to prove to them that there was a Mexican party in the Congress of the United States who were doing all in their power to aid them. ("That's the truth," "Lincoln's a traitor," etc.) That a man who takes sides with the common enemy against his own country in time of war should rejoice in a war being made on me now, is very natural. (Immense applause.) And in my opinion, no other kind of a man would rejoice in it. ("That's true," "hurrah for Douglas," and cheers.)

Mr. Lincoln has told you a great deal to-day about his being an old line Clay Whig. ("He never was.") Bear in mind that there are a great many old Clay Whigs down in this region. It is more agreeable, therefore, for him to talk about the old Clay Whig party than it is for him to talk Abolitionism. We did not hear much about the old Clay Whig party up in the Abolition districts. How much of an old line Henry Clay Whig was he? Have you read Gen. Singleton's speech at Jacksonville? ("Yes, yes," and cheers.) You know that Gen. Singleton was, for twenty-five years, the confidential friend of Henry Clay in Illinois, and he testified that in 1847, when the constitutional convention of this state was in session, the Whig members were invited to a Whig caucus at the house of Mr. Lincoln's brother-in-law, where Mr. Lincoln proposed to throw Henry Clay overboard and take up Gen. Taylor in his place, giving, as his reason, that if the Whigs did not take up Gen. Taylor the Democrats would. (Cheers and laughter.) Singleton testifies that Lincoln, in that speech, urged, as another reason for throwing Henry Clay overboard, that the Whigs had fought long enough for principle and ought to begin to fight for success. Singleton also testifies that Lincoln's speech did have the effect of cutting Clay's throat, and that he, Singleton, and others withdrew from the caucus in indignation. He further states that when they got to Philadelphia to attend the national convention of the Whig party, that Lincoln was there, the bitter and deadly enemy of Clay, and that he tried to keep him (Singleton) out of the convention because he insisted on voting for Clay, and Lincoln was determined to have Taylor. (Laughter and applause.) Singleton says that Lincoln rejoiced with very great joy when he found the mangled remains of the murdered Whig statesman lying cold before him. Now, Mr. Lincoln tells you that he is an old line Clay Whig! (Laughter and cheers.) Gen. Singleton testifies to the facts I have narrated in a public speech which has been printed and circulated broadcast over the state for weeks, yet not a lisp have we heard from Mr. Lincoln on the subject, except that he is an old Clay Whig.

What part of Henry Clay's policy did Lincoln ever advocate? He was in Congress in 1848-9 when the Wilmot proviso warfare disturbed the peace and harmony of the country until it shook the foundation of the republic from its centre to its circumference. It was that agitation that brought Clay forth from his retirement at Ashland again to occupy his seat in the Senate of the United States, to see if he could not, by his great wisdom and experience, and the renown of his name, do something to restore peace and quiet to a disturbed country. Who got up that sectional strife that Clay had to be called upon to quell? I have heard Lincoln boast that he voted forty-two times for the Wilmot proviso, and that he would have voted as many times more if he could. (Laughter.) Lincoln is the man, in connection with Seward, Chase, Giddings, and other Abolitionists, who got up that strife that I helped Clay to put down. (Tremendous applause.) Henry Clay came back to the Senate in 1849, and saw that he must do something to restore peace to the country. The Union Whigs and Union Democrats welcomed him the moment he arrived, as the man for the occasion. We believed that he, of all men on earth, had been preserved by Divine Providence to guide us out of our difficulties, and we Democrats rallied under Clay then, as you Whigs in nullification time rallied under the banner of old Jackson, forgetting party when the country was in danger, in order that we might have a country first, and parties afterwards. ("Three cheers for Douglas.")

And this reminds me that Mr. Lincoln told you that the slavery question was the only thing that ever disturbed the peace and harmony of the Union. Did not Nullification once raise its head and disturb the peace of this Union in 1832? Was that the slavery question, Mr. Lincoln? Did not disunion raise its monster head during the last war with Great Britain? Was that the slavery question, Mr. Lincoln? The peace of this country has been disturbed three times, once during the war with Great Britain, once on the tariff question, and once on the slavery question. ("Three cheers for Douglas.") His argument, therefore, that slavery is the only question that has ever created dissension in the Union falls to the ground. It is true that agitators are enabled now to use this slavery question for the purpose of sectional strife. ("That's so.") He admits that in regard to all things else, the principle that I advocate, making each state and territory free to decide for itself ought to prevail. He instances the cranberry laws, and the oyster laws, and he might have gone through the whole list with the same effect. I say that all these laws are local and domestic, and that local and domestic concerns should be left to each state and each territory to manage for itself. If agitators would acquiesce in that principle, there never would be any danger to the peace and harmony of this Union. ("That's so," and cheers.)

Mr. Lincoln tries to avoid the main issue by attacking the truth of my proposition, that our fathers made this government divided into free and slave states, recognizing the right of each to decide all its local questions for itself. Did they not thus make it? It is true that they did not establish slavery in any of the states, or abolish it in any of them; but finding thirteen states twelve of which were slave and one free, they agreed to form a government uniting them together, as they stood divided into free and slave states, and to guarantee forever to each state the right to do as it pleased on the slavery question. (Cheers.) Having thus made the government, and conferred this right upon each state forever, I assert that this government can exist as they made it, divided into free and slave states, if any one state chooses to retain slavery. (Cheers.) He says that he looks forward to a time when slavery shall be abolished everywhere. I look forward to a time when each state shall be allowed to do as it pleases. If it chooses to keep slavery forever, it is not my business, but its own; if it chooses to abolish slavery, it is its own business—not mine. I care more for the great principle of self-government, the right of the people to rule, than I do for all the negroes in Christendom. (Cheers.) I would not endanger the perpetuity of this Union. I would not blot out the great inalienable rights of the white men for all the negroes that ever existed. (Renewed applause.) Hence, I say, let us maintain this government on the principles that our fathers made it, recognizing the right of each state to keep slavery as long as its people determine, or to abolish it when they please. (Cheers.) But Mr. Lincoln says that when our fathers made this government they did not look forward to the state of things now existing; and therefore he thinks the doctrine was wrong; and he quotes Brooks, of South Carolina, to prove that our fathers then thought that probably slavery would be abolished, by each state acting for itself before this time. Suppose they did; suppose they did not foresee what has occurred,—does that change the principles of our government? They did not probably foresee the telegraph that transmits intelligence by lightning, nor did they foresee the railroads that now form the bonds of union between the different states, or the thousand mechanical inventions that have elevated mankind. But do these things change the principles of the government? Our fathers, I say, made this government on the principle of the right of each state to do as it pleases in its own domestic affairs, subject to the Constitution, and allowed the people of each to apply to every new change of circumstance such remedy as they may see fit to improve their condition. This right they have for all time to come. (Cheers.)

Mr. Lincoln went on to tell you that he does not at all desire to interfere with slavery in the states where it exists, nor does his party. I expected him to say that down here. (Laughter.) Let me ask him then how he is going to put slavery in the course of ultimate extinction everywhere, if he does not intend to interfere with it in the states where it exists? (Renewed laughter.) He says that he will prohibit it in all territories, and the inference is then that unless they make free states out of them he will keep them out of the Union; for, mark you, he did not say whether or not he would vote to admit Kansas with slavery or not, as her people might apply; ("he forgot that as usual," &c;) he did not say whether or not he was in favor of bringing the territories now in existence into the Union on the principle of Clay's compromise measures on the slavery question. I told you that he would not. ("Give it to him, he deserves it," &c.) His idea is that he will prohibit slavery in all the territories, and thus force them all to become free states, surrounding the slave states with a cordon of free states, and hemming them in, keeping the slaves confined to their present limits whilst they go on multiplying until the soil on which they live will no longer feed them, and he will thus be able to put slavery in a course of ultimate extinction by starvation. (Cheers.) He will extinguish slavery in the Southern states as the French general exterminated the Algerines when he smoked them out. He is going to extinguish slavery by surrounding the slave states, hemming in the slaves, and starving them out of existence as you smoke a fox out of his hole. And he intends to do that in the name of humanity and Christianity, in order that we may get rid of the terrible crime and sin entailed upon our fathers of holding slaves. (Laughter and cheers.) Mr. Lincoln makes out that line of policy, and appeals to the moral sense of justice, and to the Christian feeling of the community to sustain him. He says that any man who holds to the contrary doctrine is in the position of the king who claimed to govern by divine right. Let us examine for a moment and see what principle it was that overthrew the divine right of George the Third to govern us. Did not these colonies rebel because the British Parliament had no right to pass laws concerning our property and domestic and private institutions without our consent? We demanded that the British government should not pass such laws unless they gave us representation in the body passing them,—and this the British government insisting on doing,—we went to war, on the principle that the home government should not control and govern distant colonies without giving them a representation. Now, Mr. Lincoln proposes to govern the territories without giving the people a representation, and calls on Congress to pass laws controlling their property and domestic concerns without their consent and against their will. Thus, he asserts for his party the identical principle asserted by George III. and the Tories of the Revolution. (Cheers.)

I ask you to look into these things, and then to tell me whether the Democracy or the Abolitionists are right. I hold that the people of a territory, like those of a state, (I use the language of Mr. Buchanan in his letter of acceptance,) have the right to decide for themselves whether slavery shall or shall not exist within their limits. ("That's the idea," "Hurrah for Douglas.") The point upon which Chief Justice Taney expresses his opinion is simply this, that slaves being property, stand on an equal footing with other property, and consequently that the owner has the same right to carry that property into a territory that he has any other, subject to the same conditions. Suppose that one of your merchants was to take fifty or one hundred thousand dollars worth of liquors to Kansas. He has a right to go there under that decision, but when he gets there he finds the Maine liquor law in force, and what can he do with his property after he gets there? He cannot sell it, he cannot use it, it is subject to the local law, and that law is against him, and the best thing he can do with it is to bring it back into Missouri or Illinois and sell it. If you take negroes to Kansas, as Col. Jeff. Davis said in his Bangor speech, from which I have quoted to-day, you must take them there subject to the local law. If the people want the institution of slavery they will protect and encourage it; but if they do not want it they will withhold that protection, and the absence of local legislation protecting slavery excludes it as completely as a positive prohibition. ("That's so," and cheers.) You slaveholders of Missouri might as well understand what you know practically, that you cannot carry slavery where the people do not want it. ("That's so.") All you have a right to ask is that the people shall do as they please; if they want slavery let them have it; if they do not want it, allow them to refuse to encourage it.

My friends, if, as I have said before, we will only live up to this great fundamental principle there will be peace between the North and the South. Mr. Lincoln admits that under the Constitution on all domestic questions, except slavery, we ought not to interfere with the people of each state. What right have we to interfere with slavery any more than we have to interfere with any other question. He says that this slavery question is now the bone of contention. Why? simply because agitators have combined in all the free states to make war upon it. Suppose the agitators in the states should combine in one-half of the Union to make war upon the railroad system of the other half? They would thus be driven to the same sectional strife. Suppose one section makes war upon any other peculiar institution of the opposite section, and the same strife is produced. The only remedy and safety is that we shall stand by the Constitution as our fathers made it, obey the laws as they are passed, while they stand the proper test and sustain the decisions of the Supreme Court and the constituted authorities.

CHAPTER THIRTEEN

THE CAMPAIGN ENDS

The debates had ended; the campaign continued. Crowds still turned out to listen to arguments now worn bare. For a Douglas meeting at Decatur on October 18 the Democrats claimed an attendance of 6,000; at Bloomington, on the 22nd, 8,000 were present. Lincoln, speaking in smaller towns, drew proportionate audiences: 3,000 at Rushville on October 20; 2,000 at Dallas City on the 23rd; 4,000 at Macomb two days later.

The attendance was the more remarkable because the weather had become uncertain. There were bright days, as there always are in Illinois in October, but there were also days when sharp winds blew relentlessly and chill rains soaked even heavy clothing. Yet the interest of the people could not be dampened. The response at Macomb, reported by the Press and Tribune, *was typical.*[1]

QUINCY, ILL., Oct. 26, 1858

Yesterday witnessed one of the grandest demonstrations at Macomb that ever came off in this part of the State. Early in the morning the Quincy delegation, consisting of upwards of four hundred live Republicans, accompanied by the Quincy Guards and Blues in full uniform with their music, left this city to do honor to Abraham Lincoln, the champion of free principles in Illinois. The weather was dreary and foggy during the morning, but the enthusiasm of the Republican host defied the elements. All along the road crowds had assembled to greet us and swell our number, until finally the conductor was obliged to run by several stations without stopping, there not being even standing room left.

On arriving at Macomb we were received, though in a drizzling rain, by an immense crowd of the hard working Republicans of McDonough and the surrounding counties. The streets were muddy, the sidewalks slippery and things overhead decidedly damp. We were then escorted by the citizens, on foot, in wagons and on horseback to the new and commodious Randolph House, placed at the

[1] October 28.

disposal of our military companies for the day by Mr. Randolph. . . . On arriving in front of the Hotel three tremendous cheers gave us their welcome to Macomb. About this time a delegation from the northern part of the county entered the town, and in passing around the public square were attempted to be stopped by a squad of Douglas riff-raffs. An old gentleman, near sixty years of age, jumped in among them and in rather less than no time four of the drunken bullies were sprawling in the mud. We were not interrupted again during the day.

The people kept pouring in notwithstanding the rain kept pouring down. At noon Old Abe arrived escorted by a procession *over a mile long,* and was met by a similar caravan of the people of Macomb—prominent among whom were a large cavalcade of ladies and gentlemen on horseback. As soon as the procession came in sight the crowd commenced cheering, and kept it up in a continued tumult until Mr. Lincoln reached the Hotel.

At two o'clock Mr. Lincoln commenced speaking in the court house square to an audience of over four thousand persons, who stood there in the mud, and fog, and drizzle through his whole speech. Of his argument I need only say that it completed the Quincy debate in which Douglas was so unmercifully threshed, and was received with great cheers and enthusiasm.

Last-minute editorials placed the campaign in historical perspective more accurately than is usually the case with such exhortations. We quote from the Press and Tribune *for October 29.*

Tomorrow, Mr. Lincoln will terminate, so far as his personal efforts are concerned, by a speech at Springfield, the most brilliant, and, as the event will prove, most successful political canvass ever made in the country. From first to last he has preserved his well earned reputation for fairness, for honor and gentlemanly courtesy, and more than maintained his standing as a sagacious, far-seeing and profound statesman. Scorning the use of offensive personalities and the ordinary tricks of the stump, his efforts have been directed solely to the discussion of the legitimate issues of the campaign and the great fundamental principles on which our government is based. No man living has been a closer student of those principles than Mr. Lincoln; and in his numerous speeches throughout the state he has brought the result of that laborious study, and the convictions of his matured reason and sober judgment before the people with an ability, a force and an eloquence rarely equalled and that have made a deep and an ineradicable impression upon all who have heard him.

No fact has been more apparent in the canvass than that Mr. Lincoln was more than a match for his opponent. In all the elements of statesmanship, in close, compact, logical argument, in gentlemanly amenity, in control of his temper under the severest provocation, in an unfailing fund of good nature—in every quality, in short, that commends itself to the approbation of the better nature of man, on every occasion he has loomed above Mr. Douglas, immeasurably his superior. He has proved himself Mr. Douglas' superior in another respect also. He can do more work and bear it better. Strictly correct in all his habits, simple and abstemious in his manner of life, he has gone through the herculean labor of the canvass without flagging in a solitary instance, all his physical powers in full and harmonious action, his voice clear and ringing, and in all respects more fresh and vigorous than when on the 9th of July he made his first speech from the balcony of the Tremont.

Mr. Lincoln's efforts in this canvass have also made for him a splendid national reputation. Identified all his life long with the old Whig party, always in a minority in Illinois, his fine abilities and attainments have necessarily been confined to a very limited sphere. He entered upon the canvass with a reputation confined to his own state—he closes it with his name a household word wherever the principles he holds are honored, and with the respect of his opponents in all sections of the country. If it should turn out that, by fraud on the part of his opponents to override the will of a large majority of the bona fide citizens of Illinois, Mr. Lincoln shall fail of an election to the Senate, his fame is already secure.

In similar vein, the Times *summed up on October 31.*

Judge Douglas reached the city [Chicago] last evening, by the train from Rock Island. He is in excellent health and spirits. Notwithstanding his many speeches, his voice is still in excellent order.[2]

The campaign has been the most remarkable one ever conducted in a western state. On the 9th of June he made his speech at Chicago, on the 16th, while on his way to meet the State Central Committee at Springfield, he spoke at Bloomington; on the 18th he reached Springfield, and spoke there for over three hours. In the two days that ensued, he and the state committee sketched off a series of appointments for meetings extending to late in September. He then returned to this city, where he remained for a few days, and then, on the 27th of July, spoke at Clinton, De Witt county.

---

[2] Much unprejudiced evidence indicates that by the time of the Alton debate Douglas' voice was failing. For the remainder of the campaign he had great difficulty in making himself heard.

Between the 27th of July and the 21st of August he attended fifteen mass meetings held in that part of the state included in De Witt, Piatt, Edgar, Montgomery, Bond, Madison, Scott, Pike, Cass, Mason, Fulton, Peoria, and Marshall counties, and on the 21st of August met Lincoln at Ottawa in the first joint debate.

On the Tuesday following, he resumed his appointments, and from that time up to Friday, October 29, he has, upon an average, addressed mass meetings daily. He has traversed the state from one end to the other, and everywhere he has been met by hearty welcomes, and cheered with an enthusiastic good will that was of itself a reward for the [time] and labor he had expended in the Senate in defense of the people's rights. We mention these things to show our distant readers the intense interest felt in all parts of the state in the coming contest. The battle has been fought, and if we can have an honest vote on Tuesday, we will have no fault to find with the judgment of the people. The Democratic party have never had to encounter such a campaign. In front they were opposed by an unscrupulous enemy who were fighting with the desperation of men fighting for life. In addition to this, our army was assailed like that of Scott on his march to the city of Mexico, by a band who were insidiously circulating their gold and their promises of high office and rank to those who would desert their friends and betray their country. As was the case with Scott's army, some were weak enough to pocket the gold of the enemy, and turn their guns on their countrymen; but the world knows the history of that treason—the traitors were disposed of as they deserved. The Democracy of Illinois, after they have whipped the Republicans, will possibly have some drumhead court martials upon the men who have acted as traitors.

Both candidates closed with speeches in their home cities. Lincoln's last meeting took place on Saturday, October 30. The Press and Tribune *reporter contributed a final column of hyperbole.*[3]

SPRINGFIELD, Oct. 30, 1858

Never has there been such a political demonstration in central Illinois as we have now here today. Mr. Lincoln's old friends and neighbors, who have known him for twenty-five years—the Old Whigs whom he has often led to victory—old Democrats whom he has as often opposed—men of all classes and all nationalities—have been anxious for a month past to show their appreciation of the man and their contempt for his slanderers. Until today, his engagements elsewhere have forbidden his presence at home. But when it was announced that he would be in Springfield on Saturday, the

[3] November 2, 1858.

preparation for a grand reception commenced; and never since Sangamon has been a county or Illinois a state, has the centre seen such an outpouring of the people to do a citizen honor. Never, never!

I must be brief; but when I tell you and your readers that the whole county of Sangamon was in town, that we had an immense delegation from Jacksonville, another from Decatur, and that Logan and McLean counties sent us down a train of thirty-two cars packed to the roofs with live Republicans, that we had eight bands of music and an infinity of banners, you and they will have some faint idea of what the Springfield boys succeeded in doing. But all attempts to describe the irrepressible enthusiasm of the tens of thousands, to give you an idea of their triumphant shouts, to portray the mortification and rage of the Douglas men, and the vociferous jubilation of our side, would fall short of the reality. I have been through some exciting campaigns; but never have I seen men so righteously enthusiastic, so confident of victory, so determined to work for it and win it, as are our men here today. Speaking was out of the question. Lincoln tried it, and though he held at all times an audience of five thousand or more, something more demonstrative than his convincing and unimpassioned oratory was needed to satisfy the eager crowd. They formed processions in defiance of marshals and music, marched, counter-marched, and marched back again, making their banners eloquent, and the whole air vocal with their shouts. Hurra for Sangamon!

Lincoln may not have breathed the fire that his audience wanted, but there were few times in his life when he spoke more movingly than he did in his peroration.[4]

My friends, to-day closes the discussions of this canvass. The planting and the culture are over; and there remains but the preparation, and the harvest.

I stand here surrounded by friends—some *political, all personal* friends, I trust. May I be indulged, in this closing scene, to say a few words of myself. I have borne a laborious, and, in some respects to myself, a painful part in the contest. Through all, I have neither assailed, nor wrestled with any part of the Constitution. The legal right of the Southern people to reclaim their fugitives I have constantly admitted. The legal right of Congress to interfere with their institution in the states, I have constantly denied. In resisting the spread of slavery to new territory, and with that, what appears to me to be a tendency to subvert the first principle of free government itself my whole effort has consisted. To the best of my judgment I

---

[4] *Collected Works*, III, 334.

have labored *for*, and not *against* the Union. As I have not felt, so I have not expressed any harsh sentiment towards our Southern brethren. I have constantly declared, as I really believed, the only difference between them and us, is the difference of circumstances.

I have meant to assail the motives of no party, or individual; and if I have, in any instance (of which I am not conscious) departed from my purpose, I regret it.

I have said that in some respects the contest has been painful to me. Myself, and those with whom I act have been constantly accused of a purpose to destroy the Union; and bespattered with every imaginable odious epithet; and some who were friends, as it were but yesterday have made themselves most active in this. I have cultivated patience, and made no attempt at a retort.

Ambition has been ascribed to me. God knows how sincerely I prayed from the first that this field of ambition might not be opened. I claim no insensibility to political honors; but today could the Missouri restriction be restored, and the whole slavery question replaced on the old ground of "toleration" by *necessity* where it exists, with unyielding hostility to the spread of it, on principle, I would, in consideration, gladly agree, that Judge Douglas should never be *out*, and I never *in*, an office, so long as we both or either, live.

Douglas spoke for the last time on November 1, the night before the election. Chicago Democrats read the report of the meeting as the votes were being cast.[5]

In spite of the rain, an immense number of citizens assembled last night in front of Garrett Block to hear Senator Douglas on the issues to be decided today. There is no building in Chicago large enough to hold one quarter of the number there collected. From the windows and balconies of the Garrett Block were hung out almost innumerable banners and transparencies; and bonfires were blazing on State Street. When Senator Douglas ascended to the rostrum, cheers broke from the multitude that were heard all over the city. The distinguished orator proceeded to deliver an elaborate speech, which was in his usual and convincing style. It was received with the most vehement applause; and notwithstanding the inclement weather, he held the thousands of listeners in rapt attention for nearly an hour.

From this fact it is seen how earnestly the masses confide in his wisdom—how they admire his eloquence—and how deeply imbedded in their hearts is the love of Democratic principles. When he closed his address, and withdrew, such another burst of applause was seldom or never heard before.

[5] Chicago *Times*, November 2, 1858.

SPEECHES OF LINCOLN AND DOUGLAS IN THE CAMPAIGN OF 1858[1]

June 16. Lincoln at Springfield.

July 9. Douglas at Chicago.

July 10. Lincoln at Chicago.

July 16. Douglas at Bloomington.

July 17. Douglas (afternoon) and Lincoln (evening) at Springfield.

July 27. Douglas (afternoon) and Lincoln (evening) at Clinton.

July 29. Douglas and Lincoln at Monticello.

July 30. Douglas at Mattoon.

July 31. Douglas at Paris.

August 2. Douglas at Hillsboro.

August 4. Douglas at Greenville.

August 5. Douglas at Highland.

August 6. Douglas at Edwardsville.

August 7. Douglas at Winchester.

August 9. Douglas at Pittsfield.

August 11. Douglas at Beardstown.

August 12. Lincoln at Beardstown.

August 13. Douglas at Havana.

August 14. Lincoln at Havana.

August 16. Lincoln at Bath; Douglas at Lewistown.

August 17. Lincoln at Lewistown.

August 18. Douglas at Peoria.

August 19. Lincoln at Peoria; Douglas at Lacon.

August 21. First joint debate at Ottawa.

August 23. Lincoln at Henry.

August 25. Lincoln at Augusta (afternoon) and at Macomb (evening); Douglas at Galena.

August 26. Lincoln at Amboy (impromptu).

[1] This list covers only the speeches of the two candidates, not their full itineraries.

August 27. Second joint debate at Freeport.

August 28. Lincoln at El Paso (impromptu); Douglas at Turner Junction (now West Chicago).

August 30. Lincoln at Tremont.

August 31. Lincoln at Carlinville; Douglas at Joliet.

September 2. Lincoln at Clinton; Douglas at Pontiac.

September 4. Lincoln at Bloomington; Douglas at Lincoln.

September 6. Lincoln at Monticello; Douglas at Jacksonville.

September 7. Lincoln at Mattoon (impromptu) and at Paris.

September 8. Douglas at Carlinville.

September 9. Lincoln at Hillsboro.

September 10. Douglas at Belleville.

September 11. Lincoln at Edwardsville (afternoon) and at Highland (evening); Douglas at Waterloo.

September 13. Lincoln at Greenville; Douglas at Chester.

September 14. Douglas at Cairo.

September 15. Third joint debate at Jonesboro.

September 16. Douglas at Benton.

September 17. Douglas at Centralia.

September 18. Fourth joint debate at Charleston.

September 20. Douglas (early afternoon) and Lincoln (late afternoon) at Sullivan.

September 21. Douglas at Danville.

September 22. Lincoln at Danville.

September 23. Douglas at Urbana.

September 24. Lincoln at Urbana; Douglas at Onarga.

September 25. Douglas at Kankakee.

September 27. Lincoln at Jacksonville.

September 28. Lincoln at Winchester; Douglas at Hennepin.

September 29. Douglas at Henry.

September 30. Douglas at Washington (impromptu) and Metamora.

October 1. Lincoln at Pittsfield.

October 2. Douglas at Pekin.

October 4. Lincoln at Metamora; Douglas at Oquawka (afternoon) and Burlington, Iowa (evening).

October 5. Lincoln at Pekin; Douglas at Monmouth.

October 7. Fifth joint debate at Galesburg.

October 8. Lincoln at Toulon; Douglas at Macomb.

October 9. Lincoln at Oquawka (afternoon) and Burlington, Iowa (evening); Douglas at Macomb (afternoon) and Plymouth (late afternoon).

October 11. Lincoln at Monmouth; Douglas at Carthage.

October 12. Douglas at Augusta.

October 13. Sixth joint debate at Quincy.

October 15. Seventh and last joint debate at Alton.

October 16. Lincoln at Lincoln; Douglas at Gillespie.

October 18. Lincoln at Meredosia; Douglas at Decatur.

October 19. Lincoln at Mount Sterling.

October 20. Lincoln at Rushville; Douglas at Springfield.

October 21. Douglas at Atlanta.

October 22. Lincoln at Carthage; Douglas at Bloomington.

October 23. Lincoln at Dallas City; Douglas at Peoria.

October 25. Lincoln at Macomb.

October 26. Douglas at Toulon.

October 27. Lincoln at Vermont.

October 28. Douglas at Geneseo.

October 29. Lincoln at Petersburg; Douglas at Rock Island.

October 30. Lincoln at Springfield.

November 1. Douglas at Chicago.

November 2. Election Day.

INDEX

Abolitionism: Republicans charged with, 160–67, 180; Lincoln charged with, 167

Abolitionists: hold convention, xxv–xxvii, 1854 platform, 105–7; take over Republican party, 192–97, 260–63; alliance with Republicans, 226; character of, 228; manage Dred Scott case, 256, 337–38; attack Compromise of 1850, 258–59; compact with Whigs, 262–63; agitate slavery question, 399

Adams, John, admission of new states, 252

Adams, John Quincy, admission of new states, 252

Allen, Nathan, mentioned, 214

Alton (Madison Co.): designated debate site, 88; Trumbull's speech at, 236–40; debate at, 361–402; Douglas' opening speech, 362–75; Lincoln's reply, 376–96; Douglas' rejoinder, 396–402

Amboy (Lee Co.), Lincoln at, 138, 409

American party: Lincoln deplores, xxviii; in 1856 campaign, xxx–xxxi; death of, xxxvii; and Lecompton constitution, 13–14, 72

American Tract Society, division in, 388

Anti–Nebraska party: support of, urged, xxv; Lincoln candidate of, xxvi; Republicans supersede, xxix; 1854 resolutions, 305–7

Ashmun, George, Mexican War resolution, 271–72, 397

Atchison, David R., forces amendment of Nebraska Bill, xxi–xxii

Atlanta (Logan Co.), Douglas at, 411

Augusta (Hancock Co.): Lincoln at, 138, 409; Douglas at, 322, 410

Baker, Jehu, mentioned, 194, 264, 293, 298

Banks, Nathaniel Prentiss: elected speaker, xxix; Abolitionist, 226, 264

Bath (Mason Co.), Lincoln at, 98–99, 409

Beardstown (Cass Co.): Douglas at, 91–93, 409; Lincoln at, 93–94, 409

Belleville (St. Clair Co.), Douglas at, 410

Belvidere (Boone Co.), delegation at Freeport, 139

Bement (Piatt Co.): Douglas at, 85, 87–88; Lincoln at, 85

Benton (Franklin Co.), Douglas at, 232, 410

Bigler, William, and Toombs Bill, 237–38, 244

Binmore, Henry, reports campaign of 1858, xxxix

Bissell, William Henry, mentioned, 197

Black Hawk War, Lincoln in, 98

Blair, Francis Preston, Jr., emancipation plan defeated, 334, 342, 392

Bloomington (McLean Co.): Republican convention, xxx; Douglas at, 43, 403, 409, 411; Lincoln at, 182, 410

Bowen, Sherman W., mentioned, 213, 214

Breckinridge, John Cabell, Vice-President, xxx–xxxi

Breese, Sidney: opposes Douglas, 193, 261; aids Abolitionists, 194, 264

Bristow, Benjamin F., welcomes Douglas, 184–85

Bromwell, Henry P. H., welcomes Lincoln, 234

Brooks, Preston Smith: attacks Sumner, xxx; on perpetuation of slavery, 76–77, 205, 354, 393–94

Bross, William, interjections by, 152–53, 154–55, 160, 167

Brown, Benjamin Gratz, emancipation plan defeated, 334, 342, 392

Brown, John, kills proslavery settlers, xxxii

Browning, Orville Hickman: senatorial aspirations, 263; entertains

[413]

JO DAVIESS
D Galena

STEPHENSON
Freeport
Aug. 27
LD
Galena

WINNEBAGO   BOONE   McHENRY   LAKE

& Chicago Union R.R.

CARROLL

OGLE

DE KALB   KANE   COOK

Du PAGE
D Chicago
D

WHITESIDE   LEE
Chicago &   North Western R.R.
Illinois   L
Central R.R.   Amboy   Turner Junction
D

La SALLE   KENDALL   WILL
Joliet
D

ROCK ISLAND   HENRY   BUREAU
D
Rock Island   Chicago   Burlington & Quincy   R.R.
Geneseo D   Rock Island R.R.   Ottawa   GRUNDY
Aug. 21   KANKAKEE
MERCER   Valley R.R.   LD   Hennepin   Illinois R.
D
KNOX   STARK   PUTNAM
MARSHALL   Kankakee D
WARREN   L   Toulon   D Henry   LIVINGSTON   IROQUOIS
Galesburg   Oct. 7   PEORIA   Lacon
Oquawka   LD   WOODFORD   Pontiac   Onarga
Oquawka   D Metamora   D   St. Louis
Burlington, Iowa   D   L   Peoria & Bureau   L Washington   McLEAN   Oquawka   R.R.
Peoria   Monmouth   R.R.   Peoria   El Paso L
L D   Peoria   Chicago   VERMILION
HENDERSON   FULTON   Pekin   Peoria
D L   Illinois Central
HANCOCK   McDONOUGH   Tremont   Bloomington
Dallas   L   L   D
City   Macomb   Lewistown   CHAMPAIGN
D   D   MASON   LOGAN   DE WITT   Urbana   Danville
Carthage   L   L   Havana   Clinton   D   D
D   Plymouth   L   Bath   D   D L   L
Augusta   L D   Lincoln   PIATT
SCHUYLER   Rushville   MENARD   Monticello
ADAMS   BROWN   L   Petersburg   MACON   Sullivan   EDGAR
Quincy   Mount   CASS   L   RR.   D   MOULTRIE   Paris
Oct. 13   Sterling   Beardstown   SANGAMON   Decatur   D L   D
LD   D   L   Great   COLES   Charleston   L
PIKE   MORGAN   Western   Springfield   Sept. 18
L Meredosia   SCOTT   L D   CHRISTIAN   Mattoon   LD   CLARK
Pittsfield   D   Jacksonville   SHELBY   D L
D L   D   Winchester   CUMBERLAND
GREENE   MACOUPIN   St. Louis R.R.
Carlinville   MONTGOMERY   Alton   FAYETTE   EFFINGHAM   JASPER   CRAWFORD
CALHOUN   D   Terre Haute   R.R.
Gillespie   Hillsboro   I.C.R.R.   CLAY
D   D   L   RICHLAND   LAWRENCE
JERSEY   MADISON   BOND   Greenville
LD Alton Oct. 15   D L   MARION
D   Edwardsville   Highland   CLINTON   EDWARDS   WABASH
L   D L   Ohio &   Mississippi   R.R.   I.C.R.R.
ST. CLAIR   WAYNE
Belleville   D Centralia   Wabash R.
D   WASHINGTON   JEFFERSON   HAMILTON   WHITE
MONROE
Waterloo   D
RANDOLPH   PERRY   FRANKLIN   SALINE   GALLATIN
Chester   Benton   WILLIAMSON
D   JACKSON   D

UNION   JOHNSON   POPE   HARDIN
Jonesboro
Sept. 15
LD

ALEXANDER   PULASKI   MASSAC

Cairo
D